RESEARCH

PERSPECTIVES ON

SECOND LANGUAGE

ACQUISITION

RESEARCH

PERSPECTIVES ON

SECOND LANGUAGE

ACQUISITION

JOHN ARCHIBALD
UNIVERSITY OF CALGARY
AND GARY LIBBEN
UNIVERSITY OF ALBERTA

COPP CLARK LTD
TORONTO

ISBN: 0-7730-5416-2

Executive editor: Jeff Miller
Managing editor: Barbara Tessman
Editor: Camilla Jenkins
Proofreader: Susan James
Index: Christopher Blackburn
Design: Rob McPhail
Cover design: Mary Opper
Cover art: Paul Watson
Typesetting: Gallimere Graphics
Printing and binding: Metropole Litho Inc.

Canadian Cataloguing in Publication Data
   Archibald, John, 1959–
   Research perspectives on second language acquisition

   Includes bibliographical references and index.
   ISBN 0-7730-5416-2

   1. Second language acquisition.
   I. Libben, Gary, 1952–   . II. Title.
   P118.2.A73 1995   401'.93   C94-932823-5

Copp Clark Ltd.
2775 Matheson Blvd. East
Mississauga, Ontario
L4W 4P7

Printed and bound in Canada

1 2 3 4 5   5416-2   99 98 97 96 95

This book is dedicated to
David Mendelsohn and to all the
bilinguals the authors live with.

Contents

Acknowledgements

It is very difficult to acknowledge all of the people who have had a hand in influencing this kind of general textbook. Primarily we are indebted to the army of people who have conducted the research that we are reporting; they have made the field the exciting place it is. Compiling a work like this is the result of the collaboration of many people. To any we have inadvertently forgotten, we thank you.

Several years of students have struggled through earlier drafts of this textbook and we thank them for their patience and comments.

The authors' views of second language acquisition have been directly influenced by a number of people over the years. We would like to acknowledge Susanne Carroll, Birgit Harley, David Mendelsohn, and Merrill Swain. These people are, of course, not responsible for any wild infelicities that may be found in this text.

We would also like to acknowledge the tireless work of our editor, Camilla Jenkins. Camilla's keen eye for detail, consistency, and the unsupported claim has not gone unappreciated. The book is undeniably better for her contribution.

Particular thanks go to Peter Avery and David Mendelsohn for reading and commenting on what was, in hindsight, a painfully early draft. David was also the first author's first teacher of second language acquisition and is therefore responsible (though not to be held responsible) for his getting into the field. No one could have asked for a better role model as a teacher, scholar, and humanitarian.

Introduction

This book grew out of senior undergraduate courses we have both taught in the departments of linguistics at the University of Calgary and the University of Alberta. The courses have tended to cater to a mixed population: people from linguistics, education, psychology, and computer science have all wandered in at one time or another. The text is aimed at this heterogeneous crowd. We hope that it will be of interest both to linguistics majors and to people majoring in other disciplines.

There is enough here for a full-year course, but we have also used the text in a half-year course. We expect that instructors of one-semester courses will be able to choose the chapters that best suit their interests and meet their needs.

The field of second language acquisition, like its audience, is extremely diverse. No textbook can claim to be comprehensive, at least not one of this length. At times we have been very narrow in our coverage of an issue, choosing to present the details of a particular study at some length rather than to summarize a few more studies briefly. One reason for this is to give students a chance to familiarize themselves with the details of research methodology. Overall, however, the text surveys the many aspects of second language acquisition research.

The book is divided into five sections: background, second language competence, second language performance, factors affecting second language acquisition, and related issues. These allow us to address several areas of concern. We examine how second language grammars are represented in the mind, how that knowledge is implemented, and the factors that influence the representation and processing of interlanguage grammars. Most chapters include a discussion of the pedagogical implications of the research outlined. There is also a self test at the end of each chapter in the form of a cloze (fill-in-the-blanks), which can function as a kind of review. The answers are found in the appendix at the end of the book.

The text contains some key terms with which the reader should be familiar from the outset:

L1 The first language of the learner
L2 The second (or other) language of the learner
SLA Second language acquisition
Interlanguage The grammatical system of a second language learner
CLT Communicative language teaching. Characterized by a focus on meaningful communication in the L2 classroom. Does not focus on explicit grammatical instruction
Universal grammar The initial state of the language faculty of the mind

Let us conclude with a brief word about the title: *Research Perspectives on Second Language Acquisition*. There are obviously many different perspectives on something as complex as SLA: linguistic, psychological, educational, and so on. We hope to have done justice to a variety of them. Like other scientific research, study of second language acquisition is done by people, and in this book you'll meet a lot of them, although by no means all. We also hope to have demonstrated that knowledge is built via research and that conclusions are based on empirical investigation.

So you've got your road map and you know where we're going. You're going to meet some interesting people and see some interesting places in the world of SLA research. Ladies and gentlemen, fasten your seatbelts.

Background

This section presents the necessary background for a detailed investigation of second language acquisition. Chapter 1 is a general introduction to some of the issues involved in the study of second language acquisition. Chapter 2 provides an introduction to linguistic theory, which may be familiar to people with a background in the field. Chapter 3 outlines the relevant topics in language, learning, and mind. Chapter 4 discusses the whats and whys of learning a first language.

In order to entertain a sophisticated discussion of second language acquisition research, we first have to establish the necessary background in these areas.

1

......

The Study of Second Language Acquisition

This textbook is going to introduce you to the field of second language acquisition. We offer a survey of the major issues of the discipline and by doing so hope to give you some idea why we feel it is an area of considerable interest and excitement.

Perhaps obviously, we should begin by saying that the field explores issues related to how people learn additional languages. Traditionally, this has been referred to as *second* language acquisition, but it can be just as concerned with third and fourth languages. The discipline grew out of the area of second language teaching, or pedagogy. One of the earliest reasons for asking and answering questions about second language acquisition was to determine methods that would aid second language teaching. Although these are related fields—and throughout this text we will consider the pedagogic implications of the acquisition research—it is necessary to point out that the two academic disciplines have grown considerably apart. How we acquire knowledge about and ability in something as stunningly complex as language raises its own intriguing questions without necessarily drawing in the study of teaching. So, although this book presents what we believe are some of the classroom implications of the research, it will not discuss the actual pedagogy. For discussions of language pedagogy see, for example, Richards and Rodgers (1986).

1 THE ROLE OF THEORY: THE REFLECTIVE TEACHER

We do not wish to suggest that we see teaching and learning as completely unrelated activities. One of the central reasons for writing this book has been a belief that knowledge of second language acquisition theory is an important part of the education of language teachers.

The relationship between teachers and researchers, however, has not always been perceived as terribly friendly. This is expressed clearly by Derek Bickerton, commenting on the relationship between theoretical linguists and second language acquisition researchers:

> There is a pecking order within disciplines just as there is within barnyards. In linguistics, the theoretical linguist rules the roost; it is he who provides the descriptive models which, after a time-lapse of a few years, are applied to the description of natural languages by the working grammarians and phonologists on the next level down. Models that have been tried and found effective, or at least fashionable, on that level are then handed on, like second-hand clothing, to workers in the field of child language, and then, after another lapse of a year or two, they finally reach the second language acquisitionist, who is already well on the wrong side of the pure/applied line and has only language teachers to peck at (Bickerton 1983, xxi).

Let us explicitly state that we do not agree with this pecking order, and we plan to devote a considerable amount of attention in this book to showing how the study of second language acquisition is a rigorous academic discipline.

Nor have teachers always been inclined to look favourably on the pronouncements of researchers. Widdowson (1980) notes that many second language teachers express a certain amount of distrust for theory. Comments such as "I don't see how this is relevant to what I'm going to do in class," or "Just tell me what to do" are all too common. At best, he remarks, they see theory as an academic indulgence of no real consequence and at worst as something that gets in the way of good, sound pedagogy. This book looks at how theory *is* important for second language teachers, and particularly for people who are becoming second language teachers.

Widdowson makes a useful distinction between training and education. He defines training as preparation for dealing with known situations and education as preparation for dealing with unknown situations. Obviously, then, in these terms our goal is to educate teachers. The same view is expressed in the familiar saying that it is not enough for teachers to know *what* to do in a classroom but that they must also know *why*. They must understand how the things that they do in the language classroom influence language learning.

As soon as you start to ask to ask the question *why*, you enter into a rigorous consideration of such things as language, learning, and teaching. In other words, asking questions leads to theory. Throughout the book, we will be looking at various aspects of language, learning, and teaching about which research has something useful to say to those interested in second language acquisition. The following is an illustrative but not exhaustive list of the kinds of questions that research may address. It also serves as a brief overview of some of the issues covered in this text:

- Can adults learn second languages successfully?
- Is second language acquisition like first language acquisition?
- Are some people better at second language acquisition than others?
- Does error correction help language learners?
- Why do we make mistakes in a second language?
- Are some languages harder to learn than others?
- Are some linguistic features harder to learn than others?
- Does the first language help or get in the way of second language learning?
- Are bilingual brains different from monolingual brains?
- Can second language learning cause you to lose your first language?
- Is there a methodology that will successfully teach a second language?

Research on the nature of language, learning, and teaching may help us to answer some of these questions. Let's begin, then, by talking about language.

2 LANGUAGE

This section has to do with the *language* part of the term *second language acquisition*. Chapter 2 will address the issue in much greater depth; for now, let us just say that in order to have anything interesting to say about how something is learned, we need to have a reasonable description of what that something is. The science of linguistics gives us such a description. It allows us to be explicit about what is being acquired. What has to be learned, for example, when we learn the sound system of a language? What has to be learned when we learn the syntax of a language? The *knowledge* that is acquired when learning a second language must be examined in detail.

We will also address how that knowledge is implemented in a variety of circumstances. Usually, you don't just know something about your second language; you can also do something with that language. One way to discuss the various methods of utilizing linguistic knowledge is to refer to the five skills of second language use:

- talking
- pronunciation
- listening
- reading
- writing

These five skills frequently form the backbone of a program of second language instruction. Most second language learners need to be able to use their second language knowledge to do all of them.

3 LEARNING/ACQUISITION

This section is concerned with the *acquisition*[1] part of the term *second language acquisition*. What exactly does it mean to acquire something? Gregg has some delightful reflections on this question:

> It is important to remember—and surprisingly easy to forget—that when we talk about acquisition in SLA research, we are not talking about acquisition in the sense that one acquires polo ponies, Lladró figurines, or CBS, but rather in the sense that one acquires vicious habits, a taste for Brie, or a potbelly. We are talking, that is, about some sort of change in the organism resulting from its interaction with the environment (1989, 16).

Thus, when individuals acquire a second language, we are assuming that they acquire a particular kind of knowledge. This must be represented in the mind somehow, and therefore any examination of second language acquisition must make use not only of the concept of knowledge but also of *memory*. Chapter 3 deals with these concepts in more detail.

Linguistic knowledge must be represented or remembered, and it must also be accessible. When considering how linguistic information is stored, we must also consider how the individual gains access to it. One common characteristic of language use in an older subject is that lexical retrieval slows down. The word is still somewhere in the mind of the individual, but finding it in the mental closet can take a bit more time than it used to. SLA researchers often also raise the question of whether non-nativelike performance in non-native speakers reflects non-native-like knowledge (or representation), or whether it indicates a difficulty in

---

[1] Even people with little background in second language acquisition have sometimes been exposed to a terminological distinction made by a researcher named Stephen Krashen. For Krashen, *learning* and *acquisition* are two distinct processes. We are not going to go into detail at this time. Suffice it to say that Krashen viewed acquisition as a very effective unconscious learning process similar to a child "picking up" a language "naturally." He saw learning, on the other hand, as a conscious process— usually involving much focus on the linguistic form—and did not consider it very helpful in second language development. In this book we will use the terms learning and acquisition synonymously.

getting access to that information (a problem of control). Ultimately the L2 learner must gain both a representation of the second language and an ability to control or get access to that knowledge.

In discussing the concept of learning in any detail, a number of terms often arise, usually presented as opposing pairs. We would like to consider a few of these now. The question of how these processes are involved in second language acquisition will be considered in more depth in Chapter 3.

3.1 ROTE VERSUS MEANINGFUL LEARNING

The distinction between *rote* and *meaningful* learning was coined by Ausubel (1965). He suggested that people may have two rather different ways of acquiring knowledge. Rote learning involves memorizing information and storing it so that it is unrelated to existing knowledge. Memorizing phone numbers, for example, is rote learning. By contrast, meaningful learning is conceived of as the incorporation of new knowledge into an existing cognitive system.

An example from computers may help to make the distinction clear, as some people have learned to use their computers by rote and others by meaningful learning. Imagine that you wanted to retrieve a file from a remote computer and save it on your personal computer. If you were proceeding by rote, you would probably follow a list of instructions going something like this: (1) log on to remote host; (2) transfer file to local mainframe; (3) download file to personal computer. If something went wrong you would probably have no idea why. If the person who gave you the instructions originally had been proceeding by meaningful learning though, he or she would be able to make a guess at what was going on inside the machines and ask, "Was it a binary file?" Rote learning would involve memorizing the sequence of pushing buttons; meaningful learning would involve understanding what each command accomplished.

3.2 INDUCTIVE VERSUS DEDUCTIVE LEARNING

Researchers in the field of language acquisition tend to have different perspectives on the learning mechanism involved. Some maintain that language acquisition is driven by a process of *induction*. Induction involves learning by forming and testing hypotheses. Learners are exposed to certain linguistic items in the environment and have to determine the rules underlying those forms. They will generate hypotheses about these rules and test them against the occurring data. If the rules work, the hypotheses will not change; if the rules do not account for the data, then the hypotheses will be revised. If, for example, you were unfamiliar with the rules of baseball and were watching a game, you would find yourself presented with certain data and would try to find patterns. How many chances does the batter get to hit the ball? How many times can the pitcher throw it? Why does the pitcher sometimes throw the ball to first base? Why do all the players spit and scratch? As you gradually tested and refined your hypotheses about the rules of baseball, you would be learning by induction.

Other researchers maintain that language acquisition is driven by a process of *deduction*. Deductive learning involves learning from first principles, not testing hypotheses. Let's assume that we have acquired certain world knowledge that takes the following form: (1) when things are put in fire they get hot; (2) hot things are often red; (3) when we touch hot things it hurts. Now imagine that you see red-hot glass for the first time in your life. You probably wouldn't think "I wonder if touching that would hurt as much as that time I leaned on the wood stove?" Instead, drawing on your existing knowledge, you would be able to deduce what was going on. Deduction assigns a somewhat less active role to the language learner than induction does. As a result of being exposed to linguistic data, certain changes occur in the learner's mental representation. A common metaphor is that certain switches get set. The learner does not choose which switches, since the process is triggered by the linguistic environment. As we will see later, in language acquisition, the existing knowledge is often assumed to be innate.

3.3 EXPLICIT VERSUS IMPLICIT LEARNING

Currently, neuropsychologists make a distinction between *explicit* and *implicit* learning. Explicit learning takes place very quickly, perhaps with a single trial. You hear a new word in a second language, such as *capucha* (Spanish for *hood*), for example, and with one hearing you learn that word. This is contrasted with implicit learning, a slow process in which knowledge is accumulated through repetition. Under this mechanism, performance can improve but the person is usually unable to articulate why. As you become better at hitting a tennis ball, for example, you are usually unable to explain what exactly you are doing better. The improvement comes slowly, when it happens at all.

3.4 CONTROLLED VERSUS AUTOMATIC PROCESSING

When we consider learning in cognitive domains other than language, we often encounter the terms *controlled* versus *automatic* processing. Imagine yourself learning to play tennis. When you begin, you have to devote a lot of attention to remembering how to hold the racquet, how to step properly, and so on. Your play involves controlled processing.

With practice, though, you become able to perform these low-level aspects of the game unconsciously and can devote your processing capacity to higher-level concerns such as strategy. At that point, you use automatic processing to perform the basic elements of the game.

4 TEACHING

As we indicated near the beginning of the chapter, the fields of second language learning and second language teaching are quite distinct. Nevertheless, it is highly likely that instruction has a certain effect on acquisition.

Figure 1.1 presents a model of second language pedagogy that defines the areas under discussion and illustrates the context of second language teaching. The model owes a debt to Stern (1983) but has been modified to reflect the content of this book. Throughout the text, we will be looking at different aspects of this diagram, as indicated by the topics shown in the individual boxes. Traditionally, the middle level (level 2) has been referred to by such names as *applied* or *educational* linguistics. Note that an investigation of this level requires knowledge of the foundation level that feeds it (level 1). We will look at all three levels, though our focus will be on the first two.

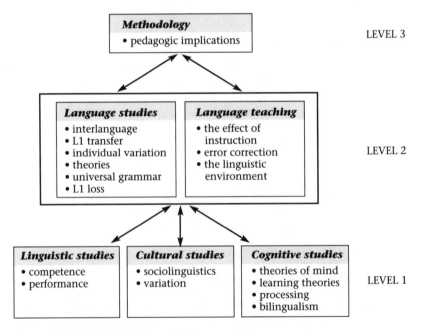

Figure 1.1   A Model of Second Language Pedagogy

5 CONCLUSION

This chapter has discussed some of the issues important to the reflective language teacher. The teacher must think about certain aspects of language, of learning, and of teaching. They are all relevant. A second language teacher needs to know about language structure, language use, and language acquisition.

CLASSROOM IMPLICATIONS

Evaluating New Materials

Every teacher must decide what materials to use in class. There may be a limited choice but there usually is one, and new materials are often available. How do teachers decide which materials are going to be suitable for their class? They consult some sort of personal theory, and may consider, among other things,

- the age of the students
- the interests of the students (possibly related to age)
- the proficiency level of the students
- the educational background of the students
- the cultural background of the students

The point is that classroom practitioners need to ask themselves "Why would I use this material?" or "Why wouldn't I use this material?" This type of decision can be well informed by theory.

Evaluating Teaching Methodologies

Teachers are also faced with the problem of deciding what sort of methodology to use in their classrooms. Usually, they are exposed to a number of different second language methodologies in their education programs and are then in the position of having to determine what works and what doesn't. What works will, of course, depend on the context in which the teaching occurs. Suffice it to say that there are many different views as to the "best" methodology. For an overview of methodologies, see Howatt (1984) or Richards and Rodgers (1986).

Evaluating Classroom Activities

What kinds of activities should go on in a second language classroom? Should we use drills, pair work, group work, or co-operative learning? How does the type of class influence the type of activity? Should teachers focus on the content to be learned or on the linguistic material to be learned? What is the role of practice in second language classrooms? All of these questions need to be seriously considered by the reflective teacher.

FURTHER READING

Brown, H.D. 1993. *Principles of Language Learning and Teaching,* 3rd ed. Englewood Cliffs, NJ: Prentice-Hall.

Ellis, R. 1986. *Understanding Second Language Acquisition.* Oxford: Oxford University Press.

Stern, H.H. 1983. *Fundamental Concepts of Language Teaching.* Oxford: Oxford University Press.

2

......

Linguistic Theory

Presented here is an overview of the basic issues in the discipline of linguistics. Students who feel comfortable with their background preparation in linguistics will most likely be able to skip, or at least skim, the chapter. Linguistics is often referred to as the scientific investigation of language. This, of course, leads us directly to the question of what language is.

1 LANGUAGE

This is an old question, and a difficult one. As with many complex areas, the more we find out about it, the more complicated it appears. It is the task of the discipline of linguistics to investigate the properties of language rigorously. We use the word *language* to denote many things. Some animals are capable of making their wants known through sounds of some sort. A bird may have one call to signal *Danger!* and another to signal *I've found food!* Is this language? A baby may have a certain kind of cry to signal hunger and another to signal pain. Most caregivers feel that this is the case. Is this language?

Language is a systematic mapping of sound onto meaning. If we hear an entirely novel sentence, we can understand it. The sentence *Four hundred and thirty groundhogs watched carefully as the farmer threw pineapples at the tourists* is most probably new to you and yet you have no problem determining its meaning. Why? Language functions according to certain shared principles known as rules, which allow us to determine meaning from a sequence of words even when we have never seen it before. The science of linguistics investigates these rules. Animal call systems do not function in this way, as animals cannot combine signals to produce new meanings. Language, then, is a uniquely human ability. Let us now examine two crucial properties of and facts about human language.

1.1 LANGUAGE IS A SYMBOLIC SYSTEM

A symbolic system involves the relationship between signs and what those signs represent. Some signs have a physical correspondence to what they represent. If you saw the signs in Figure 2.1 on doors, for example, you would probably be able to identify what they referred to; there is a resemblance between the signs and what they represent, albeit bound by culture. But what if you saw the signs in Figure 2.2? You certainly wouldn't get any information from what they resemble physically.

Figure 2.1   **Figure 2.2**

Signs that bear a physical resemblance to what they represent are called *icons*. The relationship between an icon and what it means is predictable. Signs that do not have a predictable meaning are called *symbols*. The relationship between a linguistic sign and what it means is not predictable. A linguistic sign is usually a sequence of sounds. If you hear the sequence of sounds *r-e-d*, there is nothing predictable about what it will mean. The same item is represented by different sounds in different languages:

r-o-j-o [řoxo] (Spanish)
r-o-u-g-e [ʁuž] (French)
h-ó-n-g [hoŋ] (Mandarin Chinese)[1]

The meaning of a symbol must be learned as part of a culture. Language, then, is not iconic, but symbolic. This symbolic quality of language is sometimes referred to as *arbitrariness* because the relationship between sound and meaning is arbitrary.

1.2 PRESCRIPTIVE VERSUS DESCRIPTIVE GRAMMAR

There is sometimes a bit of confusion over the term *grammar*. Two distinct schools of thought should be outlined. Some people maintain that the job of a grammar is to evaluate how a person uses language and to decide whether it is correct or not. This is a *prescriptive* view of grammar; it suggests that a grammar prescribes the way that people should use language. Prescriptive grammarians rail against new verbs (*impact* and *access*); they remind us not to split infinitives (*to* boldly *go* where no one

---

[1] The symbols within square brackets in each case represent the way that the word is pronounced, as transcribed in the International Phonetic Alphabet (IPA). We will be discussing the IPA later in this chapter.

has gone before); and they claim that an English sentence should never end with a preposition (Who do you want to talk *to*?).

The other view is known as *descriptive* grammar. A descriptive grammar does not judge someone's language use but merely describes how that person uses language in a particular context. A descriptive grammarian would not say that a sentence such as *There's three important points* is wrong but that some people in some, usually informal, situations use a contracted form of the singular verb even when there is a plural object.

The science of linguistics is based upon a descriptive view of grammar, and it is the approach that this text will maintain. In our view, second language teachers do their students a disservice by telling them that sentences such as the one above are incorrect, when the students will hear such things all the time. Teachers would better serve them to explain the circumstances in which this construction is and is not used. Grammars, then, are in the heads of learners, not in prescriptive grammar books.

2 LINGUISTICS

Linguistics has emerged in the twentieth century as a discipline dedicated to understanding language. Chomsky (1988) presents the goals of linguistics in the following manner: (1) to describe the system of knowledge of native speakers; (2) to explain how that system of knowledge was acquired; (3) to explain how that system of knowledge is used; and (4) to describe the physical mechanisms responsible for storing and processing that system of knowledge.

The achievement of these goals brings linguistics into contact with a number of other disciplines: psychology, education, and neuroscience. Linguistics shares with these fields an interest in human cognitive development, in the nature of mental representations, and in the mechanisms that underlie comprehension and production of language. Yet linguistics is a distinct discipline characterized by a particular approach to the study of language. The linguistic approach divides language inquiry into two components: formal analysis of the various levels of language, referred to as the core; and application of that analysis to various areas of inquiry. The division between the two is depicted in Figure 2.3. It should be noted that the areas of inquiry shown are only a sampling. This book is clearly focussed on one of these: language acquisition, specifically of a second language. We will find, however, that information from other areas contributes to our understanding of second language acquisition and that familiarity with formal aspects of core linguistics adds precision to our thinking about language ability.

The core	**Areas of inquiry**
Phonetics *The sounds of language*	**Historical linguistics** *How languages change over time*
Phonology *How sounds pattern in a language*	**Language acquisition** *How a language is learned*
Morphology *Word structure and formation*	**Psycholinguistics** *How language is processed*
Syntax *Sentence structure and formation*	**Neurolinguistics** *Representation of language in the brain*
Semantics *The analysis of meaning in language*	**Sociolinguistics** *The social aspects of language*

Figure 2.3   The Discipline of Linguistics

To attain a useful level of exactitude, the core areas—phonetics, phonology, morphology, syntax, and semantics—have developed rich technical vocabularies and systems of formal representation. This chapter reviews aspects of the core that are important to understanding second language acquisition research. It will not include discussion of formal semantic theories, however, because the field of semantic representation is less homogeneous than the other core areas. Also, the acquisition of L2 formal semantics has received very little attention from researchers.

3 PHONETICS

The word *phonetics* is derived from a Greek word meaning *to be spoken.* Phonetics deals with the mechanics of how sounds are made in human languages. This is usually referred to as *articulatory* phonetics.[2] Anyone who has experience with a phonetic alphabet will have some familiarity with phonetics. A phonetic alphabet is a way of visually representing sound. Each phonetic symbol represents one, and only one, sound, and each sound is represented by one, and only one, symbol. Table 2.1 shows some examples of phonetic transcription using the International Phonetic Alphabet (IPA). Note that phonetic transcriptions are indicated by enclosure within square brackets.

---

[2] *Acoustic* and *auditory* phonetics look at sound from additional perspectives. We will not be discussing these views in this book.

Table 2.1   Phonetic Transcription

Spelling	Phonetic transcription
go	[gow]
dog	[dɑg]
women	[wɪmən]
through	[θru]
bough	[baw]
one	[wʌn]

Phonetics offers us the ability to characterize speech and speech sounds, and this allows us to think about aspects of speech in a much more precise manner. One commonly recognizable characteristic of second language speech is that it is unlike native speech. Most second language learners have non-native accents. But what is accent? When you hear someone speak and you recognize an accent, what exactly are you noticing? People usually respond with such observations as "They said it wrong," "Something about the vowels," or "Something about the consonants." We tend to be quite vague in our ability to identify how the non-native speaker deviated from the native speaker norm. Phonetics provides the necessary vocabulary to describe learners' errors.

A language such as English has two dominant forms of expression: spoken and written. In this society, we tend to think of the written form when we hear the word language. And we have a much richer common vocabulary for talking about written language than we do for spoken language. When we use such terms as letter, word, sentence, and paragraph we tend to think of the printed page. Even in a language you don't know you can usually identify these aspects of a written text. Try to do the same when listening to a language you don't know.

For most people, this bias towards written language results in an impoverished vocabulary for talking about spoken language. In order to provide useful feedback to second language learners, however, we need to be able to talk very precisely about sound; we can't do it by using the vocabulary of written language. English is notorious for the poor fit between its written and spoken languages. In many languages, if you are reading a word you have never seen before, you have a pretty good idea of how to pronounce it. In English you have to gamble a bit. The letter *t* for example, is typically pronounced as in the word *tick*. But consider its pronunciation in the words *there* or *action*. The correspondence between letters representing vowels and the vowels themselves is more complex. Consider the different sounds associated with the letter *i* in the word *inviting*.

George Bernard Shaw illustrated the problems of the English spelling system with the following example. How would you pronounce the word

> The English have no respect for their language, and will not teach their children to speak it. They cannot spell it because they have nothing to spell it with but an old foreign alphabet of which only the consonants—and not all of them—have any agreed speech value. Consequently no man can teach himself what it should sound like from reading it; and it is impossible for an Englishman to open his mouth without making some other Englishman despise him. Most European languages are now accessible in black and white to foreigners: English and French are not thus accessible even to Englishmen and Frenchmen. The reformer we need most today is an energetic phonetic enthusiast: that is why I have made such a one the hero of a popular play.
>
> George Bernard Shaw
> Preface to *Pygmalion*

ghoti? Shaw argued that in English it could conceivably be pronounced [fɪš] (the word *fish*). All you have to do is pronounce the *gh* as in *enough* [f], the *o* as in *women* [ɪ], and the *ti* as in *nation* [š]. We hasten to add that Shaw used this as a demonstration of the difficulties in the English spelling system, not of his solution.

The moral of all this is that we have to treat spoken and written language on their own terms. And in order to talk about spoken language, we need to talk about phonetics.

3.1 ARTICULATORY PHONETICS: SOME KEY TERMS AND CONCEPTS

One way to understand what phonetics is trying to do is to think of asking a series of questions about a particular sound:

- Is it a consonant or a vowel?
- Where is it made?
- How is it made?
- Is it voiced or voiceless?

If we can answer all of these questions we will have a good idea of where a student's pronunciation problem lies.

Let's begin by asking the first question. Again, we probably have a strong bias towards written language when trying to answer. You may have thought that it is perfectly straightforward to tell whether something is a consonant or a vowel. "English has five basic vowels," you might say, "so everything else is a consonant." We will return to the question of how many vowels English has shortly, but first we need to clear up another source of confusion. In terms of the written language, yes, we are all pretty good at telling which written symbols represent consonants and which represent vowels. But what about in spoken language? If someone asked you how many consonants you heard in the word *thing*, what would you say? There are four written symbols for consonants, but how many consonants do you hear? Two is the correct answer: [θ] and [ŋ]. Clearly, we need to define how consonants and vowels are made, not just to memorize what the written symbols stand for.

Consonants are produced in one of two ways. They can be made with a complete blockage somewhere in the vocal tract. For example, [b] is made by bringing both lips together and blocking the air flow completely. Alternatively, they can be made with a major constriction somewhere in the vocal tract. For example, [f] is made by resting the upper teeth lightly on the lower lip and thus restricting the airflow. The air is interfered with but not blocked. To feel the difference between these two methods of making a consonant, see how long you can make an [f]. Now see how long you can make a [b]. The reason you can make the [f] for so much longer is that the air is not blocked.

These articulatory facts are important for second language learners because they might get them wrong. If a student attempts to make a sound that has a complete blockage in English but only manages to constrict the air, a non-native accent will result. It is a common mistake for Spanish speakers, for example, when trying to pronounce an English [b] between vowels, not to make a complete blockage. The word *rubber* sounds something like *ru_w_er*.[3] The converse pattern can be seen when a French speaker tries to make the English *th* sound, which demands a constriction of air rather than a blockage. A common error for Québécois speakers is to pronounce [θ] as [t], so the word *three* sounds like *tree*. Instead of constricting the airway, they are blocking it completely.

In contrast to consonants, vowels are made with a relatively free passage of air. When you say the vowel in the word *see*, which we will from this point onwards represent as [i], the air is not significantly interfered with. Different vowel sounds are produced by changing the shape of the oral cavity. The vowel [ɑ], as in *b_ough_t*, is produced by dropping the tongue to the floor of the mouth. This is therefore the sound that your physician would like you to make if he or she wants to see into your throat. The sound [i], on the other hand, is produced with the tongue very high in the mouth. Try producing [i] while looking in the mirror. You will find that your tongue blocks any view of your throat.

3.1.1 Classification of Consonants

Table 2.2 classifies a variety of consonants. It shows the place and manner of articulation and whether the consonant is voiced or voiceless.

---

[3] Actually, they produce a voiced, bilabial fricative [β] but that's beyond our concern here.

Table 2.2 Classification of Consonants

Manner of articulation	Labial	Labio-dental	Inter-dental	Alveolar	Alveo-palatal	Palatal	Velar	Glottal
Place of articulation								
Stops								
Voiceless	p			t			k	ʔ
Voiced	b			d			g	
Fricatives								
Voiceless	ɸ	f	θ	s	š		x	h
Voiced	β	v	ð	z	ž		ɣ	
Affricates								
Voiceless	pf			t^s	č			
Voiced				d^z	ǰ			
Nasals	m			n		ñ	ŋ	
Liquids				l r				
Glides	(w)					y	w	

3.1.1.1 Place of Articulation

The term *place of articulation* is probably self-explanatory. It refers to where a sound is made. This is either the place of the blockage of the airflow or the place of the major constriction. Human languages make use of the following places of articulation:

1. (Bi) Labial [p b m]
   • The lips are brought together.
2. Labio-dental [f v]
   • The lower lip and upper teeth are brought together.
3. (Inter) Dental [θ ð]
   • The tongue touches the teeth.
4. Alveolar [t d n s z l r]
   • The tongue touches the bumpy ridge right behind your upper front teeth.
5. Post-alveolar or Alveopalatal [č ǰ š ž]
   • The tongue is positioned just a bit further back, between the alveolar ridge and the hard palate.
6. Palatal [y]
   • The tongue touches the hard palate. (If you run your tongue along the roof of your mouth you will come to a point where the bone stops. Stop moving your tongue before something horrible happens. This is the hard palate.)
7. Velar [k g ŋ]
   • The sound is produced at the velum, or soft palate; the very back of the mouth.

8. Uvular (none in English)
   • The sound is produced at the tip of flesh that you see when cartoon characters scream.
9. Glottal [h]
   • The sound is made at the vocal folds. (The space between the folds is called the glottis.)

These terms can also help us to define second language learner errors. In English, the [t] sound is usually made at the alveolar ridge. In French, it is dental. So if an English speaker learning French makes an English [t], he or she will be producing a non-native accented sound. Similarly, the English [r] sound is alveolar while the French is uvular. If we get the place of articulation wrong, we will sound non-nativelike.

3.1.1.2 Manner of Articulation

The term *manner of articulation* refers to how a sound is made. This goes back to our earlier discussion of whether a consonant is made with a complete blockage or a major constriction of the air passage. Now let's look at the technical terms:

1. Stops [p b t d k g]
   • Sounds are made with a complete blockage somewhere in the vocal tract.
2. Fricatives [f v θ ð s z š ž h]
   • Sounds are made with a major constriction somewhere in the vocal tract.
3. Affricates [č ǰ]
   • These complex sounds consist of a stop + a fricative. Some phonetic alphabets make this explicit by using a combination of stop and fricative symbols: [č] = [tš] and [ǰ] = [dž].
4. Nasals [m n ŋ]
   • Sounds are made with the air coming through the nose.
5. Glides [y w]
   • Sometimes called *semi-vowels*, glides are made with just slightly more constriction than their related vowel. The glide [y] is just a bit higher than [i] as in s<u>ee</u>; [w] is just a bit higher than [u] as in t<u>o</u>. See how little you have to move your tongue to go from [i] to [y] and from [u] to [w].
6. Liquids [l r]
   • Sounds are made with more constriction than the glides but not as much as the fricatives.

Manner of articulation can also help us to understand second language learners' errors. A learner who substitutes an affricate for a glide in the sentence *What do you want?* ends up producing a [ǰ] in the middle of the utterance, as in *What do joo want?*

3.1.1.3 Voiced or Voiceless?

Notice in Table 2.2 that some of the consonants are positioned in rows labelled *voiced* while others are in rows labelled *voiceless*. This phonetic distinction has to do with what is going on in the larynx. The larynx, or Adam's apple, contains the vocal folds. This is where the voice begins, and for second language learners, it is often where accent begins. Figure 2.4 illustrates two possible positions of the vocal folds in the larynx. If the vocal folds are far apart (as in the drawing on the left), the air can flow past them without being interfered with; the vocal folds do not vibrate.[4] If the vocal folds are drawn together (as in the drawing on the right), then the vocal folds vibrate when the air from the lungs passes through. It is this vibration that we refer to as *voicing*.

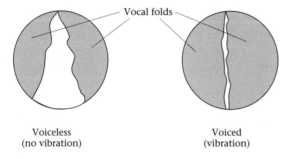

Voiceless
(no vibration)

Voiced
(vibration)

Figure 2.4   The Vocal Folds

Thus, two sounds can be made in exactly the same way with respect to place and manner of articulation but can be different in terms of what's going on in the larynx. This is where second language learners can get things wrong. They can have everything right above the larynx but use the wrong voicing value. Let's look at a specific example of how. The voiced and the voiceless consonants of English are listed in Table 2.3.

Table 2.3   Voiced and Voiceless Consonants

Voiced	b	m	v	ð	d	n	z	ž	l	r	ǰ	y	g	ŋ	w
Voiceless	p		f	θ	t		s	š			č		k		h

Notice that some sounds have voiced/voiceless pairs while others do not. There is no voiceless version of [m], for example, but there is certainly a lot that is similar between [p] and [b]. Both [p] and [b] are bilabial stops.

---

[4] It's the air flowing past that causes the vibration. Think of how the wind whistles when it blows through a crack in a door but does not whistle when it blows through an open door.

That is to say, they are both made with both lips, and both block the air completely. Yet [p] is voiceless and [b] is voiced. Similarly, [f] and [v] are both labio-dental fricatives. The only difference between these consonants is the voicing value. So imagine a second language learner who has everything right about the two consonants except the voicing. Have you ever heard a non-native speaker of English pronounce something like "I ha<u>v</u>e a bro<u>th</u>er" as [ay hæ<u>f</u> ə brʌ<u>θ</u>ər]? The sounds [f] and [θ] are substituted for [v] for [ð]. Notice that in a situation like this, the learner has correctly produced a labio-dental and an interdental fricative. What they have got wrong is the voicing; they have produced voiceless sounds rather than voiced ones.

The above example illustrates that the kinds of things second language learners do are not random; there is a system to their production. It also illustrates that abstract phonetic concepts like voicing are very real insofar as they describe the kinds of things that second language learners do. The example also has classroom implications. If we weren't aware of voicing, we might just think that the student found it hard to learn how to make the English [v] or the English [ð]. But such problems are not isolated. The student doesn't have difficulty with individual sounds but with voicing. It is the job of the second language teacher to find patterns in the students' language. Knowledge of how sounds are made will help them to find those patterns.

3.1.1.4 A Note on Non-English Sounds

Some symbols in Table 2.2 describe sounds that are not found in English. Knowing a little about these sounds can help us to understand the phonetic source of non-native accents.

First let's look at labial fricatives. The voiceless labial fricative [ɸ] is found in Japanese in words like *tofu* and *Fuji*. A voiceless labial fricative is a lot like the sound you make when blowing out a candle. Make sure that your lips don't touch. English has borrowed these words with a voiceless, labio-dental fricative [f]. An English speaker who uses a labio-dental fricative in these words produces a non-native Japanese accent.

The voiced counterpart of [ɸ] is a voiced labial fricative [β], which is found in Spanish in words like *cannibal*. English has borrowed this word with a voiced labial stop [b]. An English speaker who uses the stop instead of the fricative is perceived as having a non-native Spanish accent.

In order to understand the nature of the affricate [pf], as found in the German word *pfennig*, let us consider the nature of affricates. An affricate is a complex sound consisting of a stop followed by a fricative made in the same place. The English [č], for example, can be thought of as a [t] followed by a [š], and a [ǰ] is a [d] followed by a [ž]. In Québécois French, a word such as *petit* (little) is pronounced [pətˢi]. German uses the labial affricate, which consists of the stop [p] and the fricative [f]. If an English speaker pronounces *pfennig* with a fricative rather than an affricate [fɛnɪg], a non-native accent results.

A detailed analysis of phonetic structure, then, allows us to describe and explain certain characteristics of second language learner speech. Non-native accents can result from problems with voicing, place, or manner of articulation.

3.1.2 Classification of Vowels

Figure 2.5 presents the classification of English vowels. The major dimensions with which to classify vowels are *high/low*, *front/back*, *tense/lax* and *rounded/unrounded*. Some vowels are made with the front of the tongue, such as [i], and are referred to as front vowels. Others are made with the back of the tongue, such as [u], and are referred to as back vowels. Vowels like [i] and [u] are made with the tongue high in the mouth and are therefore classified as high vowels. Vowels like [ɑ] are made with the tongue low in the mouth and, not surprisingly, are called low vowels. Finally, vowels can be made with the lips rounded [u], or unrounded [i]. Notice what the lips do when you say a word like *boot* compared to when you say *beet*. Because vowels are made with a relatively unobstructed airway, the tongue cannot interfere much with the passage of air in the production of vowels. Figure 2.6 shows the tongue position in the mouth for four vowels.

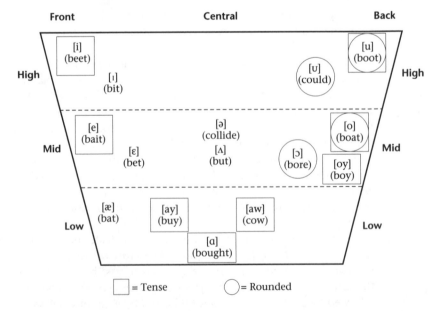

Figure 2.5   Classification of Vowels

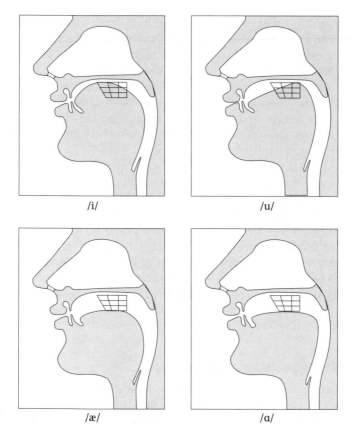

Figure 2.6   Articulatory Position of Vowels in the Mouth
Source: Adapted from Mackay (1987, 67).

If the non-native speaker gets any of these dimensions wrong, a non-native accent results. Unlike consonants, which are discrete, vowels are a continuous phenomenon. That is to say, we can glide continuously from vowel to vowel, [a i o u], in a way that we cannot do with consonants. Thus, there is a vowel sound between [i] and [e] but there is no stop consonant between [p] and [t]. Teachers must learn to diagnose students' problems in terms of the dimension they are getting wrong. Do they have a problem with the height of the vowel? The frontness? The tension? The rounding?

It should be noted that Figure 2.5 is approximate. It may not, for example, capture the exact vowel characteristics for your dialect of English. Nevertheless, it will be sufficient to provide us with a framework for understanding some of the difficulties second language learners have with the pronunciation of vowels.

In Spanish, for example, there is no high front lax vowel such as the English [ɪ] in *bit*. Spanish learners of English therefore naturally substitute the closest vowel in their repertoire, the high front tense vowel [i], when an English [ɪ] is required. This process creates one of the most salient aspects of a Spanish accent in English. When Spanish speakers say "a leetle beet" instead of "a little bit," they are systematically substituting a high front tense vowel for a high front lax (non-tense) vowel.

English speakers show similar tendencies when they try to produce vowels that are not in their repertoire. English has no high front rounded vowel such as in the French word *tu* or the German word *über*. In this case, the high back rounded vowel [u] is the closest in the English speaker's repertoire. The effect of this substitution is that English learners typically pronounce the French word *tu* so that it sounds the same as the English *two*, using a high back rounded vowel instead of a high front rounded vowel. Figure 2.5 can be useful in explaining how the vowel error may be corrected. The figure tells us that the target vowel in *tu* has all the characteristics of the English vowel [i] except that it is rounded. Now try this: say the vowel [i] with your lips rounded, as they are when you pronounce [u]. The sound you produce should be very close to the correct French vowel in the word *tu*.

3.2 PHONETICS: SUMMARY AND REVIEW

Our discussion of phonetics has focussed on the means by which speech sounds can be classified. It introduced the basic articulatory categories for consonants and vowels as well as the symbols commonly used to represent English speech sounds. Consonants can be classified in terms of place of articulation (e.g., bilabial, alveolar, velar), manner of articulation (e.g., stop, fricative), and the voiced–voiceless distinction. Vowels fall into classes based on characteristics such as high, low, front, back, tense, and rounded.

This system of classification not only allows us to describe sounds that we produce but also makes it possible to describe sounds that we either cannot produce or have never heard before. With a knowledge of phonetics it is possible to explain how sounds are made. We can say, for example, that the last consonant in the name of the German composer Bach is a voiceless velar fricative and represent the sound with a symbol [x].

This presentation has been introductory. Phonetic analysis and transcription require considerable practice, but they have a wide range of application. For second language learners in particular, knowledge of phonetics has several concrete benefits. It gives them access to the phonetic transcriptions used in dictionaries to indicate pronunciations. It gives them a way of writing down how a word is pronounced. It gives teachers a method of providing students with precise correction on their pronunciation faults. Comments such as "Speak more clearly," or "Don't swallow that sound" are not very helpful. Just as we want to give students precise feedback about their grammar by referring to such basic terms as noun, verb, agreement, and so on, so too we want to be as precise as we can in commenting on their pronunciation.

The final benefit is less tangible. There is an old story of a Zen master who was waiting patiently while a student tried to solve a problem. The student announced that he couldn't do it; that the problem was impossible. The Zen master walked over to the student and whacked him on the side of the head. Suddenly everything was clear and the student found the answer. Now, we are certainly not suggesting that physical violence is the solution to L2 pronunciation problems. Rather, we would like to propose that the whack on the side of the head can be metaphorical. Adult students especially sometimes need a new way to think about sound. They may have been pronouncing their L2 in the same way for years (what we will come to term *fossilization*). By learning about phonetics they may free themselves to make some changes in their stable system.

4 PHONOLOGY

Phonology is the branch of linguistics that considers speech sounds as they combine to make meanings. Phonology is concerned with how the phonetic sounds influence meaning. Why does *pin* differ in meaning from *bin*? Because /p/ and /b/ are what are called *phonemes* in English (indicated by enclosure within slanted lines). Different phonemes combine to produce different meanings, whereas not all phonetic changes produce changes in meaning. Consider the way you pronounce the *l* in the word *leaf* and the word *milk*. For most people, these two *l*s are made quite differently, and yet if we changed from one to the other it would not change the meaning. The result might sound like a foreign accent in English but it would still sound like *l*. These two sounds are phonetically different; they are made differently. Yet they are not phonologically different; they are not phonemes, and do not change the meaning.

The next section outlines some characteristics of English phonology relevant to the English language learner and teacher. Phonological analysis is concerned with, among other things, determining which phonetic variation is predictable in a language and which is unpredictable. Predictable phonetic variants are referred to as *allophones* of a single phoneme, whereas unpredictable phonetic variants are referred to as *separate* phonemes. Let us look at an example of each kind of variation.

4.1 PREDICTABLE VARIATION

An example of predictable variation is the voicing of liquids and glides in English. Consider how the various *l*s are made in Table 2.4.

Table 2.4

Voiced /l/	Voiceless /l/
leaf	play
fall	climb
milk	

Note that in the first column the sounds are clearly voiced [l], while in the second they are voiceless (more precisely, [l̥]). How do we know when or where to voice or devoice the /l/? Is it something that has to be memorized as part of every English word, or does a rule exist? As it turns out, there is a rule: devoice an /l/ if it occurs after a voiceless stop consonant. The distribution of voiced and voiceless /l/ is thus predictable, or complementary; they are allophones of the same phoneme and therefore the variation in sound does not affect meaning. This is usually diagrammed in the form below, in which C stands for consonant and the horizontal line represents a blank for the remainder of the word following the consonant:

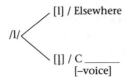

4.2 UNPREDICTABLE VARIATION

If two sounds belong to different phonemes though, their distribution is unpredictable. Consider the distribution of voiced and voiceless labial stops in Table 2.5.

Table 2.5

[p]	[b]
pin	bin
pail	bail
puck	buck

The [p] and [b] sounds obviously not only occur in the same phonetic environments but also change the meaning of a word. Therefore, /p/ and /b/ are said to be separate phonemes of English; their occurrence cannot be predicted. To understand this, try to decide whether the voiced [b] or voiceless [p] bilabial stop goes in the following blank: ___in. You can't predict. But now try to predict whether the voiced [l] or voiceless [ḷ] goes into the following blank: ___ist. You are able to predict that the /l/ should be voiced because it does not occur after a voiceless consonant.

4.3 CROSS-LINGUISTIC DIFFERENCES

Phonetic variation that is predictable in one language may be unpredictable in another, and vice versa. If we take an example from Spanish and English, we find that both languages have the phones, or sounds, [d] and [ð], but that the predictability of the two variants differs. In Spanish, [ð] is a predictable phonetic variant of /d/ occurring, let us say for now, between vowels. The [d] occurs everywhere else. The Spanish phonological system, then, looks something like this, where V stands for vowel:

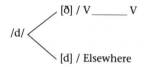

In English, however, we have different phonemes /d/ and /ð/:

Phoneme		Phone
/d/	→[5]	[d]
/ð/	→	[ð]

If we asked you to predict which phonetic variant went in the blank ___en, you would be unable to. The sound [d] would produce the word *den*; the sound [ð] would produce the word *then*.

When acquiring a second language sound system, it is therefore necessary to learn which types of phonetic variation are predictable and which are unpredictable. The mapping between phonological and phonetic representations varies from language to language.

Predictable variants can often be quite difficult to hear in your native language. Below are some examples of predictable (allophonic) variation in English useful for native speakers and people interested in teaching English phonology. An example of allophonic variation in German is also given, to show how L1 variation can affect second language learners.

---

[5] The arrows in diagrams such as this one are interpreted to read, "is realized phonetically as."

4.4 CONSONANTS

4.4.1 Five Kinds of *T*

This first point illustrates how both our spelling system and our native-speaker intuitions may block us from perceiving English in the way that our non-native students do. Consider the [t] sound in English. Table 2.2 says that the English [t] is a voiceless, alveolar stop. And it is. Usually. What a phonetic chart does not indicate is how a sound changes in a particular context.

Consider the [t] sounds in Table 2.6. Notice how they are pronounced differently in each of the columns. The words in column 1 have the "normal" alveolar [t] sound. Those in column 2 illustrate the unaspirated [t] sound. If you say the sounds in column 1 you will noticed that a puff of air comes out of your mouth when the [t] is released. (You can check this with your hand or, more excitingly, with a match). In column 2, however, there is no puff of air, no aspiration. This is because the [t] is preceded by an [s]. We may be unaware of this rule of English pronunciation: voiceless stops that follow [s] are unaspirated. The [t] sounds in column 3 are referred to as *flaps*. The most relevant characteristic of the flap is that it is voiced. Sometimes pronunciation books refer to this as *t-voicing*. In Canadian English, we tend to say these words with a voiced flap. Words like *latter* and *ladder* are pronounced similarly. If there is a difference it is probably in the length of the first vowel. Column 4 illustrates what are known as *unreleased stops*. At the end of a word or sentence, the [t] sound is unreleased. The blockage in the vocal tract is held until sound production stops. Thus, when we stop saying the word *cat* the tip of the tongue is still touching the alveolar ridge. Column 5 illustrates a [t] sound with glottalization and a nasal release. Some people can make these sounds without any contact between the tongue and the alveolar ridge; they just make a glottal stop. This stop is then released by having the air pass through the nose.

Table 2.6   Five Kinds of T

(1)	(2)	(3)	(4)	(5)
Tom	stop	butter	cat	button
tie	stone	city	but	kitten
tough	stance	pretty	combat	eaten
tune	story	letter	sit	mitten
torrid	stupid	better	format	gotten

The point here is that all of these are probably thought of by most native speakers as "kinds of *t* sounds" but phonetically they are quite different, and in predictable ways. It's not that teachers have to say to their students, "English has five different kinds of *t* sounds. Listen to know which one to use." There are rules to tell the students which [t] is appropriate. Teachers must also be aware of the kinds of differences that non-native speakers will perceive. They must learn to hear their own language through unbiased ears. Phonetic and phonological analysis helps.

4.4.2 Final Devoicing in German

German has both voiced and unvoiced consonants. If a consonant occurs at the end of a word, however, it is always voiceless. Consider the German words in Table 2.7 (where the phonetic symbol indicates the pronunciation of the underlined sound). Note that for all the forms the consonant is voiced when it does not occur at the end of the word but becomes voiceless in word-final position. Notice also that the spelling system of German preserves the underlying form (as in *bad*), not the form that is actually pronounced (*bat*).

Table 2.7   Final Devoicing in German

baden	[d]	to bathe	bad	[t]	bath
flieger	[g]	pilot	flug	[k]	flight
staubig	[b]	dusty	staub	[p]	dust
gläser	[z]	glasses	glas	[s]	glass

Like most phonological processes this one is unconscious. Native speakers of German are not consciously aware of the regularity of the process and indeed are usually not even aware of the fact that they only produce voiceless consonants in word-final position.

4.5 VOWELS

The phonetic environment, or context, can influence the production of vowels in the same way that it does the production of consonants. Below are two examples of the way in which vowels can be affected by their phonetic environment: Canadian raising and vowel reduction.

4.5.1 Canadian Raising

One of the characteristics of Canadian English is known as Canadian raising. This is a phonological phenomenon related to the sounds [aw] and [ay]. Consider the lists of words in Table 2.8. For many dialects of English, columns 1 and 2 would be pronounced with the diphthong [ay] as in *ride*, while columns 3 and 4 would be pronounced with the diphthong [aw] as in *loud*.[6] Canadian English, however, uses different

---

[6] A diphthong is a complex, vowel-like articulation in which there is a change of position of the articulators.

diphthongs in columns 1 and 2, and also distinguishes between columns 3 and 4. In column 1 the "normal" [ay] sound is used. In column 2, however, the diphthong [ʌy] is used. This diphthong has a higher starting point than [ay]. Compare your pronunciation of the words in columns 1 and 2. Chances are, if you're a speaker of Canadian English, you make different diphthongs. Similarly, in column 3, Canadian English speakers use the [aw] diphthong but in column 4 use a diphthong [ʌw].

Table 2.8   Canadian Raising

(1)	(2)	(3)	(4)
ride	right	loud	lout
live (adj.)	life	house (verb)	house (noun)
eyes	ice	cloud	clout
rise	rice		out
tribe	tripe		about

4.5.2 Vowel Reduction

The final thing to say about vowels is that their pronunciation is also affected by whether they are stressed or not. In English, stressed vowels tend to have higher pitch, greater length, and greater clarity than unstressed vowels. By greater clarity, we mean that they are recognizable as one of the vowels given in Figure 2.5. Consider the vowels in the word *battalion* [bətǽlyən]. The stressed vowel is a full vowel [æ] while the unstressed vowels have been reduced to schwas [ə]. That this is conditioned by stress can be seen when we compare the pronunciations of two related words: photograph [fótəgræ̀f] and photography [fətɑ́grəfi]. In the word *photograph*, the primary stress is on the first syllable and the first syllable has the full vowel [o]. In *photography*, the primary stress is on the second syllable (with a subsidiary stress on the final syllable), and as a result the first syllable is reduced to a schwa [ə]. Compare the other vowels in the two words and you will see the same pattern. When a vowel is stressed it receives its full phonetic value. When it is unstressed it is reduced to a schwa.

4.6 PHONOLOGY SUMMARY AND IMPLICATIONS FOR SECOND LANGUAGE ACQUISITION

This section has briefly outlined what a small part of phonological competence looks like. What we know and what we know how to do as native speakers of a language are complex on many levels. Phonological competence is no exception. Second language teachers need to be aware of the complexity in order to decide how best to help second language students attain this knowledge.

It is interesting to note that although the phonological phenomena introduced above appear to create very minor effects in speech, their presence or absence is highly noticeable to native speakers. Much of the foreign accent that native speakers perceive in the case of Spanish learners of English, for example, results because Spanish speakers do not typically reduce unstressed vowels.

German learners of English also tend to transfer the phonological processes of their language into English. Thus a very salient characteristic of a German accent in English comes from the tendency of German speakers to employ final consonant devoicing in English. German speakers often pronounce the English words *hit* and *hid* in exactly the same fashion.

Finally, we would like to mention one interesting interaction of phonological processes heard among German Canadians. It seems that in some cases a German learner can combine a phonological process from his or her native language, final consonant devoicing, with one from the target language, Canadian raising, to produce a rather curious mixture. German speakers sometimes say, for example, "I have seen it with my eyes" [ʌys]. In this case, the speaker pronounces the English word *eyes* in exactly the same fashion as *ice*. Apparently, the German final devoicing rule changes the final [z] of *eyes* into a [s]. As a result of this alteration, the word becomes susceptible to Canadian raising because it now ends with a voiceless consonant. The result is a change of the [ay] to an [ʌy], yielding the mispronunciation [ʌys].

5 MORPHOLOGY

Words are the building blocks of a language, but they are often composed of smaller units of meaning called *morphemes*. A morpheme is defined as the smallest unit of meaning. Words that do not contain any smaller units of meaning, such as *dog,* are called monomorphemic. Words that do contain smaller units of meaning are termed multimorphemic. The word *ungentlemanliness,* for example, can be shown to have the constituent morphemes *un + gentle + man + ly + ness*.

At first glance it might appear that a multimorphemic word like *rewallpapering,* as in *We were rewallpapering the basement,* is simply composed of a string of units. Further inspection reveals, however, that there is more to it:

• Not all morphemes are of the same type.
• Multimorphemic words are organized hierarchically.
• Morphology allows us to produce and comprehend new words.

5.1 NOT ALL MORPHEMES ARE OF THE SAME TYPE

The word *rewallpapering* contains four morphemes. Two of these are roots and two are affixes. The two roots combine to form the compound *wallpaper*. When morphemes combine in this way they form a unit of meaning that is greater than the sum of its parts. The word *wallpaper* is not any paper on a wall. If we close our eyes and imagine wallpaper, a specific image comes to mind.

The two affixes in the word are also distinct. The morpheme *re-* is a prefix. It is dedicated to fall in a particular position in a word. Note that this differentiates it from roots in a compound, which may be exchanged to form different meanings. The word *paperwall* is an interpretable compound with a meaning that is quite distinct from *wallpaper*. The word *wallpaper-re,* formed by using the prefix as a suffix, is uninterpretable in English because a principle of English morphology has been violated. Similarly, the affix *-ing* can only perform its function in a particular location in the word. It is dedicated to acting as a suffix, and strings such as *ing-wallpaper* cannot be interpreted.[7]

There is another important difference between the affixes *re-* and *-ing*. The former is *derivational* and the latter is *inflectional*. The *re-* affix functions to change the meaning of the word and effectively turn it into another word. The affix *-ing* doesn't seem to do the same sort of thing. It doesn't make a new word, but rather makes it possible for a word to exist in a particular context. In this case the context is a sentence that requires a progressive verb: a verb ending in *-ing*. Many linguists believe that inflectional affixes really belong to the syntax of a sentence.

A final point concerning the types of morphemes in the word *rewallpapering* deals with the process of conversion. The compound *wallpaper* is a noun, yet in this word it functions as a verb. One explanation of how conversion is accomplished is that an invisible derivational affix is added to the noun *paper* to convert it to a verb. Although this may sound mystifying, it really isn't. Affixes can change the grammatical category of words. The suffix *-al,* for example, attaches to nouns and changes them into adjectives: *nation* becomes *national* and *judgment* becomes *judgmental.* Sometimes words have the same phonetic form but different grammatical categories. The word *play,* for example, can be either a noun or a verb, and the same is true of *walk.* For reasons beyond the scope of our discussion here, it is desirable to argue that the change in grammatical category results from the addition of an affix. In this case though, the affix has no phonetic content and hence is "invisible."

---

[7] A string is a sequence of elements. We can refer to a string of phonemes such as /blæk/, a string of morphemes such as *nation + al + ity,* or a string of words such as *this is a string.*

5.2 MULTIMORPHEMIC WORDS ARE ORGANIZED HIERARCHICALLY

The considerations above have consequences for how we imagine the word to be interpreted by native speakers. It seems unlikely that native speakers consider the word *rewallpapering* to mean some mixture of the meanings of its constituent morphemes. Rather, they seem to have a hierarchical interpretation based on successively larger units. They comprehend *wallpaper* as a compound noun. The head of that compound noun is then converted to a verb. Only after it is converted is it possible to interpret the *re-* prefix as referring to the repetition of an action. Finally, the suffix *-ing* is attached to allow the word to exist in a sentence like *We were rewallpapering the basement.* Note that if the sentence context were *He ___ the basement,* a different inflectional affix would be required (*-s* or *-ed*).

This process, which is simply a representation of how native speakers understand and use multimorphemic strings, is the basis for the tree diagrams that linguistics uses to illustrate word structure. Figure 2.7 shows: (1) how the nouns *wall* and *paper* are combined to form the compound *wallpaper;* (2) how understanding *wallpaper* as a verb requires that the morpheme *paper* be converted from a noun to a verb; (3) the hierarchical arrangement of morphemes in the string *rewallpaper;* and (4) how the entire string *rewallpaper* can have an inflectional suffix attached to it so that it can fit into a sentence such as *We were rewallpapering the basement.*

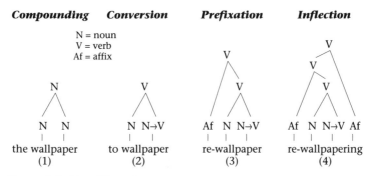

Figure 2.7   Tree Diagrams

5.3 MORPHOLOGY ALLOWS US TO PRODUCE AND COMPREHEND NEW WORDS

Understanding the relationship between how language is organized and how humans process language in the acts of comprehension and production is an important goal in the study of language. That morphemes can be organized differently in different languages suggests that humans can use morphological knowledge in a variety of ways. In many of the world's languages, morphology is so flexible that it is hard to imagine how speakers store whole words in their minds. Rather, they might produce and understand words by putting them together and taking them apart "on the fly."

Even in a language such as English, which has a relatively simple morphology, we see evidence of this. Mastery of English involves not only competence with a set vocabulary but also the ability to understand new morphological constructions using known morphemes and principles of morphology. When children are able to recognize that a Martian is somebody who lives on Mars, they are not only learning a new word but also learning about the sound changes that accompany affixation. When they realize that *ball-hockey* and *hockey-ball* mean different things they are learning about *right-headedness* in English. English compounds are referred to as right-headed because both the grammatical category and semantic features of the compound are taken from the root on the right. *Ball-hockey* thus describes a type of hockey and *hockey-ball* a type of ball. Similarly, the compound *watertight,* for example, is an adjective because the root on the right (*tight*) is an adjective.

Acquiring morphological knowledge is equally important in the area of second language learning. A learner who cannot compose and break down words during language use has not yet achieved the skills that a native speaker possesses and in this way is still handicapped in his or her language ability.

6 TRADITIONAL SYNTAX

The level of language at which we deal with how words combine and influence each other is known as *syntax*. We know that *My brothers hate dogs* means something different from *Dogs hate my brothers*. The order of the words or morphemes can alter the meaning of the sentence.

This section reviews some basic grammatical concepts in traditional terms. It will therefore not be drawing on the large literature of theoretical syntax that attempts to describe adult competence. This is a valuable literature, however, and some of its implications will be considered in Chapters 8 and 9. For now, we present some of the fundamental knowledge that teachers will find useful in order to deal with the syntax of their students: grammatical categories (Table 2.9), grammatical relations (Table 2.10), verb forms (Table 2.11), and verb tenses (Table 2.12). The information presented in the tables is by no means exhaustive.

Table 2.9   Grammatical Categories

Grammatical category (Part of speech)	Description	Example
Noun	Person, place, thing, or concept	woman, Geneva, toast, happiness
Adjectives	Describe, or modify, nouns	*fascinating* textbook, *remarkable* instructor
Prepositions	Grammatical markers indicating grammatical relations	in, out, to, by
Verbs	Action words	run, see, appear
Modal verbs	Auxiliary verbs	could, should, might
Adverbs	Describe, or modify, verbs	*frequently* drinks, *suddenly* died
Determiners[†]	Specify a particular noun	*the* dog; *a* cat; *this* wildebeest
Pronouns	Refer to other nouns. *Subject* pronouns (nominative) *Object* pronouns (accusative) *Possessive* pronouns (genitive) *Reflexive* pronouns	 I, you, she me, you, her my, mine, our myself, ourselves, her*self*[‡]

[†] The traditional term *article* is a subset of the more current term *determiner*.
[‡] Note that while *myself* and *ourselves* and most of the reflexive pronouns have the genitive pronoun as the stem, for almost all dialects of English the third person singular forms have the accusative pronoun as the stem: *him*self and *her*self.

Table 2.10   Grammatical Relations

Grammatical relation	Description	Example
Subject (Nominative)	The noun phrase to the left of the verb	*The man* on the corner is waiting for a bus. *The six plastic cups* look divine.
Direct object (Accusative)	The noun phrase after the verb	I saw *the movie*.
Indirect object (Dative)	The second noun phrase after the verb	Tom gave the books to *Bob*.

Table 2.11   Verb Forms

Base form (Infinitive)	Present participle (Progressive)	Simple past	Past participle (Perfective)
walk	walking	walked	walked
take	taking	took	taken
go	going	went	gone
have	having	had	had

Table 2.12   Verb Tenses

Tense	Description	Example
Past time		
Simple past	Used for activities that begin and end in the past	I *ate* a frog yesterday.
Past progressive	Expresses an activity that was in progress at a particular time in the past	I *was hallucinating* when the gryphons arrived.
Present perfect	Expresses activities that occurred at some unspecified time in the past	He *has driven* over the pie already.
Past perfect	Expresses an activity that occurred before another time in the past	I wasn't hungry at lunch since I *had* already *eaten* the snails.
Past perfect progressive	Refers to the duration of an activity that occurred before another time in the past	I *had been living* in Montreal for three years before I moved to Calgary.
Present time		
Simple present	For daily habits For general statements of fact	I *eat* snails every day. Water *seeks* its own level.
Present progressive	Expresses an activity that is occurring right now	I *am working*.
Present perfect progressive	Expresses the duration of an activity that is in progress	I *have been studying* for three weeks.
Future time†		
be going to		I *am going to* cry.
will		I *will* drop off the ammunition later.
Present progressive		I *am arriving* tomorrow.
Future perfect progressive	Refers to the duration of an activity that will have been completed at some point in the future	I *will have been living* in Calgary for three years next month.

† English doesn't have a future tense, but we use certain phrases to express future time.

Some basic vocabulary will also prove helpful. Verbs that are not followed by an object are called intransitive (*Bob is sleeping*). Verbs that are followed by an object are transitive (*The train hit the car*). Some verbs can be either intransitive or transitive (*Bob is studying* or *Bob is studying linguistics*). Verbs that require both a direct and an indirect object are ditransitive (*Larry gave the books to Maria*). Every verb has four forms: infinitive, progressive, simple past, and perfective, or perfect. The progressive (or continuous) form is regular, but the simple past and perfective (or completed) forms can be irregular and must be memorized.

One day, I am told, and, as it was cold,
   I suppose it occur'd in cold weather,
The NINE PARTS OF SPEECH, having no one to teach,
   Resolv'd on a PIC-NIC together.

The ARTICLE mov'd, and the PRONOUN approv'd
   That the NOUN should preside at the feast;
But the ADJECTIVE said, though the Noun might be head,
   The VERB should be none of the least.

The ADVERB cried out, "PREPOSITION, no doubt,
   Will sit at one end of the table:"
CONJUNCTION replied, "Let us sit side by side,
   And let him act as Vice who is able."

INTERJECTION said "PISH! Let me have but a dish,
   And a look at your good-humour'd faces; —
Then they who think fit may exert all their wit,
   To make a selection of places."

Now loud was the call, — ETYMOLOGY HALL!
   Run, ARTICLE; — SUBSTANTIVE, run:
My Reader, run too; and perhaps you may view
   Some scenes full of innocent fun.

The Infant's Grammar, or
A Pic-Nic Party of the Parts of Speech (1824)

Of course, there is more to syntactic competence than just knowledge of things like grammatical category. Section 7, below, will discuss some basic notions of generative approaches to syntax.

7 GENERATIVE SYNTAX

Generative syntax is the approach to syntactic structure instigated by Noam Chomsky. The theory maintains that humans have knowledge of a set of rules that allows them to generate all and only the grammatical, or well-formed, sentences in a language. One of the basic tenets of generative syntax is that sentences, like words, have an internal structure. To

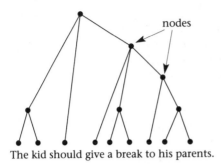

The kid should give a break to his parents.

Figure 2.8

put it another way, sentences are more than just linear strings of words. Traditional methods of sentence parsing, which involved identifying things like subjects, predicates, and direct objects, were indirectly concerned with identifying internal structure. In current syntactic models, this structure is usually represented by a syntactic tree (Figure 2.8).

Ignoring for the moment how the dots (called *nodes*) in a tree are labelled, there is an internal structure to a sentence represented this way. Certain groups of words form *constituents*. To a certain extent we have conscious intuitions about which words are grouped together. We also have a sense of which different groups of words belong to the same type. In other words, we know something about phrasal-level categories such as noun phrase (NP) or verb phrase (VP) or prepositional phrase (PP), as shown in Figure 2.9. Of course, this implies that word-level categories are also represented (Figure 2.10).

There is actually solid empirical evidence, beyond native speaker intuition, that we should represent sentences in this fashion. For example, we have morphological evidence that words do fall into grammatical, or

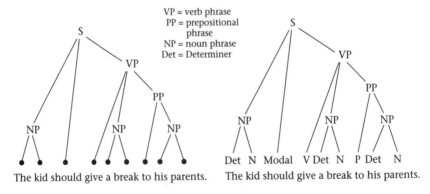

The kid should give a break to his parents.   The kid should give a break to his parents.

Figure 2.9   **Figure 2.10**

syntactic, categories. Note that many morphemes only attach to specific grammatical categories, such as English -*ed* attaching to verbs to produce past tense. It doesn't attach to other categories.[8] This gives us some sort of independent test to determine which grammatical category a lexical item belongs to. We could argue that English modal verbs (*do,* for example) form a separate grammatical category because they are not inflected for past tense in the same way as main verbs. That is to say, *shoulded, coulded,* and *musted* are ill-formed. In this way, we justify the existence of a distinct grammatical category in English: modal verbs, or modals.

We also have empirical evidence for the existence of phrasal categories such as noun phrase. Most of the evidence is syntactic. By positing the existence of phrasal-level categories, we can account for the grammaticality and ungrammaticality of certain strings. We note, for example, that only phrasal constituents can serve as sentence fragments. Consider the following exchanges (from Radford 1988):

1. *Speaker A:* Where are you going?
    Speaker B: To the movies.
               or
               The movies.

Both answers are possible because the first is a prepositional phrase and the second is a noun phrase. This can also help us to explain why certain utterances are ill-formed, as in (2):

2. *Speaker A:* What are you looking up?
    Speaker B: *Up the number.

3. *Speaker A:* What are you climbing up?
    Speaker B: Up the tree.

The reason for the grammaticality of (3) and the ungrammaticality of (2) lies in their respective syntactic structures, as shown in Figure 2.11. In the first tree we see that *up the number* is not a phrasal constituent, and

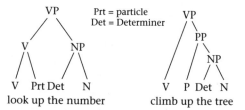

Figure 2.11   Constituent Structure of Particles versus Prepositions

---

[8] Note that when it attaches to adjectives, the phonetic realization is not the same. *Naked,* for example, is pronounced [neykəd]. If it were a verb it would be pronounced [neykt].

therefore cannot stand on its own, while in the second tree, *up the tree* is a constituent and is therefore fine as a sentence fragment.

....

7.1 PHRASE STRUCTURE

Principles that determine how a syntactic tree is built are known as *phrase structure rules* (PSRs) and traditionally take the form of the following examples:

Noun phrase (NP) → determiner + noun
Verb phrase (VP) → verb + noun phrase
Prepositional phrase (PP) → preposition + noun phrase

In more general terms, these can be represented as

NP →...N...
VP →...V...
PP →...P...

where the ellipsis dots indicate that certain unspecified elements can occur within the phrase and the N, V, and P indicate, respectively, that a noun phrase must have a noun in it, a verb phrase must have a verb in it, and a prepositional phrase must have a preposition in it. In other words, there has to be a certain connection between what is on the left side of the arrow and what is on the right side. These obligatory members of phrasal categories are known as the *heads*. The arrow is read as "rewrites as" or "expands to," so the statement VP → V NP, for example, indicates that a verb phrase can expand to, or contain, a verb plus a noun phrase (*walk + the dog*). Not every verb phrase, however, contains a noun phrase; this is just one possibility. Second language learners do not have to learn that a phrasal category has a head. It is a principle of syntax and holds for all the world's languages.

Where the world's languages do vary, though, is in the order of elements within a constituent. In English the verb is on the left of the verb phrase, for example, and the preposition is on the left of the prepositional phrase. This is not universal. There are languages in which the verb phrase has the structure VP → NP V and the prepositional phrase[9] has the structure PP → NP P.

This difference between languages is captured by the term *head*. A verb is the head of a verb phrase and a preposition is the head of a

---

[9] More accurately called a *postpositional* phrase in this case.

prepositional phrase, no matter whether they are on the left or the right side of the phrase. Languages vary in terms of whether their phrasal categories are head-left or head-right. This does have to be learned by second language learners.

7.2 SYNTACTIC MOVEMENT

The final aspect of generative syntax to be considered here is syntactic movement. Generative grammar assumes that there are different levels of syntactic representation and that when we move from one level to another in our analysis of a sentence, certain linguistic items, such as *wh* words (*who, what, where,* and so on), can also move.

To see how this works, let's consider the distribution of accusative case marking in English. English does not retain a fully productive case system. For the most part, it does not use inflections to indicate the grammatical relations of nouns within a given sentence. In other words, we can only tell whether a noun is being used as an object or a subject by its place in the sentence, not by any marker on the noun itself. Pronouns, however, are inflected. We see a difference in the pronominal forms depending on whether they are nominative or accusative (Table 2.13). This explains why we have different pronominal forms depending on whether something is the subject or the object of the sentence. In the sentence *I saw him.*, for example, the subject pronoun *I*, which comes before the verb, is in the nominative form and the object pronoun *him,* which comes after the verb, is in the accusative form.

Table 2.13 Pronominal Forms

Nominative	Accusative
I	me
you	you
he	him
she	her
we	us
they	them

Now consider how you would explain the sentence *Whom would you like to see?* Notice that the accusative form of the pronoun (*whom*) does not come after the transitive verb *see*. Perhaps our previous explanation is destroyed, and we now have to say something like this: accusative case occurs either after verbs or before them. Clearly this reduces the explanatory power considerably. It has been proposed instead that there are two levels of representation of this sentence. At one level we would find something like Figure 2.12.

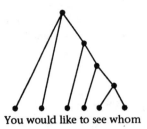

You would like to see whom

Figure 2.12   Deep Structure of "Whom would you like to see?"

To this underlying, or deep, structure a movement transformation[10] applies that moves the accusative form to the beginning of the sentence, as illustrated in Figure 2.13.[11] This analysis allows us to explain why the pronoun is in the accusative case, because at the deep-structure level of representation, it came after the transitive verb. The movement transformation changes the deep structure, generated by phrase structure rules, into the surface structure. The generative model of the grammar, then, takes the form

phrase structure rules → deep structure syntactic tree →
transformations → surface structure (modified) syntactic tree

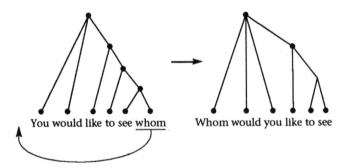

You would like to see whom   Whom would you like to see

Figure 2.13   Transforming Deep Structure into Surface Structure

The languages of the world vary in terms of where elements can move within sentences. Some languages allow certain categories to move a long way in a sentence, whereas others have much more restricted move-

---

[10] Transformations are different from phrase structure rules. Phrase structure rules *generate* syntactic trees; transformations, as their name implies, *transform* syntactic trees.

[11] The figure ignores the node labels, which are not relevant here, and another movement rule that accounts for the *would you* order in the final sentence.

ment. We will return to this in Chapters 8 and 9 in more detail. For now, it is relevant to note that this is part of the syntax that a second language learner has to acquire.

8 GRAMMATICAL SUMMARY

The basic terminology presented above is necessary in order to discuss the grammatical competence of a learner. As well, many second language learners have been taught the same terminology in their home countries. Although communicative language teaching does not emphasize formal grammatical instruction, it does include it at times. Knowledge of the fundamental vocabulary will give second language teachers access to grammar books and will help them to avoid embarrassment if a student asks a question couched in this not-so-mysterious terminology.

We have also discussed some of the principles of generative syntax. These can show us exactly what a second language learner is acquiring: sentences with a complex internal structure that includes

- word-level grammatical categories
- phrasal-level grammatical categories
- principles of phrase structure
- constraints on movement

9 CONCLUSION

This chapter has looked at some of the characteristics of phonetic, phonological, morphological, and syntactic—or grammatical—competence. As native speakers of a particular language, we are often unaware of its structural complexity. The chapter has used examples that illustrate the necessity of knowing about the structure of the linguistic code being taught.

SELF TEST

A human language is a _____ system. In other words, the rela-
(1)
tionship between the sign and the meaning or concept is
_____ . The system of knowledge that we have of a language is
(2)
known as a _____ . Chomsky suggests that the goals of lin-
(3)
guistics are to: (1) _____ the system of knowledge of native
(4)

speakers; (2) account for how it was _____ ; (3) account for
how it is _____ ; and (4) describe the physical mechanisms
(6)
responsible for _____ and processing of this system of
(7)
knowledge.

Knowledge of language includes knowledge of the phonology, morphology, and syntax. If the vocal folds are vibrating, a sound is said to be
_____ . An articulatory description of [p] is a _____ ,
(8)   (9)
_____ , _____ . The actual articulation of a sound,
(10)   (11)
however, can depend upon its phonetic _____ . In Canadian
(12)
English, [aw] becomes [ʌw] before _____ consonants.
(13)

When we look at word structure, we note that words have an internal
_____ structure. Principles of morphology capture our ability
(14)
to _____ and _____ words we've never encoun-
(15)   (16)
tered before.

Nouns, verbs, and so on are examples of _____ categories.
(17)
These word-level categories can be combined into _____ -level
(18)
categories such as NP and VP. Even though some of these constituents
can move, there are _____ on the movement. This is all part
(19)
of what the second language learner and the second language researcher
need to know.

FURTHER READING

Phonological Competence

Avery, Peter, and Susan Ehrlich. 1992. *Teaching American English Pronunciation*. Oxford: Oxford University Press.

Kaye, J. 1989. *Phonology: A Cognitive View*. Hillsdale, NJ: Erlbaum.

Morphological Competence

Bauer, L. 1988. *Introducing Linguistic Morphology*. Edinburgh: Edinburgh University Press.

Jensen, J. 1990. *Morphology: Word Structure in Generative Grammar*. Amsterdam: John Benjamins.

Syntactic Competence

Cowper, E. 1992. *A Concise Introduction to Government-Binding Syntax.* Chicago: University of Chicago Press.

Haegeman, L. 1991. *Government and Binding Theory.* Cambridge, MA: Blackwell.

Larsen-Freeman, D. and M. Celce-Murcia. 1986. *The Grammar Book.* Cambridge, MA: Newbury House.

3

......

Language, Learning, and Mind

The study of second language learning explores how individuals come to possess the knowledge and skills that constitute second language ability. Our views of the nature of second language knowledge and of how such knowledge is acquired will ultimately depend on broader conceptions of certain fundamental issues:

- What is the nature of the human mind?
- What is learning?
- What is language?

These are big questions and they undoubtedly do not have simple answers. Nevertheless, all approaches to second language learning assume particular answers to them. Often these assumptions are implicit, vague, and fragmentary. In all cases, however, they profoundly influence the kinds of phenomena considered worthy of investigation and the kinds of explanations considered plausible or implausible.

This chapter outlines some fundamental conceptions of the nature of *mind, learning,* and *language* that are relevant to the study of second language acquisition. We will find that opinions in these three areas tend to come in "packages"; a particular view of mind will only be compatible with particular views of learning and of language. The latter sections of the chapter discuss one of these packages in some depth: the theory of language and mind proposed by linguist Noam Chomsky.

1 THE INITIAL STATE OF MIND: EMPIRICISM VERSUS RATIONALISM

Humans are influenced by the forces that act upon them, but in most cases the effect of these forces is not direct. Rather, it is mediated by what we conventionally call mind: the organization of knowledge, beliefs, values, emotions, and so on that makes up our internal mental state. Just about everybody will agree that we need to posit some form of mind in order to account for human behaviour. Explanations usually take the form shown in Figure 3.1. The figure represents the view that experience acts upon the human mind and creates a system of knowledge. The development of this system influences not only the subsequent behaviour of the individual but also the effect that future experience will have.

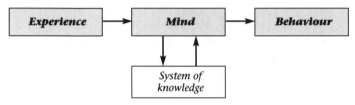

Figure 3.1   The Interaction of Experience, Mind, and Behaviour

This chapter focusses on just one of these systems of knowledge: language. How does it develop? Can a human language take any form? Can the human mind acquire any language? These questions force us to think about the beginning of knowledge acquisition in the child. If, for example, a baby's mind is essentially blank at birth and systems of knowledge are determined solely by the developing child's experience, then we should imagine that just about anything is possible. A child growing up in an English environment will acquire English; a child growing up in a Japanese environment will acquire Japanese; a child growing up in a Martian environment will acquire Martian. Under this view, the mind is essentially a sponge. It will absorb anything to which it is exposed.

A contrasting point of view is that we begin the knowledge acquisition process with a richly structured mind capable of acquiring only certain kinds of knowledge systems. In the case of language, the child comes to the world with a set of principles that make the acquisition of any natural human language easy and the acquisition of a non-human language (such as Martian) impossible, because the structure of the mind places constraints on the form that human language can take.

These positions represent two ends of a continuum in a philosophical debate that is over four hundred years old (see Mathews 1989;

Demopoulos 1989). The belief that the mind is blank at birth is commonly referred to as *empiricism* and is associated with the philosopher David Hume. The position that the mind has innate capacities is known as *rationalism* and is associated with the French philosopher René Descartes. In the seventeenth and eighteenth centuries, theories of the acquisition of concepts formed the battleground for these opposing points of view. Now, attention has shifted to acquisition of language. Language acquisition has become the arena of dispute for linguists, philosophers, and psychologists because, it is argued, it is the one domain in which we have a good, independently motivated description of *what* is learned. Thus we can tackle such issues as *how* with more success.

David Hume was a Scottish philosopher who lived from 1711 to 1776. He wrote *A Treatise of Human Nature* in his mid-twenties. Hume systematically developed John Locke's and George Berkeley's views and is known for scepticism about inferences beyond what can actually be experienced. Empiricists such as Hume assign a major role to the environment in human learning. In this paradigm, one of the most common metaphors for the mind is a tablet of hot wax. Everything in the mind is created by impressions from the outside world, from experience. This does not mean that empiricists do not endow the mind with any innate structure; they do. Nonetheless, they do not believe that this structure places any restrictions on what forms of knowledge can be acquired. The sponge-like mind is thought to be capable of representing any generalizations that might underlie the linguistic input. It is thus innately capable of inductive procedures, and there are no restrictions on the kinds of knowledge it is possible to develop. In the case of language, an individual's knowledge structure—his or her grammar—may thus take any form.

Contrasted with empiricists are rationalists such as René Descartes. Descartes was a seventeenth-century French philosopher who lived from 1596 to 1650. On 11 November 1619, he had a series of dreams that inspired him to found a new philosophical and scientific system based upon a method of doubt: "I resolved to reject as false everything in which I could imagine the least doubt, in order to see if there afterwards remained anything that was entirely indubitable." It was this that led him to pronounce, "Je pense, donc je suis" (I think, therefore I am). His works include *Meditations on First Philosophy, Geometry,* and *Discourse on Method.* Rationalists endow the human mind with many innate capabilities. A metaphor for their view of the mind is a dark museum. Whatever is in the museum is in there from the start; it just has to be found or activated. As we will see in our discussion of Noam Chomsky, the rationalist view claims that both language acquisition and the forms it is possible for actual human languages to take are severely restricted by the innate linguistic structures with which we are born.

2 LEARNING

So far the discussion has outlined two contrasting positions about the initial state of the mind. Our focus in what follows will be on how that condition is affected by experience so that a new state is created and systems of knowledge develop.

2.1 EMPIRICIST AND RATIONALIST THEORIES OF LEARNING

As one might imagine, empiricists and rationalists typically see human learning in markedly different ways. Because empiricists posit very little innate knowledge at birth, their accounts of learning place great importance on the role of the environment in shaping knowledge and on inductive learning procedures. Induction is a process of deriving generalizations about the properties of the input in the environment: the properties of things to which the human mind is exposed. It moves from the particular to the general. In the case of language, the particular is the linguistic input and the general is the linguistic rules. An inductive procedure should be able to derive the rules underlying any input.

Rationalist learning, on the other hand, proceeds by deduction. Deduction is a process of drawing conclusions from principles that are already known. It moves from the general to the particular. In the case of language, the general is known as universal grammar and the particular is language-specific grammar. Universal grammar (UG) describes the initial state of the human mind with respect to language; it is what we are born with. Rationalist learning theorists do not claim that the environment plays no role in learning, but they do argue that innate knowledge determines how the child makes sense of events in the environment.

Empiricism and rationalism are best seen as extremes at either end of a continuum rather than as discrete alternatives. In this century, three important theorists have established positions along the continuum that bring the differences between empiricism and rationalism as they relate to learning into clear focus: B.F. Skinner, Noam Chomsky, and Jean Piaget.

2.1.1 Skinnerian Behaviourism

Behaviourism is a form of empiricism. Undoubtedly the most important figure to consider in the area of behaviourism as it relates to language is B.F. Skinner. Skinner drew on the work of Ivan Petrovich Pavlov (1849–1936), who is best known for experiments in which dogs were trained to salivate in response to a tuning fork sounding. Skinner extended the work of Pavlov in his major book *The Behavior of Organisms* (1938). Backed by many experiments and hard data, Skinner applied such concepts as stimulus, response, and reinforcement and introduced the concept of *operant conditioning*. While Pavlov's classical conditioning focussed on the association between a signal (a tuning fork) and a reinforcer (food), Skinner emphasized the association between an action (such as a rat pressing a bar, or a human talking) and a reinforcer. He attempted to apply his system to language learning in 1957, when he published *Verbal Behavior*. In contrast to *The Behavior of Organisms*, *Verbal Behavior* was a completely speculative exercise. Even a cursory glance will reveal that it contains little hard data. If we return to our previous schema of human learning, we can see that a behaviourist view attempts to bypass the middle elements (see Figure 3.2).

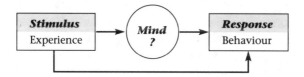

Figure 3.2   The Behaviourist View

The behaviourist position is that stimulus and response can be directly linked with no intervention from the organism. Twadell (1935) made this quite clear when he stated, "The scientific method is quite simply the convention that mind does not exist." Behaviourism, then, is a radical form of empiricism. (Other empiricist accounts of learning are less extreme, and empiricism itself has not been discredited.) Behaviourism assigns an important role to experience and considers the role of the learner minimal. Learning involves the acquisition not so much of a system of knowledge as of a set of automatic habits.

2.1.2 Chomsky and the Critique of Empiricist Learning

Even though Skinner and behaviourism influenced second-language pedagogy for many years, *Verbal Behavior* was attacked almost immediately in the academic community. The primary offensive came from Noam Chomsky, who published a review of Skinner's work (Chomsky 1959). Chomsky presented two types of criticism. The first dealt with Skinner's use of terminology such as *stimulus* and *reinforcer*. Chomsky pointed out that readers had two options in interpreting these and other terms. If they chose broader metaphorical definitions, then Skinner's theory did not add anything new to the field of language learning. If they investigated Skinner's assertion that his was a precise theory, then fundamental weaknesses were revealed. Even such basic terms as *stimulus* were not rigorously defined. It was impossible to determine what the stimulus was until the behaviour occurred. If someone looked at a red chair and said "red," for example, then the stimulus was redness. If he or she said "chair," then it was chairness. If the person said "What's your brother's name?" it would be very difficult to determine the stimulus. If its basic terms are not rigorously defined, a theory is not falsifiable.

In addition, Chomsky presented rationalist criticisms of an empiricist view. If learners are merely imitating what they have heard, for example, how can they both comprehend and produce sentences that they have never heard before? Chomsky also pointed out that there is an internal system to the learner's grammar; it is not merely a bad imitation of the adult/native grammar. Children produce forms such as *goed, comed,* and *putted,* for example, without ever hearing an adult say them. The forms are generated by the child's version of a rule for past tense formation that is different from the adult's. Chomsky's concept of a learner system, and indeed his focus on the learner, proved to have far-reaching consequences in second language acquisition research, as we shall see.

Noam Chomsky is institute professor of linguistics at the Massachusetts Institute of Technology. He is undoubtedly the most influential linguist of our time. In 1957 he published a book called *Syntactic Structures,* which revolutionized twentieth-century linguistics and ushered in the rigorous study of theoretical syntax. His publications since then have continued to reform the field of linguistics. He is responsible for such concepts as generative syntax, transformations, universal grammar (UG), and government and binding theory. He is probably the only linguist you will ever see on television. A concise formulation of Chomsky's view of Skinner's approach is reflected in a 1983 interview that he gave to *Omni* magazine:

Omni: How do you think your view differs from B.F. Skinner's behaviorist theory of language, learning, and mind?

Chomsky: Skinner used to take a relatively extreme position. At one point he held that apart from the most rudimentary functions, essentially nothing of importance was genetically programmed in the human brain. Skinner agreed that humans were genetically programmed to see and hear, but that's about all. Accordingly, he argued that human behavior was simply a reflection of training and experience. This view can't possibly be correct. And, in fact, Skinner's approach has led absolutely nowhere in this area. It has yielded no theoretical knowledge, no nontrivial principles as far as I'm aware—thus far, at any rate.

Omni: Why is that?

Chomsky: Because Skinnerian behaviorism is off the wall. It's as hopeless a project as trying to explain that the onset of puberty results from social training.

Skinner himself seemed to acknowledge some of Chomsky's points in 1988 (Catania and Harnad 1988, 364), when he came as close as he ever did to responding to Chomsky: "My book *Verbal Behavior* (1957) was an interpretation, not an explanation, and it is merely useful, not true or false." This, however, does seem to be a direct contradiction of the purported goal of the book. Skinner (1957, 12) states, "The ultimate aim is the prediction and control of verbal behavior." In an appendix to *Verbal Behavior*, we find a description of a dinner at which both Skinner and Alfred North Whitehead were present. Whitehead (1861–1947) was a mathematician and philosopher who co-authored *Principia Mathematica* with Bertrand Russell. Whitehead was skeptical of Skinner's theories and challenged him to use his theory to account for the fact that Whitehead was saying *No black scorpion is falling on this table*. Not surprisingly, Skinner had difficulty.

Soon after Chomsky's criticisms, the world of psychology began to question many of Skinner's claims. In particular, the work of David Ausubel (1965) reinforced the new discipline of cognitive psychology. A crucial distinction for Ausubel was between *rote* and *meaningful* learning. Essentially, behaviourists viewed all learning as rote: the acquisition of isolated facts, somewhat like trying to remember thousands of phone numbers. Ausubel, like Chomsky, proposed that we must not ignore the contribution of the organism to the learning process. Ausubel states, "From the standpoint of cognitive theorists, the attempt to ignore conscious states or to reduce cognition to mediational processes reflective of implicit behavior not only removes from the field of psychology what is most worth studying, but also dangerously oversimplifies highly complex psychological phenomena" (1965).

His concept of meaningful learning reflects this. For meaningful learning to take place, learners must be able to integrate the input into their existing cognitive complex. They must be able to hang new knowledge on existing cognitive pegs. McLaughlin (1987) maintains, "All learning involves restructuring of the cognitive framework by linking previously isolated procedures into a unified representation framework." We can trace this back as far as James (1890), who believed that "in mental terms, the more other facts a fact is associated with in the mind, the better possession of it our memory retains."

2.1.3 Piaget: The Middle Ground

The third theorist to be considered in this discussion of empiricist and rationalist perspectives on learning is Swiss psychologist Jean Piaget. Piaget was born in 1896 in Neuchâtel, Switzerland. He was professor of child psychology at the University of Geneva and director of the Centre for Genetic Epistemology until his death in 1980. Piaget's early studies were in zoology, specifically mollusks, but he later switched to more complex organisms. He pioneered the study of cognitive development in children. Among his works are *The Language and Thought of the Child*, *The Child's Conception of the World*, and *The Mechanisms of Perception*. Piaget described himself as an anti-empiricist. His ontological beliefs were halfway between the empiricist and the innatist (rationalist) traditions. In contrast to behaviourists, he was very much concerned with the nature of mind and the development of cognition in childhood. Nevertheless, his views also differed from the rationalist views of Noam Chomsky.

Piaget saw children as active, constructive agents who slowly progressed in a kind of perpetual bootstrapping operation. He proposed four developmental stages that children move through:

1. *Period of sensory-motor intelligence.* From birth and for a short time after babies' behaviour is automatic, or reflexive. A stimulus is received and the motor response is automatic. By the age of two, though, children have learned to make sensory-motor adjustments to their environment. Children will learn, for example, to close their eyes and draw back their heads when things come close to their faces.
2. *Period of pre-operational thought.* According to Piaget, in this stage children learn to manipulate the environment symbolically. They learn that an object that is out of sight, for example, such as a toy hidden under a blanket, still exists.
3. *Period of concrete operations.* Children's ability to understand symbols grows until they have developed an organized symbolic system. This period lasts until about thirteen years of age, and during it children's perception over-rides logic. In a well-known experiment, Piaget would show children at this stage two identical glasses with identical measures of liquid and ask them if the glasses contained the same amount. They consistently answered yes. Then the children watched as the contents of one glass were poured into a thinner, taller glass, so that the liquid level was higher. This time, according to Piaget, when asked the same question children consistently answered no.
4. *Period of formal operations.* In this stage, children are able to consider the results of activities. The period lasts throughout adolescence. Adolescents understand relations such as cause and effect and other logical connections.

Chomsky, on the other hand, sees the mind as a set of essentially pre-programmed units, each of which is equipped from the start to realize its full potential and needs only a modest environmental trigger to exhibit its abilities. He maintains that the environment has no structure, or at least none that the organism can directly assimilate. Order is imposed on the perceptual world, not derived from it. The difference in emphasis between the two can be summed up by saying that Chomsky is concerned with determining humanity's common innate endowment, whereas Piaget is concerned with describing humanity's universal path of development.

To a large extent, the differences between Chomsky and Piaget emerge from their fundamentally different views of the nature of mind. For Piaget, the mind is an all-purpose discovery tool which shows general development as the child grows older. For Chomsky, the mind is a collection of organs (just as the heart and the liver are organs). Language is one of these organs. It develops according to a biological timetable in a very specific fashion. Chomsky claims that we should not expect to discover a general learning theory any more than we would expect to discover a general growth theory.

Whether or not Piaget's theoretical accounts of cognitive development are accurate, it is almost universally agreed that he has made a very important contribution to the field of cognition. He brought the study of the child to the forefront of psychology and has provided science with a wealth of observation through his voluminous writings. Gardner (1980) summarizes Piaget's contributions:

> The phenomena he discerns offer a convincing series of snapshots of how development proceeds, but the specific terms he has devised and the models he has formulated have fared less well in the face of rigorous criticism. At most, Piaget's adventures into technical vocabulary and formal models offer a convenient way of synthesizing the enormous amount of data he has accumulated. In the end, it is his overall *vision* of how capacities relate and how knowledge in its varied forms develops that inspires workers in the field.

2.2 MEMORY: THE APPARATUS OF LEARNING

So far we have seen that different theorists can hold very different views about the fundamental nature of mind. The discussion of Skinner, Chomsky, and Piaget has shown that these views are not simply isolated in the realm of philosophy but rather, play decisive roles in theories of learning. This section focusses on another decisive component of a theory of learning: the mind's apparatus for representation. It seems clear that learning involves changes to the mind and that these changes must be represented in some form or other. In the field of psychology, where much of the work on learning has taken place, the dominant term used to refer to mental representations is *memory*. In this case, the term is used in a very restricted sense. It refers only to the representation of information in the mind and not directly to its retrieval.

The field of memory is very rich and broad. What follows outlines some of the major types of memory postulated and explores their relevance to both language representation in the mind and acquisition of a second language.

2.2.1 Short-Term versus Long-Term Memory

The word *memory* refers to the human capacity to represent information. Research by psychologists has identified two fundamental types of information representation, or storage. The first is *short-term* memory. This is the type we use when we have looked up a number in the telephone book and need to represent it in our minds long enough to dial the correct number. A key characteristic of this type of memory is that it decays rather quickly and is of limited capacity.

In 1956, George Miller published a now famous paper entitled "The magical number seven plus or minus two: Some limits on our capacity for processing information." In it he presented data and arguments indicating that human beings can consciously think about roughly seven things at a time. Now, what is particularly interesting about Miller's findings, and very relevant to second language acquisition, is that these seven things may be simple or complex. We can hold on to seven letters at a time, seven words at a time, and, under some circumstances, seven sentences at a time. The general conclusion to be drawn here is that short-term memory has a limited capacity of seven items plus or minus two, but if the items are highly organized (phonemes ordered into words, for example) they may each contain a lot of information. This characteristic of short-term memory is used in many mnemonic devices, or tricks that aid in recall. We notice, for example, that holding a ten-digit telephone number in short-term memory is rather difficult. The task becomes much easier if we organize the ten units into three: a three-digit area code, a three-digit exchange, and a four-digit number.

It is short-term memory that we use to carry on an everyday conversation. We are able to retain what was said to us long enough to respond appropriately. As soon as we have responded, however, we typically forget the particular words that were used by the other speaker and retain only the meaning of the utterance. This is an example of the rapid decay of short-term memory. It is also interesting to note that native speakers are not limited to being able to understand sentences only seven phonemes long or even seven words long. Their grammatical ability probably allows them to group phonemes quickly into words and words into phrases and phrases into larger phrases so that it is possible to represent very long utterances in short-term memory. Second language learners, on the other hand, do not have native speaker grammatical ability. In many cases a language learner's inability to understand an utterance can be traced to lack of syntactic organization and a consequent "overload" of short-term memory.

Short-term memory appears to have two primary functions. It serves as a temporary storage area for expendable representations, such as telephone numbers. It also stores representations that are going to be recoded into a more efficient and permanent form. This seems to be the role of short-term memory in conversation. The surface structure of the sentence is apparently held in short-term memory long enough to be recoded and stored in a more permanent semantic form. The relatively permanent mental repository of information is called *long-term* memory.

Representation of information in long-term memory is assumed to be qualitatively different from that in short-term memory. The information is organized, not stored in its original form. It is therefore represented in terms of its meaning more than of its physical or acoustic properties. Information introduced into long-term memory must be integrated into existing information rather than stored individually.

When information cannot be retrieved from short-term memory it is assumed to be lost, in the sense that the memory representation has decayed. When information cannot be retrieved from long-term memory on the other hand, it is assumed that the representation remains intact but that access to it has been lost.

Thus, long-term memory is what we know. The next section examines a fundamental distinction in long-term memory between what we know about our lives in the world and what we know about the world itself.

2.2.2 Semantic versus Episodic Memory

In 1972, psychologist Endel Tulving proposed a terminological distinction between *semantic* and *episodic* memory. This may capture the difference between two types of human knowledge.

Episodic memory is the memory of episodes or events in one's life. It encompasses where and when an episode occurred as well as information about the episode itself. Episodic memory is always growing. It can be viewed as a slow-moving conveyor belt carrying memories further and further back into the depths of our minds. New information is placed on the beginning of the belt. To make room for future information, new information is moved a little further back each day. It is thus assumed that childhood memories are never really lost but have been moved back so far on the conveyor belt that they are very difficult to retrieve.

Semantic memory is fundamentally different from episodic memory. It is the organized knowledge we have of the world and of the symbol system we use. It therefore contains our knowledge of language, mathematics, music, and so on. Unlike episodic memory, semantic memory contains elaborate relationships between elements and rules for the manipulation of elements. It is believed that native speakers use the knowledge contained within semantic memory to understand and produce sentences of their language. This type of knowledge allows us to solve arithmetic problems that we have never seen before and to understand sentences that we have never seen before, such as most of the ones in this text.

Any university course should effect changes in a student's semantic memory. Sometimes these are immediately evident; sometimes it takes a while for the new information to be integrated into existing structures of semantic memory. Often a student will understand how things "fit together" only after graduation.

Acquiring a second language may represent the greatest change in semantic memory possible for an adult. Successful second language acquisition requires that an entirely new system of rules and representations be developed. It also demands that the system be completely integrated into all aspects of semantic memory. One must be able to use the new language to talk about what one knows, to assimilate new knowledge, and to translate between the new language and the native language. It is clear that a deeper understanding of the structure of human semantic memory will have great consequences for understanding second language learning.

2.2.3 Working Memory

The last type of memory considered here is *working* memory. The concept of human working memory has been borrowed from research in computer science and artificial intelligence. It has been found that a computer program typically requires the ability to represent intermediate calculations in memory in order to solve a problem. This type of memory is a sort of "scratch pad."

In humans, working memory is seen as a special type of short-term memory. We use it when we solve problems or decode linguistic messages. Part of the difficulty associated with processing complex sentences can be attributed to the demands that they make on working memory resources. Processing a fairly complex and ambiguous sentence like *The cat that Bill owned and Bob fed died because he left him outside the door all night* makes high demands on working memory. When the listener actually hears the pronoun *he*, it is not clear at all whether it refers to Bill, Bob, the cat, or someone else. The various possibilities must be represented and held in working memory for future resolution. Now, when the word *him* is heard, things get even worse because the same possibilities exist. It could refer to Bill or Bob or the cat, or someone else entirely. Again, working memory resources are required to consider these possibilities, calculate possible solutions, and hold onto the various hypotheses about who did what to whom. Only when the last five words of the sentence are heard—*outside the door all night*—can the reasonable assumption be made that *he* is probably (but not certainly) Bob and that *him* is probably the cat.

Recent research has shown that impairment in working memory resulting from damage to the brain can have devastating consequences for language comprehension and production. It has also been found that using working memory for language is a highly practised skill. Much of the task of second language acquisition involves developing efficient use of working memory.

2.3 THE NEUROPSYCHOLOGY OF LEARNING

Up to now, we have been focussing on *mental* models of learning: on the mind rather than the brain. Traditionally, researchers concerned with cognition were able to develop mental models that did not necessarily refer to neurology, primarily because not enough was known about neurological structures and processes to propose a neurologically plausible model. Kandel and Hawkins note, however, that "over the past several decades, there has been a gradual merger of two originally separate fields of science: neurobiology, the science of the brain, and cognitive psychology, the science of the mind" (1992, 79).

There is a growing literature on the neuropsychology of learning, and some of it has direct application to language acquisition. Jacobs and Schumann (1992), for example, argue that the field of language acquisition should take more notice of what is going on in the neurosciences. Through a variety of technologies (such as positron emission tomography, or PET), information is being gathered on how learning takes place at a neural level. Kandel and Hawkins (1992), for example, provide a quite accessible overview of their findings: that two different types of learning, which they call *explicit* and *implicit* learning, are characterized by different molecular activity. Astonishingly, we seem to be approaching a molecular biology of learning. Although this has not led to chemical treatments in the second language classroom, neuropsychology has had an effect on certain theories of learning applied to language acquisition.

Probably the framework most influenced by neuropsychology is *connectionism*. Connectionist, or parallel-distributed processing (PDP), models are computer models designed to simulate human performance (Rumelhart and McClelland 1986a, 1986b; MacWhinney 1987a, 1987b; Spolsky 1989). They have been built to account for such diverse phenomena as word perception, memory, stereoscopic vision, and others. Connectionist researchers accept the computational metaphor of human cognition, of the mind/brain as a kind of information processor (Pylyshyn 1984; Jackendoff 1987; Carroll 1989a). They see the microstructure of human thought as a processing system composed of thousands of individual units, or nodes. Each unit is like a neuron and, like a neuron, is connected to many other units. A system of connected units can carry out a cognitive function, such as learning to navigate uneven terrain, for example, or learning the past tense of a verb.

The goal of connectionist models is to characterize how the brain performs cognitive functions at the neural level. The characterization is functional but not necessarily structural. It is therefore referred to as *functional architecture*. The proposed model is assumed to imitate the function in question and be neurologically (or structurally) plausible, but it is not necessarily accepted that humans actually have this exact kind of neural network hardware in their brains.

The basic structure of the network model is shown in Figure 3.3. The input units (on the left) contain the information that the programmer enters. If the network were to learn the past tense of verbs, for example, the input might be the verb *help* or *walk*. The output units represent the network's guess at what the output pattern should be. A training session is used to teach the model which output units should be activated in order to produce the correct pattern. During the training session, the network is presented with input/output pairs such as *walk/walked, go/went, sing/sang,* and *pray/prayed* and trained to associate them. (This is what the pattern associator does). The goal is to have the network learn to deal with novel input. After the sample training session just described, could the network predict that the correct phonetic output for *bake* [beyk] is *baked* [beykt]? How does the network learn?

It is clear that the connections allow the units in the system to interact with each other. If one unit is activated then all units attached to it are also affected. Each connection has a weight, or strength. Associations that are frequent in the input (such as *go/went*) will lead to stronger connections than infrequent pairs (such as *cling/clung*). If the weight of all the connections touching a particular node reaches a certain threshold—called the activation threshold—then the node in question is activated.

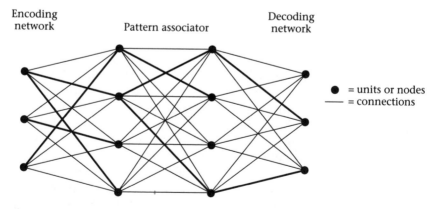

Encoding network   Pattern associator   Decoding network

● = units or nodes
—— = connections

Figure 3.3   Basic Structure of a Connectionist Model

Knowledge in a connectionist model is found in the units and is represented by a pattern of activation over the units. At any given time, then, what the system is representing (in terms of an activation pattern) is what it knows. Thus knowledge is *distributed* over the system, which is why connectionist models are also known as parallel distributed processors. They are capable of learning patterns of activation over units by modifying the weights of the connections between units. The training session allows the model to establish the correct weights to produce the appropriate output. Learning in a connectionist model is a matter of finding the right connection strengths so that the appropriate output pattern will be produced under the right circumstances. So, if the network has been trained and is then exposed to the form *cling,* it would note that it had strong connections (the heavier lines in Figure 3.3) with *ring/rang* and *sing/sang.* The best guess of the network might therefore be *clang.* A connectionist network learns on the basis of the patterns it has noted in the input. It is worth remarking that this places it firmly within the empiricist camp.

Computer models have addressed issues in both first language acquisition (Stemberger 1992) and second language acquisition (MacWhinney 1987b; Gass 1987; Kilborn and Cooreman 1987; Harrington 1987; and McDonald 1987). Rumelhart and McClelland (1986b), for example, attempt to account for one aspect of first language acquisition: past tense endings in English and their over-regularization. It is common for children learning English as a first language to move through a sequence of developmental stages in learning the past tense. In the first stage, they produce the correct forms of irregular verbs (such as *went*). This is most probably an input-driven effect resulting from rote memorization. During the second stage they overgeneralize and treat those verbs as if they were regular (*goed*). Finally, at the third stage, they treat irregular verbs as the exceptional forms they are. The sequence can be written as

went → goed → went

When children exhibit this behaviour it is often explained by saying that they have acquired the productive rule for the formation of the past tense. In other words, they have learned to produce the past tense by adding the suffix *-ed* to the verb. Rumelhart and McClelland argue on the basis of their connectionist network, however, that the representations and procedures used in language processing can be characterized without reference to rules even though the behaviour of the network may conform to a set of rules. In other words, rule-governed behaviour does not necessarily indicate that those rules are represented. The orbit of the earth is governed by rules; it is systematic and predictable. Yet this does not mean that the earth knows the equations that describe its orbit.

A connectionist network has no rule of past-tense formation. All it does is find patterns, modify connections, and activate nodes.

It is undeniable that the field of cognitive science, including second language acquisition, will continue to see a great deal of work in the connectionist paradigm. The interested reader may wish to consult Klein (1990) and Pinker and Prince (1988) for an extended discussion of the pros and cons of connectionist cognitive architecture.

2.4 SIGNIFICANCE OF LEARNING THEORY FOR SLA

The psychological theories of memory discussed above demonstrate the complexity of how information is represented in the human brain. We have seen that the way in which it is stored determines how we can use it. All human learning results in a change in memory representations, and all learning requires memory (temporary and scratch pad storage).

It may be possible to characterize language learning solely in terms of memory. Varied language teaching methods may induce students to store the second language information in different ways. Particular classroom techniques may be more or less adequate with respect to how much they encourage students to use short-term and working memory efficiently, though this remains an area for empirical research.

The connectionist perspective on knowledge representation and learning is particularly challenging. It is constructed on a neurological model of simple processors (neurons) and pathways between them. Pathways can be strengthened or weakened as a result of experience. The connectionists offer an account of language without assuming that languages, words, or meanings are actually stored as symbolic representations in the mind. For them, the mind is composed of huge networks of connections built up from experience. There are neither any language centres per se nor any principles of acquisition unique to language. The connectionist approach is thus more like the empiricist approach of Skinner than the rationalist approach of Chomsky. A connectionist account of second language acquisition makes use of general principles of reinforcement and feedback and describes the phenomenon of second language acquisition as a network reorganization.

It is important to note that connectionist, behaviourist, and Piagetian views of language acquisition share an important feature. They all assume that the mind is a general device for learning and representation. Chomsky's view of mind, however, is rather different. He proposes that the mind's organization is modular, and he employs the metaphor of mental organs to elucidate his view. Chomsky argues that mental organs work together as the organs of the body do to, say, circulate and oxygenate blood. While it is true that the heart and lungs work together, the lungs will never be able to pump blood and the heart will never be able to breathe. The section below examines modularity of mind in greater depth.

3 MODULARITY OF MIND

The question of whether the organization of mind is modular has both theoretical and practical consequences. Theoretically, the position one adopts will significantly affect how one views linguistic knowledge. Practically, the modularity hypothesis suggests that second language acquisition must take the special nature of language knowledge into consideration. It claims, for example, that highly effective techniques in teaching mathematics may be utter failures in teaching language. For these reasons, the issue of modularity currently receives a lot of attention in the philosophy of mind and in linguistics (see Garfield 1987). Chomsky sets the stage for the discussion when he says,

> There are a number of cognitive systems which seem to have quite distinct and specific properties.... The language faculty is one of these cognitive systems. There are others. For example, our capacity to organize visual space, or to deal with abstract properties of the number system, or to comprehend and appreciate certain kinds of musical creation, or our ability to make sense of the social structures in which we play a role, which undoubtedly reflects conceptual structures that have developed in the mind, and any number of other mental capacities. As far as I can see ... they appear to have quite specific and unique properties (1983, 33).

Chomsky (1984) outlines some characteristics of modular approaches to the study of mind; the metaphor of mental organs captures the idea that the various cognitive systems are separate. He notes that the traditional Cartesian view does not support the concept of modularity but instead sees the mind as "entirely indivisible." This view is also adopted by a range of people from Skinner to Piaget (which, as Chomsky notes, includes just about everyone). Piaget does assume a kind of modularity in the stages of cognitive development but for each stage the principles proposed are uniform across all cognitive domains, such as mathematics, language, vision, and so on.

As a general argument, Chomsky suggests that "every complex biological system we know is highly modular in its internal structure. It should not be a terrible surprise to discover that the human mind is just like other complex biological systems: that it is composed of interacting subsystems with their specific properties and character and with specific modes of interaction among the various parts" (1984, 16).

Probably the best known proponent of a modular view of the human mind is Jerry Fodor, particularly in his 1983 monograph, *The Modularity of Mind*. Jackendoff (1987) also maintains a modular position. In the opinion of this text, there appears to be a considerable body of evidence to support a modular view of mind, in which language is a separate cognitive domain. Thus, language acquisition must be explained with reference to principles specific to the language faculty, not by a set of principles constraining cognitive systems more generally.

EVIDENCE FROM ABNORMAL ACQUISITION

Curtiss (1988) presents some interesting evidence for the modularity hypothesis from abnormal language acquisition. She discusses the tragic case of Genie, an abused girl (see also Curtiss 1977). Genie was discovered by the authorities at the age of thirteen. Until that time she had been kept confined in an attic and had not been allowed to make any noise. Nor was anyone allowed to speak to her. In addition, she was severely malnourished when discovered. Not surprisingly, Genie had not acquired language in her state of captivity. Upon being placed in the care of the state, however, Genie received a great deal of professional help and attention.

By looking at Genie, Curtiss (1988) found some support for modularity. Genie's utterances had severe grammatical problems, such as little inflectional morphology, omission of obligatory constituents, lack of syntactic devices marking embedding, and so on:

Man motorcycle have.
Tummy water drink.
Genie bad cold live father house (Curtiss 1988, 98).

She did acquire some grammatical facts, however, such as whether verbs were transitive or intransitive. She also showed awareness of grammatical categories in that she never attached morphemes to the wrong base category. She never attached -*ing* to nouns, for example, but always to verbs. Genie showed impairment in certain structural aspects of language but not in the semantic component; evidence of a kind of modularity.

Curtiss found further support for modularity in the case of Chelsea, who also acquired her first language as an adult. Chelsea was a severely hearing-impaired adult who, due to a lack of social services, did not begin to acquire her first language until she was in her early thirties, when she was fitted with hearing aids. Chelsea appeared to have relatively normal non-linguistic cognitive and social abilities, and fairly good lexical abilities. Nevertheless, she had striking deficiencies in her syntax. Whereas Genie's sentences were semantically clear but ungrammatical, Chelsea's utterances were both ungrammatical and uninterpretable:

They are is car in the Tim.
Daddy are be were to the work.
The they (Curtiss 1988, 99).

Yet she had mastered a number of discourse connectors such as *How are you? OK,* and *Well.* Genie never managed these kinds of social formulae. Curtiss concludes that in both cases semantic acquisition, grammatical acquisition, and social abilities functioned separately.

She also cites evidence of a reverse profile: examples of individuals in whom grammar acquisition appears intact despite impairments in other components of linguistic development and despite significant and pervasive retardation. Antony had an estimated IQ of between 50 and 56, and had pervasive delays in motor, social, and cognitive abilities. His linguistic development, however, outstripped his development in all other areas. Consider such sentences as

It's not Vivian's, it's mine.
I don't want Bonnie coming in here (Curtiss 1988, 106).

Even so, his utterances were often semantically deficient and he made frequent lexical errors, substituting the word *taking* for the word *dropping,* for example. Though he used tense markings, a single marker might indicate past, present, or future. The word *baked,* for example, might be used in one sentence to indicate the past tense and in another to indicate the future. His pragmatic skills were also markedly deficient, in that he had trouble maintaining and controlling conversations. Thus, Antony presents evidence of grammar maturing independently of both other linguistic and non-linguistic faculties.

There is of course a catch to all this. If one claims that language is governed by a unique set of principles, the theory of language must include these principles and demonstrate how they explain linguistic knowledge. Chomsky's theory of language is a bold attempt in this direction and the difficulty of the task must be taken into consideration when we evaluate its success. The following sections present an overview of the Chomskyan theory of language and mind. It has evolved considerably over the past forty years. We therefore concentrate on the core ideas and insights and discuss their implications for the field of second language acquisition.

4 CHOMSKY: A THEORY OF LANGUAGE AND MIND

A theory of grammar hypothesizes about a particular type of knowledge represented in the mind/brain. The works of Chomsky (especially 1986b; 1988) emphasize the link between language and mind, and have led to the realization that theories of grammar and of language acquisition must be explicitly connected. One of the jobs of the linguist is to propose grammars that describe native speaker competence, but we must also ensure that the grammars propounded are learnable. In other words, a grammar has to be acquired by a child on the basis of the linguistic input in the environment.

4.1 LANGUAGE IS GRAMMAR

According to Chomsky, being a native speaker of English means having a grammar of English. This idea is central to his approach to language. Grammar is defined here in a very technical sense and differs considerably from the everyday meaning of the word. It is the set of rules that allows native speakers to produce and understand the sentences of their language. The grammar is the *unconscious* rule system that characterizes native speakers' knowledge.

Is there any evidence that native speakers unconsciously possess a grammar? Chomsky believes so. For him, it is fundamentally important to observe that native speakers can understand and produce original sentences. They can only do so if they possess an internalized representation of the rules required to *generate* sentences of English. If they had internalized actual sentences, native speakers would only be able to understand sentences previously known to them. Chomsky points out that the production and comprehension of novel sentences is the norm, not some exotic ability reserved for poets.

Further evidence comes from the observation that native speakers are able to judge whether particular strings of words are grammatical or ungrammatical. Again, the ability is not restricted to previously encountered sentences. Consider sentence (1), below. You have probably never seen it before but nevertheless consider it an example of an English sentence. How do you know it is English? According to Chomsky, you recognize it because it conforms to grammar rules that you possess unconsciously. Now consider sentence (2). The asterisk (*) to the left indicates that this is not a grammatical string in English. If you have also found it ungrammatical, what is the source of your knowledge? Again, the Chomskyan framework suggests that you judge this sentence to be ungrammatical because it does not correspond to your internalized unconscious grammar of English.

1. I know who the politician cheated.
2. *I know who the politician cheated the taxpayers.

It is important to note here that because both (1) and (2) are probably novel strings, native speakers can only judge grammaticality on the basis of a rule system. Again, the nature of this system appears to be unconscious. Most native speakers of English cannot say *why* (2) is ungrammatical—what rule of English grammar is violated—but they can make very consistent judgments about it. The rules involved are not the sort one learns in school. It is also very unlikely that during childhood native speakers are explicitly taught that sentences like (2) are ungrammatical.

One objection to this line of reasoning, and indeed to the entire Chomskyan view of an internalized unconscious grammar, deems assessments of the grammaticality of (2) merely to be statements that it doesn't make any sense. In other words, grammar has nothing to do with judgment of sentences. Native speakers simply consider comprehensible sentences like (1) to be English and incomprehensible sentences like (2) not to be English. The response to this comes from a consideration of sentences like (3):

3. Colourless green ideas sleep furiously.

If making sense were the criterion for grammaticality, then (3) should be ungrammatical. It is impossible to be *colourless* and *green* at the same time. *Ideas* don't have colour and they don't sleep. Even if they did, they would be unlikely to sleep *furiously*. Nevertheless, sentence (3) is perfectly good English. Notice, however, that it can be made to violate our grammars by simple deletion of the *s* in *ideas*, yielding (4). Sentence (4) is ungrammatical and it also doesn't make sense:

4. Colourless green idea sleep furiously.

To summarize, then, Chomsky claims that grammar is an abstract, unconscious rule system possessed by native speakers. This rule system generates all and only the sentences of the language.

4.2 LANGUAGE IS STRUCTURE

In Chomsky's theory, grammar is characterized as a set of rules that generate *structures*. For Chomsky, a sentence is not a string of words but rather an organization of structures. These can neither be seen nor heard but are essential to our comprehension of language. Chomsky notes that if a sentence were simply a string of words, then all identical word strings should have identical meanings. As can be seen in sentences like (5), this is not the case.

5. Visiting relatives can be boring.

The sentence is ambiguous; it can mean *I find it boring to visit relatives* or *I find it boring when relatives visit me*. It is important to observe that the source of the ambiguity has nothing to do with the meanings of the individual words. It is found in the invisible structure.

The role of invisible structure can also be seen in (6) and (7), below. Here the sentences are not identical: in (6), the adjective *eager* is used; in (7), the adjective *easy* occurs. This very simple change, however, brings with it an entire shift in the invisible structure which drastically changes the sentence's meaning. In sentence (6), *John* is the deep-structure subject of the sentence. Sentence (7) has an invisible "implied" subject (the person who pleases John) and *John* is the logical, or deep-structure, object of the sentence.

6. John is eager to please.
7. John is easy to please.

It can be seen from the examples above that characterizing language by dealing only with the surface organization of words would miss many of the important characteristics of native speaker competence. Sentences are much more than strings of words on a page. They are organized into abstract, hierarchically arranged structures, which are not physically present when we see or hear a sentence. In that case, where are they? Chomsky's answer is that they are in the mind. He sees the interesting characteristics of language not in its artifacts—newspapers, books, tape recordings, and so on—but in the minds of the people who created those artifacts and who can make sense of them. Again, the study of language is the study of the human mind.

4.3 COMPETENCE VERSUS PERFORMANCE

Those in the field of second language acquisition are typically interested in the development of second language skills. These skills can only be observed through their manifestation in the linguistic acts of speaking, listening, reading, and writing. The study of second language acquisition is therefore the study of second language *performance*.

Chomsky explicitly states that linguists should *not* deal with the study of language performance but rather with language *competence*. For him, language performance is what people *do* with language. It is therefore language activity, not language. Chomsky makes this distinction because he considers language activity to be made up of many mental abilities, only one of which is related to the mental organ for language. Language performance is influenced by self-confidence, shyness, short-term memory, nervousness, tiredness, and so on. All these factors are relevant to how effectively someone will speak, understand, read, or write, particularly in a second language. They do not, however, characterize language competence, the state of the internalized, unconscious grammar.

Chomsky claims that if we are to understand the true nature of language competence, we must consider it in the abstract, apart from the details of language performance. He does not deny that language performance is important, or worthy of study, but simply does not consider it to be the domain of linguistics. Linguists should study language, not the effects of headaches or nervousness.

Thus, Chomsky sees generative grammar as offering information about only one component of language performance. He claims that tasks such as reading involve not only language competence but also much more. Generative grammar says nothing about recognition of English letters on a page or how the eyes move across the page in scanning text. It says nothing about the memory processes involved in reading comprehension and indeed says very little about the process by which a reader extracts meaning from a passage of text.

Even in the area of syntax, the theory of generative grammar is not designed to offer any information about *how* the grammar is used in the processes of language production and comprehension. It tells us that native speakers of a language have abstract, unconscious grammars which allow them to have two distinct structural representations for sentences such as *Visiting relatives can be boring*. It does not tell us how these representations are built when someone hears a sentence. Chomsky's theory is not concerned with whether native speakers get both understandings simultaneously or one after the other.

To summarize, in all domains of language, Chomsky's theory of language deals with unconscious knowledge, not with how people use that knowledge. Of course, he would argue, before we can have a theory of how people use something, we need a theory of what that something is.

5 CONCLUSION

This chapter examined how theories of language acquisition are influenced by theories of mind. Rationalist theories emphasize the innate contributions of the learner, whereas empiricist theories place more emphasis on the role of the environment. These issues have been addressed by philosophers, psychologists, and linguists. They are also of major interest to second language teachers.

Chomsky's theory of language can best be seen as presenting a challenge for the study of second language acquisition. It tells us, essentially, that having a language necessitates having a grammar of that language. The grammar of a language is a rich, abstract system of rules. If this is an accurate characterization of native speaker competence, it offers, in effect, a characterization of the goals of second language acquisition. It claims that second language acquisition can never be as simple as learning to memorize sentences and phrases of the language. Second language acquisition can only be successful if one has acquired a generative grammar.

We are now forced to see second language acquisition as the development not only of second language skills but also of second language grammars. If we see second language acquisition as the development of a grammar, and if we hold to the Chomskyan view that human beings must develop typically human grammars, then the study of second language acquisition offers us a very privileged view of language and mind. Seen from this perspective, the second language learner who produces imperfect English is not simply making mistakes but is revealing the organization of his or her grammar of English (that is, the system that allows sentences to be generated). This grammar is different from the native speaker's because it generates different sorts of sentences, but it is nevertheless complex and abstract. During the course of second language acquisition, the learner's grammar is constantly changing. Once the process stops, the learner has reached a second language plateau. If, at this point, the learner's grammar is essentially the same as a native speaker's, then the learner has become bilingual.

Later chapters of this book will explore this perspective on second language in much greater depth and return to many of the issues discussed here.

CLASSROOM IMPLICATIONS

The theory of mind you maintain influences the kind of classroom you have. What do you think are characteristic activities of an empiricist classroom? What do you think are characteristic activities of a rationalist classroom? When would each type of activity be suitable? When, for example, would you use empiricist activities? When would you use rationalist activities?

Which aspects of second language acquisition do you think that the teacher is responsible for and which aspects do you think that the student is responsible for? Consider such things as reading, writing, listening, talking, pronunciation, accuracy, fluency, correction, practice, and so on.

SELF TEST

Theories of second language acquisition are informed by psychological theories of learning and philosophical views of the nature of the human mind. Philosophers disagree over: whether the mind is _____ (1) at birth, a view known as _____ (2) and represented by the work of Hume; or whether there is a rich _____ (3) structure at birth, as argued by philosopher _____ (4) and known as _____ (5).

Rationalist philosophers view learning as a _____ (6) procedure that derives specific knowledge from general principles. Empiricist philosophers, on the other hand, view learning as an _____ (7) process of deriving general rules from specific input data. The clearest example of a linguistic empiricist is _____ (8). Somewhere in the middle is _____ (9), who, in contrast to Chomsky, maintains a _____ (10) view of the human mind.

Learning involves memory, which is a complex construct. Humans are capable of retaining isolated bits of information in _____ (11) memory but call upon _____ (12) memory to organize knowledge. Recent advances in _____ (13) have led to a much fuzzier distinction between the science of the mind (cognitive psychology) and the science of the brain (neurobiology). This is particularly reflected in the model of cognitive architecture known as _____ (14).

FURTHER READING

Diller, K. 1978. *The Language Teaching Controversy*. Cambridge, MA: Newbury House.

4

......

Learning a First Language

This chapter describes some characteristics of the developmental path children take in acquiring a first language and certain theoretical issues in developing a theory of first language acquisition. The relationship between first and second language acquisition research is also covered. First let's look at an example of child language: "I looking the crocodiles. There. I found it. What that? I no know what names" (Samantha, aged two and a half). Clearly, child language is unlike adult language. How is it different, and why is it different?

1 WHAT DO CHILDREN DO?

A frequently asked question is, "When does language acquisition begin?" Is babbling language? Is crying? The question of crying is an interesting one. Several studies have tried to determine whether children have different cries to communicate hunger, pain, and so on. All have agreed that caregivers *cannot* tell the source of the discomfort just by listening to a cry but rely on contextual clues, such as knowing when the baby was last fed or whether there are any sharp implements within reach.

1.1 PHONOLOGICAL DEVELOPMENT

Children don't just cry, even though it seems like it sometimes. They also produce sounds that are used in human languages. Between one and two months they go through a stage known as *cooing*. Cooing is characterized mainly by the production of clear vowels ([ɪ], [ʌ], [ɛ]). These are also known by the term *happy sounds*. Somewhere between two and six months the child starts producing consonant–vowel (CV) patterns like [ʔɛ] or [gʌ]. From six months to a year the happy sounds get more complex, and the child starts to produce two-syllable reduplicated forms such as [mama] or [dada]. Once children begin to produce these forms they are said to be in the stage of *babbling*. At this point they begin to produce sound sequences with the forms CVC, CCV, and CCVC.

The first word comes in somewhere between eight months and a year and a half. For about the next ten months the child will be at the *one-word stage,* in which all utterances consist of one word. The question of which words are acquired first, though, is difficult to answer. For many children, the first words are: objects that can move by themselves (*mama, dada, dog, car*); and objects that can be manipulated by the child (*juice, milk, sock*). The first words, of course, do not arrive on the scene sounding exactly like adult forms. The phonological processes listed in Table 4.1 have been noted in child phonology (Ingram 1989; Reich 1986).

Table 4.1   Child Phonology

Process	Child form	Adult target	Process form
Syllable deletion	[mænta]	Samantha	[sa] → ∅
Reduplication	[dada]	—	[da] is duplicated
Simplification	[hɛp]	help	[l] → ∅
Substitution	[hɛč]	head	[d] → [č]
Assimilation	[fway]	try	[t] → [f] /____ [w]
Metathesis	[æks]	ask	[ks] → [sk]

These processes should be familiar to everyone who has studied phonology. It is interesting that the phonology of child language appears to be governed by the same sorts of processes as adult phonology. Obviously, though, child speech—especially at the early stages—does not sound like adult speech. Determining the cause or causes of these differences attracts considerable attention in the acquisition literature (see Archibald 1994). Two possible reasons for a child's deviant productions are:

1. The child cannot perceive the difference between the sound he or she is making and the sound the adult is making. The child perceives the sound incorrectly and produces the sound he or she is attempting.
2. The child does not have the necessary motor abilities (has not matured enough biologically) to make the target sound. The child perceives the sound correctly but produces it incorrectly.

It is not always easy to decide between these explanations. Perhaps the most important thing to realize here is that child phonology is rule governed. The rules may affect the perception or the production, or both, but the child does possess a phonological system. Second language learners also possess a phonological system. We find many examples of the same phonological processes in second language learner speech, as can be seen in Table 4.2.

Table 4.2 Phonological Processes of Second Language Learners

Process	Native target	Non-native speaker form
Syllable deletion	two hors<u>es</u>	two horse
Simplification	fixed [fɪkst]	[fɪk]
Addition	dog [dɑg]	[dɑgə]
Substitution	read [rid]	[lid]

There are several possible reasons for non-nativelike production. Just as is the case for children, the second language learner may not perceive distinctions that are important in the second language. The speaker may be producing a faithful version of an incorrect representation. It is also possible that the speaker perceives the difference but is having difficulty producing the correct sound. Both these difficulties may result from characteristics of the first language. We do tend to hear things through the filter of our first language. If you say the sound sequence [tlemor] to an English speaker, for example, it is highly likely that the speaker will hear it as [klemor], because English does not allow [tl] as a consonant cluster at the beginning of a word. Also, if you have to learn to make a new sound—such as an implosive, an ejective, or something less exotic, like a front rounded vowel—it can cause trouble. Note that the explanations proposed for the second language learner system are different from those for the child's. We cannot assume that adult second language learners lack biological maturity.

Similarity between child and adult systems may be taken as evidence of certain universal linguistic processes in both first and second language acquisition. We will return to this issue later in the text, when we look at the L1 = L2 hypothesis and the role of universal grammar in second language acquisition.

1.2 SEMANTIC DEVELOPMENT

The first words of a child do not necessarily mean the same thing as the adult words. Two common relationships between the meaning of a child word and of an adult word are semantic *overextension* and semantic *underextension*. Underextension refers to a child's use of a word to describe a smaller set of items than adult usage includes. If the child has the word *plane* but only uses it to refer to planes in the air, not planes on the ground, for example, he or she is exhibiting underextension. If the child uses the word *papa* to refer to all men with beards, on the other hand, he or she is demonstrating overextension. Overextension, or overgeneralization, is a very common process in language acquisition, and we will return to it repeatedly throughout the text.

1.3 SYNTACTIC DEVELOPMENT

A considerable amount of research has been done on the developmental stages of child language development, and a few brief comments are in order. A general progression has been proposed:

one-word stage → two-word stage → telegraphic speech

The one-word stage is self-explanatory as far as its name goes, but interesting research issues surround both the order of word acquisition and the phonological structure of those first words, although we will not go into them here. After seven to ten months of one-word utterances, children start to put words together. For the most part, these new utterances consist of two words, such as *mommy shoe*, *baby juice*, and so on. Even at this two-word stage of development, children's use of language is creative; they produce sentences that they have never heard before. The third stage involves the production of longer but still notably non-adult-like sentences: *Me want more juice*; *Daddy throw ball again*. This stage of acquisition is distinguished by the lack of grammatical function words. The content words—nouns and verbs—tend to be there, but the function words—articles and prepositions—are absent.[1] For this reason it has often been called telegraphic speech, as these are exactly the words that are left out of telegrams. There is nothing in the metaphor to suggest, however, that children are deleting words from a mental representation of a sentence, in the way that adults do from a telegram. Children most likely do not have the syntactic structure necessary to represent these items.

Again, children's speech exhibits certain similarities to the kinds of utterances we may find in the earliest stages of second language acquisition. If you have a very limited vocabulary in your second language, you start by producing extremely simple sentences. You may find yourself at a one-word stage in your responses, even though you are able to understand more complex utterances addressed to you. If you were asked in French or Spanish if you liked a place you had visited, for example, you

---

[1] There is, in fact, a burgeoning literature in first language acquisition addressing whether or not children have functional categories, but we will not get into it here. See Radford (1990), or Guilfoyle and Noonan (1992).

might well understand the question but only be able to respond *oui* or *claro*. Later, when you had acquired a few more words, you might find yourself producing telegraphic L2 speech, such as *maison intéressant* or *casa bonita*. As before, we have to discount biological maturity for these types of utterance. Assuming that the adult's L1 has determiners and prepositions (or postpositions), it is most probably not lack of biological maturation that causes the interlanguage forms. As in phonology, we note that there are similarities in both the processes and the representations found in first and second language learners' grammars but that the structures may arise for different reasons.

1.4 OVERGENERALIZATION IN LANGUAGE ACQUISITION

Overgeneralization in language acquisition is highly productive. Evidence of it is found at almost every level of linguistic structure. We hear examples of *semantic* overgeneralization. A child who uses the word *moon* to refer to all kinds of round objects, for example (*cookies, buttons,* and so on), is overgeneralizing the meaning.

We find *syntactic* overgeneralization. A child may assume that the first noun phrase (NP) of a sentence is the agent, for example, and as a result interpret sentences like *The car hit the truck* and *The car was hit by the truck* the same way, assuming that the first NP was doing the hitting. Here the child is overgeneralizing the syntactic function.

We also find examples of *morphological* overgeneralization. Children may know that you tend to make plurals in English by adding an -s to the noun and so produce forms like *cats, dogs,* and *oxes*. In this case, they do not know the appropriate irregular form and therefore overgeneralize by using the productive morpheme.

We see *lexical* overgeneralization as well. Children may produce sentences like *Should you go?* and *Want you go?* This indicates that they have not yet distinguished the two classes of verbs in English: auxiliary and main verbs. They have one lexical category where adults have two.

1.5 ORDER OF ACQUISITION

Order of acquisition in child language has received a considerable amount of attention, probably in large part because of Piaget's influence. Remember that Piaget was concerned with describing the stages in cognitive development. Psychologists interested in language acquisition seek to discover the stages of language development.

Roger Brown, working at Harvard University, was probably the first to note certain regularities in the linguistic development of children (Brown 1973). He observed that children tend to move through the same developmental stages in the same order, even though a particular stage could not necessarily be correlated with chronological age. We cannot talk about how two year olds use language because they differ considerably in their linguistic development, but we can note that children move through a sequence of stages even though their ages on reaching each stage vary, as does the amount of time they then spend at that stage.

One of the best-known parts of Brown's study discusses the acquisition of inflectional morphemes in three English-speaking children, Adam, Eve, and Sarah. Ignoring some of the morphemes he discussed, we note the following order of acquisition:

1. present progressive tense
2. plural
3. irregular past tense
4. possessive
5. regular past tense
6. third person singular present tense

A couple of comments are apropos. First, consider what it means for a form to be acquired. At what point are we willing to say that a child has acquired a particular morpheme? Researchers differ over this, of course, but one of the most common methods to determine acquisition is known as a *supplied in obligatory context* analysis (SOC). It involves looking at a transcript to determine every instance where an adult would use a requisite morpheme (as in *two cats*), and to see whether the child used the morpheme. In other words, SOC checks the obligatory contexts for a morpheme and ascertains whether the child uses that morpheme. Usually, researchers settle on a threshold of use in 80 or 90 percent of the obligatory contexts to say that a morpheme has been acquired.

Second, consider the acquisitional sequence from the list above: (2) plural, (4) possessive, (6) third person singular present. Note that in English all of these morphemes have the same phonetic realization, [s]:

Plural: *two cats*
Possessive: *Jack's book*
Third person singular present: *he walks*

We cannot explain the acquisitional sequence with reference to phonetics. That is, we cannot argue that the third person marking comes later than the plural marking because it is harder to say, as they have the same phonetic form.

Roman Jakobson (cited in Moskowitz 1978) had an interesting explanation for this. He noted that each of the three morphemes realized as [s] applies at a different level of the grammar. Plural applies at the word level. Possessive applies at the phrase level, as we can see when we look at a phrase like *the man who is standing on the corner's hat*. It is ungrammatical to mark the noun for possession: **the man's who is standing on the corner hat*. We must mark possession at the phrase level. Finally, third person subject agreement occurs at the sentence level. We need to know what the subject of the sentence is and to have some way of getting the verb to agree with the subject (see Figure 4.1[2]). This explanation is appealing because it suggests that children first become accurate on lower-level structures and gradually gain accuracy on structures of greater complexity.

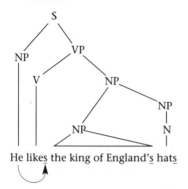

He likes the king of England's hats

Figure 4.1 Plural, Possessive, and Third Person Present

2 THEORIES OF ACQUISITION

In discussing the concept of language acquisition theories, it is useful to begin with Pinker's list of conditions that a viable theory of this nature must meet (1979):

1. The *learnability condition* is met if the theory can account for the fact that languages can be learned.
2. The *equipotentiality condition* is met if the theory does not succeed merely by being extremely narrow; forcing many things to be specified as innate when, in fact, they might be learned. The theory must be able to account for the acquisition of all languages.
3. The *time condition* is met if the theory explains how learning can take place within the time that the learner normally takes to acquire a grammar.

---

[2] Notice that the tree diagram indicates the NP *the king of England's* with a triangle rather than with lines running to each word of the phrase and specifying parts of speech. This less specific notation is standard for parts of a tree diagram that are not under discussion.

4. The *input condition* is met if the theory accounts for language learning with the typical input available to the learner.
5. The *developmental condition* is met if the theory makes correct predictions about the learner's capabilities during the course of acquisition.
6. The *cognitive condition* is met if the theory agrees with the known cognitive faculties of the learner.

2.1 HOW DO CHILDREN ACQUIRE LANGUAGE?

It is often said that acquiring language is the most complex thing we will ever do in our lives. Yet it appears to be so effortless for the child. Indeed, most of us have absolutely no recollection of what it was like to learn our first language. How is it that very young children, who do not have the motor skills to tie their shoes, the biological development to inhibit urination, or the cognitive skills to know that if one boot is on the correct foot then the other one will have to be correct too, are well on their way to acquiring complex linguistic abilities?

Many researchers argue that language is somehow special; that humans have a unique endowment which predisposes them to learn language. Chomsky has stated that language is not so much something the child actively acquires, but rather something that happens to the child. One of the first researchers to outline this theory was Eric Lenneberg, in his book *The Biological Foundations of Language* (1967).

2.2 THE BIOLOGICAL FOUNDATIONS OF LANGUAGE

Lenneberg argued that "the capacities for speech production and related aspects of language acquisition develop according to a built-in biological schedule." He maintained that there was a sensitive period—what he called a period of *resonance*—from about age two to age twelve, when children were able to acquire language effortlessly. This view of language acquisition represented a shift to a more rationalist view of the learner, placing greater emphasis on biology. Earlier views had focussed on the environment or the culture as the driver of the acquisition process.

Lenneberg presented a variety of data to support his claim. One study investigated the emergence of vocalization in infants whose parents were deaf and who were therefore not speaking to the child but signing. These children were compared with others who had hearing parents. Lenneberg argued that there were no significant differences in either the type of vocalization or the age of onset of vocalization. More recent studies have shown problems with both his age-of-onset claim (Oller and Eilers 1988) and his type claim (Kent et al. 1987), but a study on the babbling of children who used American Sign Language (Petitto and

Marentette 1991) argued that when modality is factored out, the babbling is very similar for speaking and signing children.

Lenneberg also presented evidence from aphasia. He offered data
showing that learners who suffered cerebral trauma to the left hemisphere of the brain, where much of language is controlled, displayed
varying symptoms depending on their age at the time of trauma.
Learners who experienced the trauma before puberty were able to effect a
complete recovery of their linguistic skills, whereas those who were
injured later were significantly less likely to regain full use of their language. Lenneberg argued that puberty was some kind of boundary with
respect to language learning. Children were resonant with their environment; language happened to them.

2.3 THE ROLE OF THE ENVIRONMENT

As innatist theories of language acquisition have often been criticized for
neglecting the role of the environment, we would like to discuss this
issue briefly. Chapters 16, 17, and 18 examine the role of the environment specifically with respect to second language learning. Chomsky
(1983) makes two points clearly: (1) there is something in the human
biological endowment that contributes to the growth of language in the
mind; and (2) the way in which language develops in the mind is going
to be affected by the environment.

These points should be uncontroversial. Nevertheless, to understand
this particular view of the role of environment, it is important to distinguish between *triggering* and *shaping* effects. Certain conditions in the
environment may be necessary for a given system to develop, even
though those conditions do not shape its development. Chomsky cites
the example that sheep require mother–neonate interaction in order to
develop normal depth perception. In this case, the environment has a
triggering effect on a biologically determined system. Studies investigating how the characteristics of the visual field influence the development
of the visual system, on the other hand, reveal a shaping effect. Cats who
are exposed only to horizontal lines in their visual environments, for
example, develop different visual apparatus than cats who are exposed to
both vertical and horizontal lines.

Innatist theories emphasize the triggering role of the environment. As
always, researchers are open to considering explicit proposals about how
the environment shapes such linguistic features as question formation, but
in the virtual absence of such proposals, there is little to argue against.

2.3.1 The Poverty of the Stimulus

What is known as the *poverty of the stimulus* argument bolsters the
innatist view of language. This is a classical rationale made use of by
such thinkers as Plato and Descartes. Chomsky summarizes it as follows:

"If we find that the mind is doing something in the absence of relevant experience, we have to attribute what it is doing to the intrinsic structure of the mind" (1984, 19).[3]

Lightfoot (1982) explicates the position clearly.[4] Essentially, the poverty of the stimulus is a biological style of argument used to identify genetic contributions to development and to winnow out environmental ones. It claims that childhood experience is insufficient to explain the rich, complex adult language. No matter what language they are exposed to, children learn to utter and comprehend an infinite set of sentences. As Lightfoot points out, the input is inadequate on three levels:

1. The speech that children hear does not consist solely of well-formed sentences; they also hear slips of the tongue and incomplete thoughts. Even if only 5 percent of the input data are defective, this is an immense problem. Imagine how difficult it would be to induce the rules of a chess game if 5 percent of the moves were illegal, but you didn't know which 5 percent. The input to learners does not flag which sentences are grammatical and which are ungrammatical, and yet children learn to make this type of judgment consistently.
2. Children encounter a finite range of expressions when learning language but are eventually able to deal with an infinite range of novel sentences, going far beyond what they heard in childhood, through such grammatical devices as relativization, subordination, and co-ordination. The input does not provide them with a list of every possible sentence in the language.
3. People come to know things subconsciously about their language for which no direct evidence is available in the data they are exposed to as children.

The third is probably the most important deficiency. Consider the phenomenon of *wanna* contraction in English. In certain environments the sequence *want to* can be contracted to *wanna*. Remember that when

---

[3] Chomsky also refers to this when he says, "Even knowing very little of substance about linguistic universals, we can be quite sure that the possible variety of languages is sharply limited. Gross observations suffice to establish some qualitative conclusions. Thus, it is clear that the language each person acquires is a rich and complex construction hopelessly underdetermined by the fragmentary evidence available.... [N]evertheless, individuals in a speech community have developed essentially the same language. This fact can be explained only on the assumption that these individuals employ highly restrictive principles that guide the construction of grammar. Furthermore, humans are, obviously, not designed to learn one human language rather than another.... [P]owerful constraints must be operative restricting the variety of languages" (1975, 10).

[4] Lightfoot's book has one of our all-time favourite dedications: to anybody who ever met a couple of linguists in a bar and asked them what they did for a living.

we talk about a sentence being well formed in linguistics we are not talking about prescriptive grammar rules. It is a well-supported fact that many native speakers of English contract *want* and *to*; at this point we are not discussing the social conditions under which it is appropriate. The following is an example of *wanna* contraction:

I *want to* go. → I *wanna* go.
Who do you *want to* see? → Who do you *wanna* see?

In the next example, however, the contraction is not allowed:

Who do you *want to* go? → *Who do you *wanna* go?

How does the learner arrive at the correct knowledge? There is nothing in the input to indicate that the first two sentences are grammatical and the third is not.

A Chomskyan model of syntactic structure can explain this seemingly arbitrary fact. If we look at the structure of two of the sentences, we find the following surface structures:

Who do you want to see *t*?
Who do you want *t* to go?

Remember the discussion about *wh* movement in Chapter 2. The deep structures of the preceding sentences would be something like

You want to see who?
You want who to go?

The *wh* words move to the front of the sentence but they leave behind a trace (*t*) in their original, deep-structure positions. Note that in the surface structures, the traces are in different positions:

Who do you want to see *t*?
Who do you want *t* to go?

As White (1989b) points out, *wanna* contraction is sensitive to the presence of *wh* traces. Contraction is blocked if there is a trace between *want* and *to*. Obviously this information is not available in the input as we cannot *hear* traces, yet this universal grammar knowledge that a trace is present guides the learners' behaviour. Otherwise, we would have no explanation for why the sentences *Who do you want to see?* and *Who do you want to go?* behave differently with respect to *wanna* contraction.

Another example may help to make this clear. Consider the sentence: *Who do you want to leave?* In one reading, you want someone to leave; in the other, you want to leave someone. These two different readings have different structures. The reading in which you want someone to leave has the structure

Who do you want *t* to leave?

The reading in which you want to leave someone has the structure

Who do you want to leave *t*?

The explanation we gave before would predict that *wanna* contraction is possible in the second reading but not in the first. Why? Because in the first reading *want* and *to* are separated by a trace, and therefore contraction will be blocked. This, in fact, is the case, as we see when we consider the possible answers to the question *Who do you wanna leave?* We can answer *I wanna leave my husband* but not *I wanna Bob leave*. Once again, abstract linguistic structures can help to explain our linguistic performance.

2.3.2 Negative Evidence

Another question about the input that learners receive has to do with how they learn about ungrammaticality. How do they learn what *cannot* be said, which strings are ill formed? It is conceivable that children learn what not to say by being overtly corrected. This is referred to as *negative evidence*. First language acquisition literature has addressed the issue extensively (see Pinker 1989). Note the assumptions here: (1) children get negative evidence (through correction); and (2) children make certain kinds of mistakes.

The classic study concerning the first assumption, Brown and Hanlon (1970), showed that children do not usually get corrected when they make grammatical mistakes. Braine (1971) argued that even when they are exposed to negative evidence, they ignore it. He used the following example:

Child: Want other one spoon, Daddy.
Father: You mean, you want THE OTHER SPOON.
Child: Yes, I want other one spoon, please, Daddy.
Father: Can you say "the other spoon?"
Child: Other ... one ... spoon.
Father: Say ... "other."
Child: Other.
Father: "Spoon."

Child: Spoon.
Father: "Other ... spoon."
Child: Other ... spoon. Now give me other one spoon? (1971, 160–61).

Parents usually focus on the *content* of what their children say rather than the form. So if a child says, for example, "I goed outside," the parent is more likely to respond "Why didn't you tell me?" than to launch into a grammar lesson. It has been pointed out, however, that if input were the driving force here we would expect our children to grow up speaking the truth ungrammatically. In fact, the opposite is more common.

The other kind of evidence telling us that external factors alone do not drive language acquisition is found in the kind of errors children make or, more accurately, don't make. A theory of language acquisition that relies on negative evidence considers the learner to proceed via induction, to test hypotheses about the patterns underlying the data. The learner might think, "Maybe I can say *x*," and would then be corrected if *x* were ill formed. But when we look at the things that children actually say, we find that many hypotheses do not get tested.

Consider the example of *wh* movement that we have talked about previously. As adults, we know that there are some ways in which you can move *wh* words and some in which you cannot, as shown below:

1. Who should Bob fire *t*?

2. *Which should Bob meet *t* of Tom's friends?

Children never produce sentences like (2). Therefore, their knowledge of its ungrammaticality cannot come from correction. Chomsky would argue that the knowledge comes instead from a principle of universal grammar constraining *wh* movement. Consequently, in most Chomskyan approaches to language acquisition it is assumed that negative evidence does not play a part. Children are not regularly exposed to it; they do not change their grammars when they are; and it cannot explain their final-state grammars. We will return to the implications of "no negative evidence" to second language learning in Chapter 18.

2.3.3 Caretaker Speech

Another argument often made against innatism is referred to as *caretaker speech*.[5] In this line of reasoning, the simplified speech that caretakers (often parents) address to learners provides sufficient structure for

---

[5] Also known as baby talk, motherese, or caregiver speech.

language acquisition to take place on an inductive basis. In other words, learners simply generalize patterns without the aid of genetically determined principles. Note, though, that in effect this is just switching the genetic burden to the caretaker, who "happens" to know how to lead the learner along structurally, getting more and more complex, with no overt knowledge of the structures in question. There are four major problems with the caretaker speech hypothesis (Gleitman, Newport, and Gleitman 1984):

1. Children register only part of their environment, and we have no way of knowing what each child registers. Children are not solely exposed to caretaker speech. They have input from, for example, other children, television, and other adults. This may contain ungrammatical sentences such as slips of the tongue.
2. Even if they ignore ungrammatical input somehow and only register well-formed utterances, the third data deficiency raised by Lightfoot still holds: people subconsciously know things about their language for which there is no direct evidence in the input they receive as children. We can provide further evidence of this deficiency of input by noting that there is a definite gap between what learners experience and the knowledge they attain. The child is exposed to, for example, [ðədɑgčeystðəkæt]. The adult comes to know what is represented in Figure 4.2: information that is not in the input.

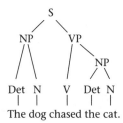

The dog chased the cat.

Figure 4.2

3. If children registered only simplified and well-formed utterances, their job would be more *difficult* as their information would be limited.
4. Newport, Gleitman, and Gleitman (1977) show that parents' speech to children has a high proportion of questions and imperatives. In this caretaker speech, declarative sentences are rarer than in ordinary speech. Yet the emerging language of children does not reflect a similar bias. This suggests that there is no simple correlation between the emerging language and the kind of language that parents direct at the children.

3 CONCLUSION

This chapter has looked at some of the major issues in child language acquisition. The major concern in this book, however, is second language learning, so why spend so much time on first language learning? One of the issues in second language research and education is the extent to which first and second language acquisition are similar. We will be discussing this explicitly later.

We are also concerned with developing a theory of second language acquisition. Much of the research in the study of second languages is heavily influenced by theories developed to account for first language acquisition. Such things as the role of feedback and of correction are of great concern to those working in the L2 field, but they arose from the L1 literature.

CLASSROOM IMPLICATIONS

Do people learning second languages do the same kinds of things as children learning first languages? Stern (1970) suggests, although he does not necessarily advocate, a series of positions for discussion:

1. In language teaching, we must practice and practice, again and again. Just watch a small child learning his mother tongue. He repeats things over and over again. During the language-learning stage he practices all the time. This is what we must also do when we learn a foreign language.
2. Language learning is mainly a matter of imitation. You must be a mimic, just like a small child. He imitates everything.
3. First, we practice the separate sounds, then words, then sentences. That is the natural order and is therefore right for learning a foreign language.
4. Watch a small child's speech development. First he listens, then he speaks. Understanding always precedes speaking. Therefore, this must be the right order of presenting the skills in a foreign language.
5. A small child listens and speaks and no one would dream of making him read or write. Reading and writing are advanced stages of language development. The natural order for first and second language learning is listening, speaking, reading, writing.
6. You did not have to translate when you were small. If you were able to learn your own language without translation, you should be able to learn a foreign language in the same way.

7. A small child simply uses language. He does not need learn formal grammar. You don't tell him about verbs and nouns. Yet he learns the language perfectly. It is equally unnecessary to use grammatical conceptualization in teaching a foreign language (Stern 1970, 57–58).

We present Stern's statements as a jumping-off point for discussion. How many of them do you think are valid? How many do you believe are invalid?

There are obvious differences between teaching children and teaching adults. Even if we were to assume that second language acquisition is just like first language acquisition, it is unlikely that we could treat adult and child learners the same way. Discuss some of the differences you would expect to find between teaching a second language to children and teaching it to adults in terms of

- topics covered (content)
- explicit grammar instruction
- what is relevant to the learners
- materials used
- methods used

In which of the following areas do you think there would be differences in the performance of children and adults?

- pronunciation
- vocabulary
- syntax (complex or simple)
- reading
- writing
- discourse skills

SELF TEST

Children move through recognized developmental _____ in
(1)
their acquisition. Clearly their language production is unlike that of
_____ . Interestingly, the same kinds of linguistic
(2)
_____ that are useful in describing adult systems appear to be
(3)
operating in child systems as well. Related to this, we note that child language is the product of a _____ . We see evidence of this in the
(4)
types of _____ that they make.
(5)

Theories of acquisition have been proposed to account for these characteristics of child language. Chomsky's theories emphasize the role of _____ (6) structures and view the environment as a necessary _____ (7) of those structures. Any theory of acquisition that views the environment as the driving force of acquisition has to confront the issue of the _____ (8) of the stimulus. Similarly, we have to be explicit about what counts as the linguistic environment. Most theories do not admit _____ (9) evidence into the learning theory.

FURTHER READING

Fletcher, P. and M. Garman, eds. 1986. *Language Acquisition.* Avon: Cambridge University Press.

Goodluck, H. 1992. *Language Acquisition.* Cambridge, MA: Blackwell.

Second Language Competence

I N this section, we enter into a consideration of what interlanguage grammars look like. Chapter 5 discusses the notion of proficiency, the final goal. What exactly are second language learners trying to learn? Chapter 6 is concerned with theories of second language acquisition. What does a theory of second language acquisition have to account for? Chapter 7 looks at the nature of an interlanguage. How, for example, does the structure of the learner's first language influence the structure of the interlanguage? Chapter 8 looks at language universals and SLA. Certain universal properties and principles of human language also influence the structure of an interlanguage grammar. Case studies presented in Chapter 9 inform us about the structure of an interlanguage in terms of phonology and syntax.

5

....

Proficiency, the Final Goal

Much of the research conducted in second language acquisition has focussed on learners' developmental stages, often by describing the form of an interlanguage grammar at a particular moment. In Chapter 3 we talked about the grammar of a native speaker. Here we note that non-native speakers have grammars too. Unlike native grammars, these interlanguage grammars vary quite a bit from person to person, influenced by such things as level of proficiency in the L2 and the nature of the L1. The interlanguage hypothesis (Selinker 1972) assumes that change is a defining characteristic of interlanguage grammar. Usually, this means that the interlanguage grammar is becoming more like the target language grammar. Clearly, this supposes that the goal of second language acquisition is the knowledge and abilities possessed by native speakers. Perhaps idealistically, we assume that the target of SLA is competence and performance indistinguishable from native speakers.

This chapter presents a detailed discussion of the final destination of language learners: proficiency. What is proficiency in a second language? We will consider it in terms of both knowledge and ability: (1) What does the learner *know*? and (2) What can the learner *do*? We can say that L2 learners want to be able to do the same things that adult native speakers of a language can do. So what can native speakers do?

As we have seen, one of the goals of descriptive linguistics is to describe the system of knowledge that native speakers possess. A generative grammar accounts for all and only the grammatical sentences of a particular language. For a non-native speaker, the interlanguage grammar is responsible for generating what the learner considers to be well- or ill-formed strings. Of course, these judgments may be different from those of a native speaker. A non-native speaker might, for example, judge the sentence *He walk to school every day* to be well-formed, or grammatical. Naturally, native speakers' judgments vary to a certain extent as well. Do you consider the following to be grammatical or ungrammatical?

It is apt for Paul to win.
How many Spanish authors do you have books by?

What this reinforces is the Chomskyan idea that grammars are individual constructs (what he calls I-languages). The word *scombroid*, for example, is definitely an English word, but if it means nothing to you it is not part of your grammar.

It is here that our concerns as second language researchers begin to diverge slightly from the concerns of theoretical linguists. For second language learners, grammaticality is not enough. In the field of second language acquisition, we must adopt a more comprehensive notion of competence than the strictly grammatical. This broader construct has come to be known as *communicative competence.*

Noam Chomsky originally coined the distinction between competence and performance. Performance describes language in use, which can be affected by such factors as emotion and fatigue. So, if someone makes a slip of the tongue—saying "backbloard" for *blackboard*, for example—we don't feel that it offers an accurate picture of what the speaker knows about English, of his or her competence. Rather, we consider it a performance error. Competence, on the other hand, is the underlying system of knowledge that the speaker possesses.

The term communicative competence was originally coined by the sociolinguist Dell Hymes (1971). Hymes felt that applied linguists needed a broader construct than linguistic competence. He originally described communicative competence as "knowing when it is appropriate to open a conversation, and how, what topics are appropriate to particular speech events, which forms of address are to be used, to whom and in which situations, and how such speech acts as greetings, compliments, apologies, invitations and complements are to be given, interpreted and responded to" (cited in Wolfson and Judd 1983, 61).

The study of communicative competence is beneficial for three reasons. It gives us a model of what native speakers know and know how to do. Second, the model shows us what second language learners are trying to learn. Third, by breaking the construct of proficiency into manageable parts, it gives us some sort of framework both for predicting where second language learners might have trouble and for evaluating those difficulties. Let us now try to formalize a model of communicative competence.

1 BACHMAN'S MODEL

Canale and Swain (1980) proposed that communicative competence consisted of four components: grammatical competence, discourse competence, sociolinguistic competence, and strategic competence. Lyle Bachman expands on this seminal work and proposes a more complex model in the same intellectual tradition. His model, shown in Figure 5.1 in a simplified form,[1] still acknowledges that using a language communicatively involves both knowledge and the ability to implement it (Bachman 1990). Bachman reminds us that it is to be thought of as a "visual metaphor" for proficiency. This chapter examines each of his proposed divisions, beginning with language competence.

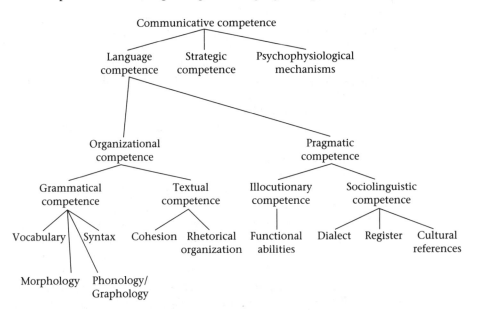

Figure 5.1   Bachman's Model of Communicative Competence
Source: Adapted from Bachman (1990).

2 LANGUAGE COMPETENCE

For Bachman, language competence has to do with the linguistic knowledge and abilities that underlie proficiency. We can immediately note that his model comprises different components from those suggested by

---

[1] Figure 5.1 does not show as much detail under illocutionary competence as Bachman's original model.

On those remote pages [of the *Celestial Emporium of Benevolent Knowledge*] it is written that animals are divided into (a) those that belong to the Emperor, (b) embalmed ones, (c) those that are trained, (d) suckling pigs, (e) mermaids, (f) fabulous ones, (g) stray dogs, (h) those that are included in this classification, (i) those that tremble as if they were mad, (j) innumerable ones, (k) those drawn with a very fine camel's hair brush, (l) others, (m) those that have just broken a flower vase, (n) those that resemble flies from a distance.

Jorge Luis Borges
Other Inquisitions

Canale and Swain. It must be acknowledged that empirical validation of any such distinctions is difficult to come by. A large-scale, five-year project known as the Development of Bilingual Proficiency (DBP) project was conducted at the Modern Language Centre of the Ontario Institute for Studies in Education (reported in Harley et al. 1990). The DBP project developed measures of grammatical, discourse, and sociolinguistic competence, but a statistical analysis of subjects' test scores did not validate the categories. Bachman and Palmer (1982), on the other hand, did find statistical support for the componential nature of linguistic competence when testing for grammatical, pragmatic, and sociolinguistic competence. Regardless of the statistical validity of divisions such as Bachman's, we believe that his model is useful, if only as a metaphor.

Bachman subdivides language competence into *organizational* and *pragmatic* competence. First let's look at organizational competence.

2.1 ORGANIZATIONAL COMPETENCE

Organizational competence is concerned with knowledge and ability related to the structural aspects of language: *grammatical* and *textual* competence. A second language learner must be able to generate well-formed structures, whether the structure in question is a syllable, a word, a sentence, or a paragraph. Broadly speaking, the term grammatical competence refers to the well-formedness of structures at and below the sentence level, whereas textual competence encompasses the construction of units larger than the sentence.

2.1.2 Grammatical Competence

It is important to remind ourselves how the word *grammatical* is being used. We might tend to think of grammatical or ungrammatical sentences when we hear the word *grammar*, although grammar refers not just to sentence-level phenomena but to the learner's system of knowledge about all aspects of the language structure. We must also be careful not to think of grammar in prescriptive terms. With that in mind, the subdivisions of grammatical competence should be familiar as the subdisciplines of linguistics: vocabulary (lexis), morphology, syntax, phonology, and graphology.

2.1.2.1 Vocabulary (Lexis)

When we know a word we know its meaning. At a certain level, it seems simple to perceive meaning. If we consider a word such as *cat*, for example, we can clearly identify that it refers to a furry feline, and regardless of the kind of feline (Manx, tabby, sleeping, playing, and so on), we accept the label *cat*. Yet many words are not as straightforward. Think about possible adjectives in English for describing someone who is not fat. *Skinny, slim,* and *emaciated* are just a few. Most people have a clear preference about the label they would like to have applied to themselves. Also consider words to describe someone who does not spend very much money: *cheap, thrifty, miserly.* Which would you rather be called? The differences among words such as these lies in their denotative (or literal) and connotative meanings. The literal meanings of words like *skinny, slim,* and *emaciated* are similar, but their connotations are quite different. The same is true for *cheap, thrifty,* and *miserly.* Some have positive connotations and others have negative ones.

The implications of connotation for the second language learner become very clear when we get to the sentence level. If a second language learner tries to say, "That large man is really thrifty," but in fact says, "That fat guy is really cheap," there is a high probability that the message received will be very different from the one intended. Speakers obviously have to grasp more than the literal meaning of a word in order to behave appropriately.

When we know a word we also know something about the kinds of syntactic structures in which it can appear. The property of a word is referred to as its *subcategorization frame.* Some verbs, for example, can appear in structures in which they are followed by a noun phrase (NP):

Randolph saw *Harry*
         $\overline{\text{NP}}$

Other verbs require two NPs to follow them:

Randolph gave *Harry the book*
         $\overline{\text{NP}}$ $\overline{\text{NP}}$

The importance of subcategorization facts can be seen in the utterance *I slept a nap this afternoon.* The meaning is transparent but the speaker doesn't have the verb subcategorized correctly. The sentence *I took a nap this afternoon* is grammatically correct, because *took* is subcategorized to be followed by an NP.

2.1.2.2 Morphology

When we know about the morphology of a word we understand its internal structure. We can determine something about the meaning of a word like *renativizations,* for example, by looking at the internal structure, even if it is the first time we've seen the word:

native	the root of the word (noun)
[nativ] ize	to make native (verb)
re [nativize]	to make native again (verb)
[renativiz] ation	the process of making native again (noun)
[renativization] s	plural form of the above noun (noun)

Knowledge of morphology can help second language learners to understand the meanings of words they haven't seen before. It can also help them with their production. In English, morphemes are constrained both in the parts of speech they can be attached to and in the parts of speech they can produce. Consider these pairs: kind, unkind; happy, unhappy; able, unable; clear, unclear. The prefix *un-* attaches to adjectives but not to nouns, as can be seen from the ungrammaticality of the following: car, *uncar; student, *unstudent. Once you graduate or drop out of school you do not become an *unstudent.* Even though its meaning may be understood in a particular context, the word is an ill-formed morphological string. This is simply a property of the English prefix. Forms like this are ruled out for structural reasons, and that knowledge can help to prevent students from generating ungrammatical forms. At first blush, it seems as if words such as *unhappiness* are counter examples to this claim, but a look at their internal structure shows that these words conform to the same principle. *Unhappiness* has the hierarchical structure shown in Figure 5.2.

Figure 5.2

The suffix *-ness* attaches to adjectives to form nouns. The prefix *un* has already attached to the adjective *happy* to form another adjective, *unhappy.* The *un-* cannot be attaching to the noun *happiness.*

It is also important to know what part of speech results from adding a suffix or a prefix. The prefix *un-* attached to an adjective (such as *clear*) to produce another adjective (*unclear*). Sometimes the part of speech changes, as in the following pairs: govern, government; assess, assessment; attain, attainment; measure, measurement. In this case we see that the suffix *-ment* attaches to verbs and produces nouns. This too is important knowledge in helping students to use words correctly.

One of the standard ways of representing the internal structure of morphologically complex words is with word trees. Word trees make clear the grammatical category of the stem and of the resulting word. A word such as *government,* for example, has the structure shown in Figure 5.3. The tree shows graphically that the affix *-ment* can only attach to verbs and that the resulting lexical item is a noun. The more complex *renativizations* is represented in Figure 5.4.

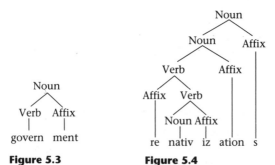

Figure 5.3   **Figure 5.4**

Not all languages are organized in this manner on the word level. Whether or not their first languages have internal word structure, however, second language learners benefit from knowledge of morphology. At times, they produce semantically clear forms that violate the morphological rules of the language. The forms below, for example, are probably interpretable but would not be used by a native speaker. Consider what makes each of the italicized words ill-formed:

I think he is *unliterate*.
That couch looks *sleepable*.
I forgot to buy all the *butters*.
She *shoulds* leave.
The walls are *chartreuser* than I thought they'd be.

2.1.2.3 Graphology

One of the structural aspects of competence that must be acquired is the graphology or writing system of a language. The writing systems of students' first languages can differ greatly in terms of both surface features, such as character form, and the deeper organizing principles. Some languages, such as Chinese, use a *logographic* writing system, in which a character or symbol represents an entire word (see Table 5.1). Other languages, such as Cree, use a *syllabic* writing system; a symbol represents a syllable (see Table 5.2). Still others, like English, Vietnamese, Russian and Arabic, use an *alphabetic* system in which the symbols stand for consonants and vowels. As Figure 5.5 illustrates, alphabetic systems manifest a great surface variety. Languages vary, then, in the level of linguistic unit that is represented by a graphic symbol: word (or morpheme), syllable, or segment.

Table 5.1   A Logographic Writing System

Phonetic determinatives

	Semantic radical	A 敖 (áo)	B 参 (cān)	C 尧 (yáo)	D 甫 (fǔ)
1	亻 'person'	傲 (ào: 'proud')	傪 (cān: 'good')	侥 (jiǎo: 'lucky')	俌 (fǔ: 'help')
2	扌 'hand'	撽 (ào: 'shake')	摻 (shán: 'seize')	挠 (náo: 'scratch')	捕 (bǔ: 'catch')
3	木 'wood'	檄 (ào: 'barge')	橬 (shēn: 'beam')	桡 (náo: 'oar')	楠 (fú: 'trellis')
4	氵 'water'	潎 (ào: 'stream')	渗 (shèn: 'leak')	浇 (jiāo: 'sprinkle')	浦 (pǔ: 'creek')

Source: Adapted from DeFrancis (1989).

Table 5.2 A Syllabic Writing System

Δ	i, ī	∇	ē	▷	o, ō	◁	a
Λ	pi, pī	V	pē	>	po, pō	<	pa
∩	ti, tī	U	tē	⊃	to, tō	C	ta
Γ	ci, cī	⊓	cē	J	co, cō	L	ca
P	ki, kī	⊄	kē	d	ko, kō	b	ka
Γ	mi, mī	⊓	mē	J	mo, mō	L	ma
σ	ni, nī	ᴗ	nē	₍	no, nō	ᴀ	na
ʃ	si, sī	↘	sē	↗	so, sō	↘	sa
↗	yi, yī	⊰	yē	⊲	yo, yō	↳	ya

Finals

ᵖ p   ⁄ t   – c   ↘ k   ᴄ m   ⌃ s   ⊃ n   • y   o w   ⁙ h   × hk   ₎ l   ₃ r

Source: Adapted from Pentland (1977).

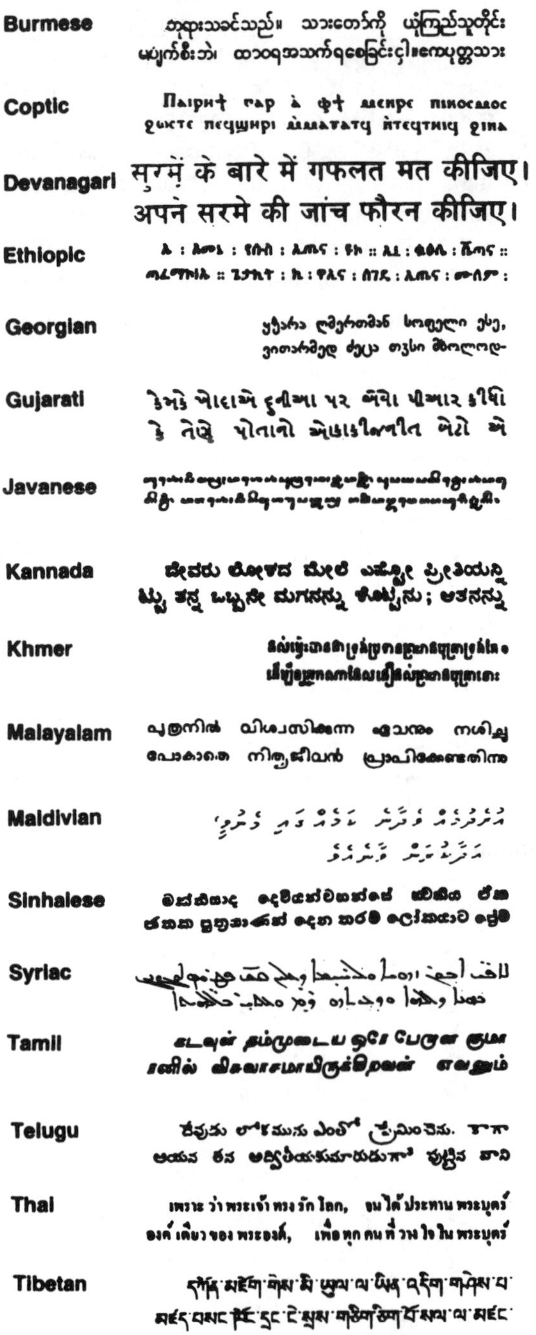

Burmese

ဘုရားသခင်သည်။ သားတော်ကို ယုံကြည်သူတိုင်း
မပျက်စီး�’ဘဲ ထာဝရအသက်ရစေခြင်းငှါ၊ပေးပွင့္သား

Coptic

Ⲡⲁⲓⲣⲏϯ ⲅⲁⲣ ⲁ ⲫϯ ⲙⲉⲛⲣⲉ ⲡⲓⲕⲟⲥⲙⲟⲥ
ϩⲱⲥⲧⲉ ⲡⲉϥϣⲏⲣⲓ ⲙ̄ⲙⲁⲩⲁⲧϥ ⲁ̄ⲧⲉϥⲧⲏⲓϥ ϩⲓⲛⲁ

Devanagari

सुर्मे के बारे में गफलत मत कीजिए।
अपने सरमे की जांच फौरन कीजिए।

Ethiopic

ል ፡ ኔመኒ ፡ ፃሰቢ ፡ ኔሠኖ ፡ ፃኑ ። ኔኗ ፡ ፁፅኔ ፡ ሸኖቴ ።
ዓሬፖዏኔ ። ፘፇኔፖ ፡ ክ ፡ ፃኔፄ ፡ ሸፃፄ ፡ ኔሠኖ ፡ ሣኖሰፖ ፡

Georgian

ყჩსჩ ღშჟჩოისჩ ხოგუღო ჟს,
ჟოთახშჟე ძსჟ თჟსო შოლლოლ-

Gujarati

ꠉꠝ꠪ ꠉꠣꠟꠣꠇ ꠖꠥꠘꠤꠀꠣ ꠙꠞ ꠅꠤꠉꠣ ꠙꠤꠟꠣꠞ ꠇꠣꠋꠠꠣ
ꠇ꠪ ꠘꠤꠎ꠪ ꠙꠥꠘꠣꠘꠥ ꠄꠥꠟꠣꠇꠠꠣꠉꠣꠋꠉ꠪ꠘ ꠇꠠꠕꠤ ꠄ

Javanese

ꦲꦤ꧀ꦤꦁꦱꦶꦫꦔ꧀ꦒꦶꦠꦸꦮꦸꦃꦲꦤ꧀ꦤꦁꦱꦶ ꦲꦤ꧀ꦤꦁꦱꦶꦫꦔ꧀ꦒꦶ
ꦲꦤ꧀ꦤꦁ ꦲꦤ꧀ꦤꦁꦱꦶꦫꦔ꧀ꦒꦶꦠꦸꦮꦸꦃꦲꦤ꧀ꦤꦁꦱꦶꦫꦔ꧀ꦒꦶꦠꦸꦮꦸꦃ

Kannada

ಕೆವರ ಕೆಲೆಕ್ಷೆ ಮೇಲೆ ಎಷ್ಟೋ ಪ್ರೀತಿಯನ್ನ
ಟ್ಟು ತನ್ನ ಒಬ್ಬನೇ ಮಗನನ್ನು ಕೊಟ್ಟನು; ಅಷ್ಟನ್ನು

Khmer

ឥស្សរៈប្រាណៈក្រៃលៃប្រៈឥស្សរៈក្រៃលៃ ។
ឥស្សរៈប្រៈឥស្សរៈក្រៃលៃប្រៈឥស្សរៈក្រៃលៃ៖

Malayalam

പുതുനിൽ വിശ്വസിക്കുന്ന ഏവനും നശിച്ച
പോകാതെ നിത്യജീവൻ പ്രാപിക്കേണ്ടതിനു

Maldivian

ﺍﺭﺭﻭﺍﺭﺭﺩﺍﺭ ﻭ ﻭﺭﺭﻭﺍﺭ ﻭﺭﺍﺭ ﻭﺭﺍﺭﺩ ﻭ ﻭﺭﺭﻭ
ﺍﺭﺭﺭﺍ ﻭﺭﺭ ﻭﺭﺭﺭﺭﻭ

Sinhalese

මෙහෙයමස් දෙම්බැන්ටම්බෙන්බෙ බම්බික ටම
ම්බක ඩම්බාම්බෙ දෙම කරම් මලේබක්බම් ම්ජ්බ

Syriac

ܠܐܠܦ ܐܚܡܕ ܐܘܣܐ ܡܚܫܒܛܐ ܘܚܫ ܩܡܐ ܘܚ ܐܝ
ܚܡܐ ܘܚܫܡܐ ܐܚܝܕܝ ܘܡ ܐܝܕܝܐ ܚܫܡܐ

Tamil

உடலும் தம்முடைய ஒரே பேறான குமா
ரனில் விசுவாசமாயிருக்கிறவன் எவனும்

Telugu

 కెవుడు లోకమును ఎంలో ప్రేమించెను. కాగా
ఆయన తన అద్వితీయకుమారుడుగాని పుట్టిన కొడ

Thai

เพราะว่าพระเจ้าทรงรักโลก, จนได้ประทานพระบุตร
องค์เดียวของพระองค์, เพื่อทุกคนที่วางใจในพระบุตร

Tibetan

དཀོན་མཆོག་གིས་འཇིག་རྟེན་ལ་ཤིན་ཏུ་དགའ་བའི་
སད་འབང་ཏེ་རང་ཏེ་སྲས་གཅིག་ཁོ་ནས་ལ་སད

Figure 5.5 Alphabetic Writing Systems
Source: Gunnemark and Kenrick (1985).

In addition to the organizing principles and form of the characters, writing systems can vary in terms of their alignment on a page. Some of the most obvious differences among graphologies are listed below, with examples of the languages that illustrate each:

- Some languages are written horizontally from right to left (Arabic, Hebrew).
- Some languages are written horizontally from left to right (English, Vietnamese).
- Some languages are written vertically from left to right (Mongolian).
- Some languages are written vertically from right to left (Chinese).
- Some languages are written vertically from bottom to top (some forms of Ancient Greek).
- Some languages are written strictly horizontally (English).
- Some languages are written with a gentle slope across the page (Arabic, Farsi).

The type of writing system that we use in the first language has an effect on the way we think about language in general. Students who come from a language with a logographic writing system are used to the idea that a written symbol represents a whole word or concept. Of course, students from these languages are able to learn that a written symbol can represent other units in other languages, but they might be expected to assume initially that words are unanalysed units, that they cannot be broken into components.

Using a syllabic writing system also seems to influence the way in which speakers think about language. Students who are accustomed to writing the combination of sounds [na] with one symbol, for example, may at first have difficulty segmenting language into consonants and vowels.

Students with an alphabetic first language may still have difficulties with the English writing system. They have many new letter forms to learn and several other factors may vary. Consider an English speaker trying to learn the alphabet of a language like Arabic, or Greek, or Hebrew. Obviously, many new forms are involved. Table 5.3 shows the many different forms of Arabic letters that must be mastered, for example.

We also find instance of slight overlap among alphabets. The words below are written in the Cyrillic alphabet and used in Russian. For the most part, the English and Cyrillic alphabets are composed of different characters, but clearly they do share some, although the written symbols correspond to different sounds:

BOP [ror] = thief
COCHa [sosna] = pine tree

This might be expected to cause English readers some trouble.

Table 5.3 Arabic Letter Forms

Phonemic Value	Final	Medial	Initial	Alone	Numerical Value	Name
ʔ	ا			ا	1	ʔalif
b	ـب	ـبـ	بـ	ب	2	bāʔ
t	ـت	ـتـ	تـ	ت	400	tāʔ
θ	ـث	ـثـ	ثـ	ث	500	θāʔ
j	ـج	ـجـ	جـ	ج	3	jīm
ḥ	ـح	ـحـ	حـ	ح	8	ḥāʔ
x	ـخ	ـخـ	خـ	خ	600	xāʔ
d	ـد			د	4	dāl
ð	ـذ			ذ	700	ðāl
r	ـر			ر	200	rāʔ
z	ـز			ز	7	zāy
s	ـس	ـسـ	سـ	س	60	sīn
š	ـش	ـشـ	شـ	ش	300	šīn
ṣ	ـص	ـصـ	صـ	ص	90	ṣād
ḍ	ـض	ـضـ	ضـ	ض	800	ḍād
ṭ	ـط	ـطـ	طـ	ط	9	ṭāʔ
̣ð	ـظ	ـظـ	ظـ	ظ	900	̣ðāʔ
ʕ	ـع	ـعـ	عـ	ع	70	ʕayn
ɣ	ـغ	ـغـ	غـ	غ	1000	ɣayn
f	ـف	ـفـ	فـ	ف	80	fāʔ
q	ـق	ـقـ	قـ	ق	100	qāf
k	ـك	ـكـ	كـ	ك	20	kāf
l	ـل	ـلـ	لـ	ل	30	lām
m	ـم	ـمـ	مـ	م	40	mīm
n	ـن	ـنـ	نـ	ن	50	nūn
h	ـه	ـهـ	هـ	ه	5	hāʔ
w	ـو			و	6	wāw
y	ـي	ـيـ	يـ	ى	10	yāʔ

Source: Adapted from Bright (1992).

Even students with an L1 that uses the *same* alphabet—French speakers learning English, for example—will have certain things to learn about the writing system. A study by Oller and Ziahosseiny (1970) found that French speakers made more spelling mistakes in English than Arabic students did because the French forms were sometimes very similar to the English ones. You can test this yourself by seeing if you stumble over the spelling of word pairs such as *plancton* and *plankton*. Which is French and which is English?

2.1.3 **Textual Competence**

Grammatical competence deals with structural aspects of language up to the sentence level. Yet obviously students are required to handle language above that level. In other words, they must deal with larger units than single sentences. *Textual* competence refers to the knowledge of how to join utterances together to form a text: two or more utterances structured according to the rules of *cohesion* and *rhetorical organization.*[2] Texts can be either spoken or written, as both genres involve combining sentences. First, let's look at cohesion.

2.1.3.1 Cohesion

Cohesion involves the overt structural links between utterances. Consider the following texts, paying special attention to the italicized elements:

> *Larry* is a really funny guy. Everybody likes *him* a lot.
> We went to *the movies and* saw *The Maltese Falcon*
> I used to drive an *MG.* I will never own another *sports car.*

Each illustrates some sort of overt link. In the first example, pronouns link utterances together. We can see that this is not merely an optional feature of a text when we violate certain principles of cohesion. Take a look at the sentences below:

> Larry is a really funny guy.
> Everybody likes Larry a lot.
> The students always rate Larry very highly in their evaluations.
> Larry, however, remains humble.

All of them are fine in terms of grammatical competence, but look what happens when we join them into a text. Unless we use some devices of cohesion, the result will look or sound odd:

> Larry is a really funny guy. Everybody likes Larry a lot. The students always rate Larry very highly in their evaluations. Larry, however, remains humble.

The same holds true for the other sentences given above. If our students never used conjunctions, for example, their texts would appear quite choppy: *We went to the movies. We saw The Maltese Falcon,* as opposed to *We went to the movies and saw The Maltese Falcon.* The first version appears much more disjointed, whether spoken or written.

---

[2] The term *utterance* is common in talking about discourse-level phenomena. A *sentence* has a precise syntactic definition. When actually using language, people do not always speak or write in grammatical sentences. Utterance is a broader term than sentence in that it does not refer to grammaticality.

Closely related to cohesion is *coherence*. These unfortunately similar terms were first coined by Halliday and Hasan (1976). Cohesion refers to the overt links characterizing a well-formed text, and coherence describes the covert links between utterances. There are no overt structural connections between sentences in the following text, for example, but semantically they are clearly related and the discourse flows well:

It's cold in here. Could you please close the window?

Textual competence does not always require overt links between the utterances; they are only one way to generate well-formed texts.

2.1.3.2 Rhetorical Organization

Rhetorical organization relates to the kind of text being generated. Different kinds of texts may have different conceptual structures. An academic essay, for example, is often described as having an introduction, a body, and a conclusion. The introduction starts generally and builds to a statement of thesis. The body consists of a series of arguments in support of the thesis statement. A work of fiction, however, is clearly not bound by the same constraints of logical construction of argumentation.

Some people claim that the rules governing these forms vary from culture to culture. When answering questions at a job interview in North America, for example, it is common to respond directly and quickly:

Interviewer: What were your duties in your last job?
Applicant: I was in charge of the research and development team for new software.

In another culture, it is conceivable that the discourse would be constructed differently:

Interviewer: What were your duties in your last job?
Applicant: It's important that everybody works together as a team. You have to support one another. No one person can really take the credit for developing a program. So, even though I was in charge of research and development, I feel that we all worked together.

While in some respects it is certainly true that such differences exist, we have never seen empirical support for greater variation between cultures than within a single culture. Nonetheless, it may be useful to be aware that the rules governing the structure of a text can vary from culture to culture.

2.2 PRAGMATIC COMPETENCE

Up to this point we have looked at the grammaticality, or structural wellformedness, of a sentence or text but have not really considered the role of context in communication. This is what constitutes the domain of *pragmatics:* the factors that make an utterance acceptable in some situations and not in others. Bachman breaks pragmatic competence into two constituents: *illocutionary* and *sociolinguistic* competence. We will deal with each in turn.

2.2.1 Illocutionary Competence

Illocutionary competence is based on the theory of speech acts. Speech act theory is concerned not with the structure of an utterance but with its function. Consider a sentence such as *The streets are like a skating rink.* Among other things, it could be

- an assertion (about the physical condition of the roads)
- a warning (to drive carefully)
- a request (not to drive at all)
- a retribution (for driving in this weather)

Even though there are several possible meanings, however, only one is intended. The intended meaning of an utterance is referred to as its *illocutionary force.*

L2 students must become adept both at expressing their intended meaning and at accurately interpreting the illocutionary force of utterances they hear. Below are two examples of someone misinterpreting the intended meaning of an utterance (either intentionally or unintentionally):

Speaker A [telephone caller]: Is your father home?
Speaker B [child answering the phone]: Yes.

Speaker A [stranger asking someone with a watch] Do you have the time?
Speaker B: Yes.

In both cases, Speaker B assumes the literal interpretation of the sentence, ignoring or not understanding the intended meaning of the speaker.

Learners must be able to perform the same speech function in a variety of ways. If they want someone to close the window, they should be able to say not just some variant of "Could you please close the window?" but also, "I think I'll get a sweater," "It's a little cold in here," or "Are you cold?" Similarly, they should be able to respond appropriately when someone addresses them with any of these utterances.

2.2.2 Sociolinguistic Competence

Sociolinguistics deals with the description and explanation of variation in language use. Bachman's model indicates geographical dialect, register, and cultural references as the components of sociolinguistic competence that second language learners must master. This chapter does not discuss aspects of regional variation but clearly language learners tend to acquire the version spoken around them. So, for example, if a non-native speaker of English hears utterances such as *Have you a car?* and *I've three dollars,* he or she will tend to acquire that particular dialect. If the same learner were to hear *Do you have a car?* and *I've got three dollars,* that would be the variation acquired.

Language use also varies according to social factors. A linguistic variant that is governed by social rather than geographical factors is known as a *register.* We find that people use language differently depending on such things as their age, sex, and socio-economic status. This type of variation can be a touchy area in terms of pedagogical implications. Before we consider that aspect, though, let us examine how sociolinguistic diversity manifests itself.

2.2.2.1 Age

Speakers of different ages use various linguistic devices to express their message. For one, they use distinct vocabulary. Examine the italicized words in the following sentences and decide whether you know anything about the age of the speaker:

> I have to buy a new *ice box.*
> We had a *gay* time.
> I have a *gay* friend.
> The concert was *lame.*

The speaker of the first two sentences would most likely be older than the speaker of the second two. This has particular relevance for second language teachers of young people. They cannot just teach their students to use language in the way that they do themselves. And they cannot tell them that their peers are speaking "bad" English. It would be just as noticeable for teenagers to talk about ice boxes as for octogenarians to refer to concerts as lame. Second language teachers must be sensitive to the communication styles of different age groups and not try to impose their own standards on other ages. On the other hand, their students must also learn to switch their language style according to the situation and realize that it may not be appropriate to write an essay with the sentence *Hopkins' use of sprung rhythm is awesome.*

2.2.2.2 Sex

In some languages men and women use different forms. In Japanese, for example, men and women employ different forms of the first person pronoun. Men are more likely to say "washi" or "boku" and women to say "atakushi" or "atashi." English is not so completely differentiated by the sex of the speaker, but in some areas it is nevertheless a sex-preferential language. Women appear to use certain words and phrases more than men do and vice versa. This is not a hard and fast rule of English but rather a tendency. Consider the following sentences and decide whether you think you know anything about the sex of the speaker:

What a charming house.
Where are my keys?
Where are my goddamned keys?

According to Coates (1986), the first sentence is more likely to be uttered by a woman, the second could be uttered by either a man or a woman, and the third is more likely to be uttered by a man. The pedagogical ramifications are problematic. Linguistic studies that refer to this phenomenon merely describe it; they do *not* mean that teachers in second language classes have to teach women to talk like women and men to talk like men. Even so, the students should probably be made aware of how their language use may be interpreted. Whether we like it or not a teenaged boy who refers to his friend's house as charming is likely to receive a negative reaction. The teacher should inform the student of this.

2.2.2.3 Socio-Economic Status

Language use also varies according to the socio-economic status of the speaker. Again, let us be crystal clear about the theoretical framework of descriptive linguistics. By describing the variation in how two populations use language, we are not judging either variant to be superior or inferior. A couple of examples from phonology should make it apparent how arbitrary judgments in this area can be.

One of the ways that dialects vary in English is whether [r] is pronounced post-vocalically, that is, after a vowel. In some—the so-called *r*-less dialects—a word like *car* is pronounced [ka:]. In others—the so-called *r*-ful dialects—the same word is pronounced [kar]. In every culture, some dialects are regarded as more prestigious than others, and the [r] sound gives us a nice picture of these distinctions. Labov (1966) conducted a study to determine who in New York had *r*-less and who *r*-ful pronunciation. He found a definite social stratification something along the following lines:

Upper-middle class always used [r]: *New York*
Lower-middle class sometimes used [r]: *New York / New Yo:k*
Working class never used [r]: *New Yo:k*

Trudgill (1974) did a similar study on dialects in Reading, England. He also found social stratification with respect to *r*-less and *r*-ful pronunciation:

Upper-middle class never used [r]: *fa:m*
Lower-middle class sometimes used [r]: *farm / fa:m*
Working class always used [r]: *farm*

Note that for both dialects there is a correlation between social class and language use but that the judgments about status are completely inverted. There is nothing inherently prestigious in a particular linguistic form such as [r]. The judgments are purely cultural.

Reflect as well on an example from the second language classroom. In Canada, some people are inclined to view *r*-less pronunciation as prestigious; teachers and students often express an affinity for "British English." Yet when a Cantonese student produces a similar form as a native speaker of British English—[ka:] for *car*, for example—the same teacher may view it as incorrect and say that the student needs work on his or her pronunciation. Arbitrary.

2.2.2.4 Register

Language use also varies according to certain characteristics of the situation: whether the communication is spoken or written, for example, or the level of formality. This is known as variation in register.

Imagine that you want to break up with someone you have been seeing for a long time. Try to decide what kind of language you would use to do this. Now think of the difference between writing and speaking this message. They would probably take quite different forms depending on the medium.

The formality of the situation also influences the style of communication. Consider the circumstances under which you would say "Hi!" or "How do you do?" When would you say "I'm afraid I'll have to ask you to leave" and when "Get out"? It is worth reminding ourselves that one type of utterance is not *better* than the other, but they are different. An analogy with fashion may help to clarify this. When attending a wedding it is usually inappropriate to wear a bathing suit. People often use this kind of statement to argue that formal language is better, but imagine the reverse of our example. Would you wear evening clothes on the beach? Formality is just as out of place in an informal situation as informality is in a formal one. Second language teachers cannot teach their students to converse with their friends in the same way that they would answer questions at a job interview. Communicative competence involves being flexible.

2.2.2.5 Cultural References

Sociolinguistic competence also involves being able to interpret cultural references in the language. When students hear utterances like those below, for example, they need a certain cultural knowledge to interpret them correctly:

We don't want this to be another *Waterloo*.
The Big Apple is getting more and more dangerous.
November 24th is *D-day* in this course.

This form of interpretation reinforces the idea that we cannot divorce language and culture, especially in the L2 classroom.

3 STRATEGIC COMPETENCE

Strategic competence involves the strategies you bring into play to maximize the efficacy of your communication. The term refers to two useful skills: communication strategies and learning strategies. Both are important for second language learners. Communication strategies are used by the learner to deal with gaps in his or her knowledge as they occur in conversation. An aspect of performance, they are designed to avoid communication breakdowns. Learning strategies, on the other hand, are designed to fill those knowledge gaps permanently, to change the competence of the learner. Learning strategies will be covered in greater depth in Chapter 15, when we explore individual differences among L2 learners. Tarone (1981) cites the following as examples of communication strategies:

1. *Paraphrase* Under the general heading of paraphrase she gives three subtypes: approximation, word coinage, and circumlocution. Approximation involves using a word that you know has approximately the correct meaning when you realize you don't have the exact word, such as using *table* when you mean *desk*. The learner may understand the distinction between tables and desks but lack the necessary vocabulary. In order to communicate, he or she uses a word that will be understood. Word coinage involves inventing a new word to fill a gap in your knowledge: *bookholder* for *bookshelf*. Circumlocution involves using a phrase to communicate what could probably be described by a word: *the plastic square where you keep your computer files,* instead of *disk*. This strategy is illustrated nicely in Nigel Barley's amusing book, *The Innocent Anthropologist,* when he described his own inability to say in Dowayo that a scorpion was in his hut. He ran screaming outside shouting the Dowayo equivalent of *hot beasts within!* The communication was successful though his reputation for idiosyncrasy remained intact.

2. *Borrowing* Both communication and learning strategies are utilized by monolingual speakers. Second language learners, though, also have the opportunity to draw on their L1 to keep communication going. Under borrowing we see two subtypes: translation and language switch. Translation occurs when we don't know the appropriate grammatical structure to use in the second language. We may translate from our first language. *Je marche le chien,* for example, is a direct translation of the English *I walk the dog,* but is incorrect in French. Language switch involves substituting a word from your first language in the hope that it will be understood by the second language listeners: *Is it cold enough outside to wear a ... sombrero?*

3. *Appeal to authority*　Sometimes when communication breaks down the learner appeals for assistance to someone who can answer the question. Phrases such as *What's this?* or *How do you say...?* are examples of appeals to authority. Looking something up in a dictionary or phrasebook is also considered an appeal to authority.

4. *Mime*　We can often make ourselves understood through mime when our second language skills let us down. Actions such as pointing, clapping, nodding, or shrugging can often help in communication. And we can all imagine how we might behave if we couldn't think of the word for *airplane* or *food* in the second language, how we might successfully mime these concepts.

5. *Avoidance*　Though it might seem counterintuitive at first, avoidance can also be a useful communication strategy. Everyone is well aware that conversations about certain topics may be beyond their abilities. If the authors of this book were asked to talk about international finance in French, for example, our linguistic abilities would not be up to the task and so we would avoid it (though not only for linguistic reasons). By steering the conversation away from certain topics we can keep it flowing smoothly.

All of these are examples of what we do when we come across a gap in our knowledge, and are an important part of communicative competence. One of the most entertaining examples of a communication strategy comes from Carlos Yorio. Yorio was a linguistics professor and a non-native speaker of English who was extraordinarily proficient in his second language. At times in conversation he would get an expression on his face that could be interpreted unambiguously as meaning *How can I possibly explain such a complex concept to idiots like you?* He later admitted that what was really going on in his head during those moments was something like, *I wonder how you say that in English?* He was covering up for a gap in his knowledge by making the listener think that he was trying to recast his thoughts to explain something better. We're not sure that instructors need to teach their students this strategy, but it certainly worked for Carlos. For a more detailed investigation of communication strategies, see Bialystok (1990) and Faerch and Kaspar (1983).

4 PSYCHOPHYSIOLOGICAL MECHANISMS

Very quickly, let's look at the last component of Bachman's model: psychophysiological mechanisms. Obviously, to be communicatively competent learners must have the necessary physical equipment to perform the tasks. They must have certain neurological, auditory, and articulatory abilities in order to function. As teachers we may not have any influence in this area unless we are specifically trained to deal with students who have impaired abilities.

5 OTHER ELEMENTS OF COMMUNICATIVE COMPETENCE

What else does communicative competence entail? This section will look at a few aspects not included in Bachman's model.

5.1 RULES OF CONVERSATION

Even though we may not be explicitly aware of them, rules govern conversation. Perhaps we become more conscious of these rules when they are violated. Consider what you would say in your first language to initiate a conversation: "I was wondering if I could talk to you about...?" or perhaps "Have you read the new Robertson Davies book?" Compare these to remarking, "How much did those shoes cost?" and "You look terrible!" How would you terminate a conversation? You might say, "Well, I've got to be going" or "I'll let you go now," as opposed to walking away without saying anything. To interrupt a conversation politely, speakers of English can interject, "Excuse me..." or "But don't you think...?" which are preferable to "That's ridiculous!"

Some interesting cross-cultural variation can be observed over *when* it is appropriate to interrupt. A characteristic of all conversations is turn taking. Conversations are co-operative ventures; as a conversation moves along, different speakers are given the floor at different times. The question is, how do we signal when we are giving up our turn? Turn taking also involves receptive ability, as we must be able to determine when someone else has finished his or her turn in order to avoid interrupting (unless we want to). We signal the end of our turn in a number of ways:

- content: *...and that's what I think* [summing up the preceding conversation]
- intonation: *...so I went home* [said with a falling intonation, or pitch contour] A rising or level intonation is generally not perceived by English speakers as signalling the end of a turn.
- pausing: *That's what Bob said* [followed by silence]

Different cultures have different acceptable pause lengths. Imagine—completely hypothetically—that English has a pause time of one second. After one second of silence, the other participants in a conversation would realize that the speaker was signalling the end of a turn. Now imagine another language with a pause time of two seconds. A native speaker of this language who was studying English would wait for a two-second silence before taking his or her turn in an English conversation, but that turn might never come because the native speakers in the conversation would be jumping in after one second. The student might well feel that English speakers are always interrupting each other and never giving him or her a chance to speak. What about a student whose first language had a pause time of half a second? She or he would hear half a second of silence and assume that the speaker was signalling the end of a turn. This learner might well be perceived by native English speakers as always interrupting. In this domain, we can see how first language transfer can actually cause others to make certain judgments about the personality of the learner.

5.2 NONVERBAL COMMUNICATION

Communicating also involves nonverbal signals. Consider the gestures you would use to convey the following messages:

- yes
- no
- come here
- I don't know
- obscene messages
- counting
- pointing
- the height of a person

We also find cross-cultural variation in these gestures. The gesture for *come here* in English tends to be made with the palm up, whether we gesture with one finger or the whole hand. In Japanese, on the other hand, the same gesture is made with the palm down. This is often interpreted by native English speakers to mean *go away*. Consider also how you count on your fingers. If you wanted to signal in a restaurant that you wanted two cups of coffee, you might hold up your index and middle finger to signal *two*. People in many other cultures, though, would hold up the thumb and index finger.

When examining nonverbal communication we must also think about such things as eye contact and physical distance. When is it appropriate to make eye contact? In some cultures, it is not considered respectful to make eye contact with someone who has a more powerful social position than you, such as your teacher. In other cultures it is considered a sign of respect to maintain constant eye contact with your teacher to show that you are paying attention. Both behaviours may be disconcerting to the native English teacher at first.

How close do you stand to people when you are talking to them? How close do you stand to someone on an elevator? The classic study in this field is by Hall (1966), who argued that cultures have different sizes of "bubbles" which represent the distance that people keep from one another. North Americans, he claimed, had a space bubble of about 20 to 24 inches. They feel uncomfortable if someone who is not intimate to them gets closer than this. Members of other cultures, though, have smaller space bubbles. You may find that students from Latin-American countries, for example, will stand much closer to you than you expect.

6 CONCLUSION

This chapter has emphasized that communicative competence in a second language is a very intricate construct involving both knowledge and ability. When discussing second language teaching, assessment, or acquisition, we always have to be aware of this complexity. Our investigations cannot focus on one just aspect of communicative competence.

CLASSROOM IMPLICATIONS

Everything that goes on in a second language classroom is influenced by the instructor's model of proficiency. If a second language teacher assumes that students need only manipulate grammar, then that is what will be done in class. If the teacher doesn't believe that students must be able to use the language appropriately, then he or she won't spend much time on pragmatics in class. An uninformed theory of proficiency might lead to an imbalanced class. A model of communicative competence allows the teacher to give second language learners a balanced program: to cover all the things they need to know; and to give them an opportunity to practise appropriate communicative tasks.

A model of communicative competence also influences how teachers assess students' proficiency. If the instructor believes that sentence-level grammar is the students' primary form of knowledge, then he or she will test them accordingly. If we are to get an accurate picture of students' wide range of knowledge and abilities, we need to consult a model of proficiency in constructing our tests.

Do you think that all aspects of communicative competence need to be taught explicitly? Do some of them come naturally?

SELF TEST

The construct of communicative competence looks at proficiency in terms of both _____ and _____ . Bachman's model
(1)   (2)
divides language competence into _____ and _____
(3)   (4)
competence. L2 learners need to know about both. Textual competence deals with structure _____ the sentence level, but this does
(5)
not imply that levels such as phonology, morphology, and syntax are unimportant. In terms of pragmatic competence, learners must be able to produce and comprehend the _____ force of an utterance.
(6)
Language use also varies according to the _____ of the situa-
(7)
tion. L2 learners need to develop _____ strategies for those
(8)
instances when their performance limitations inhibit conversation. Crucially, the teacher's view of what learners need to acquire in terms of knowledge and ability will greatly influence both L2 teaching and L2

_____ .
(9)

FURTHER READING

Bachman, L. 1990. *Fundamental Considerations in Language Testing*. Oxford: Oxford University Press.

Bialystok, E. 1990. *Communication Strategies*. Oxford: Blackwell.

Canale, M. and M. Swain. 1980. Theoretical bases of communicative approaches to second language teaching and testing. *Applied Linguistics* 1:1–47.

Theories of Second Language Acquisition

1 CHARACTERISTICS OF A GOOD THEORY

Much of the research on second language acquisition has attempted to construct a theory of second language learning that is able both to describe and to explain what second language learners do and how they do it. This chapter examines two complementary theories of second language acquisition, but before they are presented we need a framework within which to assess them. What does a "good" theory do? Stern (1983) offers the following characteristics:

1. A theory must be *useful* and *applicable*. This is more or less self-explanatory. For a theory to be useful it must apply to the area of investigation in question. A theory of second language learning, clearly, should apply to second language learners.
2. A theory must be *explicit*. According to Stern, a theory should "state and define its principal assumptions" (1983, 27). If the terms it uses are inexplicit and open to debate or confused interpretation, it is difficult to assess the claims that the theory makes.
3. A theory must be *coherent* and *consistent*. It is more than a collection of facts. A coherent theory should reveal connections among previously unrelated facts: an order or pattern to the facts. A theory should also treat phenomena consistently. A theory of second language learning that accounts quite well for the acquisition of Russian as a second language but has difficulty accounting for the acquisition of French, for example, is inconsistent.
4. A theory must be *comprehensive*. It should attempt to account for all relevant phenomena within a particular domain. The domain may be quite limited. A theory of second language listening comprehension,

for example, has to account for many aspects of its subject, but it does not need to say anything about L2 writing; it does not have to be comprehensive in that fashion.

5. A theory must be *predictive*. A good theory makes predictions about phenomena not yet observed. If we discover that Polish speakers tend to transfer their L1 rules when stressing an L2 word, for example, our theory might predict that Hungarian speakers would behave in the same way. A theory that does not make any predictions has less value.

6. A theory must be *falsifiable*. A theory that cannot be proven wrong is not highly valued. Consider the early theories of physics which explained the behaviour of bodies in motion by asserting, among other things, that rocks fell to earth because of a natural tendency to do so. This could not be disproved. Contrast this with falsifiable physical theories. If you postulate that light behaves as a stream of particles, you can make a prediction about its behaviour under certain experimental conditions—that the particles will bounce back from an impenetrable surface and scatter like billiard balls, for example—and then either confirm or disprove it. The terms and predictions of the theory are explicitly stated. The theory that the Earth was at the centre of the universe was disproved because it made testable claims and predictions.

7. A theory must be as *simple* as possible. This criterion is probably most familiar as Occam's Razor. William of Occam was a fourteenth-century philosopher who stated that entities must not be unnecessarily multiplied. Good theory is economical. When two theories can both account for observed phenomena, all other things being equal, the simpler one is preferred. We speculate that the reference to a razor in this principle comes from the metaphor of scraping away unnecessary facial hair.[1]

On the subject of evaluating theories, Chomsky makes a useful distinction between *descriptive* and *explanatory* adequacy. A theory that succeeds in delineating the observed data is descriptively adequate. This is certainly a minimal criterion. A theory should also elucidate the data, however, and if it does so it is said to have explanatory adequacy.

A theory of second language acquisition, then, should seek to describe and explain what L2 learners do. Perhaps it goes without saying that no comprehensive theory of second language learning exists. Nonetheless, a variety of theories have been proposed to account for certain parts of the SLA process. This chapter examines Schumann's and Krashen's models, but before turning to them let us first explore the role of theory in second language acquisition research generally.

---

[1] It was Bertrand Russell who said, "We must apply Occam's Razor to Plato's beard," in an attempt to simplify Plato's philosophical views.

2 THE ROLE OF THEORY IN SECOND LANGUAGE ACQUISITION RESEARCH

Ellis (1986) outlines two approaches to theory in second language research: theory-then-research and research-then-theory. The first of these involves five stages, shown in Figure 6.1. Research-then-theory involves four stages, shown in Figure 6.2. McLaughlin (1987) refers to the latter as a *prototheory* because it begins as a collection of unrelated facts. Gradually patterns may be found to connect the facts.

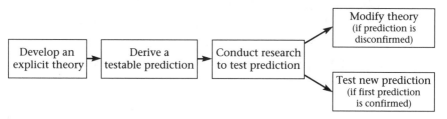

Figure 6.1   A Model of Theory-Then-Research

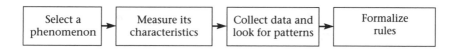

Figure 6.2   A Model of Research-Then-Theory

Both models are used in second language research. Much of the work in universal grammar proceeds as theory-then-research. Syntactic research, for example, may develop a theory of *wh* movement that explains why French speakers can move elements differently from the way English speakers do. An SLA researcher could test this theory by looking at English speakers who are learning French, to see whether the theoretical predictions are upheld.

If there is no explicit theory of a particular phenomenon, then the research-then-theory model may be followed. A researcher who wanted to understand a particular linguistic function, such as apologizing, might find that there was no accepted theory of how to apologize successfully and appropriately in a particular language. The researcher might well decide to gather a corpus of actual second language learner apologies and then try to find patterns.

3 MODELS OF SECOND LANGUAGE ACQUISITION

Broadly speaking, the process of SLA takes the form in Figure 6.3. Some theories emphasize the role of input and others focus on factors internal to the learner. We would now like to turn the discussion to two theories, or models, of second language acquisition. The first is Schumann's pidginization hypothesis (1978), also known as the acculturation hypothesis, and the second is Krashen's monitor model (1981). These two have been chosen because of their complementary nature. Schumann's model emphasizes factors that are external to the learner in an attempt to explain *why* the learner behaves in a particular fashion. Krashen's model emphasizes factors that are internal to the learner in an attempt to explain *how* the learner attains proficiency in a second language.

Figure 6.3

This is also an opportunity to begin an historical overview of the field of second language acquisition, as both models have been around for some time. More recent theories will be explored later in the text. Many of the phenomena raised by Schumann and Krashen must be addressed by any comprehensive theory of SLA.

3.1 THE PIDGINIZATION HYPOTHESIS

Schumann (1978) reports on a longitudinal study of a thirty-three-year-old Costa Rican named Alberto. Throughout the project, Alberto showed very little evidence of linguistic development in his second language, English. Schumann's goal was to discover the factors that accounted for Alberto's lack of learning. He looked at the development of three aspects of Alberto's grammar: negatives, interrogatives, and auxiliaries. From a larger population, Schumann noted the stages that second language learners usually moved through in acquiring these grammatical systems. For negatives, learners tended to follow the order given here:

1. *no* + verb (*I no want coffee*)
2. *don't* + verb (*I don't can explain*)
   - At this stage it appears that *don't* is unanalysed.[2] Learners are unaware of its internal structure, and use it as a variant of *no*.

---

[2] By referring to *don't* as unanalysed, we mean that the learner is not aware of the complex morphological nature of the word, in the same way that someone might not know that *won't* is a contraction of *will not*.

3. auxiliary + negative (*isn't, can't*)
4. analysed *do* + negative + verb (*don't, doesn't, didn't*)

Alberto remained at stage (1) throughout the project.

For interrogatives involving *wh* elements, the following path of development was observed (from Cazden et al. 1975):

1. Learners do not distinguish between word order in simple and embedded *wh* questions. Note that in a simple question such as *Where is Bob staying?* the auxiliary verb *is* and the subject *Bob* are inverted from the statement form *Bob is staying (at a hotel)*, whereas in a *wh* question embedded in a longer statement or question—*Do you know where Bob is staying?*—they are not. At stage (1) learners do not differentiate between these two types of question and do not invert the subject and auxiliary of either.

    We should point out that the main sentence does not have to have an interrogative function for it to contain an embedded question. A sentence such as *I don't know where Bob is staying* contains an embedded question in exactly the same way as *Do you know where Bob is staying?* The deep structure of *where Bob is staying* is the same for both sentences and is independent of the main sentence.
2. Learners sometimes invert simple questions. At this stage they might produce, for example, both *How can you say that?* and *Why I should go?*
3. Learners usually invert simple questions and occasionally embedded questions as well: *When should he come?* occurs alongside *I don't know when should he come.*
4. Learners distinguish fully between the two sentence types.

Alberto remained at stage (1) throughout the study.

Regarding auxiliaries, Schumann noted these stages of development:

1. Learners primarily use the auxiliary *is.*
2. Learners use *do* and *can* as well.
3. Learners achieve greater variation in auxiliary use.

Alberto remained at stage (1) throughout the project.

In general, he observed that Alberto used a reduced and simplified form of English, noting the following characteristics:

- used only *no* as a negative marker
- didn't invert questions
- used only *is* as an auxiliary
- didn't mark possessives
- regular past tense marking (*-ed*) was virtually absent

- marked plural correctly 85 percent of the time, but this could be accounted for via transfer from Spanish
- marked the progressive morpheme (-*ing*) 60 percent of the time

Schumann concluded that Alberto's reduced and simplified English was very similar in structure to a pidginized language.

A *pidgin* develops when people who speak different languages come into frequent contact, usually for reasons of business. Many pidgins developed hundreds of years ago. Portuguese speakers in Africa who wished to conduct business with Akan speakers, for example, needed to develop a way to communicate, since neither group understood the other's language. A kind of hybrid with some of the characteristics of both languages developed. Speakers from both languages were then able both to comprehend and to produce the pidgin. Pidgins are found all around the world and interestingly involve many different languages coming into contact, yet they share structural similarities:

- invariant negative marker
- few grammatical transformations
- no auxiliary verbs
- little or no inflectional morphology

The example below is from Cameroon pidgin English (Todd 1974, 70, 97):

aiɔn	no	fit	hɔt	if	yu	no	putam	fɔ	faia
↓	↓	↓	↓	↓	↓	↓	↓	↓	↓
iron	no	fit	hot	if	you	no	put + it	for	fire

An iron cannot get hot if you don't put it in the fire.
(Nothing can succeed if it is not tried.)

The similarities between the linguistic characteristics of a pidgin and of Alberto's English are clear. The question remains, though, what would *cause* Alberto's language to pidginize? To answer this, we need to consider the purposes a language serves. Smith (1972) proposed three general functions: (1) *communicative*, transmitting simple, literal information; (2) *integrative*, identifying the speaker as a member of a particular social group; and (3) *expressive*, identifying the speaker as a valued member of a linguistic group. Pidgin languages are usually restricted to the first function, and this limitation is said to cause the reduced and simplified form of language.

So how does this help us to account for Alberto's lack of development? Schumann considered three possible explanations. First, he assessed Alberto's ability. Maybe there was something physical or cognitive preventing Alberto from learning. After conducting a variety of tests, Schumann concluded that Alberto had no gross cognitive deficits that would have prevented him from learning English. Second, he considered Alberto's age. Maybe Alberto was too old to learn English in any sophisticated way. We will see in Chapter 14 that this explanation is untenable. Many adults who begin learning after puberty are able to acquire the second language. Third, he considered Alberto's *social* and *psychological distance* from target language speakers. This, Schumann believed, caused the functional restriction of Alberto's English and thus the simplified interlanguage he was using. Schumann noted that the speech of the second language learner would be restricted to the communicative function if the learner was socially and/or psychologically distant from the speakers of the target language (1976b). The following sections consider the constructs of social and psychological distance in more detail.

> I suppose hearing a language is a different way of feeling the words. I don't suppose there are synonyms really. I wonder if *moon* means exactly the same thing as *luna*. I don't suppose it does; there's a slight difference. There should be—in every word. So that to learn any language is to find out different ways of viewing, of sensing the universe, the world, or ourselves.
>
> Jorge Luis Borges
> The Royal Society of Arts, 5 October 1983

3.1.1 Social Distance

Social distance pertains to the individual as a member of one social group in contact with another social group. We might find that the social patterns of two immigrant groups were very different. Toronto, for example, has a large population of Italian speakers but relatively few Yoruba speakers. We might be able to explain different language learning patterns for these two groups in relation to their social situation. The Italian speakers will have the opportunity to do much more in the community in their first language than will the Yoruba speakers. Usually, social group in this sense is determined along linguistic lines. With respect to Alberto, his social group would be considered to be other Spanish speakers, rather than Costa Ricans or other non-native speakers.

Social distance has the effect of restricting the linguistic *input* to which the learner is exposed, and this is likely to have a negative effect on learning a second language. It is determined by several factors:

1. *Social equality* If two cultural groups are of roughly equal social status, the distance between them is minimal. If one culture is clearly dominant, however, then the social distance will be greater.
2. *Desire for assimilation* Social distance can result if either the dominant or the non-dominant culture has no desire for the non-dominant culture to assimilate.
3. *Size and cohesion of second language group* A large non-dominant culture tends to experience greater social distance than a small one. This can be tempered by the degree of cohesion. Social distance will be reduced if a large community is not very tightly knit, or cohesive.
4. *Cultural congruence* If the two cultures share many characteristics they are congruent. Congruent cultures have less social distance than do incongruent cultures.
5. *Attitudes* The attitude of each culture towards the other affects the social distance. If the cultures have largely positive perspectives then the social distance is reduced, and conversely if one culture has a negative point of view about the other the social distance is increased.
6. *Enclosure* The extent to which a community is self-contained, in terms of such things as schools, churches, places to shop, and so on, affects social distance. If the non-dominant community is self-contained, or enclosed, the social distance between the two cultures will be greater.
7. *Length of expected stay* If the non-dominant community does not intend to stay within the host culture then the social distance is increased. The intention to stay a long time reduces the social distance.

3.1.2 Psychological Distance

The construct of psychological distance relates to the individual alone, not to his or her position as a member of a social group. Schumann asserted that if the construct of social distance didn't clearly predict whether the situation was good or bad for language learning, then psychological distance would become more important. Psychological distance has the effect of restricting the amount of *intake* to the learner. Input is the data sent to the learner; intake is the data that the learner takes in. As fixed capacity processors, humans cannot process everything at once, and some input therefore never becomes intake. We might diagram this as in Figure 6.4.

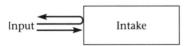

Figure 6.4 The Input/Intake Distinction

Table 6.1 summarizes the effects of psychological distance on language learning. Psychological distance is caused by culture shock, language shock, motivation, and ego permeability. Culture shock is a familiar term to most of us; it arises when the learner discovers that the problem-solving and coping strategies effective in the first culture are not working in the second (Smalley 1963). Activities that were routine at home, such as banking, shopping, travelling, and so on, now require great effort. The learner may react with fear, disorientation, anxiety, and stress, all of which divert energy from the language learning task.

Table 6.1   Characteristics of Psychological Distance

Positive	Negative
No language shock	Language shock
No culture shock	Culture shock
High motivation	Low motivation
Low ego boundary	High ego boundary

Source: Adapted from McLaughlin (1987).

Language shock comes from speaking a new language. Stengal (1939) notes that learners may be haunted by doubts about whether their words accurately reflect their ideas. They may fear appearing comic or child-like in their second language performance.

Motivation, or lack of it, can influence the psychological distance of a learner from the target language and culture as well. Gardner and Lambert (1972) distinguish between individuals who are *integratively* motivated and individuals who are *instrumentally* motivated. Learners who have integrative motivation are interested in learning the second language in order to become integrated with the second culture. Non-Japanese people living in Japan, for example, may want to understand more about the Japanese culture and way of thinking. Learners who have instrumental motivation, on the other hand, want to learn the second language for specific reasons: in order to get or keep a job with the government, for example, or to read the works of Chekhov in the original. Within Schumann's framework, integrative motivation leads to less psychological distance than instrumental motivation does because the learners feel much closer to the target culture.

The final variable that Schumann considered was ego boundaries. Basing his argument on a study done by Guiora et al. (1972), he claimed that people who had greater *ego permeability* were better second language learners. Ego permeability is related to empathy, the ability to put oneself in someone else's position. People who have low ego permeability are unable to put themselves in others' shoes; those with high ego permeability are more empathic. Thus, lack of ego permeability can result in psychological distance.

Schumann weighed the influence of all these factors in reaching this conclusion:

The learner's psychological distance will prevent him [or her] from identifying with the speakers of the target language such that he will not attempt to incorporate into his speech those linguistic features that would help to identify him as a member of the TL [target language] group. Hence, his use of the target language will be functionally restricted and, therefore, we would expect it to pidginize (1976a, 402).

One of the problems with the construct of psychological distance is that it makes the pidginization hypothesis difficult to falsify. Especially, notions of culture shock, language shock, and ego boundaries are very difficult, if not impossible, to measure. (The idea of motivation is somewhat easier to assess objectively, as we will see in Chapter 15.) If we do not have independent, objective ways of measuring these factors, we cannot say that they are *causing* linguistic pidginization.

In relating his hypothesis to Alberto, Schumann noted certain facts about the subject's lifestyle: he had few English-speaking friends and made no attempt to find any; he played only Spanish music; he "chose"[3] to work both at night and in the day rather than to attend English classes. Essentially, Alberto did not seek instruction because his English was adequate for his needs. We often reach a plateau in language learning when we can do everything we need or want to do in the second language. If we can get what we want when we order in Cantonese in a restaurant we may feel no pressure to keep improving our Cantonese. Alberto felt that he could do all he needed to, or wanted to, in English.

As part of the project, Alberto was given seven months of instruction. At the end, there was virtually no effect on his spontaneous speech, although his test performance improved. Schumann concluded that "instruction is evidently not powerful enough to overcome the pidginization engendered by social and psychological distance."

3.1.3 Modifications to the Acculturation Model

Schumann's model is helpful because it emphasizes that language learning must be viewed in a social context. It is inexplicit about the mechanisms of processing (*how* learners do what they do) but helps us to understand some of the factors that influence *why* learners do what they do. Ultimately, we will want a theory of language acquisition to account for both the how and the why.

Before moving on, however, it is useful to consider a modification made to Schumann's model by Acton (1979). Acton argued that it was

---

[3] We put this in "scare" quotes because we think it quite likely that Alberto's social position did not allow him to "choose" his employment selectively.

impossible to come up with an accurate measure of social distance for all members of a culture. He considered the *perceived* social distance of a particular member to be more important, noting that if learners perceive themselves to be either too close to or too distant from the second culture, then they will be "bad" language learners. He argued that "good" language learners maintain some distance between themselves and *both* cultures.

Kellerman (1979) also built upon Schumann's work by proposing the interesting construct of *perceived language distance*. Kellerman contended that learners had definite ideas about which languages were closer to their first language and that this might affect their second language acquisition. An English speaker might think that German is a lot like English but that Chinese is really different, for example. The learner in question may then find German easier to acquire than Chinese, in a self-fulfilling prophecy. As we will see in the next chapter, it is not at all straightforward whether elements that are similar in two languages are easier to acquire than dissimilar ones. Certainly these kinds of comparisons cannot be made for whole languages. We may have something to say about English vowels compared to Chinese vowels or English morphology compared to German morphology, but it verges on meaningless to believe simply that Chinese is difficult.

3.1.4 Evaluation of the Pidginization Theory

Let us now briefly assess Schumann's theory with respect to the criteria discussed earlier.

1. *A theory must be useful and applicable.* The model is useful in that it raises our awareness of the social milieu in which second language acquisition occurs. Schumann emphasizes the complexities of the social factors influencing the input to which the learner is exposed. The hypothesis is also clearly applicable to second language learners in a variety of social situations. It does not, however, appear to apply to foreign language learning environments where there is no cultural contact and most of the learning takes place in a classroom.
2. *A theory must be explicit.* A number of Schumann's key terms are difficult to measure objectively because they are inexplicit. Several subcomponents of both social and psychological distance, such as ego boundaries or degree of congruence, are never explicitly defined.
3. *A theory must be coherent and consistent.* Schumann's model does well in terms of both coherence and consistency. It emphasizes the role of external factors in the learning process but acknowledges that internal factors such as motivation also play a part.
4. *A theory must be comprehensive.* Schumann's theory does not address issues of second language learning in the classroom. If we noticed

similarities between the kind of language used in classrooms and that used in naturalistic settings, we would be unable to explain it with reference to the theory. The model also focusses on input and output in the learning process, tending to emphasize the form of the language produced rather than the mental representation of a grammar.

5. *A theory must be predictive.* The model clearly predicts that learners in different social situations and with different psychological make-up will have varied learning outcomes. The lack of explicitness in some of the constructs, however, makes more precise predictions difficult.

6. *A theory must be falsifiable.* The inherent problems in attempting to measure inexplicit constructs also affect falsifiability. If we want to say that x is causing a certain behaviour, we need to be able to define or measure x.

3.2 THE MONITOR THEORY

The monitor theory was proposed by Stephen Krashen. Although much criticism has been heaped upon it, a sport known as Krashen bashin', this model is included in the chapter for three major reasons. First, it has been, and continues to be, very influential, spawning such pedagogical strategies as the whole language approach. Second, in spite of its theoretical shortcomings, it has very good pedagogical implications. It does the right things for the wrong reasons. Third, Krashen claimed to provide a model of how learners do what they do, which is a nice complement to Schumann's model. Figure 6.5 illustrates the main components of the model, which will be examined in turn. Input comes into the learner, is processed, and results in speech production. Production follows one of two paths, either bypassing the monitor or being mediated by it.

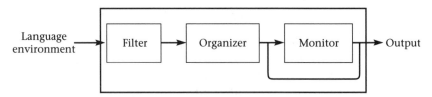

Figure 6.5   The Monitor Model

3.2.1 The Filter

The filter, also known as the affective filter, influences the input to which learners are exposed. Learners do not take in everything they hear. Certain affective factors influence their learning. Krashen's metaphor, then, is that something acts as a screen, letting certain things through and blocking others out. If the filter is lowered into place it blocks the input from becoming intake.

Krashen focussed on two factors—motivation and emotional state—and discussed how they could affect second language acquisition. He judged that lack of motivation could lower the affective filter. High motivation could raise the filter and thus allow input to flow freely into the learner. Relaxation also raises, or lifts away, the filter, leading to intake; anxiety brings down the filter, blocking the input.

3.2.2 The Organizer

The organizer is the internal processing system responsible for the learner's gradual organization of the new language system. According to Krashen, it functions "subconsciously" on "cognitive" principles. Although he used these labels, Krashen did not specify anything about the organizer's internal mechanisms; its operation remains a mystery. The lack of details is one of the biggest problems of a theory intended to address the internal mechanisms of language processing.

3.2.3 The Monitor

The third aspect of Krashen's model, and the one from which it takes its name, is the monitor. The monitor is responsible for conscious linguistic processing, which draws on knowledge obtained from reading grammar books or receiving explicit instruction in formal (prescriptive) grammar. In other words, it acts as a kind of editor of utterances. The learner formulates and may edit an utterance with reference to known rules, to see whether it is well-formed. Krashen claimed that the monitor was used when the speaker performed a task that required conscious attention to linguistic form. The ability to monitor depends on four factors:

1. Age
   • Children do not have a monitor. They are aware of what language does, not how it is structured.
2. Amount of formal instruction the learner has received
   • Monitoring requires knowledge of the rules.
3. Focus of the task
   • The task must focus on linguistic form, as opposed to communicative success.
4. Personality
   • Some learners monitor more than others.

The filter, the organizer, and the monitor, then, are the three basic components of Krashen's model. To see how it works, let us examine five hypotheses that Krashen made about second language acquisition.

3.2.4 The Acquisition/Learning Distinction

Krashen can be held individually responsible for one of the most frustrating terminological distinctions in the field of applied linguistics (right up there with cohesion and coherence). He maintained that there were two distinct ways of "getting" a language: *acquisition* and *learning*. Part of the frustration arises because English doesn't have a supercategory that would allow one to remain neutral about this distinction. Try to complete the sentence *Acquisition and learning are both kinds of....* There is no appropriate term.[4]

According to Krashen, adults have two discrete ways of developing competence in a second language. The first process, acquisition, is very similar to the way children get their first language. Children just absorb language without conscious knowledge of rules. Acquisition is knowledge *of* language. In the second process, learning, a person focusses consciously on knowledge of formal rules, knowledge *about* language. Some theorists have claimed that children acquire language but adults can only learn it. Krashen, however, maintained that adults can also acquire a second language.

He argued that the knowledge arising from acquisition was somehow deeper than the knowledge arising from learning. Acquisition led to the deep knowledge that allowed us to turn our thoughts into L2 words. For Krashen, acquisition was much more important in the scheme of things than learning. Learning functions only as a monitor, or editor, and knowledge of the formal rules of grammar plays a very limited role in L2 performance. He also maintained that knowledge developed through learning could never attain the deep status of knowledge developed by acquisition. This particular hypothesis had an enormous influence on second language classrooms; for many years the notion of teaching formal grammar in a communicative classroom became ugly. Second language teachers were made to feel embarrassed if they admitted to teaching grammar.

An obvious pedagogical implication of Krashen's hypothesis is that L2 teachers should be trying to make the learning environment acquisition rich; they should be trying to make second language acquisition much more like first language acquisition. Indeed, for a time, the amount of overt error correction that students received in many communicative second language classrooms was reduced under the influence of this theory. It has been shown that in first language acquisition, error correction tends not to affect the development of the child's linguistic system. Krashen argued that it is similarly ineffective for the adult learner.

3.2.5 The Natural Order Hypothesis

Basing his claim on a number of studies that investigated the acquisition of grammatical morphemes, Krashen maintained that there was a natural order for language acquisition. Certain structures would be acquired

---

[4] This is the only section of the book in which we will make the distinction between learning and acquisition.

before others, and the learning environment should encourage this natural order. Ever since Roger Brown (1973) reported that children tended to move through the same developmental stages when acquiring a first language, second language researchers have wondered if the same were true for L2 learners. Krashen considered the process of acquiring a second language practically identical to absorbing a first language. If this were the case, then we would expect second language learners to follow the same developmental path as first language learners. So if, for example, we noted that children tended to acquire their L1 morphemes in a given order—plural -s, possessive -s, and third person singular s,—then we could expect learners who were acquiring, as opposed to learning, a second language to follow the same path. If they didn't, Krashen asserted, they would be monitoring and interfering with the natural order. This is central to Krashen's theory. With Terrell, he produced a pedagogical guide entitled *The Natural Approach* (Krashen and Terrell 1983).

3.2.6 The Monitor Hypothesis

The monitor played such a limited role for Krashen because it could only be employed when certain situational criteria were met: the learner must have sufficient time (for most people, the demands of normal conversation do not allow enough time to monitor utterances); the learner must be able to focus on the form, rather than the meaning, of the utterance; and the learner must know the relevant rule. Krashen attempted to account for variation in second language acquisition by asserting that all speakers vary in the extent to which they use their monitors and identifying three types of monitor users:

1. *Monitor overusers* Monitor overusers attempt to monitor all the time. A symptom of this strategy is very hesitant speech, formally correct but lacking in fluency. These people are very conscious of being correct. They may even avoid communication for fear of errors.
2. *Monitor underusers* Monitor underusers are unconcerned with the formal correctness of their utterances. They are most concerned with successful communication. If the listener has understood the gist of the message, then the underuser is satisfied.
3. *Optimal monitor users* These people know when to monitor and when not to. Their fluency is not impeded by an over-riding concern with form, but when the task demands or allows it they are able to concentrate on the form of the utterance.

Carlos Yorio introduced a fourth category, the *super monitor user.* Super monitor users are exceptionally skilled performers who are able to monitor their utterances consciously even in normal conversation.

3.2.7 The Input Hypothesis

As we have seen, one of the ways of viewing second language learning is as a series of developmental stages. The learner progresses through these stages, which we will label here as S:

$$S_0 \rightarrow S_1 \rightarrow S_2 \rightarrow S_i \rightarrow S_{i+1} \rightarrow$$

Krashen claimed, "A necessary (but not sufficient) condition to move from stage i to stage i + 1 is that the acquirer understand input that contains i + 1, where 'understand' means that the acquirer is focused on the meaning and not on the form of the message" (1982, 21). How can the learner understand messages beyond his or her stage of development? According to Krashen, three factors allow us to do this: context, knowledge of the world, and extralinguistic information.

In a crucial phrase, he summarizes his hypothesis by saying that we must provide the learner with *comprehensible input*. Even though the input may be structurally or semantically beyond the ability of the student, the context can make it comprehensible. Without a context, the student may have difficulty understanding an utterance like *Paul suddenly felt morose*, but if we provide a context, the same word may be understood quite readily: *Earlier this morning, Paul's car exploded, the bank foreclosed on his mortgage, someone ran over his dog, he lost his job, and ran out of clean socks. He felt morose*. In this way we can strive to give our students comprehensible input.

3.2.8 The Affective Filter Hypothesis

As we have seen, Krashen argued that affective factors can block input from becoming intake. This hypothesis influenced second language classrooms to a considerable extent. Earlier pedagogical approaches, such as audiolingualism, emphasized drilling students with lots of grammatical information. Krashen argued that this type of instruction would neither relax students nor motivate them and as a result their affective filters would block input. Instead, he argued for a more meaning-based kind of instruction that dealt with topics relevant to learners and did not make them anxious. Teachers should strive to create a classroom atmosphere that produced relaxed and motivated students.

We can summarize Krashen's thesis into three main claims: acquisition is more important than learning; learners need to be exposed to comprehensible input; and learners must have low affective filters.

3.2.9 Criticisms of Krashen

The following briefly outlines some of the criticism levelled against Krashen's model:

1. McLaughlin (1978) argues that it is impossible to test the claims made by the model because subconscious processes like acquisition

are not open to inspection. In fact, if the only mechanism involved is subconscious, it is difficult to see what claims the model is making at all.

2. Krashen's claim that learning can never become acquisition, or that what we learn consciously will never become automatic, has been criticized by a number of people (Gregg 1984). Many cases have been cited of learned knowledge becoming automated through practice. Just consider learning how to drive a car. When one of the authors of this text was learning how to drive, he felt that it was completely impossible for a human to (1) hit the turn signal, (2) depress the clutch, (3) gear down, (4) turn the steering wheel, (5) let out the clutch, (6) watch the road for oncoming traffic, and (7) remain calm all at the same time. He now has the ability to do all of these things in what can best be described as a state of semi-consciousness (say driving late at night), with no conscious attention to detail. In other words, it has become automatic.

   In non-linguistic domains it seems clear that learned knowledge can become subconscious. It is, of course, open to debate whether the same is true of linguistic domains. Anecdotally, at least, there does appear to be a certain amount of evidence supporting the claim. Consider second language learners as they are acquiring irregular morphology. When they are first exposed to irregular forms such as *ate* or *rostra*, they have to associate them consciously with the appropriate root. Once the learner achieves a certain degree of proficiency, he or she no longer has to search consciously for the past tense of *eat* or the plural of *rostrum*. It has become automatic.

3. Krashen never outlined the actual processes responsible for acquisition or learning.

4. The only evidence for monitoring is the user's own account of trying to apply explicit rules. Can we, as language users, really distinguish applying rules from operating by feel?

5. Monitoring only accounts for production of utterances; it says nothing of perception.

6. Krashen limited monitoring to syntax, but learners can also monitor pronunciation, lexis, and discourse.

7. The model allows no role for comprehensible *output* in advancing second language development. Swain (1986) argued that receiving comprehensible input is not enough for people to learn second languages. They must also be given the opportunity to produce what she called comprehensible output. In her view, students can learn when they note that listeners do not understand what they are trying to say. When communication breaks down they have to evaluate their utterances and diagnose the problem. Swain argued that this process was beneficial and should not be overlooked.

8. Input, comprehensible or otherwise, is not enough to account for first language development. Adults come to know things for which there is no evidence in the input. The same poverty of the stimulus arguments apply to second language learning.

9. Krashen based his "natural order" hypothesis on the results of studies that looked primarily at students' accuracy on a small number of grammatical morphemes. It is a huge leap from claiming that plural marking tends to be acquired before possessive marking in English to claiming that there is a natural order of acquisition for all elements of language.

3.2.10 Evaluation of the Monitor Hypothesis

Let us apply the criteria discussed at the beginning of this chapter to Krashen's hypothesis.

1. *A theory must be useful and applicable.* Krashen's theory appears to have been very useful to second language teachers in terms of the ways it has influenced L2 classrooms. Its lack of explicitness has made it of less use to SLA researchers.

2. *A theory must be explicit.* As we have seen, the monitor model lacks explicitness in some important ways, such as in its reliance on subconscious processes. The distinction between monitor overuser or underuser says no more than that one person tends to focus on form and another tends to focus on meaning. New labels are not explicit definitions.

3. *A theory must be coherent and consistent.* Krashen's theory does appear to hang together for the most part, but his assertion that "learned" knowledge cannot become "acquired" is not consistent with known facts.

4. *A theory must be comprehensive.* Krashen's theory attempts to be comprehensive, covering second language acquisition in its entirety. It thus sets up lofty theoretical goals but does not provide enough detail for any of the claims to be closely evaluated. This is perhaps its major weakness.

5. *A theory must be predictive.* With its reliance on processes not open to conscious inspection, Krashen's theory does not lead to many empirically testable predictions. Those that have been made—such as the impossibility of learning becoming acquisition—have been tested and proven wrong.

6. *A theory must be falsifiable.* This, too, is a major problem for the monitor model. Think of recording an error in a second language learner's speech and trying to explain why it occurred. You would have to consider all of the following and more: maybe the affective filter was in

place; maybe the learner wasn't motivated; maybe the learner was monitoring too much; maybe the learner was monitoring too little; or maybe the learner didn't know the rule. One has to ask what the model *cannot* account for. It appears to be overly flexible and therefore unfalsifiable.

4 CONCLUSION

This chapter has looked at two influential models of second language development. Schumann's model emphasized the situational factors influencing *why* the learners do what they do. Krashen's model emphasized the input that learners receive and made some attempt to explain *how* they dealt with it. Any comprehensive theory of second language learning will have to account for these factors. Both models attempt to elucidate certain parts of the acquisition process and as a result shed valuable light on the enterprise. Figure 6.6 shows just what has to be explained. Throughout the book, we will continue to look at other aspects of this diagram in more detail.

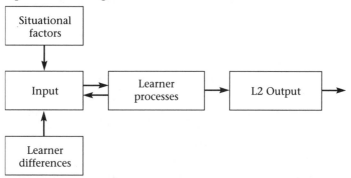

Figure 6.6   Factors Involved in Second Language Acquisition
Source: Adapted from Ellis (1986).

CLASSROOM IMPLICATIONS

The following teaching guidelines are given in Dulay, Burt, and Krashen (1982):

1. Maximize student's exposure to natural communication.
2. Incorporate a silent phase in your program.
3. Use concrete referents to make input comprehensible.

4. Devise techniques to relax students and protect their egos.
5. Include time for formal grammar for adults.
6. Learn motivations of your students and incorporate this into the lessons.
7. Create an atmosphere in which students are not embarrassed by their errors.
8. Use socially useful phrases in dialogues.
9. Certain structures should be learned first. The plural, for example, will probably be acquired before the possessive in English.
10. Do not refer to the L1 when teaching the L2.

These suggestions for a successful language classroom reinforce the idea that Krashen was advocating the right things for the wrong reasons, or for no reason. Many of them are self-explanatory, but a couple of points require comment.

The second item refers to a silent period. This is based on first language acquisition. Children learn to comprehend before they learn to produce language; they are not pressured to produce before they are ready. Dulay, Burt, and Krashen believed that the same should apply to adults learning a second language.

The fifth item seems somewhat out of place in Krashen's world, but he acknowledges that you have to give learners what they expect or their affective filters will come down. Adults often expect formal grammar lessons and Krashen therefore sanctions giving them.

The tenth item seems questionable to the authors of this text. There is very definitely a place for the first language in the second language classroom. Imagine a class of students with varying levels of proficiency: any class, in fact. One student has not understood the instructions for an activity. How do we deal with this? We could opt to keep trying ways to get that one student to understand the instructions, but this might be dull for the rest of the class. More desirably, we could ask someone in the class who speaks the student's first language to explain the instructions. Thirty seconds later the student with the initial confusion will be back into the second language, doing the activity in question. This is a completely justified use of the L1, and there are others. Try to think of them.

SELF TEST

One characteristic of a good theory is that it makes _____ (1) about unobserved phenomena. A good theory is _____ (2) (can be proven wrong) and simple (_____ (3) Razor). Two theories are

presented in this chapter. _____ emphasizes external factors,
                                    (4)
and _____ emphasizes internal ones. For Schumann, the
            (5)
process of SLA is like the process of _____ . Pidginized lan-
                                              (6)
guages and _____ share certain characteristics, such as a
                    (7)
_____ of inflectional morphology. The construct of
        (8)
_____ distance limits the learner's input, and _____
        (9)   (10)
distance limits the learner's intake.

Krashen addresses the *hows* rather than the *whys* of SLA. He assigns a
peripheral role to _____ instruction, emphasizing the natural
                            (11)
picking-up of language, which he labels _____ Krashen's
                                                (12)
model tends to be quite vague about the actual _____ that it
                                                        (13)
claims to describe, raising questions about its falsifiability and utility.

FURTHER READING

McLaughlin, B. 1987. *Theories of Second Language Learning.* New York:
    Edward Arnold.

Spolsky, B. 1989. *Conditions for Second Language Learning.* Oxford: Oxford
    University Press.

The Nature of an Interlanguage

Over the past twenty-five years and through a variety of approaches to second language acquisition, researchers have retained the basic insight that the knowledge of non-native speakers has a system. Just as researchers working in first language acquisition came to realize that child language was not simply an imperfect imitation of adult language but was instead productive and rule-governed, so too second language researchers came to recognize that non-native language was not just an impoverished version of the native language.

Both first and second language acquisition are characterized by the following schema:

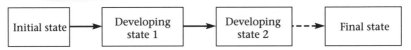

For first language learners, as we have seen, the initial state is universal grammar and the final state is adult grammar. For second language learners, the initial state is the grammar of the first language and the desired final state is the grammar of the second language.

This chapter investigates the characteristics of the intermediate, or developing, states. Selinker (1972) referred to these as *interlanguages,* a term that is commonly used today. The SLA process, then, could be conceived of as follows:

Yet this strictly linear interpretation of the acquisition process is not supported. Chapter 2 offered the example of a native speaker of German who produced the word *eyes* [ayz] as [ʌys]. We saw that within the grammar of this speaker the rules of final devoicing and Canadian raising interacted. The derivation of the interlanguage form can thus be represented as

Phonological representation	/ayz/
↓	
Rule 1. Final devoicing	ays
↓	
Rule 2. Canadian raising	ʌys
↓	
Phonetic representation	[ʌys]

Clearly, this indicates the systematic nature of an interlanguage grammar. It also suggests that

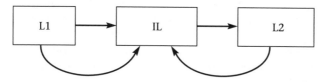

may be a more accurate representation of the SLA process. In the above diagram, the curved arrows illustrate that an interlanguage, or IL, grammar is influenced by characteristics of both the L1 and the L2. In the example of the German speaker, final devoicing came from the first language and Canadian raising from the second. To understand the nature of the interlanguage, we need to look at both sources. The chapter explores three of the major approaches to describing the nature of interlanguages: contrastive analysis, error analysis, and order of acquisition studies.

1 THE INFLUENCE OF THE FIRST LANGUAGE

We receive manifest support for the influence of the L1 when we hear a non-native accent. As native speakers, we are often able to tell what the first language of non-native speakers is. In Chapter 14, when we look at the critical period hypothesis, we will consider whether pronunciation is somehow different from other components of language. For now, we can note that at least in some domains, the L1 influence is clear.

A variety of terms are used to refer to this phenomenon. Sometimes we hear that the L1 *transfers*, sometimes that it *interferes*. The term *interference*, particularly, reflects the view of many people that the role of the first language is negative. Behaviourist learning theory has shaped this attitude. Remember from Chapter 3 that behaviourists saw language as a set of habits rather than as a system of knowledge. The first language constituted a collection of old habits that got in the way of the new habits of second language. Even though behaviourist learning theory had been discredited in the early 1960s, it continued to affect language classrooms and policy for a long time. Its influence can still be felt today. In Chapter 21, we will see the effects of the behaviourist approach on the bilingualism policy of the education system. Many students were forced to lose their first language in the belief that it was somehow getting in the way of the second language.

Transfer, however, doesn't always have to be negative. If the two languages differ over a given feature, transfer is said to be negative. If the two languages are similar with respect to a certain feature, transfer is said to be positive. Imagine yourself as a native speaker of English trying to learn French. You find yourself in a situation that is beyond your L2 abilities. You want to convey the message *I see the dog*. In an attempt to communicate, you decide to translate this sentence word for word from English into French, producing *Je vois le chien*. As it happens, this is a grammatical utterance; the transfer is positive. Soon after, you find yourself again in the position of having to speak French, and you want to say *I walk the dog*. Again, you decide to translate the English sentence word by word into French, producing *Je marche le chien*. This time, the utterance is not grammatical. Even though in some contexts the French word *marche* means *walk* in English, it cannot be used transitively (as in to walk *something*). In this case, the transfer is negative. You made a mistake. As mistakes are one of the most obvious characteristics of L2 speech, let us look at them in a bit more detail.

2 ERROR PATTERNS IN THE INTERLANGUAGE GRAMMAR

Within the behaviourist view of language, errors were considered extremely undesirable. If students in a language class made mistakes, they were to be immediately corrected before new (bad) habits could form. Errors were evidence that learning had not taken place, and the teacher had to ensure that it did. Concern with errors led to one of the most influential, and intuitively appealing, movements within second language acquisition research: contrastive analysis.

Why was, and is, contrastive analysis so attractive, especially to L2 teachers? Second language instructors are concerned with understanding why their students do the things they do. If a student says "I bought on the weekend" or "He very tall," the teacher wants to know why. Asking *why* questions is a big part of becoming a good language teacher, and one of the most commonly asked is why students are making a particular mistake. Contrastive analysis addresses that need to know; it tries to determine when errors will occur.

The driving force behind contrastive analysis was Robert Lado. In 1957, he wrote a book entitled *Linguistics across Cultures,* in which he said,

> The plan of the book rests on the assumption that we can predict and describe the patterns that will cause difficulty in learning, and those that will not cause difficulty, by comparing systematically the language and culture to be learned with the native language and culture of the student.... Those elements that are similar to [the learner's] native language will be simple for him [or her] and those elements that are different will be difficult (Lado 1957, vii, 1–2).

Again, it is easy to see why this appealed to teachers. If they knew what students would find easy, they could avoid wasting time and devote their attention to the things that learners found problematic. During the late 1950s and early 1960s, the focus of second language classrooms and research was clearly on *teaching*, as opposed to *learning*.

Wardhaugh (1970) made a distinction between two versions of the contrastive analysis hypothesis. The strong (or before-the-fact) version attempted to predict when L2 errors would occur. It assumed that the only source of error was the first language. The weak (or after-the fact) version used contrastive analysis as a kind of diagnostic only. Once the learner had produced some written or spoken language, the sample was analysed. Contrastive analysis in this case attempted to determine *which* of the errors resulted from L1 transfer. In other words, the weak version maintained that there was more than one source of error.

Once it was accepted that there was more than one underlying cause for errors, the question of when the first language would transfer was raised. Would certain factors such as level of proficiency or nature of the L1 allow us to identify when transfer was most likely to occur? Taylor (1975) claimed that beginning students made more transfer errors than intermediate students, who made more *overgeneralization* or *developmental* errors.

In Chapter 4, we saw that one of the most common kinds of mistakes for children learning a first language was overgeneralization. Remember the example of the child who overgeneralized the rule for past tense formation to produce *I goed.* This kind of mistake forces us to view errors in a new light. Rather than thinking of the error as evidence of non-learning, as behaviourists did, we must now conclude that it is, in fact, evidence that the child *is* learning. These kinds of errors are labelled developmental. Second language learners make developmental errors as well. They too may produce forms such as *I goed*, and it may have nothing to do with their first language.

In his ontogeny model, Major (1987) formally represents the influence that the developmental stage, or level of proficiency, has on the type of error the learner makes (see Figure 7.1). He claims, "At the early stages of acquisition interference processes predominate and then decrease over time, while at the early stages developmental processes are very infrequent, later they increase in frequency, and then they decrease over time" (102). The number of transfer errors thus declines as the learner progresses, whereas developmental errors start out by being infrequent, get more common in the intermediate stages, and then decrease. If we overlay the two graphs in Figure 7.1, we get a picture of the different error profiles of beginning, intermediate, and advanced students, as shown in Figure 7.2.

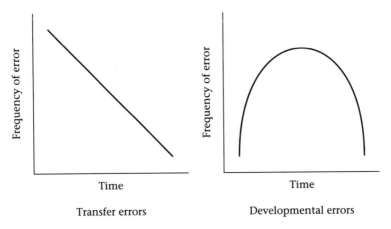

Figure 7.1   Major's Ontogeny Model
Source: Adapted from Major (1987).

This is a somewhat idealized representation, as it assumes that second language proficiency will continue to improve. It is of course possible that second language acquisition will reach a kind of plateau, referred to as *fossilization*. Saying that an interlanguage grammar has fossilized assumes that it has stopped changing, at least in a particular area. A fossilized grammar can be represented on an ontogeny model as shown in Figure 7.3.

3 CONTRASTIVE ANALYSIS

Major's model allows us to predict the kinds of errors we will find in an interlanguage if we know the level of proficiency of the learner. It doesn't have anything to say about the specific form of the IL grammar.

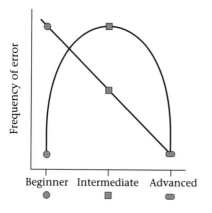

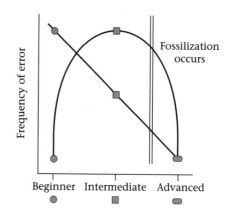

Figure 7.2   Composite Ontogeny Model
Source: Adapted from Major (1987).

Figure 7.3   Fossilization in the Ontogeny Model

Contrastive analysis explicitly attempted to explain why some elements of the L2 would cause difficulty for speakers of one L1 but not for another. The procedure was an algorithm for comparing two languages and trying to predict what the IL would look like.

There are four steps to conducting a contrastive analysis: description, selection, comparison, and prediction (Whitman 1970). First, a formal description of two languages is made or consulted. Second, a particular part of the languages is selected for analysis, such as segments (consonants or vowels). Third, the two systems are compared. Finally, areas of difficulty are predicted. If, for example, we made a contrastive analysis of Arabic and English sound systems, the facts shown in Table 7.1 would emerge.[1] This is the traditional starting point for conducting a contrastive analysis. The elements that were missing from the second language would be assumed to cause difficulty.

By comparing the sound systems of two languages we immediately note the differences. English has a voiceless bilabial stop, for example, whereas Arabic lacks it. On the other hand, Arabic has a variety of consonants made towards the back of the vocal tract. When comparing vowel systems, we can see that English has many more vowels than does Arabic. Clearly, speakers of either language would have to learn to make some new sounds if they were learning the other language. But are all new sounds equally difficult to master? There are several plausible answers:

1. Learning a new sound is hard. It doesn't matter whether it's [p] or [x].
2. Some sounds are naturally harder to make than others.

---

[1] The discussion simplifies slightly by ignoring secondary articulations in Arabic.

Table 7.1   Arabic and English Sound Inventories

Consonants

	Labial	**Dental**	**Alveolar**	**Palatal**
Arabic	b f m w	θ ð	t d s z n l r	š y
English	p b f v m w	θ ð	t d s z n l r	š ž č ǰ y

	Velar	**Uvular**	**Pharyngeal**	**Glottal**
Arabic	k g x ɣ	q	ʕ ʔ	h
English	k g			h

Vowels

Arabic	**English**
i u	i u
	e ə o
a	æ ɑ

3. Sounds that are found in many of the world's languages are easier to learn than rarer sounds. Uvulars and pharyngeals are less common than many other sounds and would therefore be relatively difficult.
4. Degree of difficulty depends on the relationship between the L1 and L2 sound systems. It might be easier to learn a system containing fewer contrasts than your L1 (English vowels → Arabic vowels) than one involving new contrasts (English velar consonants → Arabic velar consonants). These are referred to as directionality of difficulty effects.

The above possibilities demonstrate that there may be a number of potential causes of *difficulty* in L2 learning. The first step, however, is to sort out the areas of *difference*.

Let's look a little more closely at what goes on when we compare two languages. We started with the assumption that similar elements in the two languages will not cause problems but dissimilar ones will. This, in turn, is based on the presupposition that elements are either similar or different, that there are no other possibilities. In fact, when contrastive analyses were conducted (their heyday was in the early 1970s), it quickly became clear that it wasn't enough merely to talk of similarity and difference. A more finely grained analytical tool was needed to allow us to talk about *degrees* of similarity. Prator (1967) proposed the following system of classification, starting with the easiest type of correspondence between languages for the second language learner to master and getting harder. The hierarchy is based on the assumption that degree of difference corresponds to degree of learning difficulty.

Level 1 There is no difference between the element in the first language and the element in the second language. The /m/ sounds in

English and French are made in the same way, for example, and therefore would not be expected to cause problems.

Level 2 Two items in the first language converge into one item in the second language. For example, *savoir* and *connaître* in French are both translated into English as *know*. *Ser* and *estar* in Spanish are both translated as English *be*.

Level 3 A feature of the first language is absent in the second language. For example, in English questions are formed differently depending on whether or not they are embedded clauses. Consider the difference in word order in the simple question *Should he go?* and in the same question when it's embedded in the sentence *Do you think he should go?* This grammatical feature is absent from Spanish.

Level 4 An item in the first language has a different distribution from that in the second language. Spanish has the sound [ð], as in English *them* or Spanish *lado*, for example, but it only occurs in a specific phonetic environment. (Let us simplify and say that it occurs between vowels.) In English it can occur in any environment: *this*, *mother*, or *breathe*. The element is in both languages, but the distribution is different. In Spanish, [ð] is an allophone of /d/, whereas in English it's a separate phoneme.

Level 5 There is no similarity between the first language feature and the second language feature. The German [x], as in *Bach*, has no equivalent in English. English has a voiceless velar stop [k] but no voiceless velar fricative [x].

Level 6 One item in the first language diverges into two items in the second language. The meaning of the word *the* in English, for example, is represented in French by *le*, *la*, or *les*, depending on the context.

As finely grained as the hierarchy appears to be, it still has problems. It is not always straightforward to determine the level into which a particular comparison will fall. Consider the case of a Spanish speaker learning the English [r] sound. Phonetically, the English /r/ and the Spanish /r/ are quite different. The English /r/ is classified as a retroflex liquid [r], which has the tongue tip curled back in the mouth but not making contact with the roof of the mouth. The Spanish /r/ is a tapped [ɾ], in which the tip of the tongue touches the roof of the mouth near the alveolar ridge. And the Spanish /r/ has variants that the English /r/ doesn't, becoming trilled at the beginning of a word, for example, to produce [ř]. In light of all this, fairly strong arguments could be made for placing this item at level 3 (Spanish /r/ is a tap and English doesn't have that); or level 4 (English has a tap but it's a variant of /t/ not /r/); or level 5 (the English /r/ splits into two variants in Spanish: [ɾ] and [ř]). The criteria proposed are not well enough defined to predict with certainty what level of difficulty we expect.

They always teach you vocabulary and grammar rules, and you'd think that would be enough for basic survival. Once I knew enough to say "Excuse me. Could you please tell me how to get to the bus station?" in Hebrew I thought I was set. But I also needed to know how to be rude, or at least abrupt. I could never get anyone to stop long enough to hear more than "Excuse me." It took about six months before I figured out that in Hebrew you've got to get right to the point. You've got to say "Where's the bus station?" Oh, and "Excuse me" is only for apologies.

It's those tiny details that do you in: a vowel here, a consonant there. Who would think it would make such a difference? Like the time I thought I was telling my roommate that the sink was plugged again. I said "kinor." I meant *kiyor* ... big deal. But Ruthie had no idea what I was trying to say. I ask you, how hard can it be to figure out that I meant *sink*, and not *violin*? Oh, and there was the time her friends came calling, and asked if she was *yeshna* (there). I thought they were asking if she was *yeshena* (sleeping), and closed the door. They thought I was nuts. Fortunately, she woke up and explained that I was only Canadian.

Janet McDonald
Professor of Linguistics,
University of Calgary

3.1 CONTRASTIVE PRAGMATICS

One aspect of contrastive analysis that never received as much attention as contrastive linguistics was contrastive pragmatics, or cultural analysis. Lado originally claimed that analysis would be able to tell us which aspects of cultural acquisition would be easy and which difficult to acquire. In some respects, research on communicative competence has pursued this line of inquiry, as we saw in Chapter 5 when we looked at cross-cultural variation in things like gesture and pause time. We might look at culture one (C1) and culture two (C2) in terms of certain communicative situations. How do you signal that you are listening to someone in C1 versus C2? How do you greet someone politely in C1 versus C2? On a purely speculative level, we might expect the same kinds of directionality of difficulty effects as we saw in comparing sound systems, above. Would it be harder for a speaker from one culture to learn to suppress being very formal to teachers or for a speaker from another to learn to treat teachers very formally? These questions have received very little attention in either the SLA or anthropological literature.

3.2 PROBLEMS WITH CONTRASTIVE ANALYSIS

Traditional contrastive analysis had a serious problem: many predicted errors did not occur and many errors that did occur were not predicted. Yet the people working within this framework were not oversimplifying anything. Their grammatical models were sophisticated, and their method of comparison was anything but simple-minded. So why so many problems?

Contrastive analysis assumed that the only source of error was the first language; it did not acknowledge such things as overgeneralization. A number of studies were done to determine the percentage of L2 learner errors that could be traced back to the L1. Ellis (1986) provides a summary of them which clearly shows that L1 transfer is not the only source of error (Table 7.2).

Table 7.2   Percentage of Transfer Errors

Study	Percentage of transfer errors	L1 of learners (adults)
Grauberg (1971)	36	German
George (1972)	33	mixed
Tran-Chi-Chau (1975)	51	Chinese
Mukattash (1977)	23	Arabic
Flick (1980)	31	Spanish
Lott (1983)	50	Italian

Source: Adapted from Ellis (1986).

As we saw in Chapter 3, behaviourist learning theory had a great deal of trouble accounting for language acquisition. The equation of *different* with *difficult* and *similar* with *easy* proved to be a particularly problematic aspect of contrastive analysis (Ellis 1986). A simple example should clarify the problems here. Consider how the /t/ sound is made in English and French. In English, it's a voiceless alveolar stop. In French, it is classified as a voiceless dental stop; the tip of the tongue touches the teeth rather than the alveolar ridge. Now, the dental and alveolar places of articulation are very close, and contrastive analysis would therefore predict that it should be easy for English speakers to remember to make all the French /t/ sounds with the tongue touching the teeth instead of the alveolar ridge. Clearly, this is not the case. It is often characteristic of an English accent in French to produce alveolar rather than dental stops. The converse is also problematic. An English speaker studying Spanish has to learn how to make the [β] sound, a voiceless bilabial fricative found in words such as *saber*. As this is unlike anything in English—to say that it is sort of like a [b] is akin to saying that [s] is sort of like [t]—contrastive analysis predicts that this would be a difficult item for an English speaker to acquire. Again, this is not necessarily the case. English speakers tend not to confuse [β] with any other sound.

This type of problem led to another version of the contrastive analysis hypothesis: the *moderate* version. Oller and Ziahosseiny (1970) conducted a study investigating the spelling ability of ESL learners. They looked at two groups of students. The first had French as a first language (and hence a roman alphabet as a writing system), and the second had Arabic as a first language (and hence a non-roman alphabet). The strong version of the contrastive analysis hypothesis predicts that the L1 Arabic students should have more trouble with English spelling; the weak version would expect performance between the two groups to be about the same, as learners would only retreat to the L1 when they didn't know how to spell something. In fact, the French students had more trouble spelling English than did the Arabic students. Because English has borrowed a sizable vocabulary from French, it is conceivable that a French speaker could use a French word as a communication strategy in English conversation and be understood, although the words would be spelled differently. The Arabic speaker would not have the same initial advantage lexically. Oller and Ziahosseiny add to our understanding of contrastive analysis by noting that "wherever patterns are minimally distinct in form or meaning in one or more systems, confusion may occur" (1970, 186). Thus, the moderate version of the contrastive analysis hypothesis maintains that similarity can also cause errors.

Oller and Ziahosseiny conclude,

> the data of the present study lead us to conclude that as far as English spelling is concerned, the strong form of the CAH [contrastive analysis hypothesis] is probably too strong, and the weak form too weak. The strong version predicts greatest difficulty where the difficulty is apparently least, and the weak form predicts no difference in level of difficulty where there is a highly significant difference.... Apparently, knowledge of one Roman writing system makes it *more* difficult, *not less* to acquire another Roman spelling system (1970, 188).

Still, we must ask whether writing is different from speaking in this respect.

Researchers have also raised the concern that contrastive analysis is somewhat narrow in scope. In spite of Lado's original formulation, contrastive analysis tended to emphasize the grammaticality of an utterance. Shifts in both linguistic analysis and pedagogic concerns over the past fifteen years have made it clear that language involves more than merely being grammatically correct. Language functions in a social context. Consider a sentence such as *I'm wearing brown shoes.* It is clearly grammatical, but now look at it in the following context:

Speaker A: What did you do this weekend?
Speaker B: I'm wearing brown shoes.

Obviously, the grammatically correct utterance is not relevant to the situation. Second language learners must also be able to produce appropriate utterances, to say "Hi" in some contexts and "How do you do" in others. Contrastive analysis focussed on grammatical competence and had less to say about textual or pragmatic competence.

Another problem with contrastive analysis was its assumption that all learners could be treated the same way. This probably stemmed from the behaviourist learning theory underlying the technique. Behaviourism maintained that general learning principles could be postulated to account for any organism learning anything. It didn't matter if we were talking about pigeons learning to play "Take Me out to the Ballgame" on the piano or humans learning language. Learner variation was not a concern. Yet contrastive analysis revealed that not all learners behave in the same way. Not all Spanish speakers, for example, make exactly the same kinds of mistakes when they're learning English.

In spite of all of the sophisticated attempts within the framework of contrastive analysis, it was difficult to determine even the level of linguistic structure that was causing a learner's problem. Burt and Kiparsky (1972) published a book called *The Gooficon,* which listed a large number of second language learner errors classified by type, among them,

1. Surrogate subject missing: *there* and *it*
   a. Are too many people here.
   b. Is raining.
2. Simple predicate missing: *be*
   a. John tall.
   b. My sisters very pretty.
3. Object pronoun missing
   a. I bought in Japan.
4. Subject pronoun missing
   a. My mother been the first wife of our father. Always lead the other wives wherever they are invited.

At first blush it might seem straightforward to assign errors to a particular cause, but let's consider a number of other possibilities. Burt and Kiparsky assume that the sentences in (1) reveal a syntactic problem, but consider the phonetic similarities between the learner version and the target version:

> *Learner:*   Are too many people here.
> *Target:*   There're too many people here.

Most native speakers pronounce the first two words in the second sentence something like [ðər]. This form is very similar to the learner's, and most likely perceptually difficult to distinguish. Is this a syntactic problem or a perception problem? The same point arises when we consider sentence 2(b), *My sisters very pretty,* which has a form very close to *My sisters're very pretty* and sounds identical to *My sister's very pretty.* Furthermore, compare the learner sentence 1(b) and its native target version:

> *Learner:*   Is raining.
> *Target:*   It's raining.

Is the learner unaware of the distribution of expletive subjects in English,[2] or is he or she having a phonological problem in realizing consonant clusters? What if the learner had produced something like *Yesterday I miss my bus*? Would this indicate a morphological problem or a strategy of simplifying consonant clusters?

Similarly, in sentence 3(a) is it relevant that an object pronoun is missing, or has the learner mixed up the verbs *buy* and *shop*? The sentence *I shopped in Japan* is perfectly fine.

Finally, the sentences in 4(a) are interpreted as indicating difficulty understanding that English does not allow null subjects, but consider the following:

1. *A sentence:* He stepped into the street without looking. Never knew what hit him.
2. *A sign:* GET INTO LAW SCHOOL! Want to know more?
3. *A conversation:*
   Speaker A: Did you hear that salaries will be cut by 5 percent?
   Speaker B: Haven't heard about it.

All of these could conceivably be construed as instances of null subjects in English. Is the learner who produced the erroneous form having difficulty with syntax, or with the pragmatic factors that influence when English allows subjects to be dropped?

We raise these issues not to show that Burt and Kiparsky had the causes of errors wrong but that other causes are possible. Contrastive analysis proved problematic in determining the source of error because it was not explicit about non-surface aspects of linguistic structure.

---

2 *It* and *there* are often used as expletive subjects. In sentences such as *It is raining* or *There are two cats in the house* the *it* and *there* do not refer to anything but are required because English sentences need subjects.

4 TRANSFER AND INTERLANGUAGE PHONOLOGY

As we have seen, contrastive analysis is centrally concerned with how the structure of the first language will influence the structure of the interlanguage grammar. Phonology is usually considered to be the area in which L1 transfer is most obvious; we can, after all, recognize particular accents easily. French speakers do tend to say things like "It is really 'ot in 'ere" and Spanish speakers do tend to say such things as "I espeak Espanish." Both these examples can be explained by properties of the L1 phonological system. When English borrowed the word *Koran* from Arabic, for example, it replaced the uvular stop [q] with a velar stop [k]. Transfer from the L1 does appear to explain many of the characteristics of second language accent. Tarone (1987), however, presents data to support the argument that interlanguage phonology involves more than transfer alone, maintaining that the following additional processes play a part:

1. *Overgeneralization* Sometimes learners overgeneralize a sound that is not found in their L1. An English speaker learning German who uses [x] for both [x] and [ç], for example, is not transferring from L1. In German, the palatal fricative [ç] is found after front vowels and the velar fricative [x] is found after back vowels: *ich* [iç] and *Bach* [bax]. Neither of these sounds is found in English, and if a learner mastered one of the sounds and overgeneralized its application—saying both [ix] and [bax]—we could not say that the cause was L1 transfer.
2. *Approximation* The learner may approximate the L2 sound with one found in neither the L1 or the L2. An English speaker who attempts to make a Vietnamese implosive sound—in which the air goes *in* rather than out—and doesn't quite get it, makes an approximation that can't be explained by L1 transfer.
3. *Avoidance* Learners may actually be able to avoid sounds that they find particularly difficult. An English speaker learning Spanish might have difficulty with the name Jorge [xorçe], for example, and avoid it purely for phonological reasons by saying "Where is your brother?" rather than "Where is Jorge?"

Tarone also points out that there may be certain universal principles at work in second language accent. The following constraints appear to be operative:

1. *The inherent difficulty of certain target language sounds* In the field of language universals, it has been claimed that some sounds—perhaps those not found in many of the world's languages—are inherently more difficult for the human vocal tract to produce. Examples are clicks ([ʘ ǀ ǂ ǁ]), implosives ([ɓ ɗ ɠ]), and ejectives ([p' t' k']).

2. *The tendency to prefer a CV pattern*   Again drawing on language universals, Tarone argues that interlanguages may tend to reflect a universal preference for syllables in a consonant–vowel (CV) form. If a second language learner pronounces the word *pig* as [pɪgə], for example, it may reflect universal preferences rather than L1 transfer.

5 SUMMARY OF TRANSFER

The effects of the first language on the second language are still receiving a lot of attention in the literature today. (See Odlin (1989) for overviews of transfer studies.) Much of the material in Chapters 8 and 9 will examine how the L1 influences the interlanguage. The phenomenon must definitely be accounted for.

Ringbom describes transfer as "the ways in which knowledge of the mother tongue (and other languages) influences the learning of another language" (1990, 205). It is undeniable that a certain number of learner errors resemble structures of the L1 and appear to have no basis in the L2 data. Despite its problems, contrastive analysis does capture a certain part of the SLA process, and the first language does play a role. This should not really be surprising when we consider the role of existing knowledge in other cognitive domains. In an area such as mathematics, for example, we fully expect the learner to rely on extant knowledge when acquiring new. Why should language be any different? Brown makes this point when he says, "Human beings approach any new problem with an existing set of cognitive structures and ... call upon whatever prior experiences they have had and whatever cognitive structures they possess to attempt a solution" (1987, 81).

For Brown, three commonly used terms—*transfer, interference,* and *overgeneralization*—are, in fact, manifestations of the same principle, "the interaction of previously learned material with a present learning event" (81). Ringbom summarizes the current view when he says, "Today it is generally acknowledged that language transfer is an important subject of study which plays a subtle and pervasive part in L2-learning" (1990, 205). He goes on to acknowledge, however, that accepting the existence of transfer necessitates exploration of "*when* and *why* learners transfer *what*, and *how much*" (205).

Ringbom conducted a large-scale study of the acquisition of English by Finnish speakers and Swedish speakers living in Finland. Swedish is related to English but Finnish is not. The study assumed that

Swedish-speaking Finns ... would do better in any test of English than an equivalent group of Finns. It can be expected that the advantage of the Swedes who learn a related language, compared with the Finns who learn an unrelated language, will appear at all levels and stages of learning. With one minor exception, that of English spelling, this hypothesis has also been borne out in all experiments (1990, 208).

These results are consistent with the assumption that L1 learners are transferring at least some of their L1 structures into the L2. When these structures are the same, the learners produce correct forms; when the structures are different, they produce incorrect forms. It appears that some of the failure of contrastive analysis had to do with the tools of linguistic analysis available.

6 ERROR ANALYSIS

We have seen how contrastive analysis emphasized interference from the L1 as the major source of error and essentially ignored the similarities between first and second language acquisition. Drawing on work being done in first language acquisition (Brown 1973, for example) and in psychology (Piaget 1929), researchers began in the 1970s to consider that second language learners were constructing a system. The role of the learner was not nearly so passive as contrastive analysis might have led us to believe; instead, language learning was seen to be a creative process. In short, second language acquisition began to be considered in much the same way as first language acquisition.

The parallels are clear when we view language learning in the following way. For first language learners, the initial state is the state the child is in at birth and the final state is adult knowledge. For the second language learner, the initial state is the first language. The learner's task is to acquire the second language grammar. Both types of learners move along a developmental path through intermediate states that appear to share certain characteristics, systematicity in particular.

Children make errors when learning to speak their first language and nobody views it as undesirable or even strange. Corder (1967) first made this explicit when he noted that we don't even regard their speech characteristics as errors but as normal child language. Corder pushed for a similar view of second language learners. He made an interesting and useful terminological distinction between *mistakes* and *errors*.[3] Mistakes

---

[3] We will not be maintaining this terminological distinction throughout the book, but an understanding of it has useful pedagogical implications which we will consider later.

are errors in performance. Even native speakers make mistakes, and they have no significance in the study of competence because they do not give us a true picture of the underlying system of knowledge. If you were standing at the front of a classroom and said something like "I'll put an example on the *backbloard*," you wouldn't panic and think you were losing your grasp of English. You would know that you simply made a slip of the tongue. Second language learners do this kind of thing, too. Errors, on the other hand, are systematic and result from a transitional competence. It is errors that most concern the teacher in the second language classroom and the second language researcher. If a learner consistently produces sentences of the form *I wish he hadn't went outside*, we may well have reason for assuming that he or she hasn't internalized the distinction between past participle and simple past. Systematic errors give us a window onto a developing system.

Corder proposed the following stages in conducting an error analysis: (1) select a linguistic corpus; (2) identify the errors; (3) classify the errors (determine their source); and (4) evaluate the errors for teaching implications. Note the assumption in step (3) that it is possible to determine the target sentence unambiguously and therefore to determine if the utterance contains an error. A learner might produce a sentence such as *I haven't known you very long, but I love you a lot*. How do we know whether the learner really meant *love* or whether he or she meant *like*? Or a learner might write *Canadian weather designs are more fluid than in Mexico*. Is there an error in this sentence? Error classification is not necessarily straightforward. We will return to this issue in Chapter 18 when we look more closely at the issue of error correction.

6.1 PROBLEMS WITH ERROR ANALYSIS

Although error analysis fared better than contrastive analysis, it was not problem free. For one thing, it tended to make researchers and teachers too preoccupied with errors. Second language teachers do not want their classrooms to become centres for error correction and nothing more. We can also learn from the kinds of things that students get right. For another thing, error analysis tended to stress production data more than perception data although both are revealing when it comes to looking at second language learning.

Schachter (1974) proposed a compromise between contrastive and error analysis by showing how they could be useful when used together. She examined the acquisition of relative clauses by speakers of Persian, Arabic, Chinese, and Japanese. A contrastive analysis allowed her to predict that the Persian and Arabic students would have problems with pronominalization, producing utterances such as *the man who I saw him playing the flute*. The relative clause is in the right place but there is an extra pronoun. She predicted that the Chinese and Japanese students, on the other hand, would tend to produce utterances such as *the who I saw man is playing the flute,* in which the relative clause is well formed but in the wrong place. When she looked at a breakdown of actual student errors, she found the pattern shown in Table 7.3.

Table 7.3   Distribution of Errors in Relative Clause Acquisition

	Correct	Error	Total	Percentage of errors
Persian	131	43	174	25
Arabic	123	31	154	20
Chinese	67	9	76	12
Japanese	58	5	63	8

Source: Adapted from Schachter (1974, 209).

At first glance, we might think that Persian and Arabic students had more difficulty producing relative clauses because they made more errors, but notice that they also produced many more relative clauses (154 and 174 respectively) than did the Chinese (76) and Japanese (63) students. Why? Persian and Arabic have *postnominal* relative clauses while Chinese and Japanese have *prenominal* relative clauses. A Persian relative clause is thus placed after the noun (*The man who is playing the flute is my brother*) and a Japanese relative clause is placed before (*The playing the flute man is my brother*). English, like Persian and Arabic, has postnominal relative clauses. The difficulty predicted by the contrastive analysis hypothesis thus shows up not in the number of errors but in the number of relative clauses the learners attempted. The Chinese and Japanese students tried to *avoid* the relative clause construction. The Persian and Arabic speakers, though, perceived the structure to be the same and produced many more of the clauses, making pronominaliza-tion errors in the process. Error analysis cannot detect avoidance of a particular structure. It is only in combination with contrastive analysis that we can understand the Chinese and Japanese students' behaviour.

6.2 TEACHER'S ATTITUDE TO ERRORS

Yorio (1976) reminds us, "Errors are unintentional; students do not make errors because they want to, in order to upset us and make us angry." Second language teachers must always remember this. Sometimes L2 teachers might catch themselves thinking "We talked about that on Friday! How come you're still making mistakes? Weren't you paying attention?" Yorio cites the following examples of native speakers' utter-ances, taken from insurance reports describing the situation surrounding an accident, to illustrate that students *and* teachers should understand how natural it is to make errors:

Coming home I drove into the wrong house and collided with a tree I don't have.

I thought my window was down, but I found it was up when I put my head through it.

A truck backed through my windshield into my wife's face.

The guy was all over the road. I had to swerve a number of times before I hit him.

In an attempt to kill a fly, I drove into a telephone pole.

I told the police that I was not injured, but on removing my hat found that I had fractured my skull.

The pedestrian had no idea which direction to run; so I ran over him.

To avoid hitting the bumper of the car in front, I struck the pedestrian.

I saw a slow-moving, sad-faced old gentleman as he bounced off the roof of my car.

Clearly, native speakers are not always perfect in their language, thinking, or writing, Non-native speakers are no different. Yorio concludes by saying "to err is human, to forgive and understand is common sense ... and that is good pedagogy" (1981, 61). This view of errors is very much in tune with what we saw in first language acquisition. It also leads to a fundamental question: Is second language acquisition like first language acquisition? Several researchers have addressed this issue by looking at order of acquisition.

7 ORDER OF ACQUISITION

Everyone who attempts to acquire a first language is successful (except for pathological cases) but not everyone who attempts to acquire a second language achieves equal success. As we saw earlier, this has led some people to propose that we should make the second language learning environment more like the first. The underlying assumption here is that language learning is always the same; it doesn't matter whether it's a first or second language. This is referred to as the *L1 = L2 hypothesis.*

In attempting to discover whether first and second language acquisition are indeed the same, researchers have drawn much of their data from order of acquisition studies. They compared the order in which learners of a given language—children learning it as their first language and adults learning it as their second—acquired a number of morphemes or grammatical structures. Let us look at one such example.

Cazden (1972) discovered the following order of development for interrogatives in children learning English as a first language:

1. One-word utterances are used as questions.
2. Intonation questions appear regularly and some *wh* questions are formed without auxiliaries: *Where you going?*

3. *Wh* questions become productive but without inversion: *Why you are crying?*
4. Inversion appears in yes/no questions but not *wh* questions: *Are you crying? Why you are crying?*
5. Inversion appears in *wh* questions, including embedded questions: *Why are you crying? I don't know why are you crying.*
6. No inversion is used in embedded *wh* questions: *I don't know why you are crying.*

Hatch and Wagner-Gough (1975) conducted a similar investigation of adults acquiring English as a second language. They found the following sequence:

1. Questions formed by intonation alone: *You go?*
2. Tag questions appear: *You go, OK?*
3. *Wh* questions appear: *Where my book?*
4. Inversion occurs with modals: *Can I play?*
5. Inversion occurs with *be*: *Is it raining?*
6. Inversion occurs in embedded questions: *I no know what is it.*
7. Inversion disappears in embedded questions: *I no know what it is.*

There is a remarkable similarity between the two orders.

7.1 PROBLEMS WITH ORDER OF ACQUISITION STUDIES

In spite of these appealing results the studies contained some problems. There was no real methodological consensus. At what point do we say that someone has acquired a structure or a morpheme? When they use it accurately 100 percent of the time? 90 percent? Different studies adopted different thresholds. It is probably a greater problem, however, to make the leap from saying that people acquire certain morphemes in L1 and L2 in a similar order to saying that people acquire first and second languages in the same way. Yet this was precisely the leap made by some researchers. In addition, many of the grammatical analyses involved relatively superficial grammatical phenomena and did not consider whether the results could be caused by deep linguistic factors. The findings were pleasing but they didn't explain much.

Finally, the issue raised in Chapter 4 applies here. Just because we see similar surface features does not necessarily mean that they have the same underlying cause. Remember that it is characteristic of both early child first language and early adult second language that grammatical (function) words are missing:

Child L1 learner: Daddy throw ball again.
Adult L2 learner: He no want me in class.

The reasons for this performance, however, probably differ. Children are clearly influenced by both biological and cognitive maturation in a way that adults are not. Children are setting up the syntactic scaffolding necessary to produce sentences for the first time. Adults have already done this but may have trouble *using* their knowledge.

7.2 ACQUISITION PROCESSES

The issue of whether the processes or strategies involved in acquisition are the same for first and second languages has been investigated frequently. Dan Slobin (1971; 1973) proposed a series of *operating principles* for first language acquisition. He viewed the child as attempting to form hypotheses about the underlying patterns of the data in the linguistic input. The following are some of the principles that he proposed guide the child's development; the child consults them in the process of hypothesis construction:

1. Pay attention to the ends of words.
2. The phonological forms of words can be systematically modified.
3. Pay attention to the order of words and morphemes.
4. Avoid interruption and rearrangement of linguistic units.
5. Underlying semantic relations should be marked overtly and clearly.
6. Avoid exceptions.
7. The use of grammatical markers should make semantic sense.

Andersen (1987) proposed similar operating principles for second language acquisition:

1. Store any perceptually salient stretches of speech.
2. Pay attention to stressed syllables.
3. Keep track of the frequency of occurrence of every unit and pattern that you store.
4. Determine whether a newly extracted stretch of speech seems to be the same or different from anything you have already stored. If it is different, store it separately; if it is the same, take note of this sameness by increasing its frequency count by one.
5. An interlanguage system should be constructed in such a way that an intended underlying meaning is expressed with one clear invariant surface form.
6. When you cannot perceive the structural pattern used by the language you are trying to acquire, use your native language structure with lexical items from the second language.

Andersen draws on Slobin's work and clearly believes that very similar operating principles are at work in first and second language acquisition. Note, however, that both Slobin and Andersen assume the learner to be a hypothesis tester proceeding by induction. While sympathetic to the attempt to determine the processes driving language acquisition, the operating principles they propose are quite vague and do not explain how language is represented in the mind. Such statements are not falsifiable; these "theories" can account for anything. We need a theory that makes predictions capable of being disproved.

The question of whether second language acquisition is like first language acquisition, then, has been investigated by asking if learners follow the same order of acquisition and by asking if the processes underlying L1 and L2 acquisition are the same. The results of both strands of research are somewhat problematic. Chapter 8 will examine another approach to this question: universal grammar.

This chapter has shown that certain researchers have looked at the *products*—the representations or outputs—of first and second language acquisition and argued that they were the same or similar, while others have looked at the *processes* and argued that they were the same or similar. Let us conclude with John Macnamara's clear statement of the L1 = L2 hypothesis:

> Many people imagine that babies learn languages in a special manner which is different from the way older persons learn them. They miss the obvious point that for an adult to know a language is in all essentials the same as for a baby to know it. Since the product is the same, the simplest hypothesis is that the learning process is the same. Suits of clothes which look identical are probably cut from the same pattern. There is then just as much magic in an adult's learning a language as in a baby's doing so. And in the absence of all evidence to the contrary, we can safely hypothesize that it is the same magic (1975, 261).

Macnamara takes a strong position on equating the processes of first and second language acquisition. Although few today would adopt his extreme stance, its appeal is clear. It is complicated to determine in which ways first and second language acquisition in children and adults are similar and in which ways they differ. Our best hope is to conduct our research taking care to be as explicit as we can about the representations and processes involved in acquiring a second language grammar.

8 CONCLUSION

This chapter has demonstrated that second language learners often do things that native speakers do not. Much research has attempted to account for *why* they make the mistakes they do. The chapter was primarily an historical overview of relevant research studies. Some have argued that L1 interferes with the L2, whereas others contend that first and second language acquisition are similar (if not identical) processes with comparable orders of acquisition and error types. Not surprisingly, elements of both views are correct. The interlanguages of second language learners are influenced by many factors, one and only one of which *is* the first language. Subsequent chapters will investigate other influences on the structure of an interlanguage.

CLASSROOM IMPLICATIONS

Contrastive analysis influenced second language classrooms by, among other things, encouraging the search for *method*. A single method of teaching all learners, however, would only work if all learners behaved in the same fashion. As more and more evidence about the variation among learners emerged in the late 1980s (see Skehan 1991), the single-method concept was seriously endangered. Danesi comments that abandonment of the notion of method has "spawned a healthy eclectic attitude in the teaching profession" (1988, 15). He goes on to propose some neurological reasons why method *cannot* work. Yorio (1987) explicitly deals with the eclectic approach. Chapter 13 will talk more of this when we discuss learner variation.

DISCUSSION QUESTIONS

1. An interesting task to conduct in a second language class is to have students identify the errors in samples of their own writing. They will be able to find certain problems but will miss others. In light of what we have said about errors and mistakes, what would you do in response to the writing sample?
2. Look at the following sample of student writing:

   I am writing about I am lived with roommate and close relationship. I am going to write down about him whose lives with me now; He was born in London, and he has been studied psychology and sociology at university. He has BA, MA and MBA degrees with him. Now he is teacher as Social Psychology and Sociology and he write his own book. It was about psychology for people's problem and instruction. I think he's a genuis and kind. He is interested in American Sign Language in 1979. He wanted to be learned as sign language when he went to ***** and took course from level one to advanced (level four). He has been successed his own ASL since he studied at *****. He also learned it from me with total communcation. He favroites that I cook fried potatoes, frying chicken and cheescake with cherry topping. Sometimes he is funny and loves tease and always called me "Sweetie" because he loves me, and is interesting total communcate with me. Also he has been learned with deaf people for his life. He understands them well. Now he has been improved since he learned and studied ASL. I felt that we are close relationship and understand each other, share, help each other and learn each other. It is amazing.

David

Correct the errors in the preceding passage. Assume that the learner is extraordinarily thick-skinned and loves error correction. In this respect this is not a simulation of a real classroom exercise. It is highly unlikely that you would ever correct every mistake a student made, unless there were very few. After you have fixed the problems, compare the way you corrected them with the way some other students did. Where do you agree? Where do you disagree? Why do you think there wasn't complete agreement? How can we discover what the student actually *meant* to say?

3. Respond to the following quotation from Macnamara: "It would seem that homes and streets produce 'natural' language, whereas schools produce 'artificial' language, and that the variation among the students is an indication of the artificiality. Our task is to make the school more like the home and the street" (1975, 265). Remember Macnamara believed that second language learning should be like first language learning. Do you think that the classroom could be better than the street in some ways?

SELF TEST

Certain characteristics of an interlanguage grammar can be attributed to the L2 and others to the L1. It is sometimes said that the L1 _____ into the L2 (or into the interlanguage grammar). The
(1)
_____ analysis hypothesis predicted that L1 items
(2)
_____ from the L2 would cause difficulty, but not all errors
(3)
are the result of L1 transfer. Learners also make _____ errors,
(4)
which are often the result of _____ .
(5)

A finely grained contrastive analysis argued for _____ of
difference and assumed that acquisition would be harder when a single
L1 category _____ into two L2 categories than when the
opposite occurred. Traditional contrastive analysis had many weaknesses.
It was difficult to identify the _____ of error in the proposed
hierarchy. More fundamentally, the grammatical models focussed on
_____ syntactic analysis.

One feature that child grammars and interlanguage grammars share is
their _____ . Like children, L2 learners make systematic errors
and non-systematic _____ , which are caused by performance
factors. Although error analysis acknowledged more sources of error than
contrastive analysis, it had difficulty accounting for the phenomenon of

_____ .

The _____ hypothesis assumed that language learning was
all the same, regardless of whether it was L1 or L2.

FURTHER READING

Gass, S. and L. Selinker. 1992. *Language Transfer in Language Learning*.
Amsterdam: John Benjamins.

Odlin, T. 1989. *Language Transfer*. Cambridge: Cambridge University
Press.

8
......

Language Universals and Second Language Acquisition

1 LANGUAGE LEARNABILITY

One of the goals of linguistic theory is to come up with a grammar. As we have seen earlier, a grammar is a description of the linguistic knowledge of a given speaker. Obviously, a speaker's knowledge can be described in a number of ways, and methods of doing so need to be evaluated. Chomsky provides some useful terminology to evaluate proposed grammars.

A grammar is *descriptively* adequate if it satisfactorily describes the language. A grammar is *explanatorily* adequate if it goes beyond this and explains *why* the language takes the form that it does and behaves in the way that it does. These are two of the best-known criteria for judging grammars, but another one, *feasibility*, is going to be our major concern here. The criterion of feasibility demands that the grammar as it is described could be learned under realistic conditions: those that a child (or adult) actually faces. If a learner could acquire the grammar only upon exposure to the entire language, or if it required unrealistic memory capacity, the grammar would not be feasible.

The field of *language learnability* is concerned with developing feasible descriptions of grammars, in effect with the relationship between linguistic theory and language acquisition. Much of the history of generative grammar has involved revising the theory in order to produce learnable grammars. Linguists use the word *grammar* to refer not only to an individual's knowledge but also to the linguist's description of that knowledge. Clearly, the grammar of an individual is learnable, because the individual has already learned it. The field of learnability is an attempt to constrain linguists' models of grammar to those that could be learned.

Linguists want to account for how learners arrive at the correct grammar on the basis of the data to which they are exposed. Learners are exposed to a range of linguistic input and must either construct or select—depending on the learning theory assumed—a hypothesis about the patterns underlying these data. One of the facts we note about first language acquisition is that although they receive different input, all learners converge on a remarkably similar grammar. In other words, what one speaker of English knows about the language is very similar to what another speaker knows. The problem for learning theory is how to guarantee that all speakers end up converging in their knowledge. Clark (1992) illustrates this clearly when he asks us to consider a learner who has to learn a grammar with thirty parameters, or binary characteristics. This would result in 2^{30}, or 1 073 741 824, possible grammars. If the learner tested one grammar every second, it could take up to thirty years to find the right one. So how do learners end up in the same place?

In learning theory, one of the ways to ensure that this happens is to restrict the hypotheses available to the learner. Let's consider one brief example. Early models of transformational grammar had a very large number of transformations. Such names as *dative movement, do support, there insertion,* and *passivization,* just to name a few, may be familiar to you from introductory linguistics courses, depending on when you took them. If transformations are so unconstrained, however, how can a grammar invoking them be learned? These types of grammars were not learnable and so linguists made changes to reduce the power of transformations. Much of this was inspired by Chomsky's paper, "Conditions on transformations" (1973). The movement reached its peak (within this pre-parameter setting model) with the publication of Wexler and Culicover's *Formal Principles of Language Acquisition* (1980). All of this led to simpler, more general transformations and consequently, fewer of them, increasing the learnability of the grammar as the choice among transformations decreased.

Traditionally, the study of both first and second language acquisition was primarily concerned with charting the developmental path of the learner in a Piagetian fashion. Learnability research takes a different perspective. Rather than investigating the learner's developmental path, it studies the *universal endowment* of the learner. It examines the final, adult grammar and seeks to explain how that knowledge could have been attained.

2 LANGUAGE UNIVERSALS

Language universals are structures or properties that all human languages have in common. Much traditional work in this area tended to view language development as the result of inductive strategies operating on the input data. The learner was seen as a hypothesis tester guided by general learning strategies. A learner who noticed the following utterances, for example,

He should work harder.
Should he work harder?

might hypothesize that questions are formed in English by moving the verb to the front of the sentence. The operating principles proposed by Slobin (1971; 1973) and Andersen (1987), which we saw in Chapter 7, are examples of this type of research.

Much current work in the learnability paradigm disagrees with this view. Many researchers subscribe to a modular view of mind, which argues that language learning is different from other kinds of learning. This chapter looks at how *linguistic* properties (as opposed to properties of general development) can account for the development of interlanguages. First of all, let's look more closely at two distinct approaches to linguistic universals.

2.1 UNIVERSAL GRAMMAR

One of the underlying assumptions of generative grammar is that the first language learner is somehow innately equipped to learn language. Humans possess a language faculty that other species do not. At birth, humans already have certain knowledge built in that will allow them to acquire any human language quickly and flawlessly. The initial state of the language faculty is referred to as universal grammar (UG). UG addresses the convergence problem by assuming that many things found in final-state grammars do not have to be learned. This assumption also greatly restricts the hypothesis space of the learner. The correct hypothesis is selected from a small number of options given by UG.

The universal grammar (or UG) paradigm is championed by Chomsky. By examining the final state of knowledge—the adult grammar—and the input to which the learner is exposed, we determine which aspects of knowledge must be innate and which must be learned. If there is no evidence that the knowledge is found in the input and we find evidence that the same knowledge is found in adult grammars, then that knowledge must be innate. How else could it get there?

Occasionally, work within this framework is criticized for "copping out." It has been argued that it is an unsatisfying explanation to say that complex knowledge is innate. It also strikes some people as counter-intuitive to imagine that we can determine that something is universal just by looking at one language. The authors of this text disagree. To maintain that something is innate is a very strong claim. It is falsifiable and it

> It has come to our ears, what we cannot mention without shame, that you are in the habit of expounding grammar to certain persons.... [I]n proportion as it is execrable for such a thing to be related of a priest, it ought to be ascertained by strict and veracious evidence whether or not it is so.
>
> Pope Gregory I, the Great
> Letter to Desiserius, Bishop of Vienne (France)

is testable. If we were to claim, for example, that something is innate for an English speaker, then we would expect it to be universally innate. If we then found that it did not hold for a particular language, the claim would be proven wrong. It is an eminently reasonable manner in which to conduct research, and this chapter will focus primarily on the UG paradigm.

2.2 TYPOLOGICAL UNIVERSALS

UG is not the only way of looking at universals. Such people as Joseph Greenberg (1966) and Bernard Comrie (1981) have done work in *language typology*, or *typological universals*. Work within this framework examines a wide range of languages from different language families and geographical regions to see what they have in common. Researchers have found evidence for universals in such areas as word order, colour terminology, and kinship terms.

Many typological universals are stated in terms of *implicational universals* or *implicational hierarchies*. If a particular language has nasal vowels in its phonetic inventory, for example, it implies that it will also have oral vowels. There are no languages attested to have only nasal vowels. This can be written in the following form:

Oral vowels > Nasal vowels

The hierarchy thus flows in one direction only; the presence of any element implies the presence of all the elements to its left. If we examine a language unknown to us and hear a nasal vowel, we can predict that the language will also have oral vowels, but if we listen to a language and hear an oral vowel, we cannot predict whether the language will have nasal vowels.

Let us consider a more complex example. Keenan and Comrie (1977) proposed the following accessibility hierarchy for the formation of relative clauses in languages:

Subject > Direct object > Indirect object > Oblique > Genitive >
Object of comparative

A language that can form a relative clause, or relativize, out of any of the
above positions can also form relative clauses out of all the positions to
its *left* on the above hierarchy but not to the right. So, if a language can
form a relative clause out of the indirect object position, it will also be
able to relativize out of the direct object and subject positions, but we
know nothing of its ability to relativize out of the positions to the right.
Table 8.1 should make this clearer. The relative pronoun in each sentence
has the indicated grammatical function. Note that English can relativize
out of all of the positions. Other languages are more restricted, however,
and the restrictions appear to follow Comrie and Keenan's hierarchy.

Table 8.1   Relative Pronouns

Subject:	The man *who* kicked the dog....
Direct object:	The boy *whom* the man saw....[†]
Indirect object:	The boy *that* he gave a book to....
Oblique:	The house *that* she lives in....
Genitive:	The dog *whose* owner has died....
Object of comparative:	The man *that* I am richer than....

[†]The grammatical function can be seen clearly in the form *The
man saw the boy.* This is why we say it is functioning as a direct
object.

For the most part, work in this tradition has provided very interesting
data and adequate descriptions of many languages. Nevertheless, there is
little in terms of explanation of the relevant facts. As we are concerned
with both description and explanation, the UG framework is of most
interest at this time.

3 THE UNIVERSAL GRAMMAR FRAMEWORK

Primarily as a result of poverty of the stimulus arguments, it is generally
accepted that first language acquisition is driven by universal grammar.
The input data to which the child is exposed does not reveal enough
about the complexity of the knowledge to be acquired (the language),
yet the child acquires that language. This has been referred to as the *logical problem* of language acquisition (Baker and McCarthy 1981). Children
also acquire a sophisticated knowledge of what is *not* possible in a particular language.

Lydia White, in her article "Is there a logical problem of second language acquisition?" (1985b), presents the following sentences:

1. The book is dull.
2. Is the book dull?

On the basis of this input, the learner might be justified in assuming that the rule for question formation in English is: move the verb to the front of the sentence. If a learner formulated that rule and then heard a sentence such as (3), below, he or she would then produce a question in the form of sentence (4):

3. The book which is on the shelf is dull.
4. *Is the book which __ on the shelf is dull?[1]

But children never produce forms like this. They produce grammatically correct forms like (5).

5. Is the book which is on the shelf __ dull?

They seem to know without being told that rules are *structure dependent*. That is to say, rules make reference to syntactic structure, not to things such as linear order, or position in the sentence. No language has a rule that looks anything like either of the following two: to make a question move the fourth word to the front; to make a sentence negative move the second word to the end. In other words, children are not trying out all the "logical" possibilities in attempting to construct a grammar. Their hypotheses are constrained by something, and that something is most probably UG.

White (1989b) also offers data on how children learn about *wh* words in English. We know that English permits *wh* questions such as

6. Who should Bob see *t* ?[2]
7. What should Nancy buy *t* ?

Maybe the learner hypothesizes that *wh* words can move to the beginnings of sentences. The underlying representation would be

8. Bob should see who
9. Nancy should buy what

To form a questions, the *wh* word would move. But what does the movement rule look like? The simple hypothesis that the *wh* word moves to

---

[1] The blank serves as a reminder of where the verb moved from.

[2] Remember that *t* stands for *trace* and indicates the original site of the *wh* element. It can also be indicated by a blank.

the front of the sentence would not be disproved when the learner noted that the *wh* word can move even farther, as in sentences (10) and (11):

10. Who did Fred believe (that)[3] John saw *t* ?
11. What did Jane think (that) Mary bought *t* ?

If learners believed that a *wh* word could move to the beginning from anywhere in a sentence, however, we would expect them to produce sentences like (12) and (13):

12. *Who did Fred believe the rumour that John saw *t* ?
13. *What did Jane hear the news that Mary bought *t* ?

These are immediately recognizable as ungrammatical and not just because we're trying to move the *wh* word too far. We can say

14. Who do you think (that) Bill said (that) Susan saw *t* ?

Why don't learners generalize their hypotheses to generate sentences like (12) and (13)? White rejects some potential explanations and then offers a UG argument. Let's consider some of the reasons why learners don't generate these ungrammatical utterances.

3.1 SEMANTICS

Maybe learners don't produce certain sentences because those utterances don't make sense. This explanation must be rejected. Although questions like (12) and (13) are hard to understand, it cannot be for semantic reasons because the corresponding statements are perfectly straightforward:

15. Fred believed the rumour that John saw Mick Jagger.
16. Jane heard the news that Mary bought a Ferrari.

The problem with (12) and (13) must be syntactic or structural.

3.2 INPUT

Maybe learners don't generate these sentences because they've never heard them before. This cannot explain things either, as learners are constantly producing structures that they have never heard. Even at the word level, you know things about words you have never heard before. If you were presented with the "words" *blick* and *bnick* you would know

---

[3] The parentheses indicate an optional element.

immediately that *blick* is a possible English word but *bnick* is not. This is because you have knowledge of the principles that govern sound sequences in English.

3.3 NEGATIVE EVIDENCE

Perhaps learners actually do go through a phase of generating ungrammatical utterances like (12) and (13) but are then corrected. This, as already noted, is referred to as negative evidence. Chapter 18 is entirely devoted to the role of error correction in second language learning. For now, let us just note three problems with this proposed explanation: (1) first language learners *don't* make these kinds of mistakes; (2) formal correction doesn't occur that often (3) when formal correction does occur it doesn't affect children much. As a result, it is assumed that children have some kind of advance knowledge of certain universal linguistic principles which constrain the form of the grammar. These are the principles of UG. But what about second language acquisition?

3.4 UNIVERSAL GRAMMAR AND SECOND LANGUAGE ACQUISITION

The poverty of the stimulus applies to L2 input as much as it does to L1 input. Is UG still available to adult learners? This is a highly controversial question in the field of second language acquisition. The bulk of the evidence argues that universal grammar is available to adults, and the following evidence supports that position:

1. *Untenability of critical period hypothesis* The critical period hypothesis, which we will look at more closely in Chapter 14, assumes that there is an optimal time, or critical period, for the acquisition of language. If acquisition does not occur within this interval, it is too late. Anecdotally, people usually mark the end of the critical period as the onset of puberty. There is no solid evidence that adults are incapable of acquiring a second language and are therefore fundamentally different from child learners.
2. *Lack of adult UG violations* Adult speakers do not generate sentences such as *What did Jane hear the news that Mary bought?* That is to say, they do not produce sentences that violate proposed universals, possibly because adult competence is still governed by UG.
3. *Lack of L2 adult UG violations* This is probably the most contentious issue in the field. The interlanguage grammars of adult second language learners do not appear to violate linguistic universals (White 1989b; Archibald 1993). While not everyone agrees with this viewpoint (Bley-Vroman 1989), the authors of this text contend that the most compelling evidence argues *for* adult access to UG.

4 UNIVERSALS AND THE STRUCTURE OF INTERLANGUAGE

Let us now look at some empirical studies that have attempted to explain the structure of an interlanguage by drawing on some sort of linguistic universal.

4.1 RELATIVE CLAUSES

Gass (1979) looked at the acquisition of relative clauses by adult L2 learners of English and compared their rate of accuracy with the Keenan and Comrie hierarchy discussed earlier. She found a close correlation between the two. Learners were thus most accurate at relativizing the subject position, less accurate on the direct object, and so on. The only exception was the genitive position, which proved to be easier to relativize than predicted.

Gass (1982) tested to see if instruction could affect this order of difficulty. One group of students was given explicit instruction on a universally more difficult position to see if they could then generalize their knowledge to a universally easier position. They could. Another group received explicit instruction only on the easier position and they were unable to generalize their knowledge to the more difficult structures. The implications of this will be discussed in more detail in Chapter 16, which explores the effects of instruction on second language learning.

4.2 MARKEDNESS

A number of other studies have drawn on linguistic universals in light of a concept known as *markedness*. In order to understand markedness, first examine the representation of linguistic knowledge shown in Figure 8.1. UG forms the core of the grammar. The periphery contains such elements as lexical borrowings, historical phenomena, and irregular morphology. Consider the English idiom *The more the merrier*. We might believe it a core property of English that its sentences have verbs, but there is no verb in this one. It is a peripheral construction in modern English. A word such as *schmaltz*, with an initial sound sequence found only in a small number of forms, is a peripheral construction. Words with irregular morphology such as *larynx/larynges* or *go/went* are also peripheral constructions. Elements belonging to the core of a language are said to be *unmarked*; elements belonging to the periphery are said to be *marked*.

How do we determine whether a particular element belongs to the core or the periphery? How do we define markedness? In truth, many definitions have been proposed. While the concept remains an

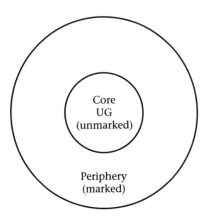

Figure 8.1   Core/Periphery Distinction

intuitively appealing one it has proved quite difficult to formalize. Markedness has something to do with naturalness, or minimal amounts of information. For some it is equated with a default value. The concept of a default value is borrowed from the field of computer science. It refers to the value assigned to a variable in the absence of relevant evidence. If you buy a modem, for example, you will find the switches already set to certain positions, the default or factory settings. You can change the settings to fit your particular needs, but in the absence of any such change, they remain in the default positions. Greenberg (1966) proposed that unmarked elements could be used in a wider range of constructions than could marked elements. Consider, for example, Table 8.2. Following the criterion, words such as *big, long, hard,* and *fast* are deemed unmarked because they can occur in a greater range of constructions than *small, short, slow*, and *soft*, which are marked.

Table 8.2   Distributional Analysis of Markedness

Can occur in interrogative	Cannot occur in interrogative
How big is it?	*How small is it?
long	short
fast	slow
hard	soft

What can markedness tell us about the structure of interlanguages? Wode (1984) argues that unmarked constructions are learned earlier than marked ones. It is here, however, that we must be very careful of circular argument. Some people actually define markedness in terms of order of acquisition, forms acquired early being unmarked and those acquired later marked. If we follow this definition, we will need some kind of external criterion to validate it. Wode claimed that the word order *subject + negative + verb phrase,* as in *my dog no bark* is the unmarked structure for negation as it is typologically the most frequent. He claimed that this type of negation appears early in the acquisition of a second language even when it is not the order of either the L1 or the L2.

Kellerman (1979) applied the concept of markedness to word meanings. He argued that a word had an unmarked core meaning and peripheral meanings that were more marked. He surveyed non-native speakers of English, and asked them to judge the grammaticality of sentences such as *I broke the glass* and *The glass broke by falling.* The speakers consistently found the first sentence more acceptable grammatically than the second. He interpreted this as an indication that *I broke the glass* reflects the core meaning of the verb *break* while *The glass broke by falling* is a more marked meaning. The unmarked assumption is that somebody physically breaks something, and anything else is more marked: *She broke my heart* and *The chair broke my fall,* for example. He suggested that the unmarked core meaning of a word will be acquired first.

4.2.1 Markedness Differential Hypothesis

Markedness theory may provide a basis for solving some of the problems of traditional contrastive analysis discussed in Chapter 7. In particular, it can help to explain why some differences between L1 and L2 lead to learning difficulty while others do not. Eckman (1977) proposed what he called the *markedness differential hypothesis,* which states that the difficult areas of the target language are those that are both different from and relatively more marked than the L1.

He begins by looking at voicing contrasts such as /t/ and /d/ in English and German. English maintains this voicing contrast word-initially, -medially, and -finally, whereas German maintains it only word-initially and -medially. Table 8.3 illustrates the pattern. When we look at learning German and English as second languages, we note a directionality of difficulty. That is to say, German speakers have more difficulty learning to make the English voicing contrast in final position than English speakers do in suppressing the voicing contrast word-finally in German. Traditional contrastive analysis says only that things that are different will be difficult; it doesn't predict any directionality of difficulty.

Table 8.3 Voicing Contrast in English and German

	English	**German**
Initially	tin, din	tasse (cup), das (the, that)
Medially	betting, bedding	baten (asked), baden (to bathe)
Finally	bet, bed	n/a

Now consider some data about English and French. French has the [ž] phoneme word-initially, -medially and -finally, while English only has it word-medially and -finally, as Table 8.4 illustrates. The English speaker learning French must learn to make a new voicing contrast ([š]/[ž] in initial position) but the French speaker learning English must learn to suppress that contrast. Yet learning the new contrast is not especially difficult for English speakers (Gradman 1971).

Table 8.4   Voicing Contrast in English and French

	English	**French**
Initially	n/a	jeune
Medially	vision	agent
Finally	garage	image

Thus we have one case (English/German) in which learning a new contrast causes difficulty and one case (English/French) in which it doesn't. Traditional contrastive analysis cannot account for this, but Eckman invokes his markedness differential hypothesis to reconcile the results. Let us begin by looking at his definition of markedness: "A phenomenon *A* in some language is more marked than *B* if the presence of *A* in a language implies the presence of *B* but the presence of *B* does not imply the presence of *A*" (1977, 60). Some examples should make this clear.

First an example from phonology. Some languages, such as Korean, have only voiceless stops ([p], [t], [k]), and others, such as English, have both voiceless and voiced stops ([p], [t], [k], [b], [d], [g]). No languages have only voiced stops ([b], [d], [g]). The presence of voiced stops implies the presence of voiceless stops, and voiced stops are therefore more marked than voiceless stops.

We can draw another example from syntax. Some languages, such as Arabic and Greek, have only agentless passives, as in the sentence *The door was closed.*[4] Others, such as English and Japanese, have both agentless and agentive passives: *The door was closed* and *The door was closed by the janitor.*[5] No languages have agentive passives without agentless passives. Therefore, agentive passives are more marked than agentless passives.

Eckman employs this concept of markedness to explain directionality of difficulty in second language learning. He argues that areas of difficulty can be predicted on the basis of a systematic comparison of the grammars of the native language, the target language, and the markedness relations. His explanation can be summed up in three points:

---

[4] This is called agentless because the agent of the action is unspecified. We don't know who closed the door.

[5] The agent of the action is specified. The janitor closed the door.

1. Areas of the target language that differ from and are more marked than the native language will be difficult.
2. The relative degree of difficulty of the areas of the target language that are more marked than the native language will correspond to the relative degree of markedness.
3. Areas of the target language that are different from but not more marked than the native language will not be difficult.

Let us return to our phonological data and see how we can explain learner behaviour. Dinnsen and Eckman (1975) proposed a universal voicing hierarchy to explain patterns in different languages. Languages such as English, Arabic, and Swedish maintain a voicing contrast initially, medially, and finally. German, Polish, and Japanese, among others, maintain the contrast only initially and medially. A third group, to which Corsican and Sardinian belong, maintains the contrast initially. Finally, languages such as Korean make no voicing contrast. The hierarchy is illustrated as

Initially > Medially > Finally

or as in Table 8.5.

Table 8.5 Voicing Contrast Hierarchy

Initially	Least marked
Medially	↓
Finally	Most marked

Remember that in the data we are trying to account for, the German speaker had difficulty acquiring an English voicing contrast, but the English speaker did not have difficulty acquiring a French voicing contrast. Seen in light of this universal hierarchy, we note that the German speaker had to learn a more marked contrast (word-final voicing) than the English speaker did (word-initial voicing), and thus the degree of difficulty conforms to Eckman's hypothesis.

While markedness is an intuitively appealing notion, it is not always easy to draw conclusions from the studies. Everyone seems to have their own definition of markedness, and in the next section we see further disagreement in the research.

4.3 STRUCTURAL CONFORMITY HYPOTHESIS

Eckman has modified his markedness differential hypothesis in more recent work, but he continues to investigate the structure of interlanguage grammars within the framework of typological universals. In Eckman (1991) he examines the acquisition of consonant clusters. He argues for what he calls the *structural conformity hypothesis,* which states that the structure of an interlanguage will conform to the universal (typological) principles found in primary languages. The universals he assumes are given below:

1. *Fricative–stop principle* If a language has at least one final consonant sequence consisting of *stop + stop* (as in *apt*), it also has at least one final sequence consisting of *fricative + stop* (as in *ask*).
2. *Resolvability principle* If a language has a sequence of three consonants in either initial or final position, which we will here call *m*, it will also have at least one subsequence consisting of *m* – 1. So the presence of a word-initial sequence such as *str*, for example, indicates that the language will also contain at least one of the subsequences *st* or *tr* in the same position.

These principles can be reformulated into implicational statements with English data (Table 8.6).

Table 8.6 Fricative–Stop and Resolvability Principles

Fricative–stop principle[†]	Resolvability principle	
pt#, kt# > ft#, sp#, st#, sk#	#spr > #sp, #pr	spt# > sp#, pt#
	kts# > kt#, ts#	pts# > pt#, ts#
	#str > #st, #tr	sks# > sk#, ks#
	skt# >sk#, kt#	pst# > ps#, st#
	#skr > #sk, #kr	kst# > ks#, st#
	sps# > sp#, ps#	

[†] # indicates a word boundary

Eckman was interested in whether the grammars of second language learners followed these implicational rules. He obtained data from eleven subjects (four native speakers of Japanese, four of Korean, and three of Cantonese). None of these languages allows consonant clusters in either initial or final position. Learners therefore have to acquire the English constraints on allowable consonant clusters. The issue is whether their inventories will violate the proposed universals. The subjects performed several tasks, ranging from reading lists of words to conversing freely.

Consider what would falsify the structural conformity hypothesis. If an individual's interlanguage grammar contained the *stop + stop* clusters (pt# or kt#) but did *not* contain the *fricative + stop* clusters (ft#, sp#, st#, or sk#), then the grammar would violate the implicational universal of the fricative–stop principle. The application of the resolvability principle to interlanguage grammars can be tested in a couple of ways. The principle could be confirmed if the grammar had the three-consonant cluster and *either* of the two-consonant clusters (#skr and #sk, for example, but not #kr). This is what Eckman refers to as *weak* support. Alternatively, it could be supported if the grammar contained the three-consonant cluster and *both* the two-consonant clusters (#skr and #sk and #kr). Eckman refers to this as *strong* support.

Table 8.7 summarizes the data on consonant cluster acquisition. Out of 524 relevant target sequences, 324 did not contain the element on the left side of the implicational universal: the three-consonant cluster. In these cases, the implicational hierarchy could not be tested but the grammar was consistent with the principle. Remember that the principle predicts that if a subject produces *str*, he or she will also produce *st* and *tr*. If the subject doesn't produce *str*, nothing is predicted. Of the remaining 200 test cases, 147 (74 percent) provided strong support, 48 (24 percent) provided weak support, and only 5 (2 percent) violated the implicational universals.

Table 8.7   Structural Conformity Hypothesis Data

	Strong support	Weak support	Consistent	False	Total
Task 1	69	11	54	1	135
Task 2	48	18	56	0	122
Task 3	29	18	85	2	134
Task 4	1	1	129	2	133
Total	147	48	324	5	524

Source: Data from Eckman (1991).

According to Eckman, these data strongly suggest that interlanguage grammars are governed by the same kind of implicational universals as primary languages and support the structural conformity hypothesis.

5 PRINCIPLES AND PARAMETERS

Much current linguistic theory is being conducted within the framework known as the principles and parameters model (Chomsky 1988). In this model, the grammar consists of universal, innate *principles*. All human beings come equipped with certain structures as a result of being human, and these enable them to acquire language. These universal principles, though, are slightly underspecified. *Parameters* must also be established according to the linguistic environment. The most common metaphor for a parameter is a light switch. The switch is set either up or down depending on the language to which the learner is exposed. Both settings of the parameter yield possible human languages.

Work within this framework, then, does not view learners as hypothesis testers; they do not select linguistic rules from among an infinite possible number. Rather, learners set the underspecified parameters of UG.

> Yet language survives everything—corruption, misuse, ignorance, ineptitude.... It is the human glory which antecedes all others. It merits not only our homage but our constant and intelligent study.
>
> Anthony Burgess
> *Language Made Plain*

Instead of searching an infinite range of possible grammars, they try to answer a few simple questions, such as whether the switch is set to position A or position B. Looking at some specific examples of principles and parameters should elucidate this process.

5.1 STRUCTURE DEPENDENCY

One of the most commonly discussed principles of UG, outlined clearly by Cook (1988), is *structure dependency*. It asserts that language relies on structural relations. In other words, sentences in all languages have an internal, hierarchical structure.

Consider the sentence *Should Bob go to the library tonight?* The formation of questions is often described in terms of movement, or transformation. The deep structure of the sentence is something like *Bob should go to the library tonight.* How does the learner represent the rule that transforms the first sentence into the second? Conceivably, the rule could dictate that the second word of a sentence moves to the beginning. This would produce the correct sentence, but imagine that the learner then applied it to the sentence *Jim and Dave went on an awesome environmental adventure.* The above rule would produce the question form **And Dave Jim went on an awesome environmental adventure?* Obviously, rules do not depend on the movement of any numbered position.

In English, we form questions by moving the auxiliary verb of the main sentence to the left of the subject, so that a sentence like *The man who is singing is your brother* generates the question *Is the man who is singing your brother?* The rule depends on syntactic structure, and this is true for all languages. Structure dependency, then, is a principle of UG. Now let's see what a parameter looks like.

5.2 THE HEAD-DIRECTION PARAMETER

Remember that principles are good at describing what is *common* among all human languages. We need parameters to capture *variation* among languages. You will recall from Chapter 2, and perhaps from earlier linguistics courses, the principles of left- and right-headedness in phrase structure rules. One of the ways in which languages vary is in the order of elements within a phrasal category. The heads can be on either the left or the right. In English, the verb is on the left of a verb phrase, as in _gave a book to David_. A preposition is on the left of a prepositional phrase, as in _to the library_. The noun phrase in a relative clause is on the left, as in _the man who had the flame-thrower_. As a result, English is said to be left-headed or head-left. This is captured in parametric terms by saying that the head-direction parameter in English is set to the left. Japanese, on the other hand, is head-right; the parameter is set to the right. Thus the verb is on the right of a VP, and the preposition (actually called a postposition, for obvious reasons) is on the right of a PP.

The head-direction parameter captures variation among languages. Again, note that both settings describe actual human languages. The task of the learner is to determine whether the language has the head-direction parameter set to left or right.

Thus, universal grammar contains principles and parameters. Two questions immediately arise if we want to apply this model to second language acquisition: (1) Do L2 learners have access to UG principles? and (2) Can L2 learners reset their parameters? Each of these will be addressed, but before that is possible we need to say a bit more about the learning theory related to parameter setting. One of the basic learning concepts is known as the subset principle.

5.3 THE SUBSET PRINCIPLE

Remember that one of the tenets of most learning theories designed to account for child acquisition of L1 is _no negative evidence_. It is generally accepted that children receive very little form-focussed activity, or correction, and that when they do they do not benefit from it. The no negative evidence assumption was also motivated by strong theoretical concerns. Probably the central question of learnability research is how the learner can attain the final grammar on the basis of the given input.

A deductive theory of acquisition seeks to constrain, or limit, the hypothesis space in order to account for two facts: (1) learners do not merely test hypotheses, as there are many perfectly reasonable hypotheses that they never entertain; and (2) all learners of a given L1 attain similar grammars. By making the supposition that language learning is driven by positive evidence only, we can constrain the learning theory and establish guidelines to ensure that the learner avoids certain hypotheses. Probably the best known formulation of this is Wexler and Manzini's subset principle: "For every parameter p and every two values i, j of p, the languages generated under the two values of the parameter are one a subset of the other" (1987, 60). In other words, the two settings of a particular parameter generate possible languages which are in a subset relationship. An example should make this clear.

White (1985b) and others have investigated a proposed null-subject parameter,[6] which can be used to illustrate the subset principle. Languages such as Spanish and Italian allow what are often referred to as null subjects. Let us begin with a simple description of this phenomenon. In Spanish, both of the following sentences are grammatical:

1. Yo hablo inglés.
   I speak English.

2. Hablo inglés.
   Speak-I English.
   I speak English.

Even when the subject pronoun is absent, the meaning of the sentence is clear, and sentences (1) and (2) therefore mean the same thing. Languages such as English and French, though, do not allow null subjects. Although sentences (3) and (4), below, are grammatical, (5) and (6) are not. The subject pronoun cannot be omitted.

3. She speaks English.
4. Ils parlent anglais.
5. *Speaks English.
6. *Parlent anglais.

The two possible parameter settings (conventionally written as [± null subject]) both generate possible languages. The languages are in a subset relation, as illustrated in Figure 8.2, where X represents the grammar of language X and Y the grammar of language Y.

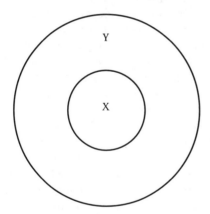

Figure 8.2   The Subset Relationship

---

[6] This parameter has actually been questioned by some researchers for a number of theoretical reasons that do not concern us here, but it will serve as a relatively clear example of how the subset principle operates.

In the case of null subjects, the smaller grammar will be generated by the [– null subject] setting (English and French). This setting forbids null subjects and can only generate sentences of the form *I speak English*. The [+ null subject] setting (Spanish and Italian) generates both forms: *Yo hablo inglés* and *Hablo inglés*. The minus setting generates a grammar which is a subset of that generated by the plus setting, as shown in Figure 8.3.

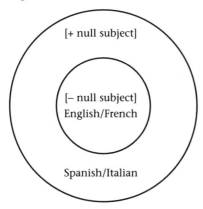

Figure 8.3   Null Subjects and the Subset Principle

The subset principle claims that learners will always innately have the setting that generates the subset as an initial or default value. This being the case, there is no need for negative evidence. Positive evidence will provide the necessary information to force a resetting of the parameter. Let us consider the two possible learning paths. If we assume that language learners comes into the world with a minus setting for this parameter, they will generate the following forms:

> I speak English.
> Je parle anglais.
> Yo hablo inglés.
> Io parlo inglese.

For English and French speakers, this turns out to be the right setting. Spanish and Italian speakers, however, also hear

> Hablo inglés.
> Parlo inglese.

The English and French speakers never hear sentences that drop the subject pronoun without changing the meaning.[7] When the Spanish and

---

[7]   Note that this section is dealing with syntactic properties rather than the characteristics of dropping subjects in certain discourse contexts, as English does.

Italian speakers actually hear sentences with null subjects, they receive positive evidence to reset the parameter.

But what of the other possible learning path? What if learners came into the world with [+ null subject] as the initial setting? They would be able to generate all the sentences below:

Yo hablo inglés.	Hablo inglés.
I speak English.	Speak English.
Je parle anglais.	Parle anglais.
Io parlo inglese.	Parlo inglese.

This time, the Spanish and Italian speakers would have the right setting, but the English and French speakers would not. To realize that their parameter setting was incorrect, they would need to be exposed to negative evidence. They would have to be told that *Speak English* and *Parle anglais* are ungrammatical as declarative sentences and we have already seen that this kind of evidence is, by and large, unavailable to children.[8] This would force our learner to think something like "Wait a minute. I have *never* heard *anybody* say 'Parle anglais.' Maybe my parameter setting is wrong." This type of learning theory, known as indirect negative evidence, cannot guarantee that all learners will get to the correct final state.

5.3.1 Subsets and Second Language Acquisition

The subset principle seems to guide first language acquisition. Clearly, we must ask to what extent it operates in second language acquisition. There are three possibilities, as argued in White (1989b):

1. L2 learners could continue to select the parameter setting that generates the subset grammar. They would return to the default settings.
2. L2 learners could transfer their L1 parameter setting into L2.
3. As some parameters generate more than two values meeting the subset condition, L2 learners may select a value that represents neither the L1 nor the L2 setting. It would not, however, violate the principles of UG.

Up until now this text has made the simplifying assumption that parameters are binary. In fact, researchers have proposed multivalued parameters in a number of linguistic domains. Without getting into the technical details of a particular parameter, we may still note the possibility of the relationships shown in Figure 8.4. At a given developmental stage, a learner may have a parameter setting that is neither that of the L1 nor of the L2 but which is still sanctioned by UG.

---

[8] It is also unavailable to most parents. Most caregivers, we are confident, could not provide corrections in terms of such things as violations of the parametric settings.

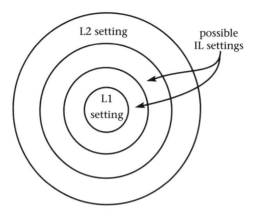

Figure 8.4   Multivalued Parameters

By looking at cases where the L1 value generates the superset and the L2 requires the subset, we might be able to obtain data to shed light on hypotheses (1) and (2), above. This is done in White (1989a), Zobl (1988), Finer and Broselow (1986), and Broselow and Finer (1991). Numerous studies have attempted to shed light on these hypotheses with respect to particular parameters. Mazurkewich (1984) argued that L2 learners did revert to the default setting. White (1989a) found evidence that learners transferred their L1 settings for a given parameter rather than reverting to a default setting. This supported the idea that L2 learners are not guided by the subset principle. Zobl (1988) reached similar conclusions when investigating a different parameter. Finer and Broselow (1986) found that learners sometimes generated natural languages—that is, did not violate UG—through parameter settings that could not be predicted by either the subset principle or L1 transfer. Broselow and Finer (1991) reached the same conclusion; sometimes the IL parameter settings were in between the L1 and L2 settings. The findings are therefore inconclusive, but as White (1989a) emphasized, the problematic nature of the subset principle in SLA does not disprove that adults have access to UG. They still generate systems that are consistent with universal grammar. The studies also show much evidence of L1 transfer.

5.4 RESETTING PARAMETERS

Even if learners do not have access to the subset principle it is natural to assume that positive evidence has an effect on adult L2 learners.[9] An English speaker learning Spanish may begin by uttering sentences something like (1) and (2):

---

[9] The work of Pienemann on teachability (1989), however, maintains that this assumption must be investigated very carefully.

1. Yo hablo inglés.
2. Yo no soy marinero.

They will never, at the beginning, produce (3) and (4):

3. Hablo inglés.
4. No soy marinero.

Once exposed to positive evidence by hearing sentences like (3) and (4), however, the learner may well realize that the L2 can do things that the L1 cannot and therefore that the current grammar must be revised.

But what about moving in the other direction? What if the learner has assumed the superset value? What kind of evidence will lead to resetting? A Spanish speaker learning English may begin by producing sentences (5) and (6):

5. I speak Spanish.
6. Speak Spanish.

Yet the learner will never receive positive evidence that (6) is ungrammatical but would have to notice that he or she had *never* heard that type of sentence. Non-occurrence does not guarantee ungrammaticality; there are many perfectly grammatical sentences that learners will never hear. L2 learners, then, may require negative evidence to revise their grammars and reset their parameters. Lightbown and Spada (1990) certainly advocate doing so, as we shall see in Chapter 18. Rutherford (1987) also illustrates the benefits of grammar teaching, error correction, and other forms of consciousness raising. It is conceivable then that negative evidence plays a different role in L2 acquisition than in L1 acquisition.

5.5 NULL SUBJECTS IN SLA: EMPIRICAL STUDIES

Having discussed some of the general issues related to second language acquisition within a UG framework, let us now turn to a more in-depth discussion of the research literature related to a particular parameter: the null subject. By looking at this phenomenon, we will gain understanding of how current UG accounts explain such things as L1 transfer, directionality of difficulty, the effects of feedback, and whether interlanguages are natural languages. Certain linguistic properties tend to cluster around null subjects. That is to say, languages that allow null subjects also have other patterns in common. Linguists, however, do not agree on which properties are directly related to the null subject parameter. Table 8.8 summarizes two positions commonly taken.

Table 8.8   Two Views of the Null-Subject Parameter

	[+ null subject] (Spanish, Italian)	**[– null subject]** (English)
Version 1 (Chomsky 1981) (Phinney 1987) (Rizzi 1982) (White 1986)	Null subjects No expletive pronouns *El esta joviendo.* Subject–verb inversion in declaratives *Vino Juan* *That*–trace sequences *Quien dijiste que __ vino?*	No null subjects Expletive pronouns *It is raining.* No subject–verb inversion in declaratives *Came John* No *that*–trace sequences[†] *Who did you say that __ came?*
Version 2 (Hilles 1986) (Hyams 1986)	Null subjects No expletive pronouns Auxiliaries and main verbs form one category *Yo quiero comer.* *Yo debo comer.*	Lexical subjects Expletive pronouns Auxiliaries are distinct from main verbs[‡] *I want to eat.* *I must to eat*

[†] The underlying structure of the English example here would be *You did say that who came.* The gaps in the surface structure indicate the original site of the *wh* element. English does not allow the word *that* to be followed by a gap, or trace.

[‡] English auxiliary verbs behave differently from main verbs in a number of ways. Main verbs can be followed by an infinitive, for example, while auxiliaries cannot. Spanish does not have this distinction.

Source: Adapted from White (1989b).

White (1986) looked at native speakers of Spanish [+ null subject] who were learning English. She had a control group of native speakers of French [– null subject] who were also learning English. Looking at the interlanguage grammars of French and Spanish speakers learning English will tell us whether the parameter settings from the L1 transfer into the L2. The results of this study are summarized in Table 8.9, in which the numbers indicate the percentage of accuracy in a grammaticality judgment task. The subjects in question might have been asked to judge the grammaticality of sentences such as the following:

Should go.
I should go.
Came Suzanne.
Suzanne came.
Who do you think that came?

Accurate responses identify either a grammatical sentence as grammatical or an ungrammatical sentence as ungrammatical.

Both Spanish and French groups were accurate in judging grammatical sentences but there were significant differences between them in terms of their accuracy on subjectless sentences. The Spanish subjects

Table 8.9   Spanish versus French Judgments on Null-Subject Phenomena

Sentence type	% of Spanish speakers' accuracy	% of French speakers' accuracy
Subjectless (ungrammatical)	61	89
With subjects (grammatical)	90	97
Verb–subject order (ungrammatical)	91	96
Subject–verb order (grammatical)	81	85
That–trace (ungrammatical)	23	35

Source: Adapted from White (1986).

were much more likely to accept these null-subject sentences than the French subjects were. This seems to indicate that the Spanish subjects were transferring into English the property of their L1 that allows null subjects. Nevertheless, there are no significant differences between the two groups on other aspects of the parameter. Both groups rejected verb–subject order in declarative sentences, and both groups accepted *that*–trace violations. In this case, the clustering of properties hypothesized by linguistic theory was not borne out by empirical study.

White believes that the examples may have been too difficult for the subjects and that they just answered *correct* when they couldn't decipher complex sentences. An additional task was assigned to try to eliminate this complexity factor. In the second task, subjects were given a declarative sentence and asked to produce a related question. They were given a sentence such as *Elizabeth believes that her sister will be late,* for example, and asked to form a question about the underlined words. The appropriate response would be *Who does Elizabeth believe will be late?* The idea was to see if the subjects would produce sentences with *that*–trace violations (*Who does Elizabeth believe that __ will be late?*). After removing subjects who could not form even simple questions correctly from the analysis, White reported the data given in Table 8.10. The Spanish subjects were significantly more likely than the French to produce a *that*–trace violation, which can be explained in terms of transferring L1 properties.

Table 8.10   Percentage of *That*–trace Violations in Spanish and French Subjects

	Correct	*That*–trace	Other errors
Spanish (n = 22)	17	71	12
French (n = 30)	20	42	38

Source: Data from White (1986).

Phinney (1987) looked at both native speakers of Spanish learning English (ESL), and native speakers of English learning Spanish (SSL). Although there are some methodological concerns with the study, the results are interesting to examine. Written data were gathered from students' free compositions and analysed for the omission of subject pronouns. Table 8.11 summarizes the results for both the ESL and SSL subjects. Two groups were studied within each population.

Table 8.11   Percentage of Omitted Subjects in ESL and SSL Groups

	ESL 1	ESL 2	SSL 1	SSL 2
Referential subject e.g. *The dog* is wet	13	6	83	65
Expletive subject e.g. *It* is hot outside	56	76	100	100

Source: Data from Phinney (1987).

The non-native speakers of English (ESL) were much more likely to omit expletive than referential subjects. Omitting expletive subjects in English is ungrammatical (*Is raining*). The non-native speakers of Spanish (SSL) on the other hand were correctly omitting expletive pronouns in their Spanish. In this case we see a directionality of difficulty phenomenon. The speakers of Spanish had more trouble resetting to the English value of the parameter than the speakers of English did resetting to the Spanish parameter. This is exactly what would be expected in terms of the subset principle, as shown in Figure 8.3, above. Positive evidence is available to the learner who resets from English to Spanish, but no positive evidence is at hand to those who must reset from Spanish to English. Thus, the directionality of difference can be accounted for by the kind of evidence necessary to reset a parameter.

5.6 DIRECTIONALITY OF DIFFICULTY

All of these concepts regarding principles and parameters together may provide some insight about directionality of difficulty in second language acquisition. White (1986; 1988b) argued that it would be easier to reset from the subset (unmarked) L1 value to the superset (marked) L2 value than the reverse because positive evidence exists for resetting in this direction.[10] Resetting from a superset to a subset value would require negative evidence. Although fairly little research has been done on the efficacy of feedback or error correction in second language acquisition, it has been claimed that L2 learners cannot make use of negative evidence (Schwartz 1987). This strong claim runs counter to Rutherford's views (1987) and obviously demands further empirical investigation. The authors of this text consider that it is easier to reset a parameter using positive evidence than it is by using negative evidence.

---

[10] Though see Phinney (1987) for counterarguments.

6 ADULT ACCESS TO UNIVERSAL GRAMMAR

The preceding section illustrated the way in which second language acquisition research draws on the construct of learners resetting *parameters*. This section investigates the role of *principles* in an interlanguage grammar. Not all researchers are convinced that adult interlanguage grammars are constrained by the principles of UG. Phrased in another way, they are not convinced that adults have access to UG.

Bley-Vroman (1989) addresses this issue extensively, suggesting that child L1 acquisition and adult L2 acquisition take place in distinct ways. He calls this the *fundamental difference hypothesis,* arguing that adult L2 learners have access only to the principles instantiated in their L1 (the indirect access model in Figure 8.5). According to this view, a feature of UG that was not triggered in first language acquisition would no longer be available to the L2 learner. If learners had acquired a first language in which gender was not triggered, such as English, then they would not have access to gender in learning a second language. Indeed, English speakers are notorious for having trouble learning languages with gender marking. Other researchers (such as White 1989b) assume the direct access model, which predicts that interlanguage grammars cannot violate principles of UG. Future empirical studies are necessary to sort out these conflicting claims. We will return to this issue in the next chapter.

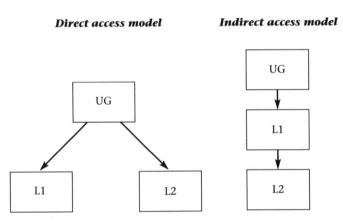

Direct access model   *Indirect access model*

Figure 8.5   Direct and Indirect Access Models

7 CONCLUSION

In attempting to get an idea, then, of what an interlanguage grammar looks like, we see that linguistic universals influence the interlanguage structure. Studies have either relied on a typological approach to universals or been conducted within a UG framework. Both are able to inform us about certain properties of the interlanguage grammar.

Considering the role of language universals has three results: (1) it forces us to think about second language acquisition in terms of the final product and of how that knowledge is acquired; (2) it offers a characterization of principles and parameters; and (3) it facilitates testable claims. The study of SLA within a UG framework promises to be a burgeoning field in the future.

CLASSROOM IMPLICATIONS

Bley-Vroman (1989) presents certain "fundamental differences" between child L1 acquisition and adult L2 acquisition. Below are the characteristics of adult L2 learning; child L1 learning is assumed to be the opposite. Discuss each of the following points:

1. *General failure* Bley-Vroman argues that adult L2 learning is usually characterized by failure. He suggests that the number of successes in adult SLA may be about equal to the number of failures in child L1 learning.
2. *Variation in processes* Adult language learning is similar to general adult skill acquisition (such as learning to play chess or tennis), in that people may learn these skills in different ways, in different orders, and with different strategies.
3. *Variation in goals* Adults may have very different goals for learning a second language, and these can influence their SLA.
4. *Fossilization* Adult grammars fossilize before attaining the target grammar.
5. *Indeterminate intuitions* Adults' intuitions about the well-formedness of L2 strings are frequently less clear than children's intuitions about L1 strings.
6. *Importance of instruction* Adult SLA can be influenced by instruction.
7. *Negative evidence* Adult L2 learners are exposed to a great deal of negative evidence.
8. *Affective factors* Adult language learning can be influenced by affective factors that do not influence L1 acquisition.

SELF TEST

When evaluating a theory of grammar, the criterion of _____ (1) demands that the grammar be learnable. A UG-based approach to language acquisition assumes that (1) learning proceeds by _____ (2) ;

and (2) there are many _____ constraints on the kinds of
(3)
grammars that can be represented by the human mind. The study of language typology makes use of _____ universals such as Oral
(4)
vowels > Nasal vowels.

Gass found a correlation between the implicational hierarchy proposed for relative clause formation and _____ of L2 acquisi-
(5)
tion. Although there are several definitions of markedness, most
researchers assume that _____ forms will be acquired early.
(6)
Eckman refines this notion and argues that L2 elements that are different
from and _____ marked than the L1 will be difficult to
(7)
acquire. His structural conformity hypothesis argues that interlanguages
are _____ languages; they do not violate typological universals.
(8)
The principles and parameters model determines markedness through
the _____ principle. Learners can reset from the subset to the
(9)
superset setting because there is _____ evidence available.
(10)
Studies of SLA and null subjects generally agree that L1 parameter settings transfer, but that the _____ of properties predicted does
(11)
not always occur.

FURTHER READING

Archibald, J. 1993. *Language Learnability and L2 Phonology: The Acquisition of Metrical Parameters*. Dordrecht: Kluwer Academic Publishers.

Cook, V. 1988. *Chomsky's Universal Grammar*. Cambridge: Blackwell.

Eubank, L., ed. 1991. *Point Counterpoint: Universal Grammar in the Second Language*. Amsterdam: John Benjamins.

Flynn, S. and W. O'Neil. 1988. *Linguistic Theory and Second Language Acquisition*. Dordrecht: Kluwer Academic Publishers.

Gass, S. and J. Schachter. 1989. *Linguistic Perspectives on Second Language Acquisition*. Cambridge: Cambridge University Press.

White, L. 1989b. *Universal Grammar and Second Language Acquisition*. Amsterdam: John Benjamins.

9

······

The Structure of an Interlanguage

This chapter describes three studies of interlanguage structure, all of which draw on linguistic theory to describe the knowledge and behaviour of second language learners. One of the studies, Ellen Broselow's "Prosodic phonology and the acquisition of a second language" (1988), looks at interlanguage phonology. Broselow investigates several patterns of L2 phonological errors and then tries to explain them. Another, Lydia White's "Island effects in second language acquisition" (1988a), looks at interlanguage syntax. The third, "Testing a proposed universal" (1989) by Jacquelyn Schachter, considers some of the same material as White's study with respect to knowledge of L2 syntax, as well as methodological issues in getting an accurate picture of that knowledge.

When we work within a particular framework of linguistic analysis we can explain and maybe even predict the errors that second language will make. This, of course, was the stated goal of contrastive analysis, and current research is attempting to address similar questions to those posed by this earlier method. This chapter demonstrates that work within a UG framework attempts to be specific about transfer, in terms of parameters, principles, syllabification, and so on. By being explicit about the kinds of abstract mental representations dealt with in current theory, a UG-based approach has potential advantages over its surface cousin, contrastive analysis. Let's begin by looking at phonological errors.

1 PHONOLOGICAL ERRORS

The first error pattern to be considered here is the break up of consonant clusters in English by native speakers of two dialects of Arabic: Egyptian and Iraqi. Table 9.1 notes the errors in a mixture of orthography and phonetics that we trust is transparent.

Table 9.1   Arabic Speakers' Pronunciation of English Consonant Clusters

English target	Egyptian production	Iraqi production
children	childiren	chilidiren
plastic	bilastic	iblastic
Fred	Fired	iFred
translate	tiransilate	itranislate

Egyptians speaking English as a second language tend to insert a vowel[1] (a phonological process known as *epenthesis*) between the two consonants of an initial cluster, or after the second of three consonants word-internally: *Fired, childiren*. Iraqis, on the other hand, insert a vowel *before* two initial consonants, or after the *first* of three medial consonants: *iFred, chilidren*. These seemingly different strategies can be explained and unified when we look at the syllabic structure of the languages involved.

The maximal syllable in both Egyptian and Iraqi Arabic multisyllabic words is consonant–vowel–consonant (CVC) or consonant–vowel–vowel (CVV). The term *maximal* indicates that although Arabic syllables can be simpler than CVC (such as CV), they cannot be more complex (such as CCVCC). An English word like *cat* [kæt] has this syllable structure. A syllable—represented by a Greek sigma, σ—has an internal structure that looks like Figure 9.1. The vowel forms the nucleus of the syllable; the consonants before the vowel are said to be in the onset of the syllable; and the consonants after the vowel are said to be in the coda of the syllable. The nucleus and the coda form the rhyme of the syllable.

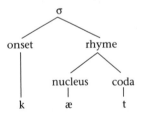

Figure 9.1   A CVC Syllable

Within this framework, then, the maximal Arabic syllable has the structure shown in Figure 9.2. English allows much more complex syllables, however, such as we see in Figure 9.3 in the word *strengths* [strɛŋkθs].

When Arabic speakers speak English, they often have to deal with syllables containing many more consonants than their first language per-

---

[1]   For Arabic speakers the epenthetic vowel is always [i].

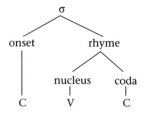

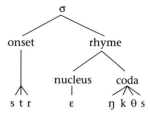

Figure 9.2   A Maximal Arabic Syllable

Figure 9.3   An English Syllable

mits. The consonants that cannot be assigned to an Arabic syllable trigger epenthesis of an additional vowel. This makes a new syllable for the extra consonant to attach to. The two dialects of Arabic differ in the direction of epenthesis with respect to the unattached consonants. Egyptian speakers insert the epenthetic vowel to the *right* of a leftover consonant, while Iraqi speakers insert it to the *left*. Let us look at one example in detail: syllabification of the word *translate* [trænslet] (see Figure 9.4).

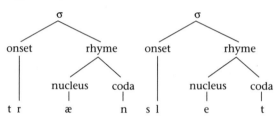

Figure 9.4   Initial Syllabification of *translate*

1.1 EGYPTIAN EPENTHESIS

An Egyptian Arabic speaker attempting to pronounce the English word *translate* is likely to use epenthesis twice: to the right of the [t] and to the right of the [s] (Figure 9.5).

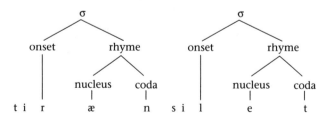

Figure 9.5   *Translate* after Epenthesis

These new vowels form the nuclei of new syllables (Figure 9.6).

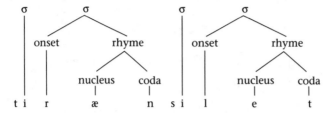

Figure 9.6 *Translate* **after Epenthesis and Resyllabification**

Now the previously unattached consonants have syllabic slots to fit into, places to attach themselves (Figure 9.7).

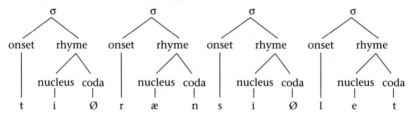

Figure 9.7 **Final Syllabification of Egyptian** *translate*

Thus, the form [tirænsilet] is the result of trying to make an English string of segments fit into an Arabic model. Let us now turn to the Iraqi form.

1.2 IRAQI EPENTHESIS

In Iraqi Arabic, the epenthetic vowel is inserted to the *left* of the unattached consonant. This produces the structure in Figure 9.8.

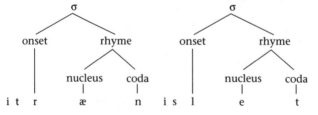

Figure 9.8 **Iraqi** *translate* **after Epenthesis**

Again, the new vowels form the nuclei for new syllables (Figure 9.9).

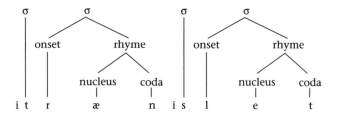

Figure 9.9   Syllabification of Iraqi *translate* after Epenthesis

Now the unattached consonants can be syllabified (Figure 9.10).

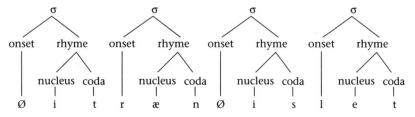

Figure 9.10   Final Syllabification of Iraqi *translate*

Once more, the student-produced form is the result of trying to make an English word fit into an Arabic phonological structure.

1.3 Arabic Monosyllables

Another error pattern noted by Broselow is caused by a constraint on monosyllabic Arabic words that only allows them take the form CVVC or CVCC. In analysing the Arabic speaker's production of words like *translate*, we stated that the maximal Arabic syllable was CVC or CVV, and this is true for multisyllabic words. (*Strengths* had a multisyllabic form as a result of epenthesis.) Monosyllabic words are different. CVVC and CVCC are referred to as *superheavy* syllables, and they constitute the minimal possible word form in Arabic. Below is an inventory of possible syllable types in Arabic, their labels, and within what type of word they can appear:

Light syllable: CV (in multisyllabic words)
Heavy syllable: CVV or CVC (in multisyllabic words)
Superheavy syllable: CVVC or CVCC (in monosyllabic words)

One analysis of the internal structure of superheavy syllables suggests that they have two rhymes, as shown in Figure 9.11. The triangle notation is a shorthand indicating that we are not concerned with the internal structure of a particular constituent, in this case the rhyme. A branching rhyme can contain either a VV sequence or a VC sequence. Figure 9.12 shows the allowable structure of a two-syllable Arabic word, which also has two rhymes and which cannot contain superheavy syllables.

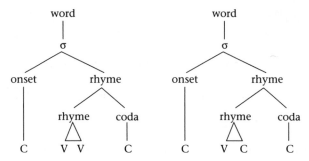

Figure 9.11   Monosyllabic Words with Superheavy Syllables

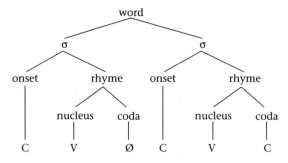

Figure 9.12   Structure of a Bisyllabic Word

This analysis allows us to make the generalization that an Arabic word, whether mono- or multisyllabic, must contain at least two rhymes. English, however, does not follow this constraint. We can see this clearly because English allows CVC words such as *bus* and *bed*. Again, when Arabic speakers produce these words, they try to fit them into Arabic phonological structure. The first thing we note is that learners tend to translate the English *tense/lax* vowel distinction into a *long/short* distinction. That is to say, they tend to pronounce English tense vowels as long vowels, as Table 9.2 shows.

Table 9.2   Lengthening of Tense Vowels

English	Arabic
teen [tin]	[tiin]
base [bes]	[bees]
road [rod]	[rood]

In English, lax vowels are always followed by a consonant.[2] When faced with a closed syllable with a lax vowel, Arabic speakers do one of two things. They either lengthen the consonant, as in the examples in Table 9.3, or they lengthen the vowel, which produces the forms in Table 9.4.

Table 9.3   Lengthening of Consonants

English	Arabic
bus [bʌs]	[bass][3]
bed [bɛd]	[badd]

Table 9.4   Lengthening of Lax Vowels

bus [bʌs]	[baas]
bed [bɛd]	[baad]

These mispronunciations all involve increasing the syllable weight of the words. The English words are heavy (CVC); Arabic speakers are making them superheavy (either CVVC or CVCC). Once more we see that the syllabic organization of the two languages is different and that learners' errors can be explained as attempts to make the English words fit into Arabic phonological rules and constraints. Linguistic theory helps to account for how that conflict is resolved by the learner.

2 SYNTACTIC PHENOMENA

Linguistic theory can also inform us about the syntactic characteristics of an interlanguage. Lydia White (1988), in her article "Island effects in second language acquisition," addresses some interesting syntactic issues. As does Broselow, White presents a certain amount of technical linguistic terminology, which must be mastered in order to understand the syntactic structure of an interlanguage. Her work also addresses some of the broader issues in second language acquisition. Second language research often asks if interlanguages are natural languages. Do they have the same structure as first languages? Are they generated by the same principles? White's article looks at one particular area of linguistic knowledge in order to test two hypotheses: (1) that adult SLA is mediated by UG; and (2) that L1 parameter settings transfer to L2.

---

[2] English has no monosyllabic words ending with any of the lax vowels.

[3] We will not consider their shift from [ʌ] to [a]. Suffice it to say it is the closest vowel Arabic has to English [ʌ].

2.1 LINGUISTIC BACKGROUND

The linguistic structures White investigates are related to *wh* movement. Remember that when we analyse a sentence such as *What do you see?* as being derived from the underlying *You see what,* the *wh* element moves from its underlying position to where it is seen on the surface. *Wh* movement in English is quite free. We can produce the following pair of sentences:

Bob likes that team.
Which team does Bob like?

English does not, however, allow certain other types of *wh* movement:

[$_S$ [$_{NP}$ John][$_{VP}$ likes [$_{NP}$ the people [$_{PP}$ in this office]]]].
*Which office [$_S$ does John like [$_{NP}$ the people [$_{PP}$ in *t* ?]]]

The labelled brackets used above are a slightly simplified version of the tree diagram in Figure 9.13. They do not show the internal structure of phrasal-level categories. The S stands for sentence. This type of notation can make certain constraints on movement very clear.

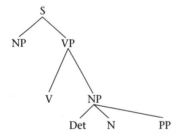

John   likes   the   people   in   this   office

Figure 9.13

We need to account for what blocks the movement in sentences such as *Which office does John like the people in?* Why does this sentence not provide a legitimate landing site for a *wh* element? In English, we cannot extract a *wh* element out an object noun complement (the PP in an object NP: *the people in this office*). Also note the following sentences:

[$_{NP}$ Your interest [$_{PP}$ in baseball]] surprised me.
*What [$_S$ did [$_{NP}$ your interest [$_{PP}$ in *t*]]] surprise me?

We cannot extract the *wh* element out of a subject noun complement (the PP in a subject NP: *your interest in baseball*). And look at the sentences below:

Mary believed [$_{NP}$ the claim [$_{S'}$ that John had won the race]].
*What [$_S$ did Mary believe [$_{NP}$ the claim [$_{S'}$ that John had won *t* ?]]]

We cannot extract a *wh* element out of a complex noun phrase (*the claim that John had won the race*). To understand why this type of noun phrase is referred to as complex, compare the two sentences below:

Mary believed the story.
Mary believed the claim that John had won the race.

The verb *believe* is followed by a noun phrase in both sentences, but the second is clearly more complex.

Finally, consider the following pair of sentences:

John wondered [$_{S'}$ whether [$_S$ Mary had chosen a good book]]
*Which book [$_S$ did John wonder [$_{S'}$ whether [$_S$ Mary had chosen *t* ?]]]

We cannot extract a *wh* element out of a *wh* clause (*whether Mary had chosen a good book*).

What at first may appear to be different restrictions on *wh* movement can be explained by quite general factors. All of the violations occur when a *wh* phrase moves *too far*. There is a constraint on all languages with syntactic movement which says that *wh* elements can cross only one *bounding node* (although the nodes that are bounding differ from language to language).[4] This rule is known as *subjacency*. Bounding nodes are syntactic constituents that can block, or bound, *wh* movement.

Now let's turn to what the term S' was introduced to accommodate. A sentence such as *I believe that Tom saw Mary* illustrates what S' represents. This sentence has a structure something like Figure 9.14. The branching S' node creates a site for complementizers (COMP) like *that* to go in relative clauses. The complementizer position allows us to describe the structure of things like relative clauses. By distinguishing S' from S, we are able to say that *Tom saw Mary* (S) is a sentence but that *that Tom saw Mary* (S') is not (from White 1989b, 112). We also note that the complementizer position can be left empty, as in *I believe Tom saw Mary*.

There is reason to believe that the higher sentence has an S' node as well to create a site for other elements, like *wh* words, to move into. The surface structure of the sentence *Who do you believe Tom saw?* for example, looks something like Figure 9.15.

The fact that different languages can move *wh* elements differently can be described in terms of parametric variation. French has different parameter settings from English with respect to subjacency. In English,

---

4 Remember that a *node* is a labelled position in a syntactic tree and that it branches.

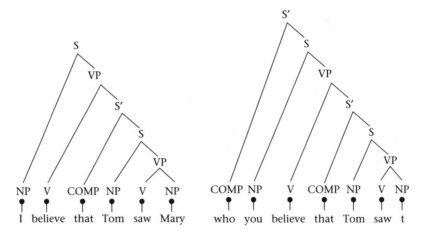

Figure 9.14   **Figure 9.15**

the bounding nodes are S′, S, NP, and PP. In French, the bounding nodes are S′, NP, and PP but not S. Consider the sentence below:

*What did John wonder whether Mary would do?

The structure is as follows:

*What [$_S$ did John wonder [$_{S′}$ whether [$_S$ Mary would do *t* ?]]]

This is ungrammatical in English because S is a bounding node. The *wh* element would have to move over more than one bounding node. The French equivalent of this sentence, though, is grammatical because the movement would only cross one bounding node (S′):

Que [$_S$ se demandait Jean [$_{S′}$ que [$_S$ Marie allait faire *t* ?]]]

This can also be seen in the grammaticality of French sentences such as the one below, in which the *wh* element (in this case, *combien*), crosses an NP node and an S node. The NP is bounding but the S is not (from White 1985a, 5):

Combien [$_S$ as tu vu [$_{NP}$ *t* [$_{PP}$ de personnes?]]]

The English equivalent is clearly ungrammatical:

*How many did you see of the people?

2.2 SUBJACENCY IN INTERLANGUAGE GRAMMARS

White looked at native speakers of French learning English as a second language to see if they would acquire knowledge of the status of S as a bounding node for subjacency in English. In other words, if French speakers can move *wh* elements in French in ways that English speakers can't in English, we might expect to see this reflected in their knowledge of English.

White's experiment was designed to determine the extent to which subjects were aware of the ungrammaticality of sentences violating subjacency. The learners were two groups of intermediate-level adult ESL students. They had to judge the grammaticality of sentences in two tasks. First they read the sentences and judged them with no time limit. Then they heard the sentences on tape and had three seconds in which to judge them. Possible responses were *acceptable*, *unacceptable*, or *unsure*. The following are some examples of the kinds of sentences the subjects had to judge in the written task:

1. Mary is frightened by stories about witches and ghosts.
   (a) Which stories is Mary frightened by?
   (b) Who do stories about frighten Mary?
   (c) About whom do stories frighten Mary?

2. Alice is friendly with a man who teaches history.
   (a) What is Alice friendly with a man who teaches?
   (b) Who is Alice friendly with?
   (c) Why is Alice friendly with a man who teaches history?
   (d) With whom is Alice friendly? (White 1988a, 169)

The sentences below were played on a tape recorder in the timed task:

1. Which movie did you guess who had gone to?
2. Last week, I read a book of which I have forgotten the name (White 1988a, 171).

Table 9.5 depicts some of the results. The numbers represent mean accuracy scores for ungrammatical subjacency violations for one native-speaker and two non-native-speaker groups. Most, though not all, of the native speakers rejected sentences such as the following:

Complex NP violation: What did Mary believe the story that John saw?
Wh clause violation: What did John wonder whether Mary would do?

Both ESL groups were quite accurate in detecting subjacency violations in complex NPs, but these are ungrammatical in French too. It is in the sentences with *wh* clause violations that we would expect to see the effects of the bounding status of S. One of the two groups achieved about the same accuracy on *wh* clause violations as they did on the complex NP violations. The other did less well, with 65 percent accuracy. This would be explained if the subjects were assuming that English, like French, did not have S as a bounding node. The explanation would lead us to expect that the first group was lower in proficiency than the second, as they showed more L1 transfer. White reports that independent tests of proficiency did not confirm this difference but that teacher reports labelled the first group as low-intermediate and the second as high-intermediate.

Table 9.5 Accuracy on Subjacency Violation Tests in Percentage

	Native speaker control group	Group 1	Group 2
Complex NPs	96	80	81
Wh clauses	91	65	80

Source: Adapted from White (1989b, 113).

White concluded that adult learners appear to be constrained by UG with respect to subjacency. Their judgments showed evidence of transfer of the L1 parameter settings insofar as sentences in which the *wh* element moved across an S were judged grammatical.

2.3 TESTING FOR KNOWLEDGE OF SUBJACENCY

Jacquelyn Schachter (1989) also examined the knowledge that second language learners had of subjacency. Her results help to illustrate the care with which conclusions have to be drawn in this field. So far we have looked at English and French, languages that have *wh* movement but differ with respect to the bounding nodes. A number of languages, Korean and Chinese among them, do not form *wh* questions by moving the *wh* word to the front of the sentence. Schachter argues that these languages are not constrained by subjacency. She attempts to answer whether the interlanguage grammars of Korean and Chinese learners of English will be constrained by this principle. If it is truly a universal principle, then these subjects too should be able to perceive subjacency violations in English, not because of their knowledge of the L1, but because of their knowledge of UG.

Schachter made two hypotheses: (1) subjects who judged grammatical sentences to be grammatical would also be able to judge subjacency violations to be ungrammatical; and (2) subjects who judged grammatical sentences to be ungrammatical, thus failing the syntax test, would not recognize subjacency violations, thus also failing the subjacency test. More concretely, this would predict that a subject who judged a sentence like *The man whom I saw yesterday is outside again today* to be ungrammatical would be unlikely to recognize a subjacency violation based on this structure. She represented the possibilities as shown in Figure 9.16.

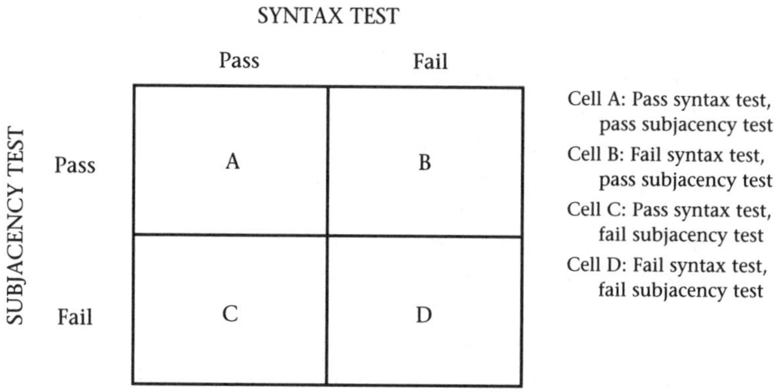

SYNTAX TEST

Pass   Fail

| | Pass | A | B |
| | Fail | C | D |

Cell A: Pass syntax test,
    pass subjacency test

Cell B: Fail syntax test,
    pass subjacency test

Cell C: Pass syntax test,
    fail subjacency test

Cell D: Fail syntax test,
    fail subjacency test

Figure 9.16   Schachter's Research Design for Subjacency Test
Source: Schachter (1989, 79).

The syntax test referred to four structures: sentential subjects, relative clauses, noun phrase complements, and embedded questions. Examples are given below:

Sentential subject:	<u>That oil prices will rise again this year</u> is nearly certain.
Relative clause:	The theory <u>(that) we discussed yesterday</u> will be on the exam next week.
Noun phrase complement:	There is a good possibility <u>that we can obtain the information elsewhere.</u>
Embedded question:	The dorm manager asked me <u>who I wanted to have as a roommate.</u>

For each structure, six grammatical sentences were presented to the subjects. Subjects who judged five of the six sentences given as grammatical were said to *pass* the syntax test. If they judged more than one of the grammatical sentences to be ungrammatical, they failed the syntax test.

The subjacency test required the subjects to judge subjacency violations of the sort given below:

Sentential subject:	*Which party did [for Sam to join *t*] shock his parents?
Relative clause:	*What did Susan visit the store [that had *t* in stock]?
Noun phrase complement:	*Who did the police have evidence [that the mayor murdered *t*]?
Embedded question:	*Who did the Senator ask the President [where he would send *t*]?

Subjects who judged five out of the six ungrammatical sentences as ungrammatical were said to pass the subjacency test. If they judged more than one of the ungrammatical sentences to be grammatical, they failed the subjacency test.

Most native speakers were in Cell A of the research design (Figure 9.16), and thus the control group supported Schachter's first hypothesis, that subjects who judged grammatical sentences to be grammatical would also be able to judge subjacency violations to be ungrammatical. This is shown in Table 9.6. Subjects who fell into Cell D of the research design satisfied the second hypothesis, that those who failed the syntax test would also fail the subjacency test.

Non-native speakers' behaviour did not support the hypotheses, as many subjects passed the syntax test but failed the subjacency test (shown in Table 9.7). They thus behaved differently from the control group.

Schachter contended that L2 learners did not have access to the subjacency principle, basing her argument on the data. When we group the structures together—sentential subjects, relative clauses, noun phrase

Table 9.6 Native Speaker Responses to Subjacency and Syntax Tests

	Sentential subjects		Relative clauses		NP complements		Embedded questions	
	pass sub.	fail sub.	pass sub.	fail sub.	pass sub.	fail sub.	pass sub.	fail sub.
Pass syntax	15	3	17	1	10	1	14	2
Fail syntax	1	0	0	1	7	1	3	0

Source: Data from Schachter (1989).

Table 9.7 Non-Native Responses to Subjacency and Syntax Tests

	Sentential subjects		Relative clauses		NP complements		Embedded questions	
	pass sub.	fail sub.	pass sub.	fail sub.	pass sub.	fail sub.	pass sub.	fail sub.
Indonesian								
Pass syntax	6	1	6	1	8	0	8	1
Fail syntax	11	2	9	4	11	1	6	5
Chinese								
Pass syntax	7	5	10	0	11	0	7	2
	7	1	6	4	9	0	9	2
Korean								
Pass syntax	3	2	5	0	2	0	3	0
Fail syntax	7	9	8	8	15	4	13	5

Source: Data from Schachter (1989).

Table 9.8   Native and Non-Native Responses to All Structures

	Native		Indonesian		Chinese		Korean	
	pass sub.	fail sub.	pass sub.	fail sub.	pass sub.	fail sub.	pass sub.	fail sub.
Pass syntax	56	7	28	3	31	8	13	2
Fail syntax	11	2	37	12	33	8	43	26

Source: Data from Schachter (1989).

complements, and embedded questions—we see that there are a large number of subjects in Cell C for all non-native groups, as shown in Table 9.8. Cell C is argued by Schachter to indicate lack of access to UG.

A couple of factors challenge Schachter's conclusion that lack of access to subjacency equals a lack of access to UG. Although non-natives behaved significantly differently than did native speakers, they did not behave significantly differently from one another. That is to say, the behaviour of the Korean subjects was not significantly different from the behaviour of the Chinese subjects, even though, in Schachter's own words, "Korean [has] ... no evidence of subjacency ... [whereas] Chinese and Indonesian show limited evidence" (1989, 84). If their behaviour was caused by their knowledge of subjacency, we would expect differences between the different L1s and we do not find this.

This leads to the second problem with Schachter's analysis. For all intents and purposes, she did not acknowledge that subjacency could be anything other than an all-or-nothing principle, that it could manifest itself slightly differently in different languages. Indeed, current work argues for the concept of multivalued parameterized subjacency, which tries to take these differences into account. By not doing so, Schachter's conclusions raise questions as well.

3 CONCLUSION

Both in phonology and syntax, we see how the theoretical framework adds depth to our understanding of second language learners' behaviour. The studies discussed in this chapter showed how linguistic theory could help to inform second language research. Broselow's study demonstrated how current phonological theory, which includes such things as hierarchical syllable structure, can reveal the characteristics of the interlanguage grammar and help to explain which properties of the L1 will influence the interlanguage phonology.

The two syntax studies were also informative, even though they drew different conclusions. White adhered to the direct access model and argued that second language learners had knowledge of subjacency. Schachter supported the indirect access model and argued that they did not. (See Figure 8.5 from the previous chapter for graphic representation of the two models.)

There is seldom total agreement in an academic field, and the study of second language acquisition is no different. By presenting some opposing studies, we hope not to have frustrated and confused you but to have emphasized that by looking closely at the linguistic models and experimental techniques employed, we may be able to get a picture of *why* the results conflict. Studies can then be designed to give one more piece of information to help resolve the confusion.

CLASSROOM IMPLICATIONS

One of the most important implications for the classroom of acquisition research couched within linguistic theory is that students' interlanguage has structure. Their performance shows evidence of a system, which the teacher must try to get an accurate picture of.

Finding Patterns
Describe the rule or rules that seem to underlie the following types of performance:

1. A student produces these sentences:
   Are you sleeping?
   Where my book is?
   I don't know where my book is.

2. A student uses these types of pronunciation (note the [d]/[ð] alternation):
   door   [dor]
   a doctor   [ə ðaktər]
   bad   [bæd]

3. A student produces these words with the stresses marked:
   astónish
   cinéma
   hurrícane
   édit
   cáncel

SELF TEST

Broselow's study looks at how L1 _____ structure can influence interlanguage grammar. In particular, she looks at how the process
of _____ breaks up L2 consonant clusters that the L1 does not
allow. Egyptian and Iraqi Arabic differ over whether the epenthetic vowel
is inserted to the left or right of an _____ consonant. In
Arabic, a word must have a minimum of two _____, whether
it is mono- or multisyllabic.

White's study looks at how the constraint known as _____
restricts syntactic _____ in a language. In English,
_____ is a bounding node while in French it is not. White
argues that L2 learners are constrained by _____ with respect
to movement. The learners appear to transfer their L1 _____
regarding bounding nodes. Contrary to White, Schachter contends that
L2 learners only have access to the subjacency information found in
their _____, not direct access to UG.

FURTHER READING

Gass, S., and J. Schachter. 1989. *Linguistic Perspectives on Second Language Acquisition.* Cambridge: Cambridge University Press.

White, L. 1989b. *Universal Grammar and Second Language Acquisition.* Amsterdam: John Benjamins.

Second Language Performance

In this section we turn from what interlanguage grammars look like to what happens when people actually *use* their grammars. Chapter 10 describes some basic issues in the field of language performance. Chapter 11 presents a model of language production and considers its implications for second language learners. Chapter 12 outlines the processes involved in language comprehension. Chapter 13 surveys variationist perspectives on SLA by looking at how interlanguage use can vary according to certain extralinguistic and linguistic factors.

Second language acquisition involves both *knowledge* and the *implementation* or *control* of that knowledge. We turn now to that second aspect.

10

···········

Language Performance

The goals of this chapter are similar to the goals of Chapter 2. That chapter introduced a number of technical terms and concepts from the fields of phonetics, phonology, morphology, and syntax, on the grounds that familiarity with these formalisms made it possible to think about language competence in a much more refined fashion. This chapter discusses some of the key ideas in psycholinguistics, the study of language performance. Familiarity with psycholinguistic constructs enhances our ability to think about reading, writing, listening, and speaking.

1 COMPETENCE AND PERFORMANCE REVISITED

It is worthwhile at the outset to return to the distinction between language competence and performance. Language performance is what we do. It is the *act* of language production and comprehension. As this text has noted in a number of places, language is a type of knowledge possessed by speakers, and we may call this knowledge language competence. With current research techniques, however, competence can only be studied through its expression in performance. We have no direct means to assess whether a learner of English "knows" a word, for example, but infer this to be the case when the learner reliably uses the word in an appropriate semantic and syntactic context and appears to understand what that word means when he or she is exposed to it.

The goal of the theoretical linguist is to characterize language competence in a succinct and elegant manner. In this way, the theoretical linguist is similar to the mathematician who attempts to provide a formal characterization of various events and processes. The study of language performance, on the other hand, is the study of the mental representations and processes involved when people engage in acts of language production and comprehension.

The following non-linguistic example may elucidate the distinction. The associative property of multiplication states that it does not make a difference which numbers are associated with one another when they are multiplied. An elegant expression of this property is that for any three numbers a, b, and c,

$$(a \times b) \times c = a \times (b \times c)$$

Most school children know this and the expression above presents a formal characterization of their knowledge. We might wonder, however, in what sense the mathematical formalism plays a role when children perform the task of multiplying three numbers. Perhaps it actually forms a component of the multiplication process; the child wonders which numbers to multiply first and then remembers the principle that it doesn't matter. Alternatively, the property of association might be merely implicit; the child multiplies in a haphazard manner and simply never encounters a situation in which it makes a difference. Finally, it might be completely unknown to the child, who nevertheless manages to perform multiplication on three numbers perfectly well. In this case, the child might think that the first two numbers must always be multiplied first. Although the belief is untrue, the child will always achieve the correct result in multiplication. A formal characterization thus does not necessarily tell us what representations and processes are employed in actual computation.

In the field of language study, we expect that as our understanding progresses, theoretical accounts of language structure will be very closely associated with representations actually employed by language users. At present, however, this is not always the case, in part because theories of language competence are constructed to be independent of modality-specific factors such as how reading differs from listening or how speaking differs from writing. They are also designed to be independent both of how representations are accessed during language comprehension and of the steps involved in moving from a message to a sentence in language production. These are not inadequacies; rather, they reflect a division of labour in the study of language.

The field of psycholinguistics is concerned with exactly the phenomena that theoretical linguistics does not treat. What happens in the mind/brain when we understand a sentence or recognize a word or speak a phrase? How are words represented in semantic memory? Do speakers construct hierarchical syntactic representations when they understand sentences? To answer these questions, psycholinguists employ a variety of experimental techniques and examine evidence from naturally occurring speech. They attempt to describe the mechanisms of language performance in terms of the representations employed and the cognitive processes that act upon these representations during comprehension and

In the speech below, Eliza Dolittle of George Bernard Shaw's *Pygmalion* is making conversation over tea in an upper-class drawing room. (The interjections of other characters have been omitted.) She has been taught by a linguist to mimic the pronunciation appropriate to this setting, but her words illustrate the importance of appropriate subject matter as well.

My aunt died of influenza: so they said. But it's my belief they done the old woman in. Why should she die of influenza? She come through diphtheria right enough the year before. I saw her through with my own eyes. Fairly blue with it she was. They all thought she was dead; but my father he kept ladling gin down her throat til she came to so sudden that she bit the bowl off the spoon. What call would a woman with that strength in her have to die of influenza? What become of her new straw hat that should have come to me? Somebody pinched it; and what I say is, them as pinched it done her in. Them she lived with would have killed her for a hat-pin, let alone a hat.

George Bernard Shaw
Pygmalion, Act III

production. This chapter introduces some central ideas from psycholinguistics and some of the evidence involved in forming and testing psycholinguistic hypotheses.

2 KEY CONCEPTS IN THE STUDY OF LANGUAGE PERFORMANCE

Much of the research into the processes of language production and comprehension can be summed up in four questions:

- What language representations are stored in the mind?
- What are the properties of these representations?
- What language representations are computed rather than stored?
- How does this computation occur?

It seems relatively unlikely that entire sentences are stored in the mind. As Chomsky has argued, most sentences are heard only once and remembering each one would require a great deal of memory. What's more, it would be a great waste of effort. Odds are that if a sentence were stored, it would never get used again. It is, therefore, reasonable to assume that sentences are computed. This brings psycholinguistic inquiry to the question of how computation occurs. Researchers are interested in determining the role that syntactic structure plays in sentence computation and the extent to which the computations involved in sentence generation are similar to those involved in sentence comprehension.

Words, in contrast to sentences, seem to be excellent candidates for storage rather than computation. A word must be learned and stored in semantic memory, and this type of storage is commonly called a vocabulary. We assume that we go to sleep with a vocabulary and wake up with the same vocabulary. But knowing that words are stored is just the beginning of the investigation. What is the form of a word's representation in the mind? How is the word's meaning represented? How is its sound? Its spelling?

Finally, let us briefly consider language representations for which the issue of storage versus computation is unresolved. Morphologically complex words such as *unhappiness* seem to allow both possibilities. They could be stored just as simple words such as *house* are stored. Or they might be computed from their morphological constituents just as sentences are computed from their constituents. A good deal of psycholinguistic experimentation has addressed this question and we will return to it in our discussion of the mental lexicon.

2.1 METAPHORS FOR MIND/BRAIN FUNCTIONING

It is important to note that strictly speaking we cannot observe the actual representations and processes involved in language performance. The terms and concepts are best seen as metaphors, as the language we use to talk about mind/brain function very often reflects the technology of our day. In the nineteenth century, when the railroad was the dominant new technology, theorists conceived of language processing as information being "shipped" from one location in the brain to another. In the early twentieth century, the metaphor of electricity flow became dominant. In the middle of this century, the mind/brain was seen as similar to a telephone switchboard, and in the latter part of this century, the prevailing metaphor has been the computer. Even the words used to frame the discussion here reflect the dominance of the computer metaphor. We speak of storage and computation, memory restrictions, and so on.

This is not a criticism but a cautionary note. Metaphors are necessary and reflect our best guesses in every generation. Nonetheless, it is important to bear in mind that they are simply aids to conceptualization. It is probably quite unlikely that our language systems are organized along the lines of a railroad, a telephone system, or a computer system, although these metaphors have led to considerable insight into language processing.

2.2 FEATURES

A central concern of psycholinguistics is the determination of the basic unit of representation for every field of language processing. Consider, for example, the sounds of our language. We have noted that speech sounds can be described in terms of discrete segments, such as [b]. We have also seen that these segments can be described in terms of their component phonetic features; [b] is a voiced bilabial stop. It is important to know whether features such as *voiced* and *stop* actually play a role in speech production and perception. Can phonetic features offer any insight into the processes involved in language comprehension and production? Tentatively, we can answer yes.

Some evidence comes from the study of naturally occurring speech errors, the "slips of the tongue" that we all make from time to time in everyday conversation. An examination of the examples in Table 10.1 reveals that features do indeed offer insights that would not be available if we were to think about speech segments or phonemes as indivisible units. In (a) and (b), for example, the speaker has not simply substituted one phoneme for another. There is a pattern here, and phonetic features offer us the means to discuss that pattern. The errors in (a) and (b) are a result of the phonetic feature *voice* being misapplied. The difference between *big* and *pig* is only a matter of voicing or not voicing the initial phoneme. The same holds true for *fat* and *vat*, *pat* and *bat*, and *girl* and *curl*. The error in (c) is particularly intriguing because we normally think of [b] and [m] as completely different phonemes, but you may recall that they differ only in terms of nasality. Otherwise, they are identical, both being voiced bilabial stops. Thus the error in (c) is a misapplication of the feature *nasality*.

Table 10.1   Naturally Occurring Speech Errors

Intended		Actually produced
(a) big and fat	→	pig and vat
(b) Is Pat a girl?	→	Is bat a curl?
(c) Cedars of Lebanon	→	Cedars of Lemanon

Source: Adapted from Fromkin (1993).

We can also see the effects of features in L2 learners' production. Learners of English as a second language typically have difficulty producing the voiced and voiceless versions of *th*, [ð] and [θ]. It is interesting to note that French speakers preserve the voicing distinction between these two sounds in English even though they are able to produce neither. Québécois speakers substitute a voiced alveolar stop [d] for the voiced dental fricative [ð] and a voiceless alveolar stop [t] for the voiceless dental fricative [θ]. Speakers of Continental French, on the other hand, substitute a voiced alveolar fricative [z] and a voiceless alveolar fricative [s]. These distinctions are illustrated in Table 10.2. This sort of evidence suggests, then, that phonetic features do play a role in language production in both first and second languages.

Table 10.2   English Pronunciation Errors Made by Québécois and Continental French

	Transcription	Québécois French	Continental French
three	[θri]	[tri]	[sri]
they	[ðey]	[dey]	[zey]

Some interesting research has revealed that features of a slightly different kind play a role in reading (Neisser 1967). Here is a simple example of one of the experiments. Subjects were shown letter strings such as those in (1) and (2) below and asked to find the letter X in each and press a reaction time key as soon as they had found it.

1. WLKMNHYTHFZWXHKL
2. RGBJPSUQBRCBXPOSU

It took longer to identify the X in string (1) than in string (2) because (1) contains only letters made of straight lines. The letter X also has only straight lines and is therefore difficult to find it when it is embedded in a list of characters with similar features. String (2), however, contains only characters containing curved lines. Against this background, the X is much easier to identify.

These results would be unexpected in a theory claiming that character recognition involves whole characters rather than features. Assuming that one processes the strings from left to right, one character at a time, a whole-character recognition model would assert that the recognition system proceeds in the following manner. At each character in the string, the processor asks, "Is this an X?" If the answer is no, the processor continues to the next character. If the answer is yes, he or she presses the button. If such a model were correct, the operations required to find the X in strings (1) and (2) would be identical and there should be no difference in reaction time between the two. That there *is* a difference suggests that the strings are instead processed feature by feature.

A number of areas thus provide evidence that the fundamental units of language processing may be very small: phonetic features as opposed to phonemes, or lines as opposed to letters. This has led many researchers of language processing to view language structure in much the same way that theoretical linguists do, as structures in which small features combine to form successively larger units of representation. Features form phonemes, phonemes form morphemes, and morphemes form words.

Recently, however, some connectionist theorists have presented a radical challenge to these approaches (Seidenberg and McClelland 1989).

You will recall from Chapter 3 that connectionist theorists use computer simulations to model both the neuron-like processing units in the brain and the way in which connections between such simple processing units can yield the complex representations and processes that we attribute to the mind. Seidenberg and McClelland's connectionist model of word recognition proposes that there are *only* features; that the mind does not represent higher units such as words at all. This is an important challenge, for if it were proven correct, it would force a drastic revision of conceptions of language representation. Most views of language processing still assume that although features play a role, higher level symbols such as words and phrases also exist in the mind.

The field provokes considerable debate and controversy but two things are clear: features are important, and we are often deceived by our intuitions about the units of language. Second language learners may think that they are acquiring the ability to produce new sounds but in fact be learning to recombine phonetic features. They may believe that they have acquired a new word but instead be developing new connections among conceptual features, sound features, and perhaps visual features. This fundamentally affects how we conceive of second language acquisition. When we think above the level of features, it seems that second language acquisition involves learning new things: new phrases, new words, new sounds, perhaps a new alphabet. When we think about these new things at the level of features, however, there is really nothing new at all. The acquisition of new phonemes is a reorganization of associations among phonetic features, and learning new words is again simply a matter of reorganization. Even learning a new writing system involves not learning new characters but developing reorganized associations among line and curve features.

2.3 BOTTOM-UP AND TOP-DOWN PROCESSING

The interplay of *bottom-up* and *top-down processing* in language performance is fundamental. Bottom-up processing is driven solely by properties of the stimulus. In our example of the detection of the letter X in a string, we were only talking about bottom-up processing. We claimed that recognition of the letter X proceeded by first considering the line feature and then working our way up to the level of the whole letter. This approach seems to make sense when the letter is to be recognized in a meaningless list of letters. But what about the recognition of the *x* in *fox*? In this case, a complete line-by-line feature analysis would not be necessary. The language processor should be able to predict to some extent that the last letter of this word is *x*. This type of prediction is called top-down processing.

Top-down processing makes proofreading a very difficult task. Typographical errors are missed in proofreading because the mind is fixing the errors as they are read. In effect, proofreaders believe that they have seen the correct character. The confusing information in this case is supplied by top-down processing, which is characteristic of normal reading. A common technique to improve proofreading is to cut off top-down processing by reading in an abnormal fashion; that is, without comprehension. Some proofreaders suggest reading a text from the end to the beginning because it interferes with the extraction of meaning and therefore the opportunity for top-down processes to interfere.

Another example of the role of top-down processing is shown in Figure 10.1. The words in the figure are most often read as THE CAT. If you examine the middle character in each of the two words, however, you will see that they are the same. If you did, in fact, perceive the phrase THE CAT, then your mind transformed the middle character (which doesn't correspond to any real letter in the English alphabet) into an H for one word and an A for the other. Clearly, top-down processing is responsible for these transformations.

TΛE CΛT

Figure 10.1

A final example of top-down processing is given in Figure 10.2 below. If you perceive this word to be FED, then again you have demonstrated how high-level information can affect the perception of letters. In this case, however, you have also demonstrated how processes involved in reading operate in parallel. How did you know that the first letter was F? Well, if you respond that you knew the first letter was F because the middle letter is E, then how did you know that the middle letter was E? Surely, not because the first letter was F! In this example we can see that the perception of the F and E must occur simultaneously, or in parallel. In comprehension, the human mind does not wait for one operation to be complete before going on to the next.

Figure 10.2

2.4 THE FREQUENCY EFFECT

We have all heard that practice makes perfect. This is one of those bits of knowledge that are so well known and so obvious that few of us have stopped to wonder why they might be true. Why is it, for example, that an L2 word you have used only rarely is harder to recall and harder to say than a word you have used many times? If a word is simply a representation in semantic memory, the number of times it has been used should not make a difference.

What about activities, as opposed to representations? Let us take hitting a tennis ball as an example. Why does practice in hitting tennis balls improves one's tennis ability? After all, each new tennis ball comes at you from a slightly different angle, at a different height, and at a different speed. In this way, each hit is a unique event. In principle, practice should not make a difference. We all know, however, that it does, and this is what needs to be explained.

Clearly, to make any sense of the apparent paradox in the effect of practice on hitting tennis balls, understanding sentences, or any other complex activity, we must think in terms not of the activity as a whole but of its components. Although all sentence comprehension events are unique, they must make use of common operations and units of representation. The extent to which a particular unit or operation is repeatedly used is the measure of its frequency, and in the psycholinguistic literature, the term *frequency effect* is often used to describe the positive effect that practice has on performance.

By far most research on the frequency effect has studied single-word comprehension and production. There are two reasons. It is relatively easy to study the effects of single-word frequency because a number of published frequency counts of various languages are available. These have been compiled simply by taking texts from many sources and counting the number of times a given word occurs in, say, a sample of a million words. The result is a frequency count such as the one produced by Kucera and Francis (1967). The ten most frequent words are given in Table 10.3.

Table 10.3   Ten Most Frequently Used English Words

Word	Frequency per million
the	69 971
of	36 411
and	28 852
to	26 149
a	23 237
in	21 341
that	10 595
is	10 099
was	9 816
he	9 543

Source: Data from Kucera and Francis (1967).

The other reason that word frequency has been investigated to a great extent is that the frequency of a word was shown fairly early on to affect the speed with which it was both recognized (Rubenstein, Garfield, and Millikan 1970) and read aloud (Forster and Chambers 1973). In subsequent research, the frequency effect has been shown to be extremely robust. Frequency is by far the most important determinant of how easy it is to recognize or produce a word.

Why might this be the case? Early on it was thought that the frequency effect resulted from the same pathways in the brain being activated over and over again. These pathways were imagined to be somewhat like paths in a forest; the more often they were travelled, the deeper and more well-worn they got. In other models (such as Forster 1976), the words in an individual's vocabulary were represented in a long list, with the most frequent words at the top and the least frequent at the bottom. When looking for a word, the person would search the list from top to bottom.

An influential explanation for the frequency effect was first proposed by Morton (1969) in his logogen model. In this model, each word is associated with a logogen, which acts like a smoke detector. Each logogen is sensitive to a particular blend of smoke—a particular word. When the smoke of that blend is encountered, the alarm sounds and word recognition occurs. The logogen model claims that a frequent word has activated the alarm many times. The more often an alarm is activated, the easier it becomes to activate it again. Less smoke is required to activate the alarm and the smoke needn't be exactly of the specific mixture. To put it in logogen terms, a frequent word develops a lower activation threshold. The logogen model provides a natural account of how we read both THE CAT in Figure 10.1 and the characters in Figure 10.3.

W RD

Figure 10.3

Probably the first word that comes to mind upon seeing Figure 10.3 is *word*. Of course, the missing letter could also have been *a*, giving the word *ward*. According to the logogen model, *word* has precedence over *ward* because it is more frequent in the English language and therefore has a lower activation threshold. The word *word* also has a lower activation threshold because of the context. Because this text deals with word recognition, the lexical entry for *word* has been activated many times in this chapter. In fact, it has thus far been used fifty-four times.

Variations and developments of the logogen model have been very important in modelling the frequency effect. In the field of second language processing, it has been claimed that the interference a second language learner experiences from the words in his or her first language may actually be a manifestation of the frequency effect. Some models of bilingual processing assume that interference is really an inability to suppress "trigger happy" logogens from the L1.

2.5 PARSING

We have claimed many times in this book that the concept of a hierarchical syntactic structure is required to explain how sentences are understood. The structure of words and sentences has been represented with hierarchical tree diagrams. These representations are understood to be the product of the comprehension process, but how are they built up *during* the process? In the psycholinguistic literature, the process has been referred to as *parsing*. The abstract device that researchers believe actually builds these structures is called *the parser*.

The intention here is not to review individual proposals for the architecture of the parser, but simply to discuss the general idea and give some indication of how a parser might work. For this reason, we turn to the phenomenon that is best known for pointing out the need to postulate a parser distinct from a grammar. Consider the following sentence:

1. The horse raced past the barn fell.

Sentences such as this are called *garden path sentences*. After reading it a couple of times, you probably still find it difficult or perhaps impossible to understand. For some reason, your parser is leading you down the garden path to an incorrect syntactic analysis. In fact, the sentence is perfectly grammatical and is simply a result of deleting some optional elements from the sentence below:

2. The horse <u>that had been</u> raced past the barn fell.

It is, in fact, very much like (3):

3. The horse led past the barn fell.

Do you get it now? Frazier (1987) presents a number of garden path sentences and argues that the difficulty people have in understanding them can tell us a good deal about sentence parsing. Here are two more:

4. The reporter saw her friend was not succeeding.
5. Since Jay always walks a mile seems like a short distance to him.

Both (4) and (5) typically result in temporary misanalyses.

Frazier (1987) has proposed that these effects result from principles of parsing called *minimal attachment* and *late closure*. The principle of minimal attachment states that we do not postulate new syntactic nodes unless it is clear we absolutely have to. The principle of late closure states that we prefer to attach new words to the clause currently being processed as we proceed through a sentence from beginning to end.

Application of these principles as we process sentences (1), (4), and (5) results in impossible analyses and we therefore have to go back and try to understand them again

It is the principle of minimal attachment that makes *The horse raced past the barn fell* difficult to understand. The correct syntactic structure for the sentence is given in Figure 10.4. We have a difficult time coming up with this representation because we are unwilling to posit the extra S node above the string *raced past the barn*. Instead, we typically come up with a representation such as the one in Figure 10.5.

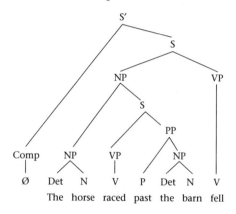

Figure 10.4[1]

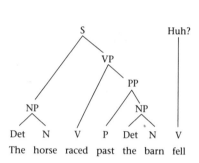

Figure 10.5

This discussion of parsing brings up both a general and a specific point in the study of language performance. Generally, an understanding of language requires formal analyses of language structure and psycholinguistic analyses of processing mechanisms. As the study of parsing reveals, we need to know not only what representations are created but also how they are created. Specifically, processing strategies or habits are not always optimal. The parser's strategies work for most sentences but not for all. Once the parsing strategy is well ingrained, however, it is very difficult to change. Second language learners bring to the task of L2 sentence processing a set of strategies that may not be optimal. These strategies are unconscious and well practised, and adjusting them is a formidable task.

2.6 THE MENTAL LEXICON

It has been estimated that a native speaker of English knows about seventy-five thousand words. How are these words stored in the mind? The concept of a mental lexicon begins with the common observation

---

[1] For ease of explication, empty nodes in the lower clause have been omitted.

that individuals can readily perform the various functions of actual dictionaries. Native speakers of a language can easily and naturally translate between the different domains of speech, print, and meaning in the performance of common tasks such as reading aloud. In addition, native speakers tend to exhibit dictionary-like indexing abilities in generating lists of words that rhyme or lists of words that begin with a particular sound.

Given these observations, the need to postulate a psychologically real mental lexicon of word forms becomes apparent. How is this store of words organized, arranged, and accessed? As far as the representation of information in the mental lexicon is concerned, there are at least three possibilities (see Figure 10.6). The first claims that the mental lexicon contains all the words an individual knows. Thus, it would contain an entry for the word *watch*, an entry for the word *watching*, and an entry for the word *watches*. We will refer to this as the whole-word hypothesis. The second, which we will call the morphological hypothesis, claims that the mental lexicon is organized in terms of morphemes and therefore does not contain any complex entries. Each entry can contain only one morpheme, or meaning unit. Thus the mental lexicon would not have an entry for *watching* but separate entries for the root *watch* and the suffix *-ing*. The third hypothesis proposes that the mental lexicon

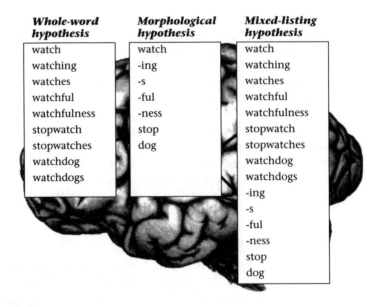

Figure 10.6   Three Views of the Lexicon

contains all morphological units: word and morphemes. We will call this the mixed-listing hypothesis.

As can be seen in Figure 10.6, the morphological hypothesis is somewhat more efficient than either the whole-word or the mixed-listing hypothesis in that it requires fewer entries. Nevertheless, it necessitates the development of special procedures in comprehension to break a complex word such as *watching* into its components so that the entries *watch* and *-ing* could be activated in the mental lexicon.

The mixed-listing hypothesis appears to be the least efficient. It, too, would require special computational mechanisms to disassemble and assemble complex words. It also results in the largest number of entries and the greatest amount of clutter in the mental lexicon. Even so, it has received the most experimental support because it is able to account for some fundamental facts about words and word processing. Language users are able to understand complex words that they have never encountered before. Think of the word *dogwatcher*. You are unlikely to have seen it before but you can understand it nevertheless. The only way this is possible is for individual morphemes to be represented in your mental lexicon. So, the whole-word hypothesis must be inadequate. Now think of the word *bullseye*. If you know what it means, then you can process it quite easily. If, on the other hand, you do not know that the whole string refers to the center of a target, then knowing the meaning of the constituent morphemes *eye* and *bull* isn't going to help you very much. Evidence of this sort tells us that the morphological hypothesis is also inadequate.

The organization of the mental lexicon and the manner in which it is accessed have formed the meeting point for many issues in psycholinguistics: the fundamental unit of representation; the information contained in a lexical entry (what you know when you know a word); and how words are parsed in comprehension. On this last point there have been a number of proposals for English (Libben 1992, 1994; Taft 1981; Taft and Forster 1976). As with sentence parsing, an understanding of how word parsing works and to what extent parsing strategies are language specific may tell us a great deal about what second language learners must acquire when they encounter a new language.

We would expect that in second language acquisition, greater reliance would be placed on word parsing because many complex words are new to the learner. A learner of English as a second language may know the meanings of *un-*, *forget*, and *-able*, for example, but be required to conduct a morphological parse to understand the word *unforgettable*.

Another important point is that languages have different types of morphology. The acquisition of a language that differs morphologically from the L1 may force fairly drastic changes to the organization of a learner's mental lexicon and word-parsing strategies. Native speakers of German seem to have no difficulty processing words like

Sonntagnachmittagfamilienspaziergang, which contains nine morphemes and means roughly *a Sunday afternoon family stroll.* An English learner of German might wonder how they find all the pieces; the acquisition of German seems to require not only learning new words and new morphemes but also acquiring enhanced skills in morphological parsing.

A perhaps even more extreme example is what might happen when a speaker of English tries to acquire a morphologically agglutinating language like Turkish. Hankamer (1989) has remarked that Turkish words are formed by stringing along so many morphemes that if all the full forms of the language were represented, the mental lexicon would have to contain billions of words. Consider the following Turkish noun:

Bayramlaşamadiklarimiz

/ bayram	–	laš	–	á	–	ma	–	dɨk	–	lar	–	imɨz /
holiday	– reciprocal	– negative	– negative	– object	– plural	–	first
		inabilitive			particle	noun	person
							plural
							possessive

"Those of our number with whom we cannot exchange the season's greetings."

Although memorizing full words is a strategy that works quite well for English, it would be impossible for Turkish.

3 SOURCES OF EVIDENCE IN LANGUAGE PROCESSING

The sections above have discussed some of the more important issues and concepts in the study of language processing, but that is only half the story. Psycholinguistics is defined not only in terms of its area of inquiry but also in terms of its methods. Most information about how language is processed has come from studying language users as they produce or comprehend language. In some cases, special experimental procedures are required to elicit the kinds of data relevant to testing particular hypotheses. In other cases, we can look at naturally occurring speech for clues about the processes involved in production.

Below is a brief overview of the kinds of methods that psycholinguists employ. It provides the necessary background for the discussion of research on production and comprehension in Chapters 11 and 12.

3.1 SPEECH ERRORS

We have seen that naturally occurring speech errors such as (1), below, can tell us something about the extent to which features play a role in speech production:

1. big and fat → pig and vat

As we will see in Chapter 11, researchers such as Garrett (1984) have built entire models of language production from speech error data. These theorists look not only at phonetic errors but also at errors such as (2):

2. It tended to turn out → It turned to tend out

In this example, the past tense marker -*ed* is left in the correct place even though the roots *tend* and *turn* have been reversed. This sort of error reveals that individual morphemes have independent positions in sentence planning.

Speech errors can also tell us something about how words are associated in our mental lexicons. Consider (3) and (4):

3. That's a horse of a different colour. → That's a horse of a different race.
4. He has too many irons in the fire. → He has too many irons in the smoke.

These errors are essentially semantic and reveal how the intended activation of one word can result in the activation of its semantic neighbour instead.

How do researchers collect these errors? Well, it takes a good deal of effort and patience. They listen to talk shows, read first drafts of manuscripts, and in general never leave home without a pencil and notepad.

Clearly, speech error analysis offers important evidence in the study of language processing, but it does have a number of disadvantages. Researchers have to wait until an error occurs; they do not have any control over when and where errors will be created. As well, speech error data do not make it easy to test hypotheses. We might wonder after examining the error in (4), in which the speaker said *smoke* for *fire*, whether people are also inclined to say *fire* when they mean *smoke*. This is difficult to answer if all you can do is sit around and wait for an error to occur. The next section examines techniques to answer specific questions such as this. All these techniques are experimental in the sense that they involve controlling and manipulating the environment and observing subjects' responses to these manipulations under controlled conditions.

3.2 RESPONSE TIME AND ACCURACY

What do psycholinguistic experiments actually measure? Let's say you are learning English as a second language and we want to know which types of sentences are easy for you to understand and which are difficult. The obvious thing to do would be to make up a test in which you are required to indicate your comprehension of sentences by, say, picking out from an array of pictures the one that best represents the meaning of each sentence. For this experiment, we might pick five active voice sentences (*The cat bit the dog*), five passive sentences (*The dog was bitten by the cat*), and five cleft sentences (*It was the dog that the cat bit*). Now what would we measure? It seems reasonable simply to count up the number of correct answers for each type of sentence and to see whether there is a difference in the number correct for the various types of sentences. In other words, we would measure your response accuracy. Our hypothesis would probably be that you would do better on simple active sentences than on passives, and better on passives than on cleft sentences.

Now, let's say we wanted to do the same experiment with native speakers of English, because we suppose that they too will find active sentences easier than passives and passives easier than clefts. Here we run into difficulty because native speakers would probably get all the items correct, even though some would be more difficult than others. To get around this problem, we could measure their speed of response. Even if native speakers end up getting all the answers right, we can hypothesize that some sentence types, because they are more difficult to parse, would require more time. In this case what we measure—the dependent variable in our experiment—is response time rather than response accuracy.

You may have noted in the brief discussion of the frequency effect that response time is very often used as a dependent variable in psycholinguistic experiments. Native speakers will recognize frequent words such as *ridiculous* correctly. They will also recognize infrequent words such as *ubiquitous* correctly, but it will take them longer. Both response time and response accuracy are considered to be measures of difficulty. Response time, however, is a more sensitive measure and is therefore used quite often.

3.3 PRIMING EFFECTS

One way to find out whether the words *smoke* and *fire* are related in the mental lexicon is to conduct what is known as a priming experiment. A subject is first shown one word (the prime word) and then another (the target word). Using the logogen model, we might hypothesize that if the prime word were related to the target word in the mental lexicon, it would take less time to read the target word aloud because the neighbouring prime word would lower the activation threshold for the target word. We would therefore expect a shorter response time to *fire* if it were preceded by the word *smoke* than if it were preceded by an unrelated word, such as *table*. This is exactly what typically happens; prior presentation of *smoke* facilitates recognition of the word *fire*. This is termed the semantic priming effect.

This sort of experimental technique gives the researcher much more control than is possible in the analysis of naturally occurring speech errors. It can also be used to examine many other questions about how language elements are associated in the mind. Of special interest in the study of second language acquisition is whether priming effects occur across languages. De Groot (1993) summarized a number of studies that showed priming effects operating both between and within languages for subjects with a reasonable degree of fluency in their second language. In other words, if you are a French learner of English as a second language, your mental lexicon gets reorganized so that *fire* and *feu* both prime *smoke*.

3.4 INTERFERENCE EFFECTS

Just as we can learn something from the effects of priming, we can also learn something from the effects of interference. A classic procedure, called the Stroop technique, represents some very clever experimentation and is also highly revealing of the fundamental characteristics of language comprehension.

The technique was first reported by Stroop in 1935. In the original version, subjects were presented with a colour word such as *blue*. The word was written in red ink, and the subjects were required simply to name the colour of the ink and to ignore the meaning of the word. This is a very difficult task. Subjects' response times are slow and they make errors because of the interference coming from the meaning of the word. The results of many experiments employing this technique and other variants all tell us the same thing: You cannot turn your language processor off. Figure 10.7 shows a version of the Stoop test for you to try. Try simply to name the shapes out loud. You will note that even though you have prepared for this task, it is more difficult to name the shapes on the left than the ones on the right. The meanings of the words are impossible to suppress, and those on the left interfere with the identification of the shapes.

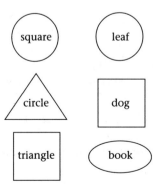

Figure 10.7 The Stroop Technique

What would happen if you were learning German and the test employed German words? Would you experience the same Stroop effect? Unsurprisingly, it turns out that you would not. Somehow, the activation from your second language is not as strong and therefore does not create as much interference (see Figure 10.8).

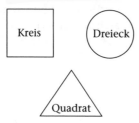

Figure 10.8   The Stroop Technique in a Second Language[2]

Even though the interference from a second language is not as strong, however, you cannot shut it out. Numerous experiments have shown that interference effects are present no matter how things are arranged. If the words are in German and you have to name the shape in English, you suffer interference; if the situation is reversed, you also suffer interference; if you do the whole thing in German, you still suffer interference.

This is only one type of interference effect but it should provide you with a flavour of the logic behind this kind of research. It is unlikely that developing a vocabulary in a second language involves the development of a new and separate lexicon. If this were so, it would be possible to shut one down and you would not experience interference from German words when you were required to name shapes in English. Cross-language interference suggests that words of the two languages are stored together in a system with no off switch.

4 CONCLUSION

This discussion of language performance has set the stage for the treatment of language production and comprehension in the following two chapters. It has covered a number of core concepts and techniques in the study of language processing. All of these enhance our ability to address the questions that were brought up at the outset of the chapter:

- What language representations are stored in the mind?
- What are the properties of these representations?
- What language representations are computed rather than stored?
- How does this computation occur?

---

[2] *Kreis* = circle; *dreieck* = triangle; *quadrat* = square.

Definitive answers are simply not yet available, but even the tentative answers we do have greatly increase our understanding of second language acquisition. What the learner acquires, after all, is the ability to *do* things in a second language. It seems relatively clear that speaking, listening, reading and writing in L2 cannot involve the creation of new language processing systems unrelated to those used for L1. On the other hand, it also seems clear that L1 representational and computational systems are modified through the acquisition of a second language. Second language acquisition does not involve building a new mental lexicon but changing the old one.

Another point of importance is how both accuracy and response time are associated with underlying processing difficulty. In the field of second language acquisition, these ideas relate directly to the two overt characteristics used to assess proficiency: fluency and accuracy. Fluency is of course also a measure of speed. In the next chapter, we will see how models of speech production can be used to predict and understand the accuracy–fluency trade-off in second language acquisition.

CLASSROOM IMPLICATIONS

Second language teaching methods can have very different views on the amount of explicit instruction provided to the learner and the type of practice that the learner should be engaged in. Consider the following issues:

1. How do the second language teaching methods with which you are familiar differ with respect to
   - encouraging learners to become aware of component phonological, visual, morphological, syntactic, and semantic features of structures in the target language?
   - encouraging primarily bottom-up or top-down processing?
   - providing the learner with explicit parsing strategies?
2. Do you think that the vocabulary of second language learners is subject to frequency effects? How do you think classroom practices can affect the organization of the learner's target language lexicon?

SELF TEST

A full understanding of language requires that we consider both language _____ and language _____ . The field of
    (1)   (2)
_____ is concerned with language performance.
    (3)

Psycholinguists are interested in which representations are stored in the mind and which are _____ . It is important to note, however,
(4)
that the terms we use to describe mind/brain functioning are simply

_____ .
(5)

The study of speech _____ can tell us a good deal about
(6)
the fundamental units of language processing. The smallest of these units are called _____ . Language processing may be seen as an
(7)
interplay between _____ and _____ processing.
(8)   (9)
Morton's _____ model provides an account of how the
(10)
_____ effect may be related to activation thresholds. The
(11)
study of how syntactic structures are built during sentence comprehension is called _____ .
(12)

The dominant current view of the elements contained in the mental lexicon claims that both _____ and _____ are rep-
(13)   (14)
resented. In psycholinguistic research, both _____ and
(15)
_____ are considered to be measures of difficulty. The
(16)
_____ effect refers to the phenomenon of prior presentation
(17)
of one item facilitating recognition of a subsequent item. The
_____ technique is an example of an interference effect. The
(18)
effect tells us that language processing is _____ .
(19)

FURTHER READING

Berko Gleason, J. and N. Bernstein Ratner. 1993. *Psycholinguistics*. Orlando, FL: Harcourt Brace Jovanovich.

Garman, M. 1990. *Psycholinguistics*. Cambridge: Cambridge University Press.

Language Production

Language production may take many forms. It may be spoken, written, typed, or signed, but the spoken form is by far the most common. Most people never learn sign language; many never learn to write. This chapter explores language production as it is expressed in speech, capturing the principles of production that are most applicable across age groups, cultures, and languages.

What is speaking? We would all probably agree that speaking is the means by which we communicate our thoughts to other people. We will use this commonsense definition as a starting point to develop a model of speech production. A preliminary model can be represented by the box-and-arrow notation in Figure 11.1, which sets the agenda for this chapter: to investigate the contents of the empty box.

Figure 11.1   A Preliminary Model of Speech Production

The box is empty because we know that intermediate processes must transform a message into sound, but the nature of these processes is available neither to introspection (as perhaps the message is) nor observation (as the sound output is). How, then, can the contents of the box be investigated? As long as the speech production system is working perfectly and is consistently producing speech output that faithfully represents the speaker's intended message, it is next to impossible to determine the intermediate processes in speech production. When the system produces an error, however, we can analyse the error to determine what went wrong in the production process and therefore what the components of the process might be. This chapter is concerned primarily with production errors and the ways in which the study of speech errors has contributed to understanding production.

1 SECOND LANGUAGE SPEECH ERRORS

Second language speech typically contains speech errors, where errors are defined as a deviation from the target language norm. The field of *error analysis* addresses the significance of learner errors. Within the field, errors are often characterized in terms of the level of language at which they occur: errors of word selection (lexical errors); of word structure (morphological errors); of sentence structure (syntactic errors); and of sound patterns (phonological errors).

What is the status of these different error types? Are they just convenient means of attaching labels to the speech of language learners or do they actually reveal the processes that *produce* the errors? The psycholinguistic approach to error analysis divides it roughly by the error types just mentioned. Consider the following example of interlanguage speech:

Can you me borrow two dollars?
Meaning: Can you lend me two dollars?

The sentence clearly contains a word selection error. Did the second language speaker actually attempt to select an item from a store of words corresponding to the meaning *lend* but end up choosing the wrong one (*borrow*)? The body of evidence considered here claims that this is so.

The evidence suggests discrete stages in the process of speaking, which correspond to discrete levels of language. Thus, there is a stage of processing at which the word *lend* or *borrow* is selected on the basis of its match to a set of semantic features, a stage at which the word *dollars* is created from the components *dollar + s,* and a stage at which the word *me* is inserted into a particular position in the sentence. Its position in the learner's utterance does not conform to the target language norm and it is thus a syntactic error.

The source of error might be found in second language competence: the representation of linguistic knowledge in semantic memory. If so, we assume that the learner has not yet acquired the appropriate principle of English syntax that disallows the placement of the pronoun *me* before the verb in a sentence of this sort. If, on the other hand, the error has its source in linguistic performance, then we assume that the relevant syntactic knowledge is present but that the cognitive and motor mechanisms carrying out this knowledge have not performed perfectly. The relevant mechanisms in this case would calculate the appropriate positions and insert words into them as they are uttered.

You might be sceptical at this point about whether it is possible for a second language speaker to have perhaps perfect competence and still produce grammatically incorrect sentences. Two observations are relevant to this issue. The first is that L2 production is typically quite variable; most learners produce syntactically correct sentences on some occasions and incorrect sentences of the same type on others. If we were to claim that the incorrect sentences resulted from lack of knowledge, then we would be at a loss to explain how the learner ever produces the correct form. Surely it is unlikely that he or she would know the rule on one day and not on another. Such a claim would be contrary to the general view that knowledge is relatively permanent and unchanging. To consider the opposite, we don't usually think of *acquiring* a bloody nose; it's an unstable phenomenon. One of the key assumptions in the field of error analysis is that systematic errors—those consistently produced by the learner—reflect the nature of the learner's grammar, whereas unsystematic errors are attributable to performance factors.

ANOTHER VIEW OF LANGUAGE PRODUCTION...

The object of this work is to place before the reader, in as *concise* and *clear* a manner as possible, the *practical* working of this *new* and *true* theory of *perfect voice production.*

This theory, which has taken upwards of twenty years' continuous and persistent study to perfect, the author claims to have *originated;* as it *differs entirely, on all the most vital points, from any other method hitherto advanced!*

... The theory is based upon such a solid foundation of scientific investigation and experiment, every feature, phase, and detail of the question endorsing and upholding the other—no single point being at variance with another—the whole being in perfect accord and harmony with itself—and that whole being nothing more nor less than a reflex of true and perfect nature, *in the fullest meaning of the word*—that we say it would be impossible to dispute, or in any way gainsay it, either as a whole or in any particular.

Alfred Augustus North
Proemial Note
Voxometric Revelation, 1896

The second observation supporting the view that competence and performance are distinct comes from native speech. Native speakers, by definition, have perfect competence in their language. Should we then predict that their speech production will also be perfect? Surely not. Analysis of native speaker speech reveals many lexical, morphological, syntactic, and phonological errors. These cannot be caused by lack of competence but must instead reflect the computational processes that are relevant to language production. Presently, the most influential psycholinguistic models of speech production are based on analysis of speech errors, or "slips of the tongue." The section below examines one such model, proposed by Merrill Garrett (1976; 1980; 1984). It is intended to account for the patterns of speech error in native speakers but also has important consequences for the characterization of second language speech.

2 GARRETT'S MODEL OF SPEECH PRODUCTION

Garrett's model is based on analysis of thousands of naturally occurring errors in the speech of native speakers of English. He noted that errors are of four major types: semantic substitution, word exchange, sound exchange, and stranding. Garrett contends that each type reveals the computational processes used at a particular stage in sentence planning and production. To get a flavour of the reasoning in this approach, we will consider Garrett's analysis of the first two error types.

Semantic substitution usually involves exchanging a word for its opposite. The speaker intends to say "good" but instead says "bad," or intends to say "up" but instead says "down." Garrett suggests that these errors in lexical selection reveal how words are organized in our minds. Words are arranged in meaning clusters. If you dip into your store of words for a particular lexical item and are less than exact, chances are that you will erroneously select a close neighbour of the word you were looking for. Because words are organized in semantic memory along semantic lines, the erroneously selected word will have a strong semantic association with the intended word. It seems that the strongest such association is opposition. This is easily demonstrated in simple word-association tasks. You hear a word and are asked to say the first word that comes into your mind. If you hear the word *black*, for example, you would probably immediately say "white." You would choose a word with an opposite meaning, not one with a similar meaning, such as *brown* or *dark*.

The second of Garrett's error types is word exchange. These are errors such as

He put the pot in the soup
Intended meaning: He put the soup in the pot.

I'll floor the polish
Intended meaning: I'll polish the floor.

It is interesting to note that word exchanges always occur between words in different phrases. Above, the words *pot* and *soup* are exchanged. They are both nouns but are not in the same phrase. In the other example, an element in a noun phrase is exchanged with an element in a verb phrase.

This can be explained by considering the steps involved in sentence production. Garrett claims that a sentence begins with a message, which is not in linguistic form. It begins to acquire a linguistic form when we organize its concepts according to the vocabulary of our language. To do this we select lexical items, or "packages of meaning," from our mental lexicon. After we have selected the appropriate lexical items and determined the semantic relationships among them, we begin to construct a sentence structure. This is made up of phrases, which we might imagine to be empty containers. Once the containers are in place, the selected lexical items are dropped into them. Garrett asserts that dropping words into the wrong containers causes word exchanges such as those in the two sentences above. Because each container is a phrase, his model provides a very natural account of why word exchange errors always involve words showing up in the wrong phrases.

Reasoning in the above fashion, Garrett constructed a model of speech production to account for the patterns of speech errors commonly produced by native speakers (see Figure 11.2). It is essentially the same as the one with which the chapter began, except that it contains a set of intermediate levels of representation between a message and the sound of a sentence.

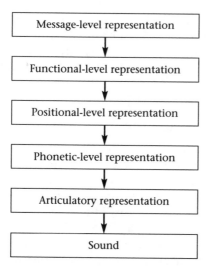

Figure 11.2. Garrett's Model of Speech Production
Source: Adapted from Garrett (1984, 174).

To highlight the main features of the model, let's examine the steps involved in producing a specific sentence: *I arrived in Paris yesterday.* In this particular case, we imagine the message to be something retrieved from the episodic memory of the speaker. It is transformed into a linguistic representation by recoding the general message-level concepts into specific word meanings. At this stage of processing the relation of the selected words to one another is also determined. In this case, it is established that the sentence will centre around the verb *to arrive*. The word *I* will represent the person who did the arriving and the word *Paris* will represent the location of arrival. Finally, *yesterday* will represent the time of arrival. Once these processes have been completed, the message-level representation has been transformed into a functional-level representation.

The functional level is then transformed into the positional level by the creation of a syntactic structure for the sentence, which determines that the first word in the sentence will be *I*, the second will be *arrived*, and so on. At this point, the phonological representation for each word is established and the words are dropped into the (usually) appropriate sentence positions.

The next set of procedures determines phonological factors for the utterance rather than for individual words. This involves such elements as sentence stress and intonation. Once this is completed the message has reached the phonetic level of representation.

The final procedures in the process of sentence production calculate the motor movements required to utter the sentence. This results in the articulatory representation, which, when executed, produces the sound of the sentence.

Garrett's model clearly leaves many details of the speech production process unexamined. Nevertheless, it offers a framework within which to discuss discrete components of production and is extremely important for understanding the different types of difficulties encountered by second language learners.

2.1 SECOND LANGUAGE SPEECH PRODUCTION

A model of speech production such as Garrett's allows us to reconsider, in a more rigorous fashion, the general question of proficiency in a second language. The first step in the model is to formulate concepts in terms of the "packages of meaning," which correspond to the vocabulary of a language. What happens when one learns the vocabulary of a second language? Is it necessary to acquire a new set of processes to gain access to and produce different "meaning bundles"? In other words, do we have to develop a new functional level of representation? To become a true bilingual, one probably does have to evolve a new set of procedures. Most second language learners, however, never become true bilinguals, quite possibly in part because they do not develop new procedures and representations but instead continue to use first language "boxes" in production.

As long as learners continue to use the first language procedures for developing the functional level of representation, we would expect that they will often use words inappropriately in the target language. When a speaker of English wishes to talk about someone with whom he or she is relatively well acquainted, he or she will often select the word *friend*, which corresponds to a particular meaning package. Now, suppose the English speaker happens to be learning German and wishes to talk in German about someone with whom he or she is relatively well acquainted. Selecting the English meaning package for this concept and then producing the German word *Freund* would result in a second language error. The speaker would have used the wrong—that is, the English—packaging system. In German, the word *Freund* refers to someone with whom you are very familiar and therefore corresponds to a much smaller meaning unit than does *friend* in English.

To avoid errors of this sort the learner must develop a new, separate lexical system at the functional level for the second language (Figure 11.3). To the extent that the learner does not do so, he or she will experience first language interference when speaking in the target language although the errors may be covert for the most part.

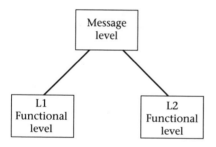

Figure 11.3   Separate Lexical Meaning Systems for Each Language

The severity of the interference can be represented in Garrett's model as degrees of overlap between the two systems. If the learner fails to develop *any* new processes at the functional level, he or she will produce the second language using only first language word meanings. We expect that this is possible and indeed may characterize the majority of language learners. At other levels of the production process, however, it seems that the learner *must* create a separation between processes and representations in the two languages in order to develop proficiency in the target language. At the positional level, for example, if the learner does not develop a new box specific to the second language, he or she will produce target language sentences with first language word order. This was perhaps the case in the learner utterance considered earlier: *Can you me borrow two dollars?*

The issue of overlap between first and second language production processes applies to every level of representation in Garrett's model. At the phonetic level, for example, overlap in the phonological processes of sentence creation results in what is perceived as a strong foreign accent. At the articulatory level, a high degree of overlap results in the inability to produce specific target language sounds (such as [θ] or [ð] in English).

It is apparent, then, that production models make our understanding of second language speech errors concrete. Specifically, Garrett's model ties errors to distinct stages of sentence creation and allows us to formalize L2 proficiency as the development of computational procedures appropriate for the target language. It also permits us to consider second language speaking proficiency as a collection of independent components. A particular learner may develop a high degree of proficiency at the functional and positional levels, for example, but not at the phonetic level. Similarly, three second language learners might all show speech production difficulties but for three entirely different reasons. A common difficulty in the fluency of speech output may be caused by slowness at any level of representation in the speech production process. For the purposes of language remediation, it is essential to know which component is responsible for the difficulty.

Let's now explore the usefulness of production models for distinguishing between correctness and fluency in second language speech. We will also discuss how particular components in the production process can be isolated by comparing learner production across modalities.

3 ACCURACY AND FLUENCY

We have seen above that speech production may be viewed as a series of processes which create a number of discrete levels of representation between a message and speech output. These processes are summarized below.

3.1 MESSAGE- TO FUNCTIONAL-LEVEL CONVERSION

These processes essentially convert non-linguistic thought to linguistic thought. They select appropriate lexical items for particular concepts and determine thematic relations among lexical items.

3.1.1 Accuracy

The accuracy of the procedures that convert message-level representations to functional-level representations in second language speech can be influenced by both competence and performance factors. If the learner has developed a functionally distinct lexicon for the target language but that lexicon is still in an impoverished state, then the appropriate lexical items for particular concepts are often unavailable. This state of affairs typically results in circumlocution. Accuracy will also be impaired if the learner is using the L1 semantic lexicon to express concepts.

The dominant performance factor affecting accuracy in message- to functional-level conversion involves "slips of lexical selection." The mechanisms of lexical access are less well-practised for the target language than for the first language and are therefore more prone to error. These errors are semantic and produce inappropriate, but semantically related, words such as *borrow* instead of *lend*.

3.1.2 Fluency

Lack of fluency at this stage of processing is caused by developmental inefficiency of the procedures of lexical access in the target language. Although quite a bit is known about the mechanisms of lexical access in language comprehension, a great deal less is known about the mechanisms that organize concepts into words for the purposes of speech production. It remains unclear, for example, why the word-finding processes in speech production are so vulnerable. Word-finding difficulties form part of the clinical picture in virtually all forms of aphasia (language disturbance as a result of damage to the brain), and, as we probably all know from personal experience, word-finding processes are greatly disturbed under conditions of nervousness, tiredness, and the like. We therefore expect that a significant proportion of fluency difficulties in second language speech can be attributed to disturbances in the efficiency of lexical access, but an exact formulation of the nature of fluency at this level awaits further research.

3.2 FUNCTIONAL- TO POSITIONAL-LEVEL CONVERSION

The processes involved in conversion from the functional to the positional level are responsible for doing what we generally refer to as *syntax* and *morphology*. For the most part, the actual details of the processes remain unknown. Garrett suggests that, for native speakers of English, the structure of a sentence is worked out as a "skeleton" into which lexical items are inserted. He posits that this skeleton contains the syntactic structure of the sentence as well as particular affixes and function words. Thus, in the case of the sentence *The boy played in the yard,* the words *boy, play, in,* and *yard* would be inserted into boxes 1, 2, 3, and 4 respectively in Figure 11.4. Garrett's proposal assumes that function words play a very large role in determining the structure of a sentence. It also claims that words like *played* are put together at this point in the production process, from the elements *play* and *-ed*.

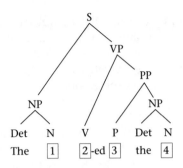

Figure 11.4   Positional Skeleton

According to Garrett, postulation of structures such as that in Figure 11.4 is necessary to account for the fourth error type: stranding. The sentence *The boy yarded in the play* exhibits such an error. Stranding is caused in essentially the same way as word exchange errors. Words are dropped into the wrong boxes. In this case, *play* was dropped into box 4 instead of box 2 and *yard* was dropped into box 2 instead of box 4. The affix *-ed*, however, has been "stranded" in its original position in the sentence. Garrett claims that the phenomenon of stranding occurs because the affix is part of the sentence skeleton and therefore cannot move.

3.2.1 Accuracy

At this stage of processing, identical accuracy errors can be caused by either competence or performance. Accuracy errors at this stage involve a word in the wrong place (syntactic errors) and/or in the wrong form (morphological errors). If the learner makes an error because he or she possesses syntactic or morphological rules that do not correspond to those of the target language, it is a matter of linguistic competence. If, on the other hand, the rules are present but the learner has made a word exchange error or a stranding error, as native speakers do, then the error is one of performance. These two sources can be distinguished on the basis of systematicity; the unsystematic errors are really mistakes, and are attributed to performance.

Accuracy errors can also occur because the mechanisms that build the structures into which lexical items are inserted have failed. Garrett's model asserts that affixes and function words play a crucial role in the development of sentence structures in native speakers. It is commonly observed, however, that the speech of language learners, especially in communicative settings, is characterized by an absence of appropriate function words and affixes. It is possible, then, that at the earlier stages of developing bilingualism, language learners use a fundamentally differ-ent means of creating sentence structure, one that does not rely on function words and affixes. If this is the case, several observations of second language syntax may be more easily accounted for.

The L2 learner's approach to building sentence structure could be driven primarily by lexical selection and the assignment of thematic roles. In the sentence above, for example, the learner would select *boy, play,* and *yard,* and establish that *boy* is the agent, *play* is the action, and *yard* is the location of the action. Rather than build a hierarchical syntactic structure for the sentence such as the one in Figure 11.4, the learner may then simply apply what he or she considers to be the normal order of thematic roles in English to produce *Boy play yard.*

This is a very common sort of production in learner speech. It contains all the sentence items except those considered to be part of the sentence skeleton in Figure 11.4, so if the learner knows that the verb *play* requires an animate agent and some sort of theme, he or she could produce *Boy play yard.*

It is interesting to note that this sort of sentence is also produced by people who have suffered language loss as a result of damage to a particular section of the frontal lobe of the brain. This condition is known as *agrammatism,* or loss of grammar. Researchers such as Caplan and Futter (1986) maintain that agrammatic patients have lost the ability to build sentence skeletons and therefore do exactly what language learners might do in sentence production.

3.2.2 Fluency

The fluency of processes that create the positional level is related to the complexity of the representation to be computed, the efficiency of the computational procedures, and the number of times the accuracy of these procedures is checked.

It is not surprising to find that second language production fluency is typically related to sentence length and complexity. Simpler sentences are easier to compute. This seemingly obvious statement, however, predicts the complexity–fluency trade-off often found in the speech of *fossilized* second language acquirers. It is said that learners are fossilized when there is no further change in their grammars and they become fluent in the fossilized version of the target language. If it is indeed the case that all fossilized grammars are simpler versions of the target language grammar, then it should be easy for the learner to become extremely fluent in the *created* language. This fluent fossilization is often characterized in the immigrant character roles of television situation comedies.

Exactly the opposite type of second language speaker has developed a knowledge of the target language that closely approximates that of the native speaker but has not yet developed efficient and automatic means of utilizing it to create target language sentence structures. In listening to second language speakers of this sort, one gets the subjective impression of sentences being slowly and painfully constructed in accordance with a set of grammatical well-formedness rules. Note that the slowness results from poorly practised syntactic skills rather than from conscious evaluation of the *results* of syntactic operations.

The learner who appears to be constantly checking the results of his or her sentence construction processes is even less fluent. Monitoring of this sort reflects intact competence but rather shaky confidence in the performance procedures. This characterization seems correct because if the learner did not "know" the appropriate rules of the language, he or she would have no criteria for testing the correctness of production.

3.3 POSITIONAL- TO PHONETIC-LEVEL CONVERSION

The processes involved in conversion from the positional to the phonetic level perform the phonological operations that give all the elements in a sentence their correct phonetic values. The kinds of phonological operations required at this stage not only build phonologically correct words from the sequence of morphemes created at the positional level but also organize those words into the appropriate phonological form for the particular sentence being constructed.

Consider the formation of the word *played* in the sentence *The boy played in the yard*. It was claimed above that the suffix *-ed* was present in the sentence skeleton at the positional level and that the word *play* was inserted into this skeleton. We have assumed that at this point the phonological form of the word *play* is determined. But what about the phonological form of the suffix *-ed*? In English, this suffix has three forms: [d] as in *pulled*; [t] as in *picked*; and [ɪd] as in *needed*. What determines the form the suffix will take? If the last consonant of the word to which the suffix attaches is voiced, then the form [d] will be used. If the last consonant is voiceless, then *-ed* will have the sound [t]. Finally, if the last consonant of the word is *-d* or *-t* then the *-ed* suffix will have the sound [ɪd]. It is clear that in the context of the performance model under consideration, the choice of correct suffix form must occur *after* the positional level, because it is only at that level that *play* and *-ed* are put together. Thus, for *The boy played in the yard* the sound of the word *played*, [pley] + [d], is calculated by the phonological processes that create the phonetic level of representation.

These processes also determine that the word *the* in both positions in this sentence does not have the long vowel sound that would occur if the first consonant of the next word were a vowel (compare pronunciations of *the apple* and *the potato*). Again, the phonological processes can occur only after all the words in the sentence are in place. Finally, the processes calculate sentence stress and intonation, ensuring that a question sounds like a question and an answer sounds like an answer.

3.3.1 Accuracy

Inaccuracy at this level of processing is commonly attributed to interference from the phonological system of the L1. As noted already, we are treating such interference as the result of failure to develop appropriate target language rules.

At this level of processing, it is difficult to distinguish between errors caused by competence deficits and those caused by performance deficits. On the one hand, failure to develop the appropriate phonological rules for the target language seems to be a matter of competence. On the other, it appears that all of phonology is tied to some sort of motor plan for the speech organs, the organs of speech performance. In either case, lack of accuracy at this level of processing forms the prototypical image of speech difficulty: the foreign accent in the target language.

3.3.2 Fluency

The primary determinant of fluency at this stage of processing seems to be monitoring. Learners who frequently stop to evaluate whether they have "pronounced it correctly" produce speech that is perceived as both slow and unnatural. Here again, however, we assume that competence is intact and constitutes the internal standard against which the learner checks his or her production.

3.4 PHONETIC-LEVEL TO ARTICULATORY REPRESENTATION CONVERSION

Here the phonetic-level representation is acted upon by a set of procedures that determine the exact motor movements required to utter the sentence.

3.4.1 Accuracy

You might wonder at this point how the procedures at this level differ from the phonological ones discussed above. Although accuracy errors at both levels create what is perceived as a foreign accent, the nature of the errors reveals that articulatory rules differ from phonological rules in two ways.

First, articulatory errors are generally much more local than phonological ones. They are limited to accuracy on particular phonemes (such as the English *th*). Second, the speaker cannot monitor articulatory errors. Many L2 learners of English have difficulty producing the English vowel schwa, for example, which is found in the word *information*. Most often the second language speaker believes that he or she is producing the sound correctly but is not, and is therefore making an articulatory error. When the difference between the target language sound and the actual production is pointed out, the learner typically reports not being able to hear any difference.

3.4.2 Fluency

Lack of fluency at this stage of processing produces slow and effortful speech. This sort of speech is also found in Broca's aphasia, a linguistic disturbance associated with damage to a particular area of the brain. In both second language and aphasic speech, errors attributable to difficulty at this level have to do with sound *execution*, not sound *planning*.

4 CONCLUSION

This chapter has presented the process of language production as a series of steps through which a non-linguistic message is transformed into speech output. We have described one model in some detail and discussed the ways in which the representations and processes it postulates may organize and clarify our thinking about second language acquisition.

It is important to note that Garrett's model of speech production is not the only one. Influential models have been developed by Fromkin (1971) and Levelt (1989). Although these differ from Garrett's in some significant details, they nevertheless provide us with the same step-by-step picture of the language production process, in which the second language learner can show strengths and weaknesses at distinct levels.

The chapter has also argued that speech accuracy and speech fluency are not unitary phenomena. To understand the characteristics of second language speech, it is more relevant to speak of accuracy and fluency at each level of language processing. Differences in fluency are primarily related to performance factors, whereas differences in accuracy may be related either to performance or to competence.

CLASSROOM IMPLICATIONS

Discussion Questions

1. The discussion of Garrett's model in this chapter assumes that a single individual can have only one message level. Do you think second language learners can develop culture-specific and language-specific ways of thinking and thus two message levels?
2. Why do you think some learners naturally pay more attention to L2 fluency and others to L2 accuracy?
3. This chapter suggests that second language production ability requires the development of new knowledge structures and perhaps processing mechanisms. What sorts of activities would provide the learner with the relevant production practice?

4. Do you think that specific second language production exercises could be developed to target specific aspects of the production process in Garrett's model? What sorts of exercises could target, for example, functional- to positional-level conversion?

SELF TEST

_____ model of speech production is designed to account for
         (1)
speech _____ . In this model, a message is converted to a
              (2)
sound representation through a series of steps. Lexical items are selected

for production at the _____ level. They are inserted into a
                          (3)
syntactic skeleton at the _____ level. An analysis of second
                                 (4)
language production with this model suggests that different abilities

have different implications for fluency and _____ at each
                                                    (5)
level. In general, _____ is a reflection of both competence and
                         (6)
performance, whereas _____ is mainly a reflection of the
                               (7)
learner's performance abilities.

FURTHER READING

Berko Gleason, J. and N. Bernstein Ratner. 1993. *Psycholinguistics*. Orlando, FL: Harcourt Brace Jovanovich.

12

Language Comprehension

Language comprehension is how we obtain meaning from the surface form of language received through our senses. In the case of listening comprehension, the surface form is auditory. In the case of reading, it is visual.

In many ways, the processes of language comprehension are better understood than those of language production because it is much easier to design experiments to investigate comprehension. The comprehension process begins with a stimulus, a word or sentence on a page, for example. The experimenter can manipulate stimuli and thus control the input to the processing system. In production, however, the process is assumed to begin with a non-linguistic message in the mind of the speaker. Clearly, the experimenter can have no control over this type of representation. Indeed, it is not even possible for the speaker to give us any information about the nature of the non-linguistic message. By telling us about it, the speaker would be forced to convert it into linguistic form.

This chapter addresses the question of how language comprehension works, concentrating, for several reasons, on comprehension in reading. Considerably more research has been done on language processing in the visual modality than in the auditory modality, primarily because it is easier for researchers to control and manipulate a visual stimulus on a computer screen than it is to control and manipulate an auditory stimulus. As well, understanding research on speech comprehension requires in-depth discussion of the technical aspects of acoustic phonetics, which is beyond the scope of this text. Finally, language comprehension through reading is particularly interesting for second language acquisition because learners often have to read from completely new writing systems.

Some of the questions addressed in this chapter are specific to reading. Do we read letter by letter? Do we sound out words when we read silently? Other issues are independent of whether language is being received through the auditory or the visual channel. Asking how people understand complex words or sort out the organization of information in sentences, for example, involves questions about high-level cognitive processing.

1 BASIC CHARACTERISTICS OF LANGUAGE COMPREHENSION

The discussion of language production in Chapter 11 focussed on the sequential process by which a non-linguistic message is converted into an acoustic representation. Can we say, then, that comprehension is the reverse of production? If so, does language comprehension simply proceed through a set of intermediate representations such as those in Garrett's model, but in reverse? It appears not. Although comprehension and production are two sides of the language performance coin, they have significant differences.

First, the processes involved in many aspects of language comprehension are parallel rather than sequential. In listening to a sentence, for example, the listener is typically analysing phonemes, performing lexical access, analysing the syntax of the sentence, and attempting to determine the overall sentence meaning, all at the same time.

Second, in the process of production the speaker begins with an abstract message and converts it into a concrete series of motor operations. Thus, in models such as Garrett's, information flows in a single direction from message to sound. In comprehension, however, we find that information can flow in both directions. In other words, it employs both bottom-up and top-down processing. Low-level concrete representations are used to create higher level abstract representations, but high-level representations may also be used to aid in low-level operations. If you happen to have close friends who do you the favour of finishing all your sentences for you when you are talking to them, then you have some experience with this phenomenon. A friend who knows how your sentences will end is able to use low-level information coming from the senses, such as the sound of the first few words in a sentence, to form high-level (in this case, semantic) representations. The friend can also simultaneously use high-level knowledge about English syntax, the topic of conversation, your speech style, your views, and so on to generate low-level representations: the rest of the words in the sentence.

1.1 LANGUAGE COMPREHENSION IS EASIER THAN PRODUCTION

Presupposing that language comprehension involves both bottom-up and top-down processes allows us to address an apparent paradox in language performance. It is a well-documented observation that language production is more difficult than language comprehension. Most second language learners can understand more than they can express. In first language acquisition, children understand words and messages before they can produce them. The passive vocabularies of native speakers are larger than their active vocabularies. And finally, in the case of language disturbance following brain damage, comprehension is typically better than production.

On first thought, it seems that this should not be the case. In language production, the speaker or writer is in control. He or she can decide which words or syntactic structures to avoid and which ones to use, and can produce them at his or her own pace. None of these options is available to the language listener or reader. In comprehension, you must take what is presented to you and deal with it. You can neither choose the words that someone else will use nor control the rate of speech in a movie or the speed with which the credits on the screen roll by.

So why is comprehension easier? Perhaps it really isn't easier but it's easier to cheat. Many second language learners report that they often nod or give facial cues to indicate comprehension but are in fact thinking: "I have no idea what you are saying, but I'll be able to figure it out eventually." Alternatively, the criteria for "correct" comprehension may not be as stringent as those for correct production. We can see or hear when an utterance is not produced correctly, but it is more difficult to find out whether it is understood correctly. Lastly, the processes involved in comprehension may be inherently more efficient than those involved in production.

On this last point, the simultaneous use of many sorts of high- and low-level cues may make it easier for a listener or reader to extract the meaning of an utterance. Or perhaps what appear to be disadvantages in comprehension are really advantages. The necessity for listeners or readers to deal with whatever they are exposed to may force the language comprehension system into a state of very high efficiency in which processing is fast, automatic, and unconscious. Each of these features is briefly reviewed in the following sections.

1.2 LANGUAGE COMPREHENSION IS FAST

Most of us can read much faster than we can speak. The average adult reads at a rate of about 250 words per minute. It takes about one-quarter of a second to recognize a word, depending on what measure of recognition is used. Understanding spoken language of course takes much longer because the speed is limited by the amount of time it takes for a word or sentence to be spoken. The evidence suggests, however, that like reading, speech perception is very fast.

The significance of word recognition speed becomes apparent when we reflect that word recognition must involve many operations to isolate a presented word from among the over seventy-five thousand in a native speaker's vocabulary and extract its properties. Conscious operations are much too slow for this. In order for language comprehension to occur in the time that it does, its basic operations must be automatic and unconscious.

1.3 LANGUAGE COMPREHENSION IS OBLIGATORY

Perhaps the most important characteristic of language comprehension is also the most obvious. You cannot choose not to understand a word that you know. This point has already been made in connection with the Stroop technique in Chapter 10 and will also be relevant to the discussion of bilingualism in Chapter 20, but it is important enough to warrant additional discussion here. Speakers have complete control over whether or not to speak. You can think of a word or sentence and then choose whether or not to say it. Now contrast this with the complete lack of conscious control that you have when information is going in the opposite direction. No matter how hard you try, you cannot suppress the comprehension of a word you know. Try it with the word in italics coming up: *clock*. Odds are, you were not very successful. Now, try *not* to understand this sentence: *On Tuesdays, she likes to eat chicken.* The only way to avoid understanding it is to avoid looking at it. As soon as you do look, the obligatory, or automatic, processes of sentence comprehension take over.

This observation has implications for our conception of language comprehension in second language acquisition. Anyone who has tried to acquire another language remembers the tremendous strain and conscious effort that comprehension required in the early stages. These conscious activities may constitute the necessary precursors to development of the automatic processes that characterize language comprehension, but they are also qualitatively different from the unconscious and automatic processes we have been describing in this section.

1.4 MECHANISMS OF LANGUAGE COMPREHENSION ARE SHIELDED FROM CONSCIOUSNESS

Not only do listeners or readers have little control over language comprehension, but they also have very little conscious awareness of the processes they employ to achieve comprehension. Consider the case of reading: Our intuitions about what our eyes do while reading are not very accurate. We have the subjective impression that our eyes move smoothly across the page of text, but try observing someone reading a book or newspaper. You will see that their eyes do not move smoothly at all but in a series of jerks, called saccades. In each saccade, the eyes dart across part of the page. During a saccade, which lasts about fifteen thousandths of a second, you see nothing. The periods between saccades are called fixations. During these fixations, the eyes are stationary and, in effect, take a snapshot of a set of words.

Not only the physical operations in language comprehension are shielded from consciousness. Our subjective intuitions also mislead us over the higher processes involved in language comprehension. Consider the sentence *John found several spiders, roaches, and bugs in the room.* This seems fairly straightforward. You probably did not notice that the word *bug* is ambiguous; it can mean either a type of insect or a covert listening device. Experimental evidence has demonstrated that even in a sentence like this, in which there is a very strong contextual bias towards one reading of the word, both meanings are activated in the reader's mind. The inappropriate meaning gets discarded at a later stage of processing and never reaches the level of conscious awareness (Swinney 1979).

2 READING

A great deal of language comprehension occurs through the medium of print. It is difficult to imagine a university course without readings or textbooks (although many would probably like to try). Indeed, a life without reading ability is cut off from a good part of this society.

This is a new development. It has been estimated that humanity has been in possession of spoken language for about a hundred thousand years. Written language has been around for only five thousand of those years. In all but the past couple of hundred, only a very small percentage of the population could read or write. Reading ability is definitely a newcomer on the cognitive scene.

The process of reading has been very well studied in the fields of psychology, education, and psycholinguistics. University libraries typically hold scores of volumes and academic journals on reading, in part because of the importance placed on reading in our society and therefore in the education process. The problem of illiteracy has received a great deal of attention in recent times because the standards of literacy are ever increasing. At one time, literacy meant the ability to read the Bible and write your name. Now it includes skills such as being able to read road signs while piloting a vehicle at 100km per hour in heavy traffic. Nevertheless, the study of reading ability holds great appeal to researchers for another reason. It offers an important view of how the mind works and how language is organized.

Writing systems are human inventions, which accounts for their great variety. Chapter 5 discussed the ways in which a different writing system can pose substantial problems for the L2 learner. Written characters can represent phonemes, syllables, or morphemes. The writing system can be organized to read from left to right, right to left, top to bottom, or bottom to top.

Given this amount of variation, it is reasonable to suppose that learning to read in a second language requires considerable adjustment to the psychological processes described above as fast, obligatory, and unconscious. As we have noted in many places in this text, the first step to understanding how an L2 learner acquires new knowledge and skills is to explore *the nature of the system* to be learned. Our discussion begins with an exploration of what is currently known about the psychological processes involved in reading English.

2.1 PSYCHOLINGUISTIC METHODS FOR THE INVESTIGATION OF READING

Although researchers can control many aspects of the stimulus when studying language comprehension, they cannot observe the results of comprehension directly. They cannot see someone understanding. They have therefore been forced to develop a number of indirect and often very clever techniques to study the operations involved in reading.

2.1.1 Lexical Decision Tasks

The *lexical decision* task is probably the most widely used technique in the psycholinguistics of word recognition. Subjects are presented with a series of words and asked to decide for each whether it is really a word of their language. The subjects respond by answering either yes or no for each word. Table 12.1 contains a lexical decision experiment for you to try. You will probably get most or all of them correct.

Table 12.1   Lexical Decision Task

	Word	Decision	
1.	dog	Y	N
2.	flig	Y	N
3.	wrath	Y	N
4.	glib	Y	N
5.	ring	Y	N
6.	rmuz	Y	N
7.	pad	Y	N

Answers: Y, N, Y, Y, Y, N, Y

The value of the lexical decision task is based on the assumption that in order to decide whether a character string is a word, you must attempt to access that word in your mental lexicon. If activation occurs, you respond yes; if it does not, you respond no. In real lexical decision experiments, response time, rather than response accuracy, is the important measurement. Words are presented one at a time on a computer screen, and the subject presses one of two keys to record a response. The computer records the amount of time in milliseconds that elapses between the appearance of the word on the screen and the subject's response.

Average response time to a common word by a college student is about 600 milliseconds (six-tenths of a second). In such experiments, it is typically found that it takes less time to respond correctly to words such as *dog* or *ring* than to words such as *wrath* or *glib*. This is the frequency effect discussed in Chapter 10. More frequent words take less time to access. You may also have noticed that it was easier to judge that *rmuz* was not a word than to judge that *flig* was not. Lexical decision experiments often reveal that words such as *flig*, which is at least phonetically possible in English, are rejected more slowly than words such as *rmuz*, which contains an initial consonant cluster that would never be allowed in English.

Second language learners produce many more errors in lexical decision tasks than do native speakers. They know fewer words and are therefore generally inclined to respond yes when the correct answer is no. Their answers are also considerably slower than those of native speakers. Interestingly, their lexical decision response times are correlated with their general proficiency. As we might expect, the acquisition of unconscious phonological and orthographic knowledge is one of the by-products of vocabulary development.

One final note concerning the lexical decision response times of second language learners is of considerable interest. In a series of experiments, Mägiste (1982; 1985) reported that Spanish speakers who had learned English, English speakers who had learned German, and Swedish speakers who had learned German took more time to recognize words than monolingual speakers of any of these languages. This is not terribly surprising for their second languages, but it is quite counter-intuitive that their lexical decision speeds should decrease in their first languages. Mägiste found that the decrease was most apparent for low-frequency words and suggested that the process of second language acquisition simply increases the size of one's vocabulary, so that the individual has many more words to choose from in a lexical decision task.

The lexical decision technique is sometimes used in experiments that simply compare response times to different classes of stimuli, such as frequent versus infrequent words or nouns versus verbs. In other experiments, it is used to measure the effects of facilitation (in a priming experiment, for example) or the effects of interference. The technique is easy to use and has produced very reliable results. One important criticism levelled at it, however, is that it measures activities that are not necessarily part of the normal reading process.

2.1.2 Naming Latency

The technique of measuring *naming latency* is sometimes used to overcome the difficulties associated with lexical decision. The set-up is very much like that for lexical decision; a word appears on the screen of a computer. In this case, however, the subject's task is to read the word aloud as quickly as possible. The computer records the amount of time elapsed between the presentation of the word on the screen and the time that the first puff of air hits the microphone into which the subject is required to speak.

2.1.3 Word-by-Word Sentence Presentation

Although lexical decision and naming latency work very well for the study of how people read single words, they cannot tell us very much about reading sentences. A technique in which sentences are presented one word at a time in the centre of a computer screen can be used instead. In these experiments, subjects press the space bar on the keyboard when they have read a word and are ready for the next. At that point the word disappears and the next appears in the same spot. The computer records the amount of time taken for each bar press.

A very interesting use of this technique is reported by Stine (1990). She presented subjects with long, complex sentences such as *The Chinese, who used to produce kites, used them in order to carry ropes across the rivers.* Figure 12.1 displays the bar-pressing times in milliseconds between each

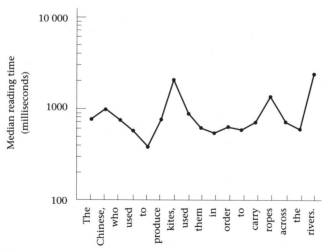

Figure 12.1   Word-by-Word Reading Times
Source: Adapted from Stine (1990).

of the words in this sentence. The times are not equal across all points in the sentence but instead show a scalloped pattern. The poorer readers were slower than the better readers, but all took extra time at phrase and clause boundaries. The results reinforce the view that the syntactic structure of a sentence plays a role in reading. Stine interpreted these findings to suggest that the pauses between syntactic chunks reflected the extra time that subjects needed to incorporate new chunks into the overall structure of the sentence. She also found that the magnitude of the delay increased towards the end of the sentence, where new chunks needed to be incorporated into an increasingly complex structure.

Stine's study also compared the reading of older people to that of younger adults. She found that the younger adults, who were on the whole better readers, showed proportionally longer pauses towards the end of the sentence. She argued that the younger adults allotted the required time to integrate new lexical and syntactic information, whereas the older readers did not. According to Stine, this judicious allocation of processing time allows for better comprehension. The technique has never to our knowledge been used with second language learners. It would be interesting to see, however, whether language learners show the same scalloping of bar-pressing times. This would allow investigation of the parcelling of sentence constituents by second language learners to see if it differs significantly from that displayed by native speakers in the same task. The magnitude of the peaks would also indicate points of confusion and second language processing complexity.

2.1.4 Eye Fixation

Rapid eye movements, or saccades, move the reader to the next fixation point in a line of text. During a saccade, the reader sees only a blur. The information that the reader receives is picked up during fixations. Much of our knowledge about the process of reading has come from tracking these eye movements: examining how many times readers fixate on words, when they fixate, and under what conditions they back up to take another snapshot.

Just and Carpenter have worked with this technique for many years. They have found that fluent readers make many stops during the processing of a sentence. Each fixation picks up a target word and some adjacent words. Fluent readers make many fixations in a sentence and typically fixate on 80 percent of the content words and about 40 percent of the function words (1987, 37). Good readers spend about a quarter of a second on a fixation and generally make only forward saccades. As can be seen in Figure 12.2, poor readers show longer fixations and tend to make backward saccades much more often. The backward saccades are generally considered to be indicators of miscomprehension or difficulty. Boxes represent points of fixation and numbers within boxes indicate duration of fixation in milliseconds. Arrows represent direction of saccades.

Good readers

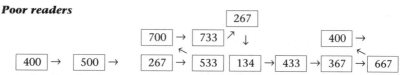

... makes the short wave enthusiast resort to the study of such seemingly ...

Poor readers

... makes the short wave enthusiast resort to the study of such seemingly ...

Figure 12.2   Saccades and Fixations
Source: Adapted from Just and Carpenter (1987, 27).

Eye monitoring requires some specialized apparatus. Figure 12.3 displays the set-up of Just and Carpenter's reading laboratory. The subject is seated in front of a computer screen. A low-intensity infra-red beam of light is bounced off the subject's eyeball and registered on a video camera. The image from the video camera is digitized and fed to a computer

Figure 12.3   Reading Laboratory
Source: Just and Carpenter (1987, 59).

which is also controlling the display of characters on the screen. The computer calculates where on the screen the subject is currently fixating.

3 RECOGNIZING AND UNDERSTANDING SINGLE WORDS

So far, we have reviewed the techniques used to investigate how language is processed in the visual modality. This section examines how these techniques and others have been used to increase our understanding of what happens when a language user sees a word. We will incorporate these research findings into a model of single-word reading and discuss second language reading acquisition in the context of the model.

3.1 THE ROLE OF INDIVIDUAL LETTERS

It is an obvious and important characteristic of written words in an alphabetic system such as English that they are made up of individual letters. It is commonly observed that it is very difficult to distinguish the individual sounds of a word that you hear in a second language, or even to hear the boundaries between words. This is not the case for reading, at least not in English, as the letters that form the constituents of a word are easy to isolate. Do people understand written words by first distinguishing and processing the individual letters? Yes and no. As we have seen, language comprehension employs both bottom-up (letter to word) and top-down (word to letter) information.

Just and Carpenter (1980) used the eye fixation technique to find out whether readers process individual letters. They reasoned that if words are processed letter by letter, then longer words would demand greater fixation times than shorter words. This is exactly what they discovered. Fixation time was increased by about 30 msec for each letter in a word.

The findings suggest a model in which individual letters are processed to make up words. Nevertheless, evidence that this view is too simplistic comes from an experiment conducted by Reicher (1969). It was found that individual letters are recognized more accurately when they form part of a word than when they are presented in isolation. This has been called the *word superiority effect*, and it suggests that top-down information from the whole word aids the letter recognition process.

Another highly convincing bit of evidence about the role of top-down information in reading comes from the following sort of experiment. In the passage below, try to cross out all the instances of the letter *t* as quickly as you can:

Smoke was rising here and there among the creepers that festooned the dead or dying trees. As they watched, a flash of fire appeared at the root of one wisp, and then the smoke thickened. Small flames stirred at the bole of a tree and crawled away through leaves and brushwood, dividing and increasing. One patch touched a tree trunk and scrambled up like a squirrel. The smoke increased, sifted, rolled outwards. The squirrel leapt on the wings of the wind and clung to another standing tree, eating downwards. The fire laid hold on the forest and began to gnaw (Healy 1976).

It contains forty instances of the letter *t*. Native speakers of English take an average of forty-seven seconds to complete the task and miss about seven of the *t*s. The most common error is to miss the *t* in the word *the*, of which there are eleven. Healy argued that people cannot find this *t* because they process *the* as an entire word, by its overall shape. His interpretation is strengthened by another experiment he conducted, in which the words of the passage were scrambled so that there was no linguistic structure to the sentences. Readers still made the majority of errors on the word *the*.

Some years ago, one of the authors of this text conducted an experiment in which beginner and advanced learners of English as a second language were presented with Healy's passage. Both groups were more accurate on the task than were native speakers. Beginning ESL students made only three errors and advanced learners made an average of five. The advanced learners behaved like native speakers in that the majority of their errors were on the word *the*. The beginners, however, did not show this tendency. They seemed to process every word the same way.

Observation of ESL learners on this task suggests that top-down information is only available after a certain degree of proficiency is achieved. This makes sense if one considers that the word *the* is the most frequent in the English language. It is so common that it can be recognized by overall shape alone, but only after considerable experience with the language.

So, we have evidence that some words are recognized in terms of their overall shape. It is unlikely, however, that word recognition is simply a pattern-matching operation. We do not have pictures of words in our heads, nor is it likely that we have pictures of letters. If the latter were the case, reading different print fonts would be much more difficult than it actually is; consider the variations in Figure 12.4. As well, try reading the sentence in Figure 12.5. Clearly, if word recognition involved matching a representation on a page to a picture in your mind, reading the text in mixed type would be next to impossible. In fact, once you get used to it, this type of reading becomes very easy. Indeed, Coltheart and Freeman (1974) found that lexical decision response times to words typed in this fashion were only 12 msec slower than response times for words in lower case print.

If letters were pictures, this would be pretty difficult.
If letters were pictures, this would be pretty difficult.
If letters were pictures, this would be pretty difficult.
If letters were pictures, this would be pretty difficult.

Figure 12.4

ThIs iS aN ExAmPlE oF tExT iN UpPeR aNd LoWeR cAsE. NoTiCe hOw tHiS gEtS eAsIeR aS yOu Go oN.

Figure 12.5

To sum up, a word is actually a tightly woven association of letter features. Fluent readers make use of both letter information and whole-word characteristics in order to identify words as quickly as they do. Language comprehension processes occur in parallel and successful second language acquisition involves the ability to process many aspects of language structure simultaneously.

3.2 THE ROLE OF SOUND

When children learn to read, they already have a well-developed linguistic system. They can typically produce and comprehend relatively complex sentences and have extensive vocabularies. Acquiring reading ability requires the integration of a new skill into an existing system of linguistic performance. Children begin to read by sounding out words letter by letter, or by learning the sound of the overall word. Do they ever lose their reliance on the phonological representation with which the word is associated? Fluent readers feel that they read by directly converting print into meaning, rather than having to convert printed words into phonological representations first. As we have found throughout our discussion of language performance, however, one's subjective intuitions are not necessarily accurate indicators of the unconscious processes constituting language comprehension. Experimentation often reveals unexpected results.

In 1971, Rubenstein, Lewis, and Rubenstein reported on a lexical decision experiment like that in Table 12.2. They found that subjects took longer to respond no to items such as (3) and (5) than to items such as (2). If you sound out items (3) and (5) you will find that they sound like the words *fox* and *blood* respectively. Stimuli of this sort are called *pseudohomophones*. The researchers reasoned that the only way in which the increased response time for these items could be explained was to assume readers actually converted the character strings into sound representations. Presumably, the correspondence between these sound representations and those of real words made the lexical decision task harder.

Table 12.2   Lexical Decision Task with Pseudohomophones

	Word	Decision	
1.	bribe	Y	N
2.	blig	Y	N
3.	phocks	Y	N
4.	wall	Y	N
5.	blud	Y	N

Answers: Y, N, N, Y, N

Another bit of evidence in favour of the view that sound plays a role in reading comes from what is known as the *regularity effect.* This can be explained by considering words such as *yacht, choir,* and *gnaw,* which have irregular spelling-to-sound correspondences in English. The word *yacht* should probably be pronounced [yæčt], but it is not. It has been found in a number of studies that it takes longer to respond to irregularly spelled words in a lexical decision task. Recall that the subject simply sees a word and presses a response button. If readers access their mental lexicons directly from the printed word, the spelling-to-sound properties of a word should not make a difference. But they do. So, again, we have evidence that even fluent readers of English access the sound of words while reading silently.

The regularity effect suggests that we hold a set of rules or patterns in our minds which represent the regular sound–spelling correspondences in our language. This conclusion must be tempered, however, by the finding of Mark Seidenberg and his colleagues that the regularity effect only occurs with low-frequency words (Seidenberg et al. 1984). Frequent irregularly spelled words such as *of* or *have* do not show the effect. In addition, it seems obvious that although readers may convert print into sound for low-frequency words or for words they have never seen before, they must also make use of the visual properties of words. Otherwise, it would be impossible for them to get the different meanings of homophones such as *pair* and *pear* as they read.

Now, what do we know at this point? Even accomplished readers use some system for converting a printed word into a sound representation, but they also seem to be able to process words in a directly visual manner. These observations have led researchers to hypothesize that reading involves parallel visual and phonological routes.

3.3 A MODEL OF WORD READING

Figure 12.6 summarizes the data on reading discussed so far. The model is to be read from top to bottom and indicates that words are processed through routes (a) and (b). Models of this sort are called *horse-race models* because they assume that both routes are active all the time and that whichever one proves faster will be responsible for the final comprehension. Readers process words through a direct visual route and also convert them into sound representations. Most of the time, the visual route is faster, and access to the mental lexicon is primarily based on the visual properties of the stimulus. For infrequent and unfamiliar words, however, the direct visual route is slower, and lexical access is based on the results of phonological analysis from route (b). Thus the model accounts for the regularity effect, the pseudohomophone effect, and also the evidence that readers access meaning directly. Note also that bottom-up and top-down information about the role of individual letters and sounds in reading is captured by the feedback loop flowing from the mental lexicon back to the letter representations and phonological representations.

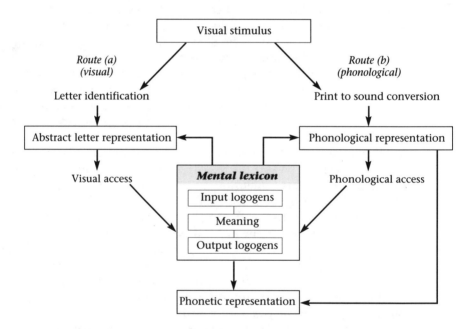

Figure 12.6   A Two-Route Model of Word Reading

The representation of the mental lexicon in this model makes use of the concept of logogens, discussed in Chapter 10. Recall that a logogen can be seen as a unit with an activation threshold. This threshold is related to the frequency of the unit—how often the word represented by the logogen is in the input—and to contextual factors. When the activation threshold is surpassed as a result of information coming in from either the phonological or the visual route, the logogen "fires" and the word is recognized. The division of the mental lexicon into both input and output logogens represents the claim that the mind holds separate representations for a word's input and output forms.

Support for the two-route model can be derived from several curious and interesting observations of the ways in which brain damage impairs reading ability, specifically in English. Loss of reading ability following brain damage is called *acquired dyslexia*. Various types of acquired dyslexia have been described in the literature. People with *surface dyslexia* can only read through the phonological route. They have difficulty understanding the difference between homophones (*pear, pair*; *rose, rows*), and read regularly spelled words much more successfully than irregularly spelled ones. People with *phonological dyslexia* can read frequent and familiar words aloud with understanding. Their reading is unaffected by spelling regularity or word length, but they are unable to read unfamiliar words or non-words (like *blig*) aloud. Finally, people with *visual dyslexia* misread visually similar words (*deal, dial*) and mistake letter identities (*big* → *dig*).

The two-route model of reading offers a straightforward account of the three forms of acquired dyslexia. Surface dyslexia can be considered as a loss of the ability to use route (a), the visual route. These dyslexics show difficulty with homophones because homophones require the use of visual information. They also tend to misunderstand irregularly spelled words, thinking, for example, that *bear* means *beer*. Phonological dyslexics, on the other hand, cannot use route (b). They cannot read either neologisms or words that are new to them because they require use of spelling–sound correspondences, and they have difficulty with infrequent words, for which route (a) is not very well practised. Finally, visual dyslexia can be seen as an impairment in establishing the abstract letter representations for a word. These dyslexics show errors similar to those produced by beginning readers (reading *father* for *farther*, for example).

Caplan (1993) offers a good discussion of the motivation for a two-route model of reading and also surveys additional research findings. As it is presented here, the model contains only those details relevant to second language reading.

3.4 WORD READING IN A SECOND LANGUAGE

The acquisition of second language English reading ability can be profitably explored in the context of the two-route model, as we look at the new skills and adjustments accompanying development of word recognition facility in a new writing system. Of course, a good many second language learners are not simply acquiring a new system for reading when they learn to read in English as a second language. They are also becoming literate for the first time. Discussion of these learners will be deferred to Chapter 19, which focusses on the effects of literacy.

3.4.1 Learning New Letter Identities

Clearly, L2 learners of English whose L1 uses the Latin alphabet have some advantage in developing English reading skills. When learners' native orthography is different, we expect the basic principles of contrastive analysis to apply. When there is partial overlap between the systems of writing, the learner may suffer considerable interference. An English learner of Russian might have difficulty because the Cyrillic alphabet shares visual segments with the English system but has different phonetic values. The Russian word *ponom*, for example, would be very confusing because although it looks to an English reader as though it should be pronounced [ponom], it is actually pronounced [ropot].

Another source of interference emerges when the two systems of writing encode different units of language. Moving from a logographic system to an alphabetic one, or from a syllabary to an alphabetic script, requires the acquisition of not only a new set of symbols but also a new principle of orthographic representation.

3.4.2 Learning Grapheme-to-Phoneme Conversions

The reading literature on the exact nature of the mechanisms that allow a reader to convert print into sound reflects a great deal of controversy. Some researchers have suggested that a set of spelling–sound rules are employed. Others have contended that we work out the sound of a familiar word on the basis of analogy with words we already know. Still others have accounted for spelling–sound regularities within the architecture of connectionist networks.

Whatever the mechanism happens to be, it is clear that spelling–sound correspondences are among the first second language reading skills that a learner of English must acquire. In an orthography such as English, this is not a simple task. The English spelling system does not have a transparent relationship between sounds and letters and is therefore inadequate as a system for phonetic transcription. Some letters, such as *x*, are associated with two sounds (in this case [ks]), and some sounds, such as [θ] or [ð], are associated with two letters (*th*). Most important, English has a *deep orthography*. English spelling often represents not the surface sound structure of a word but its underlying morphological structure. Consider the words *please* and *pleasure*. If English had a shallow orthography, these words would have quite different spellings because they sound quite different. The deep orthographic system of English maintains a similar spelling for them so that their morphological relationship remains clear. This is probably an aid to reading through route (a), but is a disadvantage to route (b) and a source of frustration for L2 learners.

3.4.3 Development of the Visual Route

The visual route is the means by which a word is identified through converging information from its letter components and overall shape. Evidence suggests that the operation of the visual route is dependent on the frequency of the word and therefore simply the amount of exposure a reader has had to it. The recognition vocabulary of a reader is assumed to have a logogen structure in which recognition units develop thresholds for activation on the basis of frequency.

The implications for second language reading ability in English or any other language are straightforward: efficient use of the visual route requires repeated and frequent exposure. Reading silently with comprehension develops the efficiency of the input logogen system; reading aloud also develops the efficiency of the output logogen system.

3.4.4 Relative Use of the Visual and Phonological Routes

Many of the world's highly varied writing systems have developed independently of one another. Reading and writing systems are human inventions and therefore probably not subject to the same biological constraints that listening and speaking might be.

In a very broad and early study, Gray (1956) compared eye fixations and reading speeds of readers of fourteen different languages. Gray examined only very general characteristics of reading but found that, on the whole, readers of different languages do pretty much the same things. The eye fixation patterns of readers of very different writing systems had the same general characteristics and exhibited only slight variation in the average number. We thus have reason to believe that when a reader of one language approaches the task of reading a second, the same general scanning mechanisms can be positively transferred.

There is also reason to believe that the basic model of two-route reading applies to all writing systems that have been studied. It is therefore unlikely that a second language reader would have to develop a new route to reading. Nevertheless, different writing systems require the reader to make more or less use of either the visual or the phonological route.

The Serbo-Croatian writing system has received a lot of attention because it has an almost perfectly *shallow* system of orthography, possessing completely regular sound–spelling correspondences. Turvey, Feldman, and Lukatela (1984) have argued that Serbo-Croatian readers make exclusive use of the phonological route in reading, which means that they would have to acquire visual reading ability when learning English as a second language. Seidenberg and Vidanovic (1985), however, found that readers of Serbo-Croatian can also use the direct visual route when reading Serbo-Croatian. Seidenberg and Vidanovic's conclusions have been found to apply to many languages. Although it was initially assumed that a logographic system like Chinese, for example, would require only visual processing, experimental evidence has revealed that both phonological and visual information are used in reading Chinese characters.

Japanese has also received a great deal of attention. It is one of relatively few writing systems to make use of two different systems of writing: a logographic *kanji* system and *kana* syllabary. Again, research suggests that although the differences between the writing systems dispose readers to place greater reliance on one route or another, both systems make use of both routes. (See Besner and Hildebrandt (1987) and Paradis, Hagiwara, and Hildebrandt (1985) for a review of Japanese reading research.)

So, the Japanese, Chinese, or Serbo-Croatian learner of English would have to adjust the relative use of phonological and visual information when acquiring English reading ability. Because these adjustments would be made in different directions depending on the L1, we suspect that the cross-linguistic differences in reading give rise to language-specific "reading accents." A reading accent in this case would be similar to a production accent in that the accent incorporates elements of more than one language.

3.4.5 Summary: The Two-Route Model

The cross-linguistic evidence and other research on reading suggest that the two-route model offers a good framework for understanding both the reading process and the kinds of skills and adjustments a second language learner must develop. It must be stressed, however, that the version of the model used in this chapter ignores a number of processes and issues relevant to a full account of reading. While it seems necessary to postulate a phonological route to the lexicon to account for readers' ability to pronounce words they have never seen before, for example, it is not clear that use of the route accounts for all the phonological effects observed in reading. For relatively well-known words, the phonological information may actually come from representations in the lexicon after a word has been recognized through the visual route.

4 READING AND UNDERSTANDING SENTENCES

As noted in the discussion of language competence, a sentence is more than a series of words, so it should not be very surprising to find that reading a sentence is much more than simply reading its lexical constituents. Nevertheless, a lot of the relevant ground about sentence processing has already been covered: top-down and bottom-up processing; sentence parsing; the experimental techniques dominant in psycholinguistic study of sentence reading; and, of course, the research on single-word reading. This section brings it all together. As you might imagine, many, many, models of sentence reading have been proposed. Each has its strengths and weaknesses and if there is anything we have learned about language research, all of them will turn out to be inadequate in the long run. Of the various alternatives, this discussion focusses on the model proposed by Rayner and Pollatsek (1989) because it is clear, relatively simple, and makes reference to the issues under examination here.

4.1 OBLIGATORY AND AUTOMATIC CREATION OF REPRESENTATIONS IN READING

Like word recognition, fluent sentence processing must be seen as fast, automatic, obligatory, and unconscious. We cannot suppress the construction of linguistic representations at any level of language structure. Four different research studies provide evidence in this direction.

Swinney (1979) presented subjects with sentences such as *John found several spiders, roaches, and bugs in the room.* Recall that the key word here is *bugs*. Do subjects get both meanings? Swinney found that in a lexical decision task following presentation of the sentence, response times for words related to either meaning (such as *spy* or *insect*) were faster than those for unrelated words. In other words, the presence of *bug* primed both interpretations independent of sentence context.

Tanenhaus, Leiman, and Seidenberg (1979) conducted a very similar experiment using naming latency as the experimental measure. Again, they found that for a sentence such as *The entire audience rose*, the word *rose* primed both *stood* and *flower,* providing evidence that all semantic representations for a word are activated.

In a study of morphological ambiguity, Libben (1994) investigated whether the principle of multiple representations extends to the formal aspects of word structure. He presented subjects with words such as *seathorn, fangear, seatrim,* and the like. All of these compound words have two separate parsings (*seathorn* → *sea thorn* or *seat horn*). Libben found that in a lexical decision task, response times for these ambiguous words were greater than response times for matched novel compounds such as *seabrim*. He concluded that both representations of the ambiguous compounds were activated.

Finally, Tanenhaus, Carlson, and Seidenberg (1985) put forth interesting arguments and data to support the view that, at the sentence level as well, subjects automatically and obligatorily construct multiple linguistic representations for structurally ambiguous strings.

We therefore begin with the idea that when the reader processes a sentence, all the structural representations that can be created, are created. In second language acquisition, the learner's interlanguage grammar probably limits the automaticity of such creation more than any other factor. Thus, in our view, a learner's sentence processing ability is best predicted by the language structures that the learner knows. This seems particularly reasonable in light of findings by Gray (1954) and Just and Carpenter (1987) that in terms of overall perceptual activity, the psychological processes in sentence reading do not differ a great deal from language to language when they do *not* involve creating linguistic structure. Creating structural representations must therefore depend on the reader's store of lexical and syntactic knowledge about the given language.

4.2 A MODEL OF SENTENCE READING

The model represented in Figure 12.7 provides a framework in which issues of language performance and competence can be discussed. It is based primarily on eye fixation research. The model is read from top to bottom, and circled units represent observable activities: eye fixations and saccades. Operations that we cannot observe but suspect must exist are represented in rectangles. The boxes with rounded corners represent representations and processing in memory. The model makes use of two types of memory. Long-term memory is where the lexicon, the representation of the meaning of the text, and knowledge of the world are located. Operations such as parsing, thematic processing, and inner speech are located in working memory.

If we begin at the top of the model, we are beginning at a point of eye fixation in a sentence. At this point, two operations are going on: *parafoveal* and *foveal processing*. Parafoveal processing is the term for the "corner of the eye" glimpses of what is coming up next. This information is blurry but detailed enough to guide the target for the next saccade jump. Foveal processing deals with the word on which the eye is currently fixated. (The fovea of the eye is the centre of greatest visual acuity.) Routes (1) and (2) on the left of the model correspond to routes (a) and (b) of the two-route model for reading.

Information following lexical access is passed on to the parser and the thematic processor. Rayner and Pollatsek see the parser as a purely syntactic device that uses input from the lexicon to produce a structural representation for the sentence. In their model, the parser uses the principles of *minimal attachment* and *late closure,* which we saw in Chapter 10.

The thematic processor is an independent processing unit that constructs a semantic representation for the sentence based on information from the lexicon and knowledge of the world. The thematic processor can use real world knowledge to evaluate the results of the parser and "ask it to do another parse." Yet it cannot intervene in the parsing process or help the parsing module do its job. In other words, it cannot prevent the parser from getting "garden pathed."

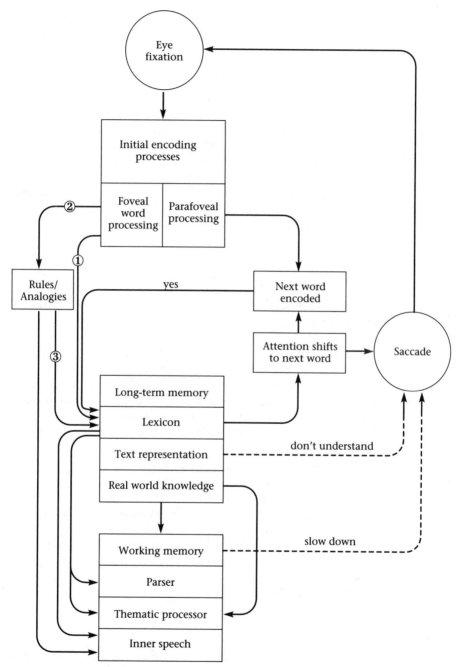

Figure 12.7 A Model of Sentence Reading
Source: Rayner and Pollatsek (1989).

The inner speech module in working memory is the area in which the actual sequence of words in the sentence is temporarily stored. Rayner and Pollatsek assume that the nature of this temporary storage is phonological. The function of the inner speech module is to allow the sentence to be replayed if comprehension fails.

The analysis that takes place in the various subcomponents of the model builds a text representation in long-term memory. This is essentially the permanent storage of meaning. Like most psycholinguistic models of reading, Rayner and Pollatsek's is quite sketchy on the details of meaning representation. To be fair, however, that is an underdeveloped area in much of the psycholinguistic work on language processing.

Finally, the activities represented on the right-hand side of the model allow extended eye fixations or regressive saccades to occur in cases of miscomprehension. These operations account for the different eye fixation patterns of good and poor readers (see Figure 12.2).

5 IMPLICATIONS FOR SLA: COMPREHENSION PROCESSES AND PITFALLS

This chapter has covered a lot of technical material. You will probably agree by now that the human ability to perform even the simplest tasks of language comprehension is truly astounding. Appreciating the complexity of the phenomenon makes it easier to understand why language processing must be unconscious and automatic. It is also easy to see why it probably cannot be taught in the traditional sense of the word; partly, of course, because the process *is* unconscious but also because language comprehension is not really a single activity. Rather, it is the name we give to a multitude of separate activities that feed information to one another and benefit from processes at numerous different levels. We have seen this in the case of word recognition and sentence comprehension.

Reflecting on many of the phenomena frequently observed in second language comprehension should put us in a better position to interpret them. The sections below consider some very common second language abilities and difficulties and discuss them in terms of the research and conclusions presented thus far.

5.1 READING ALOUD

Consider the task of reading text aloud in a second language. If you have done this, you know that it is fairly difficult. If you have heard non-native speakers of English read texts aloud, you have probably recognized that their reading is characterized by incorrect intonation patterns, hesitations, and errors. They sound as though they have no idea what the text they are reading means. In a sense, this is true. When native speakers read aloud, their eyes are far ahead of their mouths. By processing language far ahead of production, fluent readers are not really reading the words that they are speaking. Rather they are *repeating* the sentences they have just processed. Beginning second language learners are simply not yet able to get ahead of their production. If readers must sound out words segment by segment, they are taking computational resources away from their ability to parse the sentence or to get the integrated meaning of the text. Thus the intonation errors that learners produce in reading can be seen as a result of comprehension that is not far enough ahead of production and of the great demands that low-level word processing requires when it is not yet fully automatic.

It is interesting to note that as second language learners improve in their reading ability they often start making errors they did not make before. A beginning L2 learner of English would probably read the sentence *He who waits has his dinner served cold* slowly and with a number of sound–spelling correspondence errors. As learners become more proficient readers, they show increased ability to derive the correct pronunciation of a word from phonological representations (output logogens) in the mental lexicon. Thus their sound–spelling correspondence ability improves and some mispronunciations disappear. Yet other errors start to show up as a result of the newly developed fast and automatic processing. Instead of simply reading the words on a page aloud, more advanced learners read sentences as native speakers do, forming an internal representation and converting it into speech production. When this happens, they begin to produce errors that reflect the nature of the interlanguage grammar. The sentence might then be read aloud as *He who wait have his dinner serve cold.* The example is fictitious, but it indicates the qualitative difference between the conscious reading of beginners and the start of automaticity for advanced learners. The nature of errors often reflects which side of the watershed the learner is on.

5.2 UNDERSTANDING BACKGROUND CONVERSATION

We have all experienced the difficulty of trying to talk in a crowded restaurant where you cannot shut out the conversation of the couple at the next table. If you have ever been in a restaurant in a foreign country, you also know that you are completely undistracted by adjacent conversations. In fact, it seems to require a special effort to understand background conversation in a second or foreign language. As is discussed in Chapters 10 and 20 of this book, there is good reason to believe that you cannot turn off language comprehension. That the French at the next table in Paris doesn't distract you cannot be explained by the fact that you are speaking English at your table. Rather, if your French is not particularly strong, the activation thresholds for the French logogens you do have will be very high. In addition, comprehension will require extra, conscious inferential processes to fill in the gaps in your French knowledge. Thus, unless you really attend to the French at the next table, you will not use these processes, your French logogens will not fire, and you will not understand what is being said. As you become more proficient in French, you will find that you become more and more distracted. Such is the cost of bilingualism.

5.3 GETTING SUBTLE MEANINGS AND JOKES

Some years ago, one of the authors of this text was talking to a visiting professor from Europe. He had a thorough command of English and seemed to have no difficulty conducting lectures in his second (actually third) language and understanding what was said to him. When he was complimented on his English ability he responded that he actually had great difficulty comprehending what people really meant, in particular the subtle, indirect language that academics often use. "It's frustrating," he said. "I can walk in English, but I can't dance!"

Much of the difficulty language learners have in understanding subtle messages or determining whether a statement is serious is undoubtedly related to cultural factors: the real world knowledge represented in Rayner and Pollatsek's model of reading. Cultural knowledge allows the native speaker to use top-down information and to rule out implausible interpretations of the message.

Jokes are by far the most difficult things to understand in a second language. They, too, often trade on shared expectations and culturally defined world knowledge. On the formal side of language processing, linguistically based jokes place great requirements on automatic parallel access to formal representations. If parallel unconscious activation of logogens does not occur—if both meanings of a word are not activated—the joke doesn't work.

Puns are a good example of this principle. We know some terrible punsters. Just give them a key word and they'll keep going long past the point at which nausea normally sets in. Here's what happened after starting them off with the word *egg*:

Speaker A: Eggs? I don't know any egg jokes. Would you accept a *yoke*?
Speaker B: Oh no, this is going to be *egg*scruciating.
Speaker A: No, you mean *egg*sasperating.
Speaker B: OK, how about this egg joke? To *beat* or not to *beat,* that is the question.
Speaker A: That's an egg joke?
Speaker B: Sure, I think it's a line from *Omelette*.

Aside from being a good example of very bad humour, this also demonstrates how phonological information is made available in reading and how logogens in the mental lexicon can be related to one another in networks of shared features. One cannot learn any real strategies for getting these puns. They simply work because of the automatic and obligatory activation of semantic, phonological, and visual features that make up the linguistic representations of a fully acquired language performance system.

5.4 PROCESSING LANGUAGE AND CHEWING GUM AT THE SAME TIME

Language comprehension has been described above as a set of tightly interwoven but autonomous activities involving feature detection, word recognition, and sentence parsing. For the native speaker, these are fast, automatic, obligatory, and unconscious. Nevertheless, because the computations are extremely complex they do consume mental resources. We have all noticed that it is more difficult to comprehend complex material if we are tired and that unfamiliar material is harder to process than familiar material. When driving in heavy traffic, we are less able to pay attention to what our passengers are saying. Presumably our computational resources are limited and language computation must compete with other demands.

Someone acquiring a second language, of course, experiences much greater competition. The more conscious language processing is, the more it demands of our mental resources. Although no research has investigated this, it can be expected that the degree to which a language learner's comprehension system is automatic is specific to the individual subcomponents of comprehension. A learner could have well-developed word recognition ability, for example, but a relatively slow and conscious system for syntactic parsing. Another learner could show the opposite profile. We still know relatively little about the exact nature of the computational (working memory) resources made use of by individual language processes, but it seems reasonable to assume that an individual learner's language comprehension strengths and weaknesses will determine what sorts of other tasks interfere the most with second language processing.

6 CONCLUSION

Language comprehension is a complex, covert activity that requires a great deal of exposure and practice. The system develops as the language user's cognitive system adapts to deal with the demands of the real-time processing of spoken and written language. Second language learners cannot expect to acquire comprehension facility without considerable exposure. It is probably the difference in exposure that accounts for the often noted qualitative difference between foreign language learners and second language learners. The comprehension systems of the former are typically underdeveloped relative to their production systems simply because the learners have not been exposed to the target language under conditions of normal use.

The process of language comprehension in native speakers has been examined using a variety of psycholinguistic techniques, generating a good deal of evidence and numerous hypotheses and explanatory models. We expect that over the next decade many of these research techniques will be applied with the same rigour to word recognition and sentence processing by second language learners. The psycholinguistics of second language acquisition still has many more questions than answers.

CLASSROOM IMPLICATIONS

Discussion Questions

1. Should second language comprehension be practised in the classroom under ideal conditions, with nothing else competing for the listener's attention, or under conditions that more closely approximate everyday situations, with background noise and so on?
2. This chapter claimed that comprehension was easier than production. Can you think of types of second language learner for whom the opposite would be true? What would cause such students to find production easier than comprehension?
3. Can you think of specific second language reading exercises that would individually target either the visual or the phonological route?
4. This chapter has discussed some fairly elaborate experimental techniques for the study of language comprehension. Do you think that any of these could be used in the development of more accurate and useful tests of second language ability?

SELF TEST

Language comprehension usually refers to the processes of reading and
_____ . The operations involved in language comprehension
(1)

are shielded from the _____ mind of the language user. Two
(2)
experimental techniques used to study word recognition are
_____ and naming latency. The study of sentence reading has
(3)
relied heavily on the use of eye fixation studies. These studies have
revealed that poor readers show longer and more frequent
_____ . Poor readers also show more regressive
(4)
_____ . The two-route model of reading claims that there are
(5)
two routes to reading, a visual route and a _____ route. The
(6)
model has been used to account for data both from normal reading and
from reading deficits in acquired _____ . In Rayner and
(7)
Pollatsek's model of reading, semantic and _____ structures
(8)
for a sentence are calculated independently. Thus the _____
(9)
cannot use real world knowledge to help it with garden path sentences.

FURTHER READING

Berko Gleason, J. and N. Bernstein Ratner. 1993. *Psycholinguistics.*
Orlando, FL: Harcourt Brace Jovanovich.

Caplan, D. 1993. *Language: Structure, Processing, and Disorders.* Cambridge,
MA: MIT Press.

Rayner, K. and A. Pollatsek. 1989. *The Psychology of Reading.* Englewood
Cliffs, NJ: Prentice-Hall.

13

Variationist Perspectives on Second Language Acquisition

Language variation is most commonly addressed in the field of sociolinguistics. Indeed, it is a central concern of sociolinguistics to determine which situational or social factors influence variation in language use. We might note, for example, that people use different variations of a particular form. You might say *working* as [wərkɪŋ] in some situations and as [wərkɪn] in others. A standard model of linguistic competence assumes that our knowledge of a lexical item has a single phonological form. One would assume that the stored form of *working* was [wərkɪŋ]. The study of language variation investigates the factors that determine this kind of variable performance. Who says [wərkɪn]? When do they say [wərkɪŋ]? Later in this chapter we will investigate cognitive explanations of language variation, but a number of external variables such as socio-economic status have been identified as influences on this phenomenon.

Wolfram (1969) reported on several linguistic characteristics of Detroit English. One variant feature was the realization of final consonant clusters in words such as *mist* and *wild*. Some speakers had a marked tendency to simplify these clusters by deleting the second member, producing [mɪs] and [wayl]. Wolfram noted that there was clear social stratification underlying the phenomenon, as shown in Table 13.1. Regardless of age, subjects with lower socio-economic status simplified their consonant clusters more often.

Table 13.1   Percentage of Simplified Consonant Clusters

	Age 10 to 12	Age 14 to 17	Adult
Upper middle class white	6.7	4.7	8.6
Upper middle class black	18.0	15.9	10.2
Lower middle class black	33.0	27.4	23.5
Upper working class black	47.2	50.0	48.5
Lower working class black	58.4	46.7	53.4

We also see variation within an individual. A person will simplify some but not all of the consonant clusters. As well, situational factors such as formality influence variation. We tend to use different lexical items in formal and informal situations. Contrast when you might use the words *pugnacious* and *feisty*. In informal situations people also tend to use non-standard grammatical structures more often.

So, variation occurs both between social groups and within an individual. Clearly, this is reminiscent of second language learners. It appears that the intersection of the fields of language variation and second language acquisition will be a profitable one. This chapter focusses on the variation seen within an individual.

1 VARIABLE RULES

Traditional linguistic rules are not designed to account for variation among individual speakers. Consider a phonological rule that looks something like this:

$$/l/ \rightarrow [ɫ] / V \_\_$$

The rule explains why we find variation in the kinds of /l/ sounds produced by native English speakers; we get an alveolar (clear) [l] before vowels and a velarized (dark) [ɫ] after vowels.[1] This is complementary distribution. Nevertheless, the formulation of the rule does not lead us to expect that individuals will vary in implementing it. If the structural description of the rule is met, then the rule has to apply.

We run into the same problem when trying to account for variation within a speech community. A traditional linguistic rule could describe what was going on with the Detroit consonant clusters with the following rule:

$$C \rightarrow \emptyset / C \_\_$$

If we saw that this phenomenon was socially stratified, we would predict that members of certain social groups would have the rule and members of other social groups would not, but we would not be able to talk about differing *probabilities* of implementation. The rule would either have to apply or not apply.

To address these problems, sociolinguists—or variationists—have introduced the notion of a new type of linguistic rule: the variable rule. Without being overly concerned about notation developed to represent

---

[1] More accurately we might note that we get the velarized [ɫ] in syllable codas but the alveolar [l] in syllable onsets.

it, let us just say that the variable rule is probabilistic. It incorporates the probability of its own implementation. We might imagine a rule saying that a speaker will simplify a consonant cluster 50 percent of the time to look something like this:

$$C \rightarrow \emptyset / C \_\_ (50\%)$$

This, then, is one way to describe the variation in both communities and individuals. It implies that knowledge doesn't vary; a rule still exists, but now it incorporates patterns of implementation. Again we are concerned with both knowledge and the ability to implement or control that knowledge.

2 VARIABILITY IN SECOND LANGUAGE LEARNERS

It has long been noted that the forms second language learners use vary according to a number of factors. A learner may sometimes use the form *went* and at other times the form *goed*. This phenomenon had not received a systematic treatment until recently (Eisenstein 1989; Gass et al. 1989; Preston 1989).

The work on second language learners builds on the foundation of work done on native speakers. Reid (1976) reported on variation in Scottish children (see Figure 13.1). Eleven year olds were observed in four styles to see whether they pronounced the *-ing* morpheme as [ɪŋ] or as [ɪn]. The more casual the situation, the more often the [ɪn] variant was observed. The more a task focussed on form, the closer the speech was to the standard dialect.

Most formal			*Most casual*
⊩◄	|	|	➤⊩
Reading	Interview	Peer group	Playground

-ing as [ɪn]   14   45   54   59

Figure 13.1   Percentage of Non-Standard Variants in Different Contexts
Source: Adapted from Reid (1976).

Non-native speakers also appear to be affected by these situational factors. They may be more accurate—closer to the native speaker standard—in a grammatical exercise than in casual conversation. According to Tarone (1989), it is casual conversation, also known as the vernacular, that provides the best window on an interlanguage grammar. She argues that the vernacular reveals the learner's true knowledge and ability.

2.1 VARIABLE COMPETENCE OR VARIABLE PERFORMANCE?

Ellis (1989b) points out that although everyone acknowledges the existence of variation, some people ascribe it to performance and others to competence. Clearly, Chomsky would argue that variation is due to performance. Competence, by definition, is invariable. You either know something or you don't, but your ability to get access to or to implement that knowledge can vary according to stress, fatigue, and so on. For Chomsky, these are performance factors. Viewing knowledge as mental representation, we can illustrate this stance as follows. If you have a mental representation of a word, you cannot choose not to understand it, and if you do not have a mental representation of it you cannot choose to understand it. Your mental representation is invariable.

Ellis, on the other hand, argues for what he calls *variable competence*. It is immediately obvious that he is not using the word *competence* in a Chomskyan sense. He sees variation as part of the mental representation. Situational factors appear to be able to affect how knowledge is stored. Some of the terms that Ellis invokes are useful for describing characteristics of second language speech and so are given below. He begins by distinguishing between *free* and *systematic* variation within an individual. Remember, though, that language production involves more than just speaking your competence.

2.1.1 Free Variation

Free variation is the performance variation within an individual. It is unsystematic and has two possible sources: performance lapses such as slips of the tongue; and haphazard implementation of competing rules. Ellis offers as an example of competing rules the two utterances *No look my card* and *Don't look my card,* produced by the same speaker, in the same setting, in the same session. He suggests that the learner has two rules for negating sentences and that these are in competition. One rule is to negate by putting *no* at the beginning of the sentence and the other is to negate by combining the auxiliary *do* with the word *not.* The learner is still trying to determine the correct rule for English negation; sometimes one rule will be invoked, sometimes the other. The result is unpredictable variation.

One of the problems with Ellis's characterization of free variation, though, is that he does not have any systematic observation to back up the claim that the variation really is random. One robust finding of sociolinguistics is that people are unreliable judges of their own performance. You might think that you freely alternate between *the data are* and *the data is,* but careful observation might well reveal a pattern. We cannot rely on intuitions regarding variation.

Let us assume for the moment, though, that there truly is free variation and spend some time investigating Ellis's account of it. He suggests three different causes of the competing rules that lead to free variation:

1. *Internal versus target norms* Conflict between the form that the interlanguage grammar generates and the form that the learner notices in the input. On a lexical level, the learner might think, for example "She said *nonsystematic* but I would have said *unsystematic*. I wonder which one is right?" On a syntactic level, the learner might notice the sentence *Do you think Jane should go?* and wonder why *Jane* and *should* were not inverted. These competing norms can result in random variation.

   Nevertheless, this does not imply that competence varies. A learner such as the one described above, we would argue, at no time has either a nativelike representation for the word *systematic* or a nativelike understanding of inversion. It's not that the competence varies but that it is different from a native speaker's.

2. *Variable rules in target variety* The second language learner will hear speech in a variety of social situations and from speakers belonging to a variety of social classes, and the input will therefore exhibit variation. Second language learners exposed to the Detroit dialect discussed earlier, for example, would sometimes hear consonant clusters simplified and sometimes not. They would have to try to determine the cause of the variation and until they did, it is likely that their own output would vary.

   Even in a standard dialect of English, this kind of variation is present. A learner will hear both *Bob is tall* and *Bob's tall*, depending on the formality of the context. Note, too, that the learner will have to discover the syntactic restrictions on where contractions such as this can occur. We can say "Bob's tall," but not "Dan's taller than Bob's." We have to say "Dan's taller than Bob is." Grammatical function words tend not to be contractible at the ends of sentences. Thus, contraction is sometimes governed by syntactic factors and sometimes by situational ones. While the learner sorts this out, his or her output will probably vary.

3. *Reaction to target varieties* Input preferences of the learner. Second language learners may decide, for example, that input from the teacher is preferable to input from other native speakers. Preferences are not absolute, though, and the learner may also produce forms from other social groups.

2.1.2 Systematic Variation

According to Ellis, systematic variation within individuals can be caused by: (1) linguistic context, such as allophonic variation; (2) discourse context, such as variation according to register; and (3) social context, such as socially stratified variation. Allophonic variation is not discussed here, as it is the product of linguistic competence. Rather, we will focus on the other two factors, which fall into the realm of sociolinguistics. As we saw when we looked at native speakers, the forms used in a particular register or by a particular social group exhibit patterns. The alternation of forms like *talking* and *talkin'* is systematic in relation to the formality of the situation or the socio-economic status of the speaker. It may well be the case that non-native speaker variation arises from the same causes.

Labov (1966) noted that *attention to form* can also lead to systematic variation within an individual because someone who is paying attention to the form is more likely to use standard structures than someone who isn't. Labov defined the vernacular as the variety of language that emerges when the speaker is paying the least attention to form. In his view, adopted by Tarone (1989), a style continuum emerges, as illustrated in Figure 13.2. Variation in the production of second language speakers could thus be explained by how much attention the speaker was paying to the form of the output. A second language learner who produces *working* as both [wərkɪŋ] and [wərkɪn] is thus assumed to be in a social situation that triggers attention to form when producing [wərkɪŋ] and in one that does not when producing [wərkɪn].

Figure 13.2   The Style Continuum
Source: Adapted from Tarone (1989).

Ellis (1987) reported that learners' accuracy on using *-ed* was greater the more time they were allowed to write a text. This seems consistent with behaviour governed by processing factors rather than by knowledge, and with the idea that knowledge is not in itself variable. To illustrate this, think of a second language learner given two tasks:

1. In the next minute, write a paragraph describing what you had for breakfast.
2. As homework tonight, write a paragraph about your favourite memory as a child.

The learner might well respond to the first task with the following:

> This morning I was late so I no have time for eating. I drink some coffee and walk to school.

The same learner could respond to the second task as follows:

> When I was very young, I remember a time when my whole family walked up a mountain. We drank orange juice and ate sandwiches.

In this scene from George Bernard Shaw's *Pygmalion,* we see how the linguist, Professor Higgins (the Note Taker), is able to detect differences between groups on the basis of their pronunciation:

> *Flower Girl:* You just shew me what youve wrote about me ... what's that? That aint proper writing. I cant read that.
> *The Note Taker:* I can.... How do you come to be up so far east? You were born in Lisson Grove.
> *Flower Girl:* Oh, what harm is there in my leaving Lisson Grove? It wasn't fit for a pig to live in; and I had to pay four-and-six a week.
> *Bystander:* Do you know where *I* come from?
> *The Note Taker:* Hoxton.
> *Bystander:* Well who said I didn't? Bly me! you know everything, you do....
> *Gentleman:* How do you do it, if I may ask?
> *The Note Taker:* Simply phonetics. The science of speech. Thats my profession; also my hobby.... You can spot an Irishman or a Yorkshireman by his brogue. *I* can place any man within six miles. I can place him within two miles in London. Sometimes within two streets.

George Bernard Shaw
Pygmalion, Act 1

The first text contains a number of errors, whereas the second, written without time pressure, is more accurate. From the same learner we see *drink* and *drank, walk* and *walked.* Does the learner know the past tense or not? Considering what we have said about knowledge before, it seems inconsistent to say that the writer knows the past tense at home but not at school. Clearly it is more likely that the situation affected the learner's ability to retrieve the knowledge. The variation was probably caused by processing factors.

2.2 A COGNITIVE VIEW OF VARIATION

Hulstijn (1989) accepts that interlanguage variation is ruled by processing factors rather than by fluctuations in actual knowledge. He first acknowledges the agreement among most researchers that such things as situation and task can affect how much attention a language user will pay to form. The degree of attention to form, in turn, causes variation in production. Hulstijn is explicit about the mechanism through which social situation affects a cognitive change in an individual—varying attention to form—which causes the variation in output. This seems entirely more plausible than the unspecified mechanism that Ellis invokes to allow the social situation to affect mental representation.

Hulstijn reconsiders output variation within the cognitive framework of information processing. Those who apply the theory of information processing to second language acquisition maintain that L2 acquisition begins with controlled processing. A learner of German as a second language whose first language is English, for example, may have to devote a lot of conscious processing to making sure that the verb in an embedded clause goes at the end of the sentence. Learners' early forms do not necessarily resemble those of the target language because humans have limited processing capacity. We cannot process everything on all levels at once. Only by making some processing automatic can we expand our range of processing ability. By making such factors as character recognition automatic in reading a foreign writing system, for example, we free ourselves to process such higher level attributes as biases in the writing style. It is difficult to determine if a writer is presenting both sides of a debate fairly when we have to work to remember the difference between *b* and *d*. Attention to form, then, focusses on the elements that require controlled processing. Conversely, the vernacular style results from automatic processing. For Hulstijn, it is not style of speech but type of processing that determines variation.

To the authors of this text, the information processing explanation is much more satisfying than the sociolinguistic explanation. The sociolinguistic school has been very good at demonstrating variation in output, the phenomenon that must be accounted for. It has been less successful at proposing explanations for the observed data.

Drawing on what we know of the cognitive abilities of humans, it seems entirely consistent to say that we set up mental representations of linguistic structures and that our manipulation of this knowledge can be affected by a variety of processing or performance factors. Rather than talking of variable competence, then, it appears more accurate to talk of L2 speech as the product of the same kinds of performance factors as we have discussed throughout Section 3 of this text.

3 TENSE MARKING

Let us turn now to a discussion of an interesting case study of systematic variation in second language learners. Wolfram (1989) investigated variation in second language tense marking. He observed that one of the most commonly noted characteristics of second language learner speech is the absence of morphologically marked tense, as found in *Last year we visit my friend*. It has also been widely noted that tense marking in second language acquisition is highly variable. In other words, the same speaker who uttered the preceding sentence would also be capable of producing *Last year we visited my friend* on certain occasions. The problem is how to explain the variation. Wolfram draws on Labov's work and argues that variation in tense marking can be constrained by both internal linguistic factors and external social factors.

Wolfram and Hatfield (1984) conducted an empirical investigation of a Vietnamese community in Northern Virginia. They interviewed thirty-two subjects for approximately an hour each on past events, such as things they had done in their homeland and the circumstances that had led to their resettlement in the United States.

Wolfram and Hatfield broke down the English past tense morpheme into its various phonetic realizations: [t] as in *missed*, [d] as in *played*, and [ɪd] as in *treated* (Table 13.2). They also investigated whether the morpheme's appearance in a regular consonant cluster—as in [kɪkt]—affected its chance of being unmarked. Finally, they considered the various irregular instantiations of the past tense: suppletive forms such as *went*; internal vowel changes, as in *came*; instances of internal vowel change plus suffix, as in *kept*; and replacive final consonants as in *made* (Table 13.3). Table 13.2 shows how the thirty-two subjects marked tense; all the irregulars are grouped into a single category. The total columns indicate the number of past tense items used in the speech data for which Standard English speakers require a marked past tense form. The unmarked columns indicate the number of times the speakers did not mark the past tense on these forms.[2]

Table 13.2   Variation in Phonetic Realizations of Past Tense Marking

Residency	1–3 years			4–7 years		
Verb type	Total	Unmarked	Percent unmarked	Total	Unmarked	Percent unmarked
Irregular	2768	1501	54.2	2078	590	28.4
Regular [ɪd]	66	58	87.9	110	83	75.5
Regular [d]	198	182	91.9	123	95	77.2
Regular cluster (C + [t])	524	506	96.6	351	286	81.5

Source: Data from Wolfram and Hatfield (1984).

The percentage of unmarked forms decreased as residency increased; the longer the subjects were resident, the more they marked past tense. Both groups exhibited a consistent pattern over which forms of the past tense they were most likely to leave unmarked. Regular forms were less likely to be marked than irregular forms. The past tense was most likely to

---

[2] This has nothing to do with a theory of markedness, only with whether tense markings are overtly used.

be unmarked when it occurred after another consonant, as in a word such as *kicked* [kɪkt]. This was also true of sequences in which the following word began with a consonant cluster. The phrase *missed school,* for example, was more likely to be unmarked than *missed autumn.* Clearly, the linguistic context of both the word and the phrase influenced the marking of past tense; the variation was systematic. A similar pattern emerged in the realizations of the irregular past forms, as shown in Table 13.3.

Table 13.3 Variation in Realizations of the Irregular Past

Residency	1–3 years			4–7 years		
Verb type	Total	Unmarked	Percent unmarked	Total	Unmarked	Percent unmarked
Regular	818	777	95.0	584	464	79.5
Replacive	381	351	92.1	255	131	51.4
Modal[†]	158	131	82.9	124	53	42.7
Internal vowel	930	495	53.2	557	177	31.8
Vowel + suffix	824	367	44.5	506	151	29.8
Suppletive	643	283	44.0	760	131	17.2

[†] can/could, for example
Source: Data from Wolfram (1989).

While it seems unlikely that all of the differences between classes are statistically significant, they are comforting in the sense that the patterns for both groups are the same. Regulars are unmarked more frequently than irregulars, and a pattern of marking frequency emerges for the different types of irregulars. Wolfram (1985) explained this by invoking a principle of *perceptual saliency:* the more distinct the past form is from the present form, the more likely it is to be marked for tense. He noted, though, that the subjects of the study demonstrated considerable individual variation.

Wolfram's data support the idea that interlanguage variability is systematic and that the cause of the systematicity is linguistic in nature. Interestingly, too, it seems that irregular forms are an integral part of early interlanguage grammars and not a late acquired peripheral element.

4 REGULAR AND IRREGULAR MORPHOLOGY IN INTERLANGUAGE GRAMMARS

Wolfram's study has shown us that regular and irregular forms behave differently when it comes to output variation. This section investigates the cognitive mechanisms that may be responsible for the differences between regular and irregular morphology in interlanguage grammars.

Clearly, native speakers have a subclass of words in which regular morphology applies and a subclass in which it doesn't. The non-native speaker has to acquire this distinction. Pinker (1993) proposes the existence of very different cognitive mechanisms underlying the generation of regular and irregular forms. Again we note a cognitive explanation for linguistic variation.

Let us begin by looking at the idea of linguistic rules. Rules have long been postulated as a way to account for the productivity of human language. As George Miller put it, language is an infinite system learned by beings with finite brains (Pinker 1993). Miller estimated that speakers know how to produce or comprehend at least 10^{20} sentences and that it would take a million centuries (two thousand times the age of the earth) to hear them all. Clearly we have not memorized them but have some mental machine capable of creating or analysing novel combinations. Miller argued that when they speak or comprehend, people are not working by association but by computation. In other words, they do not simply associate the utterance with others previously heard, but compute its structure independently.

As suggested in Chapter 3, the field of language acquisition has recently seen an onslaught of connectionist models, such as Rumelhart and McLelland (1986b), which are claimed to learn rule-like behaviour through associative learning, without rules. The claim made for these models is that they overgeneralize in much the same way as children learning language: they attempt to produce novel forms on the basis of prior experience. Pinker (1993) suggests that with the advent of connectionist models we can no longer treat the mere existence of linguistic productivity as evidence for rules in the head. He seeks to distinguish between the kind of productivity provided by rules and the kind provided by associative networks.

4.1 ASSOCIATIVE VERSUS RULE-DRIVEN PRODUCTIVITY

Pinker argues that neither rules alone nor neural or connectionist networks alone adequately account for linguistic productivity. He argues for two morphological subsystems in the mind, one using rules and the other using a network. The first is responsible for producing regular forms and the second for producing irregulars. The following discussion looks at the behaviour of both irregular past tense forms such as *go* and *went* and irregular plural forms such as *tooth* and *teeth*.

Traditionally, it has been argued that a speaker develops a regular morphological system by learning rules and an irregular system by rote learning. This does not account for the patterns found within an irregular class such as *spring/sprang/sprung* or *drink/drank/drunk*. True rote learning would be reserved for forms like *be/was*. Irregulars must be partially systematic. Chomsky and Halle (1968) proposed irregular rules to account for this, and thus provided a unified rule-based account of regular and irregular forms. Without formalizing it, we can say that an irregular rule would apply to a particular subclass of forms. It would therefore not be accidental that the past tense of *keep* is *kept*, for example, and the past tense of *creep* is *crept*. A rule would account for the pattern. Connectionist models also propose a unified account but they do not sanction rules. Instead, they posit a *pattern association network,* which would associate *drink* and *drunk* in the same way as *walk* and *walked.*

Pinker's theory of language has both a computational component for dealing with rules and representations, and an associative memory system. Under this model, the learner computes regular past tense forms by rule but memorizes irregulars as pairs of words with linkages stored in an associative memory structure. If this is the case, irregular forms should be affected by properties of associative memory, such as sensitivity to frequency, similarity, and so on, while regular forms should not.

In addition, irregular forms should serve as input to word-formation processes while regular forms should be output. These processes are generally thought of as combining items stored in the mental lexicon. If we have lexical entries for verb forms and affixes such as *drop, kick,* and *-ed* (past tense), we don't need to store the complex form *dropkicked* lexically. Complex forms are said to be the output of word-formation processes. Irregular forms, on the other hand, are thought to have their own lexical entries. We would have separate entries for nouns like *tooth* and *teeth,* for example, rather than a rule that computes *teeth* from *tooth.* The irregular form can also be the input for word-formation processes, as in the complex form *teethmarks.*

4.2 THE PSYCHOLINGUISTICS OF REGULAR VERSUS IRREGULAR MORPHOLOGY

4.2.1 Frequency

If irregular forms are memorized then they should be better remembered the more they are encountered. We know that children make errors such as overgeneralizing the regular past tense marking more often for verbs that their parents use less frequently. For adults, low-frequency irregulars co-exist with regulars, so they might alternate in their use of *slew* and *slayed,* for example, and judge both to be acceptable. We note that low-frequency forms tend to become regular over the centuries (*auditorium* → *auditoriums*). Surviving irregulars are high frequency (*sheep* → *sheep*).

Regular inflection, though, is different. Native speakers do not judge low-frequency regular verbs (such as *infarcted*) to be unusual morphologically. Native speakers are significantly faster at giving the past tense of high-frequency irregulars (*go*) than of low-frequency ones (*smite*), but this doesn't hold for regulars (*walk* versus *defenestrate*).

4.2.2 Compounding

Pinker notes that compounding is fed by stored words and we therefore expect irregular but not regular inflection to be on the left side of compounds. Thus, *mice-infested,* and *teeth-marks* are well formed, but **rats-infested* and **claws-marks* are not. Children from age three to five have this pattern. When asked questions such as, "What do you call a monster that eats mice?" a *mice-eater* was the response 90 percent of the time. The parallel question, "What do you call a monster that eats rats?" provoked the answer *rats-eater* only 2 percent of the time.

4.3 SECOND LANGUAGE LEARNERS AND INFLECTIONAL MORPHOLOGY

Do adult second language learners show evidence of the distinct subsystems just described? To investigate this question we conducted a pilot study in which five non-native speakers performed two different tasks. In the first, the subject had to generate verbally the past tense for invented forms or low-frequency verbs. The results are shown in Table 13.4, where an I indicates that subject did something irregular, and an R indicates that regular morphology was applied. From these data, a pattern from most to least regular emerges, as shown in Table 13.5 reading from the top down. The numbers in parentheses indicate regular responses.

Table 13.4   Past Tense Marking for Invented and Low-frequency Verbs

	Non-native speaker				
Word	**1**	**2**	**3**	**4**	**5**
spling	I	I	I	I	I
smite	R	R	I	R	I
ploamph	R	R	R	R	R
plip	R	R	R	R	R
slay	I	R	R	R	R
strow	I	I	R	I	I
beel	R	R	R	R	R
zoop	R	R	R	I	R
stride	I	I	I	R	I

The results were very much in line with the performance of native speakers item by item, but the non-native speakers behaved quite differently from native speakers on the second task. Here, they had to judge the acceptability of certain compounds, shown in Table 13.6.

As we saw earlier, according to Pinker (1993), native speakers tend to accept compounds that have irregular morphology in the left element (*mice-infested*) but not those with regular morphology (*rats-infested*). The

Table 13.5   Responses from Most to Least Regular

Number of regular responses	Answers
plip (5)	plipped
ploamph (5)	ploamphed
beel (5)	beeled
zoop (4)	zooped/zope
slay (4)	slayed/slew
smite (3)	smited/smote
stride (1)	strode/strided
strow (1)	strew/strowed
spling (0)	splang

Table 13.6   Acceptability of Compounds

	Native speakers	Non-native speakers				
		1	**2**	**3**	**4**	**5**
mice-infested	OK	OK	OK	OK	OK	OK
rats-infested	X	OK	OK	OK	OK	OK
teeth-marks	OK	OK	OK	OK	OK	X
claws-marks	X	OK	OK	OK	OK	X
men-bashing	OK	X	X	X	X	OK
guys-bashing	X	X	X	OK	X	OK

OK = acceptable form
X = unacceptable form

data in Table 13.6 indicate that although this is true for native speakers it does not hold true for non-native speakers. Nevertheless, although the non-native speakers behaved differently from native speakers on this task, they exhibited a pattern in their judgments. With one exception, the subjects consistently accepted or rejected pairs. If the regular was judged acceptable, the irregular was also judged acceptable. If one was considered unacceptable, the other was too. It is conceivable that the forms were being judged with reference to semantic criteria, but we did not investigate this.

Pinker (1993) has argued that careful investigation of something as basic as irregular and regular past and plural morphology reveals the necessity of both an associative and a computational component of human language. Neither rules nor associations can do everything. This, in turn, may help us to explain some of the varied performance we see in second language learners. Whether they produce regular or irregular morphology, for example, may reflect deeper properties of the human cognitive apparatus, such as whether associative memory or linguistic rules are being used. We might diagram some of the factors related to variation as in Figure 13.3.

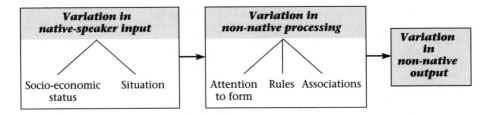

Figure 13.3   Sources of Variation in Non-Native Speech

5 CONCLUSION

This chapter has addressed the issue of variation in second language production. We have seen that variation may be caused by cognitive, linguistic, or sociolinguistic factors. This is not surprising when we consider that language *use* obviously involves cognition, language, and society. Variationist perspectives allow us to get a broader picture of just what second language performance looks like.

CLASSROOM IMPLICATIONS

Given that second language learner performance is variable, discuss the implications for second language assessment. How do you know that your picture of a given student's proficiency is accurate?

One of the major empirical findings of sociolinguistic research is that language use varies according to certain social factors. What implications do you think this has for second language instruction? Which social dialect do you think you should teach? Which register do you think you should teach?

SELF TEST

One of the major concerns of the field of sociolinguistics is

_____ . We can see linguistic variation both within a speech
(1)

community and in an _____ . One mechanism to account for
(2)

this variation is the _____ . Several factors have been proposed
(3)

to account for variation in second language acquisition, such as context and task. Researchers disagree over whether variation is the result of _____ (4) or _____ (5) factors. Attention to _____ (6) has been examined as one performance factor. Hulstijn argues that the vernacular results only from _____ (7) processing. Wolfram's case study revealed that L2 learners tended not to mark tense on _____ (8) verbs.

Pinker distinguishes between two cognitive mechanisms used in language processing: _____ (9) and _____ (10) . The pilot study done by Archibald and Libben indicates that L2 learners reveal judgments on irregular tense marking that are _____ (11) to native speakers.

FURTHER READING

Eisenstein, M., ed. 1989. *The Dynamic Interlanguage: Empirical Studies in Second Language Variation.* New York: Plenum Press.

Gass, S., C. Madden, D. Preston, and L. Selinker, eds. 1989. *Variation in Second Language Acquisition: Psycholinguistic Issues.* Clevedon, UK: Multilingual Matters.

Preston, D. 1989. *Sociolinguistics and Second Language Acquisition.* Oxford: Blackwell.

Factors Affecting Second Language Acquisition

This section discusses various factors that influence the construction of second language grammars. Chapter 14 considers whether the age of the learner has an effect on the interlanguage grammar. Chapter 15 explores individual differences in SLA. The role of affective and cognitive factors is investigated. Chapter 16 outlines the research on the effects of instruction. Do instructed learners set up different grammars from those of uninstructed learners? Chapter 17 looks at the effects of environment. Different learners are exposed to different kinds of input. We will consider whether this environmental variation affects the interlanguage grammar. Chapter 18 looks at the effects of feedback to see whether adult learners' exposure to it has a lasting effect on their grammar.

The Effects of Age

The effect of age on second language learning has received considerable attention in second language research, and almost everyone has an opinion about it. Does age affect second language development? The issue is most often considered within the context of what has come to be known as the *critical period* hypothesis. The hypothesis maintains that there is a period during which language acquisition takes place naturally, or effortlessly, and after which something happens to make acquisition difficult, or at least different. Much of the early research was predicated on the assumption that children were somehow better at or more naturally disposed to second language learning than were adults. Throughout the chapter we will return to the question of whether this supposition is justified.

1 CRITICAL PERIODS

There is considerable evidence for the existence of critical periods in many biological domains. Imprinting in birds is probably one of the best-known examples. It is only during a limited time that a bird can form an attachment to its mother; after the critical period has passed, it's too late. Another example comes from bird song. In order for the white-crowned sparrow to be able to produce the adult song, it must hear that song in the first ten to fifty days of its life. If the bird is exposed to the song only in the first ten days or only after a hundred days no learning occurs.[1] Laboratory experiments on kittens also show evidence of a critical period. Kittens raised in an environment containing only horizontal

---

[1] If the bird hears the song in the first fifty to a hundred days, partial learning takes place.

lines do not develop the necessary physical receptors to perceive vertical lines. Even if they are moved to an environment with vertical lines after a certain time, it is too late. Clearly, there are critical periods for development, during which the environment can play a significant role. The question remains, though, whether there is a critical period for linguistic development.

2 A BIOLOGICAL CRITICAL PERIOD

People often assume a *biological* critical period, a biological reason for a supposed change in behaviour. Lenneberg (1967) drew on the work of Penfield (1965) to propose a critical period for first language acquisition. He observed that "the capacities for speech production and related aspects of language acquisition develop according to a built-in biological schedule.... [L]anguage development thus runs a definite course on a definite schedule; a critical period extends from about age 2 to age 12, the beginning and end of *resonance*" (3–4). By resonance, Lenneberg meant that the child was somehow in tune with the environment. Metaphorically, the child would resonate with language.

In the late 1960s and early 70s, one of the most common ways of explaining the critical period was through research on *brain lateralization*. We have known for some time that the brain is divided into two easily distinguishable halves: the left hemisphere (LH) and the right hemisphere (RH). Although they are distinct, they are joined by a bundle of fibres known as the *corpus callosum*. Neurological and neurolinguistic research has shown that different activities are processed in different parts of the brain. In other words, neural activity is localized. Most people process much of language in the left hemisphere. The right hemisphere handles such things as spatial perception. The term *lateralization* describes this phenomenon of the two hemispheres performing different types of function.

Penfield (1965) reported that children who suffered LH damage before the age of ten or twelve were able to recover their speech ability, whereas older children suffered permanent language loss. Children with RH damage suffered minimal language disorder. His explanation was that younger children were able to transfer the language ability from the LH to the RH in the event of damage, whereas older children (and adults) were not. This characteristic of the brain is often referred to as *plasticity*; the younger brain is plastic in that it can adapt to damage. As the brain matures, the argument goes, its ability to transfer its functions from one hemisphere to the other gradually decreases.

Several people argued that the brain became more lateralized as it matured. Penfield (1965, 392) argued that lateralization was complete by puberty: "After ... [puberty], the speech centre cannot be transferred to the cortex of the lesser side [the RH] and set up all over again. This 'non-dominant' area that might have been used for speech is now occupied with the business of perception."

2.1 THE BIOLOGICAL CRITICAL PERIOD AND L2 ACQUISITION

Scovel (1969) attempted to apply these findings to second language acquisition. He noted, as had many other researchers, that although children appear to be able to acquire nativelike pronunciation in the second language, most adults do not. For Scovel, it was too great a co-incidence to ignore that both brain lateralization and ability to acquire an accent-free L2 were limited by the onset of puberty. He argued that the difficulty adults had in mastering a second sound system was caused by the completion of lateralization. This has obvious implications for L2 teachers. Should they teach pronunciation to adults? Should they teach adults at all?

Studies covering everything from *voice onset time* (VOT) to subjacency are now looking very closely at *what* is acquired in order to assess the abilities of adults. In spite of the breadth of coverage, conclusions on the subject are still controversial. To make sense of conflicting results and interpretations, Long (1990) distinguishes between the *whether* question and the *where* question. The *whether* question is concerned with such issues as whether adults have an initial advantage over children at the outset of learning and whether children's ultimate attainment outstrips adults'. The *where* question is concerned with which aspects of grammar might be affected by a critical period.

Cook (1991) makes an important point. He remarks that many researchers appear to look down their noses at a bilingual's use of the L2. We refer to it as an interlanguage, in which the L2 grammar has not yet reached the stage of proficiency of a native speaker. We think of the bilingual's competence as being somehow deficient. Would it not make more sense, he says, to think of a monolingual's competence as deficient for being monolingual? According to Cook (1991), multicompetence is the global norm, and we should think of it that way.

2.2 CRITICISMS OF THE BIOLOGICAL EXPLANATION

As we have seen, Lenneberg claimed that lateralization was a slow process beginning around age two and completed by puberty. Krashen (1973) re-examined Lenneberg's data, however, and found that all of the children who recovered their language actually suffered their cerebral trauma before the age of *five*. He therefore argued that lateralization was complete by age five, not by puberty. If this is so, and children from five to puberty can still acquire nativelike speech, then lateralization cannot mark the end of a critical period or be responsible for accented speech. Scovel (1981) responded to this by noting that we must be careful to distinguish between *emergence* and *completion* of lateralization. If lateralization is not complete until puberty, we can still use it as the basis of the critical period hypothesis.

Other problems are also associated with the construct. Segalowitz (1983) states unequivocally that lateralization does not increase with age. He studied children from ages two to seven and found no increase in lateralization at all. Other studies (such as Molfese et al. 1975) have shown LH dominance in newborn speech perception. There is even some evidence for lateralization before birth. All of this implies that seeing lateralization as a maturational process is problematic. Segalowitz (1983) also contends that lateralization and plasticity are not related, that we should not think of lateralization as signifying that part of the brain is "used up" or "filled" just because it is specialized for a particular activity.

The concept of lateralization itself may not be quite as unassailable as some researchers believe. Several studies have shown that cognitive strategies can influence lateralization. Learners who are taught in different ways, for example, process analytical tasks differently. Tasks presented in a traditional style tend to be processed in the LH, whereas tasks presented in a conversational style tend to be processed in the RH.

We are thus forced to reconsider whether we should be concentrating so much time on the relevance of lateralization to language learning. Jacobs states, "It must always be remembered that things easy to measure are not necessarily important and those not measurable may be very important" (1977, 163).

Walsh and Diller propose a modified biological explanation of the critical period, restricting it to the issue of pronunciation:

> Lower-order processes such as pronunciation are dependent on early maturing and less adaptive macroneural circuits, which makes foreign accents difficult to overcome after childhood. Higher-order language functions, such as semantic relations, are more dependent on late-maturing neural circuits, which may explain why college students can learn many times the amount of grammar and vocabulary that elementary school students can learn in a given period of time (1981, 18).

Their claim would explain why age-related effects in second language are most notable in pronunciation.

3 UNIVERSALITY OF THE CRITICAL PERIOD

Scovel (1969) makes the claim that three factors are true of all speech communities: (1) children can acquire nativelike L2 pronunciation; (2) few adults can; and (3) adults can recognize a foreign accent in their native language. These assumptions imply the universality of a critical period. Hill (1970), however, presented some data that compel us to question assumptions (2) and (3) and, by extension, whether the critical period is indeed universal.

Whereas Scovel and Lenneberg were primarily interested in the *biological* aspects of the critical period, Hill used cultural data to counter the biological explanation. She argued that learning an L2 to nativelike proficiency is perfectly ordinary in many societies. To support her view, Hill reviewed Sorensen's (1967) discussion of Amazon Basin tribes in an area where twenty-four mutually unintelligible languages were spoken, representing four language families. In this society, a person must marry someone from another tribe, who therefore speaks another language. Sorensen asserted that the adults were remarkably successful at learning an L2. He specifically rejected the claim that members of this society were forgiving in their assessment of L2 performance, arguing instead that they were quite severe in their evaluations. This is important because we must ask ourselves whether the blame for pronunciation problems should be assigned to speakers or to listeners.

It is easy to see how the problem might lie with the speaker, but how can we say that it lies with the listener? Consider a situation in which your knowledge of languages X and Y is functional but minimal and, in your eyes, at about the same level of proficiency. You speak language X to a group of native speakers, and they remark that they didn't realize you could speak X so well. You speak language Y to a group of native speakers, and they respond by correcting you or switching to English. Could it be that some cultures are harsher judges than others of second language performance? Is it possible that English speakers are very hard on non-native speakers when it comes to pronunciation?

Hill also believed that some societies were probably less able to recognize foreign accents. She pointed to Southern India—home to numerous languages coming from different families but through language contact having much in common in their phonetic inventories—and argued that people in this region were not able to recognize a foreign accent. This was contrary to Scovel's third assumption.

To sum up, the biological critical period hypothesis has encountered several problems. The primary physical correlate proposed to account for lateralization doesn't do so. Behaviour claimed to be universal may not be. Just because a behaviour is not invariant, however, does not

ACUTE ACCENTS

Vindication may be nigh for foreign teaching assistants whose students whine about the unintelligibility of their instructors' accents. According to a study done by a University of Georgia professor, the communication gap may have less to do with fractured vowels than with how their students feel about foreigners.

Donald Rubin, professor of language education and speech communication, tape-recorded a four-minute lecture given by an Ohio-born white woman, then played the tape back to two separate groups of undergraduates in two different rooms. In each room he projected a slide of a woman he identified as the lecturer; in one room the woman pictured was white, in the other she was Chinese. "To avoid confounding ethnicity with physical attractiveness," Rubin wrote in his report, "both models were similarly dressed, were of similar size and hairstyle, and were photographed in the same setting and pose (standing at a lectern in front of a chalkboard)."

The students who thought the lecture was being given by the Chinese woman scored lower on a listening-comprehension test than those who thought the lecture was given by a Caucasian. The first group scored about the same as a third group that had listened to a lecture actually given by a Chinese T.A. with a heavy accent. The students who thought the speaker was foreign also rated her teaching skills lower than those who thought she was American.

In another experiment, Rubin had two Chinese T.A.s record short lectures twice, first exaggerating their accents, then down-playing them. He found that undergraduates who listened to the tapes couldn't tell the difference.

Rubin's findings may affect more than the egos of teaching assistants, since many universities have by now invested significant amounts of time and money in pronunciation-improvement programs for their foreign T.A.s. Pronunciation workshops are often mandatory. A professor of speech-language pathology at Northeastern University recently developed a talking software program that has foreign T.A.s sitting at Macintoshes and imitating, over and over, a standard English "model voice." Many states have even passed laws requiring colleges and universities to test the proficiency of all teaching assistants' English, and to arrange remedial education for those who flunk.

Rubin now thinks these efforts miss their mark. "There's no point in trying to teach the T.A.s to sound like Tom Brokaw," he says. "It won't happen, and even if it did, their students would still be prejudiced against understanding them." A better solution, he says: "Try to improve students' attitudes about being taught by foreigners. After all, today's T.A.s are tomorrow's professors."

Sue Young Wilson
Reprinted from *Lingua Franca*

invalidate a biological explanation of a phenomenon. Scovel (1988) notes that exceptional behaviour is to be expected statistically in a normal distribution.

4 A COGNITIVE CRITICAL PERIOD

Not all investigations of the critical period focus on biology or culture. Older and younger learners clearly differ in their cognitive capacities; older learners are able to comprehend language as a formal system. Halliday (1975) summed this up by saying that a child responds to what a language *does*, not what a language *is*. Rosansky (1975) investigated cognitive factors as a possible explanation for the differences between child and adult ability to learn a second language.

Working within a Piagetian framework, Rosansky saw the young child, up to and including Piaget's concrete operations stage, as lacking flexible thinking, being self-centred (egocentric), unaware of language acquisition, and cognitively open. She believed that these exact qualities were responsible for the success of younger learners. With the onset of abstract thinking (Piaget's formal operations stage) at about age twelve, the profile of the learner is remarkably different. The older learner thinks flexibly, becomes decentred, and holds strong social attitudes about the L1 and the L2. According to Rosansky, then, the awareness that comes with age inhibits natural language learning.

4.1 CRITICISMS OF THE COGNITIVE EXPLANATION

In spite of the intuitive appeal of Rosansky's proposal, it has the same trouble accounting for Hill's data as the biological explanation does. Do Amazon Basin children never reach formal operations? That is unlikely. Like the theory of a biological critical period, the cognitive explanation assumes a significant difference between child and adult behaviour. As we will see, with the exception of pronunciation, adults may be just as capable of acquiring a second language as children are. Rosansky's theory cannot explain why the critical period only seems to affect pronunciation and not other areas of language. A larger scale criticism could be levelled at the Piagetian framework within which Rosansky worked. This is not the place to undertake such a critique, but the interested reader might wish to consult Gardner (1983).

5 A SOCIOCULTURAL CRITICAL PERIOD

The third explanation for a critical period is sociocultural. Brown (1980) proposed that second language acquisition was related to acculturation. He argued that we cannot consider what it means to learn a second language without looking at what it means to learn a second culture, and proposed four stages of acculturation:

1. *Euphoria*   The second culture seems wonderful; the differences between your first and second culture are exciting and new. (*Wow, the trains run on time!*, or *Wow, you don't need a licence to drive!*)
2. *Culture shock*   The second culture begins to feel strange; the differences that before seemed exciting now seem annoying. (*There's so much bureaucracy here!* or *Everything is so disorganized!*) Feelings of hostility towards the second culture may emerge.
3. *Anomie*   Originally a term coined by Emile Durkheim in 1897, anomie refers to a feeling of homelessness. After a certain amount of time, immigrants may not feel at home in *either* culture. They feel like outsiders in their second culture, yet when they visit their first culture they don't feel as if they belong there either. They find that wherever they are, they want to go home.
4. *Recovery*   The fourth stage of acculturation is a feeling of being comfortable in either culture.

According to Brown, the beginning of stage (3), anomie, is the ideal time to acquire the second language because at this stage the person experiences the optimal cognitive and affective tension to produce the necessary pressure to learn. At stage (2) the pressure may be too overwhelming; at stage (4), it may be too weak. But what happens if the learner separates his or her linguistic and cultural development? A learner who gets to stage (4) and feels comfortable in the second culture without having mastered the second language will fossilize. On the other hand, a learner who masters the language without achieving recovery will never feel a part of the second culture. In the ideal situation learners' linguistic and cultural development are linked, enabling them to master the language and feel comfortable with the culture.

This model is useful only for *second* language contexts (such as learning English in Canada), not for *foreign* language contexts (learning English in Japan), because foreign language contexts obviously do not involve acculturation. It is pleasing nonetheless because, unlike biological and cognitive explanations, it acknowledges that adults *can* acquire proficiency in a second language.

6 WHY PRONUNCIATION SEEMS DIFFERENT

Why has the lion's share of attention in the critical period hypothesis literature been devoted to pronunciation? Chapter 5 noted that many diverse elements made up the construct of proficiency. Pronunciation, or phonological competence, is just one branch of a leafy tree. Why should this branch behave differently from all the others?

It is well documented that many great performers in diverse fields—music, dance, skating, and so on—began to develop their skill in childhood. This seems especially significant when the skill involves muscular dexterity, and the articulation of human speech uses lots of muscles. Is the critical period hypothesis just a muscular concern? Do adults have difficulty mastering a second phonology because their muscular performance has degenerated? It is obviously true that pronunciation has a muscular component, which syntax and other levels of linguistic structure are certainly lacking. Numerous studies have investigated this question.

Neufeld (1979; 1988), showed that adults can acquire nativelike pronunciation if they are taught in a certain way. Students who had no previous exposure to a particular language—in this case, Inuktitut—were trained on certain aspects of its pronunciation. They listened to the language for a considerable time at a language lab, and were *not allowed to repeat* the sounds they heard. After some time they were permitted to produce the sounds and their production was rated by native speakers of Inuktitut as being either nativelike, near-nativelike, or non-nativelike. Many of the students were judged nativelike. Neufeld argues that if they had been allowed to produce sounds early on, their inaccurate production would have contaminated the acoustic image of the target sound. Their own output would also serve as input to them. Crucially, however, the students had had no prior exposure to the language and thus had no acoustic image of the target sounds. Within the constraints of this prerequisite, the experiment showed that adults could attain nativelike proficiency in some L2 sounds.

The work of Flege (1981) is also seminal in the field of adult pronunciation. To understand the linguistic phenomenon he investigated, voice onset time (VOT), we need to digress a bit.

6.1 VOICE ONSET TIME

Voice onset time (VOT) refers to a certain aspect of the production of stop consonants. After a voiceless stop is released, a measurable amount of time elapses before the vocal folds start vibrating for the production of the following vowel. Consider a word like *paw*. The [p] is voiceless and the [ɑ] is voiced. From the time the lips come apart to release the stop there is a delay before the voicing of the vowel starts. This is the voice onset time of [p]. Different languages have different VOTs. English has a relatively long delay after the release of voiceless stops [p], [t], and [k]; other languages, such as Spanish and Arabic, have much shorter delays. This is illustrated in the Figure 14.1.

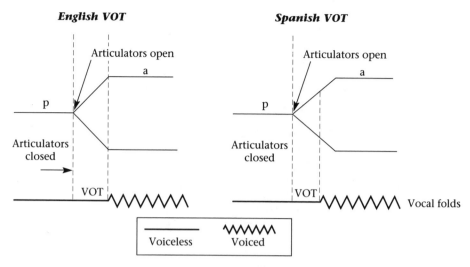

Figure 14.1   English versus Spanish Voice Onset Time

6.2 CROSS-LINGUISTIC IMPLICATIONS

Flege (1981) looked at Arabic speakers who were learning English as a second language. He examined their production of $[p^h\ t^h\ k^h]$[2] in English and found that their VOT was somewhere between Arabic and English. This shows that L2 speakers *can* alter their pronunciation somewhat, but raises the question of why they stop. Voice onset time is a matter of degree; it can be longer or shorter. The data reveal that L2 speakers move a certain distance along the continuum from L1 VOT to L2 VOT, but how do we analyse their production of phonological phenomena that are not continuous? If a Spanish speaker pronounces the word *have* [hæv] as [xæv], for example, how can we possibly view it as an intermediate phenomenon?

6.3 PRONUNCIATION OF VOWELS

Flege and his colleagues have also done some interesting work on acquisition of second language vowels (Bohn and Flege 1992). The results suggest that adults are able to acquire new vowel contrasts but that some contrasts are harder to acquire than others. The ease or difficulty could be determined by something about the acoustic space of the first language. To understand what that means, let's go back and look at the familiar vowel quadrilateral, shown in Figure 14.2.

---

[2] The superscript ʰ indicates aspiration, the puff of air that can follow voiceless stops.

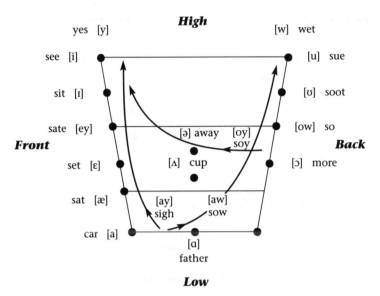

Figure 14.2   The English Vowel Quadrilateral

We are probably most used to thinking of the chart as a representation of vowel articulation. Without too much of a mental shift, though, we can think of it as a representation of the acoustic space that the phonology of a language uses for contrast. Remember that in order for two sounds to function as phonemes in a given language they must contrast: _seat_ [sit] versus _sit_ [sɪt]. In order for the sounds to contrast, they must have distinct acoustic images. The acoustic space of a five-vowel system looks something like Figure 14.3. The diagram shows a certain amount of acoustic space around each vowel. We can produce slightly different sounds and still have them perceived as belonging to a particular category, because the sounds that we produce do not impinge on any other categories. Once we cross over a boundary, the sound is perceived as a different vowel.

Consider now the hypothetical example of a learner whose L1 has the three-vowel system shown in Figure 14.4. Imagine further that the learner has to acquire some of the sounds of the English vowel system, say [ɪ], [e] and [æ]. According to Flege, learners will have no difficulty acquiring L2 sounds that are notably _different_ from their L1 (sounds for which the L1 acoustic space leaves a lot of room), but they may have difficulty with sounds that are _similar_ to their L1 (for which the L1 acoustic space leaves little room). This view predicts that the learner from the three-vowel L1 would have less difficulty acquiring English [e] than either English [ɪ] or [æ]. English [ɪ] and [æ] are quite similar to sounds in the L1 acoustic space, and it would therefore be difficult to establish them as contrastive in the interlanguage grammar. English [e] is quite distinct in the L1 acoustic space, however, and would therefore be able to contrast with other sounds easily.

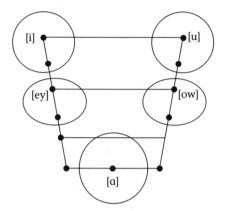

**Figure 14.3   The Acoustic Space of a
Five-Vowel System**

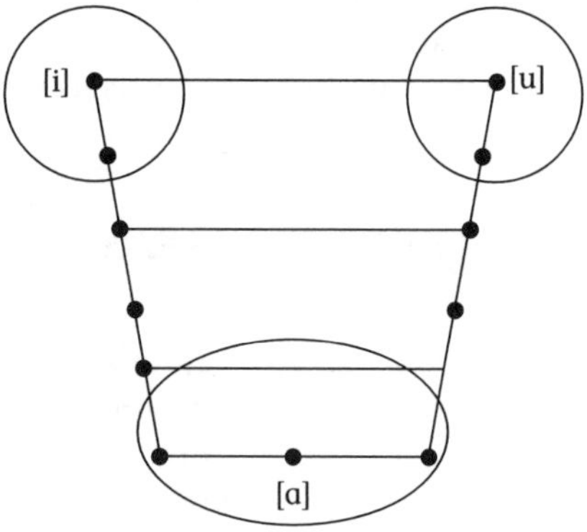

**Figure 14.4   The Acoustic Space of a
Three-Vowel System**

6.4 ACQUISITION OF STRESS

Archibald's research (1993), though not primarily conducted with the question of a critical period in mind, also has implications in this area. His research on how second language learners acquire the stress patterns of a new language shows that many of their errors are the product of L1 transfer; they often stress a word according to the rules of their first language. Yet we would be hard pressed to say that this has muscular causes. The evidence still makes a case for the distinction of pronunciation. The adults did retain a certain amount of non-native stress, but we cannot explain it in the same way as we did segmental phenomena such as the acquisition of new consonants or new vowels. Learning to make a new consonant or vowel clearly involves learning to place the articulators in new positions. The stress errors of non-native speakers could not be caused by placing the articulators incorrectly, which suggests that we are not able to explain adult second language learners' retention of foreign accent by muscular phenomena. Musculature may have more effect on segmental phonology than on suprasegmental phonology.

Archibald's studies also showed that the non-native speakers placed stress correctly most of the time; both their production and perception of stress were quite good. So while the errors that they did make could be attributed to L1 transfer, the subjects' pronunciation was relatively unaccented in terms of stress.

The studies by Neufeld, Flege, and Archibald discussed above all indicate that the prognosis for adult second language learners may not be as gloomy as was originally thought. Adults do appear able to change their phonological systems. They may not always reach nativelike proficiency in their pronunciation, but they can learn to make new distinctions. We therefore need to investigate both the factors that could stop learners reaching the final targets and the assumption that children are better than adults at certain aspects of second language learning.

7 THE RATE OF LEARNING

Ellis (1986) makes a useful distinction between studies that investigate the *rate* of acquisition and studies that investigate the *route*. Do children and adults go through the same developmental stages? Studies (Ervin-Tripp 1974) show that age does not affect the route of SLA; children and adults process linguistic data in the same way. It is an entirely different question to consider whether age affects the rate of SLA, and most studies examining the effects of age have been concerned with rate: the speed of learning and of ultimate attainment.

Age does seem to affect the rate of language learning. Snow and Hoefnagel-Höhle (1977) argue that adolescents have the best rate of learning, as shown in Figure 14.5. The only exception to this appears to be in the area of pronunciation, where Snow and Hoefnagel-Höhle found that adolescents were not any better than children.

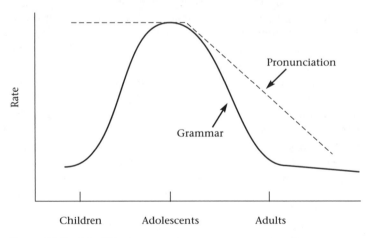

Figure 14.5   Age Effects

Pronunciation does seem to be correlated best with age of onset of learning the second language rather than length of exposure to it (Oyama 1976) but in general, the longer the exposure to the L2, the more nativelike the proficiency. As Hatch (1983) notes, however, this may be more true for overall communicative ability than for grammatical or phonological accuracy. The longer a person is exposed to a second language, the more communicatively adept they become, but accuracy in pronunciation is best correlated with onset of learning.

8 THE QUESTION OF ULTIMATE ATTAINMENT

Long (1990) issued a challenge to everyone interested in the notion of critical periods. He asserted the need for documented evidence of subjects who began learning their L2 after puberty and attained nativelike proficiency: subjects who were indistinguishable from native speakers. Undisputed examples of this kind of adult competence would clearly disprove the critical hypothesis. Several important studies have attempted to find that evidence.

Johnson and Newport (1989) examined the English language proficiency of forty-six native Korean and Chinese speakers who had arrived in the United States between the ages of three and thirty-nine. Age of arrival was considered to be their first exposure to English. All subjects had to have at least five years exposure to English and to have lived in the United States for at least three years continuously prior to the time of the test. The subjects who arrived in the United States at an early age had a significant advantage over late arrivals. Johnson and Newport measured proficiency with a grammaticality judgment test on a range of English structures: past tense, particle movement, plural, subcategorization, third person singular, auxiliaries, present progressive, yes–no questions, determiners, *wh* questions, pronominalization, and word order. Figure 14.6 summarizes the results. The maximum possible score was 276.

The later the subject was exposed to the language, the lower the score. In other words, the study suggests that children have an advantage over adults in acquiring a second language. Johnson and Newport summarize their results:

> Subjects who arrived in the United States before the age of seven achieved native performance on the test. For arrivals after that age, there was a linear decline in performance up through puberty. Subjects who arrived in the United States after puberty performed on the average much more poorly than those who arrived earlier. After puberty, however, performance did not continue to decline with increasing age (1989, 90).

In a similar study, Newport (1990) investigated subjects who were learning American Sign Language (ASL) as a second language. She found that for certain aspects of ASL there were clear age-dependent effects.

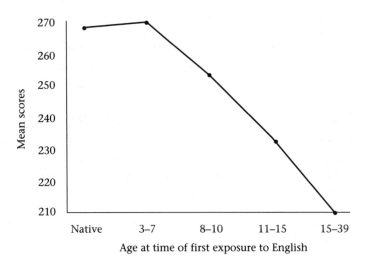

Figure 14.6   Relationship Between Age at First Exposure to English and Score on Test of English Grammar
Source: Data from Johnson and Newport (1989).

Figures 14.7 and 14.8 summarize her results. *Native* learners were exposed to ASL from birth by their deaf signing parents; *early* learners were first exposed to ASL between the ages of four and six by their deaf peers at school; *late* learners were first exposed to ASL after age twelve when they entered school, or made deaf friends, or married deaf spouses. There were no age-dependent effects for basic word order but significant age-dependent effects for morphology. The actual morphological features looked at are not crucial to this discussion. The graphs indicate that although age did not affect general communicative ability as reflected by basic word order, it did affect specific morphological aspects as measured on seven tests of ASL morphology.

In another influential study related to ultimate attainment, Coppieters (1987) compared the grammaticality judgments of twenty native speakers of French with those of twenty-one speakers who had acquired French as adults and were judged by native speakers to speak it at near-nativelike proficiency. Coppieters argued that although they appeared nativelike, the non-native speakers behaved significantly differently from the native speakers on certain linguistic tasks, as we will see when we examine Birdsong's study. He concluded that even proficient non-native adults revealed non-nativelike characteristics when their knowledge was probed deeply.

Birdsong (1992) expanded Coppieters' study in an attempt to respond to Long's challenge to produce some non-native speakers who could perform like native speakers even though they began their learning after

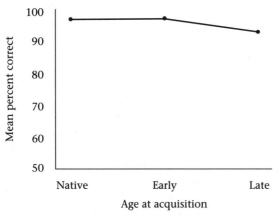

Figure 14.7   Scores on Basic Word Order for ASL Learners
Source: Data from Newport (1990).

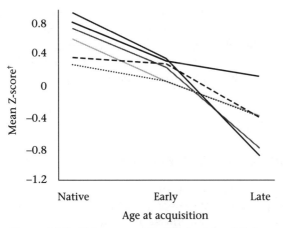

Figure 14.8   Z-Scores on Morphology for ASL Learners
[†] A z-score is a standardized measure allowing comparison of scores on different tasks. Zero on the y-axis represents an average score. Note that the early group performed near average, the late group performed below average, and the native group performed above average.

Source: Data from Newport (1990).

puberty. Three tasks were administered to the non-native speakers: (1) an ambiguity preference task; (2) an acceptability judgment task; and (3) an interpretation task involving the word *bien,* which we will not address here. He looked at twenty native speakers of English who were near-native speakers of French, and twenty native speakers of French. The subjects were comparable in terms of sociological and educational factors. As in Johnson and Newport's study, the non-natives had to have resided for three years continuously in the host country prior to testing.

Birdsong's results suggest that native and non-native speakers do not diverge dramatically in their acceptability judgments. Judgments were made on seventy-six sentences; the native and non-native groups differed significantly on seventeen items (approximately 22 percent). Even though as a group, the non-natives deviated from the native norms, Birdsong argues that these data "constitute little support for the notion of generalized competence differences between natives and near-natives" because fifteen of the twenty non-native speakers' performance fell within the performance range of the native speakers. This is at odds with Coppieters' study, which found that *none* of the non-native speakers performed in the range of native speakers.

On the ambiguity preference task, the subjects were asked to indicate which meaning of an ambiguous sentence they preferred. An English example would be something like *The duck was ready to eat.* Is it more likely that the duck is hungry or that the duck is cooked? Natives and non-natives differed significantly on only one sentence out of twenty.

The picture that emerges from Birdsong's study is not as clear cut as the one we saw arise from Coppieters' or Johnson and Newport's. Obviously, this research issue has not been resolved, but Birdsong's results suggest that the notion of an unstoppable critical period is not yet supported. Certain individuals appear to be able to perform like native speakers.

9 REASONS FOR A CRITICAL PERIOD

Let us examine two explanations of why a critical period might exist. The first was proposed by Tom Scovel in his 1988 book, *A Time to Speak.* He argues for the existence of a critical period for speech but not for language, and presents an interesting account of why that critical period comes to an end at puberty. He looks at the phenomenon from the perspective of sociobiology, the field that attempts to discover the biological bases of social behaviour. Scovel draws on Wilson's (1975) division of animals into two groups—R-strategists and K-strategists—based on rate of population density plotted against rate of population growth.[3] Table 14.1 outlines their characteristics.

Scovel claims that the critical period for speech is part of our biological endowment because it enhances our status as K-strategists. As evidence, he notes that humans are highly auditory animals; they rely

---

[3] Although neither Wilson nor Scovel make the connection, it seems that these characteristics are much in line with what biologists refer to as *altricial* and *precocial* animals.

Table 14.1 R-Strategists and K-Strategists

R-Strategists	K-Strategists
asocial	highly social
mature rapidly	mature slowly
short life span	long life span
(e.g., fleas)	(e.g., humans)

more heavily on the oral/aural channel than on any other sense for social organization. He argues that speech and language evolved much more definitely from hearing the sounds of the human voice than from seeing the gestures made by the face and body. Strong evidence for the primacy of sound is seen in the large number of innate sound discrimination abilities humans possess. Babies are able to distinguish voiced from voiceless sounds, for example.

Scovel also asks what adaptive or selective advantage there is for having acoustic feature detectors[4] programmed into human DNA chains. He answers that they not only allow rapid acquisition of the phonology system but are instrumental in *vocal identification,* by which he means the ability to identify groups as opposed to individuals. This is an important trait, according to Scovel, and to explain why, he turns to sociobiology. Sociobiologists consider the costs and benefits of a particular trait. Scovel claims that we must go back to when the hominids, or anthropoids (from which we descend), were competing with members of another genus, the hominoids (to which the great apes belong). How could they tell each other apart? They didn't have distinctive scents or remarkable plumage or special songs, but they did have their voices, and their voices served as a means of identification. This ability allowed them to recognize who was a member of their own group and who was a stranger. For Scovel, this is why recognizing accents is useful. It stems from a time when we needed to know who was a stranger.

As for why puberty ends this critical period, Scovel speculates that once sexual maturity is attained, it is vital that humans be able to select mates who will carry on their genetic material. Members of both groups at puberty would have established their own accents and their ability to perceive others' accents. The individuals who had done so would have a better chance at passing on their genes to the next generation.

Hurford (1991) proposes the second explanation, in a somewhat similar vein. He set up a computer simulation in which a population was created and the individuals in it were made to live, reproduce, and die in regular ways. He assumed that acquiring language conferred some sort of selectional advantage on an individual. In other words, individuals who had acquired language were more likely to survive and pass on their genes. Therefore, he argues, the longer the period of one's life in which

---

[4] By feature detectors, he means innate discrimination abilities.

one possesses the whole of the native language, the greater the advantage. He asserts that a built-in critical period guarantees possessing language for a longer time. Individuals who did not have critical periods would stretch their learning over more time. Without going into the details of his computer model, we can point to his conclusion that individuals who had a critical period built in survived more often than individuals who did not. Thus, he argues that a critical period seems to confer a selectional advantage on the individuals who possess it. In some ways, this is very similar to Scovel's conclusion.

10 ADULT L1 ACQUISITION AND THE CRITICAL PERIOD

One more source of evidence for a critical period should be explored: adult first language acquisition. Sadly, several cases have been documented of people who have been deprived of exposure to language throughout their childhood. Perhaps this cruel experiment of nature will tell us once and for all whether there is a critical period. Can an adult learn a first language? It so, then there is no evidence for a critical period.

Curtiss (1988; 1977) discussed the tragic case of Genie, an abused girl, as we saw in Chapter 3. Genie's performance is sometimes used as evidence either for or against the critical period. People who want to argue for a critical period point to the fact that she had severely impaired linguistic abilities. People who want to argue against show that she did learn how to communicate. We would question the relevance of this kind of data to the question at hand. Genie suffered many traumas at the hands of her abusers. To say that her performance is explicable merely as the result of her age is questionable. She had so many troubles, it is impossible to say that she didn't (or did) learn language because, or in spite of the fact that, she was past a certain age.

All in all, the documented cases of adult first language acquisition are problematic because the subjects have been affected by so many other factors, in terms of abuse and deprivation, that it is impossible to generalize the findings from this population to a normal group.

11 CONCLUSION

The effect of age on second language acquisition is still a controversial question. Studies continue to report widely divergent results. It is highly likely that we will find age-dependent factors affecting various aspects of language (vocabulary, phonology, morphology, and so on) differently. At any rate, it has become clear we cannot just *assume* that children will be better second language learners than adults in all linguistic domains.

In terms of general communicative ability, we have not seen clear age-related effects and have suggested that length of exposure predicts overall ability better than age of onset does. In the domain of specific syntactic and morphological characteristics, we have the conflicting results of Johnson, Newport, and Coppieters on the one hand and Birdsong on the other. The domain of phonology exhibits the strongest evidence for age-related effects but these may be more notable in segmental phonology. Aspects of the musculature of articulation and the acoustics of perception may help to explain this.

CLASSROOM IMPLICATIONS

Danesi's Bimodal Processing

Danesi (1988) investigates some of the pedagogical implications of brain research for the second language classroom. He begins by noting that in recent times, the *method* concept of L2 teaching has lost prominence. In the 1970s, particularly, a flurry of new methodologies was proposed: suggestopedia, total physical response, the natural approach, and the like. In the 1980s and 90s, though, a more eclectic approach to second language teaching became the norm. Single methods had addressed only one method of language processing and had been unsuccessful generally, a new awareness of learner diversity emerged, and teachers decided to rely on what was working in the classroom rather than what was prescribed by curriculum designers. Yorio (1987) described this with the metaphor of *multiple bridges*. If teachers have only one bridge, or method, to get learners where they want to go—to a state of proficiency—then only a certain number of learners will arrive there. If, however, they have multiple bridges, or an eclectic approach, more learners will get where they want to go.

Danesi asks whether anything in brain research justifies this eclecticism and concludes that the approach is supported. As we have seen, the brain is divided into two recognizable hemispheres. Both hemispheres interact in language learning. Danesi refers to left-hemisphere processing as L-mode and right-hemisphere processing as R-mode. Table 14.2 indicates some of the characteristics of each type of processing. Language processing, he claims, is *bimodal;* it draws on both hemispheres, as can be seen in Table 14.3.

Table 14.2   L-mode and R-mode Processing

L-Mode Traits	R-Mode Traits
understanding literal meaning	understanding metaphor
speech	spatial perception
verbal memory	visual memory
intellectual tasks	intuitive tasks
convergent thinking	divergent thinking
directed thinking	free thinking
analytical thinking	relational thinking
sequential thinking	multiple thinking
analysing parts	synthesizing parts
taking things apart	putting things together

Source: Data from Danesi (1988).

Table 14.3   The Bimodal Nature of Language Processing

L-Mode	R-Mode
processes syntax and morphology	processes prosodic structure (pitch, intonation, stress)
processes literal meaning	processes metaphorical meaning, connotation
detects and corrects errors	understands humour
processes text	processes context

Source: Data from Danesi (1988).

According to Danesi, teaching should therefore try to stimulate both L-mode and R-mode strategies. We can do this by contextualizing analytic tasks, supporting instruction with visual aids, and using realia and literature in the class. Thus, much of what we do in a communicative classroom is supported by Danesi's research.

SELF TEST

The effect of age on SLA has been looked at in a number of ways, usually in terms of whether some sort of _____ period exists.
(1)
Lenneberg argues that this period is governed, most generally, by
_____ and, more specifically, by brain _____ .
(2)   (3)
Researchers disagree, however, over _____ this process is com-
(4)
plete, and consequently whether it is responsible for L2 accent. Hill argues that it is governed by _____ , because observed age
(5)
effects did not appear to be _____ . Brown proposes a
(6)

_____ cause: a result stemming from the individual's
   (7)
_____ . Much of the attention in this area has been devoted to
   (8)
the effect of age on _____ . Studies by Newport and her col-
                              (9)
leagues, though, showed age-related effects in the area of
_____ as well. Birdsong's study, on the other hand, argued
   (10)
that non-native and native speakers could behave _____ .
                                                         (11)
Both Scovel and Hurford argue that a critical period would bestow some
kind of _____ advantage on the organism.
              (12)

FURTHER READING

Flynn, S. and S. Manuel. 1991. Age-dependent effects in language acquisition: An evaluation of "critical period" hypotheses. In *Point
   Counterpoint: Universal Grammar in Second Language*, ed. L. Eubank,
   117–46. Amsterdam: John Benjamins.

Harley, B. 1986. *Age in Second Language Acquisition*. Clevedon, UK:
   Multilingual Matters.

Scovel, T. 1988. *A Time To Speak: A Psycholinguistic Inquiry into the Critical
   Period for Human Speech*. New York: Newbury House.

Singleton, D. 1989. *Language Acquisition: The Age Factor*. Clevedon, UK:
   Multilingual Matters.

15

....

Individual Differences in Second Language Acquisition

This chapter discusses some of the many ways in which second language learners can differ. One of the simplifying assumptions of the contrastive analysis hypothesis was that all learners with the same L1 behaved in the same fashion, and in the field of L2 pedagogy many methodologies assumed that there was one way to teach all learners. In the past twenty years, however, research has shown that second language learners vary in numerous ways. This, of course, has pedagogical implications. If everyone learns differently, how do we teach them all?

Let us start with an investigation of individual variation in second language acquisition. Usually, this kind of issue is phrased in the form of a question: Does *x* make the learner better at SLA? To answer, we need to be very explicit about three things: (1) what *x* is; (2) what it means to be *better;* and (3) which aspects of SLA we are referring to. Figure 15.1 illustrates learner variation. This chapter looks at most of the variables shown and begins with *affective* factors.

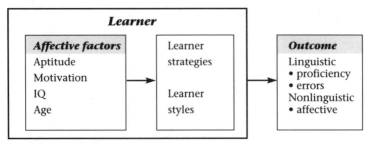

Figure 15.1   Aspects of Learner Variation
Source: Adapted from Skehan (1991).

1 AFFECTIVE VARIABLES

As intuitively appealing as research into learner differences is, the area is difficult to delineate. In general, qualities such as aptitude, motivation, anxiety, self-confidence, and so on have been the focus of research, but they are hard to define and measure. The research has therefore had some conflicting results. As Ellis (1986) pointed out, most affective factors are really just convenient labels for clusters of behaviours, and different researchers use the terms in different ways. The ensuing discussion does not describe in detail how these variables can be explicitly defined or tested. Affective factors have to do with the emotional side of the personality rather than the intellectual.

1.1 SELF-ESTEEM

Studies of self-esteem rely on the definition that it is an individual's personal judgment of his or her own worth. Often, three levels of self-esteem are distinguished:

1. *Global self-esteem* This refers to an individual's overall sense of worth in all activities and situations. It is thought to be a relatively stable aspect of our personality, not subject to daily change.
2. *Situational self-esteem* This refers to assessment of self in a particular type of situation. Do you have higher self-esteem when playing golf or when solving math problems, for example? Do you feel better about yourself at home or at work? Everyone feels different levels of self-esteem in different situations.
3. *Task self-esteem* This refers to an even smaller focus of analysis, on particular tasks within a given situation. Imagine that you're playing golf. Do you have the same sense of self-esteem when driving as when putting? In school, do you have the same sense of self-worth in anthropology as in linguistics?

It should be immediately obvious that determining which level of self-esteem a particular activity involves will be difficult and quite subjective. Consider aspects of second language learning and teaching. We would probably argue that second language learning is influenced by *situational* self-esteem. People often make statements like "I'm no good at learning other languages" (sometimes with a strange tone of pride in their voices). Yet when we consider the subskills of second language learning—listening, reading, talking, writing, and pronunciation—it seems that the *task* level is also involved. Think of your own second language ability. Do you have a better sense of self when reading the language or when writing it? Are these distinct tasks? This is probably relevant to teaching, too. Would you feel more confident teaching grammar or teaching pronunciation? Any test that claims to measure a particular level of self-esteem is going to have to justify its placement of activities at particular levels.

Heyde (1979) studied the effects of the three levels of self-esteem on performance of an oral production task. She found that all three levels correlated positively with performance on this task, but the highest correlation was between *task* self-esteem and oral performance. That is to say, if the subject scored highly on a test of self-esteem related to a particular task, then that subject was likely to do better on that task.

Heyde's study shows that when self-esteem is high, learners perform better on linguistic tasks. Should L2 teachers focus on improving self-esteem or on improving language proficiency? And does high self-esteem cause language success or does language success cause high self-esteem? In statistical terms, the correlation between two factors does not indicate a causal relation. Correlation is not causation! There might be a near perfect correlation between an individual's age and the price of gas; as one goes up, so does the other. Nevertheless, one is not causing the other. The question remains: How are self-esteem and language ability related?

1.2 INHIBITION

Some learners are more inhibited than others. Inhibition, referred to here in its everyday sense, is obviously closely related to self-esteem and we have to ask ourselves whether these are really two independent factors. Hands down the most talked-about study related to inhibition was done by Guiora, Beit-Hallahmi, Brannon, and Dull (1972) on alcohol. Ask yourself whether your second language gets better after a drink or two, or whether you just think it's getting better but your listeners would not notice any improvement or indeed may notice things getting worse. If you're ever around a group of second language learners who drink, ask them their opinions on the subject. You can bet they'll have them.

Guiora claimed that the human ego, or sense of self, includes something called a *language ego*. By this he meant that our sense of identity is closely tied to the language we speak. Many people report feeling that they have different personalities in the different languages they speak. Following Guiora's metaphor, the language ego is a kind of wall around the identity of the learner. To learn a new language, we need to be able to let down that wall, to lower our inhibitions. Otherwise the language ego may block our attempts to acquire the second language.

With this theoretical background, Guiora and his colleagues conducted a study to investigate the effects of alcohol on L2 pronunciation.

All subjects were given an initial test on their ability to pronounce Thai. After this measurement, they were given drinks with varying amounts of alcohol in them. The subjects were not told how much alcohol they were receiving. After a few drinks, the subjects' pronunciation skills in Thai were measured again.

Subjects who had no alcohol showed no improvement in their pronunciation. Subjects who had one drink improved their pronunciation. Subjects who had two drinks improved even more, but those who had three drinks started to deteriorate. Guiora concluded that there was a direct connection between inhibition and pronunciation. He argued that alcohol lowered the inhibition of the subjects and thus their performance improved.

Again, as intuitively appealing as this appears, it raises some questions, among them the problem of confusing correlation with causation. Alcohol is a muscle relaxant, which may explain why pronunciation improved. Perhaps relaxed muscles perform better, in which case the change could not be ascribed to lowered inhibition. As well, it is not certain that pronunciation is an adequate indicator of overall language proficiency. Just because the subjects' pronunciation improved, are we justified in saying that inhibition affects language ability altogether? Maybe it just affects pronunciation, but Guiora extended his conclusion about pronunciation to language as a whole.

As something of an aside, we should note that Guiora did a follow-up study to look at the effects of Valium on pronunciation (Guiora, Acton, Erard, and Strickland 1980). It showed no significant correlation. Schumann and colleagues (1978) tested the effects of hypnotism on L2 performance and found that the deeper subjects rated their trances, the better their performance had been. Any sort of external measure of relaxation, such as heart rate or breathing, failed to correlate with improved performance. If such drastic attempts to reduce inhibition as Valium and hypnotism fail to indicate improvement clearly, how can we hope that less dramatic measures will do so?

These studies raise some questions for the L2 teacher. Should teachers encourage their L2 students to drink before or during class? Should tranquillizers become part of the L2 teacher's teaching kit? Can teachers lower the inhibitions of their students? What activities or techniques would lower your inhibition in an L2 environment?

1.3 RISK TAKING

It is often reported anecdotally that "good" language learners are willing to take risks or to guess and that "bad" language learners are often unwilling to contribute to an activity unless they are certain that they know the correct answer. The difference may reflect the educational backgrounds of the students: whether the education systems of which they are a product encouraged risk takers or penalized them.

Beebe (1983) conducted a study on risk taking and second language learning. She asked herself what the possible penalties were for taking risks in a second language class. What was the learner risking if he or she got things wrong? Her list included factors both inside and outside the classroom. In class, the risks were a bad grade, failing an exam or a course, getting laughed at by a classmate or the teacher, being embarrassed, and being punished. The last two also applied outside, as did looking ridiculous, being unable to be understood, not being able to care for oneself or one's family, and losing one's identity.

Second language learners must risk some things, no matter how comforting we try to make our classrooms, and our society. Lest anyone think that students do not run the risk of embarrassment in our society, consider this story. One of the authors of this text was teaching ESL in an institution and assigned an advanced talking class to go out into the streets and conduct a survey. At one store a student, a very proficient speaker of English, was told to "go away and come back when you can speak English."

Beebe's study, however, did not show a correlation between high risk taking and high success in L2 learning. She argued that the best language learners were not *high* risk takers but *moderate* risk takers; they did not take wild risks. As Rubin (1975) noted, the good language learner is not only willing to make guesses but does so accurately.

Obviously, risk taking is related to self-esteem. A person with high global self-esteem is not going to worry as much about making a mistake as a person with relatively low self-esteem. Beebe asserts that her study has implications for fossilization. She believes that fossilization may be caused by an unwillingness to take risks. Learners may be happy sticking with a routine that works rather than trying out something new. Consider how you might feel about learning a new technique of doing something on your computer. Imagine that someone watches you, for example, move a block of text from one place to another and says, "There's another way to do that, you know." Is your reaction more likely to be "Oh good, I was looking for a better way to do this. Thank you." or "Touch my keyboard and you're dead! Things will just get screwed up and I'll lose everything! Go away!"? Are you a fossilized computer user?

In every class some learners are high risk takers and some are low risk takers. Both extremes have their benefits and drawbacks. High risk takers often keep the class lively and talkative. They may place more personal emphasis on fluency rather than accuracy. But they can drive the teacher crazy. How does a teacher tame the high risk taker? How do they make them more accurate guessers? Low risk takers are perhaps more concerned with accuracy rather than fluency. They may be able to produce more reflective comment and accurate language. But getting them to talk can be like pulling teeth. How do teachers encourage low risk takers? Consider one more question. How would you teach learners to guess from context?

1.4 ANXIETY

Anxiety, too, is difficult to define but we have all experienced it. Scovel (1978) defined anxiety as "a state of apprehension, a vague fear." Like self-esteem, anxiety can be experienced at different levels:

1. *Trait anxiety* is a characteristic of someone's whole personality. The person has a tendency to be anxious about almost everything. Charlie Brown comes to mind.
2. *State anxiety* is concerned with a particular situation or event. A normally calm and collected person might tense right up when confronted with a certain task, such as using a computer.

Scovel (1978) adopts the distinction proposed by Alpert and Haber (1960) of *debilitative* versus *facilitative* anxiety. Debilitative anxiety causes a deterioration in performance; facilitative anxiety causes an enhancement. We are inclined to think of anxiety as a totally undesirable trait, but this may not be the case. People in a wide range of disciplines talk about "getting up" for a performance or a game. Athletes, actors, dancers, public speakers, and perhaps even teachers often display a certain amount of anxiety before the big moment. Actors often comment that they have bad performances when they are not nervous beforehand and that the trick is to channel the tension into good energy. Anxiety runs the risk of being particularly debilitative for musicians; you don't want your hands shaking when you're playing the violin. To combat this, some musicians take beta blockers, a drug meant to reduce anxiety. We have heard such musicians comment that they never give really bad performances when on beta blockers, but they never give really good performances either. Without the tension, musicians say, they never really shine.

Bailey (1983) links facilitative anxiety with *competitiveness*. She claims that anxiety causes some learners to become more competitive and spurs them on to greater success. It is an empirical question—it could be answered by testing—whether there are actually two kinds of anxiety or whether anxiety is experienced in differing degrees.

Second language teachers often hear assertions that relaxed learners learn better. Indeed, this was the cornerstone of methodologies like suggestopedia and theories of acquisition such as Krashen's. But is anxiety always a bad thing in a language class? When would you find anxiety facilitative? Would you be more likely to see it as facilitative in hindsight? Does this have implications for language testing? For report cards?

1.5 EMPATHY

Guiora and his colleagues (1972) also stated that there was a correlation between a subject's empathy and his or her success in L2 pronunciation. Empathy is the ability to understand what another person is thinking or feeling in a given situation. The assertion is related to Guiora's idea of language ego, and to the concept that learning an L2 requires the speaker to adopt a different sense of self. For Guiora, the ability to feel empathy goes hand in hand with good second language learning. Other studies, though, such as Naiman, Fröhlich, Stern, and Todesco (1978), did not find a correlation.

Even if we assume the results found by Guiora and his colleagues to be correct, we have got to ask a few questions about their relevance to the classroom. Can you teach empathy? Can you learn empathy? Maybe people are either empathic or not and teaching cannot make a difference.

1.6 EXTROVERSION

Another way in which learners vary is in their degree of extroversion or introversion. Again, we will stick with the commonsense definitions of these terms and assume that an extroverted personality is more outgoing than an introverted, reserved one. All in all, the studies on extroversion have produced mixed results. Kezwer (1987) provides a survey of the literature (Table 15.1). Studies in which extroverted subjects were found to have an advantage indicate a correlation between extroversion and performance.

Table 15.1   Survey of Studies on Extroversion

Study	Effect of extroversion
Cathcart, Strong, and Wong Fillmore (1979)	advantage
Chastain (1975)	mixed
Naiman et al. (1978)	no advantage
Pritchard (1952)	advantage
Rossier (1976)	advantage
Scheibner-Herzig et al. (1984)	no advantage
Strong (1983)	advantage
Suter (1977)	no advantage
Swain and Burnaby (1976)	no advantage
Tucker, Hamayan, and Genesee (1976)	advantage

Source: Data from Kezwer (1987).

Studies have also argued for a correlation between extroversion and *lack* of success at second language learning. Busch (1982) found that in a population of adults learning English in Japan, the introverts were significantly better than extroverts in their pronunciation. One limitation of this study is that it did not also consider the fluency of the subjects. The personality of learners often manifests itself in an emphasis on either accuracy or fluency in a second language. It would not be surprising if the subjects identified as introverts in Busch's study had a preference for accuracy and were not as fluent in their L2 use. Perhaps the extroverts were more concerned with fluency.

As with many of these variables, we have to be very clear what we mean by the word *better* if we are asking whether introverts are better than extroverts at second language learning. Better at what? Better in what way? We also have to consider the medium of communication. Extroversion may be a useful trait when we are conducting certain kinds of oral interactions, but is it going to be helpful when listening, or reading, or writing?

The validity of a test instrument will influence the results. Kezwer (1987) provides examples from some tests of extroversion, revealing the diversity of these instruments. Consider the questions below from different tests. Part of the problem in determining the effect of *x* on second language learning is that the construct *x* is so vague that any test used to measure it will be quite imprecise.

> The Omnibus Personality Inventory is composed of true or false questions in the following form:
>
> > I take an active part in group or class discussions.
> > I do not introduce myself to strangers at social gatherings.
> > I hesitate to borrow money or personal belongings from others.
> > I prefer to work with others rather than alone (Heist and Yonge 1962).
>
> The Eysenck Personality Inventory is composed of yes/no questions such as those below:
>
> > Do you stop and think things over before doing them?
> > Do you often do things on the spur of the moment?
> > Are you mostly quiet when you are with other people?
> > Do you like playing pranks on others? (Eysenck and Eysenck 1963)
>
> The Marlowe-Crowne Social-Desirability Scale had the following kinds of questions:
>
> > Before voting, I thoroughly investigate the qualifications of all the candidates.
> > I sometimes feel resentful when I don't get my way.
> > I always try to practice what I preach.

> There have been times when I was quite jealous of the good for-
> tune of others (Crowne and Marlowe 1964).
>
> Source: Cited in Kezwer (1987).

The question of whether extroverts or introverts are better second language learners is intricately tied to pedagogy. Cultures have different
norms and expectations of how it is appropriate to behave in the classroom. Many students will be accustomed to a teacher-centred or teacher-
dominated classroom, in which their only role is as a passive receptacle
of knowledge. Certainly, current trends in communicative language
teaching do not encourage students to behave in this fashion. This compels us to ask whether a particular methodology can penalize a certain
kind of student. Does communicative language teaching penalize introverted students? Should teachers try to create extroverts in their classroom? Is a silent period, which provides a time to be silent in the L2 at
the beginning stages, appropriate? Does this methodology take cultural
variation into account?

1.7 MOTIVATION

Learners can vary in the amount or type of motivation they have for
learning the second language. Are motivated learners better than unmo-
tivated learners? Are there different kinds of motivation? Gardner and
Lambert (1972) made the distinction between *integrative* and *instrumental*
motivation in second language acquisition, which we saw in Chapter 6.
A person with integrative motivation wants to learn the second language
in order to integrate into the other culture or to gain an appreciation of
it. A person with instrumental motivation wants to learn the second language for a specific reason, such as meeting an M.A. language require-
ment or getting a good job.

Gardner and Lambert (1959) studied English speakers learning French
in Quebec and argued that integrative motivation led to greater success
in second language learning. The results appear tied to context, however,
because Lukmani (1972) found in a study of EFL learners in India that
instrumental motivation was more closely connected with success in L2
learning. Obviously, when we are talking of learning a *foreign* language as
opposed to a *second* language, there is no culture to integrate into.[1]

---

[1] Learning English in Canada outside of Quebec, for example, is referred to as learning English as a *second* language (ESL) because the dominant language of the culture is the one being taught. The students are exposed to the target language
outside the classroom. Learning English in Japan, for example, is referred to as learning English as a *foreign* language (EFL). Students are not exposed to the target language outside the classroom.

Gardner, Day, and MacIntyre (1992) examined second language vocabulary learning in a computer laboratory. They were interested in the effects of both integrative motivation and anxiety on learning new words. Subjects were given a questionnaire to determine their levels of motivation and anxiety. They had to rate statements such as those below:

When I was taking French, I really worked hard to learn the language.
I wish I were fluent in French.
I wish I had never studied French.
French is an important part of any school program in Canada.
I would like to know more French Canadians.
French Canadians have no reason to be proud of their culture.
I would feel calm and sure of myself if I had to order a meal in French in a French restaurant.
I was always afraid other students would laugh at me if I spoke up in French class.
I always avoid speaking in public if possible (201, 202).

Scores on these tests could later be used to see if level of motivation or anxiety was correlated with success on the learning task.

Subjects were treated in two ways: in one group anxiety was induced and in the other it wasn't. The anxiety group received the following instructions on the computer monitor:

We are going to videotape you while you learn the French words in order to evaluate your behaviour. Although it is common for people to become anxious when being videotaped, please do not let this bother you. We are interested in your reactions while you are learning French words and it is necessary to have the video recorder running (203).

The subjects in the control group were not videotaped and did not receive these instructions. Subjects in both groups were asked to indicate their level of anxiety on a thermometer on the computer screen before the learning trials began.

Subjects were told that they had six trials to learn twenty-six rare French nouns. The words were presented as English/French pairs. In each trial, the subject was presented with an English word and asked to type in the French translation. Figure 15.2 illustrates the results. The vertical axis indicates the vocabulary acquisition score. Each of the twenty-six items could earn a possible three points, for a perfect score of seventy-eight. If subjects had to learn the form *le chat,* for example, they would receive one point for getting the article right, two points for getting either the noun correct or the article correct and a reasonable approximation of the French noun, or three points for the exact response. The accuracy scores were noted for each subject on each trial and compared with their scores on the questionnaire. Subjects who scored above the mean in terms of integrative motivation were said to have high IM and those who scored below to have low IM. The high IM group was found to be significantly more accurate than the low group. There was no significant difference between subjects who had anxiety induced and those who did not.

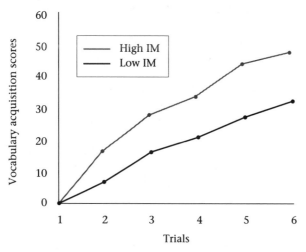

Figure 15.2   Vocabulary Score by Integrative Motivation
Source: Data from Gardner, Day, and MacIntyre (1992).

Figure 15.3 shows another interesting finding, that the amount of time taken on each trial was also associated with the level of motivation. Integratively motivated students started off by taking more time to view the stimulus words than did the non-integratively motivated students. By trial three, however, the reverse was true. The integratively motivated students seemed to be motivated to such an extent that their speed of learning increased. The study found no significant difference in amount of time taken, though, between the anxious group and the non-anxious group. Gardner and his colleagues argue that, in general, integrative motivation is correlated with success in second language learning because it reflects an active involvement in language learning.

As in the preceding study, the subjects in Gardner and MacIntyre (1991) were administered a questionnaire to determine integrative motivation. Different from the preceding study was the experimental treat-

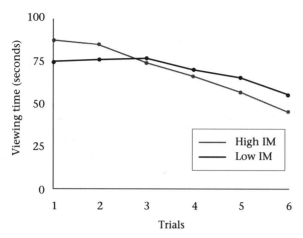

Figure 15.3   Viewing Time by Integrative Motivation
Source: Data from Gardner, Day, and MacIntyre (1992).

ment, which controlled for incentive, or instrumental motivation. Gardner and MacIntyre designed a test similar to the one just discussed but offered the members of one group $10 each if they performed well—got 24 out of 26 words correct—on the final trial of the test. The test was not concerned with anxiety. Figure 15.4 shows the results. That both instrumental and integrative motivation can be successful can be seen when we overlay one factor with the other on a single graph, as shown in Figure 15.5. The scores of the integratively motivated subjects from the first study were almost identical to those of the instrumentally

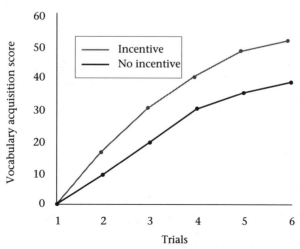

Figure 15.4   Vocabulary Acquisition by Incentive Condition
Source: Data from Gardner and MacIntyre (1991).

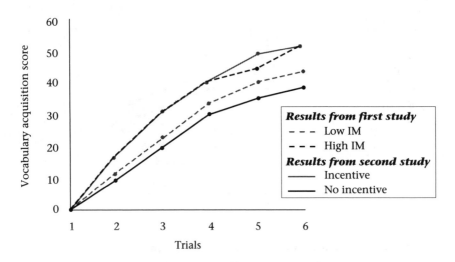

Figure 15.5   Instrumental and Integrative Motivation
Source: Data from Gardner, Day, and MacIntyre (1992) and Gardner and MacIntyre (1991).

motivated subjects from the second study (those with high incentive). The major distinction seemed to be between subjects who had no type of motivation, either instrumental or integrative, and subjects who had either kind of motivation.

1.8 ATTITUDE

Gardner and Lambert (1972) also pointed out the connection between attitudes and motivation. Someone with a good attitude towards a second language or culture is likely to be more motivated to learn that language or become a member of that culture than someone with a negative attitude. Imagine a Canadian who is strongly opposed to official bilingualism trying to learn French. There is a good chance that this person would not be terribly motivated. We can view the chain as follows:

attitude → motivation → success in SLA.

To understand how attitudes can affect either second language learning or second language teaching, consider the following selection of questions from the Foreign Language Attitude Survey for Teachers (FLAST), an instrument designed by Sandra Savignon (1983). Just as teachers' attitudes can affect what goes on in the L2 class, so too can students' attitudes affect their judgment of what is going on in that L2 class.

FOREIGN LANGUAGE ATTITUDE SURVEY FOR TEACHERS (FLAST)

Directions: For each of the following questions decide whether you strongly agree, agree, have no opinion, disagree, or strongly disagree, and check the appropriate box.

1. Mastering the grammar of a second language is a prerequisite to developing oral communication skills.
   strongly agree ☐ ☐ ☐ ☐ ☐ strongly disagree

2. Gestures and other kinesics should be taught and evaluated as an integral part of language acquisition.
   strongly agree ☐ ☐ ☐ ☐ ☐ strongly disagree

3. It is important for students to learn rules of grammar.
   strongly agree ☐ ☐ ☐ ☐ ☐ strongly disagree

4. German and French are harder to learn than Spanish.
   strongly agree ☐ ☐ ☐ ☐ ☐ strongly disagree

5. It is of primary importance that student responses in the target language be linguistically accurate.
   strongly agree ☐ ☐ ☐ ☐ ☐ strongly disagree

6. The sound system of the foreign language should be taught separately and at the beginning of the first sequence of instruction.
   strongly agree ☐ ☐ ☐ ☐ ☐ strongly disagree

7. Dialogue memorization is an effective technique in the process of learning a second language.
   strongly agree ☐ ☐ ☐ ☐ ☐ strongly disagree

8. One cannot teach language without teaching the culture.
   strongly agree ☐ ☐ ☐ ☐ ☐ strongly disagree

9. The teaching of listening and speaking skills should precede reading and writing.
   strongly agree ☐ ☐ ☐ ☐ ☐ strongly disagree

10. Foreign-language teachers need not be fluent themselves to begin to teach effectively for communication.
    strongly agree ☐ ☐ ☐ ☐ ☐ strongly disagree

11. When a student makes syntactical errors, this should be accepted by the teacher as a natural and
    strongly agree ☐ ☐ ☐ ☐ ☐ strongly disagree

inevitable part of language acquisition.

| 12. | If L1 teachers taught grammar as they should, it would be easier for us to teach a second language. | strongly agree ☐ ☐ ☐ ☐ ☐ strongly disagree |
| 13. | Language learning should be fun. | strongly agree ☐ ☐ ☐ ☐ ☐ strongly disagree |

Source: Savignon (1983).

Can teachers motivate students? How? Can teachers accommodate students with different types of motivation? How can teachers deal with negative attitudes revealed in class? How would you respond as a teacher if a student said any of the following: "I don't want to be in that group. Chinese students can't speak English"; "Why should I have to listen to them speak Spanish all the time?"; "I visited France once. All the people were rude to me"? One of the roles of the second language teacher is to dispel linguistic or cultural myths. The classroom is a sheltered place in which to do this. If the teacher doesn't, someone outside the classroom may do it in a much more aggressive fashion.

1.9 PROBLEMS OF MEASUREMENT

Ellis (1986) raised two important points with respect to measuring affective variables. Most tests designed to do so involve self-rating of some kind. The subject might have to rate him or herself in response to a statement such as *I usually talk too much,* for example. Ellis points out that these tests are often culturally biased and difficult to interpret cross-culturally. Consider a subject responding to the sentence *Disobedience to the government is sometimes justified.* Imagine the views of people from El Salvador, Canada, France, and Ethiopia about their respective governments. Can we really compare their answers without considering their background?

As well, Ellis notes that test answers may well reflect what the subject thinks the researcher wants to hear. Imagine that you had to respond to the statement, *I read classical literature (a) often (b) rarely (c) never.* Even though researchers explain that there are no right answers on these kinds of questions, subjects will often give answers that they believe make them look good.

The research to date has not shown a clearly defined effect of personality traits on second language acquisition, probably because problems emerge in defining the terms and designing reliable and valid instruments to measure the qualities under observation. The area is one of considerable intuitive interest to practitioners. Unfortunately, the research is not straightforward.

2 COGNITIVE VARIABLES

Contrasted with affective variables are cognitive variables. Whereas affective factors relate to the emotional side of a person, cognitive factors relate to the intellectual side. Cognitive variables include cognitive style, intelligence, aptitude, and learning strategies. *Cognitive style* refers to a relatively stable aspect of an individual's cognitive make-up. That is to say, we each have a particular cognitive style no matter what the situation, and we do not alter it. *Intelligence* is difficult to define and measure, but we can say that there are different forms of intelligence, which the learner can make use of for different types of learning. *Aptitude*, like cognitive style, is a stable construct. We might think of it as a special talent for a particular type of learning. *Learning strategies* (or cognitive strategies) are specific ways in which an individual attempts to acquire new knowledge. Although our cognitive style is more or less unchanging, we alter our cognitive strategies according to the situation. Each of these variables is examined below.

2.1 COGNITIVE STYLE

Many cognitive styles have been proposed but this section will introduce only two: *field dependence* and *tolerance of ambiguity*. Cognitive psychology outlines these factors in an attempt to explain something about an individual's cognitive functioning. Note that second language acquisition research conducted in this area presupposes a non-modular view of mind; a proposed "general" cognitive factor is assumed to be relevant to language learning. A modular view would suggest that a factor relevant to one cognitive module is not necessarily relevant to any other. For the most part this text has maintained a modular position, but in order to give an accurate picture of the state of the art in the second language field it is necessary to discuss these alternative views.

2.1.1 Field Dependence

A cognitive style is usually binary. In the case of field dependence, an individual is either field dependent or field independent. If your cognitive functioning is *not* impaired by distracting background information then you are field independent. You are able to separate the relevant information from the background field of irrelevant information. In terms of problem solving, you are probably able to find a particular image (say, Waldo) in a picture quickly. In other cognitive domains, you may be able to read and concentrate on a moving bus or train without being distracted. Maybe you can study with loud noise around you. On the other hand, if you tend to take in the whole picture rather than focussing on certain parts then you are most likely field dependent.

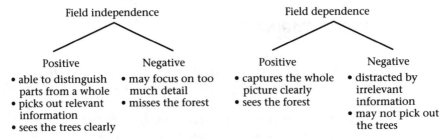

Figure 15.6   Field Independence and Dependence

There are positive and negative characteristics to both styles. Figure 15.6 illustrates the good and bad points of field independence and dependence. Field independent people tend to be more independent, competitive, and self-confident. Field dependent people tend to be more socialized and empathic.

A few studies have looked at the relationship between field dependence and second language acquisition. Naiman and colleagues (1978), in their good language learner study, found that field independence correlated positively with success in the second language classroom. Judging from the dominant teaching style at the time, we should keep in mind that the classroom under study probably favoured analytical tasks and competition. We could argue that field independent learners will be more accurate and hence judged as successful in certain types of language classrooms. It is possible that field dependent learners tend to favour fluency over accuracy and will be more successful in terms of broader communicative competence as a result of their greater empathy. A number of studies have noted that children are predominantly field dependent. This would fit in nicely if we wanted to argue that children were better than adults at learning second languages.

2.1.2 Tolerance of Ambiguity

Someone who is tolerant of ambiguity is receptive to information that is not consistent with his or her current cognitive system. The application of this cognitive style to language learning is obvious. Learning a second language always involves assimilating a great deal of contradictory information. Table 15.2 offers some hypothetical instances of ambiguity experienced by a learner of English.

Learners have different ways of responding to ambiguity. Some learners are quite intolerant of it (*What a stupid language!*); others accept that not everything can be described by an exceptionless rule. It appears that successful second language learning requires the learner to be tolerant of ambiguity. Both Naiman and colleagues (1978) and Chapelle and Roberts (1986) found a positive correlation between tolerance of ambiguity and success in second language learning.

Table 15.2   Assimilating Contradictions

What your teacher tells you	What you hear the next day
"You make plurals by adding -s"	child/children
"You make past tense by adding -ed"	take/took
"Tag questions are negative if the main clause is positive. You say 'It's raining, isn't it?' for example."	"You know Mel Gibson, do you?"

What the word means in English	What it means in L1
embarrassed	*embarasado* (Spanish) = pregnant

2.1.3 Summary of Cognitive Styles

It is very difficult to define and measure cognitive style. Can we really characterize styles across cognitive modules? And can we really be sure that we have valid tests? Does a test claiming to measure tolerance of ambiguity actually measure it? Until accurate tests become feasible and valid, it is difficult to see research in this domain moving beyond the anecdotal. It may well describe certain learner behaviour but it does not go very far in explaining it.

Children and adults have quite different metalinguistic awareness...

Father: Let's start with grammar.... Parse this sentence please. "The boy hit the ball with the bat." Well?

Son: I don't know what you mean.

Father: Parse this sentence. Analyse it grammatically. Come on. What is the subject?

Son: Oh, easy! Baseball.

Father: No, Frank. But tell me this, what is the object?

Son: To hit the ball with the bat.

Father: Away you go Frank, I'll be right there.

David Archibald
Schofield: The Sleepless Tiger, Act I, scene v

2.2 INTELLIGENCE

As with affective variables and cognitive styles, there is once again an inherent problem of definition and measurement in looking at the effects of intelligence on second language acquisition. Are people with high intelligence better second language learners? A question framed in this way compels us to be clear about how to determine who has high intelligence and who doesn't. There is, of course, something called an IQ test, which is often used to measure intelligence, but using one for this purpose is problematic. Gould (1981) discusses the issue in depth, but we will only consider it briefly.

Gould argues, first, that IQ tests are not sensitive to certain cultural differences. Some questions taken from real tests—*How tall is the average Canadian male?* and *How many nickels in a dime?* for example—do not reveal intelligence as much as knowledge of a particular culture. We will return to this problem in Chapter 21 when we look at minority language education. Second, Gould refers to the *reification of intelligence*. By this he means the assumption that intelligence is a single, quantifiable thing. If we want to ask whether people of high intelligence are better at second language acquisition, we need to be able to say that person x has intelligence of 4 whereas person y has intelligence of only 2, and then check their respective second language proficiency.

Gardner (1983) proposed an interesting alternative to this reified view in his book, *Frames of Mind: The Theory of Multiple Intelligences*. He describes seven forms of knowing, which give us a much broader view of the nature of intelligence:

1. Linguistic intelligence
   • ability to use language
2. Logico-mathematical intelligence
   • ability to solve logical problems
3. Spatial intelligence
   • ability to handle the environment and form mental images of reality
4. Musical intelligence
   • ability to perceive and create pitch and rhythm patterns
5. Bodily kinesthetic intelligence
   • fine motor movement; athletic prowess
6. Interpersonal intelligence
   • ability to understand others
7. Intrapersonal intelligence
   • ability to see oneself

Gardner suggests that by looking only at the first two, as standard IQ tests do, we ignore a great deal of valuable human ability. Gardner may have given us a new way of looking at variation in second language learning, too. Which aspects of second language learning do you think each of the intelligences would be useful for? Musical intelligence, for example, might help us to master prosodic phonology, or intonation.

A few studies have investigated the relation of IQ to second language proficiency. Genesee (1976) found that IQ score was related to the development of academic second language skills (reading, grammar, vocabulary) but not to oral production skills (as judged by native speakers). Ekstrand (1977) found that IQ scores had low correlation with listening comprehension and oral production but higher correlation with reading comprehension and free writing.

Although these results appear inconclusive, there is a way to reconcile them. Cummins (1984) makes the distinction between two different kinds of language proficiency: basic interpersonal communication skills (BICS); and cognitive academic language proficiency (CALP). He suggests that although everyone acquires BICS to the same level in their first language, the level of CALP they achieve varies. There is also considerable overlap between the constructs of BICS and context-embedded language use and of CALP and context-reduced language use. Academic language use tends to be context-reduced, and everyday language use tends to be context-embedded. The term context-embedded refers to language that allows someone to predict or determine a considerable amount of meaning from the situation alone. If you are at a hockey game and the fan next to you leans over and says something, you already have ideas about possible meanings. The empirical studies suggest a correlation between IQ score and context-reduced language use (or CALP), but no correlation with context-embedded language use (or BICS).

2.3 APTITUDE

For many years, researchers have been interested in discovering whether good second language learners possess a special quality that bad second language learners lack. This property is most often termed *aptitude*. Skehan (1991) suggests that it assumes the existence of a talent for learning languages that is independent of intelligence or previous learning experiences, relatively stable within an individual, and varies from person to person. Aptitude is not necessarily thought of as a single construct. Carroll (1965) broke it down into four components:

1. *Phonemic coding ability*: not simply the capacity to make sound discriminations, but also to code foreign sounds in such a way that they can be recalled later.
2. *Associative memory*: the ability to bond or make connections between stimuli (native language words) and responses (target language words).
3. *Grammatical sensitivity*: the ability to recognize the functions that words fulfill in sentences (*not* the ability to analyse sentences overtly).
4. *Inductive language learning ability*: the ability to examine language materials and from this to notice and identify patterns of correspondence and relationships involving either meaning or syntactic form (cited in Skehan 1991, 277).

Skehan (1991) suggests that different second language learners emphasize different factors among the four, leading to variation in both the process and the product of language acquisition.

Skehan (1989) conducted a very interesting study to follow up Gordon Wells's Bristol Study. Wells (1986), discussed in detail in Chapter 19, reported on a longitudinal study of first language acquisition that attempted to determine the effects on children of such things as socio-economic status and input from parents and teachers. In 1985, Skehan administered tests of foreign language aptitude to the students whose first language acquisition Gordon Wells had studied. At the time, the students were between the ages of thirteen and sixteen. He also collected information on the subjects' foreign language achievement, as measured by school marks.

Skehan noted significant correlations between the students' first language abilities described in Wells's study and both their foreign language aptitude and their performance in foreign languages at school. Wells had argued that one of the significant variables among first language learners was their ability to handle context-reduced language. Skehan suggested that students who were succeeding at foreign languages in high school could also handle context-reduced language. This might have been related to the way in which second languages were taught in school, where context-reduced language is emphasized.

Wells also found that later achievement at school could be significantly predicted by looking at a child's knowledge of literacy at the start of school. Children who arrived at school with general knowledge of how print worked were more likely to succeed at school than those who did not. The same was true for foreign languages in this population. Skehan speculated that if second languages were taught less like other subjects, we might not see this correlation. He argued, then, that foreign language aptitude was a combination of the four factors proposed by Carroll and skill at handling language without a rich context.

Skehan's results suggest that variation in ability to deal with context-reduced language may reflect not the subject's intelligence but something about the first language environment, such as how often the child was read to at home. Also, the study implies that if foreign language classes in school did not favour context-reduced language proficiency, we might not see the difference between groups of students. Students who have difficulty dealing with context-reduced language in either L1 or L2 may not find context-embedded language, or basic communication skills, so difficult in their L2. Clearly, this is borne out by the fact that many, probably most, bilinguals do not write essays or read academic texts in their second language but instead use the language to communicate in everyday situations.

2.4 LEARNING STRATEGIES

A great deal of attention has recently been devoted to the strategies that learners use when trying to learn something new in a second language. As was discussed in Chapter 5, a learner uses communication strategies to keep communication going when there is a gap in his or her knowledge. *Learning strategies,* on the other hand, are designed to fill that gap permanently. According to Weinstein and Mayer, a learning strategy is designed to "affect the learner's motivational or affective state, or the way in which the learner selects, acquires, organizes, or integrates new knowledge" (1986, 315). Obviously, second language learners need to be able to use both kinds of strategies.

Much learning strategy research has been conducted within cognitive learning theory, which maintains that language learning is a complex cognitive skill described by general principles of learning. As happens when we acquire any complex skill—learning to play chess, for example—we use strategies that influence our success or failure.

Learning strategies are usually divided into three types: *metacognitive*, *cognitive*, and *social/affective*. Metacognitive strategies involve planning, monitoring, or evaluating learning. Thinking that you should pay attention to what a teacher writes on the board because it is probably important is an example of a metacognitive strategy. Cognitive strategies operate directly on incoming information to organize or restructure it, by classifying words according to their attributes or meaning, for example. Social/affective strategies involve the ways in which someone interacts in a social environment, such as co-operating with other learners. In a study of beginning ESL students, Chamot and O'Malley (1990) noted numerous learning strategies, shown in Table 15.3.

Table 15.3 Learning Strategies in the Classroom

Strategy Name	Strategy Description	Strategy Definition
Metacognitive strategies		
Planning		
Advance organization	Preview Skim Gist	Previewing the main ideas and concepts of a text; identifying the organizing principle
Organizational planning	Plan what to do	Planning how to accomplish the learning task; planning the parts and sequence of ideas to express
Selective attention	Listen or read selectively Scan Find specific information	Attending to key words, phrases, ideas, linguistic markers, types of information
Self-management	Plan when, where, and how to study	Seeking or arranging the conditions that help one learn
Monitoring		
Monitoring comprehension	Think while listening Think while reading	Checking one's comprehension during listening or reading
Monitoring production	Think while speaking Think while writing	Checking one's oral or written production while it is taking place
Evaluating		
Self-assessment	Check back Keep a learning log Reflect on what you have learned	Judging how well one has accomplished a learning task

Table 15.3   Continued

Strategy Name	Strategy Description	Strategy Definition
Cognitive strategies		
Resourcing	Use reference materials	Using reference materials such as dictionaries, encyclopedias, or textbooks
Grouping	Classify Construct graphic organizers	Classifying words, terminology, quantities, or concepts according to their attributes
Note-taking	Take notes on idea maps, T-lists, etc.	Writing down key words and concepts in abbreviated verbal, graphical, or numerical form
Elaboration of prior knowledge	Use what you know Use background knowledge Make analogies	Relating new to known information and making personal associations
Summarizing	Say or write the main idea	Making a mental, oral, or written summary of information gained from listening or reading
Deduction/ induction	Use a rule/Make a rule	Applying or figuring out rules to understand a concept or complete a learning task
Imagery	Visualize Make a picture	Using mental or real pictures to learn new information or solve a problem
Auditory representation	Use your mental tape recorder Hear it again	Replaying mentally a word, phrase, or piece of information
Making inferences	Use context clues Guess from context Predict	Using information in the text to guess meanings of new items or predict upcoming information
Social/Affective strategies		
Questioning for clarification	Ask questions	Getting additional explanation or verification from a teacher or other expert
Co-operation	Co-operate Work with classmates Coach each other	Work with peers to complete a task, pool information, solve a problem, get feedback
Self-talk	Think positive	Reducing anxiety by improving one's sense of competence

Source: Chamot and O'Malley (1994).

Empirical studies involving questionnaires, interviews, and other techniques have demonstrated that different language learners use different strategies, but are certain patterns of strategy use preferred? Is there any correlation between second language ability and learning strategy?

O'Malley and Chamot (1990) observed that advanced students used a much wider range of learning strategies than did beginners and argued that foreign language aptitude was really the result of optimal strategy use, not a stable cognitive trait.

Before we can ask whether there is a correlation between x and L2 proficiency, however, we need an explicit description of x. Current literature is trying to standardize the list of learning strategies. If this is accomplished, the causal connection can be investigated but it is not yet possible to do so.

3 EXCEPTIONAL LANGUAGE LEARNERS

A few studies have looked at exceptionally good language learners in detail. Obler (1989) presented a case study of a subject called CJ. CJ learned several languages after puberty and was judged to have gained nativelike proficiency in all of them. These judgments were confirmed by native speakers and included an evaluation of his pronunciation. Obler was interested in investigating why CJ was so good at learning second languages.

It emerged, among other facts, that CJ displayed what is known as the *Geschwind cluster* of characteristics. Norman Geschwind was a neurologist who noted (Geschwind and Galaburda 1987) that at a particular time during fetal development a certain balance of hormonal levels consistently resulted in individuals who were left-handed, had a twin, had allergies, and were homosexual. CJ displayed all of these traits. Geschwind had observed that the hormonal balance of the fetus affected the developing endocrinological system as well as the areas of the cortex related to language. Thus, according to Obler and Geschwind, there could be a very real biological reason for CJ's profile of abilities. His overall intellectual ability as measured by a standard IQ test was not out of the ordinary, but he was exceptionally strong in vocabulary, acquisition of new codes, and perception of formal patterns. His visual/spatial ability appeared to be below normal and his musical ability was average. His verbal memory was outstanding.

Obler argued that there was something special about CJ's brain which made him suited to being an exceptional L2 learner. While traditional left-dominance of the brain might allow people to learn second languages *well*, Obler maintained that truly exceptional ability was limited to those with more *bilateral* organization. That is to say, only those individuals with less dominance than usual by the left hemisphere will be exceptional.

4 GOOD LANGUAGE LEARNERS

Various researchers have produced lists of the qualities exhibited by good language learners. Some are offered here to conclude the chapter. According to Rubin (1975), the good language learner

- is a willing and accurate guesser
- has a strong drive to communicate
- is uninhibited
- attends to form
- practises by seeking out conversations
- monitors his or her own speech and the speech of others
- attends to meaning

According to Stern (1975), the good language learner

- has a personal learning style or positive learning strategies
- has an active approach to the learning task
- has a tolerant and outgoing approach to the target language and empathy with its speakers
- has technical know-how about how to tackle a language
- has strategies of experimentation and planning with the object of developing the new language into an ordered system and of revising this system progressively
- is consistently searching for meaning
- is willing to practise
- is willing to use the language in real communication
- has self-monitoring ability and critical sensitivity to language use
- is able to develop the target language more and more as a separate reference system and is able to learn to think in it

Finally, according to Ellis (1986), the good language learner will

- be able to avoid developing negative anxiety and inhibitions in response to the group dynamics of the learning context
- seek out all opportunities to use the target language
- make maximum use of the opportunities afforded to practise listening to and responding to speech in the L2 addressed to him and to others, attending to meaning rather than to form
- supplement learning derived from direct contact with speakers of the L2 with learning derived from study techniques (such as making vocabulary lists) and involving attention to form
- be an adolescent or an adult rather than a young child, at least during the early stages of grammatical development
- possess sufficient analytic skills to perceive, categorize, and store the linguistic features of the L2, and also to monitor errors
- possess a strong reason for learning the L2 (which may reflect an integrative or an instrumental motivation) and also develop a strong "task

motivation," responding positively to the learning tasks chosen or provided
- be prepared to experiment by taking risks, even if they make him or her appear foolish
- be capable of adapting to different learning conditions

Clearly, the definitive list of characteristics has not been and may never be developed. The lists above are not only a summary of the research but also a starting point for discussion.

5 CONCLUSION

Without a doubt, learners vary and so do interlanguages. The beginning of this chapter suggested a framework for discussing individual variation in second language learning: Does *x* make the learner better at SLA? It also called for explicitness in determining what *x* was, what it meant to be *better*, and which aspects of SLA were being referred to. We have looked at such *x* factors as self-esteem, extroversion, empathy, field dependence, and aptitude, to name a few. In almost every case, there is no straightforward definition of *x*. Nor is it always easy to determine what being better at a particular aspect of language entails. Can someone be better than another person at L2 morphology? Finally, we cannot really predict if a particular psychological factor will affect some areas of communicative competence and not others. Would you expect risk taking, for example, to affect pronunciation more than it affects textual competence? If so, why?

The literature on individual variation in second language acquisition tackles a very fuzzy area, but this is not necessarily bad. True, we are not yet able to explain or predict how psychological factors will be correlated with second language ability, much less any causal relationships, but we are gathering more and more interesting data within the framework. The data will one day have to be explained, not just described. We leave the last word to Kevin Gregg: "Variation is, rather, like the aurora borealis: a fascinating and puzzling phenomenon" (1990, 379).[2]

CLASSROOM IMPLICATIONS

The study of variation in second language learning has made it very clear that people do things in different ways. In light of this conclusion, do you think individual instruction would be better than class instruction?

---

[2] Gregg was arguing against the idea of variable competence and suggesting that variation should be part of a theory of interlanguage performance. Although his comment is therefore taken rather out of context, it applies here too.

Would it be feasible to group students by some category other than proficiency level, such as cognitive style or affective variables? How would you feel if your second language teacher did that? Is it the domain of second language teachers or of psychotherapists to try changing students with respect to affective factors? Do teachers have the training to do so? Do they have the right?

SELF TEST

L2 learners can vary in a number of significant ways. _____
(1)
variables are concerned with the emotional side of SLA. Certain factors probably cluster in an individual. Low self-esteem, for example, may be correlated with inhibition and _____ to take risks. The anxi-
(2)
ety that SLA can cause might influence the _____ of the
(3)
learner. _____ motivation has been shown to correlate with
(4)
success in SLA.

Non-emotional factors such as _____ style also vary from
(5)
learner to learner. Studies done on the effects of the relationship between general _____ and language _____ have led to less
(6)   (7)
clear results.

Learners also vary in the _____ they use to fill gaps in their
(8)
L2 knowledge. (The learner uses _____ , on the other hand, to
(9)
keep communication going.)

All in all, the question of whether x makes someone a better L2 learner is not straightforward. Although some _____ have
(10)
been established, causal relations are much less certain.

FURTHER READING

Skehan, P. 1991. *Individual Differences in Second Language Learning.* London: Edward Arnold.

Stevick, E. 1989. *Success with Foreign Languages.* Englewood Cliffs, NJ: Prentice-Hall.

CHAPTER 16

The Effects of Instruction

The next three chapters deal with different factors external to the learner. Second language learners are exposed to the L2 in a variety of environments, and researchers are interested in investigating how this variation affects learning. This chapter discusses research on the effects of instruction, looking at the environment of the classroom. Chapter 17 examines the environmental characteristics known as input and interaction. In or out of a classroom, learners are exposed to numerous input types and styles of interaction. Chapter 18 explores feedback: a type of response to the learner that mixes instruction, input, and interaction. Second language learners often receive feedback on their performance, frequently in the form of error correction. The next three chapters, then, are thematically related, dealing with the linguistic environment of the learner. We turn now to a discussion of the classroom environment.

One of the major concerns of many people engaged in second language acquisition research is the effect of instruction on second language learning. Ultimately, researchers would like to determine which classroom characteristics lead to successful learning. This text has not yet considered *teaching* in much detail but we can begin to do so in the model of classroom teaching shown in Figure 16.1.

The model illustrates how complex a construct instruction is. When we ask whether it influences SLA, we need to be explicit about the meaning of instruction. Most often, it describes what goes on inside of language classrooms, and many factors are involved. Both teachers and students bring different knowledge and experience to the classroom, which will influence the teaching and learning that take place.

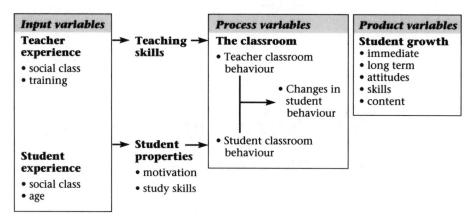

Figure 16.1   A Model of Classroom Teaching
Source: Adapted from Dunkin and Biddle (1974).

This chapter deals primarily with the *process* variables in the classroom box of Figure 16.1. In other words, we will be looking at the nature of teacher and student behaviour in real classrooms. Clearly, there is no isomorphic relationship between what the teacher teaches and what the student learns. Their varied backgrounds cause students to take different meanings from the same teaching. Certain types of research try to establish generalizations, however, by looking at how particular kinds of instruction affect groups of learners.

The main issue in this field is whether language instruction helps learning. In a study devoted to answering just that question, Long (1983) concluded that instruction does help, all other factors being equal. If you are planning to be a second language teacher, perhaps you can breathe a sigh of relief at this point. Long argued that instruction can contribute more positively to acquisition than can naturalistic exposure. Nevertheless, the issue has to be looked at more closely. We need to consider which features of classroom instruction lead to improvement of which aspects of which learners' development. It is clear that some activities may aid the acquisition of certain aspects of language, such as pronunciation or vocabulary, without affecting others. Table 16.1 lists the results of eleven studies investigating whether instruction makes a difference and a twelfth showing that exposure is a positive factor.

1 SECOND LANGUAGE CLASSROOMS

Chaudron (1988) summarizes three major issues in the field of second language pedagogy: learning from instruction, from teacher talk, and from interaction in the classroom. The remainder of this chapter invest-

Table 16.1   Studies on the Effect of Instruction

Studies showing that instruction helps

Brière (1978)
Carroll (1967)
Chihara and Oller (1978)
Krashen, Jones, Zelinski, and Usprich (1978)
Krashen and Seliger (1976)
Krashen, Seliger, and Hartnett (1974)

Ambiguous cases

Fathman (1976)
Hale and Budar (1970)

Studies showing that instruction does not help

Fathman (1975)
Mason (1971)
Upshur (1968)

Study showing that exposure helps

Martin (1980)

Source: Data from Long (1983, 375).

igates some research that falls into the first category; Chapter 17 deals at length with the second and third.

The question of whether instruction affects learning has been debated for some time. Krashen (1981) argued that the effect of instruction was limited. He contended that the main role of the classroom was to provide the learner with *comprehensible input*. Formal instruction, however, especially instruction focussed on grammatical form, would have no long-term beneficial effects on the learner's development. Long (1983) disagreed with Krashen, maintaining that one advantage of instruction over naturalistic contexts[1] was its treatment of language as an object. He believed that metalinguistic awareness was useful and led to better management of complex linguistic rules. Pienemann (1989), whose work is discussed later in this chapter, argued that instruction could speed up learners' progress but could not cause them to deviate from their pre-ordained "natural" learning paths.

A great deal of research has been devoted to investigating the characteristics of teacher talk. Teacher talk is the language that second language teachers use to talk to their students. It is of primary interest to determine which characteristics of teacher talk aid second language learning.

Interaction in the classroom is closely related to the issue of teacher talk. Learners in L2 classrooms are not only exposed to modified input

---

[1] It is a traditional dichotomy to talk of *classrooms* versus *natural* or *naturalistic* contexts. We are not entirely convinced that classroom time is filled with unnatural acts but will adopt the standard terminology.

THE ENGLISH LESSON

[Scene iv. The French King's palace]
Enter Katharine and Alice, an old gentlewoman.

Kath.   Alice, tu as été en Angleterre, et tu parles bien le langage.
Alice.   Un peu, madame.
Kath.   Je te prie, m'enseignez; il faut que j'apprenne à parler.
          Comment appelez-vous la main en Anglois?
Alice.   La main? elle est appelée de hand.
Kath.   De hand. Et les doigts?
Alice.   Les doigts? ma foi, j'oublie les doigts; mais je me souviendrai.
          Les doigts? je pense qu'ils sont appelés de fingres; oui, de
          fingres.
Kath.   La main, de hand; les doigts, de fingres. Je pense que je suis le
          bon écolier; j'ai gagné deux mots d'Anglois vîtement.
          Comment appelez-vous les ongles?
Alice.   Les ongles? nous les appelons de nails.
Kath.   De nails. Écouter; dites-moi, si je parle bien: de hand, de
          fingres, et de nails.
Alice.   C'est bien dit, madame; il est fort bon Anglois.

William Shakespeare
Henry the Fifth, Act III, scene iv

---

but are also involved in modified interactions. Long (1983) asserts that these are, in fact, more important to learners than the modified input.

2 MORPHEME ACQUISITION IN NATURALISTIC AND INSTRUCTED LEARNERS

Pica (1983) focussed on some of the differences among three learning contexts: naturalistic, instructed, and mixed second language learning. She worked with native speakers of Spanish who were learning English as a second language. Six subjects were chosen for each learning context, exhibiting a fairly wide range of proficiency. She determined the subjects' level of proficiency by looking at the developmental stage each had reached in producing English negation.

The developmental path shown in Figure 16.2 has been proposed for learning English (Cazden et al. 1975). During the first stage of development, learners tend to negate sentences by placing the word *no* in front of the verb, as in *I no want more* or *He no say that.* At the second stage, they begin to use *don't* but show no knowledge of its morphological complexity. They produce sentences like *They don't go there, He don't say that,* and *I don't study tomorrow.* At the third stage, they show that they have analysed the internal structure of *don't* by using the other forms of *do + not,* such as *They don't go there, He didn't say that,* and *She doesn't like me.*

No + verb	Unanalysed *don't* + verb	Analysed *don't*
Beginners	Intermediate	Advanced

Figure 16.2   Developmental Stages of English Negation

Each subject was interviewed about the same range of topics, thus controlling for possible contextual variation, and approximately one hour of free speech was transcribed and analysed. Let us look now at Pica's techniques of analysis.

2.1 SOC ANALYSIS

As we saw in Chapter 4, an SOC analysis looks at a given linguistic element that is *supplied in obligatory contexts.* Pica examined nine grammatical morphemes in the speech of learners and determined whether they used each morpheme where it was obligatory for a native speaker. The plural morpheme, for example, is obligatory in a construction like *I have two brothers.* If we want to get a picture of how well a particular subject uses the English plural, we identify all the places in the transcript where a native speaker would have used the plural and then check whether the non-native speaker did.

All of the groups behaved very similarly with respect to this type of analysis. It did not appear that the learning context significantly affected learner behaviour when all nine morphemes were analysed. Pica did, however, find some differences in two morphemes. The instruction-only group scored 19 percentage points higher—that is, were more accurate— on plural -*s* than were the other two groups. Also, the instruction-only group scored 38 percent and 41 percent higher than the naturalistic and mixed groups on third person singular -*s.*[2] Pica notes that both of these morphemes have transparent form–function relationships. It is clear and well-defined what the morphemes look like and do. Not all aspects of language are this transparent. She suggests that in those aspects of the grammar that have transparent form–function relationships, instruction is particularly effective.

---

[2] As in *She walks to work every day.*

2.2 TLU ANALYSIS

Pica also conducted what is known as a TLU analysis of the subjects' language: a *target-like use* analysis. This involves looking not just at accurate use in obligatory contexts but also at use in *non-obligatory* contexts. Let us look at two hypothetical learners to see what the different analytical techniques reveal. Imagine that by examining both learners' transcripts for use of the plural morpheme in obligatory contexts (SOC), we find numerous phrases such as those listed in Table 16.2.

Table 16.2   Plural Morphemes in SOC Analysis

Subject (1)	Subject (2)
two cats	two cats
some dogs	some dogs
all the babies	all the babies

Both subjects supply the plural -*s* in about 95 percent of obligatory contexts. It would therefore be tempting to conclude that they both have equal and advanced control over the plural -*s* marker. But now we conduct a TLU analysis to investigate *every* instance in which the subjects use the plural -*s*. We find phrases of the sort shown in Table 16.3. We can see that Subject (1) is making errors on the plural -*s* that Subject (2) is not. Subject (1) does not seem to have acquired the distinction between count nouns and mass, or non-count, nouns in English. Thus, the TLU test gives us another view of the competence of the subjects.

Table 16.3   Plural Morphemes in TLU Analysis

Subject (1)	Subject (2)
two cats	two cats
some dogs	some dogs
all the babies	all the babies
some informations	some information
two medicines	two doses of medicine
all the sugars	all the sugar

TLU analysis of Pica's data revealed an interesting difference between the instruction-only group and the other two groups. Pica found that learners who had never received formal instruction in the L2 tended to *omit* grammatical morphemes such as past tense -*ed*, whereas classroom learners tended to *overapply* this type of morphological marking. She distinguished between two types of overapplication: overgeneralization errors, such as *She taked a ride on the bike;* and overuse in non-obligatory contexts, such as *I studied them now.*

All learners made all types of errors, but the instructed learners made the overapplication errors significantly more often than the uninstructed learners. Learners in the mixed context performed like the uninstructed learners when they were at low proficiency levels but became more like instructed learners as their proficiency increased.

Pica drew two conclusions:

1. Similarities in morpheme difficulty across the three learning contexts suggest that much of second language acquisition depends on variation among learners, not contextual factors.
2. Instruction affects L2 production by triggering overuse of grammatical morphology, and by inhibiting ungrammatical constructions.

She cautions that no conclusions regarding rate of acquisition or ultimate attainment can be drawn from her study.

3 RELATIVE CLAUSE FORMATION IN NATURALISTIC AND INSTRUCTED LEARNERS

Pavesi (1984) compared relative clause formation in instructed and naturalistic learners. The instructed learners were forty-eight Italian high school students, aged fourteen to eighteen, who had received an average of four years of grammar-based English language instruction in Italy and who had no informal exposure to English. The naturalistic learners were thirty-eight Italian workers in Edinburgh, aged nineteen to fifty, who had received either no formal English instruction at all or only a minimal amount. They had been in Britain an average of six years. The two groups were non-equivalent in a number of ways—age, hours of exposure to English, and socio-economic status among them[3]—which made it difficult to determine causal relationships. Nonetheless, some interesting facts emerged.

Pavesi analysed relative clause formation. Remember the work of Keenan and Comrie (1977) describing some universal patterns in relative clause formation, which we looked at in Chapter 8 of this text. They claimed that there was a universal hierarchy of grammatical relations out of which relativization could take place, and described this in terms of an implicational hierarchy:

Subject > Direct object > Indirect object > Oblique > Genitive > Object
    of comparative

---

[3] The instructed learners were younger. The naturalistic group was exposed to much more English, had lower status, and less education.

As we saw in Chapter 8, a language that can form a relative clause out of any of the above positions can also form one out of all the positions to its *left* in the hierarchy but not necessarily to the right. So, if a language can form a relative clause out of the indirect object position, it will also be able to relativize out of the direct object and subject positions, but we know nothing of its ability to relativize out of the positions to the right.

Pavesi found that the school students outperformed the naturalistic learners. They did better on less marked structures (the ones to the left in the hierarchy) than on more marked structures (the ones to the right), and they were much more successful at relativizing the marked end of the scale than were the naturalistic learners.

Another difference between the two groups was in the *kind* of errors that they made. The two groups made different use of resumptive nominals and pronominal copies in their relative clauses. The following examples make those terms clear. Naturalistic learners showed significantly more noun retention—or resumptive nominals—in the relative clause than did the instructed learners, as in *The man who I am looking at the man is my father.* The noun phrase is retained in the relative clause. The instructed learners, on the other hand, used significantly more pronominal copies than the naturalistic learners, as in *The man who I am looking at him is my father.* Neither Italian nor English allows either of these structures.

Pavesi claims that the instructed group's superior performance derives from the greater amount of *complex* input that they received in their second language classroom. This explanation is not entirely satisfying, however, because we do not know whether the complex input was salient to the subjects. Clearly, exposure to complex input is not enough. If it were, we would simply have to immerse ourselves in complex language in order to pick it up. The learner must also be able to *process* the input.

It is possible, however, that formal instruction gives learners the ability to focus their attention on certain aspects of the complex input selectively. Humans are very good at paying selective attention to input forms. On hearing a text in a second language, you would probably be able to listen for every occurrence of a plural morpheme *or* every occurrence of the progressive morpheme *or* every occurrence of a subjunctive, but you would most likely be unable to listen for every occurrence of all three. Instruction on a particular structure, or function, may well allow you to focus your attention selectively on that element. In this way, instruction may help to make complex input more accessible to the listener.

Schmidt and Frota (1986) suggest in a study of L2 learners' diaries[4] that in order to acquire a given form, the learner needs to be *aware* of it

---

[4] In a diary study, a second language learner keeps a diary of impressions during a learning experience, usually over several months, which researchers then study.

in the input. It is not sufficient for the form to be taught, drilled, and in the input. The learner must also notice it. Ellis (1990), discussed later in the chapter, suggests that instruction may help the learner to notice certain forms in the input.

4 EFFECT OF INSTRUCTION ON ACQUISITION SEQUENCES

Patsy Lightbown and several colleagues in Montreal conducted a number of studies looking at the effect of instruction on acquisitional sequences (Lightbown 1983; Lightbown, Spada, and Wallace 1980). They undertook both longitudinal and cross-sectional studies on francophone children aged eleven to seventeen who were learning English as a second language. Few of the students had much contact with English outside the classroom. In the first year of the study, Lightbown looked at 175 children in Grades 6, 8, and 10. The next year, one hundred of the same children participated in the study while they were in Grades 7, 9, and 11. As Pica did, Lightbown investigated grammatical morphemes like plural -s, progressive -ing, and so on.

As Pica would have predicted, the subjects made large numbers of overuse errors, such as *The girls want a cookie* when describing a picture of one girl. The study found no significant correlation between frequency of items in the teacher's speech or in the classroom materials and either the frequency or accuracy of students' use of these grammatical morphemes. That is to say, if one teacher used a higher number of plurals than another, students in the first class were not likely to use more plurals or to use them with greater accuracy than students in the other class.

The Grade 6 class received intensive formal instruction on -ing early in the school year. This led to frequent use of -ing by the students throughout the year even though it was relatively *infrequent* in classroom language after the period of formal instruction. The students tended to overuse -ing, but after other verb forms such as simple present and imperatives were introduced, neither of which has overt morphological marking,[5] both overuse and *accurate* use of -ing declined. The students tended to favour the uninflected forms of the verb. Interestingly, these uninflected forms are generally also favoured by uninstructed learners right from the start. Lightbown concluded that, in this case, instruction appeared to alter acquisition only temporarily and quite trivially.

---

[5] I *walk* to school every day (simple present); *Walk* over here! (imperative); I am *walking* home from work today (progressive).

5 EFFECT OF INSTRUCTION ON THE RATE OF ACQUISITION

A study done by Gass (1982) supports the claim that instruction can speed up the rate of second language acquisition. Gass applied Keenan and Comrie's hierarchy not to languages but to individuals. She provided an experimental group with explicit instruction on relativization on the object of the preposition (what Keenan and Comrie call *oblique*). A control group received instruction on relativization only in subject and object positions. The experimental group showed significant improvement not just on relativization of objects of a preposition, but also on all positions to the left on the implicational hierarchy. This is exactly what the hierarchy predicts. Languages and individuals appear to be behaving in the same way. The control group did *not* show a similar improvement on items to the right on the hierarchy. Again, this is what the hierarchy would predict.

Gass's study shows that explicit instruction is able to speed up second language learning but does not say that the acquisitional sequence can be altered. No subjects were able to relativize out of, say, subject and genitive positions; nobody skipped a stage. It is of course interesting to ask why this might be. All of these forms occur in the input to the learner outside of the classroom. The effect of instruction could be either to change the learner's ability to focus on certain aspects of the input or to change the input so that the learner is exposed to the most useful input. Further research would have to be conducted to tease apart these alternatives.

6 THE TEACHABILITY OF LANGUAGE

We turn now to the work of Manfred Pienemann. Pienemann (1989) investigates what he calls the *teachability* of language. He views this as the flip side of learnability. Many linguists are concerned with developing a model of the grammar that can be learned; Pienemann wants to know if language can be taught. Central to Pienemann's research is the idea of general stages of acquisition through which all learners must pass. He gives examples from the acquisition of German word order. The stages of acquisition described below have been determined for German as a second language as a result of large-scale projects done by Jürgen Meisel, Harald Clahsen and Manfred Pienemann (Meisel, Clahsen, and Pienemann 1981) on foreign migrant workers in Germany:

Stage 1, Canonical order Learners of German as a second language—particularly, but not solely, Romance language speakers—start out with the hypothesis that German word order is subject + verb + object (SVO). They produce sentences like *Die kinder spielen mim ball* (The children play with the ball), which is for the most part correct if we ignore the preposition.

Stage 2, Adverb preposing At this stage, learners can correctly move adverbs to the beginning of the sentence and produce utterances like *Da kinder spielen* (There children play). All sentences that the learners produce at this stage with adverb preposing are ungrammatical, however, since standard German requires the verb to be in second, not final, position, as in *Da spielen kinder.*

Stage 3, Verb separation At this stage, learners are able to produce sentences that separate the auxiliary and main verbs. This verb separation is obligatory in standard German. They can produce sentences like *Alle kinder muß die pause machen* (All children must the break have).

Stage 4, Inversion Now subjects are able to produce sentences in which the subject and inflected verbal element are inverted after a preposed adverb, as in *Dann hat sie wieder die knoch gebringt* (Then has she again the bone bringed).

Pienemann claims to have documented these developmental stages thoroughly and we will adopt them here. The question arises, though, *why* this should be the developmental sequence. Pienemann relies mainly on non-structural, processing explanations for the observed sequences. These psychological processes are never explicitly stated, a major weakness in his work but one we will not dwell on here.

He argues that the canonical order of stage (1) is psychologically the simplest way of marking underlying grammatical relations. The learner moves through the developmental stages as proficiency increases. Pienemann claims that adverb preposing occurs early because it is easier to move an element into the beginning of a sentence, a psychologically salient position. Psycholinguistic experimentation has shown that people are better able to remember words at the beginning of a sentence than those within the sentence. The ranking of saliency appears to be

Initial > Final > Internal

Verb separation occurs before inversion because it entails moving an element into sentence-final position, which is more salient than internal positions.

Pienemann argues that second language teaching should make the most of this natural order, but he also maintains that instruction cannot alter the sequence. He conducted an experiment to see if second language learners could, in fact, "beat" the sequence as a result of formal instruction. He worked with ten Italian-speaking children who were learning German as a second language. All of the subjects' interlanguages were between stages (1) and (3). The subjects were taught inversion, a structure from stage (4). The subject Teresa, whose development was at stage (1), did not succeed at learning inversion productively, whereas Giovanni, whose development was at stage (3), did succeed.[6] Pienemann asserts that learners at stages (1) or (2) cannot process structures from stage (4). Somehow, they are not ready.

Pienemann's work, then, is consistent with Gass in demonstrating that instruction can accelerate the developmental progression although it cannot alter the route of acquisition. The work is inconsistent with Gass, however, in not implying that instruction on the more marked elements of an implicational hierarchy will necessarily lead to improvement in the less marked forms. For Pienemann, some forms may just be too complex for a particular learner to process.

One problem with this study and, indeed, with many studies on the influence of instruction, is that the effects may not be immediate. We all probably know the feeling of looking back years later on something that a Grade 10 English teacher or a second-year linguistics professor said and thinking, "Now I get it!"

7 THE DEVELOPMENTAL SEQUENCE

Rod Ellis is a researcher who has devoted much time to investigating classroom second language acquisition. Ellis (1989a) did a study of the acquisition of German word order, conceived to test some of Pienemann's claims. Ellis wanted to investigate whether naturalistic and classroom second language learners moved through the same developmental sequence. He looked at thirty-nine adult classroom learners who were totally reliant on the classroom for their L2 input. In other words, they were *foreign* rather than *second* language learners.

Working within the framework of four developmental stages proposed by Pienemann—canonical SVO order, adverb preposing, verb separation, and inversion—Ellis added the structure verb-end. In German, finite verbs are placed in final position in all embedded clauses, as in *Ich trank das Glas Milch, während ich den Brief schrieb* (I drank the glass of milk while I the letter wrote). He plotted these developmental stages on an implicational hierarchy:

SVO > Adverb preposing > Verb separation > Inversion > Verb-end

---

[6] This discussion focusses on two of the subjects only, as examples demonstrating the argument.

The study investigated the three final word orders: verb separation, inversion, and verb-end. The thirty-nine subjects were students taking German courses in their first year of university. The mean age of the learners was twenty-one, and they had varied L1 backgrounds of Spanish, English, French, Mauritian Creole, and Arabic. The subjects were divided into five different groups taught by five different teachers, and there was therefore no uniformity in their instruction. Regular class-room observation revealed, however, that similarities in the style of instruction outweighed differences. None of the groups received specific instruction in the three word-order rules under investigation, but the grammatical structures they were taught in class often required applica-tion of these rules.

All five groups were exposed to the word orders in the sequence (1) inversion, (2) verb separation, (3) verb-end. Ellis also looked at the amount of emphasis placed on each item as reflected in homework exer-cises and textbook coverage. Here the groups varied. Table 16.4 ranks the structures that received the most attention for each group. Thus the order of introduction of structures did not correspond to the naturalistic developmental sequence cited in Pienemann, and the amount of empha-sis did not correspond to the degree of difficulty evidenced in the natu-ralistic sequence. Ellis wished to answer a question. Since the instruction was running counter to the naturalistic order, would the learners show another developmental pattern? Would instruction affect the route of their development?

Table 16.4 Word-Order Structures

Groups A and B		Groups C and D		Group E[7]	
Verb-end	27[†]	Verb separation	33	Verb separation	24
Verb separation	22	Verb-end	24	Verb-end	15
Inversion	6	Inversion	13	Inversion	7

[†] Number of references made to the structure during the course
Source: Data from Ellis (1989a).

The students were given a task in which each member of a pair had to describe a picture to his or her partner. Together the two pictures formed a story. The pairs each had to work out their story and then produce a narrative outlining it. This task was administered once at the end of the first term (after eleven weeks) and again at the end of the second term

---

[7] Ellis discusses Group E separately from C and D even though the emphasis was the same because their instruction placed the discussion of verb-end quite separately from the other structures, six weeks after verb separation. Groups C and D, on the other hand, considered all three relevant structures at regular intervals. The empha-sis in Groups A and B was different.

(after twenty-two weeks). A cross-sectional analysis made when the task was administered for the second time supported the hierarchy of

Verb separation > Inversion > Verb-end

That is to say, all learners who mastered verb-end constructions also mastered inversion and separation and students who mastered inversion also mastered separation.[8] A longitudinal analysis revealed that most of the learners progressed as expected along this developmental path. One subject appeared to regress over this time and lost the most difficult structure.

Ellis's study appears to show that instruction does not affect the route of acquisition. This is consistent with the explanation proposed in Chapter 8 that much of second language acquisition is governed by internal mechanisms rather than by the input.

Ellis (1986) summarizes the research on the effects of formal L2 instruction on second language learning as follows: (1) it has positive effects on the *rate* of acquisition; (2) it has positive effects on the *ultimate attainment* in L2; (3) it does not appear to affect the *developmental sequence*. We should note that most studies have looked at very narrow aspects of second language competence, and it is therefore difficult to generalize to larger issues of communicative competence.

8 THE EFFECT OF TYPE OF INSTRUCTION

So far, we have not considered the consequences of different types of instruction. VanPatten and Cadierno (1993) look at the effects of two sorts of instruction, which they label instruction as manipulation of the output (traditional instruction) and instruction as focussed input processing (processing instruction). In order to understand the distinction, let us look at their conception of second language acquisition, shown in Figure 16.3. They conceive of SLA as three sets of processes. First, *input processing* converts input to intake. The second set of processes, which we

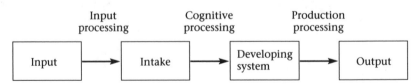

Figure 16.3   A Model of Second Language Acquisition
Source: Adapted from VanPatten and Cadierno (1993).

---

[8] Ellis considered success to be correct use 75 percent of the time.

could call cognitive processing, involves restructuring and parameter setting and converts intake into the developing system. The third set of processes, production processing, converts the acquired competence into output. In the model, then, the processes are represented by arrows; they move the learner from one box to the next.

Input processing, according to VanPatten and Cadierno, involves "strategies and mechanisms that promote form–meaning connections during comprehension" (1993, 226). They assert that traditional L2 instruction, on the other hand, focusses on the manipulation of learner output. A lesson traditionally involves the teacher explaining a grammatical concept and the learner practising the structure. Figure 16.4 represents this instruction focus.

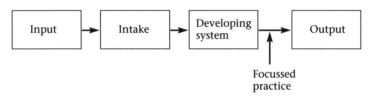

Figure 16.4   A Model of Traditional Instruction

If the purpose of traditional instruction is to alter the developing system, it is a questionable vehicle according to the model. How can practising the output affect the developing system? Instead, VanPatten and Cadierno argue, instruction should seek to influence the developing system by changing the way that input is processed, as shown in Figure 16.5.

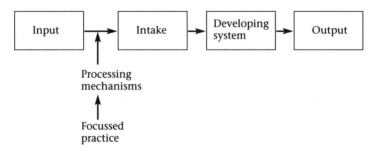

Figure 16.5   A Model of Processing Instruction

8.1 A PROCESSING STRATEGY

One of the input processing strategies observed by VanPatten and Cadierno is a general tendency for speakers to assume that in a sequence of NP + V + NP, the first NP will be assigned the role of agent and the second will be assigned the role of, in their terms, object. Indeed, this has been shown to be a productive strategy for English-speaking children at about age five. They interpret passive sentences as if they were active. Given the sentence *The truck was hit by the car,* children assume that *the truck* was the agent and ignore the passive morphology.

Other than in passives and a few other constructions, the assumption works quite well for English, but it doesn't work so well for Spanish. Spanish allows the orders SVO, SOV, OVS, and OV. The English sentence *The man follows the woman,* for example, could be translated as either *El señor sigue a la señora* (The man follows to the woman) or *A la señora la sigue el hombre* (To the woman her-OBJ follows the man). Spanish also has clitic object pronouns, which must occur *before* a simple finite verb. The subject may be placed before or after the verb. The English sentence *The man follows her,* for example, could be translated into either the form *El señor la sigue* (The man-SUBJ her-OBJ follows) or the form *La sigue el señor* (Her-OBJ follows the man-SUBJ). In both cases, the clitic object pronoun *la* must come before the finite verb *sigue,* although the subject *señor* can either precede or follow the verb.

English speakers learning Spanish tend to assume that the first NP is an agent. In other words, they interpret *La sigue el señor* as **She follows the man,* when, as we have seen, it means *The man follows her.*

VanPatten and Cadierno examined the effect of explicit instruction on input processing, looking at three groups of subjects receiving: (1) traditional instruction in object pronouns; (2) processing instruction in object pronouns; and (3) no instruction in object pronouns. The subjects were eighty students in six second-year university Spanish classes at the University of Illinois. Classes were randomly assigned to the three groups. The researchers constructed two different instructional packets, traditional and processing, to teach clitic direct object pronouns.

The traditional instruction presented grammatical explanations and then moved the subjects from mechanical, form-oriented practice to more communicative practice, as in this example:

> With another student, make up and answer questions following the model.
>
> Model: *Comer en tu casa* ("to eat at your house")
>
> > *¿Cuándo me invitas a comer en tu casa?*
> > "When are you going to invite me to eat at your house?"
> >
> > *Te invito para el sábado.*
> > "I'll invite you over for Saturday."
>
> 1. *cenar en tu casa* ("to dine at your house")
> 2. *almorzar* ("to lunch") (VanPatten and Cadierno 1993, 230).

Processing instruction, on the other hand, involved teaching how to *interpret* OVS strings (in which the O was either a full noun or a clitic object pronoun). The explicit instruction contrasted the subject and object of a verb and emphasized that Spanish allows OVS sequences. In the following activity, for example, the subjects had to demonstrate that they had assigned the correct roles to the NPs:

Listen as your instructor reads a sentence. Select the best interpretation from the English renderings.

1. a. My parents call me.
   b. I call my parents.

(Instructor reads aloud: *Me llaman los padres.*) (VanPatten and Cadierno 1993, 231).

At no point did processing instruction involve the production of the pronoun form by the learners. Essentially, then, the difference between the two groups was in the type of practice they undertook.

All three groups were given pre- and post-tests on their ability to interpret and produce object pronouns. The interpretation task was to match an appropriate picture with a sentence like *Lo saluda la chica* (Him greets the girl → The girl greets him). The production task, again based upon a visual cue, was to produce an appropriate sentence, given a context such as *El chico piensa en la chica, y entonces ...* (The boy is thinking of the girl, and then ...). As there were no significant differences between the groups in the pre-test, it could be argued that any differences in the post-test were the result of the instructional treatment. Table 16.5 summarizes the results.

Table 16.5   Results of Traditional and Processing Instruction

Interpretation

- Processing instruction better than no instruction (p = .0001)
- Processing instruction better than traditional instruction (p = .0001)
- No significant difference between traditional and no instruction (p = .12)

Production

- Traditional instruction better than no instruction (p = .0001)
- Processing instruction better than no instruction (p = .0001)
- No significant difference between processing and traditional instruction.

Source: Data from VanPatten and Cadierno (1993).

The processing group did well not only on interpretation, which it had practised, but also on production, which it had not. Even though they never produced the object clitics during instruction, these subjects performed as well as those in the traditional-instruction group. This is not surprising in light of the assumption that changing input processing should affect the developing system. What might be slightly surprising, however, is that the group who received traditional instruction performed as well in production as the processing group. The model of SLA presented by VanPatten and Cadierno (1993) suggests that we would not expect output practice to have any effect on the system. The question remains why the traditional group did as well as the processing group.

9 COGNITIVE THEORY

So far, we have looked at a number of individual studies on instructed second language learning. Ellis (1990) has proposed what he calls an integrated theory of instructed second language acquisition, which is examined below. To understand Ellis's theory, we must first be familiar with cognitive theory and its relation to second language instruction. For the most part, cognitive theory works within a non-modular view of mind; it attempts to discover general principles of learning, not just those concerned with language learning. Cognitive theory seeks to explain three principal aspects of learning: (1) how knowledge is initially represented; (2) how the ability to use this knowledge develops; and (3) how new knowledge is integrated into the existing cognitive system. We focus here on the second and third aspects.

9.1 USING KNOWLEDGE

Ellis adopts Weinstein and Mayer's position (1986) that new knowledge is acquired in two steps. First the learner selects features of the environment to attend to and transfers this information into short-term memory. Then the learner acquires some or all of these features by transferring the information into long-term memory. But how do learners achieve *control* over that new knowledge? Two accounts of the process have attracted attention in the L2 field. The first centres on different types of processing.

9.1.1 Controlled versus Automatic Processing

A number of researchers distinguish between mental operations that a person is able to perform effortlessly and automatically and those that can only be performed with considerable difficulty and relatively slowly. The first type is known as *automatic* processing while the second type is known as *controlled* processing. Learning involves making access automatic to information that before was only available through controlled processing. When first learning a skill such as swimming, for example, you must use controlled processing. Once you know how, it becomes automatic.

This type of automatization is necessary because the learner has limited processing capacity and needs to free mental operations to deal with new information. In the domain of second language acquisition, when you learn to read a new writing system you are using controlled processing to decode the script. As you gain in proficiency, the lower-level processes become more automatic. Right now in English you probably do not have to concentrate on decoding the letters; you can focus on the meaning.

9.1.2 Declarative versus Procedural Knowledge

Another framework for considering how learners get control of knowledge focusses not on the processing but on the knowledge itself. Anderson (1985) distinguishes between *declarative* and *procedural* knowledge. Declarative knowledge involves knowing *that*. It consists of such information as facts and definitions of words. We know, for example, that Ottawa is the capital of Canada. Procedural knowledge, on the other hand, is knowing *how*. This is the ability to implement knowledge. We might know how to bake a cake or ride a bicycle. Anderson identifies three stages in the learning process:

1. *The cognitive stage* At this stage, the learner makes use of conscious activity and the knowledge acquired is typically declarative.
2. *The associative stage* The learner detects errors in the original declarative knowledge and corrects them. The knowledge is proceduralized.
3. *The autonomous stage* Performance at this stage becomes more or less automatic and errors disappear. Performance occurs below the threshold of consciousness.

Obviously, the *processing* explanation of learning (controlled versus automatic) and the *knowledge* explanation (declarative versus procedural) have much in common. Similarities can be seen between controlled processing and declarative knowledge and between automatic processing and procedural knowledge. Proponents of controlled processing, however, maintain that it does not have to take place consciously. Declarative knowledge, by contrast, is conscious.

9.2 INCORPORATING NEW KNOWLEDGE

How is new knowledge incorporated into an existing cognitive system? It involves a certain amount of restructuring of the knowledge system. As McLaughlin points out, "there is more to learning a complex cognitive skill than automatizing sub-skills" (1987, 136). A learner needs to have structure to the information. Think back to when you were first learning about phonetics. You started out with a certain knowledge of how sounds were made. You knew that, say, [b] and [d] were made differently. But once you learned about place and manner of articulation and about voicing, you restructured your knowledge about sounds. You could now think of [b], [d], and [g] as similar in some way, whereas before you couldn't. By learning something you restructured your existing system.

9.3 COGNITIVE THEORY AND SECOND LANGUAGE LEARNING

Several researchers have attempted to apply cognitive learning theory to L2 acquisition. Probably the most fully worked out application is that of Ellen Bialystok. Bialystok (1981, 1982) maintains that language learning is not afforded special status in human development; language is processed just like any other type of information. She describes language proficiency with reference to two dimensions: an *analysed* factor and an *automatic* factor. The analysed factor is the extent to which the learner is aware of the structure of his or her linguistic knowledge, although not necessarily consciously. The automatic factor is the relative access the learner has to that knowledge. The two factors are independent. Knowledge gains in automaticity as learning takes place. Figure 16.6 illustrates Bialystok's model.

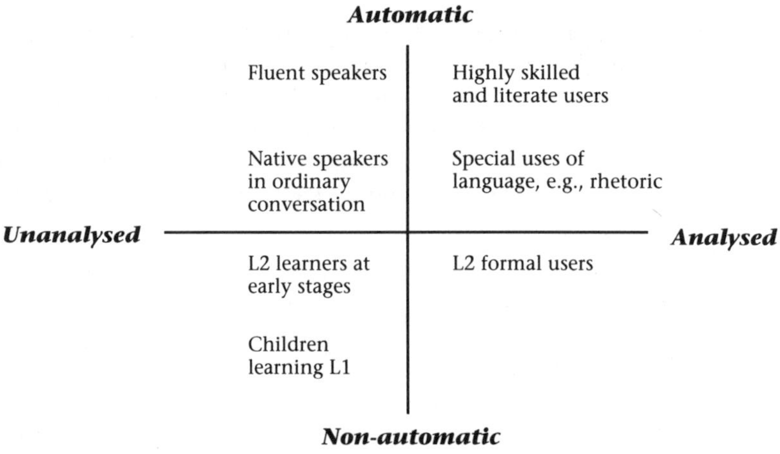

Automatic

	Fluent speakers	Highly skilled and literate users
	Native speakers in ordinary conversation	Special uses of language, e.g., rhetoric
Unanalysed		*Analysed*
	L2 learners at early stages	L2 formal users
	Children learning L1	

Non-automatic

Figure 16.6   Bialystok's Model of Language Proficiency
Source: Adapted from Bialystok (1981).

Individual learners are more likely to concentrate on one factor or the other, not both at the same time. Some learners emphasize automaticity while others concentrate on analysing their knowledge. The learning context can also influence the kind of acquisition that takes place, which in turn can affect production. Classroom learners tend to stress the analytic dimension; naturalistic learners are apt to focus on automaticity.

9.3.1 Cognitive Theory and Instructed L2 Learning

Attempting to apply cognitive theory to the classroom raises issues of the relationship between practice and automaticity, between classroom interaction and procedural knowledge, and between formal instruction and analysed knowledge. If, for example, you have analysed knowledge of how active sentences become passive, you are aware of the formal operations performed. If your knowledge is unanalysed, you simply use the passive voice. Regarding the first of these, McLaughlin (1987) maintains that practice is the key to developing automaticity. He believes that errors occur because the learner has not yet made performance automatic and doesn't have time to use controlled processing.

On the second issue, the relation of classroom interaction to procedural knowledge, cognitive theory indicates that the second language classroom should provide adequate opportunities for learners to correct errors in their declarative knowledge. Classroom interaction should involve not simply acquiring knowledge *that* but also knowledge *how*.

On the third issue, cognitive theory posits that formal instruction can help to increase the learner's analysed knowledge. Focus on form in the classroom facilitates restructuring of the cognitive system and helps learners to assimilate new knowledge.

9.3.2 Problems with Cognitive Theory and L2 Learning

Ellis (1990) argues that although it is a useful framework, cognitive theory offers inadequate explanation for several aspects of second language acquisition. He points out two areas of difficulty in its account of L2 learning: acquisitional sequences and explicit knowledge.

That instruction appears unable to alter the developmental sequence is problematic for cognitive theory. The principles of learning predict that the environment will have a greater impact on the learning sequence than it actually does. The theory also makes no predictions about which items of knowledge will develop first. Linguistically, we can propose explanations for developmental sequences such as the production of *Why you are crying?* before *Why are you crying?* Because cognitive theory assumes that language acquisition is the same as any other type of learning, however, it has nothing to say about specific linguistic structures. Cognitive theory may well tell us more about performance than it does about competence.

Ellis maintains that cognitive theory is also quite vague about the role of explicit knowledge in learning. Explicit knowledge is consciously represented in the mind of the learner and can therefore be articulated. Implicit knowledge is below the threshold of consciousness and cannot be articulated. You probably know explicitly why the sentence *I saw three dog over there* is ungrammatical. You can say what rule or principle it violates. You probably only know implicitly why the sentence *What did Jane hear the news that Mary bought?* is ungrammatical. You are unlikely to know what rule or principle has been violated. A theory of *instructed* second language learning should have something to say about the relationship between explicit and implicit knowledge but cognitive theory does not. Can explicit knowledge become implicit? Can implicit knowledge become explicit?

10 AN INTEGRATED THEORY

Ellis's integrated theory attempts to explain how instruction provides the learner with the data necessary to construct an interlanguage. For the most part, Ellis is adopting cognitive theory as an explanation for second language acquisition, but he modifies it slightly to address the shortcomings just discussed. Below are some premises of the theory.

10.1 KNOWLEDGE IS DIFFERENTIATED

Explicit and implicit knowledge are different in kind and are stored separately in the brain. Explicit knowledge is declarative and can be consciously retrieved. Implicit knowledge is subconscious and procedural, though not necessarily fully automatic. According to Ellis, only implicit knowledge proceeds along a consistent developmental path.

10.2 CONTROL IS SEPARATE FROM KNOWLEDGE

Ellis argues that knowledge and implementation of it are distinct. He also asserts that controlled processing applies to both explicit and implicit knowledge. Newly acquired knowledge tends to be accessed via controlled processing, but with sufficient opportunities for real practice it can be processed more rapidly and efficiently. This is consistent with cognitive theory.

10.3 TYPES OF INSTRUCTION AND OF KNOWLEDGE

Working from these assumptions, Ellis attempts to describe how instruction and knowledge are related. He maintains that different kinds of instruction result in different kinds of L2 knowledge. Nevertheless, he points out that while we may expect to find relationships between *form-focussed* instruction[9] and explicit knowledge and *meaning-focussed* instruction and implicit knowledge, they are not straightforward. Form-

---

[9] Form-focussed instruction concentrates on the structural properties of the language, such as syntactic, morphological, and phonological forms.

focussed instruction does seem to facilitate the acquisition of explicit knowledge, but it can also lead to the acquisition of implicit knowledge, as we will see in the next section. As we saw in Pienemann's work, the learner moves along to the next developmental stage regardless of the instruction given. Explicit instruction did not provide the explicit knowledge necessary to skip a developmental stage.

For Ellis, the major benefit of meaning-focussed instruction is that it supplies the learner with input for processing. It gives the learner an opportunity to generate comprehensible output, which, as the next chapter details, is an important consideration. Finally, meaning-focussed instruction helps learners to develop control of their knowledge. By practising in "real operating conditions," they learn to implement their knowledge and fill in its gaps.

10.4 THE ROLE OF EXPLICIT KNOWLEDGE

Ellis maintains that explicit knowledge (which may be the result of form-focussed instruction) does not turn into implicit knowledge but can, however, aid acquisition of implicit knowledge. Through explicit knowledge, the learner notices the gap between his or her own output and the input. Someone learning English as a second language, for example, may receive a lesson focussing on mass and count nouns and the next day, after saying "I have some informations on that" and hear someone else say "That's a lot of information." As a result of the explicit knowledge, the learner may notice the gap between the output (*informations*) and the input (*information*) and be able to acquire this implicit knowledge sooner.

For Ellis, then, explicit knowledge plays a very valuable role in L2 learning and should not be ignored in the second language classroom. It may help learners to pay selective attention to certain features in the complex input. In this way, Ellis's claims are consistent with those of VanPatten and Cadierno (1993), who asserted that instruction should attempt to change the way the learner processes the input.

10.5 SUMMARY

Ellis claims that his theory is able to explain why instruction fails to alter the developmental sequence (explicit knowledge cannot become implicit) and why instruction results in faster learning (it helps the learner notice the gap between the form of the output and of the input). Figure 16.7 summarizes his integrated theory. The model describes a situation in which the learner, not the teacher, is in charge of the learning. Yet the teacher has a major role to play in providing opportunities for meaning-focussed communication—and hence acquisition of implicit knowledge and controlled processing—and helping the learner to develop explicit knowledge through form-focussed instruction.

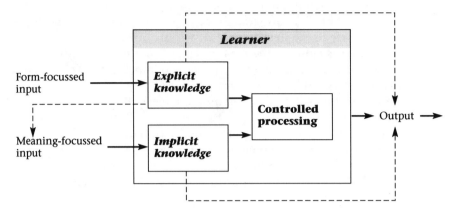

Figure 16.7   Ellis's Integrated Model
Source: Adapted from Ellis (1990).

11 CONCLUSION

This chapter has discussed the effect of instruction on second language acquisition from several different perspectives. We looked both at case studies investigating various aspects of learners' grammatical competence and at one attempt to build a more general model. The next chapter will continue in this vein as we look at the effects of the linguistic environment to which learners are exposed.

CLASSROOM IMPLICATIONS

People have been learning second languages, and teaching second languages, for a very long time. It is natural to wonder about the connection between the two. It is also normal for second language teachers to question whether what they are doing in the classroom helps the learners or not. It is pessimistically claimed that people have been learning second languages successfully for thousands of years and that it's only when teachers get involved that the success rate plummets. Do you agree or disagree?

Clearly, the effect of instruction on language acquisition raises several questions. Do you think classrooms are unnatural places to learn languages? Can we make the classroom more like the natural environment? What balance do you think is appropriate between form-focussed and meaning-focussed instruction? Is it the same for all learners? Consider proficiency, interests, and the like. Can teachers actually hinder second language learning?

SELF TEST

Studies looking at the effects of instruction on SLA have shown that the L2 classroom is quite a complex environment. Pica compared _____(1)_____ and classroom learners, using both _____(2)_____ and _____(3)_____ analyses and argued that there were certain differences between the two groups. Classroom learners tended to _____(4)_____ morphological markings. Lightbown argued that instruction had only a _____(5)_____ effect on L2 learners. Gass argued that instruction could _____(6)_____ acquisition but not cause stages to be skipped. This is consistent with the work of Pienemann, reflected in his _____(7)_____ hypothesis. Ellis's classroom replication of Pienemann's study _____(8)_____ that the natural order was unaffected by the input. VanPatten and Cadierno argued that effective instruction should focus on the way the learner _____(9)_____ input.

Ellis's integrated theory of instructed SLA draws on _____(10)_____ theory, which assumes a _____(11)_____ view of mind. He suggests that type of instruction (_____(12)_____ - or _____(13)_____ -focussed) has an effect on the type of knowledge acquired (_____(14)_____ or _____(15)_____).

FURTHER READING

Bialystok, E. 1981. Some evidence for the integrity and interaction of two knowledge sources. In *New Dimensions in Second Language Acquisition Research*, ed. R.W. Andersen, 62–74. Rowley, MA: Newbury House.

McLaughlin, B. 1987. Cognitive Theory. Chapter 6 of *Theories of Second-Language Learning*, 133–53. New York: Edward Arnold.

McLaughlin, B. 1990. Restructuring. *Applied Linguistics* 11:113–28.

McLaughlin, B., T. Rossman, and B. McLeod. 1983. Second-language learning: An information-processing perspective. *Language Learning* 33:135–58.

17

The Effects of the Environment

This chapter examines several aspects of the linguistic environment that can affect second language acquisition. Specifically, it looks at the kind of input to which second language learners are exposed and the kind of interaction in which they are involved. To envision where we are and where we are going, consider the diagram in Figure 17.1. We have looked at some characteristics of both second language output and the individual learner. This chapter investigates the input the learner receives—the environment—and the ways in which the learner interacts with that environment.

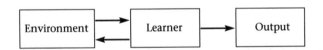

Figure 17.1.   A Simplified Model of SLA

Just as in first language acquisition research, a body of literature in the L2 field tries to explain acquisition as a product of the input, but remember the problems about this hypothesis for L1 acquisition. This is the issue of *motherese* or *caretaker speech*. Some people argue that children are taught their first language by their caregivers, that the input *causes* acquisition to take place, but the argument confuses correlation with causation. In our culture, at least, we speak differently to children than we do to adults. All children are exposed to a kind of simplified input. There is therefore a definite correlation between (1) being spoken to like a child and (2) acquiring a first language. That much is uncontroversial. The claim that (1) *causes* (2), however, is suspect, involving a number of problems which we will quickly review.

1. Children only attend to part of their linguistic environment and we have no way of knowing what they are attending to.
2. Children are exposed to input from people other than their caregivers.
3. The input to which they are exposed is deficient in important ways. Certain information is completely lacking in the input, yet children come to possess that knowledge.
4. The structures that children hear first (questions and imperatives) are not the structures they produce first (declaratives).
5. Not all cultures use baby talk, or motherese.

So, in first language acquisition, the question of whether the input *causes* the development to occur or whether it *triggers* certain things in the learner is not straightforward. We will see the same kind of controversy in the second language acquisition literature.

1 FOREIGNER TALK

The way that native speakers talk to non-native speakers is known as *foreigner talk*. One of the first studies to investigate foreigner talk was Ferguson (1975). He asked a group of native speakers to write down how they thought they would communicate the sentiments below to a non-native speaker. Try for yourself:

> I am asking you to tell me how you think an English-speaking person might act in trying to communicate with some non-English speakers. The person whose speech I want you to describe is acting as the spokesman for a group of three and he is addressing a group of non-English speakers who are obviously non-European and illiterate. They may have heard some English before but they are not really able to understand or speak it. I will read you a sentence in normal English, and I want you to write down the way you think the English speaker might say it.
>
> *Sentences*
> 1. He's my brother, he's not my father.
> 2. Did you understand what she said?
> 3. Yesterday I saw him and gave him some money.
> 4. He always carries two guns.
>
> Please write some version that approximates how you might say these things to the non-native speakers (Ferguson 1983, 392).

Ferguson claims that foreigner talk is really an imitation of the way non-native speakers speak. He noted the following patterns in the native speakers' responses:

1. Omissions
   - *the* was often omitted
   - *to be* tended to be omitted
   - inflectional suffixes (plural, possessives, and so on) were omitted
   - conjunctions were omitted
2. Expansions
   - full imperatives (<u>You</u> *come back tomorrow.*)
   - added tag (*... OK? ... right?*)
3. Replacements
   - all negatives became *no*
   - sometimes *I* was replaced by *me* (*Me help you?*)
   - *do* in questions was replaced by rising intonation (*You need help?*)

The study was seminal and triggered a whole new area of inquiry, but it did have some problems. The methodology did not reveal what people actually *do* when talking to non-native speakers, only what they *think* they would do. One subject recast the sentence about guns to include the word *firesticks*. It seems highly unlikely, no matter how many John Wayne movies the native speaker had seen, that he or she would really use *firesticks* in an effort to clarify, although perhaps such incredulity is naïve.

Hatch (1983) suggests that foreigner talk has the same functions as motherese. It promotes communication, establishes an affective bond between the native and non-native speakers, and serves as an implicit teaching mode. She suggests that the characteristics of foreigner talk emerge as the native speaker simplifies and clarifies in response to non-native speaker feedback. If the non-native speaker doesn't understand the message, the native speaker makes further adjustments.

Others have suggested that the simplicity of foreigner talk provides the learner with what Krashen (1981) refers to as comprehensible input. As we have seen, for Krashen comprehensible input is the most important element of second language learning; we only learn a language when we understand messages in that language. One problem of viewing comprehensible input as the driving force behind second language acquisition was raised by Swain (1985). She argued that learners also needed the opportunity to generate comprehensible *output*. If a second language learner attempts to communicate and the listener fails to understand, then the speaker is forced to analyse the output to determine what was causing the problem. Swain asserts that this conscious analysis helps the learner to progress. Simplified input alone will not result in communicative competence in a second language.

1.1 INPUT OUTSIDE THE CLASSROOM

Long (1981) points out that many studies describing foreigner talk have failed to collect baseline data for comparison. A study examining how native speakers talk to non-native speakers in, say, bus stations, for example, may not have collected the necessary data on how native speakers talk to *native speakers* in bus stations. Without such data, foreigner talk studies are difficult to interpret.

Ellis (1986) proposes three types of foreigner talk:

1. Talk consisting only of *functional* adjustments, with no *formal* simplifications. The speaker uses only direct requests such as *May I shut the window?* for example, and not indirect suggestions such as *Are you cold?*
2. Talk consisting of both functional and *grammatical* input adjustments. Even though the input is modified, all of it is grammatical. The speaker uses only direct requests and simplifies them (*I'll shut the window, OK?*)
3. Talk consisting of functional, grammatical, and *ungrammatical* input adjustments. Some of the input is thus ungrammatical, as in *I shut window?*

He contends that the first type is the most common and the third the least. Factors such as the proficiency of the learner, the roles and ages of the participants, and the topic of conversation will determine the type of foreigner talk used. The third type of foreigner talk is significantly different from motherese, which does not often contain ungrammatical input. Table 17.1 outlines some of the major characteristics of foreigner talk.

1.2 INTERACTION OUTSIDE THE CLASSROOM

The input that a second language learner receives is determined not solely by the native speaker but also by the learner. As Hatch suggests, the non-native speaker provides feedback—such as signalling whether the message has been understood—which determines the nature of the subsequent native-speaker input (see Figure 17.2). We therefore have to look at the discourse that native and non-native speakers construct together. In doing so, we enter the subdiscipline of linguistics known as *discourse analysis*.

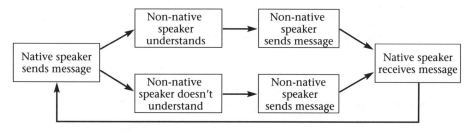

Figure 17.2   The Negotiation of Meaning

Table 17.1   Characteristics of Foreigner Talk

Lexical	Grammatical	Ungrammatical
Lexis	• Restricted vocabulary size • Difficult items replaced with more frequently occurring items • Fewer pro forms • Repetition of words • Use of analytic paraphrases (e.g., Do you have a tool for hitting this nail?) • Use of gesture	• Use of foreign or foreign-sounding words (e.g., I want to buy it. <u>Savvy</u>?)
Grammar	• Fewer contractions • Overall shorter utterance length • Grammatical relations made explicit (He asked to go → He asked if he could go) • Co-ordination preferred to subordination • Topics moved to the beginnings of sentences (I like John → John, I like him) • Fewer *wh* questions and more yes/no questions • More uninverted questions (You like John?) • More "or-choice" questions (Did you go out this weekend, or stay at home?) • More tag questions • More present (versus non-present) temporal markings	• Omission of: copula, *it, do,* verb inflections • Use of interlanguage forms (*no* + verb)

Source: Adapted from Ellis (1986).

A major feature of conversations involving L2 learners is the combined effort of native and non-native speakers to overcome communicative difficulties. This is known as the *negotiation of meaning*. Table 17.2 illustrates some of the characteristics of native/non-native speaker interaction used outside the classroom to avoid communication breakdown, focussing on the functional adjustments made by the native speaker.

2 INPUT IN THE CLASSROOM

In a second language classroom, obviously, the L2 learner will be exposed to different kinds of input from those in a naturalistic setting. The lan-

THE EFFECTS OF THE ENVIRONMENT 367

Table 17.2 Characteristics of Native and Non-Native Speaker Interaction

Type	Description	Example
More "here-and-now" topics	NS refers to objects and events that are readily observable	NS: Are you going to work? *not* NS: How 'bout those Blue Jays?
More topic-initiating moves	NS starts a conversation topic by asking a question or making a comment	NS: That's a nice jacket.
More confirmation checks	NS attempts to elicit confirmation that a NNS utterance has been correctly heard or understood	NNS: I went to cinema. NS: The cinema?
More comprehension checks	NS attempts to establish that the NNS is following what he or she is saying	NS: It was raining cats and dogs. Do you follow?
More clarification requests	NS attempts to get the NNS to clarify an utterance that the NS has not understood	NNS: She very long. NS: Sorry?
More self-repetitions	NS repeats part or all of his or her own previous utterance	NS: He got stuck in the window trying to get in. He got stuck.
More other-repetitions	NS repeats part or all of the previous NNS utterance without seeking confirmation	NNS: I went to the cinema. NS: Yeah. You went to the cinema.
More expansions	NS expands the previous NNS utterance by supplying missing formatives or by adding new semantic information	NNS: I wear a sweater. NS: Yes, you're wearing a red sweater.
Shorter responses	NS limits the length of his or her response to an NNS question or comment	NNS: What do you teach? NS: Linguistics.

Note: NS = Native speaker; NNS = Non-native speaker
Source: Adapted from Ellis (1986).

guage a teacher uses to address a non-native student is called *teacher talk*. Ellis (1986) presents the following characteristics of teacher talk:

1. formal adjustments at all levels of language
   - reduced syntactic complexity
   - standard pronunciation
   - use primarily of common lexical items
2. no ungrammatical modifications (unlike foreigner talk)
3. functional adjustments
   - frequent comprehension checks
   - fewer requests for clarification than foreigner talk contains
   - frequent repetition, prompting, and expansions

The conversation below is taken from *The Importance of Being Earnest*, by that master of interaction, Oscar Wilde.

Gwendolyn: Quite a well-kept garden this is, Miss Cardew.
Cecily: So glad you like it, Miss Fairfax.
Gwendolyn: I had no idea there were any flowers in the country.
Cecily: Oh, flowers are as common here, Miss Fairfax, as people are in London.... May I offer you some tea, Miss Fairfax?
Gwendolyn: Thank you. [aside] Detestable girl! But I require tea!
Cecily: Sugar?
Gwendolyn: No, thank you. Sugar is not fashionable any more.

Cecily looks angrily at her, takes up the tongs and puts four lumps of sugar into the cup.

Cecily: Cake or bread and butter?
Gwendolyn: Bread and butter, please. Cake is rarely seen at the best houses nowadays.
Cecily: [cuts a very large slice of cake and puts it on the tray] Hand that to Miss Fairfax.
Gwendolyn: You have filled my tea with lumps of sugar, and though I asked most distinctly for bread and butter, you have given me cake. I am known for the gentleness of my disposition and the extraordinary sweetness of my nature, but I warn you, Miss Cardew, you may go too far.... From the moment I saw you I distrusted you. I felt that you were false and deceitful. I am never deceived in such matters. My first impressions of people are invariably right.
Cecily: It seems to me, Miss Fairfax, that I am trespassing on your valuable time. No doubt you have many other calls of a similar character to make in the neighbourhood.

Oscar Wilde
The Importance of Being Earnest, Act

Long and Sato (1983) found that teachers tended to dominate the talk in second language classrooms, and that the range of functions to which students were exposed was quite different from that in a naturalistic setting. Although teacher talk is similar to foreigner talk in many ways, it is unlikely to be as finely tuned to the needs of the non-native speaker because it is a one-to-many rather than a one-to-one interaction. In using foreigner talk, the native speaker can assess the abilities of the non-native speaker and adjust his or her speech accordingly. Second language teachers cannot aim at everyone's proficiency level.

2.1 INTERACTION IN THE CLASSROOM

Of course, L2 classrooms are not merely a forum for teacher monologues. Many studies investigating classroom discourse (Coulthard and Montgomery 1981; Sinclair and Brazil 1982; Sinclair and Coulthard 1975) have focussed on what is known as *three-phase* discourse: (1) the teacher *initiates;* (2) the pupil *responds;* (3) the teacher supplies *feedback.* Also known as IRF communication, its stages go something like this:

Teacher: What are you doing this weekend? (Initiates)
Student: I is going to Banff. (Responds)
Teacher: You *is* going? (Feedback)

This kind of discourse appears to be very common in second language classrooms. Gremmo, Holec, and Riley have argued that IRF communication is so unlike anything that goes on outside the language classroom that students receive a very distorted view of interaction and a very limited range of functions: "When we analyze classroom discourse, it becomes clear that the very presence and participation of the teacher distorts the interaction to such an extent that it no longer provides even the basic raw materials from which a learner can construct his competence" (1978, 63).

3 CONTENT LANGUAGE TEACHING

It is common now to talk about *content language teaching*, a pedagogic trend that is relevant here. The methodology focusses on introducing certain content in the language classroom—an historical subject, for example—and using language simply as the medium of instruction, not as the topic itself. This is reminiscent of Stern's description (1984, 4) of French immersion as teaching *in* French, not teaching *of* French. French immersion is content language teaching. One of the arguments for this kind of instruction is that it exposes students to a more natural discourse than IRF communication.

Swain (1988) cautions that content language teaching is not necessarily good language teaching. It can be, but it doesn't have to be. She asks us to consider the following possibility. If we wanted our students to learn something about how the past tense is formed and used in a language, we could approach it in either of two ways. We could simply tell the students how the past tense is formed and used, or we could pick an historical theme and by talking about things in the past use a lot of past tense verbs. But examine the transcript of a history lesson designed to do just that:

Teacher: It [Europe] *didn't have* sugar cane. Why *didn't* they *have* sugar cane? Mary?
Student: It's too cold.
Teacher: It's too cold. Another word for "the weather"?
Student: The climate is not good (Swain 1988, 71).

A discussion that started out in the past tense ended up in the present. As Swain points out, this could send very confusing signals to the students about how English uses tenses. Pedagogically, it probably makes history appear exciting and relevant to talk about it in the present tense but linguistically, it could be detrimental.

4 COMPARING NATURAL AND CLASSROOM ENVIRONMENTS

This chapter has so far talked about naturalistic and classroom environments as if they were opposites but that may not be the best way to think about them. It's a common metaphor to think of the language classroom as the place where you get practice before going out into the real world. Comparisons are sometimes drawn between learning a second language and learning how to play tennis. To learn to play tennis you have to practise your shots and play with friends before you get out there and compete in tournaments. Maybe classrooms help learners do the same when learning a second language. Perhaps, then, we should think of classrooms and natural environments not as opposites but as places that provide varying degrees of the same sort of input and interactions. The kind of teaching that goes on in the classroom can make it more or less naturalistic. Table 17.3 illustrates some of the characteristics of different types of second language classrooms with respect to the interactions found there.

Although these broad descriptions hold, there is considerable variation within a classification. It is conceivable, for example, that you could find two immersion teachers holding strongly differing views. Teacher A, believing that the classroom focus should be solely on meaningful communication, might never give grammar lessons. Teacher B, asserting that a focus on developing communicative competence includes grammatical accuracy, might give grammar lessons in the belief that it will be too late if students don't achieve accuracy early on. We can idealize and homogenize the notion of the L2 classroom to a certain extent, but there will always be variation depending on the individual teacher.

Table 17.3   Characteristics of the Classroom

Type of classroom	Characteristics	Comparison with natural setting
The foreign language classroom	• Focus likely to be on language form, rather than meaning • L2 unlikely to be used for classroom management or for genuine social purposes	• Potentially least like a natural setting • Little negotiation of meaning
The second language classroom	• Many interactions still focus on form, rather than meaning • L2 functions as the medium of instruction as well as the goal, and is therefore used for a wider range of discourse functionsthan in the foreign language classroom	• More like a natural setting • Some chance for negotiation of meaning
The subject classroom (where the learner is placed in a class with native speakers	• Focus on meaning, rather than form • Input unlikely to be adjusted, unless numbers of L2 learners high	• Resembles exposure in natural settings (unmodified input) • Very little negotiation of meaning
The bilingual classroom (in which L2 learners receive instruction through both L1 and L2)	• Mixed focus: sometimes on form, sometimes on meaning • No need for learners to attend to L2 if the same content is taught in L1 and L2, and hence no L2 intake • Adjusted input occurs if L2 used to teach different subjects	• Potentially strong resemblance to natural setting, if learners have to attend to L2 • Negotiation of meaning likely
The immersion classroom (in which a class of L2 learners are taught through medium of L2)	• Focus on meaning in L2 subject lessons • Input likely to be simplified • IRF exchanges may still predominate	• Strongest resemblance to natural settings • Plenty of opportunity for negotiation of meaning, particularly if teaching is learner centred

Source: Adapted from Ellis (1986).

5 SELECTION OF INPUT

Beebe (1985) warns that we must not fall into the trap of viewing non-native speakers as passive recipients of native speaker input. Learners are active participants in choosing their preferred target language model according to their own value system. Even as native speakers we may be familiar with this kind of phenomenon. Have you ever heard anyone say that British English is "better" or "clearer" than Canadian English? Or that so and so *only* speaks a "dialect" of a particular language? Inherent in these terms is a predilection for one source over another. Beebe looks at these input preferences in second language learners. She divides them into what she calls *marked* and *unmarked* choices. The unmarked choice is the more frequent, basic, or expected situation.

5.1 UNMARKED INPUT PREFERENCES

5.1.1 Peers over Teachers

Drawing on both sociolinguistic (Labov 1972) and SLA (Milon 1975) studies, Beebe argues that students acquire the dialect of their peers, not of their teachers; they prefer their peers' speech. Milon claims that students have receptive knowledge of their teachers' dialect but that productive knowledge, if it occurs at all, does not come until the students are older. Milon's study describes a seven-year-old Japanese boy who immigrated to Hawaii and learned the Hawaii creole English dialect of his peers rather than the standard English of his teachers. When he moved to a middle-class neighbourhood, where his peers spoke standard English, he was found to be using standard English after one year. Current peers thus seem to be given preference over former peers, and there is also some indication that males are more influenced by peer groups than are females (Milroy 1980; Trudgill 1972).

5.1.2 Peers over Parents

It is a very common pattern to see children acquiring the language of their peers rather than of their parents. In terms of second language acquisition, it is common for second or third generation immigrants not to acquire the language of their parents at all. We see the same phenomenon within a single language. Children acquire the dialect of their peers, not their parents. If a parent speaks Scottish English and the children are raised in Alberta, the chances are that the children will not grow up speaking Scottish English, although they will most likely have a passive knowledge of it. The same preference is likely to be true of young second language learners. Not all input is created equal.

5.1.3 Higher-Prestige over Lower-Prestige Groups

While it is true that learners tend to acquire the language of their peers or own social group, if a learner decides to acquire the features of another variant of a particular language it is most likely to be that of a higher prestige group. If a speaker of African American Vernacular English (AAVE) decides to adopt the features of another dialect, for example, he or she will probably adopt standard English, not Hispanic English.

The same applies to ESL learners. A non-native speaker of English who is exposed to input that includes Canadian English, British English, and Jamaican English, for example, is likely to make a choice based on the social prestige of the dialect.

5.2 MARKED INPUT PREFERENCES

Although the above patterns are the most common, they are not the only preferences reported in the literature. Labov (1972b) cites evidence of some black adolescents acquiring the standard English of their teachers and of the white mainstream society. Poplack (1978) cites instances of bilingual Puerto Rican adolescents preferring AAVE to Hispanic English.

Thus, we see a wide range of speaker preferences. It seems that learners actively though not necessarily consciously choose the input model they prefer. Some of the studies above referred to second dialect acquisition but they can be extended to second language acquisition. We can visualize speaker choices on the scale shown in Figure 17.3. Different learners will be found at different places.

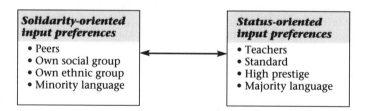

Figure 17.3 Solidarity- versus Status-Oriented Input Preferences

6 TEACHER TALK AS INPUT

What about the input in language classrooms? Wong Fillmore (1985) addresses the issue of when teacher talk *works* as input, examining the influence of instructional language and other teaching practices on language learning. She notes that not all children who are non-native speakers succeed in learning English as a second language, even though they're exposed to it at school. For many students of limited English proficiency, school is the only place where they come into regular contact with English speakers. This can be further complicated by the fact that in many school districts, many mainstream classrooms do not have very many students whose first language is English, and the non-native speakers thus may not engage in regular interaction with native speakers. Wong Fillmore noted a great variety in how well classrooms worked for language learning, and proposed the factors described in the sections below to account for the differences.

Her descriptions of teaching activities and language use raise some eyebrows among people who have been exposed to second language pedagogy training. The phrase *learner-centred* comes up a lot in training programs for teachers of a second language, with reference to both curricula and classrooms. Wong Fillmore seems to be undeniably arguing for a *teacher-centred* classroom. Remember, though, that she is describing a situation in which students are not exposed to much English outside the classroom and do not have many native speakers with whom to interact within the classroom. When these criteria are met, it may well be that teacher-centered classes serve a very useful purpose. This also describes the EFL classroom. ESL learners, of course, vary in the amount of English to which they are exposed, depending on such factors as social distance. For those learners who receive very little L2 input outside the classroom, teacher-centred instruction may be useful.

6.1 LESSONS THAT WORK AS INPUT

Lessons that work are formal and have clear boundaries:
- Boundaries marked by changes in location, props, and so on, such as moving to the school library for reading activities
- Beginnings and ends marked by formulaic cues such as the clock striking

They are regularly scheduled events:
- Scheduled time for activity
- Scheduled place for activity

They have a clear format from day to day:
- Clear instructions, lesson phases clearly marked by directions such as "First we're going to read the story silently and then we'll read it aloud together."

They demonstrate clear and fair turn allocation for student participation
- Lots of turns for each student
- Systematic turn allocation used at least some of the time
- A variety of response types invited or elicited

6.2 TEACHER TALK THAT WORKS AS INPUT

The talk involves clear separation of languages:
- No alternation or mixing

The talk emphasizes comprehension and communication:
- Use of demonstration and enactment to convey meaning
- New information presented in context of known information
- Heavy redundancy

The talk uses entirely grammatical language, appropriate to the particular activity:
- Avoidance of complex structures
- Repeated use of same sentence patterns or routines
- Use of paraphrases for variation

The talk exhibits richness of language use:
- Goes beyond books, letting students tell or write their own stories
- Plays games with language, such as making up rhymes

The talk tailors elicitation questions to allow for different levels of participation from students.

7 STUDENT REACTIONS TO TEACHER TALK

We would like to conclude this chapter with a view of teacher talk from the learner's perspective. Lynch (1988) discusses the affective factors related to teacher talk, maintaining that in his own second language learning experience he is used to being treated like an idiot. In his words, "before you can be a wit in a foreign language you inevitably have to pass through the stage of being a half-wit" (113). A brief anecdote should illustrate this familiar state. A man involved in a French immersion program in Quebec was billeted with a family. One evening, they were sitting around the television watching some intellectually stimulating show that featured a giant duck. In his best French, the man said something like "Regardez le grand canard!" (Look at the big duck!). One of the family members responded with a condescending tone, the French equivalent of "It's a man dressed as a duck." As if somehow the poor learner thought that this was a genetically engineered animal.

Lynch's study involved playing a tape for non-native speakers of English. On it a native speaker told a story, adopting an "overkill" strategy of teacher talk. You are probably familiar with this as the kind of talk you hear from someone who has taught kindergarten for fifty-five years and just can't switch it off any more. In this version, the listener was assumed to be a non-native speaker. Then they listened to another tape of the same story being told to a native speaker. The subjects had to answer questions about both the speaker and the listener. Table 17.4 lists the listeners' perceptions, demonstrating that if we are not careful the learner may perceive inappropriate teacher talk as condescending, the way you talk to a child or someone who is not very intelligent. On the other hand, note that the learners judged the same speaker to be friendlier. What can seem friendly to an unknown listener can seem condescending to you.

Table 17.4   Listeners' Perceptions

	Responses to native-speaker version	Responses to non-native-speaker version
The speaker is:	• older • not so friendly • not so clear • faster	• younger • friendlier • clearer • slower
The listener is:	• older • intelligent	• younger • less intelligent

8 CONCLUSION

The common terminology of "classroom" versus "naturalistic" environment seems to assume that the classroom is somehow unnatural, that instruction could only get in the way. This was certainly Krashen's assumption (1981). Communicative language teaching tries to make the classroom more like the broader environment in terms of the range of discourse and functions to which the second language learner is exposed. Recently, then, classrooms have experienced a shift from a traditional to a more naturalistic environment and from teacher-centred classes to student-centred classes.

In light of the evidence in this and the preceding chapter, however, it seems that classroom instruction can provide clear benefits. Simplified input gives learners the opportunity to selectively attend to and process the complex L2 input. Second language teachers obviously cannot talk to absolute beginners as if they were native speakers; they begin by simplifying their input. Yet they must keep in mind that learners must eventually be able to understand unsimplified input. If the student can only understand teacher talk then no favours have been done. We are reminded of the student who received an A grade in Intermediate Russian and went to Russia, only to discover that she could not understand what people were saying. "No one spoke Intermediate Russian," she said. Classroom instruction can help to avoid this situation by steering clear of oversimplified input.

As with many other aspects of classroom methodology, the pendulum swings back and forth between an emphasis on explicit instruction and a complete absence of it, and the extremes are rarely realistic for the classroom. Should classrooms be like the naturalistic environment? The evidence suggests that structured second language classrooms *are* good for certain things. Certainly, Wong Fillmore has shown that teacher-centred classes, teacher talk, and particular activities can have beneficial effects on L2 learning in some situations.

A comprehensive investigation of second language acquisition must include a look at the environment of the learner. This chapter has described studies examining the characteristics of the input and interaction to which L2 learners are exposed. As Ellis (1986) points out, the research to this stage has been more descriptive than explanatory. Nonetheless, it has allowed us to identify some characteristics of a good language learning environment.

CLASSROOM IMPLICATIONS

Ellis (1984) presents the following characteristics of an optimal learning environment:

1. A high quantity of input directed at the learner
2. The learner perceives a need to communicate in the L2
3. Independent control of the propositional content by the learner (e.g., control over topic choice)
4. Adherence to concrete input, at least initially
5. The performance of a range of speech acts by both the native speaker or teacher and the learner
6. Exposure to a high quantity of "extending" utterances (e.g., requests for clarification, confirmation, paraphrases, etc.)
7. Opportunities for uninhibited practice, which may provide the scope to experiment with new forms

Discuss these characteristics with respect to the second language classroom.

SELF TEST

The linguistic environment of L2 learners consists of modified _____ and _____ . The way in which native speak-
(1)   (2)
ers address non-native speakers is referred to as _____ talk.
(3)

Unlike the caregiver speech addressed to children, it can sometimes be
_____ . The modifications affect all linguistic levels. Native
(4)
speaker/non-native speaker discourse is also different from discourse
between native speakers. The participants in this conversation are
engaged in _____ of meaning as they construct a discourse.
(5)
As well, the _____ of particular functions differs from that of
(6)
interactions between native speakers. It has been argued that this type of
interaction is difficult to achieve inside a _____ .
(7)

L2 learners are not passive recipients of input; they have certain
_____ about which input sources they value. They may also
(8)
judge inappropriately modified input to be _____ .
(9)

FURTHER READING

Gass, S. and C. Madden. 1985. *Input in Second Language Acquisition*.
Rowley, MA: Newbury House.

18

....

The Effects of Feedback

This chapter concludes our discussion about the effects of the linguistic environment, begun in Chapter 16. Specifically, it focusses on the issue of feedback in the classroom. Although native speakers may occasionally provide correction or a mini grammar lesson, two things happen more in classrooms than in naturalistic environments: (1) overt error correction and (2) explicit instruction on formal aspects of the language structure. The second of these is known in the literature as focus-on-form instruction. We will look at research that tries to determine whether either error correction or focus on form helps second language learners progress. Together, these two techniques are known as feedback. Feedback is one kind of information provided in the language class; it is a subset of instruction, and a sizable literature is devoted to it. Let's begin by looking at error correction.

1 A MODEL FOR ERROR CORRECTION

Figure 18.1 illustrates a metaphor for the role of error correction in the learning process (Brown, 1987). Error correction takes place at the "cognitive feedback" traffic light. A red light is a signal to the non-native speaker that there is some problem with his or her message. Too many red lights can cause the learner to break off the attempt at communication. If we are constantly told that we are performing a task inadequately, it is a common human reaction to say the equivalent of "I'm taking my ball and going home." We may well decide that if we can't do it well, we're not going to do it at all. On the other hand, Brown argues that too many green lights can result in fossilization. If no one ever tells the learner that certain messages are not well formed, then how, we might ask, will he or she ever come to be aware of it?

The learner begins by expressing a message and getting some affective, or emotional, feedback from the situation. If the feeling is negative (–), the learner may abort trying to get the message across. If the affective atmosphere is neutral (0) or positive (+), the learner will continue to try to communicate. He or she may then receive some cognitive feedback, such as error correction. If the feedback is positive (a green light), the learner continues communicating. If it is negative (a red light) or cautious (a yellow light), the learner may loop back and consider ways to reformulate the original message.

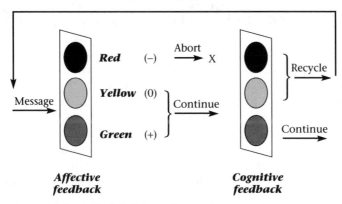

Figure 18.1   A Model of Error Correction
Brown, H. Douglas, *Principles of Language Learning and Teaching*, 2nd ed. © 1987, p. 192.   Reprinted by permission of Prentice-Hall, Inc., Englewood Cliffs, NJ.

L2 teachers must walk a fine line between providing too much error correction and too little. Most learners, however, do expect their errors to be corrected. When we notice an error, then, how should we respond? According to Brown (1987), the teacher must develop a feel for the best option in a particular situation. Long (1977) attempts to formalize the decision-making process (Figure 18.2).

1.1 DECIDING WHETHER TO TREAT ORAL ERRORS

Let's look in more detail at some of the decisions teachers make. Much of the following discussion is based on Allwright and Bailey (1991). If a teacher does notice an error, the first thing he or she has to do is decide whether to treat it or not. Whether the learner has previously been exposed to the form or function involving the error will play a part in that decision. If it is likely that the student in question has never been exposed to the item, then is it unfair to penalize them for not knowing it? Teachers vary over how they react to an error. If the student produces a stigmatizing or embarrassing error it will most likely lead to immediate treatment, though not necessarily in front of the whole class. One of the authors of this text had a Polish-speaking student who commented that whenever he tried to say the word *teeth*, people laughed. Consider his target pronunciation: [tiθ]. Now, this student did not have the tense/lax

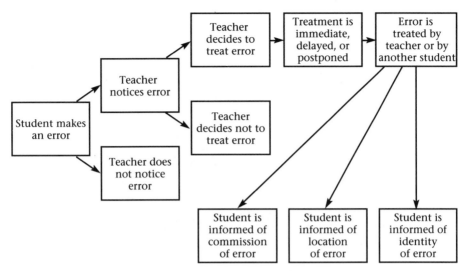

Figure 18.2 A Model of Error Correction
Source: Adapted from Long (1977).

vowel distinction, and [i] → [ɪ]. Nor did he have the voiceless interdental fricative, and [θ] → [t]. We leave it to the enterprising reader to determine why his output raised a smile or two.

Ludwig (1982) documented a hierarchy in teachers of German, Spanish, English, and French. Non-native teachers judged errors most severely, native speakers (non-teachers) judged the least severely, and native teachers were somewhere in the middle. Obviously, there will be individual variation within these categories.

1.2 DECIDING WHEN TO TREAT ORAL ERRORS

In Long's framework (see Figure 18.2), the difference between *delay* and *postpone* is length of time. *Delaying* a response involves giving feedback in the same lesson; *postponing* a response involves a longer wait. At times, teachers may decide to correct an error immediately, although they run the risk of interrupting the natural flow of communication. Doing so too often may dampen students' willingness to communicate. On the other hand, if teachers wait too long before treating errors the feedback may not be as effective. Imagine that on Monday, a teacher notices that a number of students are making mistakes on subject–verb agreement with two-part verbs, producing statements such as *He come backs tomorrow* and *She look ups the number.* Things will not be as fresh in the students' minds if the teacher waits until the following week to treat these errors.

In what situations do you think you would postpone treatment? When would you provide treatment immediately? Do you think all

People have been giving one another feedback for a long time. In the excerpt below, Polonius speaks to his son, Laertes.

> Yet here, Laertes? Aboard, aboard, for shame!
> The wind sits in the shoulder of your sail,
> And you are stayed for. There—my blessing with thee,
> And these few precepts in thy memory
> Look thou character. Give thy thoughts no tongue,
> Nor any unproportioned thought his act.
> Be thou familiar, but by no means vulgar.
> Those friends thou hast, and their adoption tried,
> Grapple them unto thy soul with hoops of steel;
> But do not dull thy palm with entertainment
> Of each new-hatched, unfledged comrade. Beware
> Of entrance to a quarrel, but being in,
> Bear't that th'opposéd may beware of thee.
> Give every man thy ear, but few thy voice;
> Take each man's censure, but reserve thy judgment.
> Costly thy habit as thy purse can buy,
> But not expressed in fancy; rich not gaudy,
> For the apparel oft proclaims the man,
> And they in France of the best rank and station
> Are of a most select and generous chief in that.
> Neither a borrower nor a lender be,
> For loan oft loses both itself and friend,
> And borrowing dulls th'edge of husbandry.
> This above all, to thine own self be true,
> And it must follow as the night the day
> Thou canst not then be false to any man.
> Farewell. My blessing season this in thee!

William Shakespeare
Hamlet, Act I, scene iii

errors are equally serious? What are some serious errors? What are some trivial errors? Do you think teachers disagree over the seriousness of a particular error? Would you postpone or treat immediately the following errors: *I have two cat at home, He come backs tomorrow, I've moved into a new bachelor department?* What factors would influence your decision?

1.3 DECIDING HOW TO TREAT ORAL ERRORS

It may not be a bad thing that errors can be treated in several ways, if we consider the amount of individual variation in second language acquisition. It is highly likely that different learners will prefer different error

treatments. An eclectic approach to classroom activity may well be justified in this domain. Chaudron (1977) provides a long list of possible
error treatments, given in Table 18.1.

Table 18.1   Chaudron's Typology of Feedback

Term	Definition	Example
Ignore	Teacher (T) ignores Student's (S) error, goes on to other topic, or shows acceptance of content.	
Interrupt	T interrupts S utterance following error or before S has completed it.	
Delay	T waits for S to complete utterance, before correcting.	
Acceptance	Simply approving or accepting word (usually as sign of reception of utter-ance), but T may immediately correct a linguistic error.	
Attention	Attention getter; probably quickly learned by Ss.	T: Be careful. Think about it.
Negation	T shows rejection of part or all of S utterance.	T: No, that's not it.
Provide	T provides the correct answer when S has been unable or when no response is offered.	S: Fifty, uh ... T: Percent.
Reduction	T utterance employs only a segment of S utterance.	S: I'm bery tired. T: Very ...
Expansion	T adds more linguistic material to S utterance, possibly making more complete.	S: It was good. T: Everybody thought it was good?
Emphasis	T uses stress, repetition, or question intonation, to mark area or fact of incorrectness.	S: A thousand. T: A thousand?
Repetition with no change	T repeats S utterance with no change of error.	S: I'm bery tired. T: You're bery tired.
Repetition with no change and emphasis	T repeats S utterance with no change of error, but emphasis locates or indicates fact of error.	S: He didn't went home. T: He didn't *went* home?
Repetition with change	Usually T simply adds correction and continues to other topics. Normally only when emphasis is added will correcting change become clear, or will T attempt to make it clear.	S: He breaked the glass. T: He broke the glass.

Table 18.1 Continued

Term	Definition	Example
Repetition with change and emphasis	T adds emphasis to stress location of error and its correct formulation.	S: He breaked the glass. T: He *broke* the glass.
Repeat	T requests S to repeat utterance, with intent to have S self-correct.	
Repeat (implicit)	Procedures are understood that by pointing or otherwise signalling, T can have S repeat.	
Loop	T honestly needs a replay of S utterance, due to lack of clarity or certainty of its form.	
Prompt	T uses a lead-in cue to get S to repeat utterance, possibly at point of error; possible slight rising intonation.	S: I'm bery … T: (interrupts) … bery?
Clue	T reaction provides S with isolation of type of error or of the nature of its immediate correction, without providing correction.	S: The Incas grow corn. T: *Grow?* Present tense?
Original question	T repeats the original question that led to response.	
Altered question	T alters original question syntactically, but not semantically.	
Questions	Numerous ways of asking for new response, often with clues, etc.	
Transfer	T asks another S, or several, or class to provide correction.	
Acceptance	T shows approval of S utterance.	
Repetitions	T attempts reinforcement of correct response.	
Explanation	T explains why response is correct.	
Return	T returns to original error maker for another attempt, after transfer. A type of verification.	
Verification	T attempts to assure understanding of correction; a new elicitation is implicit or made more explicit.	
Exit	At any stage in the exchange T may drop correction of the error, though usually not after explicit negation, emphasis, etc.	

Source: Adapted from Chaudron (1977).

We can divide treatment into three major categories. The teacher can inform the learner *that* an error has been made, inform the learner of the *location* of the error, or inform the learner of the *identity* of the error. Each of these options places less cognitive demand on the learner than the previous one. If the learner is told only that an error has been made, then he or she has to do considerable work to identify what the error is. If the teacher identifies the error, then obviously the learner will not have to do that work.

The teacher has to take a wide range of factors into account to determine whether the learner should expend considerable cognitive energy or not. Such elements as proficiency, inhibition, analytic ability, learner expectations, and so on play a part here. How do you believe these would influence error correction? In which situations would you identify the error and in which would you say that an error had occurred? When would you ignore an error?

There are many taxonomies of error correction, and the interested reader can consult the primary sources. The construct of error correction is not a simple one, as can be seen from the numerous factors presented above.

1.4 DECIDING WHO WILL TREAT ORAL ERRORS

Errors can be corrected by the learner, peers, or the teacher. The options can be used for different ends, but if the teacher selects peer correction he or she must ensure a supportive classroom atmosphere in which no one is allowed to laugh at another student. This is important. Sometimes errors can be funny, if they involve an absurd misunderstanding or something obscene, but it is important for students to know that mistakes are natural in all human learning. Second language learning is no exception. The old saying that people learn by making mistakes is particularly true in the classroom, and no one should feel stupid or foolish for making errors there.

2 TECHNIQUES FOR TREATING ERRORS

2.1 THE GARDEN PATH TECHNIQUE

One particular technique of error correction has received a fair amount of empirical investigation. Tomasello and Herron (1988) introduced a methodology they called the *garden path* technique, in which learners were actually induced to make errors so that they could be corrected in a systematic fashion. Students learning French as a second language, for example, would be presented with the following paradigm:

grand (big) → plus grand (biggest)
fort (strong) → plus fort (strongest)

Then they would be given the form *bon* (good) and asked to produce the superlative. In all likelihood, the students would say **plus bon* (best), which is incorrect but logical given their input. They would then be overtly corrected and told that the correct form is *meilleur*. The study focussed on this type of overgeneralization error, which Tomasello and Herron claimed could be effectively treated by the garden path technique.

Another Tomasello and Herron study (1989) treated transfer errors with the garden path technique. The subjects were thirty-two students taking a university course in Introductory French. The study centred on eight structures in French that deviate from the pattern found in English:

1. The elimination of the article before a profession
   French: Je *suis* actrice.
   English: I am *an* actress.
2. The use of a direct object after the verb *écouter* (to listen)
   French: J'*écoute* la radio.
   English: I listen *to* the radio.
3. The use of the verb *avoir* (to have) to express age
   French: J'*ai* vingt ans.
   English: I *am* twenty years old.
4. The use of the verb *aller* (to go) rather than *voyager* (to travel) when destination is mentioned
   French: Je *vais* à Paris chaque été.
   English: I *travel* to Paris every summer.
5. The use of three different verbs, *prendre, emporter,* and *emmener,* where English has only *to take*
   French: Je *prends* un taxi.
      J'*emporte* mon passeport quand je voyage.
      J'*emmène* un ami quand je voyage.
   English: I *take* a taxi.
      I *take* my passport when I travel.
      I *take* a friend when I travel.
6. The use of two verbs, *visiter* and *rendre,* to express the concept of visiting
   French: Je *visite* Paris.
      Je *rends visite* à mes amis parisiens.
   English: I *visit* Paris.
      I *visit* my Parisian friends.
7. The use of two verbs, *savoir* and *connaître,* to express the concept of knowing

French: Je *sais* la date de la mort de J.F. Kennedy.

Je *connais* Elizabeth Taylor.

English: I *know* the date of J.F. Kennedy's death.

I *know* Elizabeth Taylor.

8. The use of the verb *aller* (to go) and not *conduire* (to drive) when destination is mentioned.

French: Je *vais* à New York en voiture.

English: I *drive* to New York.

Half of the structures were assigned to the garden path technique—(1), (4), (6), and (7)—while the other half were taught "normally" (see Figure 18.3). The garden path technique revealed a significant advantage ($p < .05$). Thus, Tomasello and Herron assert that the technique facilitates accurate acquisition of L2 structures often involved in L1 transfer errors. The study also views errors as logical, natural, and ultimately beneficial to the learner. Success was measured by a translation task from the L1 to the L2.

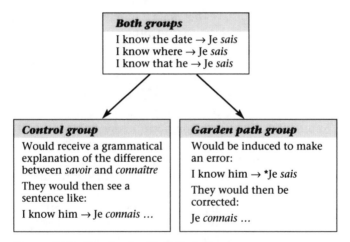

Figure 18.3   The Garden Path Technique

2.2 NEGATIVE FEEDBACK AND LINGUISTIC GENERALIZATIONS

Carroll and Swain (1993) have addressed the broader issue of whether feedback is useful to second language learners when it comes to forming linguistic generalizations. They investigated various types of negative feedback to see how they affected learner behaviour, looking at a hundred Spanish-speaking adults who were being taught the English dative alternation. This is a characteristic of English syntax by which certain verbs allow the following alternation:

Harold gave a painting to the museum.
Harold gave the museum a painting.

Not all verbs, however, can alternate in this fashion:

Harold donated a painting to the museum.
*Harold donated the museum a painting.

People learning English as a second language have to learn which sub-classes of verbs can alternate and which cannot.

Subjects in the Carroll and Swain study were given different types of feedback during the learning process. They were first trained by seeing pairs of alternating sentences. Next they were shown novel utterances in the form *Harold faxed a message to Henry* and asked to guess whether an alternative was permissible and if so what its form would be. They were told that some but not all of the items would alternate. Subjects were divided into five groups. Group A was treated with explicit hypothesis rejection; whenever subjects made a mistake they were given a linguistic (or metalinguistic) explanation about the class of verbs to which the alternation applied. Group B received explicit utterance rejection; whenever subjects made a mistake they were told that they were wrong. Group C was treated with modelling that incorporated implicit negative feedback; whenever subjects made a mistake they were given a reformulated correct response. Group D received indirect metalinguistic feedback; whenever subjects made a mistake they were asked if they were sure their answers were correct. Group Z received no treatment.

Interestingly, all of the treatment groups behaved significantly differently from the untreated group on both the training task and the guessing task. In addition, Group A performed significantly better than all other groups,[1] as can be seen in Figures 18.4 and 18.5.

The study showed a learning effect that seemed attributable to negative feedback. The negative feedback could be either direct or indirect and affected both the training session and the generalizations formed by the learners, as evidenced in the guessing session. Feedback, then, does appear able to affect second language learners.

3 COMPLEXITY OF ERROR CORRECTION

Woods (1989) argues that there are two main sources for the complexity of the error correction issue: (1) deciding that an error has occurred and interpreting it; and (2) being fair, consistent and correct in treatment of the error.

---

[1] Except Group C in the first recall session.

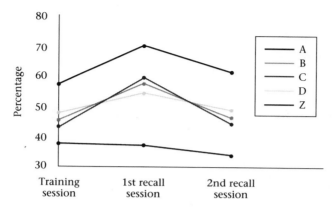

Figure 18.4   Mean Percentage of Correct Responses for Training Tasks
Source: Data from Carroll and Swain (1993).

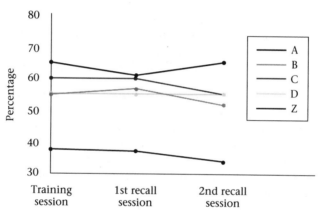

Figure 18.5   Mean Percentage of Correct Responses for Guessing Tasks
Source: Data from Carroll and Swain (1993).

3.1 HOW TO DECIDE WHAT AN ERROR IS

Underlying the notion of error is the assumption that the language in question has a correct standard form. Without a standard, how could we possibly judge what constitutes an error? But what is the standard? Some teachers believe that we should expect the standard of native-speaker English from our non-native speakers and that any deviation is an error. Others believe that L2 learners should not be expected to reach native-speaker proficiency, and they therefore have in mind some abstract norm as the standard. Still others believe that even native speakers make errors and they therefore have an abstract standard more rigorous than native speech, against which all speakers are measured. We can conceive of this hierarchy as follows:

Abstract native speaker standard
- We speak in sentences.
- Every utterance is grammatical.
- We do not make performance errors.

Native speaker standard
- Native speaker usage is taken as the standard.
- If native speakers say it, it's alright for non-native speakers to say it.

Abstract non-native speaker standard
- The teacher judges whether the non-native speaker's usage is "reasonable" compared with an image of how non-native speakers use the language.

It seems that even the notion of "correct" English is difficult to pin down.

Furthermore, if we want to have a standard for the language, we must distinguish between spoken and written forms. In informal talk we can say things like *I dunno* and *Wanna go?* but we would probably not write them in an academic essay. Similarly, in an academic essay we might write,

> One of the dominant concerns of current linguistic theory is to produce grammars that are feasible, or learnable. Often the learnability of grammars is determined philosophically (Mathews 1989) or mathematically (Wexler and Culicover 1980). But it is also enlightening to see whether a particular theoretical construct, which may meet the mathematical criteria for learnability and be a good model of adult knowledge, can also account for observed phenomena in the acquisition of this construct.

The preceding text would sound decidedly odd in conversation, but both it and informal talk are "correct." We need to keep this in mind when assessing non-native speaker performance. If we judge informal spoken performance by formal written standards we will be inconsistent. Remember, too, that there is also formal spoken language and informal written language. So, how do we decide what an error is?

Woods maintains that error correction springs from a combination of the way we *think* we speak and the way we think we *should* speak. We therefore notice, or correct, the errors for which we know the rules. Depending on a teacher's training, these may be the prescriptive grammar rules about things like not ending sentences with prepositions. Woods argues that we tend to focus on errors that are easy to label, to correct, and to give a rule for.

Consider the following paragraph, which was produced by a non-native speaker:

Thai (family) style is much more serious and (official) compared to Canadian style. In this case, I would like to mention (respecting manner.) For example, Thai children usually speak to their parents respectfully. They never try to (tease) their parents with funny words or impolite words. However, Thai parents (firstly) think about their relationship bound to their children most of the time (whenever conflicts come.) Consequently, divorce rate in Thailand is less than in Canada (Woods 1989, 63).

The circles are intended to draw your attention to those items; they are not part of the original. The author of this paragraph was enrolled in an advanced ESL writing class. Woods comments that the report was well done overall; the student made a clear and well-organized demonstration of important cultural differences between certain areas of Thai and Canadian life. Yet, the passage contains several potentially correctable items. What do you think of the words and phrases "family style," "official," "firstly," and "tease"? And consider the phrase "respecting manner." Does the student mean "with respect to" or "giving respect"? Does "manner" mean "the way something is done" or "manners"? Would you identify these as errors? Also remember that this is a written text and you therefore have time to think about these things. Imagine if this were an oral session and you had to decide what feedback to give as the student was speaking.

3.2 CONSISTENCY IN TREATMENT OF ERRORS

Even if there are many ways to identify errors, can we hope to achieve consistency in our treatment of them? Can we at least pick one method of correcting student errors and stick with it? It certainly appears to be difficult. The following is a modified version of an exchange from Allwright (1975):

Teacher: When's your birthday, Alvaro?
Alvaro: Twelfth November.
Teacher: OK. Now Santos, when's your birthday?
Santos: Fourteenth of September.
Teacher: No. Listen: *the* fourteenth. Again…

There are many reasons why this type of exchange can be justified peda-gogically. The two students may react to error correction very differently, for example, or they may be at different levels of proficiency. But con-sider how learners might interpret the exchange. They might conclude that we need *the* with *September* but not *November*, or that we need *the* with *14th* but not *12th,* or that the presence of *of* requires the presence of *the,* and so on. Any of these would make sense of the teacher's seeming grammatical inconsistency. Clearly, when we take into account classroom factors such as learner variation, content, and context, we cannot strive for perfect consistency in error correction.

4 FOCUS ON FORM

Explicit error correction is not the only type of feedback. Students may also receive explicit instruction on the formal aspects of the language, known as focus on form. VanPatten (1988) cites several sources supporting a predominant focus on form, at least initially. The American Council on the Teaching of Foreign Languages (ACTFL) Proficiency Guidelines, for example, state, "We encourage ... [the students] to realize that they must *first acquire linguistic building blocks and tools* and then, as soon as possible, begin to use the tools to put the blocks together." The guidelines clearly emphasize the necessity for accuracy of form and assume that form comes before function.

VanPatten then alludes to support for the communicative approach. Communicative language teaching minimizes the emphasis placed on grammar in the early stages of learning, focussing instead on successful communication. Considering these conflicting views, VanPatten explores the role of grammar instruction and linguistic accuracy. Particularly, he is concerned with whether we need linguistic accuracy from the beginning of the learning process. He uses the term *focus on form* to refer to both explicit grammar instruction and instruction that emphasizes linguistic accuracy.

4.1 FOSSILIZATION

Probably the best known advocates of early focus on form are Higgs and Clifford (1982). They argue that if the learner is rewarded for linguistically inaccurate but communicatively successful utterances, there is a real danger of fossilization. Higgs says, "Postponing linguistic accuracy is an approach which promises a terminal profile" (1984, 7). This is, indeed, an interesting claim but, VanPatten asks, what evidence do they present? None. Higgs and Clifford rely on phrases like "experience shows us", and "experiential data," which tell us virtually nothing about their research design. We do not know how many learners they examined, how many fossilized learners they identified, how the students were taught, what their backgrounds were, or for how long they were observed. The learners in question might not, in fact, have fossilized but instead might have reached a plateau of development. As VanPatten says, if you watch a snail cross the street, in three minutes it hasn't moved, but in three hours it's gone.

Other studies arguing that communicative language teaching at early stages leads to fossilization are also questionable. Pellerin and Hammerly (1986) argued that French immersion resulted in fossilized speech, but their study had only six subjects and it is difficult to generalize from such a small sample. As well, the data they cite do not support fossilization. The subjects were followed from Grade 1 to Grade 4 for their improvement on five grammatical items. They showed improvement on three of the five items and dramatic improvement on one of them; the error rate went from 81 percent to 1.5 percent. On the one category that does not show improvement, verb forms, Pellerin and Hammerly don't indicate what kinds of errors subjects were making when first assessed and then later, so we don't know if the same errors were sticking around or if new errors emerged. This is crucial knowledge if we want to claim fossilization. In another category, an error rate of 9 percent (or a success rate of 91 percent) was classified as fossilized. None of this is to say that fossilization in second language learning does not exist. Nonetheless, we have to look carefully at the data cited as support for the claim that communicative language teaching is the cause.

4.2 INSTRUCTION AND ACCURACY

Several studies have argued that focus on form is useful to beginning learners, that it can improve their accuracy. VanPatten, though, has well-founded reservations about some of the conclusions drawn. He has re-analysed Pica's (1983) study, discussed in Chapter 16, in which she claimed that instructed second language learners were more accurate on certain grammatical morphemes than were naturalistic learners. VanPatten argues that Pica did not control for differences between Spanish dialects. The classroom learners spoke Mexico City Spanish, whereas the naturalistic learners spoke Caribbean Spanish. Caribbean Spanish tends to delete syllable-final -s, but Mexican Spanish retains it. A phrase such as *las gallinas* (the chickens) is pronounced with the final -s in both words in Mexico but as something like *la gallina* in Caribbean Spanish. The speakers of Mexican Spanish in Pica's study would do much better on English -s morphemes (plural, third person singular, and possessive) as a result of L1 transfer than would the speakers of Caribbean Spanish.

4.3 ERROR CORRECTION AND ACCURACY

VanPatten also addressed the question of whether error correction improves the accuracy of students, claiming that "not one study clearly demonstrated that error correction made a significant difference"

(1988, 253). Lalande (1982) argued that error correction did have beneficial effects, but VanPatten comments that the standard deviation of the group receiving correction in Lalande's study increased after treatment, indicating a very diverse set of responses. It seems that error correction did not help all of the subjects. Semke (1984) showed that an *absence* of error correction did not lead to lower proficiency levels.

VanPatten argues that this is consistent with a view of the learner as information processor. Humans can only attend to a limited amount of information at a single time. When our capacity for information becomes overloaded, some information cannot be processed and gets dumped. The result is error. Error correction is just more information that has no way of being processed. VanPatten concludes by arguing that there is no evidence that focus-on-form instruction helps beginning learners achieve greater accuracy.

It is easy to understand why classroom teachers would present focus-on-form instruction in an attempt to increase the accuracy of students' production, but VanPatten demonstrates that the connection between the two is not easily established.

4.4 POSITIVE AND NEGATIVE EVIDENCE IN THE CLASSROOM

One way we can synthesize the preceding discussions of correction and focus on form is to look at another article, this time by Lydia White. White (1991) investigates the role of positive and negative evidence in the L2 classroom. Correction is referred to as negative evidence because it provides the learner with information about what is ungrammatical in the target language. Focus-on-form instruction is referred to as positive evidence because it provides the learner with information about what is grammatical in the L2. It is difficult to determine the efficacy of focus on form in part because it offers the same kind of evidence as the naturalistic environment, in the form of grammatical utterances. A series of articles investigates the role of positive and negative evidence in second language acquisition.

White (1991) points out that most theories of L1 learnability assume "no negative evidence." That is to say, children aren't usually exposed to negative evidence and when they are they don't make use of it. In general, however, adults are exposed to a lot more negative evidence than children are. Do they make use of it? White conducted an empirical investigation of French speakers learning English adverb placement. From this study she argues that negative evidence was a useful source of input.

Let's begin by comparing adverb placement in French and English. Both allow the orders *subject + verb + object + adverb* (SVOA) and *adverb + subject + verb + object* (ASVO):

SVOA: Jean boit son café rapidement.
SVOA: John drinks his coffee quickly.
ASVO: Prudemment Jean a ouvert la porte.
ASVO: Carefully John opened the door.

Furthermore, both languages allow adverbs after an auxiliary verb:

S Aux AVO: Jean a souvent visité le musée.
S Aux AVO: John has often visited the museum.

Nevertheless, the two languages have differences. In English, we do not find the order SVAO, but in French it's well formed:

Marie regarde souvent la télévision.
*Mary watches often television.

The order SAVO is not permitted in French but it is in English:

*Marie souvent regarde la télévision.
Mary often watches television.

In summary, we find the pattern shown in Figure 18.6.

Figure 18.6   Adverb Placement in French and English

The similarities and differences can be explained with reference to a parameter of universal grammar. White based her analysis on Pollock's (1989) proposals regarding verb movement. In French, all finite verbs are subject to a movement that is only permitted in English with the auxiliary verbs *have* and *be*. The verb movement, called verb raising, is obligatory in French but blocked in English. The underlying word order for French and English is SAVO and then the verb may move up the tree. As a result, SVAO is fine in French but SAVO is not, and SAVO is acceptable in English but SVAO is not. Table 18.2 summarizes this information.

Table 18.2   Verb Raising in French and English

French	English
Verb raising [Y]	Verb raising [N]
SVAO Jean boit rapidement le thé.	*SVAO John drank quickly the tea.
*SAVO Jean souvent regarde la télévision.	SAVO John often watches television.

4.4.1 Learnability and Second Language Acquisition

It is widely assumed in the literature that L2 learners may initially assume their L1 parameter settings as a basis for the L2 grammar. Later, they may come to reset their parameters. White argues that negative evidence may play a part in this parameter resetting. Her subjects had French as the L1 and English as the L2, so they had to learn that the L2 allows SAVO and does not allow SVAO. White attempted to explore what might trigger a resetting of the parameter.

Positive evidence should be available for the first element—that SAVO is permissible—because the L2 allows a range of structures that do not occur in the L1. In other words, the learner will hear grammatical English sentences in which verb raising did not take place, such as *He suddenly left the room*. Even if the learner has the initial setting or assumption that SAVO is not allowed, there will be positive evidence in the input to show that this is mistaken.

The second element—that SVAO is not permissible in English—is not as straightforward. What if the learner assumes that SVAO sequences, such as *He drank quickly his coffee*, are grammatical in the L2 as they are in the L1? These sentences do not occur in English, but White argues that the input of other sentences may give the impression of completely free adverb placement in English:

SVOA: John drinks his coffee quickly.
ASVO: Carefully John opened the door.
S Aux AVO: John has often visited the museum.
SAVO: Mary often watches television.

Logically, we might expect negative evidence to make a difference on SVAO structures. White proposes the following hypotheses:

1. L2 learners will initially assume the L1 parameter settings, leading them to believe that SVAO is acceptable in English but that SAVO is not.
2. Negative evidence will help them to realize that SVAO is not grammatical. Positive evidence alone will not help them to realize this.
3. Learners' judgments will cluster as predicted by the parameter. A learner will either have *SAVO and SVAO (if verb raising is [Y]) or SAVO and *SVAO (if verb raising is [N]).

4.4.2 The Experiment

White's experiment was conducted on two Grade 5 and three Grade 6 ESL classes in Quebec. One Grade 5 and two Grade 6 classes received explicit instruction on what English adverbs did. One Grade 5 and one Grade 6 class were not instructed explicitly on adverb placement, but were given instruction on question formation. It was assumed that question formation activities would give them ample positive evidence of English adverb placement but no negative evidence. Both groups were pre-tested on knowledge of adverb placement in English. Then the experimental groups received their explicit instruction in adverb placement, and the other groups received their explicit instruction in question formation. Both groups were re-tested on knowledge of adverb placement. A delayed post-test was administered at the end of the program and again after a year to see if any long-term effects emerged. All subjects had to perform a grammaticality judgment task, a preference task (in which they had to choose their preferred sentence), and a manipulation task (in which they had to form a sentence using the words on cards). White also used a control group to see how native English speakers responded to the test items.

4.4.3 Results

The adverb and question groups behaved differently on all tasks assigned them but there were no significant differences between Grade 5 and Grade 6. Figure 18.7 illustrates the performance on the grammaticality judgment task on the SVAO order, which is ungrammatical in English. The mean SVAO score represents the number of errors made. The maximum possible was sixteen.

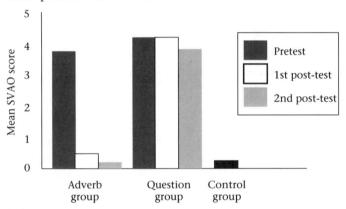

Figure 18.7   SVAO Error Scores
Source: Adapted from White (1991).

Prior to instruction there were no significant differences between the two experimental groups. They were both significantly different from the native control group. After instruction there was a significant difference between the adverb group and the question group. There was now no significant difference between the adverb group and the native control group. These patterns were maintained in the post-tests.

Significant differences were also found between the adverb group and the question group over the SAVO order (which is fine in English, and for which positive evidence is available). White maintains that similar trends were found in the preference and manipulation tasks as well, though we won't go through those here.

Her results seem to support the first two hypotheses: (1) that French learners assume English allows verb raising; and (2) that negative evidence appears to help them reset. The follow-up study revealed, however, that the adverb group did not retain knowledge over a long period (one year). In Figure 18.8, note how the follow-up error scores shoot up. In light of this evidence, we may have to revise our support of hypothesis (2) to indicate that negative evidence helps in the short but not the long term. White also suggests that the question group might not have got enough positive evidence about adverb placement. When she listened to the tapes of the classes, adverbs did not occur very frequently.

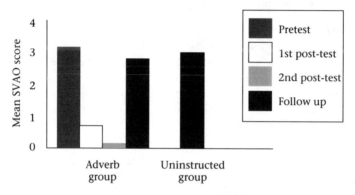

Figure 18.8   Follow-up Study SVAO Error Scores
Source: Adapted from White (1991).

The third hypothesis, about clustering, is not borne out. Clustering predicted that subjects would not accept both SVAO and SAVO, but they did. White suggests that this might occur because movement for French *non-finite* verbs is optional and the learners assumed that movement for English *finite* verbs is optional. This solution is speculative and requires further empirical study to assess.

As we saw in Chapter 8, although parameter settings have many advantages as an approach to the study of second language acquisition, the clustering of grammatical properties predicted by linguistic theory is not confirmed by study of interlanguage grammars.

4.5 FOCUS ON FORM IN A COMMUNICATIVE CONTEXT

To conclude this chapter we will examine a study that might provide the evidence VanPatten was looking for about the role of grammar instruction and linguistic accuracy. Lightbown and Spada (1990) argue that focus on form within the context of meaningful communication works better than instruction that either avoids focus on form or avoids meaningful communication.

Lightbown and Spada observed four intensive ESL classes in Quebec for twenty hours each. A macro-level analysis revealed that all four classes were primarily communicative in their approach. Classroom interaction focussed on meaning rather than form the majority of the time. They provided the breakdown shown in Table 18.3.

Table 18.3   Time Spent Focussing on Form

	Percent
Class 1 (Grade 5)	29
Class 2 (Grade 5)	13.5
Class 3 (Grade 6)	11
Class 4 (Grade 6)	13.5

Source: Data from Lightbown and Spada (1990).

The teachers almost never taught traditional grammar lessons and rarely presented rules about the target language structure. The form-focussed behaviour was usually a response to either an error or a student request. Each teacher tended to emphasize slightly different grammatical items. Class 1, for example, spent considerable time on *there is* and *there are* and other grammatical items, whereas Class 4 rarely discussed grammar but dealt with vocabulary in detail. Lightbown and Spada wondered whether there was any connection between the form of the learner language and the items that the teachers emphasized. Table 18.4 shows student accuracy on six grammatical items. Note that the significant differences, indicated by lines joining the different classes, are always between Class 4 and some other class.[2] It does seem that Class 4, the one in which grammar instruction rarely occurred and the focus on form emphasized vocabulary, behaved differently from the other classes, often significantly differently.

Lightbown and Spada concluded that "form-based instruction within a communicative context contributes to higher levels of linguistic knowledge and performance." And that is probably as good a summary as any of the classroom implications of this research.

5 CONCLUSION

The issues of error correction and focus on form have an inherent interest for second language teachers. We want to know if what we do is having any effect on the learners. There is still room for a considerable amount of empirical research to try to answer this question but we can

---

[2] Significant differences between groups cannot be determined by comparing percentage scores alone. Statisitical tests are run on the raw data, and take into account variation both within and between groups.

Table 18.4   Percentage of Students Showing Accuracy on Grammatical Items

	Class 1 (Grade 5)	Class 2 (Grade 5)	Class 3 (Grade 5)	Class 4 (Grade 6)
Accuracy on plural -*s*	50.20	59.04	58.63	37.36
Accuracy on progressive -*ing*	28.21	13.16	14.80	5.44
Zero accuracy on -*ing*	29.2	56	50	76
Accuracy on adjective/noun placement	74.63	88.74	74.71	58.96
Accuracy in use of possessive	74.00	62.90	56.00	42.00
Correct use of both *his* and *her* at least once	34.78	16.00	32.14	0

safely state that learners expect it, teachers do it, and, in a communicative context, it seems to help. Carroll and Swain's study (1993) showed that feedback (including implicit feedback) had a beneficial effect on learners' performance, but White's study (1991) forces us to question whether the effect will last beyond the short term.

CLASSROOM IMPLICATIONS

1. How would you respond if you were teaching a class and a student said, "I want you to correct every mistake I make"?
2. Do you think that correcting written work is different from correcting oral work? In what ways? In which form would you offer more corrections? Which type of correction do you think is more effective?
3. Do you think that transfer occurs from corrections on a written assignment to spoken language?
4. Would you make use of peer correction in your class? Why or why not?

SELF TEST

Error correction and _____ grammar instruction clearly happen in L2 classrooms. L2 teachers have to make many rapid decisions about whether and _____ to treat a student error. Long's model and Chaudron's model illustrate the complexity of the decisions,
(1)
(2)

and show that there is no _____ way to correct errors. The
(3)
_____ technique, in which students are actually _____
(4)   (5)
to make errors which are then corrected, appears to be effective in some
situations. Carroll and Swain examined the effects of different types of
feedback and noted that _____ evidence had a significant
(6)
effect on learners. They also showed that _____ explanations
(7)
were the most effective.

Woods points out that it is difficult at times to _____ an
(8)
error and impossible for a teacher to be entirely _____ in
(9)
treatment of errors. White argues that negative evidence can have an
effect on interlanguage grammars but that the effect may be

_____ .
(10)

FURTHER READING

Mendelsohn, D. 1991/92. Feedback instruments. *TESOL Journal* 1 (2):
25–30.

Related Issues

This section examines issues related to second language acquisition. Chapter 19 looks at the consequences of literacy and illiteracy, focussing on the social repercussions. Chapter 20 investigates bilingualism and how two languages are stored in the brain. Chapter 21 looks at bilingual education. Heritage language programs, French immersion, and the use of American Sign Language are all important issues in the bilingual classroom. Chapter 22 looks at first language attrition. Under certain circumstances, it appears as if the price of second language acquisition is the loss, or attrition, of the first language. This chapter discusses the influence of the L2 on the L1. Chapter 23 provides brief summaries of all the preceding chapters.

19

....

The Social Consequences
of Literacy

Chapter 5 discussed some of the ways in which languages can represent their spoken languages visually, and Chapter 12 looked at psycholinguistic and cognitive issues related to reading. As many, perhaps most, of the world's languages do not have written systems, linguists have argued that reading and writing are not necessary attributes of human language and therefore not central to linguistic study. Nevertheless, many language learners have to learn how to read in their second language, and it therefore deserves a certain amount of attention in the study of L2 acquisition.

This chapter differs from the rest of the text in two ways. It is primarily concerned with the *social* consequences of a given ability—in this case reading—and it centres on children rather than adults. Whether immigrant children learn to read well in their second language has far-reaching consequences for their success in school. The primary research in this chapter focusses on monolingual children, but the discussion covers the implications for non-native speakers as well. Let us begin by asking what literacy is.

1 WHAT IS LITERACY?

Bell (1990) edited a collection of papers that dealt with a variety of issues related to L2 literacy. A number of researchers were asked what exactly learners were attempting when they tried to become literate in a second language.

David Barton, a British specialist in adult literacy, talks about what a person who is not literate in his or her first language needs to learn. In many parts of Western culture, children learn about literacy almost from birth;

they may be told stories or read to even though they are not actually reading themselves. Barton believes that in this way children learn *about* literacy; they learn that a book is not a toy but a means to generate other worlds to talk about. His point is that children learn a lot about literacy that is not explicitly taught. Adults who have to acquire literacy for the first time in a second language also have to acquire knowledge about literacy.

Jim Cummins, a leading researcher of bilingual education, believes that literacy is emancipatory; that it is power. For him, students must be actively engaged in analysing the information in the text and relating it to their own lives. Within this framework, learners generate their own knowledge rather than passively receiving others'. Cummins argues that it makes sense to introduce literacy in the learner's stronger language when feasible, as this permits him or her to be more involved in the learning. (Clearly, this is not possible if the student's first language has no writing system.) Literacy skills acquired in the stronger language will transfer to the weaker language. He acknowledges that though this approach has well-documented success for children, little research has been done with adults.

David Olson is a cognitive scientist specializing in literacy. He begins by, if not debunking, at least minimizing the traditional assumption that literacy is the keystone of a civilized society. People have argued that learning to read and write is necessary to higher forms of intellectual activity (see, for example, Logan 1986). Olson calls this the *literacy myth*. He asserts that literacy is essentially a metalinguistic activity which turns language into an object of awareness. In learning to read, children become aware that their language is made up of sounds, words, and sentences. Literacy brings language into consciousness.

Researchers can take very different perspectives on what literacy is. Those just mentioned are concerned with the socio-political aspects of reading.

2 READING IN DIFFERENT WRITING SYSTEMS

One of the most common questions second language teachers have when they notice that a student is having trouble reading in the second language is whether the problem is based on language or on reading itself. The bulk of research suggests that if you know how to read in your first language you will be able to transfer those skills into the second language. We only learn to read once. Yet humans learn to read an astonishing variety of written systems, as we saw in Chapter 5, and the learner may well have to master a completely new system.

When the first and second languages have different writing systems, learners do not tend to confuse the level of representation involved.

(Remember that logographic systems represent the morpheme with a symbol, syllabic systems represent the syllable, and alphabetic systems represent the segment.) Chinese speakers learning English, for example, do not assume that English letters represent words. Confusion can arise, however, when the L1 and L2 use the same basic writing system but with certain differences. Consider the case of Turkish and English, which are both alphabetic. In the English system, the phonetic variants of a morpheme are not reflected in the spelling:

wish<u>ed</u> → [t]
fizz<u>ed</u> → [d]
fitt<u>ed</u> → [əd]

In Turkish, the spelling reflects the phonetic changes:

gel<u>di</u> → [di] (he/she came)
al<u>dı</u> → [dɨ] (he/she took)
gör<u>du</u> → [du] (he/she saw)

In both the English and Turkish examples the past tense morpheme is underlined. Speakers of Turkish who are learning the English writing system have to learn to suppress certain phonetic contrasts. Learning to read and write in a new language, then, can involve the acquisition of both high- and low-level skills.

3 INTERACTING WITH A TEXT

Reading involves more than decoding the words on a page. To acquire literacy we must learn to interact with a text and construct meaning from it. Reading is a process of interaction between the text and the reader. Traditionally, reading and listening were referred to as the *passive* skills, contrasted with the *active* skills of talking and writing. Most people now do not think of reading and listening as purely receptive. The reader actively creates information in the process of restructuring the text. Variables such as the reader's background knowledge can influence the meaning created, and different readers can get different things out of the same text. The acquisition of literacy, then, involves both decoding the text and interacting with it.

4 THE BRISTOL STUDY

We would now like to turn to an investigation of the consequences of literacy by looking at the work of Gordon Wells. In a massive longitudinal study, Wells (1986) followed the progress of a representative sample of children in Bristol, England, from a very early age to see if there was a relationship between their family background, or socio-economic status (SES), and their oral or written language ability. The study examined first language acquisition but it sheds light on the situation of many second language learners as well. Wells tracked thirty-two children for nine years.

The correlation found between achievement and family background is shown in Table 19.1, according to the age at which the children were assessed. At two and at three and a half the children were assessed on oral language exclusively. Recordings of conversation at home were analysed for such things as range of meanings expressed, forms used to express them, and functions for which speech was used. The three year olds were also given a comprehension test of both words and sentences. Teachers made comprehensive assessments of the children when they entered school at age five, again at age seven, and finally at age ten. The test at age five was to measure "readiness for school." It included a word comprehension test, an oral comprehension test that involved acting out a story, a test of hand–eye co-ordination, and a test of knowledge of literacy that determined whether the children recognized letters, their own names, and so on. At age seven, the word comprehension test was given again along with tests of reading comprehension. At age ten, the children were tested again for reading comprehension and also for mathematical ability. They had to perform a number of writing tasks as well. At each age, the results of all tasks were combined to give an overall achievement score.

Table 19.1   Linguistic Achievement and Socio-Economic Background

Age	Correlation
2	.24
3.5	.29
5	.66[†]
7	.58[†]
10.25	.59[†]

[†] Correlations were significant at the .01 level (very significant).
Source: Data from Wells (1986, 136).

What do the results signify? At the two times when the children were assessed in their preschool years, there was no significant correlation between their oral language ability and their family background. As soon as they were assessed at school, from age five on, however, the strength of the relationship increased. This suggests that the shift in assessment from purely oral skills to skills associated with literacy put some children at a disadvantage. It was always the children at the lower end of the socio-economic scale, those from working-class families, who did poorly. Immediately, we must ask why.

4.1 LINGUISTIC DISADVANTAGE

Researchers had noted before the Bristol study that children of working-class families had significantly more frequent difficulty at school than did children from families with higher socio-economic status, but they had not discovered why. Initially, it was felt that working-class children had fewer linguistic resources than their middle-class peers and were, as a result, less able to participate in the largely linguistic activities of the classroom.

With this diagnosis, the obvious remedy was to provide these children with compensatory educational programs to equip them with the skills it was believed they lacked. This was part of the justification of the Head Start program in the United States. Such programs have tended to focus on oral language on the supposition that this would remedy general linguistic deficits and thus improve literacy skills.

In Britain, Basil Bernstein (1971) offered another explanation for the disadvantage experienced by children of a lower SES, arguing that the differences between middle- and working-class children lay not in their linguistic *knowledge,* or competence, but rather in the way they *used* their language. According to Bernstein, lower SES families tend to use a *restricted* linguistic code in which much of the speaker's meaning is implicit, assumed to be shared or tied to the context. Other researchers (Cummins and Swain 1986), refer to this as context-embedded language. If you were in a restaurant, for example, and a waiter came over to speak to you, the context would tell you that the utterance was probably not "Any comments on the *Critique of Pure Reason*?" In certain contexts, we know what to expect. Middle-class families, on the other hand, tend to use, in Bernstein's terms, *elaborated* linguistic code. An elaborated code relies less on the context to convey information. This is what Cummins calls context-reduced language.

Much academic language and indeed much educational activity, is largely concerned with context-reduced language use. The words you are reading now convey information that is largely unpredictable from the context. Middle-class children, then, are accustomed to context-reduced language in their home environment and have little trouble succeeding in a school where many of the academic activities depend on this type of language use. Lower SES children, according to Bernstein, are not accustomed to context-reduced language and therefore have difficulty adapting to school expectations.

William Labov (1972a) proposed another explanation. Labov is a noted sociolinguist who specializes in urban dialects. He observed that although lower SES children often appeared to be linguistically disadvantaged in the classroom, they showed perfectly normal linguistic ability when interacting with their peers on the playground. Their verbal skills were not, however, expressed in the standard dialect. Labov argued that these children did not lack language but rather were disadvantaged in situations that demanded the use of Standard English. Their dialect did not match the dialect valued by their teachers.

With these varying explanations for the problem in mind, let us return to the Bristol project.

4.2 RESULTS FROM THE BRISTOL STUDY

As we have already seen, one of the most interesting results from this study was the absence of significant differences between middle- and working-class children up to age five. There were no notable differences with respect to their rate of development, range of meanings expressed, or range of functions: in other words, in either quantity or quality of conversational experience. Thus, the Bristol study refutes Bernstein's idea of class-associated differences in ways that parents talk with their children. Wells argued that teachers unconsciously treated children of different socio-economic status differently. Although children did not come labelled with a particular SES badge, such factors as dialect, parents' occupations, and the neighbourhood in which a child lived were reliable clues and appeared to influence teachers' expectations. Where there were high expectations, teachers were more likely to encourage children to express their ideas spontaneously and at length. Where there were low expectations, children were given few opportunities to initiate or sustain a topic of conversation.

Wells thus contended that with different opportunities, children perform differently. Even with the best intentions, the teacher can interact with a child in such a way that the child is caused to appear linguistically deficient. Consider the following conversation between Teacher A, Rosie, and another child. Rosie, at this time, has just started school:

Child: Miss, I done it.
Teacher: [to Rosie] Will you put it at the top?
Child: Miss, I done it, look. [several seconds' pause]
Teacher: [to Rosie, pointing with finger at card] What are those things?
Child: Miss, I done it. Miss, I done it. [Rosie drops something, then picks it up.]
Teacher: [to Rosie] What are those things?
Child: Miss, I *done* it.
Teacher: [referring to skis in picture] *D'you know* what they're called? [Rosie shakes her head.] What d'you think he uses them for?

[Rosie looks at the card. The teacher turns to the other child's calendar.] It's very nice. After play, we'll put some ribbons at the top.

Child: What?

Teacher: Ribbon at the top to hang them up by. Would you put all the cards together now? Put the cards together.

Child: Oh.

Teacher: [to Rosie, pointing at the skis on the card]: What's ... what are those? [Rosie looks blank.] What d'you think he uses them for?

Rosie: [rubbing one eye with the back of her hand] Go down.

Teacher: Go down, yes, you're right; go on. [Rosie rubs both of her eyes with the backs of her hands.] What's the rest of it? [Puts down card] You have a little think and I'll get, er, get the little calendar for you. I think you're sitting on.... Right. [Points to calendar.] Could you put some glue on the back there? [Rosie takes the calendar from the teacher.] He uses those to go down.... [five-second pause] Is it a hill or a mountain?

Rosie: A hill.

Teacher: A hill, yes. And what's on the hill?

Rosie: Ice.

Teacher: Yes, ice. They're called skis.

Child: Miss.... [The teacher leaves to deal with the other children. When she returns, Rosie has finished her calendar.]

Teacher: That's lovely, and afterwards we'll put some ribbon.... What d'you think the ribbon's for? [Points to calendar with pencil and looks at Rosie. Six-second pause.]

Rosie: For Father Christmas.

Teacher: [bending closer to Rosie, looking into her face] Sorry?

Rosie: [looking away from teacher] For Father Christmas.

Teacher: For Father Christmas? [Straightens slightly from bending position and looks at the card, pointing at it again with hand] If you want to put it up on the wall, you have a little piece of ribbon long enough to hang it up by (Wells 1986, 96–97).

In this conversation we note that Rosie appeared to understand little of what the teacher was saying and only produced five utterances herself. All of her utterances were simple phrases. From this sample it might appear justified to assume that Rosie was somehow linguistically deprived. But look at the following conversation between Rosie and Teacher B:

Rosie: I am tall said the tower.

Teacher: [correcting her] Chimney.

Rosie: Chimbley.

Teacher: [pointing at picture] It's a big factory chimney, isn't it?

Rosie: I don't like....
Teacher: [pointing at illustration with pencil] There's a lot a smoke coming out of the top.
Rosie: [pointing at picture of chimney] I don't like that one.
Teacher: You don't like it? [Rosie shakes her head.] Why not?
Rosie: I only like little ones.
Teacher: Have you got a chimney in your house? [Rosie nods emphatically.]
Child: And me.
Teacher: [to Rosie] D'you have smoke coming out of the top? [Rosie nods emphatically.] Mm? [Rosie nods her head again. The teacher turns the page, then closes the book.] What's underneath the chimney, then, that makes the smoke come out?
Child: I know, fire.
Teacher: [to Rosie] Mm?
Rosie: Fire.
Teacher: Is it? Have you got a fire then?
Child: Miss, can I have this one?
Teacher: [to Rosie] Which room's the fire in? [Shifts gaze to other child] Yes. [Looks back to Rosie.]
Rosie: In the front one.
Teacher: Is it? So it keeps you warm? Lovely.
Rosie: And I got a bed.
Teacher: Where's your bed?
Rosie: E's upstairs.
Teacher: Anybody else got a bed in your room?
Rosie: Carol got a bed and Kelvin [very softly] and Carol.
Teacher: Uh-huh. What about Donna?
Rosie: Donna, we're sharing it.
Teacher: You're sharing with Donna, are you? [Rosie nods her head emphatically.] D'you have a cuddle at night?
Rosie: Yeh, and I ... when I gets up I creeps in Mummy's bed.
Teacher: For another cuddle? [Rosie nods.] Oh that's nice! It's nice in the morning when you cuddle (Wells 1986, 98).

In this conversation, she responded to the teacher's questions and volunteered information. Her utterances were much more complex and she appeared to be quite a different child. Wells asserted that the teachers themselves caused these different types of response and suggested that Teacher A turned a friendly conversation into an interrogation when Rosie couldn't respond properly (probably due to a lack of exposure to the subject of the picture: skiing). Teacher B allowed Rosie to talk about something she knew: her home. The difference in performance was striking.

Let us now return to the question of why lower SES children should have difficulty at school.

4.3 KNOWLEDGE OF LITERACY

Wells gave all of the children a knowledge-of-literacy test. Even though children may not know how to read, they still may know *about* literacy. The test had two parts. In the first, each child was presented with an illustrated storybook called *Sand,* about going to the beach. The researcher handed over the book upside-down and back-to-front and noted whether the child knew to reposition it. The researcher then asked questions like "Can you show me a word?" and "Can you show me a sentence?" In the second part of the test, the researcher gave the child a sheet of paper on which all the letters of the alphabet were printed in upper and lower case, in random order. The child was then asked to name or sound any letter that he or she could recognize. Wells claims that these two parts provide a reliable estimate of how much a child knows about the conventions of written language.

The results of this test at age five can predict later assessments of school achievement. Children who scored poorly on the test were likely to have less success later on in school. Children who obtained relatively high scores on a test of knowledge of literacy were more likely to have parents who read more, owned more books, and read more to them. In turn, these children were more likely to show an interest in literacy, ask about meanings, and ask about letter shapes.

For all of these literacy-related measures in the preschool years, Wells found a significant correlation with family background. If the lower SES children did suffer from a disadvantage, it was therefore in the limited exposure to literacy-related activities as measured by the absence of books in the home and the low frequency of reading to the child. These children came to school with a very limited understanding of the purposes of literacy and little knowledge of how to get meaning from print. This may well explain their poor performance in school.

But Wells does not place *blame* on the parents for this state of affairs. He asks us to look at the phenomenon in a larger social context. Consider the children of a middle-class family. These children enter school familiar with reading and writing even though they cannot read or write themselves. With this start, they have become independent readers and writers by age seven or eight. At eighteen they usually go to college or university and then to middle-class occupations that require literacy skills. Their regular work and leisure activities allow their children to see the value of literacy. Their children come to school knowing about literacy, and the cycle continues. But now consider the children of a working-class family. These children enter school knowing little of literacy. Often they will have difficulty learning how to read and write. Perhaps, they will lose confidence in their ability to learn. The children may be placed in a remedial stream and become disenchanted with the whole institution of education. These children may leave school before graduating and get jobs with few literacy requirements. Their activities with their children do not include reading and writing. Their children enter school knowing little of literacy, and the cycle of educational disadvantage is repeated. This is clearly not true for every case, but the broad picture remains.

Margaret Donaldson (1978) comments,

> What is going to be required for success in our educational system is that [the child] should learn to turn language and thought in upon themselves. He [or she] must become able to direct his own thought processes in a thoughtful manner. He must become able not just to talk, but to choose what he will say, not just to interpret but to weigh possible interpretations. His conceptual system must expand in the direction of increasing ability to represent itself. He must become capable of manipulating symbols.

As we saw David Olson argue at the beginning of the chapter, this is what literacy involves. When children listen to stories and discuss them with adults they have the opportunity to reflect on their own experience. It also encourages them to explore the language of the text through the world of their imagination. This is admirable preparation for context-reduced language use.

5 IMPLICATIONS FOR SECOND LANGUAGE LEARNERS

We have dealt at length with the social consequences of literacy in acquiring a first language. Children who arrive at school with little knowledge of literacy seem much more likely to have problems. By extension, this is true for second language learners. Children who come to school without knowledge of literacy in their first language will most likely find themselves in the same situation as the working-class children of Well's study.

Thus, the acquisition of literacy skills has immense social consequences for non-native-speaking children. If they are not exposed to literacy activities in the home before they enter school in either the L1 or the L2, these children are likely to have little knowledge of literacy, and this does not bode well for their future in school. Success in school appears to be intimately tied to literacy, and literacy skills seem closely correlated with socio-economic factors. A wide range of problems that bilingual children of lower SES encounter at school has much more to do with social factors than with cognitive factors like intelligence or bilingualism.

6 ADULT LITERACY

Lest we think that literacy problems affect only children, let us conclude this chapter with a brief look at some facts about adult literacy. The Southam Report (1987) provided some worrying statistics related to illiteracy in Canada:

- 8 percent of Canada's adult population is almost completely illiterate (1 000 000 people)
- 16 percent is functionally illiterate (3 000 000 people)
- illiteracy is higher among men than among women
- illiterates earn two-thirds the income of literates
- one out of six working Canadians is illiterate
- 70 percent of illiterates live in cities
- 70 percent of illiterates were born in Canada
- 40 percent of illiterates are under 45
- 8 percent of university graduates are functionally illiterate

These figures do not take into account people in prison, transients, people in mental institutions, native people on reserves, or people living north of the 60th parallel. If these people were included, the Southam Report estimates that another 500 000 would be taken into account in the survey. The test items in this study included items such as understanding the dosage on cough syrup, signing the correct place on a social insurance card, circling the expiry date on a driver's licence, and circling the long distance charges on a phone bill. Someone who is functionally illiterate would have difficulty performing these tasks.

The figures make us aware of the extent of the problem. If this many native speakers have reading problems then how many non-native speakers do? For adults, too, the social cost of illiteracy is high: less money, less job satisfaction, less chance to prepare their children for better literacy skills. Obviously, illiteracy is going to affect adult second language learners as well. In today's social climate, the kinds of jobs available to someone with limited literacy skills are very restricted. Difficulty reading and writing English will certainly restrict the non-native speaker's ability to find employment.

If some, though not all, immigrant children have problems in school, and if some, though not all, immigrant adults have low-prestige jobs, we need to look primarily at social factors for an explanation. Bilingualism itself is not a disadvantage, as we will see in the next two chapters.

7 CONCLUSION

Literacy can be approached from a number of perspectives, all of which have relevance to the second language learner. We can look at it cognitively, socially, or politically. Cognitively, we have seen that the reader and the text interact to restructure a text and arrive at a unique meaning; reading is not passive. Socially, we have seen that literacy is connected to SES. Politically, we have seen that literacy and power are intimately tied together. It can affect the kinds of jobs adults get and the kind of education their children get. Reading is not just something you do. Literacy can affect who you are.

CLASSROOM IMPLICATIONS

Discuss the ways in which you think a lack of literacy skills in English would affect a second language learner living in an English-speaking country. Try to imagine yourself in a similar position. To simulate the experience, look at the Hebrew alphabet and its English transliteration, given in Table 19.2, and then try to rewrite the sequences of letters that follow into correct Hebrew form. Hebrew does not transcribe vowels in its orthography. The consonant strings are written from right to left.

Table 19.2   The Hebrew Alphabet

Name	Printed letter	Script form	Phonological form
alef	א	)c	ʔ
bet, vet	ב	බ	b or v
gimel	ג	૮	g
daled	ד	૱	d
heh	ה	ꜰ	h
vav	ו	I	v
zayin	ז	౩	z
chet	ח	ᴅ	x
tet	ט	ᴄ	t
yod	י	I	y
kaf, chaf	כ	ᴐ	k or x
lamed	ל	૬	l
mem	מ	N	m
nun	נ	ᴶ	n
samech	ס	o	s
ayin	ע	ᴕ	ʕ
pe, fe	פ	ᴐ	p or f
kof	ק	ᴩ	k
tsade	צ	ᴣ	t^s
resh	ר	ᴐ	r
shin, sin	ש	e	š or s
tav	ת	ᴐ	t

1. hu katav sefer
   He wrote a book.

2. hi ohevet glida
   She likes ice cream.

3. hem racu el hagan
   They ran to the garden.
   Note: *c* = [tˢ]

4. yeš la kelev
   exist to-her a dog
   She has a dog.

5. kar li
   cold to me
   I'm cold.

SELF TEST

The phenomenon of literacy, essentially a cognitive activity, can also be placed within a _____ context. As Cummins points out, liter-
(1)
acy is _____ . Children and adults who do not acquire literacy
(2)
skills are likely to live in a very different social world from people who do. Evidence suggests that reading skills acquired in the _____ will transfer to the _____ ; we learn to read
(3)   (4)
only once. The ways in which a spoken language maps onto the written language varies; a written character can represent a _____ ,
(5)
_____ , or _____ . Becoming literate also involves
(6)   (7)
learning how to _____ with a text and construct its meaning.
(8)
   In his Bristol Study, Gordon Wells noted that there was a correlation between _____ and achievement at school. He argued that
(9)
children from working-class families did not have _____ and
(10)
that this affected their performance at school. Teachers had _____ expectations for these children, as well.
(11)

FURTHER READING

Alderson, J.C. and A.H. Urquhart, eds. 1984. *Reading in a Foreign Language*. New York: Longman.

Bell, J., ed. 1990. *ESL Literacy*. Special issue of *TESL Talk* 20 (1). Toronto: Queen's Printer.

Bernhardt, E. 1991. *Reading Development in a Second Language*. Norwood, NJ: Ablex Publishing.

Bertelson, P., ed. 1987. *The Onset of Literacy*. Special issue of *Cognition*. Cambridge, MA: MIT Press.

Carrell, P., J. Devine, and D. Eskey. 1988. *Interactive Approaches to Second Language Reading*. New York: Cambridge University Press.

Harrington, M. and M. Sawyer. 1992. L2 working memory capacity and L2 reading skill. *Studies in Second Language Acquisition* 14:25–38.

20

....

Bilingualism

The result of successful second language acquisition is bilingualism. This chapter discusses research on the nature of bilingualism and in particular on the organization of two languages in the mind.

1 DEFINITIONS OF BILINGUALISM

If you look up the word *bilingual* in a dictionary, you are likely to find a definition like this one: "A person capable of using two languages especially with equal or nearly equal facility" (*Webster's New World Dictionary,* 1976). Definitions of this sort are in tune with the general societal view that a bilingual is someone who has perfect command of two languages. The fact is, however, that very, very few bilinguals have perfect and equal command of both languages. Considerations of this sort have prompted researchers such as Macnamara (1967) to define bilingualism in maximally weak terms as minimal competence in one of the four language skills—listening comprehension, speaking, reading, and writing—in a language other than the mother tongue. In the view of this text, the first definition is too strong because it excludes most of the individuals we might want to study and the second definition is too weak because it does not distinguish between a bilingual and a second language learner. A discussion of bilingual individuals and the organization of two languages in one mind might therefore begin with a moderate definition: a bilingual is a person who has a functional command of two languages and whose linguistic competence is in a stable state. Note the key point in this definition that the bilingual is no longer a learner; his or her linguistic systems are in a stable state that is good enough to allow the individual to function in both languages.

Nevertheless, this definition is just a beginning. As Paradis (1986) and Hamers and Blanc (1989) have pointed out, no matter how good a definition of bilingualism is, it will never be good enough to capture the many forms that bilingualism takes. Bilingualism is inherently multi-dimensional; a bilingual may be balanced, having equal proficiency in both languages, or subordinate, having unequal proficiency. The degree to which a bilingual is balanced is independent of how proficient the bilingual is in absolute terms. Immigrants to North America, for example, often find after a number of years that they are equally proficient in their mother tongue and in English but speak neither of them with nativelike competence. In the case of English, their competence has fossilized below the native speaker norm and in the case of their mother tongue, they have lost proficiency through disuse. Even bilinguals who can be said to be balanced often do not have competence equally distributed across the different levels of language. A bilingual may have nativelike pronunciation but a relatively small vocabulary in one language and non-nativelike pronunciation and a very large vocabulary in the other language.

Asymmetries can also be found in other dimensions of bilingualism. A bilingual's competence can be said to be relatively equal in the two languages but domain specific. He or she may have near perfect competence in one language for the purposes of casual and domestic discourse, for example, but be relatively poor at using that language in formal and professional settings. The bilingual's other language may show exactly the opposite configuration: relatively poor proficiency in home settings but very high proficiency for professional purposes. We all know people like this. They typically grew up speaking one language at home but went to school in another language which they now use solely in their professional lives.

Diversity among bilinguals has made the study of bilingualism relatively complex and also very important to understanding several fundamental issues in the study of language. This chapter shows how qualitative differences in types of bilingualism are related to the manner in which a second language is learned and in which both languages are used. We will also find that the study of bilingualism allows us to think about what it really means to *have* a language. It is not possible to distinguish between having linguistic ability and having a language if one looks only at monolinguals. A bilingual, however, presumably has both general linguistic ability and specific representations for two languages. How are these languages represented in one mind? How does the bilingual activate one language rather than the other? What is going on when bilinguals get together and converse in mixtures of their two languages (*The movie, c'étais pretty good. Mais, at this point j'en ai ras l'bol*)?

The following sections summarize the answers that research on bilingualism has provided to date for the questions above. They do not provide a complete review of the many dimensions of bilingualism but focus on those aspects of the subject with the greatest importance for second language acquisition: (1) how bilinguals' qualitative differences are related to their history of second language acquisition; (2) whether different types of second language acquisition can affect how languages are stored in the brain; and (3) how the two languages of a bilingual are organized so that he or she is able to use one at a time, translate between them, or switch from one language to the other.

2 QUALITATIVE DIFFERENCES IN BILINGUALISM

By far the most influential characterization of the qualitative differences among bilinguals is the *compound–co-ordinate dichotomy* proposed by Ervin and Osgood (1954). In their seminal paper, they described two types of bilinguals. The compound bilingual has two means of linguistic expression but only one system of meaning. The co-ordinate bilingual has language-specific meanings associated with each of his or her languages. The differences between these two types of bilingual organization are illustrated in Figure 20.1.

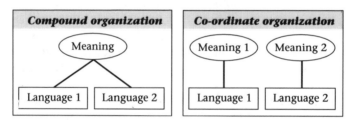

Figure 20.1   Compound and Co-ordinate Organization of the Bilingual Brain

For Ervin and Osgood, co-ordinate bilinguals are the true bilinguals because they have native-like meaning associations for the words of each language. To illustrate, we can return to an example brought up in Chapter 11. Recall the differences between the meanings of the words *friend* in English and *Freund* in German. We pointed out that the German word is used only for individuals who would be called close friends in English. In Ervin and Osgood's framework, the compound bilingual would have only one meaning representation for these words. The single-meaning representation might be the German one, the English one, or perhaps a blend of the two. The co-ordinate bilingual would actually have two separate semantic representations, one for the English word *friend* (a positive, familiar relationship) and one for the

German word *freund* (a familiar relationship involving personal commitment).

Ervin and Osgood argued that the development of co-ordinate bilingualism is related to the context of second language acquisition and language use. A child who grows up using two languages in the same environment, speaking both languages to the same person and frequently mixing languages in conversation, is likely to develop a compound system. He or she will not really have native semantic associations for either language. If a child grows up in an environment in which the two languages are separated, however, he or she will probably develop a co-ordinate system. Ervin and Osgood speculated that a co-ordinate system would develop if, for example, a child growing up bilingually spoke only one language to each parent. From an early age, the child would develop functionally separated systems corresponding to a "Mommy language" and a "Daddy language." In cases of second language acquisition, it was suggested that speaking one language at home and another at school in an immersion classroom would also lead to co-ordinate bilingualism. Finally, translating from one language to the other was seen as detrimental to the development of co-ordinate systems. In the second language classroom, learners should be forced to use inductive reasoning to develop independent semantic representations for expressions in the target language.

Since its original formulation, the compound–co-ordinate dichotomy has been the subject of many theoretical and experimental investigations. In general, it has been found that the original idea was essentially correct. A correlation exists between the separation of languages during second language acquisition and the extent to which the mental representations for these languages are also separated. Defined in terms of context of acquisition, compound bilinguals show greater interference at various levels of language: semantic, syntactic, phonological, and so on. It seems relatively clear at this point, however, that the idea of a dichotomy—two types of bilinguals—expresses the actual states of bilingualism in an overly simplified fashion. Researchers now generally agree that compound and co-ordinate bilinguals are best seen as representing two extremes on a continuum.

Our discussion of compound and co-ordinate bilingualism has raised two important points. First, bilinguals can show fundamentally different forms of cognitive organization. Second, the organization of a bilingual's linguistic system is shaped by the way in which his or her second language is acquired. In other words, how you learn a second language makes a real difference in the kind of bilingual you might become. It is important to ask at this point how far the application of this idea extends. Are we talking about the functional organization of language use or the actual organization of languages in the brain of a bilingual?

3 THE BILINGUAL BRAIN

The human brain isn't much to look at. It weighs about 1400 grams and has the consistency of Jell-O. Yet it is in all likelihood where all the things that we know are represented. Philosophers, psychologists, linguists, and neuroscientists in this century have considered it very important to ask whether the things that we treat as units in our everyday life are also represented as units in the brain. Our common experience tells us, for example, that there are differences among various emotions: fear, love, hate, and so on. Does your brain know this? Are there separate representations for each emotion?

The questions to be asked about the bilingual brain are very similar. We recognize in everyday life that differences exist among languages, and we have defined a bilingual as someone in possession of two languages. If the brain knows this, it should be possible to isolate the brain structures and functions associated with one language or the other. The research summarized below has attempted to determine whether, as far as the brain is concerned, the notion of individual language has any reality.

3.1 BILINGUAL APHASIA

Most of what is known about how language is represented in the brain has come from the study of language deficits that accompany brain damage, or aphasia. In 1861, Paul Broca reported the case of a patient who had lost the ability to speak. When the patient died, his brain was brought to autopsy and a large area of cell damage, called a lesion, was found in the frontal area of the left hemisphere of the brain. Paul Broca argued that, based on this evidence, the faculty of speech must be located in the damaged area. This brain region has since been called Broca's area and many hundreds of cases have been reported in which damage to it resulted in slow, halting speech and the omission of words, a condition now known as Broca's aphasia.

A second type of aphasia was reported in the 1870s by Carl Wernicke following study of patients who had damage to the posterior portions of the left hemisphere. These patients showed relatively fluent speech but it rarely made sense. In contrast to Broca's aphasics, they also had considerable difficulty comprehending language. Wernicke claimed that this posterior portion of the left hemisphere was the area in which the meanings and forms of words are stored and therefore language comprehension takes place. Again the nineteenth-century observations have been supported by many subsequent reports in the clinical literature. The brain area and the corresponding aphasia have been

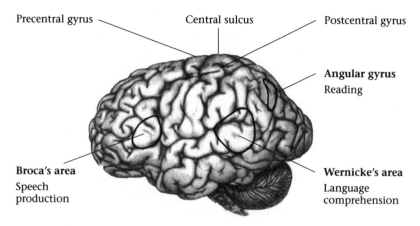

Precentral gyrus   Central sulcus   Postcentral gyrus

Angular gyrus
Reading

Broca's area   Wernicke's area
Speech   Language
production   comprehension

Figure 20.2   Areas of the Brain

been termed Wernicke's area and Wernicke's aphasia, respectively. Figure 20.2 illustrates the location of these areas in the left hemisphere of the brain.

An interesting question arises from this research. What form does aphasia take in bilingual patients? Is it possible for only one language to be damaged or are both always affected to the same extent? Paradis (1977) conducted an extensive review of the literature on bilingual aphasia and found it by far the most common occurrence for both languages to be damaged to the same extent, in proportion to the patient's original proficiency. In a few cases, however, only one language was disturbed, suggesting that at some level of brain organization, different languages have different representations.

Most monolingual patients show considerable recovery following damage to the brain. The extent of recovery depends on the cause of the brain damage, the size of the lesion, the age of the patient, and the type of treatment that the patient receives. In almost all cases, however, recovery from aphasia is never complete. The patient shows very good progress at first but eventually levels off, retaining some residual language disturbance. In cases of bilingual aphasia, the same pattern is usually seen and most often, the patient's two languages are recovered in parallel. In some cases, however, only one language is recovered. This has been termed *selective recovery* by Paradis (1977). Languages can also be recovered in succession. Perhaps most strangely, some patients have recovered languages in an antagonistic fashion. On some days, the patient can speak L1 but not L2 and on other days L2 but not L1.

Although it is extremely difficult to determine subsequent to aphasia how a patient acquired a second language initially, the available data suggest that non-parallel recovery is most common among co-ordinate bilinguals, those who acquired their two languages in different settings. Again, how you learn a second language makes a difference.

Cases of non-parallel recovery in bilingual aphasia provide additional evidence that, at some level of brain organization, languages can be distinguished. But the cases do not tell us what determines the language that is going to be preferentially recovered or exactly how individual languages are represented in the brain.

A number of answers to the first question have been proposed over the past hundred years. Ribot (1881) claimed that the L1 would be recovered best. Pitres (1895) argued that it would be the language in which the patient was most proficient. Goldstein (1948) proposed that it would be the language of the hospital environment. Each of these proposals accounts for the recovery patterns of some bilingual aphasics but not others. If there is an underlying principle that determines which language will be preferred in recovery, it is neither simple nor obvious.

What about the second question, about how a language is represented in the brain? The answer is not yet known, but several compelling observations and hypotheses have been advanced. In 1978, in a paper entitled "The bilingual brain," Ojemann and Whitaker reported a number of studies in which the brains of bilingual patients were explored through the technique of electrode stimulation. All these patients were soon to undergo brain surgery, usually for epilepsy. Prior to their surgery, the locations of various functions were mapped by inserting electrodes into the brain and stimulating the area with a small charge of electricity. The result of such stimulation is temporary disturbance of functioning in the affected brain area. Ojemann and Whitaker found that it was possible to affect only one of the patient's languages in particular brain areas. They also found that it was possible to disrupt some second language functioning by stimulating the right hemisphere and reasoned that the L1, which was always the stronger language, was represented in a more efficient manner in the brain. They also reported that the probability of being able to isolate only one language by electrode stimulation was related to the manner in which the second language was acquired. Patients who could be classified as co-ordinate bilinguals showed greater cortical separation between their two languages. For compound bilinguals, any electrical stimulation caused disturbances in both languages.

Although the Ojemann and Whitaker study made a huge impact on the field, not everyone accepted its conclusions. The researchers were generalizing from the organization of diseased brains to that of normal bilingual brains, and it remains unclear how valid such generalization is. All the subjects of the study underwent neurosurgery, which is usually the last and most drastic option in treatment. Of course, this problem is not limited to Ojemann and Whitaker's research. All the aphasia research reported so far in this chapter has involved analysing cases of brain damage to develop a hypothesis about the organization of two languages in the brain prior to the onset of aphasia.

3.2 RIGHT HEMISPHERE INVOLVEMENT IN SECOND LANGUAGE ACQUISITION

Since Paul Broca's discovery in the 1860s it has been claimed that, at least for right-handed people, language is represented in the left hemisphere of the brain. Fortunately, there are easier ways to test this hypothesis than by electrode stimulation or by the study of aphasia. The most common procedure in the past has been *dichotic listening*. In this technique, a subject wears headphones and is presented with one word in his or her left ear and another word in the right ear. For almost all right-handed people, the word heard in the right ear will seem clearer and louder because the neural pathways from the right ear lead to the left hemisphere of the brain and the neural pathways from the left ear lead to the right hemisphere (see Figure 20.3). Because the left hemisphere is specialized for language, the result is a right-ear advantage (REA). If you are right-handed, you have probably noticed that you prefer to hold a telephone receiver to your right ear. This isn't only because your right hand is stronger. Try switching sides during a telephone conversation. You will find that understanding what the other person is saying seems to require more effort when you are listening through your left ear.

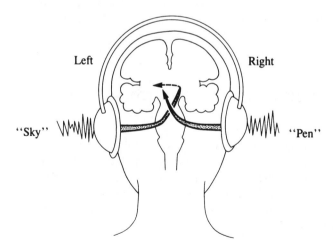

Figure 20.3   The Dichotic Listening Technique

Using the dichotic listening technique with bilingual subjects, Albert and Obler (1978) found a decreased REA for a subject's second language.

They argued that, in contrast to L1, the second language is represented across both hemispheres of the brain; the involvement of the right hemisphere in second language use is related to the more conscious manner in which the L2 is learned and to the use of both linguistic and non-linguistic strategies in L2 proficiency.

Vaid (1983) claimed that the extent of right-hemisphere involvement in the use of a second language depends on how that language was acquired. She argued that if L2 was acquired in an informal setting the right hemisphere would be involved to a greater extent. With formal explicit instruction, however, the bilingual's L2 would be even more localized in the left hemisphere than would the L1. As pointed out by Krashen, Seliger, and Hartnett (1974), the emphasis that some types of formal language instruction place on analytical techniques and deductive learning, for which the left hemisphere is naturally specialized, may be a factor.

3.3 SUMMARY OF THE BILINGUAL BRAIN

Our discussion of the bilingual brain has touched upon a very broad and important area of inquiry. The evidence to date suggests that distinct languages have distinct representations in the brain, although this does not necessarily mean that one language is localized in a particular area and the other is localized in another. In addition, studies of right hemispheric involvement in bilingualism have shown that the use of a second language involves a variety of strategies and processes that may require involvement of brain areas other than the classical language centres first identified by Broca and Wernicke.

4 THE FUNCTIONAL ORGANIZATION OF TWO LANGUAGES IN ONE MIND

How are the languages of a bilingual organized in the mind to meet the needs of bilingual functioning? A bilingual needs to keep languages separated during language processing, to translate between languages, and to voluntarily switch languages. Some of the more important experimental findings in this area and recent models of bilingual organization are considered below.

4.1 THE SWITCH HYPOTHESIS

Consider the words *information, pain,* and *chat.* These are relatively common English words, but they are also French words. The first looks the same and has equivalent meanings in English and French, but in French it is pronounced [āfɔrmasyɔ̃]. The second word, *pain*, is the French word for *bread*, pronounced [pã]. The third word, *chat*, is French for *cat*, pronounced [ša]. Even if you are a French–English bilingual, you probably initially read the words in English. How were the French meanings and pronunciations suppressed? In other words, how did you manage to keep the English and French separated? The most intuitively appealing answer is that the appearance of the words in an English context biased your interpretation towards the English pronunciations and meanings.

Many researchers in the field of bilingualism (such as Kolers 1966 and Macnamara and Kushnir 1971) have proposed that the best metaphor to explain this phenomenon is of an input switch. The switch opens one channel while closing off access to the other. When reading or listening in an English context, the switch would be set to English. If there were a clear indication in the input stream that a new language is present, however, the switch would be moved to the other position.

The input switch hypothesis was based on a series of experiments in which subjects were required to read textual passages that switched languages periodically. Macnamara compared reading times for such mixed-language passages to reading times for passages of identical meaning in which there were no changes of language. He and his colleagues found that subjects took longer to read the mixed-language passages and paused at the point of language change. He calculated that the input switch required 0.2 seconds to operate.

The existence of an input switch is intuitively pleasing and seems to accord with the introspections of bilinguals. Nonetheless, subsequent experimentation has uncovered substantial evidence against the hypothesis. The history of this hypothesis offers a particularly good illustration of how the appealing hypotheses in the field of language processing are often the untenable ones. It turns out that both channels of a bilingual's language processing system are always open, although he or she is not consciously aware of it. There *is* no input switch.

Chan, Chau, and Hoosain (1983) found that subjects took no extra time to switch languages in Chinese–English bilingual texts when the changes of language occurred at natural syntactic boundaries. Hamers and Lambert (1974) found that when English–French bilinguals were presented with words such as *chat* and *pain* in an English word list, both meanings of the words were activated. They presented English–French–German trilinguals with a list of English words and asked them to translate it into German. Some of the words were possible forms in both English and French, such as *chat*, *pain*, and *ail*. Hamers and Lambert found that even though subjects knew that all the words in the list were English, some translated the English word *chat* as *Katze*, the German word for *cat*. They interpreted this as evidence that both the English and the French meanings were activated when a subject saw the word.

The evidence favouring the view that both input systems of the bilingual are always "on" is very much in tune with the characterization of language comprehension presented in Chapter 12 of this text. It seems that for bilinguals as well as monolinguals, the language input system is organized so that all possible representations of meaning are automatically activated. Just as it is impossible for a monolingual to shut off his or her language system and "choose" not to understand a word, it is also impossible for multilinguals to shut off comprehension of any of their languages.

4.1.1 The Output Switch and Language Tagging

Although the input switch metaphor for bilingual comprehension has been rejected by researchers of bilingual processing, the concept of an *output* switch has fared considerably better. Bilinguals typically have considerable strategic control over their language output. In monolingual situations they can speak in one language while completely shutting off output in the other language. When required to translate, they can comprehend an utterance in one language and express it in the other. Finally, particularly in bilingual communities, individuals can engage in what is termed *code switching*. This process involves switching fluently from one language to the other during speech, between and even within sentences, as in the previous example, *The movie, c'étais pretty good. Mais, at this point j'en ai ras l'bol.*

This last example of code switching may be interpreted as the rapid movement of an output switch from one position to the other, but an alternative explanation has gained considerable acceptance in recent years. Albert and Obler (1978) suggested that a bilingual's two language systems might best be imagined as a set of *tags* associated with elements of each language. In this view, a bilingual has a vocabulary that is typically much larger than that of the monolingual. Like the monolingual lexicon, the bilingual lexicon consists of words tagged with their various properties—noun, verb, formal, taboo word, and the like—but for the bilingual, one of these tags identifies a word as belonging to, say, English or French. The idea of tags for individual elements of a language, as opposed to stores or boxes that encapsulate the language as a whole, easily accounts for the finding that bilinguals take longer than monolinguals to name pictures (Mägiste 1979). Because all the words they know are in a single store, they simply have more words to choose from.

The idea of language tags for words and linguistic structures has become part of theories of bilingual processing such as those proposed by Paradis (1993a) and Green (1986). Green's model of language processing is particularly intriguing because it presents an account of bilingual behaviour among both normal bilinguals and bilingual aphasics. The next section briefly sketches his model.

4.2 GREEN'S MODEL OF ACTIVATION AND CONTROL

Green's model of bilingual processing can best be understood if we reflect first on two basic questions. First, what happens when mono-linguals make speech errors such as *He was strying to improve*? Green believes that the error *strying* occurs when the representations for *trying* and *striving* both get activated and one cannot suppress the other. Bilinguals also make errors of this sort, as in *I love the flowers of springling*. In this case, the English word *spring* and the German word *Früling* were both activated. The inability of one word to win out over the other results in a blended output in speech. Second, what happens in succes-sive and antagonistic recovery from bilingual aphasia? Clearly the lan-guage that a bilingual cannot produce is not really lost; it is exceedingly unlikely that the language is actually relearned following aphasia. A more likely interpretation is that one language is suppressed by the other during the recovery pattern.

Green claims that when a bilingual chooses to produce only one lan-guage, elements from the chosen language also suppress output from the other language. The inability of elements from one language to suppress elements of the other characterizes mixing in bilingual aphasia—using elements of two languages in a single utterance—and also interference among bilinguals and second language learners. In the case of very imbalanced bilingualism, the L2 may not be strong enough to suppress the L1, but the L1 may easily suppress the L2. The result is interference in the weaker language.

Finally, Green's framework offers a very interesting account of fluent code switching and translation. When the words and structures of both languages are active, code switching results. Translation also requires ele-ments from both languages to be activated, but in this case the language from which the bilingual is translating suppresses its own output. This form of self-suppression stops the bilingual from simply repeating utter-ances in a language instead of translating them.

Green thus attempts to bring the various aspects of normal and impaired bilingual functioning under one theoretical explanation. He also asserts that there is no qualitative difference between bilingual and monolingual language processing. All of language processing involves the activation of some representations and the suppression of others. If you are asked to read the word *wind* aloud, both [wɪnd] and [waynd] will automatically be activated. Normally, [wɪnd] will have the stronger acti-vation and will suppress the output of [waynd], in part because of con-text, frequency, and perhaps some advantage that nouns have over verbs. Green suggests that the same forces are at work in bilingual lan-guage processing. The bilingual's ability to engage in monolingual speech, translation, and code switching is a matter of regulating and controlling the activation of language units.

5 CONCLUSION

The study of bilingualism is the study of the final product in second language acquisition. It allows us to concentrate in a somewhat different manner on questions about how two languages are represented and processed in the mind. Throughout most of this text language has been discussed as a process of development. Here we have focussed on a relatively stable system of representation.

The character of language representation in bilingualism is nonetheless tied to characteristics of second language acquisition. The difference between compound and co-ordinate bilingualism derives from the context of second language acquisition. Indeed, as our discussion of the bilingual brain has suggested, the manner of second language acquisition can have an influence on the organization of a second language in the brain. In this fashion, the study of bilingualism is an integral component of the study of second language acquisition. By considering both the process and the product of second language acquisition, we can explore various methods and contexts of language learning in an attempt to determine what difference they make in determining the nature of the final state of bilingualism.

CLASSROOM IMPLICATIONS

The truth of the matter is that very few learners who begin the second language acquisition process become bilinguals. Do you think that it is nevertheless reasonable to design programs of second language instruction with the goal of developing bilingualism?

This chapter has made the claim that whether a bilingual is more compound or more co-ordinate depends to a great extent on the manner in which second language acquisition takes place. It is assumed, for example, that if a learner engages in language mixing during the acquisition process he or she will probably develop a compounded system of language organization. Strict separation of the languages, on the other hand, is assumed to foster a more co-ordinate system of organization. What role do you think a language teacher can play in influencing whether learners' language systems develop as more compounded or co-ordinated? Specifically, what sorts of materials and classroom activities would support the development of co-ordinate bilingualism?

SELF TEST

A bilingual is a person who has functional command of two _____ (1) and whose linguistic _____ (2) is in a steady state. Two types are often discussed: the _____ (3) bilingual and the co-ordinate bilingual. The co-ordinate bilingual is said to have separate _____ (4) representations for each of his or her two languages. Many of the clues we have concerning the organization of two languages in the brain come from the study of bilingual _____ (5). Some researchers have claimed that the _____ (6) hemisphere of the brain plays a special role in second language acquisition. Some have also suggested that bilingual comprehension requires the postulation of an input _____ (7). This view is no longer held by many, but the existence of an _____ (8) switch remains plausible. _____ (9) model of activation and control presents an alternative view of why mixing occurs and how elements of one language can suppress activation of the other language.

FURTHER READING

Hamers, J. and M. Blanc. 1989. *Bilinguality and Bilingualism*. New York: Cambridge University Press.

Paradis, M. 1993b. Multilingualism and aphasia. In *Linguistic Disorders and Pathologies: An International Handbook*, ed. G. Blanken, J. Dittmann, H. Grimm, J.C. Marshall, and C-W. Wallesch, 278–288. New York: Walter de Gruyter.

Bilingual Education

The previous chapter discussed how two languages might be stored in one brain and how the manner of acquiring the second language can affect bilingual storage. We saw the relationship between the kind of input that the learner was exposed to and the kind of mental representation set up.

Educators, too, have been concerned with the relationship between how bilinguals are taught and how much they learn. This chapter discusses several aspects of bilingual education. It first addresses the issue of how knowledge of a minority language affects the acquisition of a majority language. Then it looks at majority language users who are attempting to learn a minority language. The terms minority and majority languages are socially defined. For a native speaker of Greek who is attempting to learn English in Canada, for example, Greek is the minority and English the majority language.

A minority language speaker faces two major challenges: learning the majority language and maintaining the minority language. Historically, a certain amount of tension between these two goals has been reflected in bilingual education programs. There are undeniable social advantages to acquiring the majority language, and the education system has always attempted to promote this. More arguments tend to arise over the role of minority language maintenance in advancing majority language acquisition. Broadly speaking, two positions can be adopted, described below with reference to the education of children:

1. Maintaining a minority language will cause confusion. If we want children to learn the majority language, the minority language should be discouraged. Bilingualism bewilders children and they don't do as well in school. If we want them to learn English, they should be immersed in English.

2. Maintaining a minority language will result in bilingualism, and there are advantages to knowing more than one language. Students taught in their first language may be able to transfer this knowledge to their second language. If we want them to learn English, first language instruction may help.

As opposed as these two positions appear, they actually contain a point of agreement. If the education system wants to create monolinguals, it uses monolingual instruction. If it wants to create bilinguals, it uses bilingual instruction. Many of the theoretical and practical aspects of bilingual education are presented in Cummins and Swain (1986). Let us now turn to the historical perspective that they provide.

1 AN HISTORICAL PERSPECTIVE

It is uncontroversial to say that the dominant attitude in the first half of the century in Canada was that immigrants should give up their own language and culture and assimilate to the "Canadian" way of life. Harney and Troper (1975) quote a 1913 speaker at a church congress: "Any traces of foreign values were eradicated in the process of impressing on students the Canadian values of punctuality, regularity, obedience, industry, cleanliness, decency of appearance and behaviour, regard for the rights of others and respect for law and order." From this perspective, bilingualism was a deeply negative, undesirable force in the child's development.

This began to change in the second half of the twentieth century. In 1971, in the report of the Royal Commission on Bilingualism and Biculturalism, the federal government of Canada adopted a policy of multiculturalism within a bilingual framework, which acknowledged that there was a place in the culture for immigrants to maintain aspects of their first culture.

Across Canada, instruction in languages other than French and English is currently offered in the public school system. There are bilingual programs in elementary schools in Ukrainian, Punjabi, German, Arabic, and Hebrew, to name a few. The cultural and educational climate has certainly changed since the earlier part of this century.

1.1 HERITAGE LANGUAGE PROGRAMS

Heritage language programs are also known as L1, or minority, language maintenance programs. They are designed to allow minority language students to keep their first languages. L1 maintenance is really a question of the price we are willing to have our students pay for acquiring L2 proficiency. Is it reasonable to ask them to give up their first language in order to learn a second? What will the consequences be? This is not a peripheral issue to education. Over 50 percent of the population of several Canadian school boards, in Toronto and Vancouver, particularly, has English as a second language. Handscombe (1989) brings home some of the implications of this in an article on mainstreaming: putting ESL students in with so-called mainstream learners. She reminds us that if over 50 percent of the students are non-native speakers then they *are* the mainstream. It is not a question of whether the school system should respond to this changing society but how it should respond.

1.2 ACCULTURATION PATTERNS

One of the issues involved in minority language maintenance is clearly the acculturation of immigrants. Lambert (1967) identified four ways in which minority students could work out conflicts between the language and culture (L & C) of the home and the school:

1. *Rejection of home L & C and identification with Canadian L & C* On the positive side of this profile, we find rapid second language acquisition. On the negative side, we find diminished familial harmony. If minority language students reject their heritage, it is going to precipitate a certain amount of tension between generations. This profile leads to students who cannot talk to their grandparents and who may reject many of their parents' values.
2. *Rejection of Canadian L & C and identification with home L & C* This pattern tends to result in difficult second language acquisition, but may well have the benefit of retaining familial harmony.
3. *Inability to identify with either L & C* This condition appears to be similar to what Durkheim (1897) called *anomie* in his book *The Suicide*. Anomie is a feeling of not belonging, in this case, of not belonging to either culture. As we saw in Chapter 14, Brown (1987) has argued that this is very good for second language learning. Nevertheless, it does not seem to be an entirely pleasurable psychological state. One would not like to endure it for prolonged periods.
4. *Identification with both home and Canadian L & C* This profile tends to enhance familial harmony and result in proficiency in both languages. These people are able to respect both cultures and to function in both languages.

In light of this taxonomy, Lambert argued that students should be encouraged to maintain *dual* heritage. They should not be forced to reject their first language and culture.

2 BILINGUAL CLASSROOMS

In the language classroom the issue of dual heritage is usually addressed in terms of how much emphasis the first language should receive. Cummins and Swain (1986) point out the two contrasting assumptions that can be made here:

1. Humans have a fixed capacity for language, like a room of a certain size. That space can be filled by either one or two languages. If you choose to fill it with two, there will be less space for each. Less space is equated with less proficiency.
2. Humans have a capacity for language that can be expressed in one or more languages. The storage space underlying one is the same size as that underlying any other.

The major implication of the first view is that increased proficiency in the L1 will lead to a diminished ability in the L2 and that instruction in the L1 will not increase knowledge of the L2. So, what effect does instruction in the first language have on minority language children? Will it result in less room for the majority language? Several empirical studies provide some answers to the question.

2.1 THE ROCK POINT NAVAJO STUDY

Before a bilingual education program was started in 1971, children on the Rock Point Navajo reserve were two years behind United States norms in English reading by the end of Grade 6. This was in spite of intensive training in English as a second language. The new program used Navajo as the major medium of instruction from kindergarten through Grade 2. From Grade 2 to Grade 6, Navajo continued to be used for between 25 and 50 percent of instruction. English was gradually introduced.

At the end of Grade 6 the students who went through this bilingual program were assessed again. This time they were performing slightly *above* the U.S. norms in *English* reading. Clearly, the instruction provided in their first language, Navajo, had no adverse effects on their L2 performance. Rather, it greatly improved their performance in English.

2.2 THE SODERTALJE PROGRAM

Another study examined the linguistic skills of Finnish children living in Sweden. Finnish children who were enrolled in Swedish-only programs—that is, who were immersed in the majority language—were found to perform worse in Finnish than 90 percent of Finnish children in Finland,

and worse in Swedish than about 90 percent of Swedish children. They had very limited linguistic skills in both of their languages.

Again, a bilingual education program was instituted and Finnish became the major language of their instruction from kindergarten to Grade 3. At the end of Grade 6 they were tested again, and they were performing in both Finnish and Swedish at about the same level as Swedish-speaking children in Finland. Again, this is a marked improvement, though we are not given the data to evaluate precisely.

2.3 THE BRADFORD PUNJABI MOTHER TONGUE PROJECT

A one-year bilingual education program for five-year-old native speakers of Punjabi was instituted in Bradford, England. The children had little or no knowledge of English at the start of the project. Approximately seventy students were randomly assigned (a rare luxury in educational research) to either the experimental bilingual instruction group or the control monolingual English instruction group. After one academic year, they were evaluated on non-verbal tasks and both English and Punjabi verbal tasks. No group differences were observed on the non-verbal ability measures. Both the monolingual and the bilingual instruction successfully taught non-verbal skills. But what about verbal performance? The bilingual group tended to perform better in Punjabi than the control group. Performance in English in the two groups was equal. Clearly, using the L1 as an initial medium of instruction had no detrimental effects on L2 development.

2.4 THE SAN DIEGO SPANISH–ENGLISH IMMERSION PROGRAM

This project was implemented in 1975 in San Diego city schools. Sixty percent of the subjects had Spanish as their L1 and 40 percent had English. Instruction was predominantly in Spanish from pre-school to Grade 3. After Grade 3, half the time was spent in English and half in Spanish. Some English instruction was provided throughout the educational program: twenty minutes per day at pre-school; thirty minutes at kindergarten and Grade 1; and sixty minutes at Grades 2 and 3.

The evaluation of these students showed that they lagged somewhat behind grade norms in both Spanish and English reading skills throughout elementary school, but by Grade 6 they were performing *above* grade norms in both languages.

Bilingual education doesn't have to cause loss of the first language, the experience of what Lambert calls *subtractive* bilingualism. Minority language children are able to add a language, or undergo *additive* bilingualism, and maintain their abilities in both languages. This has implications for the education of non-native speakers. It has long been observed that minority language children are academically at risk in monolingual, majority language schools. Because they do not fully comprehend their instruction when they first arrive in school, they often miss some important early concepts and start to lag behind their monolingual peers. Instruction in the minority language, which fosters additive bilingualism, can stop this lag from the beginning.

3 THE THRESHOLD HYPOTHESIS

Why did so many early studies on bilingualism conclude that it was bad for children, and why do so many recent studies argue for its benefits? Drawing on the compound–co-ordinate continuum discussed in the last chapter, we can say it seems that the studies were investigating different kinds of bilinguals. Cummins and Swain (1986) propose what they call the *dual threshold* hypothesis to account for the variation in student performance (see Figure 21.1). They argue that bilingual children may have to attain thresholds of linguistic competence in both languages in order to avoid general cognitive disadvantages. If they attain a relatively high level of proficiency in both languages, they will have cognitive advantages. We can think of the thresholds as marking the borders between below-average proficiency, average proficiency, and above-average proficiency. Bilingual children who do not achieve at least the lower threshold of proficiency in both languages may suffer cognitive deficits, as shown on the left in Figure 21.2, below. These people have been referred to as semilinguals because they do not function well in either language. The position of the arrows in the figure is not meant to mark an exact level of proficiency, merely the level with respect to the thresholds. A monolingual's proficiency could be average or above average without attaining the cognitive advantages of the bilingual.

The semilingual is likely to have cognitive deficits, the monolingual, who may in fact have minimal knowledge of some L2, will be cognitively

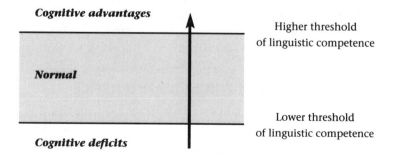

Figure 21.1   The Dual Threshold Hypothesis

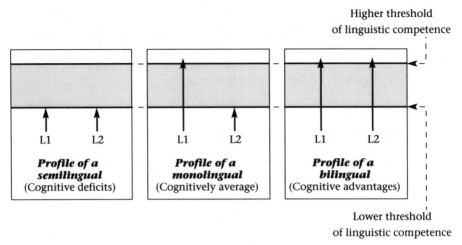

Figure 21.2   Profiles of Varying Degrees of Bilingualism

average, and the bilingual will experience certain cognitive advantages. Cummins (1981) cites the following benefits of being bilingual above the second threshold:

- ability to analyse and become aware of language
- overall academic language skills
- general conceptual development
- creative thinking
- sensitivity to the communicative needs of the listener

These thresholds are not empirically measurable as they stand in Cummins's model—they cannot be assessed with a TOEFL score—but conceptually they do allow us to reconcile some seemingly conflicting results. Because of the historical emphasis on conformity to the majority language and culture and the lack of minority language support in the school system, earlier studies may well have been investigating the population we now call semilingual. Later studies have looked at both semi- and bilinguals. The different populations explain the different results. The patterns shown in Figure 21.2 appear plausible.

4 MORE ARGUMENTS FOR L1 MAINTENANCE

Alladina (1986) summarizes the arguments for L1 maintenance as follows:

1. *Psychological* In any teaching environment, the self-esteem of the child is crucial. Language and identity are closely related. By giving

status and recognition to the home language, we help the child to develop his or her own sense of self-concept and self-esteem.

2. *Economic* Knowledge of another language has economic advantages in today's world market, particularly in conglomerated economic areas such as Europe and North America.

3. *Legalistic* It is a basic right of the child to have access to L1 instruction. The 1977 Council for European Communities directive states, "Member states, in accordance with their national circumstances and legal systems, take appropriate measures to promote, in co-ordination with normal education, teaching of the mother tongue and culture of origin for the children who are dependents of any worker who is a national of another member country" (1986, 13).

4. *Academic curiosity* Many people will argue that knowledge of another language is good for you; it's character building. Linguistic diversity is good.

5 BILINGUALISM AND SPECIAL EDUCATION

It is interesting to look at the relationship between bilingualism and special education. Cummins (1984) is devoted entirely to this question. It appears that non-native speakers of English are proportionately over-represented in special education classrooms, perhaps largely because tests administered to these students are misused or misinterpreted. The history of intelligence testing has not been kind to non-native speakers. Cummins quotes Goddard on the "success" of immigration screening tests: "The number of aliens deported because of feeble-mindedness ... increased approximately 350% in 1913 and 570% in 1914.... This was due to the untiring efforts of the physicians who were inspired by the belief that mental tests could be used for the detection of feeble-minded aliens" (1917, 271). Many minority language children are "deported" to special education classes, or remedial streams, never to return.

Most schools reflect the middle-class, monolingual, monocultural values of the majority society. IQ is assessed in relation to these norms. So, even though most educators no longer view the IQ score as a measure of innate ability, most do consider it a measure of academic potential. A low score can lead to remedial streaming. Now, imagine how students from other cultures do when asked questions in their second language. This is not the time to go into an extended discussion of IQ tests (see Gould 1981). Suffice it to say that whatever these tests measure among minority language students should not be labelled *intelligence*.

Psychological assessments of non-native speakers may also be misused. The psychologists doing the testing often do not take the students' second language background into account in any significant fashion. Consider the following case study reported by Cummins (1984). Student PR was referred for psychological assessment because he was experiencing difficulty in regular Grade 1 work even though he was repeating the grade. The principal noted that "although PR was in Portugal for part [six months] of the year there is a suspicion of real learning disability." The psychologist commented, "Psychometric rating ... places PR in the dull normal range of intellectual development. Assessment reveals performance abilities to be normal while verbal abilities fall in the mentally deficient range. It is recommended that PR be referred for resource room placement for next year and if no progress is evident by Christmas, a learning centre placement should be considered." This illustrates the abuses to which psychological assessments can be subject. It does not seem at all unreasonable that a child from a non-English background who has spent six months of the previous year in Portugal should perform very poorly on an English verbal IQ test. Yet rather than admitting that no conclusions can be drawn about the child's academic potential, the psychologist validated the teacher's "suspicion" of a learning disability by using inappropriate terminology such as "dull normal" and "mentally deficient." Neither teacher nor psychologist made any reference to the fact that the child was learning English as a second language, and both considered the child's English proficiency satisfactory enough to perform the test, on what basis we do not know. There was no discussion of how this "mentally deficient" child performed in Portuguese.

A study done in Alberta investigated the progress of minority language students in high school. Watt and Roessingh (1994) looked at students in a high school with a population of 1500. Forty percent—600 students—did not speak English as their first language. Between 1989 and 1993, they tracked 232 ESL students through high school. They found that 74 percent of these students dropped out (Table 21.1).

Table 21.1   Drop-out Rate of ESL High School Students

Proficiency at beginning of high school	Drop-out rate (in percent)
Beginner	95.5
Intermediate	70.0
Advanced	50.0

Source: Data from Watt and Roessingh (1994).

Interestingly, the drop-out rate varied significantly according to the student's proficiency at the start of high school. The study noted that 50 percent of beginners exited the educational system permanently within the first twelve months of entering high school. Among the forty-four successful graduates, twenty-nine were twenty or older or had received more than three years of ESL support. The provincial government is now proposing changes to the system that would limit ESL programs to three years and make only students under twenty eligible for them. If we were to re-analyse the earlier data by removing from consideration the students who were over twenty and received more than three years financial support, then we would find that just 6 percent of ESL students would have graduated: a drop-out rate of 94 percent. Clearly, administrative policy can have a negative effect on minority language students' performance.

Minority language children's proficiency can be promoted in school at no cost to the development of proficiency in L2. The use of L1 as a medium of instruction allows the students to benefit fully from interaction with the teacher. Concepts developed in L1 can be transferred to the L2. The education system can treat minority language students in a way that does not disadvantage them and that results in additive bilingualism. Historically, this has not always been the case. Let us hope that we can learn from past mistakes.

6 FRENCH IMMERSION

Minority language students are not the only ones involved in learning second languages. We turn now to a major phenomenon of bilingual education: French immersion. The first French immersion program was in St. Lambert, Quebec, in 1965. The impetus came from a group of parents in the area. The instigators were very concerned that such an experimental program be carefully evaluated and researched. They wanted to know, for example, whether immersing their children in French would have a detrimental effect on their English. As a result, French immersion programs have yielded some of the best studied classroom environments in history. Researchers such as Wallace Lambert at McGill University and Merrill Swain, Sharon Lapkin, and Birgit Harley at the Ontario Institute for Studies in Education have contributed a wealth of knowledge. Tables 21.2 and 21.3 indicate how the French immersion phenomenon has spread across Canada in terms of the number of students and of schools involved.

What is French immersion? In a French immersion class, all of the students are non-native speakers of French, so although they are immersed in a new language, no one in the class is a native speaker, with the possible exception of the teacher. In this way immersion contrasts with submerging non-native speakers of English in the so-called mainstream English-only classes.

H.H. Stern (1984) noted that French immersion is teaching *in* French, not teaching *of* French. In French immersion, the students learn French

Table 21.2 Enrollment in French Immersion Programs

	1991–1992			1992–1993		1993–1994
	Total school enrollment[a]	Immersion enrollment	Percentage enrolled in immersion	Boards with immersion[c]	Immersion enrollment[b]	Boards with immersion[c]
British Columbia	537 254	27 780	5.17	45	28 000	44
Alberta	493 632	28 000	5.67	41[d]	29 200	41[d]
Saskatchewan	197 237	10 851	5.50	22[d]	11 000	23[d]
Manitoba	191 516	19 669	10.27	25	20 000	25
Ontario	1 872 516	137 000	7.32	91	140 000	91
Quebec	97 216	32 000	32.91	15	33 000	15
New Brunswick	93 663	14 987	16.00	12	15 000	12
Nova Scotia	162 123	5 500	3.39	9	5 700	9
Prince Edward Island	24 007	3 511	14.62	4	3 690	4
Newfoundland	124 821	5 165	4.14	13	5 200	13
Yukon	5 410	391	7.23	1	410	1
Northwest Territories	15 468	423	2.73	3	450	3
Totals	3 814 863	285 277	7.48	280	291 650	280

[a] Does not include students for whom the regular language of instruction is French.

[b] Statistics Canada estimate.

[c] Department of National Defence Boards and private schools not included.

[d] Lloydminster is counted in both Saskatchewan and Alberta.

Source: Canadian Parents for French (1994).

Table 21.3   Number of Students in French Immersion

	1977–1978	1980–1981	1983–1984	1986–1987	1987–1988	1988–1989	1989–1990	1990–1991
British Columbia	1 301	4 368	9 807	18 744	21 404	24 292	26 900	27 984
Alberta	7 601[a]	11 291[a]	14 523	21 194	22 779	24 921	26 182	28 200
Saskatchewan	407	1 603	4 018	7 503	8 398	9 476	10 440	10 713
Manitoba	1 667	4 286	9 090	14 619	16 395	17 779	19 024	19 604
Ontario	12 764[b]	46 638	65 310	98 809	108 000	116 697	125 000[c]	135 900
Quebec	17 754	17 800[c]	17 833	18 391[d]	18 750	19 000[c]	28 717	30 800
New Brunswick	3 179	5 532	11 009	15 368	15 458	16 452	16 425	17 100
Nova Scotia	127	590	894	2 421	3 490	4 410	4 900	5 343
Prince Edward Island	541	1 280	1 833	2 514	3 033	3 165	3 271	3 371
Newfoundland	95	392	970	2 621	2 979	3 641	3 980	4 715
Yukon	—	35	171	291	318	342	360	369
Northwest Territories	—	37	151	261	310	366	380	404
Totals	45 436	93 852	135 609	202 736	221 314	240 541	265 279	284 503

[a] Unofficial figure provided to Canadian Parents for French by the provincial ministries.
[b] Includes only programs in which French is the language of instruction at least 75 percent of the time.
[c] Statistics Canada estimate.
[d] Lloydminster is counted in both Saskatchewan and Alberta.

Source: Canadian Parents for French (1994).

while learning something else. Usually, it is contrasted with *core* French programs, which employ the "traditional" daily forty-minute language classes stressing formal instruction. French immersion places less emphasis on formal language instruction, though there is some focus on form. French immersion is also inherently different from minority language programs. In the former, students from the majority language (English) are learning a minority language (French); in the latter, minority language students (such as Navajo) are learning the majority language. These differences produce different results. If we find that students who are immersed in French do quite well at learning French, does this suggest that Navajo students should be immersed in English to learn English? As we have seen, it does not. The situations are not directly comparable.

6.1 TERMINOLOGY

A variety of terms are used to refer to particular types of French immersion. In *full immersion,* all instruction is initially in French. Instruction later becomes bilingual, usually after the first three years. *Partial immersion* involves an almost even split of French and English right from the start. *Early immersion* begins in kindergarten or Grades 1 or 2. *Middle immersion* begins in Grade 4. *Late immersion* begins in Grade 6 or 7. Middle or late French immersion is usually preceded by conventional French language instruction; students are not just tossed into the deep-end of the language pool.

6.2 COMMON QUESTIONS ABOUT IMMERSION

The following questions and answers are drawn from Swain and Lapkin (1982) and Lapkin and Swain (1990).

6.2.1 Does Immersion Affect the Students' First Language Skills?

Lapkin and Swain (1990, 640) report: "The use of standardized tests of English achievement in hundreds of program evaluations conducted over the past twenty years has permitted researchers to dispel fears of the possible negative impact of French-medium instruction on the first language development of anglophone students." In terms of skills related to literacy, students of early, middle, and late programs may all lag behind monolingual English students. Early total and early partial immersion students' lag lasts until the end of Grade 3. For late immersion students, the lag is shorter or does not occur at all. After Grade 3, most early immersion students perform as well as non-immersion students, and early total immersion students perform better than their English-educated counterparts (Harley, Hart, and Lapkin 1986). These lags in

English language are not evident in oral/aural skills. French immersion students also perform as well or better than their monolingual peers in other school subjects.

6.2.2 Do They Learn French?

Early total immersion students attain near-native proficiency in listening and reading comprehension. On a French achievement test they performed as well as a class of francophone students in Montreal. Their speaking and writing skills remain non-nativelike, though proficient (Genesee 1987). Early immersion students perform consistently better in French than late immersion students in all four skill areas but not at the level of native francophones (Day and Shapson 1989). Wesche (1989) suggests that the differences between early and late immersion disappear for those students who continue to study French in university.

Lapkin, Hart, and Swain (1991, 11) also argue for the overall advantage of early immersion programs: "With respect to French language outcomes, results suggest that the middle immersion program studies yield less consistent levels of performance than early immersion." The best students of middle immersion may be as good as the best in early immersion, but their range of proficiency is much greater.

To get an idea of how late and middle immersion students perform, let us compare their results on tests of listening comprehension. Swain and Lapkin (1982, 47) provided data on a late immersion class (Table 21.4). The maximum score possible was twenty-two and the numbers indicate group averages. By Grade 12 the late immersion students had not reached nativelike proficiency.

Table 21.4 Late Immersion Comprehension Test Scores

Grade 8	Grade 10	Grade 11	Grade 12	Francophone Grade 12
8.82	12.00	14.29	14.40	17.96

Source: Adapted from Swain and Lapkin (1982).

Compare this to the results on a listening comprehension test cited in Lapkin, Hart, and Swain (1991, 22). The early immersion classes scored an average of 11.09, the middle immersion classes scored 8.42, and the francophones scored 11.73. In this case, the maximum score was 15 and again the numbers indicate group means. We can see that the early immersion students are performing at a nativelike level, whereas the middle immersion students are not.

6.2.3 How Do the Students View Themselves?

Early total immersion students consider themselves more skilled in French than middle and late immersion students do (Lapkin, Swain, and Shapson 1990). As most of their experience is in the classroom, however, it is unclear to what extent their self-assessment would be valid for out-of-class performance.

6.2.4 How Does Immersion Compare with Core French?

Immersion students' performance in French is almost always significantly better than core students'.

6.2.5 How Do Native Francophones Perceive Immersion French?

Early total immersion students' spoken French is generally assessed favourably on global acceptability judgments by both francophone adults and children.

6.3 THE IMMERSION INTERLANGUAGE

The aspect of French immersion students' language proficiency that probably attracts the most attention is the persistence of certain grammatical or sociolinguistic errors. It is often noted, for example, that immersion students have difficulty with gender assignment (Carroll 1989a), with the *tu/vous* distinction between informal and formal second person pronoun use, and with polite conditionals such as *Je voudrais* (I would like). The issue of developing sociolinguistic competence in an immersion classroom has received attention. Some researchers believe that increasing the interaction between students and native French speakers other than the teacher is the key (Hanna et al. 1980; McLean et al. 1983).

Researchers continue to investigate the interlanguage of immersion students. Some, such as Hammerly (1989), criticize the immersion interlanguage for its common grammatical errors. Yet researchers are not the only ones with opinions about immersion. The students themselves have something to say.

6.4 WHAT THE STUDENTS THINK

Lambert and Tucker (1972) offer answers to some questions about immersion students' attitudes (see Table 21.5). The table compares the attitudes of immersion and core French students towards their respective programs. In almost every case, immersion students' reactions to French became more favourable as they moved from Grade 4 to Grade 5, while core French students' reactions became more negative.

6.5 SUMMARY OF FRENCH IMMERSION

Like any aspect of the public education system, French immersion programs attract at least their fair share of criticism (see Hammerly 1989). Criticisms tend to focus on what French immersion students cannot do.

Table 21.5 Immersion and Core French Students' Attitudes

Grade		Immersion		Core French	
		4	5	4	5
1. Do you enjoy studying French the way you do at school?	Very much	45[†]	52	18	16
2. Would you rather go to an all English school?	Yes, very much	3	4	31	46
3. I enjoy school as it is.		75	68	31	27
4. Is too much time spent on French?	Right amount	75	80	63	37
5. Do you want to continue learning French?	Very much	70	84	55	37
	Never again	0	0	12	19

[†] Percentage of students agreeing with the response

Source: Data from Lambert and Tucker (1972).

Let's focus instead on what they can do, which seems to make more sense. French immersion programs appear to be producing students who have fully developed English proficiency, who often have cognitive advantages, and who possess near-nativelike abilities in French. Those seem to be noteworthy results.

One might wonder whether immersion programs appear so successful because the children who would not succeed drop out and return to the English program. This appears not to be the case. Hart, Lapkin, and Swain (1989) studied children who were transferring out of immersion and noted that the profile of parents who chose to withdraw their children was remarkably similar to that of parents choosing to leave their children in at the elementary level. It does not appear that children with particular family backgrounds are more disposed to drop out. Nor does it seem that children of below average intelligence are at a disadvantage in French immersion. If IQ were more important to success in immersion programs than in regular English programs we would expect to see a closer relationship between IQ and academic achievement in the immersion program. Swain (1975) found this not to be so. The relationship between IQ and achievement scores was the same for immersion children and children in English programs. All in all, it is clear that immersion programs are not just for the gifted.

7 AMERICAN SIGN LANGUAGE

American Sign Language (ASL) is used as an important mode of communication among deaf people in the United States and Canada. Geographical factors have also led to the creation of some other signed languages, French Canadian Sign Language, Alaskan Native Sign Language, and Nova Scotia Sign Language among them.

At first, we might think that since signed languages employ the hands and eyes to communicate rather than the mouth and ears they would differ significantly from spoken languages, but beyond the obvious difference in medium they do not. Signed languages have the same components as spoken languages: morphology, syntax, semantics, and even phonology. Though the phonology is not implemented by the vocal tract, a signed symbol can be broken into smaller units, analogous to phonological features, such as hand configuration and hand orientation.

ASL is a language in its own right. It is not some kind of manual version of English. ASL has different phonology, morphology, syntax, and vocabulary from English. There is a signed language known as Signing Exact English (SEE), however, which is a manual representation of English and hence very different from ASL.

If someone who has no knowledge of sign language watches deaf signers engaged in conversation, they see rapidly moving hands making shapes in space. One of the most common assumptions is that these gestures are mimetic, or iconic: that they imitate what they represent. This interpretation is quickly proved faulty when the watcher cannot understand the conversation even if it is performed very slowly.

7.1 ACQUISITION OF ASL

There are some very good reasons why the acquisition of language in deaf subjects should be of interest to us here. ASL is the first language of about 10 percent of the deaf population, who learn it at home from a deaf parent. For these children, learning English involves acquiring a second language. Most deaf children, however, do not have deaf parents and therefore first learn ASL when they go to school. These children tend to have difficulty achieving native-like fluency in English. They are inclined to have errors in their English similar to those of other students learning ESL.

7.2 METHODS OF EDUCATING DEAF STUDENTS

One of the most difficult problems deaf children face is the acquisition of language. They frequently have poor oral English skills and low reading levels. Recently, teachers of deaf students have come to accept signing in the classroom more often than in the past, when they usually required students to draw on residual hearing and to perform in spoken language. Nonetheless, they tend to favour signed languages other than ASL, such as SEE or some other English-based sign language. It seems that there are numerous reasons for the lack of acceptance of ASL in deaf classrooms, many of them political, but no one has investigated the possibility that it be used as the medium of instruction for teaching English. Remember Cummins and Swain's (1986) research on bilingual education programs, which showed that instruction in the first language does not lead to a diminished ability in the second language. Let's look at the options available in deaf education.

Traditionally, deaf education emphasized spoken English as the medium of instruction. Students were taught to lip-read and received hearing aids to make use of residual hearing. They were also expected to express themselves orally. Some programs combined manual communication with spoken English. In these, teachers spoke and signed simultaneously. This is a characteristic of one of the dominant schools of deaf education, the methodology known as *total communication*. ASL is permissible in total communication but tends not to be used much because most teachers of the deaf are not deaf themselves and therefore use a signed English. The most uncommon kind of program uses manual communication solely.

Several studies show that manual teaching methods work significantly better than oral teaching methods. Manual programs are rare in North America but more common in Sweden and Britain. These countries also have bilingual programs: in Swedish and Swedish Sign Language, and in British Sign Language and English. Total communication involves two versions of English, one spoken and one signed. Bilingual programs involve two truly different languages.

7.3 BILINGUAL EDUCATION THEORY

More than 90 percent of deaf children have hearing parents. The parents are not fluent in the language that these children have the means to understand. Generally, the children arrive at school with minimal communication skills. They are thus unlike hearing children, who begin school with mastery of one language. For hearing minority language children, we argued that their L1 should be incorporated into their education program. For deaf children, which language should be considered their L1? Since researchers have now acknowledged that ASL is a natural language, it seems that models of bilingual education proposed for two spoken languages can also be applied to deaf education. By and large, this has not happened in the education system for a number of reasons. First, it takes time to change the attitude that ASL is not really a language but just some kind of complex mime. Second, many teachers of the deaf are not native users of ASL. Third, there are no published ASL curriculum guides.

Let's review the benefits of bilingual education programs. Cummins and Swain (1986) argued that experience in either language could benefit the whole cognitive development of the child. They also argued that children needed a well-developed L1 before they could gain proficiency in the L2. This has clear implications for education of deaf children. Deaf children have consistently performed far below their hearing peers throughout school. But deaf children of deaf parents perform significantly better than deaf children of hearing parents, suggesting that deafness is not the only cause of the poor performance. Rather, it may have something to do with the development of L1 skills. Deaf children are not just suffering from lack of *English* input but from lack of any linguistic input that could aid their cognitive development. Certainly, deaf children of deaf parents would benefit from a bilingual education program. Strong (1988) argues that deaf children who have *hearing* parents and who are in a residential school would also benefit from this type of instruction.

7.4 DEAF CHILDREN AT RESIDENTIAL SCHOOLS

Strong (1985) examined the sign language use of nineteen young deaf children aged four to seven, in a residential school. Eleven of the children had deaf parents; eight had hearing parents. All of the subjects were deaf from birth and had no other impairments. Four subjects were in preschool; eleven were in kindergarten; four were in Grade 1. Three of the four teachers were hearing and one (the preschool teacher) was deaf. The school espoused total communication; the teachers spoke and signed in SEE simultaneously. The children were videotaped at regular intervals throughout the school year, and the tapes were studied to determine whether the children's signs were more often in SEE or in ASL.

The vast majority of utterances were in ASL even though not all of the children entered school knowing ASL. The children appeared to be much more motivated to use the language of their peers than that of their teachers. It appears, then, that ASL is the most appropriate full language system available to the deaf. Even in a residential school, children develop signing that is more like ASL than like English.

7.5 AN EXPERIMENTAL BILINGUAL PROGRAM

Strong (1988) took a first step in creating a bilingual education program in ASL and English. ASL was considered the primary language and English the secondary language. The goals of the program were to develop and expand ASL skills and then use that language as a medium for teaching English, and to develop both an awareness of ASL and English as equal but separate languages and an ability to recognize some of the differences between them. He developed a curriculum especially suited to deaf students. For example, characters in the texts did not talk on the telephone or overhear conversations. The experimental class was taught by a native user of ASL who was bilingual in English.

The lessons were conducted in ASL but also designed to teach something about English. The empirical results of the program are not yet available, but parental response has been favourable. Administrative response has ranged from tolerant to enthusiastic. We await the results of Strong's bilingual education project expectantly as we note that deaf children who are schooled in traditional programs using either an oral approach or total communication perform well below their hearing peers. Perhaps this will be one way to help them improve their performance.

8 CONCLUSION

Cummins (1981) presents the following conclusions about bilingualism and bilingual education:

1. Minority language children whose L1 proficiency on starting school is well developed will usually have little difficulty acquiring high levels of English proficiency. Children whose overall conceptual abilities in both L1 and L2 are poorly developed, however, are likely to experience difficulty in school.
2. When both languages are well developed, bilingualism seems to benefit some aspects of children's intellectual functioning. When neither language is well developed, children are often at a disadvantage at school.

CLASSROOM IMPLICATIONS

Bilingual Education

Cummins and Swain (1986) describe three principles that underlie successful bilingual education:

1. *First things first* Ensure that the child's home language is adequately developed before worrying about progress in a second language. The L1 is instrumental to the emotional and academic well-being of the child; its development must be seen as a high priority in the early years of schooling.

2. *Bilingualism through monolingualism* Two languages can be presented to the students in two ways: concurrently, by frequent shifting back and forth between languages within a lesson or activity; or separately, by a criterion such as time (English in the morning, for example), or person (Maureen teaches in Spanish), or subject (math is in English and geography is in French).

Cummins and Swain argue that separated use of the two languages is to be preferred. In a concurrent-style classroom, children can ignore the language they don't understand and wait until the one they do understand comes. There is no motivation to try to understand what is being said in the new language. Separation of the two languages also makes both students and teachers work harder. (Teachers have more of a challenge in preparing clear lessons. Separation is probably less demanding on linguistic resources though, as switching back and forth between languages can be exhausting.)

They also promote separation because the two languages may not receive equal time in a concurrent class. Even though teachers often *feel* that they are using the two languages equally, they may not be. One study showed that teachers who believed they were using English and Spanish about the same amount in class were in fact using English 72 percent of the time and Spanish only 28 percent of the time. And these were teachers whose L1 was Spanish! The separation method tended to result in equal amounts of Spanish and English.

3. *Bilingualism as a bonus* As we saw before, there are benefits to being bilingual. We can let our students know the political, economic, cultural, linguistic, cognitive, and personal benefits that arise from being bilingual.

SELF TEST

One of the main questions that research on bilingual education addresses is whether instruction in one language has a _____ effect on

(1)
the other. In heritage language and French immersion programs, the concern is whether instruction in the _____ language will

(2)
result in diminished proficiency in the _____ language. The

(3)
almost unanimous answer in the research studies is _____ .

(4)
Bilingual students, in fact, are claimed to have certain cognitive

_____ over their monolingual peers. Cummins accounts for

(5)
this with his _____ hypothesis.

(6)

Without L1 support, minority language students face a very high
_____(7)_____ rate in high school. Bilingual programs also appear to
have implications for non-hearing students whose first language is
_____(8)_____ . The results from French immersion programs suggest
that immersion students have _____(9)_____ ability in their
_____(10)_____ skills but recognizably _____(11)_____ ability in their
_____(12)_____ skills.

FURTHER READING

Cummins, J. and M. Swain. 1986. *Bilingualism in Education.* New York: Longman.

Fase, W., K. Jaspert, and S. Kroon. 1992. *Maintenance and Loss of Minority Languages.* Amsterdam: John Benjamins.

Strong, M., ed. 1988. *Language Learning and Deafness.* Cambridge: Cambridge University Press.

22

....

First Language Attrition

This chapter considers several issues surrounding the effect of learning a second language on the first language. In certain situations, learning the L2 can have an adverse effect on the L1. If, for example, an immigrant goes for many years without speaking his or her L1, aspects of it can be lost. This process is known as language *attrition*. The field can be divided into four types of attrition (Van Els 1986):

1. Loss of first or primary language within the environment of that language (dialect loss or loss of L1 through aging)
2. Loss of the L1 in an L2 environment (loss of native language by immigrants)
3. Loss of the L2 in an L1 environment (foreign language loss)
4. Loss of the L2 in L2 environment (second language loss by aging immigrants)

This chapter focusses mainly on the second type.

1 ATTRITION IN BILINGUALS

First language attrition in bilinguals is an area of interest for several reasons. Like second language acquisition, attrition tells us something about what happens when two languages come in contact in one person. It is also a testing ground for theories of linguistic universals and markedness. Do they account for attrition as well as acquisition? If more marked items are acquired later, are they the first to be lost? Can we predict or explain why certain items are lost first? Attrition also has the potential to tell us something about the relative permanence of acquisition and the conditions that result in either language maintenance or language loss.

Research in language acquisition and language attrition must explain how generalizations and overgeneralizations are learned and then *unlearned* in the emerging grammar. We know that in acquiring the L1 grammar, children often produce overgeneralized forms such as *I getted it* or *I eated them*. Eventually, though, they retreat from these overgeneralizations and arrive at the correct adult grammar. Language attrition is concerned with a similar problem. How are previously acceptable utterances unlearned? At one stage in a person's life the L1 utterances are obviously part of his or her system of knowledge, but at a later stage that system of knowledge changes. The speaker begins to use utterances that are not grammatical in the L1. When the L2 has completely replaced the L1, *language death* has occurred.

Much traditional L2 research has been concerned with language transfer: the influence of the L1 on the L2. The domain of language attrition research is the effect of the L2 on the L1.

1.1 WHEN DOES ATTRITION OCCUR?

The following psychological or sociological factors seem to be conducive to L1 loss:

1. The amount of time the speaker spends using the L1 is decreased.
2. The speaker draws upon the L1 in fewer contexts and for fewer purposes than formerly. If a first language is restricted to the basic communicative function and is neither integrative nor expressive, it is likely to suffer attrition.
3. The L1 is subordinate to the L2 in the target culture. This point draws on Schumann's work on pidginization (1978), referred to in Chapter 6. Schumann was trying to classify the sociolinguistic factors that would not be conducive to L2 learning. His framework seems amenable to description of an environment conducive to L1 loss as well. Remember Schumann's argument that social distance between two cultures would result in a poor second language learning environment. Turning this around, we can say that when the L1 is non-dominant, the L1 culture not enclosed, the length of stay considerable, and so on, the chances of attrition are greatest.

1.2 LINGUISTIC CHARACTERISTICS OF ATTRITION

Let us now turn to an investigation of what language loss looks like. Language attrition is often selective; it may affect certain parts of the grammar and not others. Yet it does not seem to be random. The unlearning of an L1 appears to be a rule-governed phenomenon. First let's look at some lexical phenomena.

You are unlikely to lose your entire L1 lexicon at one time. Preston (1982) proposes several *sites* that are likely to undergo attrition. Some of the high-attrition sites he suggests are low-frequency items, unique items, opaque items, synonymous items, and irregular items:

1. *Low-frequency items* Remember from Chapter 10 that frequency is one of the organizing principles in the structure of the lexicon. Psycholinguistic investigation has shown that people treat high-frequency lexical items, such as *food,* differently from low-frequency items, such as *pusillanimous.* If you haven't been using the L1 in a long time, low-frequency vocabulary items may be lost.
2. *Unique items* These exist in the L1 but not the L2. If the L2 doesn't have a word for *nopales* (a type of cactus), for example, and a Spanish speaker hasn't been using the L1 for a long time, he or she might lose this word.
3. *Opaque items* You may well lose more of your ability to recall semantically opaque items like *vet* than of your ability to recall semantically transparent items like *animal doctor.* The word *vet* gives no clue to its meaning.
4. *Synonymous items* Imagine that the words *donkey* and *mule* are synonymous to you. If you do not use your first language for a significant period then one of these synonyms may become lost to you.
5. *Irregular items* As the first language is lost, irregular items tend to become regularized. Even if you managed to recall the lexical item *ox,* for example, you might well pluralize it as *oxes,* not remembering the irregular form *oxen.* As we saw in Chapter 13, if irregular forms are the product of associative memory, then the strength of association will decline with disuse. The over-regularized form would be generated by the rule system.

Nevertheless, all of these forms would probably be comprehensible to you, even if you had lost your ability to produce them. If you heard the exclamation *Look what those pusillanimous donkeys did to my oxen! Where is the vet?* you might understand it.

2 LEXICAL CHARACTERISTICS: A CASE STUDY

We turn now to a case study of L1 attrition described in Olshtain and Barzilay (1991). The study focusses on lexical retrieval difficulties in adult first language attrition. Primary language attrition in adults is likely to occur when the subjects have been uprooted from their L1 context and transferred to a new language environment. In this context, the L2 is the dominant language of the culture and the L1 is somehow restricted in function. Various factors can influence the erosion of the L1: the degree of functional restriction, the prestige of the L1 in the particular community, the social distance between the first and second cultures, and the degree of individual acculturation.

Olshtain and Barzilay investigated a group of American immigrants to Israel who continued to maintain English as their dominant language even after ten or twenty years of being in Israel. They examined the attrition of the L1 (English) in the L2 (Hebrew) environment. Some of the subjects had acquired near-native proficiency in Hebrew but most only used it to fulfill their immediate needs. All continued to use English for reading, entertainment, and professional functions.

In Israel, English is considered to be a language of high prestige and great usefulness and therefore worth knowing. According to most definitions and expectations, we would not expect a great deal of attrition in this context. Nevertheless, Olshtain and Barzilay noted that lexical retrieval processes seemed to be slightly impaired in the L1.

The most likely items to suffer from language attrition are infrequent, specific nouns. Sharwood Smith (1983) refers to this "reduction in accessibility" as one of the primary characteristics of L1 attrition. The subjects in question have difficulty recalling certain words. In natural communication, they may well avoid the problem by means such as paraphrase or code switching, which can make it difficult to determine the actual limitations on their L1 use. Olshtain and Barzilay therefore designed an experiment that would not allow the subjects to evade particular words.

Their study compared fifteen Americans living in Israel and six Americans living in the United States. At the time it was conducted, the American Israelis had been living in Israel a minimum of eight years and a maximum of twenty-five. Their ages ranged from twenty-three to fifty-five. Data were collected by having the subjects tell two frog stories by Mercer Mayer: *Frog, Where Are You?* and *A Boy, a Dog, and a Frog* (1969). In these books, a story is conveyed without any text. The subjects in both groups were asked to look through the entire book and then to tell the story. Even though they had a fair amount of freedom in the task, they could not avoid certain lexical items that were repeated throughout the story. The researchers targeted five words for special attention: *jar, gopher, cliff, deer,* and *pond*.

For the most part, the American Israelis had no trouble telling the frog stories. They did, however, have difficulty with the five targeted words mentioned above. In order to tell the story successfully, they could not avoid the words so they had a number of options available to them: circumlocution or paraphrase, replacement of the word with one similar in meaning (probably primed by the target word), or conscious effort to retrieve the word. The subjects employed all three strategies, but the final two were preferred. This is not to say that the monolinguals performed perfectly homogeneously. They showed some variation in the task but not as much as the bilinguals, as indicated in Table 22.1.

Table 22.1 Monolingual and Bilingual Word Choice

Target word	Monolingual choices	Bilingual choices
pond	pond, swamp	pond, swamp, water, body of water, pond of water, puddle of water, riverbed, ocean, puddle
deer	deer, stag	deer, stag, antelope, elk, little animal
gopher	gopher, groundhog	gopher, groundhog, skunk, chipmunk, mole, hedgehog, muskrat, rabbit, squirrel
cliff	cliff, precipice	cliff, precipice, mountain, little hill
jar	jar	jar, bottle, bowl, jug

Source: Data from Olshtain and Barzilay (1991).

All the American Israelis in the study exhibited some kind of reduction of accessibility in their English. They were also aware that a more appropriate word existed which they used to know but now had to search for actively. They often said things like "I forgot the word" or "I forgot my English."

In this excerpt, A woman talks about her husband, Billy, who is missing in action in World War II. Consider the parallels to language attrition:

When I think about those times, I can almost see Billy again. At least, I can see his eyes. I can see his hands. And his teeth. He has perfect teeth. Not like mine. That's something else we fought about. [Pause] But the rest of the picture—is in shadow. [Pause] Listen. If they want to make the Hollywood blockbuster of all time—one of those stories of tragic romance—sure to have every woman in the theatre reaching for her hanky—they should tell the story of a woman—whose husband goes away—but he goes away one piece at a time. First an arm vanishes. Then a leg. Then his eyes. His hands. His teeth. Finally she can't remember what he looked like—at all. [Pause] That's what hurts. [Pause] That's what's peculiar. [Pause] Losing him—a little at a time.

John Murrell
Waiting for the Parade

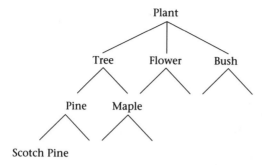

Figure 22.1 Hierarchical Structure of a Semantic Field

Generally, lexical attrition is characterized by a more restricted available lexical stock, and some items are therefore less accessible for retrieval in production. These items are probably available for comprehension; broad meanings are often retained although specific word meanings may be reduced.

Although Olshtain and Barzilay don't talk about it, we think it likely that Berlin's (1978) folk taxonomy may have some relevance here. If we consider a semantic field as having a hierarchical structure, it may look something like Figure 22.1. A subject might select an inappropriate word from a higher level (*tree* instead of *pine,* for example), from a lower level (*pine* instead of *tree*), or from the correct level (*maple* instead of *pine*). If he or she had trouble retrieving a particular lexical item, then something from nearby in the hierarchy would be selected.

Berlin's model reveals that there is a hierarchical structure to a semantic system. When people try to retrieve a word from memory they may miss the target by a bit, but they do so in a structured fashion. The subjects who used *swamp* for *pond* were at the right level, while those who used *water* for *pond* were choosing a word from a higher level.

3 MORPHOLOGICAL CHARACTERISTICS: A CASE STUDY

Kaufman and Aronoff (1991) examine some of the morphological characteristics of first language attrition. They looked at the developmental attrition of L1 (in this case Hebrew) in a young child placed in an L2-dominant environment (in this case English). The subject was a native speaker of Hebrew from Israel who entered the United States at age 2;6 (two years, six months). At age 2;7 she attended nursery school for three hours a day, three times a week, in English. At age 2;8 she attended another English school seven hours a day, five days a week. At home, Hebrew was the exclusive language used by both parents and by her six- and eleven-year-old sisters.

Kaufman and Aronoff divided her developmental progression into four stages:

1. *Onset of attrition* (2;9–3;1): characterized by L2 verbal insertions into an L1 morphosyntactic context.
2. *Bilingualism* (3;1–3;2): characterized by native-like proficiency in both languages, appropriate for the subject's age level. The L1 was still developing and productive, as evidenced by normal developmental errors.
3. *L1 disintegration* (3;2–3;5): marked by the disintegration of the L1 verbal system. This was accelerated by the child's unwillingness to speak Hebrew.
4. *Reconstruction* (3;5–4;6): characterized by reconstruction of an idiosyncratic grammar for Hebrew based largely on L2 structures.

Let's look at these stages a little more closely.

3.1 ONSET OF ATTRITION

For this subject, the attrition process began by affecting the lexicon. She would insert an English word into a Hebrew sentence, treating it morphologically and syntactically like a Hebrew word:

Ima	t-oxl-i	et	ha-apple	šel-i
Mommy	2.FUT-eat-2fs	OM	the-apple	of-me[1]

Mommy, eat my apple.

In order to discuss what the subject did, we need to say a little bit more about Hebrew verb morphology. Semitic morphology is characterized by the interaction of consonantal verb roots with primarily vocalic derivational templates. The basic meaning is expressed by the root morpheme, and related forms of the word are created by adding different vowel patterns. Consider the root *k-t-v,* for which we find the related forms shown in Table 22.2. In addition to these morphological templates, or *binyanim*, there are also derivational and inflectional affixes. Verbs agree with the subject noun in person, number, and gender.

---

[1] 2 = second person, FUT = future, f = feminine, s = singular, OM = object marker

Table 22.2   Related Forms for Single Hebrew Root

katav[2]	wrote
nixtav	was written
(h)ixtav	dictated
(h)itkatev	corresponded

During the onset of attrition, we can see that the subject dealt with English words as Hebrew words. In Table 22.3, for example, we see her forms of English verbs. In this stage, the L2 verbs are treated as L1 verbs and inflected accordingly.

Table 22.3   Treatment of English Verbs during Onset of Attrition

L2 verb	Child's form	Child's L2 verb root
clean	*a*-kliyn	k-l-n
blow	bala-*ti*	b-l
flush	*la*-flaš	f-l-š
step	*le*-step	s-t-p

Source: Data from Kaufman and Aronoff (1991).

3.2 THE BILINGUAL STAGE

The period of balanced bilingualism for this subject was very short, a single month (3;1–3;2). It was characterized by fluency in both languages and an increase in *code switching*, switching from one language to another between sentences. In this case it was regardless of the input at home, all of which was in Hebrew. The subject also engaged in *code mixing*, switching from one language to another within a single sentence. These switches consisted almost exclusively of L2 words inserted into L1 sentences, as shown in the 3;1 example below:

> First I want to bring the paper and then I bring two papers. Where my other papers? *ulay ani e-ese al ze. ani rak e-mca iparon ve-*crayon *ani rak roc-a li-rot efo. ani crix-a iparon, ulay* crayons.
>
> … maybe I 1sFUT-do on this. I just 1sFUT-find pencil and-crayon, I just want-fs to-see where I need-fs pencil, perhaps crayons.[3]

Note that the L1 syntax is still intact. At this stage in the child's development the L1 is still productive, as we find normal overgeneralization errors.

---

[2] The velar stop [k] and the velar fricative [x] alternate in ways that are beyond the scope of this discussion; the root is the same in all these forms.

[3] 1 = first person, s = singular, FUT = future, f = feminine

3.3 THE DISINTEGRATION STAGE

At this stage we begin to see disintegration of the L1 morphology and syntax. In addition, the child appears to be losing interest in the L1, claiming, "I don't like to speak Hebrew." The child's utterances are becoming L2 dominant, even though her parents and siblings continue to use the L1 exclusively. At this stage, we start to see L1 verbal insertions made into an L2 frame. The insertions consist of deviant but recognizable forms of the L1 verbs. They are, however, uninflected, as shown in this 3;6 example:

> I'm *me-nagev*-ing myself. I want to *i-nagev* myself. Can you *it-labeš* me?
> (*n-g-v* = drying   *l-b-š* = dressing)

The forms found in utterances such as this are neither normal adult Hebrew nor normal developmental errors found in monolingual Hebrew-speaking children. Clearly, the child's L1 morphology is disintegrating (see Table 22.4).

Table 22.4   Forms during Disintegration Stage

Child's form	Adult form
me-nagev-*ing*	me-nagev-et
i-nagev	le-nagev
it-labeš	le-(h)albiš

Source: Data from Kaufman and Aronoff (1991).

3.4 THE RECONSTRUCTION STAGE

At this stage, the variety of possible verb forms in Hebrew gives way to a single idiosyncratic verbal template. The subject generalized all L1 verbs to the form iCaCe(C), as in *inagev* (wipe). She used this form of the verb in all contexts. The form was then treated as an L2 stem and as a result conformed to the morphosyntax of the L2 environment, but it still retained an L1 phonetic form:

> (3;7) My room is *isader*-ed [arranged].
> (4;0) Daddy, *ixamem* [warm] this for me.

The complex L1 morphological system has been reduced to a single form. It is interesting to note that even at this final stage, the child's speech was perfectly comprehensible to her family. The study allows us to see that L1 attrition is not achieved in a single crushing blow; it proceeds by stages.

4 RECAPITULATION AND REGRESSION

Having explored the characteristics of L1 attrition, let us now turn to some of the explanations proposed for the phenomenon (de Bot and Weltens 1991).

In 1941, Roman Jakobson tried to link three processes of language change: historical change, first language acquisition, and language loss due to brain damage. The connection between historical change and L1 acquisition is usually labelled the *recapitulation hypothesis,* and the connection between language acquisition and language loss is called the *regression hypothesis.* Simply stated, these hypotheses assume that if a language changes over time by going through the developmental stages *a b c d e f* and so on, children will go through the same developmental stages as they acquire the language. Conversely, someone in the process of losing the language first loses *f,* then *e,* then *d, c, b,* and *a.*

4.1 RECAPITULATION

Let us first look at recapitulation. Jakobson believed strongly in the idea. Recapitulation was originally proposed by Haeckel in 1868 as an hypothesis about biogenetics, captured in the phrase, "Ontogeny recapitulates phylogeny." According to this theory, an *individual* proceeds along the same developmental path as the *species* did in the course of evolution. The example usually trotted out to illustrate this—and we will be no different—is that human embryos have gills at an early stage of development. This is supposed to mirror a stage in the evolution of the species when we all had gills. Although we will not go into the details here, it appears that modern biology wholeheartedly *rejects* the notion of recapitulation. The hypothesis assumes two things that modern evolutionary theory does not: that evolution is gradual, and that evolution moves from the simple to the complex (see Gould 1989).

Problems also arise in the application of this hypothesis to language. It is hotly disputed whether language acquisition and historical change are continuous and move from simple to complex. In fact, we can't even agree on how to measure linguistic complexity.

4.2 REGRESSION

Regression is the name given to the view that the order of language loss mirrors the order of language acquisition; in other words, that those items acquired first will be lost last. Several studies on the language of the elderly are relevant here.

Clyne (1981) looked at Dutch and German immigrants in Australia who showed a tendency to revert to their first language and lose their second language (English) as they grew older. This is referred to as *L1 reversion,* and it may well be linked to the level of proficiency obtained in the L2. De Bot and Clyne (1989) and Neisser (1984) assume that there is some sort of essential threshold of proficiency which makes the language immune to attrition. Subjects who were above the threshold did not regress; subjects who were below it did. This is, of course, no real explanation, but it must be accounted for.

Does regression apply to foreign language loss? If we learn Japanese in a classroom in Calgary, for example, will we lose those elements learned most recently if we stop using Japanese? Olshtain (1986) studied native speakers of Hebrew who had acquired near-nativelike proficiency in English while living abroad. She predicted that these subjects were very likely to suffer gradual attrition of the L2 (English) when they returned to their native, Hebrew-dominant environment, and claimed that their English use would be characterized by two things: variability in the application of marked rules (such as *go → went*); and reduced accessibility of specific lexical items.

For one aspect of subjects' language loss, she found that the regression explanation held. The younger subjects, aged five to eight, began the study able to correctly produce many irregular English verb forms, such as *went.* Soon after they returned to Israel though, they were overgeneralizing to forms like *goed.* Remember that in L1 acquisition of English it is common to see children moving through the developmental stages

went → goed → went

Olshtain argued that these subjects were exhibiting regression. Nevertheless, not all the subjects followed this pattern. The older ones, aged eight to fourteen, did not exhibit regression in any constructions. Clearly, the results are inconclusive.

Olshtain asserted that literacy might have been a factor. The older learners had a strong grounding in L2 literacy and continued to read in English upon their return to Israel. It is likely that their literacy continued to give them L2 input and thus halted the attrition process. Literacy might also affect how the L2 is stored in the brain. There appears to be a connection between knowledge of the L1 writing system and ability to retain that L1 even after it has been abandoned for many years. A person who learned to read and write in the L1 and then emigrated to another country and as a result stopped using that language seems to have less difficulty recovering it after many years than one who did not learn to read or write in the L1. This explains some of the differences in the performance of, say, three year olds (who have trouble recovering) and five year olds (who don't).

Even so, we are still a long way from sorting out whether attrition mirrors acquisition, as we do not have an accepted methodology or linguistic framework for determining *when* something has been acquired. Without this we are still unable to talk of order of acquisition or attrition in any really interesting fashion. The universal grammar distinction between *core* and *periphery* might facilitate a prediction here. Remember that certain grammatical items or rules are thought to be part of the core grammar and others to be peripheral. We can see how the regression hypothesis might predict that elements of the periphery would be lost first. The core would remain less permeable to change or loss. A UG-based analysis of L1 attrition would also allow us to ask whether the decaying L1 obeys linguistic universals. Is it a natural language? Again, the similarities between acquisition and attrition research are clear.

4.3 IS A LANGUAGE REALLY LOST?

Sharwood Smith (1989), working within a framework of *competence* versus *control,* investigated the interesting question of whether the first language really is lost in cases such as those we have been examining. Perhaps the knowledge is still there but the subject is having difficulty gaining access to or controlling that knowledge. Native-speaker competence might still be intact, but the mechanisms for manipulating that competence may have undergone some change. Sharwood Smith argued that for subjects who were able to judge the grammaticality of L1 sentences correctly or to self-correct, instances of the L2 influencing the L1 might reflect changes in control rather than in competence. While this is certainly an interesting avenue of investigation, Sharwood Smith presents no empirical study to inform us.

5 CONCLUSION

This chapter has shown that full bilingualism is not necessarily a permanent state. If certain conditions are met, someone may well lose particular aspects of the first language. In one case study, access to knowledge was shown to be affected, specifically in lexical retrieval. In another, the representation of linguistic knowledge was affected, as demonstrated in the loss of L1 morphology. In the case of the Americans living in Israel, social factors most probably led to attrition by restricting L1 input. In the case of the young Israeli girl living in the United States, psychological factors probably led to attrition through restricted L1 input and intake.

This is of course speculative; because we lack a comprehensive theory of acquisition, we cannot have a comprehensive theory of attrition. We must begin by simply describing the phenomenon and noting that attrition can affect both representation and process. Again, the similarity between first and second languages can be seen: both can be lost. It has been argued that interlanguage grammars are less stable than primary language grammars (Adjémian 1976). If there is a difference in the stability of L1 and L2 grammars, however, it is one of degree not of type.

CLASSROOM IMPLICATIONS AND BEYOND

First language attrition has an impact that is felt far beyond the classroom. No education affects the student solely inside the school. Language education in particular has an influence on the life of the whole family. Submersion programs,[4] in which minority language students are thrown in with native speakers, are designed to turn the students into monolingual English speakers as quickly as possible. Especially for very young children, the process can have negative consequences for their home life. Students should be encouraged to identify with both the target language and culture *and* their first language and culture. They will thus gain proficiency in two languages rather than one and maintain familial harmony through respect for their dual heritage.

It is common for minority language students submerged in regular classes without linguistic support to lose their first language, greatly restricting their communication with their parents and grandparents. We must remember that the school system cannot teach the students everything they need to know about morals and values. Children still need parents.

Educators must ask themselves whether they really want to put a policy in place—as several school boards have recently done—that could result in a large population of students losing parental guidance because they no longer share a language. What price are we willing to attach to the students learning English? Should they pay with the loss of their first language? Should they pay with loss of respect for their parents?

The United States has a program called Head Start from which other countries could learn. In some states, children who do not have English as a first language are given a "head start" by being put into an English-only program as young as age three. This too is designed to turn them into monolingual English speakers as quickly as possible. Recently, Wong Fillmore (1991) surveyed twelve hundred families with children in these early childhood education programs about the effects on their family life. Sixty-four percent reported that the programs had had a negative impact on their family. *Sixty-four percent!* In a comparison group that received instruction in both their first and second languages (Spanish and English) only 10 percent reported negative effects. Clearly, language attrition is not just about language.

---

[4] Also known as sink-or-swim, or mainstreaming.

SELF TEST

One possible consequence of acquiring an L2 is loss of the L1. Several factors appear to encourage this, among them, _____ amount (1) of time using the L1 and a _____ range of functions utilized (2) in the L1. In addition, certain linguistic _____ are more likely (3) to undergo attrition, such as _____-frequency items and (4) semantically _____ items. Olshtain and Barzilay (1991) pre- (5) sent evidence that lexical _____ may be affected by attrition (6) although lexical storage may not be. Kaufman and Aronoff looked at the attrition of L1 _____ . They noted that a child's L1 verb system (7) was reduced to a single _____ . (8)

Various models have been proposed to try to explain attrition, though none have done so completely satisfactorily. Olshtain (1986) argued that there was some evidence for the _____ hypothesis. Other (9) researchers speculate that _____ is somehow able to block (10) attrition even over long periods of disuse of the L1.

FURTHER READING

Seliger, H. and R. Vago. 1991. *First Language Attrition*. Cambridge: Cambridge University Press.

Lambert, R. and B. Freed, eds. 1982. *The Loss of Language Skills*. Rowley, MA: Newbury House.

Summary

This chapter, such as it is, offers the executive summary, the highlights of what we have talked about throughout this book.

Chapter 1: The Study of Second Language Acquisition The study of second language acquisition requires a sophisticated understanding of language, learning, and teaching, and is relevant to second language teachers.

Chapter 2: Linguistic Theory Among other things, the second language learner must acquire *knowledge* of language, which is a complex understanding on many different levels, such as phonology, morphology, syntax. This model of a grammar can benefit both researchers studying acquisition and teachers attempting to facilitate acquisition and assess proficiency.

Chapter 3: Language, Learning, and Mind People acquire knowledge and ability in differing ways, using mechanisms such as induction, deduction, and memory. A theory of acquisition must be explicit about the form in which knowledge is represented in the mind and how that knowledge got there.

Chapter 4: Learning a First Language The study of first language acquisition has revealed that children move through developmental stages en route to native-speaker competence, and that the intermediate stages are systematic. The kinds of representations and processes involved in L1 acquisition and the theoretical machinery invoked by linguists—such as no negative evidence—have had a clear influence on the study of second language acquisition.

Chapter 5: Proficiency, the Final Goal Communicative competence is a complex construct. Second language learners must acquire the competence to produce language above and below the sentence level that is accurate and appropriate to the context. This has implications for both the teaching and the testing of a second language.

Chapter 6: Theories of Second Language Acquisition A comprehensive theory of second language acquisition must incorporate a wide range of internal and external factors. Input processing is an example of the former, and social conditions are an example of the latter.

Chapter 7: The Nature of an Interlanguage   An L2 learner grammar is systematic, though non-nativelike. Some non-nativelike characteristics may be caused by L1 influence.

Chapter 8: Language Universals and Second Language Acquisition   A learner's interlanguage is constrained by certain linguistic universals: universal grammar, language typology, and implicational universals. These can tell us something about the ease or difficulty of learning certain structures. Learning to make a less marked distinction such as initial voicing contrasts, for example, may be easier than learning to make a more marked distinction such as final voicing.

Chapter 9: The Structure of an Interlanguage   A linguistic investigation of such things as phonological and syntactic structures reveals some of the organizing principles of an L2 learner grammar, such as syllable structure and syntactic movement.

Chapter 10: Language Performance   Psycholinguistics is the study of language performance: the processes and representations used in language comprehension and production.

Chapter 11: Language Production   Production can be described as a series of steps in which a non-linguistic message is transformed into language output.

Chapter 12: Language Comprehension   Language comprehension is fast, unconscious, automatic, and obligatory.

Chapter 13: Variationist Perspectives on Second Language Acquisition   Second language performance can vary according to both extralinguistic factors, such as attention to form, and linguistic factors, such as whether morphology is regular or irregular. We saw more variation in regular than in irregular forms because the first are computed and the second are stored in the lexicon.

Chapter 14: The Effects of Age   Adults and adolescents *can* acquire a second language though it will most likely be accented.

Chapter 15: Individual Differences in Second Language Acquisition   There is a great deal of individual variation in second language acquisition strategies. Numerous cognitive, affective, and biological factors—such as field dependence, anxiety, and age, respectively—make different second language learners behave in different ways. It is still unclear which ways are best.

Chapter 16: The Effects of Instruction   Instruction can make a difference to second language acquisition. It may speed up learning and help learners process complex input, though the effects may not be long-lasting.

Chapter 17: The Effects of the Environment   Modified input (teacher talk) and modified interaction (foreigner talk) may be helpful to the L2 learner. They can provide comprehensible input.

Chapter 18: The Effects of Feedback   Focus on form within a communicative context leads to improved accuracy for L2 learners. Implicit negative evidence may also aid in acquiring generalizations.

Chapter 19: The Consequences of Literacy   Literacy is a complex cognitive skill with enormous social and political consequences. A child or adult who does not develop literacy skills is at a decided disadvantage in today's society. Underdeveloped literacy in the L1 can lead to problems in an L2 school.

Chapter 20: Bilingualism   A bilingual has a functional command of two languages. Bilinguals vary in terms of the mental organization of their two languages.

Chapter 21: Bilingual Education   A well-developed L1 is crucial to succeeding in an L2 school. Submersion in the L2 is not the only route to proficiency in the L2. Additive bilingualism is possible. Not surprisingly, bilingual instruction results in bilingualism more often than monolingual instruction does.

Chapter 22: First Language Attrition   Aspects of both first and second languages can be lost in certain circumstances. When there are limited opportunities to hear or use the L1, functional restriction results. This can lead to attrition.

Acquiring a second language may be the most complex cognitive act we perform as adults. In this book we hope to have made the reader aware of some of this complexity. We have also addressed some of the methodological issues that make trying to get a picture of second language competence and performance so challenging and exciting. Second language acquisition is an immense and fertile academic field; parts of it are quite wild and others are well cultivated. A single researcher tends to get to know a small area intimately, but a lot can be learned from leaning on the fence and talking to your neighbours. This book has offered a kind of satellite photo of the landscape. Obviously, some detail is lacking, but we hope that we've made up for it by presenting the big picture as clearly as possible.

So you've had a tour of the SLA world, and we trust that you've discovered some of the places that interest you most. We like it here.

Appendix

SELF-TEST ANSWERS

....

CHAPTER

2 Linguistic Theory
1. symbolic 2. arbitrary 3. grammar 4. describe 5. acquired 6. used 7. storing 8. voiced 9. voiceless 10. bilabial. 11. stop 12. environment 13. voiceless 14. hierarchical 15. produce 16. comprehend 17. grammatical 18. phrasal 19. constraints

3 Language, Learning, and Mind
1. blank or empty 2. empiricism 3. innate 4. Descartes 5. rationalism 6. deductive 7. inductive 8. B.F. Skinner 9. Jean Piaget 10. non-modular 11. short-term 12. long-term 13. neuropsychology 14. connectionism

4 Learning a First Language
1. stages 2. adults 3. processes 4. grammar or system 5. errors 6. innate 7. trigger 8. poverty 9. negative

5 Proficiency, the Final Goal
1. knowledge 2. ability 3. organizational 4. pragmatic 5. above 6. illocutionary 7. formality 8. communication 9. testing

6 Theories of Second Language Acquisition
1. predictions 2. falsifiable 3. Occam's 4. Schumann's theory 5. Krashen's theory 6. pidginization 7. interlanguages 8. lack 9. social 10. psychological 11. formal 12. acquisition 13. process

7 The Nature of an Interlanguage
1. transfers 2. contrastive 3. different 4. developmental 5. overgeneralization 6. degrees 7. split 8. type or source 9. surface-level 10. systematicity 11. mistakes 12. avoidance 13. L1 = L2

8 Language Universals and Second Language Acquisition
1. feasibility 2. deduction 3. innate 4. implicational 5. ease or difficulty 6. unmarked 7. more 8. natural 9. subset 10. positive 11. clustering

9 The Structure of an Interlanguage
1. syllable 2. epenthesis 3. unsyllabified/unattached 4. rhymes 5. subjacency 6. movement 7. S 8. UG 9. parameter settings 10. L1

10 Language Performance
1. competence 2. performance 3. psycholinguistics 4. computed 5. metaphors 6. errors 7. features 8. top-down 9. bottom-up 10. logogen 11. frequency 12. parsing 13. morphemes 14. words 15. response time 16. accuracy 17. priming 18. Stroop 19. automatic

11 Language Production
1. Garrett's 2. errors 3. functional 4. positional 5. accuracy 6. accuracy 7. fluency

12 Language Comprehension
1. listening 2. conscious 3. lexical decision 4. eye fixations 5. saccades 6. phonological 7. dyslexia 8. syntactic 9. parser

13 Variationist Perspectives on Second Language Acquisition
1. variation 2. individual 3. variable rule 4. competence 5. performance 6. form 7. automatic 8. regular 9. associative memory 10. rules 11. similar

14 The Effects of Age
1. critical 2. biology 3. lateralization 4. when 5. culture 6. universal 7. sociocultural 8. acculturation 9. pronunciation 10. morphology 11. indistinguishably 12. selectional

15 Individual Differences in Second Language Acquisition
1. Affective 2. unwillingness 3. motivation 4. High 5. cognitive 6. intelligence 7. aptitude 8. learning strategies 9. communication strategies 10. correlations

16 The Effects of Instruction
1. naturalistic 2. SOC 3. TLU 4. overapply 5. temporary 6. speed up 7. teachability 8. confirmed 9. processes 10. cognitive 11. non-modular 12. form 13. meaning 14. explicit 15. implicit

17 The Effects of the Environment
1. input 2. interaction 3. foreigner 4. ungrammatical 5. negotiation 6. frequency 7. classroom 8. preferences 9. condescending

18 The Effects of Feedback
1. explicit 2. how 3. single 4. garden path 5. induced 6. implicit negative 7. metalinguistic 8. identify 9. consistent 10. temporary/short term

19 The Consequences of Literacy
1. social/socio-political 2. emancipatory/power 3. L1 4. L2 5. phoneme 6. syllable 7. word 8. interact 9. family background/socio-economic status 10. knowledge of literacy 11. lower

20 Bilingualism
1. languages 2. competence 3. compound 4. semantic 5. aphasia 6. right 7. switch 8. output 9. Green's

21 Bilingual Education
1. negative 2. minority 3. majority 4. no 5. advantages 6. dual threshold 7. dropout 8. ASL 9. near-nativelike 10. receptive 11. non-nativelike 12. productive

22 First Language Attrition
1. decreased 2. restricted 3. sites 4. low 5. opaque 6. access/retrieval 7. morphology 8. form/pattern 9. regression 10. literacy

References

Acton, W. 1979. Second language learning and perception of difference in attitude. Ph.D. diss., University of Michigan, Ann Arbor.

Adjémian, C. 1976. On the nature of interlanguage systems. *Language Learning* 26:297–320.

———. 1982. La spécificité de l'interlanguage et l'idéalisation des langues secondes. *Grammaire Transformationelle: Théorie et Méthodologies*. Paris: Université de Paris VIII.

Albert, M.L. and Obler, L.K. 1978. *The Bilingual Brain*. New York: Academic Press.

Alderson, J.C. and A.H. Urquhart, eds. 1984. *Reading in a Foreign Language*. New York: Longman.

Alladina, S. 1986. Language communities in Britain. *Language Issues,* 1 (Spring): 13–16.

Allwright, R. 1975. Problems in the study of the language teacher's treatment of learner error. In *On TESOL 1975*, 96–109. Washington, DC: TESOL.

Allwright, R. and K. Bailey. 1991. *Focus on the Language Classroom: An Introduction to Classroom Research for Language Teachers*. Cambridge: Cambridge University Press.

Alpert, R. and R. Haber. 1960. Anxiety in academic achievement situations. *Journal of Abnormal and Social Psychology* 61:207–15.

Andersen, R. 1989. The theoretical status of variation in interlanguage development. In *Variation in Second Language Learning*, vol. 2, ed. S. Gass, C. Madden, D. Preston, and L. Selinker, 46–64. Clevedon, UK: Multilingual Matters.

Anderson, J. 1985. *Cognitive Psychology and Its Implications*. New York: W.H. Freeman.

Archibald, J. 1991. *Language Learnability and Phonology: The Acquisition of L2 Metrical Parameters*. Ph.D. diss., University of Toronto, Toronto.

———. 1993. *Language Learnability and L2 Phonology: The Acquisition of Metrical Parameters*. Dordrecht: Kluwer Academic Publishers.

———, ed. 1994. *Phonological Acquisition and Phonological Theory*. Hillsdale, NJ: Lawrence Erlbaum.

Asher, J. and R. Garcia. 1969. The optimal age to learn a foreign language. *Modern Language Journal* 53:334–41.

Ausubel, D. 1965. Introduction to Part One. In *Readings in the Psychology of Cognition*, ed. R.C. Anderson and D. Ausubel. New York: Holt, Rinehart, and Winston.

Avery, P., and S. Ehrlich. 1992. *Teaching American English Pronunciation*. Oxford: Oxford University Press.

Bachman, L. 1990. *Fundamental Considerations in Language Testing*. Oxford: Oxford University Press.

Bachman, L. and A.S. Palmer. 1982. The construct validation of some components of communicative proficiency. *TESOL Quarterly* 16(4): 449–65.

Bailey, K.M. 1983. Competitiveness and anxiety in adult second language learning: Looking at and through the diary studies. In *Classroom Oriented Research in Second Language Acquisition*, ed. H. Seliger and M.Long, 67–103. Rowley, MA: Newbury House.

———. 1985. Classroom-centered research on language teaching and learning. *Beyond Basics: Issues and Research in TESOL*, ed. M. Celce-Murcia, 96–121. Rowley, MA: Newbury House.

Baker, C.L. 1979. Syntactic theory and the projection problem. *Linguistic Inquiry* 10:533–81.

Baker, C.L. and J.J. McCarthy, eds. 1981. *The Logical Problem of Language Acquisition*. Cambridge, MA: MIT Press.

Bauer, L. 1988. *Introducing Linguistic Morphology*. Edinburgh: Edinburgh University Press.

Beebe, L. 1983. Risk-taking and the language learner. In *Classroom Oriented Research in Second Language Acquisition*, ed. H. Seliger and M. Long, 39–66. Rowley, MA: Newbury House.

———. 1985. Input: Choosing the right stuff. In *Input in Second Language Acquisition*, ed. S. Gass and C. Madden, 404–14. Rowley, MA: Newbury House.

Beebe, L. and H. Giles. 1984. Speech accommodation theories: A discussion in terms of second language acquisition. *International Journal of the Sociology of Language* 46:5–32.

Bell, J., ed. 1990. *ESL Literacy*. Special issue of *TESL Talk*. 20 (1). Toronto: Queen's Printer.

Berlin, B. 1978. Ethnobiological classification. In *Cognition and Categorization*, ed. E. Rosch and B.B. Lloyd. Hillsdale, NJ: Lawrence Erlbaum.

Berko Gleason, J. and N. Bernstein Ratner. 1993. *Psycholinguistics*. Orlando, FL: Harcourt Brace Jovanovich.

Bernhardt, E. 1991. *Reading in a Second Language*. Norwood, NJ: Ablex Publishing.

Bernstein, B. 1971. *Class, Codes, and Control*. Vol. 1. London: Routledge and Kegan Paul.

Bertelson, P., ed. 1987. *The Onset of Literacy*. Special issue of *Cognition*. Cambridge, MA: MIT Press.

Berwick, R. 1985. *The Acquisition of Syntactic Knowledge*. Cambridge, MA: MIT Press.

Besner, D. and N. Hildebrandt. 1987. Orthographic and phonological codes in the oral reading of Japanese kana. *Journal of Experimental Psychology: Learning, Memory, and Cognition* 13:335–43.

Bialystok, E. 1981. Some evidence for the integrity and interaction of two knowledge sources. In *New Dimensions in Second Language Acquisition Research*, ed. R.W. Andersen, 62–74. Rowley, MA: Newbury House.

———. 1982. On the relationship between knowing and using linguistic forms. *Applied Linguistics* 3:181–206.

———. 1990. *Communication Strategies*. Oxford: Blackwell.

Bickerton, D. 1983. *Roots of Language*. Ann Arbor: Karoma.

Birdsong, D. 1992. Ultimate attainment in second language acquisition. *Language* 68(4): 706–55.

Bley-Vroman, R. 1989. What is the logical problem of foreign language learning? In *Linguistic Perspectives on Second Language Acquisition*, ed. S. Gass and J. Schachter, 41–68. Cambridge: Cambridge University Press.

Bohn, O-S. and J. Flege. 1992. The production of new and similar vowels by adult German learners of English. *Studies in Second Language Acquisition* 14 (2): 131–58.

Braine, M. 1971. On two types of models of the internalization of grammars. In *The Ontogenesis of Grammar*, ed. D. Slobin, 153–88. New York: Academic Press.

Brière, E. 1978. Variables affecting native Mexican children's learning Spanish as a second language. *Language Learning* 28:159–74.

Bright, W., ed. 1992. *International Encyclopedia of Linguistics*. New York: Oxford University Press.

Broca, P. 1861. Remarques sur le siège de la faculté de la parole articulée, suivies d'une observation d'aphémie (perte de parole). *Bulletin de la Société d'Anatomie* (Paris) 36:330–57.

Broselow, E. 1986. Prosodic features in the perception of word boundary position in a foreign language: A pilot study. In *Festschrift for Sol Saporta*, ed. Brame, Contreras, and Newmeyer. Seattle: Noit Amrofer.

———. 1988. Prosodic phonology and the acquisition of a second language. In *Linguistic Theory in Second Language Acquisition*, ed. S. Flynn and W. O'Neil, 295–308. Dordrecht: Kluwer Academic Publishers.

Broselow, E. and D. Finer. 1991. Parameter setting in second language phonology and syntax. *Second Language Research*. 7(1):35–60.

Brown, H.D. 1980. The optimal distance model of second language acquisition. *TESOL Quarterly* 14:157–64.

———. 1987. *Principles of Language Learning and Teaching*. Englewood Cliffs, NJ: Prentice-Hall.

———. 1993. *Principles of Language Learning and Teaching*. 3rd ed. Englewood Cliffs, NJ: Prentice-Hall.

Brown, R. 1973. *A First Language: The Early Stages*. Cambridge, MA: Harvard University Press.

Brown, R. and C. Hanlon. 1970. Derivational complexity and the order of acquisition in child speech. In *Cognition and the Development of Language*, ed. J. Hayes, 11–53. New York: John Wiley.

Burt, M. and L. Kiparsky. 1972. *The Gooficon*. Rowley, MA: Newbury House.

Busch, D. 1982. Introversion–extroversion and the EFL proficiency of Japanese students. *Language Learning* 32:109–32.

Canada. 1967–1970. *Royal Commission on Bilingualism and Biculturalism*. Ottawa: Queen's Printer, 1967–1970.

Canadian Parents for French. 1994. *The Immersion Registry 1993/94*, ed. Judy Gibson. Calgary: Canadian Parents for French.

Canale, M. 1983. From communicative competence to communicative language pedagogy. In *Language and Communication*, ed. J.C. Richards and R. Schmidt, 2–25. London: Longman.

Canale, M. and M. Swain. 1980. Theoretical bases of communicative approaches to second language teaching and testing. *Applied Linguistics* 1:1–47.

Cancino, H., E. Rosansky, and J. Schumann. 1975. The acquisition of the English auxiliary by native Spanish speakers. *TESOL Quarterly* 9:421–30.

Caplan, D. 1993. *Language: Structure, Processing, and Disorders*. Cambridge, MA: MIT Press.

Caplan, D. and C. Futter. 1986. Assignment of thematic roles to nouns in sentence comprehension by an agrammatic patient. *Brain and Language* 27:117–34.

Carrell, P., J. Devine, and D. Eskey. 1988. *Interactive Approaches to Second Language Reading*. New York: Cambridge University Press.

Carroll, J.B. 1965. The prediction of success in foreign language training. In *Training, Research, and Education*, ed. R. Glaser, 87–136. New York: Wiley.

————. 1967. Foreign language proficiency levels attained by language majors near graduation from college. *Foreign Language Annals* 1:131–51.

Carroll, S. 1989a. Second language acquisition and the computational metaphor. *Language Learning* 39(4): 535–94.

————. 1989b. Language acquisition studies and a feasible theory of grammar. *Canadian Journal of Linguistics* 34(4): 399–418.

Carroll, S. and M. Swain. 1993. Explicit and implicit negative feedback: An empirical study of the learning of linguistic generalizations. *Studies in Second Language Acquisition* 15(3): 357–86.

Catania, C. and S. Harnad. 1988. *The Selection of Behavior.* New York: Cambridge University Press.

Cathcart, R.W., M.A. Strong, and L. Wong Fillmore 1979. Social and linguistic behavior of good language learners. *On TESOL '79*, ed. C. Yorio, K. Perkins, and J. Schachter, 267–74. Washington, DC: TESOL.

Cazden, C. 1972. *Child Language and Education.* New York: Holt, Rinehart, and Winston.

Cazden, C.H., H. Cancino, E. Rosansky, and J. Schumann. 1975. Second language acquisition in children, adolescents and adults. *Final Report.* U.S. Department of Health and Welfare.

Chamot, A.U. and J.M. O'Malley. 1994. *The CALLA Handbook: Implementing the Cognitive Academic Language Learning Approach.* Reading, MA: Addison-Wesley.

Chan, M.C., H.L.H. Chau, and R. Hoosain. 1983. Input/output switch in bilingual code switching. *Journal of Psycholinguistic Research* 12:407–16.

Chapelle, C. and C. Roberts. 1986. Ambiguity tolerance and field independence as predictors of proficiency in English as a second language. *Language Learning* 36:27–45.

Chastain, K. 1975. Affective and ability factors in second language acquisition. *Language Learning* 25:153–61.

Chaudron, C. 1977. A descriptive model of discourse in the corrective treatment of learners' errors. *Language Learning* 27:29–46.

————. 1988. *Second Language Classrooms.* New York: Cambridge University Press.

Chihara, T. and J. Oller. 1978. Attitudes and attained proficiency in EFL: A sociolinguistic study of adult Japanese speakers. *Language Learning* 28:55–68.

Chomsky, N. 1959. A review of B.F. Skinner's *Verbal Behavior. Language* 35:26–58.

————. 1973. Conditions on transformations. In *A Festschrift for Morris Halle,* ed. S. Anderson and P. Kiparsky, 232–86. New York: Holt, Rinehart, and Winston.

————. 1975. *Reflections on Language.* New York: Pantheon.

————. 1981. *Lectures on Government and Binding.* Dordrecht: Foris.

————. 1983. Noam Chomsky's views on the psychology of language and thought. In *Dialogues on the Psychology of Language and Thought; Conversations with Noam Chomsky, Charles Osgood, Jean Piaget, Alric Neisser and Marcel Kinsbourne,* ed. R.W. Rieber, 29–64. New York: Plenum Press.

————. 1984. *Modular Approaches to the Study of Mind.* San Diego: San Diego State University Press.

————. 1986. *Knowledge of Language.* New York: Praeger.

————. 1988. *Language and Problems of Knowledge.* Cambridge, MA: MIT Press.

Chomsky, N. and M. Halle. 1968. *Sound Patterns of English.* Cambridge, MA: MIT Press.

Clark, R. 1992. The selection of syntactic knowledge. *Language Acquisition* 2 (2): 83–150.

Clyne, M. 1981. Second language attrition and first language reversion among elderly bilinguals in Australia. In *Sprachkontakt als Ursache von Veranderugen der Sorach-und Bewusstseinsstruktur: eine Sammlung von Studien zur sprachlichen*

Interferenz, ed. W. Meid and K. Heller, 25–32. Innsbruck: Institut fur Sprachwissenschaft.

Coates, J. 1986. *Women, Men, and Language.* New York: Longman.

Coltheart, M. and R. Freeman. 1974. Case alternation impairs word recognition. *Bulletin of the Psychonomic Society* 3:102–4.

Comrie, B. 1981. *Language Universals and Linguistic Typology.* Chicago: University of Chicago Press.

Cook, V. J. 1988. *Chomsky's Universal Grammar.* Cambridge: Blackwell.

———. 1991. The poverty-of-the-stimulus arguments and multicompetence. *Second Language Research* 7(2): 103–17.

Coppieters, R. 1987. Competence differences between native and fluent non-native speakers. *Language* 63: 544–73.

Corder, S.P. 1967. The significance of learners' errors. *IRAL* 5:161–70.

Coulthard, M. and M. Montgomery. 1981. *Studies in Discourse Analysis.* London: Routledge and Kegan Paul.

Council for European Communities. 1977. Cited in Alladina (1986).

Cowper, E. 1992. *A Concise Introduction to Government-Binding Syntax.* Chicago: University of Chicago Press.

Crowne, D.P. and D. Marlowe. 1964. *The Approval Motive: Studies in Evaluative Dependence.* New York: John Wiley.

Cummins, J. 1981. *Bilingualism and Minority-Language Children.* Toronto: OISE Press.

———. 1984. *Bilingualism and Special Education: Issues in Assessment and Pedagogy.* Clevedon, UK: Multilingual Matters.

Cummins, J. and M. Swain. 1986. *Bilingualism in Education.* New York: Longman.

Curtiss, S. 1977. *Genie: A Psycholinguistic Study of a Modern-Day "Wild Child."* New York: Academic Press.

———. 1988. Abnormal language acquisition and the modularity of language. In *Linguistics: The Cambridge Survey,* ed. F. Newmeyer, 96–116. Cambridge: Cambridge University Press.

Danesi, M. 1988. Neurological bimodality and theories of language teaching. *Studies in Second Language Acquisition* 10(1): 13–32.

Day, E.M. and S. Shapson. 1989. Provincial assessment of French immersion programs in British Columbia, Canada. *Evaluation and Research in Education* 2(3): 1–17.

de Bot, K. and M. Clyne. 1989. Language reversion revisited. *Studies in Second Language Acquisition* 11:167–77.

de Bot, K. and B. Weltens. 1991. Recapitulation, regression and language loss. In *First Language Attrition,* ed. H. Seliger and R. Vago, 31–52. Cambridge: Cambridge University Press.

Dechert, H., ed. 1990. *Current Trends in European Second Language Research.* Clevedon, UK: Multilingual Matters.

DeFrancis, J. 1989. *Visible Speech: The Diverse Oneness of Writing Systems.* Honolulu: University of Hawaii Press.

De Groot, A. 1993. Word-type effects in bilingual processing tasks: Support for a mixed representational system. In *The Bilingual Lexicon,* ed. R. Schreuder and B. Weltens. Philadelphia: John Benjamins.

Demopoulos, W. 1989. On applying learnability theory to the rationalism–empiricism controversy. In *Learnability and Linguistic Theory,* ed. R. Mathews and W. Demopoulos, 77–88. Dordrecht: Kluwer Academic Publishers.

Descartes, R. 1664. *L'homme.* Paris.

Dickerson, L. 1975. The learner's interlanguage as a system of variable rules. *TESOL Quarterly* 9:401–7.

Diller, K. 1978. *The Language Teaching Controversy*. Cambridge, MA: Newbury House.

Dinnsen, D. and F. Eckman. 1975. A functional explanation of some phonological typologies. In *Functionalism*, ed. R. Grossman et al. Chicago: Chicago Linguistic Society.

Donaldson, M. 1978. *Children's Minds*. Oxford: Oxford University Press.

Dresher, E. 1992. Acquiring stress systems. Paper presented at the DIMACS symposium. MIT.

Dulay, H., M. Burt, and S. Krashen. 1982. *Language Two*. Chicago: University of Chicago Press.

Dunkin, M. and B. Biddle. 1974. *The Study of Teaching*. New York: Holt, Rinehart, and Winston.

Durkheim, E. 1897. *Le suicide*. Paris: F. Alcan.

Eckman, F. 1977. Markedness and the contrastive analysis hypothesis. *Language Learning* 27:315–30.

———. 1991. The structural conformity hypothesis and the acquisition of consonant clusters in the interlanguage of ESL learners. *Studies in Second Language Acquisition* 13(1): 23–42.

Eisenstein, M., ed. 1989. *The Dynamic Interlanguage: Empirical Studies in Second Language Variation*. New York: Plenum Press.

Ekstrand, L. 1977. Social and individual frame factors in second language learning: Comparative aspects. In *Papers from the First Nordic Conference on Bilingualism*, ed. T. Skutnabb-Kangas. Helingstors Universitat.

Ellis, R. 1984. *Classroom Second Language Development*. Oxford: Pergamon Press.

———. 1986. *Understanding Second Language Acquisition*. Oxford: Oxford University Press.

———, ed. 1987. *Second Language Acquisition in Context*. Englewood Cliffs, NJ: Prentice-Hall.

———. 1989a. Are classroom and naturalistic acquisition the same? A study of the classroom acquisition of German word order. *Studies in Second Language Acquisition* 11(3): 305–28.

———. 1989b. Sources of intra-learner variability in language use and their relationship to second language acquisition. In *Variation in Second Language Acquisition: Psycholinguistic Issues*, ed. S. Gass, C. Madden, D. Preston, and L. Selinker, 22–45. Clevedon, UK: Multilingual Matters.

———. 1990. *Instructed Second Language Acquisition*. Oxford: Basil Blackwell.

Ervin, S.M. and Osgood, C.E. 1954. Second language teaching and bilingualism. *Journal of Abnormal and Social Psychology,* supplement, 49:139–46.

Ervin-Tripp, S. 1974. Is second language learning like the first? *TESOL Quarterly* 8:111-27.

Eubank, L., ed. 1991. *Point Counterpoint: Universal Grammar in the Second Language*. Amsterdam: John Benjamins.

Eysenck, H.J. and S.B.G. Eysenck. 1963. *Eysenck Personality Inventory*. San Diego: Educational and Industrial Testing Service.

Faerch, C. and G. Kaspar, eds. 1983. *Strategies in Interlanguage Communication*. London: Longman.

Fase, W., K. Jaspert, and S. Kroon. 1992. *Maintenance and Loss of Minority Languages*. Amsterdam: John Benjamins.

Fathman, A. 1975. The relationship between age and second language productive ability. *Language Learning* 25:245–53.

———. 1976. Variables affecting the successful learning of English as a second language. *TESOL Quarterly* 10:433–41.

Ferguson, C. 1975. Toward a characterization of English foreigner talk. *Anthropological Linguistics* 17 (1): 1–14.

———. 1983. Toward a characterization of English foreigner talk. In *Second Language Learning: Contrastive Analysis, Error Analysis, and Related Aspects*, ed. B. Robinett and J. Schachter. Ann Arbor: University of Michigan Press.

Finer, D. and E. Broselow. 1986. Second language acquisition of reflexive-binding. *Proceedings of the North Eastern Linguistic Society* 16, University of Massachusetts at Amherst, Graduate Linguistics Student Association, Amherst.

Flege, J.E. 1981. The phonological basis of foreign accent: A hypothesis. *TESOL Quarterly* 15:443–55.

———. 1987. A critical period for learning to pronounce foreign languages. *Applied Linguistics* 8:162–77.

Fletcher, P. and M. Garman, eds. 1986. *Language Acquisition*. Avon: Cambridge University Press.

Flick, W. 1980. Error types in adult English as a second language. In *New Approaches to Language Acquisition*, ed. B. Ketterman and R. St. Clair. Heidelberg: Julius Groos.

Flynn, S. and S. Manuel. 1991. Age-dependent effects in language acquisition: An evaluation of "critical period" hypotheses. In *Point Counterpoint: Universal Grammar in the Second Language*, ed. L. Eubank, 117–46. Amsterdam: John Benjamins.

Flynn, S. and W. O'Neil. 1988. *Linguistic Theory and Second Language Acquisition*. Dordrecht: Kluwer Academic Publishers.

Fodor, J. 1983. *The Modularity of Mind*. Cambridge, MA: MIT Press.

Forster, K.I. 1976. Accessing the mental lexicon. In *New Approaches to Language Mechanisms*, ed. R.J. Wales and E. Walker. Amsterdam: North Holland.

Forster, K.I. and S.M. Chambers. 1973. Lexical access and naming time. *Journal of Verbal Learning and Verbal Behavior* 12:627–35.

Frazier, L. 1987. Sentence processing: A tutorial review. In *Attention and Performance XII: The psychology of reading*, ed. M. Coltheart. London: Lawrence Erlbaum.

Fromkin, V. 1971. The nonanomalous nature of anomalous utterances. *Languages* 47:27–52.

———. 1993. Speech production. In *Psycholinguistics*, ed. J. Berko Gleason and N. Bernstein Ratner. Orlando, FL: Harcourt Brace Jovanovich.

Gardner, H. 1980. Foreword to *Language and Learning: The Debate between Jean Piaget and Noam Chomsky*, ed. M. Piatelli-Palmarini. Cambridge, MA: Harvard University Press.

———. 1983. *Frames of Mind: The Theory of Multiple Intelligences*. New York: Basic Books.

Gardner, R. and W. Lambert. 1959. Motivational variables in second language acquisition. *Canadian Journal of Psychology* 13:266–72.

———. 1965. Language aptitude, intelligence and second language achievement. *Journal of Educational Psychology* 56(4): 191–99.

———, eds. 1972. *Attitudes and Motivation in Second Language Learning*. Rowley, MA: Newbury House.

Gardner, R.C., J.B. Day, and P.D. MacIntyre. 1992. Integrative motivation induced anxiety and language learning in a controlled environment. *Studies in Second Language Acquisition* 14(2): 197–214.

Garfield, J.L. 1987. *Modularity in Knowledge Representation and Natural-Language Understanding*. Cambridge, MA: MIT Press.

Garman, M. 1990. *Psycholinguistics*. Cambridge: Cambridge University Press.

Garrett, M. 1976. Syntactic processes in sentence production. In *New Approaches to*

Language Mechanisms, ed. R.J. Wales and E. Walker. Amsterdam: North Holland Press.

———. 1980. Levels of processing in sentence production. In *Language Production*, ed. B. Butterworth. Academic Press.

———. 1984. The organization of processing structure for language production: Applications to aphasic speech. In *Biological Perspectives on Language*, ed. D. Caplan, A.R. Lecours, and A. Smith. Cambridge, MA: MIT Press.

Gass, S. 1979. Language transfer and universal grammatical relations. *Language Learning* 29:327–44.

———. 1982. From theory to practice. In *On TESOL '81*, ed. W. Rutherford and M. Hines, 129–39. Washington DC: TESOL.

———. 1987. The resolution of conflict among competing systems: A bidirectional perspective. *Applied Psycholinguistics* 8(4): 329–50.

Gass, S., and C. Madden. 1985. *Input in Second Language Acquisition*. Rowley, MA: Newbury House.

Gass, S., C. Madden, D. Preston, and L. Selinker, eds. 1989. *Variation in Second Language Acquisition: Psycholinguistic Issues*. Clevedon, UK: Multilingual Matters.

Gass, S., and J. Schachter 1989. *Linguistic Perspectives on Second Language Acquisition*. Cambridge: Cambridge University Press.

Gass, S. and L. Selinker. 1992. *Language Transfer in Language Learning*. Amsterdam: John Benjamins.

Genesee, F. 1976. The role of intelligence in second language learning. *Language Learning* 26:267–80.

———. 1987. *Learning through Two Languages*. Rowley, MA: Newbury House.

———. 1988. Neuropsychology and second language acquisition. In *Issues in Second Language Acquisition*, ed. L. Beebe, 81–112. Rowley, MA: Newbury House.

George, H. 1972. *Common Errors in Language Learning: Insights from English*. Rowley, MA: Newbury House.

Geschwind, N. and A. Galaburda. 1987. *Cerebral Lateralization*. Cambridge, MA: MIT Press.

Gibson, J. See Canadian Parents for French.

Gleitman, L., E. Newport, and H. Gleitman 1984. The current status of the motherese hypothesis. *Journal of Child Language* 2:43–79.

Goddard, H.H. 1917. Mental tests and the immigrant. *Journal of Delinquency* 2:243–77.

Goldstein, K. 1948. *Language and Language Disturbances*. New York: Grune and Stratton.

Goodluck, H. 1992. *Language Acquisition*. Cambridge, MA: Blackwell.

Gould, S.J. 1981. *The Mismeasure of Man*. New York: W.W. Norton.

———. 1989. *Wonderful Life*. New York: W.W. Norton.

Gradman, H. 1971. Limitations of contrastive analysis predictions. *Working Papers in Linguistics* 3:11–15.

Grauberg, W. 1971. An error analysis in the German of first-year university students. In *Applications of Linguistics*, ed. G. Perren and J. Trim. Cambridge: Cambridge University Press.

Gray, W.S. 1956. *The Teaching of Reading and Writing: An International Survey*. Paris: UNESCO.

Green, D. 1986. Control, activation and resource: A framework and a model for the control of speech in bilinguals. *Brain and Language* 27:210–23.

Greenberg, J. 1966. *Universals of Language*. Cambridge, MA: MIT Press.

Gregg, K. 1984. Krashen's monitor and Occam's razor. *Applied Linguistics* 5:79–100.

———. 1989. Second language acquisition theory: The case for a generative perspective. In *Linguistic Perspectives on Second Language Acquisition*, ed. S. Gass and J. Schachter, 15–40. Cambridge: Cambridge University Press.

———. 1990. The variable competence model of second language acquisition and why it isn't. *Applied Linguistics* 11(4): 364–83.

Gremmo, M., H. Holec, and P. Riley. 1978. Taking the initiative: Some pedagogical applications of discourse analysis. *Mélanges pédagogiques*. Nancy: University of Nancy, CRAPEL.

Guilfoyle, E. and M. Noonan. 1992. Functional categories and language acquisition. *Canadian Journal of Linguistics* 37(2): 241–72.

Guiora, A.Z., W. Acton, R. Erard, and F. Strickland. 1980. The effects of benzodiazepine (valium) on permeability of ego boundaries. *Language Learning* 30:351–63.

Guiora, A., B. Beit-Hallahmi, R. Brannon, and C. Dull. 1972. The effects of experimentally induced changes in ego status on pronunciation ability in a second language: An exploratory study. *Comprehensive Psychiatry* 13:421–28.

Haeckel, E. 1868. *Natürliche Schöpfungsgeschichte*. Berlin: Georg Reimer.

Haegeman, L. 1991. *Government and Binding Theory*. Cambridge, MA: Blackwell.

Hale, T. and E. Budar. 1970. Are TESOL classes the only answer? *Modern Language Journal* 54:487–92.

Hall, E. 1966. *The Hidden Dimension*. New York: Doubleday.

Halliday, M.A.K. 1975. *Learning How to Mean*. London: Edward Arnold.

Halliday, M.A.K. and R. Hasan. 1976. *Cohesion in English*. London: Longman.

Hamers, J. and M. Blanc. 1989. *Bilinguality and Bilingualism*. New York: Cambridge University Press.

Hamers, J.F. and W.E. Lambert. 1974. Bilingual reactions to cross-language semantic ambiguity. In *Bilingualism, Biculturalism and Education*, ed. S.T. Carey. Edmonton: University of Alberta Printing Department.

Hammerly, H. 1989. *French Immersion: Myths and Reality*. Calgary: Detselig Enterprises.

Handscombe, J. 1989. Mainstreaming: Who needs it? In *Multicultural Education and Policy: ESL in the 1990's*, ed. J. Esling, 18–35. Toronto: OISE Press.

Hankamer, J. 1989. Morphological parsing and the lexicon. In *Lexical Representation and Process*, ed. W. Marslen-Wilson. Cambridge, MA: MIT Press.

Hanna, G., A.H. Smith, L.D. McLean, and H.H. Stern. 1980. *Contact and Communication: An Evaluation of Bilingual Student Exchange Programs*. Toronto: OISE Press.

Harley, B. 1986. *Age in Second Language Acquisition*. Clevedon, UK: Multilingual Matters.

Harley, B., P. Allen, J. Cummins, and M. Swain, eds. 1990. *The Development of Second Language Proficiency*. Cambridge: Cambridge University Press.

Harley, B., D. Hart, and S. Lapkin. 1986. The effects of early bilingual schooling on first language skills. *Applied Psycholinguistics* 7(4): 295–322.

Harney, R. and H. Troper. 1975. *Immigrants: A Portrait of the Urban Experience, 1890–1930*. Toronto: Van Nostrand Reinhold.

Harrington, M. 1987. Processing transfer: Language-specific processing strategies as a source of interlanguage variation. *Applied Psycholinguistics* 8(4): 351–78.

Harrington, M. and M. Sawyer. 1992. L2 working memory capacity and L2 reading skill. *Studies in Second Language Acquisition* 14:25–38.

Hart, D., S. Lapkin, and M. Swain. 1989. Early and middle French immersion programs: Reports on the substudy of attrition. OISE Modern Language Centre, Toronto. Mimeo.

Hatch, E. 1983. *Psycholinguistics: A Second Language Perspective.* Rowley, MA: Newbury House.

Hatch, E. and J. Wagner-Gough. 1975. Explaining sequence and variation in second language acquisition. In *Papers in Second Language Acquisition,* ed. H. Brown, 39–57. Ann Arbor, MI: Language Learning.

Healy, A.F. 1976. Detection errors on the word *the*: New evidence on reading units. *Journal of Experimental Psychology* 2: 235–42.

Heist, P. and G. Yonge. 1962. *Omnibus Personality Inventory.* New York: The Psychological Corporation.

Heyde, A. 1979. The relationship between self-esteem and the oral production of a second language. Ph.D. diss., University of Michigan, Ann Arbor.

Higgs, T.V., ed. 1982. *Curriculum, Competence and the Foreign Language Teacher.* Lincolnwood, IL: National Textbook Company.

———. 1984. Language teaching: The quest for the Holy Grail. In *Teaching for Proficiency,* ed. T.V. Higgs, 1–9. Lincolnwood, IL: National Textbook Company.

Higgs, T.V. and R. Clifford. 1982. The push toward communication. In *Curriculum, Competence and the Foreign Language Teacher,* ed. T.V. Higgs, 57–79. Lincolnwood, IL: National Textbook Company in association with ACTFL.

Hill, J. 1970. Foreign accents, language acquisition, and cerebral dominance revisited. *Language Learning* 20: 237–48.

Hilles, S. 1986. Interlanguage and the pro-drop parameter. *Second Language Research* 2:33–52.

Hornstein, N. and D. Lightfoot, eds. 1981. *Explanation in Linguistics: The Logical Problem of Language Acquisition.* New York: Longman.

Howatt, A.P.R. 1984. *A History of English Language Teaching.* Oxford: Oxford University Press.

Huebner, T. 1983. *A Longitudinal Analysis of the Acquisition of English.* Ann Arbor: Karoma.

Hulstijn, J.H. 1989. A cognitive view on interlanguage variability. In *The Dynamic Interlanguage: Empirical Studies in Second Language Variation,* ed. M. Eisenstein, 17–31. New York: Plenum Press.

Hurford, J.R. 1991. The evolution of the critical period for language acquisition. *Cognition* 40:159–201.

Hyams, N. 1986. *Language Acquisition and the Theory of Parameters.* Dordrecht: Reidel.

Hymes, D. 1971. *On Communicative Competence.* Philadelphia: University of Pennsylvania Press.

Ingram, D. 1989. *First Language Acquisition.* Cambridge, MA: MIT Press.

Jackendoff, R. 1987. *Consciousness and the Computational Mind.* Cambridge, MA: MIT Press.

Jacobs, J. 1977. An external view of neuropsychology and its working milieu. In *Language Development and Neurological Theory,* ed. S. Segalowitz and F. Gruber. New York: Academic Press.

Jacobs, B. and J. Schumann. 1992. Language acquisition and the neurosciences: Towards a more integrative perspective. *Applied Linguistics* 13(3): 282–306.

Jakobson, R. 1941. *Kindersprache, Aphasie und allgemeine Lautgesetze.* Uppsala: Almqvist and Wiksell.

James, W. 1890. *The Principles of Psychology,* Vol. 1. New York: Henry Holt.

Jensen, J. 1990. *Morphology: Word Structure in Generative Grammar.* Amsterdam: John Benjamins.

Johnson, J.S. and E.L. Newport. 1989. Critical period effects in second language learning: The influence of maturational state on the acquisition of English as a second language. *Cognitive Psychology* 21:60–99.

———. 1991. Critical period effects on universal properties of language: The status of subjacency in the acquisition of a second language. *Cognition* 39:215–58.

Just, M.A. and P.A. Carpenter. 1980. A theory of reading: From eye fixations to comprehension. *Psychological Review* 87:329–54.

———. 1987. *The Psychology of Reading and Language Comprehension*. Boston: Allyn and Bacon.

Kandel, E.R. and R.D. Hawkins. 1992. The biological basis of learning and individuality. *Scientific American* 267(3): 78–87.

Kaufman, D. and M. Aronoff. 1991. Morphological disintegration and reconstruction in the first language attrition. In *First Language Attrition,* ed. H. Seliger and R. Vago, 175–88. Cambridge: Cambridge University Press.

Kaye, J. 1989. *Phonology: A Cognitive View*. Hillsdale, NJ: Erlbaum.

Keenan, E. and B. Comrie. 1977. Noun phrase accessibility and universal grammar. *Linguistic Inquiry* 8:63–99.

Kellerman, E. 1979. Transfer and non-transfer: Where are we now? *Studies in Second Language Acquisition* 2:37–57.

Kent, R.D., M.J. Osberger, R. Netsell, and C.G. Hustedde. 1987. Phonetic development in identical twins who differ in auditory functions. *Journal of Speech and Hearing Disorders* 52:64–75.

Kezwer, P. 1987. The extroverted vs. the introverted personality and second language learning. *TESL Canada Journal* 5(1): 45–58.

Kilborn, K. and A. Cooreman. 1987. Sentence interpretation strategies in adult Dutch–English bilinguals. *Applied Psycholinguistics* 8(4): 415–31.

Klein, W. 1990. A theory of language acquisition is not so easy. *Studies in Second Language Acquisition* 12(2): 219–32.

Kolers, P. A. 1966. Reading and talking bilingually. *American Journal of Psychology* 79:357–76.

Krashen, S. 1973. Lateralization, language learning, and the critical period: Some new evidence. *Language Learning* 23:63–74.

———. 1981. *Second Language Acquisition and Second Language Learning*. Oxford: Pergamon.

———. 1982. *Principles and Practice in Second Language Acquisition*. Oxford: Pergamon Press.

Krashen, S., C. Jones, S. Zelinski, and C. Usprich. 1978. How important is instruction? *ELT Journal* 23:257–61.

Krashen, S. and H. Seliger. 1976. The role of formal and informal linguistic environments in adult second language learning. *International Journal of Psycholinguistics* 3:15–21.

Krashen, S., H. Seliger, and D. Hartnett. 1974. Two studies in adult second language learning. *Kritikon Literarum* 3:220–28.

Krashen, S. and T. Terrell. 1983. *The Natural Approach*. Hayward, CA: Alemany Press.

Kucera, H. and W.N. Francis. 1967. *Computional Analysis of Present-Day English*. Providence RI: Brown University Press.

Labov, W. 1966. *The Social Stratification of English in New York City*. Washington, DC: Center for Applied Linguistics.

———. 1972a. *Sociolinguistic Patterns*. Oxford: Basil Blackwell.

———. 1972b. *Language in the Inner City*. Philadelphia: University of Pennsylvania Press.

Lado, R. 1957. *Linguistics across Cultures*. Ann Arbor: University of Michigan Press.

Lalande, J. 1982. Reducing composition errors: An experiment. *Modern Language Journal* 66:140–49.

Lambert, W. 1967. A social psychology of bilingualism. *The Journal of Social Issues* 23:91–109.

Lambert, W. and G. Tucker. 1972. *Bilingual Education of Children*. Rowley, MA: Newbury House.

Lapkin, S., D. Hart, and M. Swain. 1991. Early and middle French immersion programs: French language outcomes. *Canadian Modern Language Review* 48(1): 11–40.

Lapkin, S., M. Swain, and S. Shapson. 1990. French immersion research agenda for the 90s. *Canadian Modern Language Review* 46(4): 638–74.

Larsen-Freeman, D. and M. Celce-Murcia. 1986. *The Grammar Book*. Cambridge, MA: Newbury House.

Lasnik, H. 1989. *Essays on Restrictiveness and Learnability*. Dordrecht: Kluwer Academic Publishers.

Lenneberg, E. 1967. *Biological Foundations of Language*. New York: Wiley.

Levelt, W. 1989. *Speaking: From Intention to Articulation*. Cambridge, MA: MIT Press.

Libben, G. 1992. Front-end serial processing in complex and compound words: The APPLE model. *Proceedings of the Fourteenth Annual Conference of the Cognitive Science Society*, 945–50. Hillsdale, NJ: Lawrence Erlbaum.

———. 1994. How is morphological decomposition achieved? *Language and Cognitive Processes* 9(3): 369–91.

Lightbown, P. 1983. Exploring relationships between developmental and instructional sequences in L2 acquisition. In *Classroom Oriented Research in Second Language Acquisition*, ed. H. Seliger and M. Long, 217–43. Rowley, MA: Newbury House.

Lightbown, P. and N. Spada. 1990. Focus-on-form and corrective feedback in communicative language teaching: Effects on second language learning. *Studies in Second Language Acquisition* 12(4): 429–48.

Lightbown, P., N. Spada, and R. Wallace. 1980. Some effects of instruction on child and adolescent ESL learners. In *Research in Second Language Acquisition*, ed. R. Scarcella and S. Krashen. 162–72. Rowley, MA: Newbury House.

Lightfoot, D. 1982. *The Language Lottery*. Cambridge, MA: MIT Press.

Littlewood, W. 1981. Language variation and second language acquisition theory. *Applied Linguistics* 2(2): 150–58.

Logan, R. 1986. *The Alphabet Effect*. New York: St. Martin's Press.

Long, M. 1977. Teacher feedback on learner error: Mapping cognitions. In *On TESOL '77*, ed. H. Brown, C. Yorio, and R. Crymes, 278–93. Washington, DC: TESOL.

———. 1981. Questions in foreigner talk discourse. *Language Learning* 31:135–57.

———. 1983. Does second language instruction make a difference? A review of the research. *TESOL Quarterly* 17(3): 359–82.

———. 1990. Maturational constraints on language development. *Studies in Second Language Acquisition* 12(3): 251–86.

Long, M. and C. Sato. 1983. Classroom foreigner talk discourse: Forms and functions of teachers' questions. In *Classroom Oriented Research in Second Language Acquisition*, ed. H. Seliger and M. Long, 268–85. Rowley, MA: Newbury House.

Lott, D. 1983. Analysing and counteracting interference errors. *ELT Journal* 37(3): 256–61.

Ludwig, J. 1982. Native-speaker judgements of second language learners' efforts at communication: A review. *Modern Language Journal* 66:274–83.

Lukmani, Y. 1972. Motivation to learn and language proficiency. *Language Learning* 22:261–73.

Lynch, A.J. 1988. Speaking up or talking down? *English Language Teaching Journal* 42(2): 109–16.

McDonald, J. 1987. Sentence interpretation in bilingual speakers of English and Dutch. *Applied Psycholinguistics* 8(4): 379–414.

Mackay, I. 1987. *Phonetics: The Science of Speech Production*. College-Hill Publication. Boston, MA: Little, Brown.

McLaughlin, B. 1978. The monitor model: Some methodological considerations. *Language Learning* 28:309–32.

———. 1987. *Theories of Second Language Learning*. New York: Edward Arnold.

———. 1990. Restructuring. *Applied Linguistics* 11:113–28.

McLaughlin, B., T. Rossman, and B. McLeod. 1983. Second-language learning: An information-processing perspective. *Language Learning* 33:135–58.

McLean, L.D., R.E. Traub, and V.A. Gaudino. 1983. *Cultural Ambassadors: Monitors in Core-French Classes*. Toronto: OISE Press.

Macnamara, J. 1967. The bilingual's linguistic performance. *Journal of Social Issues* 23:58–77.

———. 1975. Comparison between first and second language learning. *Working Papers on Bilingualism* 7:71–94.

Macnamara, J. and S. Kushnir. 1971. Linguistic independence of bilinguals: The input switch. *Journal of Verbal Learning and Verbal Behavior* 10:480–87.

MacWhinney, B., ed. 1987a. *Mechanisms of Language Acquisition*. Hillsdale, NJ: Lawrence Erlbaum.

———. 1987b. Applying the competition model to bilingualism. *Applied Psycholinguistics* 8:315–28.

Mägiste, E. 1979. The competing languages of the multilingual: A developmental study of decoding and encoding processes. *Journal of Verbal Learning and Verbal Behavior* 18:79–89.

———. 1982. Automaticity and interference in bilinguals. *Psychological Research* 44:29–43.

———. 1985. Development of intra- and interlingual interference in bilinguals. *Journal of Psycholinguistic Research* 14:137–54.

Major, R. 1987. Foreign accent: Recent research and theory. *IRAL* 15:185–202.

Martin, G. 1980. English language acquisition: The effects of living with an American family. *TESOL Quarterly* 14:388–90.

Mason, C. 1971. The relevance of intensive training in English as a foreign language for university students. *Language Learning* 21:197–204.

Mathews, R. 1989. On the plausibility of rationalism. In *Learnability and Linguistic Theory*, ed. R. Mathews and W. Demopoulos, 51–76. Dordrecht: Kluwer Academic Publishers.

Mathews, R. and W. Demopoulos, eds. 1989. *Learnability and Linguistic Theory*. Dordrecht: Kluwer Academic Publishers.

Mayer, M. 1969. *Frog, Where Are You?* and *A Boy, a Dog, and a Frog*. New York: The Dial Press.

Mazurkewich, I. 1984. The acquisition of the dative alternation by second language learners and linguistic theory. *Language Learning* 34:91–109.

Meisel, J., H. Clahsen, and M. Pienemann. 1981. On determining developmental stages in second language. *Studies in Second Language Acquisition* 3(2): 109–35.

Mendelsohn, D. 1991/92. Instruments for feedback in oral communication. *TESOL Journal* 1 (2): 25–30.

Miller, G. 1956. The magical number seven, plus or minus two. *Psychological Review* 63:81-97.

Milon, J. 1975. The development of negation in English by a second language learner. *TESOL Quarterly* 8:137–43.

Milroy, L. 1980. *Language and Social Networks*. Oxford: Blackwell.

Molfese, D.L., R.B. Freeman, and D.S. Palermo. 1975. The ontogeny of brain lateralization for speech and non-speech stimuli. *Brain and Language* 2:356–68.

Morton, J. 1969. Interaction of information in word processing. *Psychological Review* 76:165–78.

Moskowitz, B.A. 1978. The acquisition of language. *Scientific American* (Nov.): 92–108.

Mukattash, L. 1977. Problem areas in English syntax for Jordanian students. Ms. University of Amman, Jordan.

Naiman, N., M. Fröhlich, H. Stern, and A. Todesco. 1978. *The Good Language Learner. Research in Education 7*. Toronto: OISE Press.

Neisser, U. 1967. *Cognitive Psychology*. New York: Appleton-Century-Crofts.

———. 1984. Interpreting Harry Bahrick's discovery: What confers immunity against forgetting? *Journal of Experimental Psychology: General* 113:32–35.

Neufeld, G. 1979. Towards a theory of language learning ability. *Language Learning* 29:227–41.

———. 1988. Phonological asymmetry in second-language learning and performance. *Language Learning* 38(4):531–59.

Newport, E. 1990. Maturational constraints on language learning. *Cognitive Science* 14:11–28.

Newport, E., E. Gleitman, and L. Gleitman. 1977. Mother, I'd rather do it myself: Some effects and non-effects of maternal speech style. In *Talking to Children: Language Input and Acquisition*, ed. C. Snow and C. Ferguson, 109–49. Cambridge: Cambridge University Press.

Newport, E. and T. Supalla. n.d. Critical period effects in the acquisition of a primary language. University of Rochester, Rochester, NY. Typescript.

North, A.A. 1896. *Voxometric Revelation*. London: Authors' and Printers' Joint Interest Publishing.

Obler, L. 1989. Exceptional second language learners. In *Variation in Second Language Acquisition: Psycholinguistic Issues*, ed. S. Gass, C. Madden, D. Preston, and L. Selinker, 141–59. Clevedon, UK: Multilingual Matters.

Odlin, T. 1989. *Language Transfer*. Cambridge: Cambridge University Press.

Ojemann, G.A. and H.A. Whitaker. 1978. The bilingual brain. *Archives of Neurology* 35:409–12.

Oller, D.K. and R.E. Eilers. 1988. The role of audition in infant babbling. *Child Development* 57:441–49.

Oller, J. and S.M. Ziahosseiny. 1970. The contrastive analysis hypothesis and spelling errors. *Language Learning* 20:183–89.

Olshtain, E. 1986. The attrition of English as a second language: A case of Hebrew speaking children. Tel Aviv University, Tel Aviv. Typescript.

Olshtain, E. and M. Barzilay. 1991. Lexical retrieval difficulties in adult language attrition. In *First Language Attrition*, ed. H. Seliger and R. Vago, 139–50. Cambridge: Cambridge University Press.

Olson, L. and S.J. Samuels. 1973. The relationship between age and accuracy of foreign language pronunciation. *Journal of Psycholinguistic Research* 66:263–67.

O'Malley, J.M. and A.V. Chamot. 1990. *Learning Strategies in Second Language Acquisition*. Cambridge: Cambridge University Press.

Oyama, S.C. 1976. A sensitive period for the acquisition of a phonological system. *Journal of Psycholinguistic Research* 5:261–83.

———. 1978. The sensitive period and comprehension of speech. *Working Papers on Bilingualism* 16:1–17.

Paradis, M. 1977. Bilingualism and aphasia. In *Studies in Neurolinguistics*, ed. H. Whitaker and H. Whitaker. New York: Academic Press.

————. 1986. Foreword to *Language Processing in Bilinguals: Psycholinguistic and Neuropsychological Perspectives*, ed. J. Vaid. Hillsdale, NJ: Erlbaum.

————. 1993a. Linguistic, psycholinguistic, and neurolinguistic aspects of interference in bilingual speakers: The activation threshold hypothesis. *International Journal of Psycholinguistics* 9(2): 135–45.

————. 1993b. Multilingualism and aphasia. In *Linguistic Disorders and Pathologies: An International Handbook.*, ed. G. Blanken, J. Dittmann, H. Grimm, J.C. Marshall, and C-W. Wallesch, 278–88. New York: Walter de Gruyter.

Paradis, M., H. Hagiwara, and N. Hildebrandt. 1985. *Neurolinguistic aspects of the Japanese writing system*. Orlando, FL: Academic Press.

Patkowski, M. 1980. The sensitive period for the acquisition of syntax in a second language. *Language Learning* 30:449–72.

————. 1990. Age and accent in a second language: A reply to James Emil Flege. *Applied Linguistics* 11:73–89.

Pavesi, M. 1984. The acquisition of relative clauses in a formal and informal setting. *Language Learning in Formal and Informal Contexts*. Dublin: IRAAL.

Pellerin, M. and H. Hammerly. 1986. L'expression orale aprés treize ans d'immersion française. *Canadian Modern Language Review* 42:592–606.

Penfield, W. 1965. Conditioning the uncommitted cortex for language learning. *Brain* 88(4): 787–98.

Penfield, W. and L. Roberts. 1959. *Speech and Brain Mechanisms*. New York: Atheneum Press.

Pentland, D. 1977. *Nēhiyawasinahikēwin: A Standard Orthography for the Cree Language*. Saskatoon: Saskatchewan Indian Cultural College.

Petitto, L.A. and P.F. Marentette. 1991. Babbling in the manual mode: Evidence for the ontogeny of language. *Science* 251:1493–96.

Phinney, M. 1987. The pro-drop parameter in second language acquisition. In *Parameter Setting*, ed. T. Roeper and E. Williams, 221–38. Dordrecht: Reidel.

Piaget, J. 1929. *The Child's Conception of the World*. London: Routledge and Kegan Paul.

Piatelli-Palmarini, M., ed. 1980. *Language and Learning: The Debate between Jean Piaget and Noam Chomsky*. Cambridge, MA: Harvard University Press.

Pica, T. 1983. Adult acquisition of English as a second language under different conditions of exposure. *Language Learning* 33:465–97.

Pienemann, M. 1989. Is language teachable? Psycholinguistic experiments and hypotheses. *Applied Linguistics* 10(1): 52–79.

Pinker, S. 1979. Formal models of language learning. *Cognition* 1:217–83.

————. 1989. *Language Learnability and Cognition: The Acquisition of Argument Structure*. Cambridge, MA: MIT Press.

————. 1993. The central problem for the psycholinguist. In *Conceptions of the Human Mind: Essays in Honor of George A. Miller*, ed. G. Harman, 59–84. Hillsdale, NJ: Lawrence Erlbaum.

Pinker, S. and A. Prince. 1988. On language and connectionism: Analysis of a parallel distributed processing model of language acquisition. In *Connections and Symbols*, ed. S. Pinker and J. Mehler, 73–194. Cambridge, MA: MIT Press.

Pitres, A. 1895. Étude de l'aphasie chez les polyglottes. *Revue de médecine* 15:873–99. Translated by M. Paradis in *Readings on aphasia in bilinguals and polyglots*, 23–49. Montreal: Didier.

Pollock, J.-Y. 1989. Verb movement, universal grammar and the structure of IP. *Linguistic Inquiry* 20:365–424.

Poplack, S. 1978. Dialect acquisition among Puerto Rican bilinguals. *Language in Society* 7:89–103.

———. 1980. Sometimes I'll start a sentence in English *y termino en español*: Towards a typology of codeswitching. *Linguistics* 18:581–618.

Prator, C. 1967. Hierarchy of difficulty. Classroom lecture given at UCLA, Los Angeles. Cited in Brown (1987).

Preston, D. 1982. How to lose a language. *Interlanguage Studies Bulletin* 62: 64–87.

———. 1989. *Sociolinguistics and Second Language Acquisition*. Oxford: Blackwell.

Pritchard, D.F.L. 1952. An investigation into the relationship between personality traits and ability in modern languages. *British Journal of Educational Psychology* 22:147–48.

Pylyshyn, Z.W. 1984. *Computation and Cognition*. Cambridge, MA: MIT Press.

Radford, A. 1988. *Transformational Grammar*. Cambridge: Cambridge University Press.

———. 1990. *Syntactic Theory and the Acquisition of English Syntax*. Oxford: Blackwell.

Rayner, K. and A. Pollatsek. 1989. *The Psychology of Reading*. Englewood Cliffs, NJ: Prentice-Hall.

Reich, P. 1986. *Language Development*. Englewood Cliffs, NJ: Prentice-Hall.

Reicher, G. 1969. Perceptual recognition as a function of meaningfulness of stimulus material. *Journal of Experimental Psychology* 81 (2): 274–80.

Reid, E. 1976. Social and stylistic variation in the speech of some Edinburgh schoolchildren. MLitt thesis, University of Edinburgh, Edinburgh.

Ribot, T. 1881. *Les maladies de la mémoire*. Paris: Librarie Germer Baillière.

Richards, J. and T. Rodgers. 1986. *Approaches and Methods in Language Teaching*. Cambridge: Cambridge University Press.

Riley, P. 1977. Discourse networks in classroom interaction: Some problems in communicative language teaching. *Mélanges pédagogiques*. Nancy: University of Nancy, CRAPEL.

Ringbom, H. 1990. Effects of transfer in foreign language learning. In *Current Trends in European Second Language Research*, ed. H. Dechert, 205–18. Clevedon, UK: Multilingual Matters.

Rizzi, L. 1982. *Issues in Italian Syntax*. Dordrecht: Foris.

Robinett, B.W. and J. Schachter, eds. 1983. *Second Language Learning*. Ann Arbor: University of Michigan Press.

Rosansky, E. 1975. The critical period for the acquisition of language: Some cognitive developmental considerations. *Working Papers on Bilingualism* 6:92–102.

Rossier, R. 1976. Extroversion–introversion as a significant variable in the learning of oral English as a second language. Ph.D. diss., University of Southern California, Los Angeles.

Rubenstein, H., L. Garfield, and J. Millikan. 1970. Homographic entries in the internal lexicon. *Journal of Verbal Learning and Verbal Behavior* 9:487–94.

Rubenstein, H., S. Lewis, and M.A. Rubenstein. 1971. Evidence for phonemic recoding in visual word recognition. *Journal of Verbal Learning and Verbal Behavior* 19:645–57.

Rubin, J. 1975. What the "good language learner" can teach us. *TESOL Quarterly* 9(1): 41–51.

Rumelhart, D. and J. McClelland, eds. 1986a. *Parallel Distributed Processing: Explorations in the Microstructure of Cognition*. Cambridge, MA: MIT Press.

———. 1986b. On learning the past tense of English verbs. In *Parallel Distributed Processing: Explorations in the Microstructure of Cognition*, ed. D. Rumelhart and J. McClelland, 216–71. Cambridge, MA: MIT Press.

Rutherford, W. 1987. *Second Language Grammar: Learning and Teaching*. New York: Longman.

Savignon, S. 1983. *Communicative Competence Theory and Classroom Practice.* Reading, MA: Addison-Wesley.

Schachter, J. 1974. An error in error analysis. *Language Learning* 24:205–14.

———. 1989. Testing a proposed universal. In *Linguistic Perspectives on Second Language Acquisition*, ed. S. Gass and J. Schachter, 73–88. Cambridge: Cambridge University Press.

Scheibner-Herzig, G., A. Thiele, G. Jelinek, and S. Kokoschka. 1984. A study of foreign language achievements and personality variables in 15 year old pupils. *ITL Review of Applied Linguistics* 65:43–56.

Schmidt, R.W. and N.G. Frota. 1986. Developing basic conversational ability in a second language. In *Talking to Learn,* ed. R.R. Day, 237–326. Rowley, MA: Newbury House.

Schumann, J. 1976a. Second language acquisition research: Getting a more global look at the learner. *Language Learning* Special issue 4:15–28.

———. 1976b. Second language acquisition: The pidginization hypothesis. *Language Learning* 26:391–408.

———. 1978. *The Pidginization Process: A Model for Second Language Acquisition.* Rowley, MA: Newbury House.

Schumann, J., J. Holroyd, R. Campbell, and F. Ward. 1978. Improvement of foreign language pronunciation under hypnosis: A preliminary study. *Language Learning* 28:143–48.

Schwartz, B. 1987. *The Modular Basis of Second Language Acquisition.* Ph.D. diss., UCLA, Los Angeles.

Schwartz, B. and M. Gubala-Ryzak. 1992. Learnability and grammar reorganization in L2 acquisition: Against negative evidence causing the unlearning of verb movement. *Second Language Research* 8(1): 1–38.

Scovel, T. 1969. Foreign accents, language acquisition, and cerebral dominance. *Language Learning* 19:245–54.

———. 1978. The effect of affect on foreign language learning: A review of the anxiety research. *Language Learning* 28:129–42.

———. 1981. The effects of neurological age on nonprimary language acquisition. In *New Dimensions in Second Language Acquisition Research,* ed. R.W. Andersen, 33–42. Rowley, MA: Newbury House.

———. 1982. Questions concerning the application of neurolinguistic research to second language learning/teaching. *TESOL Quarterly* 16:323–31.

———. 1988. *A Time to Speak: A Psycholinguistic Inquiry into the Critical Period for Human Speech.* Rowley, MA: Newbury House.

Segalowitz, S. 1983. *The Two Sides of the Brain.* Englewood Cliffs, NJ: Prentice-Hall.

Seidenberg, M.S. and J.L. McClelland. 1989. A distributed development model of word recognition and naming. *Psychological Review* 96:523–68.

Seidenberg, M. and S. Vidanovic. 1985. Word recognition in Serbo-Croatian and English: Do they differ? Paper presented at the annual meeting of the Psychonomic Society, Boston, MA.

Seidenberg, M.S., G.S. Waters, M.A. Barnes, and M.K. Tanenhaus. 1984. When does irregular spelling or pronunciation influence word recognition? *Journal of Verbal Learning and Verbal Behavior* 23:383–404.

Seliger, H.W., S. Krashen, and P. Ladefoged. 1975. Maturational constraints in the acquisition of second language accent. *Language Sciences* 36:20–22.

Seliger, H. and R. Vago, eds. 1991. *First Language Attrition.* Cambridge: Cambridge University Press.

Selinker, L. 1972. Interlanguage. *IRAL* 10:210–31.

Selinker, L. and D. Douglas. 1985. Wrestling with "context" in interlanguage theory. *Applied Linguistics* 6:190–204.

Semke, H. 1984. Effects of the red pen. *Foreign Language Annals* 17:195–202.

Sharwood Smith, M. 1983. On explaining language loss. In *Language Development at the Crossroads,* ed. S. Felix and H. Wode, 49–69. Tübingen: Gunter Narr.

———. 1989. Crosslinguistic influence in language loss. In *Bilingualism across the Lifespan: Aspects of Acquisition, Maturity, and Loss.* ed. K. Hyltenstam and L. Obler, 185–201. Cambridge: Cambridge University Press.

Sinclair, J. and D. Brazil. 1982. *Teacher Talk.* Oxford: Oxford University Press.

Sinclair, J. and M. Coulthard. 1975. *Towards an Analysis of Discourse.* Oxford: Oxford University Press.

Singleton, D. 1989. *Language Acquisition: The Age Factor.* Clevedon, UK: Multilingual Matters.

Skehan, P. 1989. *Individual Differences in Second Language Learning.* London: Edward Arnold.

———. 1991. Individual differences in second language learning. *Studies in Second Language Acquisition* 13(2): 275–98.

Skinner, B.F. 1938. *Behavior of Organisms: An Experimental Analysis.* New York: Appleton-Century-Crofts.

———. 1957. *Verbal Behavior.* New York: Appleton-Century-Crofts.

Slobin, D., ed. 1971. *The Ontogenesis of Grammar.* Academic Press.

Slobin, D. 1973. Cognitive prerequisites for the development of grammar. In *Studies of Child Language Development,* ed. C. Ferguson and D. Slobin, 175–208. New York: Holt, Rinehart, and Winston.

Smalley, W. A. 1963. Culture shock, language shock and the shock of self discovery. *Practical Anthropology* 10:49–56.

Smith, D. 1972. Some implications for the social status of pidgin languages. In *Sociolinguistics in Cross-Cultural Analysis,* ed. D. Smith and R. Shuy. Washington, DC: Georgetown University Press.

Snow, C.E. 1983. Age differences and second language acquisition: Research findings and folk psychology. In *Second Language Acquisition Studies,* ed. K. Bailey, M. Long, and S. Peck, 141–50. Rowley, MA: Newbury House.

———. 1987. Relevance of the notion of a critical period to language acquisition. In *Sensitive Periods in Development: An Interdisciplinary Perspective,* ed. M. Bornstein, 183–209. Hillsdale, NJ: Erlbaum.

Snow, C.E. and M. Hoefnagel-Höhle. 1977. Age differences and the pronunciation of foreign sounds. *Language and Speech* 20:357–65.

Sorenson, A. 1967. Multilingualism in the Northwest Amazon. *American Anthropologist* 69:670–84.

Southam Report. 1987. *Broken Words.* Toronto: Southam Newspaper Group.

Spolsky, B. 1989. *Conditions for Second Language Learning.* Oxford: Oxford University Press.

Stemberger, J.P. 1992. A connectionist view of child phonology: Phonological processing without phonological processes. In *Phonological Development,* ed. C. Ferguson, L. Menn, and C. Stoel-Gammon, 165–190. Timonium, MD: York Press.

Stengal, E. 1939. On learning a new language. *International Journal of Psychoanalysis* 2:471–79.

Stern, H.H. 1970. *Perspectives on Second Language Teaching.* Toronto: OISE.

———. 1975. What can we learn from the good language learner? *The Canadian Modern Language Review* 34:304–18.

———. 1983. *Fundamental Concepts of Language Teaching.* Oxford: Oxford University Press.

———. 1984. The immersion phenomenon. *Language and Society* 12:4–7.

Stevick, E. 1989. *Success with Foreign Languages*. Englewood Cliffs, NJ: Prentice-Hall.

Stine, E.A.L. 1990. On-line processing of written text by younger and older adults. *Psychology and Aging* 5:68–78.

Strong, M. 1983. Social styles and the second language acquisition of Spanish speaking kindergartners. *TESOL Quarterly* 17:241–58.

———. 1985. A study of sign language among young deaf children. Paper presented at 19th annual TESOL convention, New York.

———, ed. 1988. *Language Learning and Deafness*. Cambridge: Cambridge University Press.

Stroop, J.R. 1935. Studies of interference in serial verbal reactions. *Journal of Experimental Psychology* 118:643–61.

Suter, R.W. 1977. Predictors of pronunciation accuracy in second language learning. *Language Learning* 26 (2): 233–53.

Swain, M. 1975. More about primary French immersion classes. *Orbit* 27:13–15.

———. 1983. *Understanding Input through Output*. Paper presented at 10th University of Michigan conference on applied linguistics, Ann Arbor, Michigan.

———. 1985. Communicative competence: Some roles of comprehensible input and comprehensible output and its development. In *Input in Second Language Acquisition*, ed. S. Gass and C. Madden, 235–56. Rowley, MA: Newbury House.

———. 1986. Bilingualism without tears. In *Bilingualism in Education*, ed. J. Cummins and M. Swain, 99–110. New York: Longman.

———. 1988. Manipulating and complementing content teaching to maximize second language learning. *TESL Canada Journal* 6(1): 68–84.

Swain, M. and B. Burnaby. 1976. Personality characteristics and second language learning in young children: A pilot study. *Working Papers in Bilingualism* 11:76–90.

Swain, M. and S. Lapkin. 1982. *Evaluating Bilingual Education*. Clevedon, UK: Multilingual Matters.

Swinney, D. 1979. Lexical access during sentence comprehension: (Re)-consideration of context effects. *Journal of Verbal Learning and Verbal Behavior* 18:645–59.

Taft, M. 1981. Prefix stripping revisited. *Journal of Verbal Learning and Verbal Behavior* 20:289–97.

Taft, M. and K.I. Forster. 1976. Lexical storage and retrieval of polymorphic and polysyllabic words. *Journal of Verbal Learning and Verbal Behavior* 15:607–20.

Tanenhaus, M.K., J.M. Leiman, and M.S. Seidenberg. 1979. Evidence for multiple stages in the processing of ambiguous words on syntactic contexts. *Journal of Verbal Learning and Verbal Behavior.* 18:429–40.

Tanenhaus, M.K., G. Carlson, and M.S. Seidenberg. 1985. Do listeners compute linguistic representations? In *Natural Language Parsing*, ed. D. Dowty, L. Karttunen, and A. Zwicky. Cambridge: Cambridge University Press.

Tarone, E. 1981. Some thoughts on the notion of communicative strategy. *TESOL Quarterly* 15:285–95.

———. 1983. On the variability of interlanguage systems. *Applied Linguistics* 4(2): 142–63.

———. 1984. The role of the syllable in interlanguage phonology. In *Theoretical Issues in Contrastive Phonology*, ed. S. Eliasson, 63–72. Heidelberg: Julias Groos Verlag.

———. 1985. Variability in interlanguage use: A study of style-shifting in morphology and syntax. *Language Learning* 35:373–403.

———. 1987. The phonology of interlanguage. In *Interlanguage Phonology: The*

Acquisition of a Second Language Sound System, ed. G. Ioup and S. Weinberger, 70–85. Cambridge, MA: Newbury House.

———. 1989. Accounting for style-shifting in interlanguage. In *Variation in Second Language Acquisition: Psycholinguistic Issues*, ed. S. Gass, C. Madden, D. Preston, and L. Selinker, 13–21. Clevedon, UK: Multilingual Matters.

Taylor, B. 1975. Adult language learning strategies and their pedagogic implications. *TESOL Quarterly* 9:391–99.

Todd, L. 1974. *Pidgins and Creoles*. London: Routledge and Kegan Paul.

Tomasello, M. and C. Herron. 1988. Down the garden path: Inducing and correcting overgeneralization errors in the foreign language classroom. *Applied Psycholinguistics* 9:237–46.

———. 1989. Feedback for language transfer errors: The garden path technique. *Studies in Second Language Acquisition* 11:385–95.

Tran-Chi-Chau. 1975. Error analysis, contrastive analysis and students' perception: A study of difficulty in second language learning. *International Review of Applied Linguistics* 13:119–43.

Trudgill, P. 1972. Sex, covert prestige and linguistic change in the urban British English of Norwich. *Language in Society* 1:179–95.

———. 1974. *The Social Differentiation of English in Norwich*. Cambridge: Cambridge University Press.

Tucker, G.R., E. Hamayan, and F. Genesee. 1976. Affective, cognitive and social factors in second language acquisition. *Canadian Modern Language Review* 32:214–26.

Turvey, M.T., L.B. Feldman, and G. Lukatela. 1984. The Serbo-Croatian orthography constrains the reader to a phonologically analytic strategy. In *Orthographies and Reading*, ed. L. Henderson. London: Erlbaum.

Twadell, W.F. 1935. On defining the phoneme. In *Readings in Linguistics (1957)*, ed. M. Joos, 55–80. Chicago: University of Chicago Press.

Upshur, J. 1968. Four experiments on the relation between foreign language teaching and learning. *Language Learning* 18:111–24.

Vaid, J. 1983. Bilingualism and brain lateralization. In *Language Function and Brain Organization*, ed. S.J. Segalowitz. New York: Academic Press.

Valian, V. 1990. Null subjects: A problem for parameter-setting models of language acquisition. *Cognition* 35:105–22.

Van Els, T. 1986. An overview of European research on language attrition. In *Language Attrition in Progress*, ed. B. Weltens, K. de Bot, and T. Van Els. Dordrecht: Foris.

VanPatten, B. 1988. How juries get hung: Problems with the evidence for a focus on form in teaching. *Language Learning* 38(2): 243–60.

VanPatten, B. and T. Cadierno. 1993. Explicit instruction and input processing. *Studies in Second Language Acquisition* 15(2): 225–44.

Vigil, N.A. and J. Oller. 1976. Rule fossilization: A tentative model. *Language Learning* 26:281–95.

Walsh, T. and K. Diller. 1981. Neurolinguistic considerations on the optimum age for second language learning. In *Individual Differences and Universals in Language Learning Aptitude*, ed. K. Diller, 3–21. Rowley, MA: Newbury House.

Wardhaugh, R. 1970. The contrastive analysis hypothesis. *TESOL Quarterly* 4:123–30.

Watt, D. and H. Roessingh. 1994. ESL dropout: The myth of educational equity. *Alberta Journal of Education Research* 40(3): 283–96.

Weinstein, C.E. and R.E. Mayer. 1986. The teaching of learning strategies. In *Handbook of Research on Teaching*, ed. M.C. Wittrock, 315–27. New York: Macmillan.

Wells, G. 1986. *The Meaning Makers: Children Learning Language and Using Language to Learn*. Portsmouth, UK: Heinemann.

Wernicke, C. 1874. The aphasic symptom complex: A psychological study on a neurological basis. Breslau: Kohn and Weigert. Reprinted in *Boston Studies in the Philosophy of Science*, vol. 4, ed. R.S. Cohen and M.W. Wartofsky. Boston, MA: Reidel.

Wesche, M. 1989. Long-term outcomes of French immersion education: A follow-up study at university. Paper presented at OMLTA conference, Toronto.

Wexler, K. and P. Culicover. 1980. *Formal Principles of Language Acquisition*. Cambridge, MA: MIT Press.

Wexler, K. and M.R. Manzini. 1987. Parameters and learnability in binding theory. In *Parameter setting*, ed. T. Roeper and E. Williams, 41–76. Dordrecht: Reidel.

White, L. 1985a. The acquisition of parameterized grammars: Subjacency in second language acquisition. *Second Language Research* 1:1–17.

———. 1985b. Is there a logical problem of second language acquisition? *TESL Canada Journal* 2(2): 29–41.

———. 1986. Markedness and parameter setting: Some implications for a theory of adult second language acquisition. In *Markedness*, ed. F. Eckman, E. Moravscik, and J. Wirth. New York: Plenum Press.

———. 1988a. Island effects in second language acquisition. In *Linguistic Theory and Second Language Acquisition*, ed. S. Flynn and W. O'Neil, 144–72. Dordrecht: Kluwer Academic Publishers.

———. 1988b. Universal grammar and language transfer. In *Learnability and Second Languages: A Book of Readings*, ed. J. Pankhurst, M. Sharwood Smith, and P. Van Buren. Dordrecht: Foris.

———. 1989a. The principle of adjacency in second language acquisition: So L2 learners observe the subset principle? In *Linguistic Perspectives on Second Language Acquisition*, ed. S. Gass and J. Schachter, 134–58. Cambridge: Cambridge University Press.

———. 1989b. *Universal Grammar and Second Language Acquisition*. Amsterdam: John Benjamins.

———. 1990. Second language acquisition and universal grammar. *Studies in Second Language Acquisition* 12(2): 121–34.

———. 1991. Adverb placement in second language acquisition: Some effects of positive and negative evidence in the classroom. *Second Language Research* 7:133–61.

———. 1992. On triggering data in L2 acquisition: A reply to Schwartz and Gubala-Ryzak. *Second Language Research* 8(2): 93–119.

Whitman, R. 1970. Contrastive analysis: problems and procedures. *Language Learning* 20:29–41.

Widdowson, H. 1980. The use of theory. Extracts from the Gretta Smith memorial, University of London, England.

Wilson, E. 1975. *Sociobiology: The New Synthesis*. Cambridge, MA: Harvard University Press.

Wode, H. 1984. Some theoretical implications of L2 acquisition research and the grammar of interlanguages. In *Interlanguage: Proceedings of the Seminar in Honour of Pit Corder*, ed. A. Davies, C. Criper, and A.P.R. Howatt. Edinburgh: Edinburgh University Press.

Wolfram, W. 1969. *A Sociolinguistic Description of Detroit Negro Speech*. Washington, DC: Center for Applied Linguistics.

———. 1985. Variability in tense marking: A case for the obvious. *Language Learning* 35:229–53.

———. 1989. Systematic variability in second-language tense marking. In *The Dynamic Interlanguage*, ed. M. Eisenstein, 187–97. New York: Plenum Press.

Wolfram, W. and D. Hatfield. 1984. Tense marking in second language learning: Patterns of spoken and written English in a Vietnamese community. *Final Report*, National Institute of Education Grant.

Wolfson, N. and E. Judd. 1983. *Sociolinguistics and Second Language Acquisition*. Rowley, MA: Newbury House.

Wong Fillmore, L. 1985. When does teacher talk work as input? In *Input in Second Language Acquisition*, ed. S. Gass and C. Madden, 17–50. Rowley, MA: Newbury House.

———. 1991. A question for early-childhood programs: English first or families first? *Education Week*, 19 June.

Woods, D. 1989. Error correction and the improvement of language form. *TESL Canada Journal* 6(2): 60–73.

Yorio, C. 1976. Discussion of "Explaining sequence and variation in second language acquisition." *Language Learning* Special issue 4:59–63.

———. 1981. The teacher's attitudes to student errors. In *TEAL Occasional Papers* (Spring). British Columbia Teachers' Association.

———. 1987. Building multiple bridges: Eclecticism in language teaching. *TESL Canada Journal* 5(1): 91–100.

Zobl, H. 1988. Configurationality and the subset principle. In *Learnability and Second Languages: A Book of Readings*, ed. J. Pankhurst, M. Sharwood Smith, and P. Van Buren. Dordrecht: Reidel.

———. 1989. Modularity in adult L2 acquisition. *Language Learning* 39:49–79.

Index